MACROECONOMIC THEORY

MACROECONOMIC THEORY

Dr Sunil Bhaduri
(Hon.) Senior Lecturer in Economics
Middlesex University, London

New Central Book Agency (P) Ltd
LONDON
HYDERABAD ERNAKULAM BHUBANESWAR
NEW DELHI KOLKATA PUNE GUWAHATI

NCBA

REGD OFFICE

8/1 Chintamoni Das Lane, Kolkata 700 009, India.
email: ncbapvtltd@eth.net

OVERSEAS

NCBA (UK) Ltd, 149 Park Avenue North, Northampton, NN3 2HY, UK
email: ncbauk@yahoo.com

EXPORT

NCBA Exports Pvt. Ltd, 212 Shahpur Jat, New Delhi 110 049
email: ncbaexports@ncbapvtltd.com

BRANCHES

212 Shahpur Jat
New Delhi 110 049
email: ncbadel@ncbapvtltd.com

Shop Nos. 3 & 4, Vinayak Towers
681/B Budhwar Peth, Appa Balwant Chowk
Pune 411 002
email: ncbapune@ncbapvtltd.com

Shop No. 15, Bharati Towers, Ground Floor
Forest Park, **Bhubaneswar** 751 001
email: ncbabub@ncbapvtltd.com

House No. 3-1-315, 1st Floor
Nimboliadda, Kachiguda, **Hyderabad** 500 027
email: ncbahydb@ncbapvtltd.com

GSS Shopping Complex, 1st Floor
Opposite College Post Office, Convent Road
Ernakulam 682 035
0484-4021054/53

Radhamayee Complex (Second Floor)
Opp. SBI, Panbazar, Jaswanta Road
Guwahati 781 001
email: ncbaguwahati@ncbapvtltd.com

MACROECONOMIC THEORY • Dr Sunil Bhaduri

First Published: 1999
Reprinted: 2002, 2012, 2015

PUBLISHER
New Central Book Agency (P) Ltd
8/1 Chintamoni Das Lane, Kolkata 700 009

TYPESETTER
Ray Computer, Kolkata

PRINTER
New Central Book Agency (P) Ltd
Web-Offset Division, Dhulagarh, Sankrail, Howrah

COVER DESIGNER
Angik

PROJECT SUPERVISOR
Usha Ranjan Bhowmik and Prabhat Jas

ISBN 978 81 7381 756 4

Price ₹ 415.00

PREFACE

This book covers the Economics (Honours) syllabi of various universities in West Bengal, India and in many universities outside India, especially universities in South East Asia, Africa and England. This book will also cater to the needs of M. Com. students of various universities in India and outside India where M. Com. is taught. Students of M.A. course in Economics in various universities will also find this book useful as background reading. In addition, students preparing for various competitive examinations like I.E.S, I.A.S, W.B.C.S, will find this book useful as well. It would be helpful for people who intend to take professional examinations.

The book starts from fundamental concepts and deals with all the topics extensively. Mathematical tools and techniques have been used whenever necessary for the purpose of exposition. Even when mathematics have been used, attempts have been made to explain economic significance as thoroughly as possible. Besides, diagrammatic presentations have been provided as extensively as possible.

Although poets and story-writers may get pleasure from the sheer act of writing and publishing, text-book writers are pleased if their work is read, understood and enjoyed by students. However, a text-book like this cannot claim originality except for redefining or reorienting the mode of presentation of the materials. Standard text-books on the subject have been consulted and used in writing this book. For advanced students a list of reference books has been presented at the end of the book.

This book integrates both the classical and Keynesian economics. The prominent role of Keynesian approach to economic fluctuations in this book is a testament to the influence and importance of Keynesian revolution — some economists forgot the role of classical economists in providing the right answer to many fundamental questions. This book incorporates many of the contributions of the classical, the Keynesian, the new classical economists and the new Keynesians. Substantial coverage is given also to the IS -LM model of aggregate demand, the short-term trade-off between inflation and unemployment, and theories of wage and price rigidities.

Almost all chapters contain exercises for students to practice. Every efforts were made to keep the book as brief as possible, because of my experience as a student, I know that long books are less likely to be read. My goal is to offer the clearest, most uptodate, most accessible course in the fewest words possible.

Students of macroeconomics are concerned with economic policy which should be guided by research, hard-headed reasoning and statistical analysis. Economic policy should be *for the people* but not *by the people* in the sense that it should not be decided by majority voting but by the minority of researchers.

While writing this book, I benefited from comments of many colleagues and friends. I wish to thank those who read and commented on a large part of the manuscript, especially Mr. Sanjay Majumder of L.S.E.

The staff of New Central Book Agency and the publisher, Mr. Amitava Sen, also deserve thanks for their support, cooperation and help in publishing this book in time. I am also grateful to Dr. H. K. Saharay for his help and encouragement to publish this book.

Finally, I wish to thank my wife, Kalpana, and son, Indranil, for their help and support without which this book could not have been completed.

However, the author bears the full responsibility for all errors and omissions.

25 December, 1998

Sunil Bhaduri
Middlesex University
London

CONTENTS

	Pages
Chapter 1 : Introduction	3- 10
Chapter 2 : Basic Concepts	11- 22
Chapter 3 : National Income Accounting	23- 44
Chapter 4 : Equilibrium in the Goods Sector	45- 64
Chapter 5 : Equilibrium in the Money Sector	65- 92
Chapter 6 : The Goods and Money Sectors together	93-102
Chapter 7 : Macroeconomic System	103-116
Chapter 8 : The Complete Keynesian Model	117-143
Chapter 9 : Keynes Versus the Classicists	144-153
Chapter 10 : Aggregate Demand	154-178
Chapter 11 : Income Determination with Government Sector	179-208
Chapter 12 : The Consumption Function	209-230
Chapter 13 : Investment Demand	231-255
Chapter 14 : The International Trade Sector	256-276
Chapter 15 : The Mundell-Fleming Model	277-292
Chapter 16 : Inflation and Unemployment	293-326
Chapter 17 : The Theory of Real Business Cycles and Economic Fluctuation	327-344
Chapter 18 : The Theory of Economic Growth	345-371
Chapter 19 : The Debates over Government Debt	372-381
Chapter 20 : International Institutions	382-401
Appendix : Notes on Figures	403-442
Glossary	443-459
Bibliography	461-463
Index	465-470

MACROECONOMIC THEORY

1 INTRODUCTION

Economics is a social science which seeks to explain the economic basis of human society. Our purpose here is to identify the basic economic problems encountered by all societies and to focus attention on the basic concepts which modern economists employ in their attempts to analyse this problem. We start our study of the economy as a whole and in this book we consider many of the world's most pressing macroeconomic problems—problems like present unemployment, rapid inflation, balance of payments difficulties, economic stagnation, etc. In order to analyse these problems, we must first identify and consider the determinants of the main aggregates in the economy. The most important aggregates are : (a) the economy's total output of goods and services, (b) the total demand for this output, (c) total employment in the economy, (d) the general price level, (e) the rate of growth in the economy and (f) the balance of payments. It is important to gain a good understanding of the meaning of these aggregates.

Distinction between Microeconomics and Macroeconomics

Economic theory is broadly divided into two branches—microeconomics and macroeconomics. The term 'micro' comes from the Greek word *mikros* which means small. Accordingly, *microeconomics studies the activity of the individual units in the economy*. It is essentially a theory of decision-making which deals with the problems of maximisation or minimisation of an objective function of a decision-taking unit within the constraints imposed upon it. Its subject-matter is the interactions of the behaviour patterns of various decision-taking units, as they are reflected in the market. In microeconomic model, households choose their purchase to maximise their utility (satisfaction), and firms make production decisions to maximise profits. Prices are formed in the markets where the outcomes of separate individual behaviours are coordinated. How each price is formed, how different prices are related to each other, etc., are the central problems of micro-theory. Price and quantity of each product, demand and supply of each product and factor, demand and supply of each decision-taking unit and similar other things are the primary economic variables that are dealt with in micro-theory.

Again, the term 'macro' comes from the Greek word *makros* which means large. Thus, *macroeconomics is concerned with the behaviour of the economy as a whole* — with booms and recessions, the economy's total output of goods and services and the growth of output, the rate of inflation and unemployment, the balance of payments and so on. Macroeconomics studies the interaction of many households and firms, but macro and micro are inextricably linked. When we study the economics as a whole, we must consider the decisions of individual economic actors. For example, to understand what determines total consumption spending, we must think about a family decision as to how much to spend today and how much to save for the future. Since aggregate variables are simply the sum of the variables describing many individual decisions, macroeconomics is inevitably founded in microeconomics.

The distinction between microeconomics and macroeconomics is artificial since aggregates are derived from the sums of individual figures. Yet the distinction is justified because what is true for individual in isolation, may not be true for the economy as a whole. For example, an individual may become richer by saving than spending. However, if all individuals save more and spend less, the nation as a whole does not become richer. If every individual in the economy saves more than before the national income falls — this is the paradox of thrift in macroeconomics. The distinction is also justified because of the methodological differences in the two branches of economics. Microeconomics uses the partial equilibrium analysis where the ceteris paribus assumption is made. Thus, when the price of a commodity is determined, it is assumed that other things remain unchanged. To have an overall idea about the totality of economic activities, we might take resort to the Walrasian General Equilibrium Analysis in which all markets and all individual quantities would be presented simultaneously with all their interrelations. All the individual quantities would, then, be derived from the behaviours of all decision-making units. Each and every differential of individual behaviour would exhibit its proper role in the social integral.

Macroeconomics is a young and imperfect science. It was first introduced by R. Frisch in 1933. Before that macroeconomics was known as income theory and microeconomics as price theory. The price theory was mainly concerned with the determination of individual prices, whereas macroeconomics is concerned with the determination of the equilibrium level of income and employment in the economy. This does not mean that income concepts are neglected in microeconomics and prices are neglected in macroeconomics. Microeconomic theory is mainly concerned with the determination of factor incomes such as wages, rent, interest and profit. Similarly, macroeconomics is also concerned with the determination of the price level. Where microeconomics is concerned with the determination of relative prices, macroeconomics determines the absolute price level. Again, while microeconomics determines the relative factor shares, macroeconomics determines the aggregate income level. We study macroeconomics not only to explain economic events but also to improve economic policy. The monetary and fiscal tools of Government can influence the economy and macroeconomics helps policy-makers to evaluate policies. Macroeconomists are asked to explain the economic world as it is and to consider what it could do to improve the situation.

Subject Matter of Macroeconomics

There is no clear-cut division between micro- and macro-economics. The scope of macroeconomics can be stated by giving a list of most important problems with which it is concerned. As noted before, macroeconomics is concerned with the behaviour of the economy as a whole. The subject matter of macroeconomics is income and employment, inflation, balance of payment problems etc. which occur in milder forms all the time. The purpose of macroeconomics is to present a logical framework for the analysis of these phenomena. What does determine income and employment? What does determine the price level? How are these related? What policies can be used to affect them and how do they work? These are some of the questions the analytical framework presented here is meant to handle. Real income, employment, the price level and the balance of payments are determined by the interaction of decisions made by the individuals when solving their economic problems; decisions about the consumption and investment, decisions about the allocation of wealth among alternative assets, decisions about how much labour to hire and supply, and many others. Though these decisions are interdependent, it is useful to subdivide the economy into various sectors of decision-making in order to examine what forces operate in each sector before looking at the interdependence among them.

The division between micro and macro is a matter of convenience. It is convenient to make distinction, because (1) the method of analysis is different and (2) the problems are also different. The basic microeconomic problem is the determination of structure of relative prices and the basic theory is that of demand and supply. The basic macroeconomic problem is the determination of the *flow of income* and the basic theoretical structure is the model of the *circular flow of income*. For this reason, we should know the circular flow of income concept :

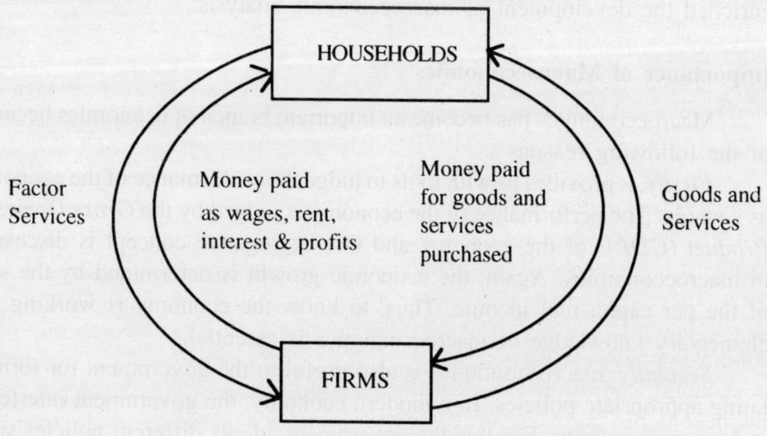

Fig. 1.1 Simple Circular Flow Diagram

We assume that, in the economic system, production takes place in the firm sector and the individuals consume what is produced in the firm sector. The individual owners of factors of production supply factor services to the firms and receive income in return. They spend this income to buy goods and services from firms. These transactions generate flow of goods and services in one direction and a flow of money in the other direction. Money in return flows from firms to households in return for factor services provided by households. Money also flows to firms in return for the output purchased from firms. These flows are given in Fig. 1.1 in the previous page.

In such a simple economy, there are only two groups of decision-takers, households and firms. Each group earns all its income by selling goods and services to the other groups and each group spends all of its income by buying goods and services from the other group. Households earn their income by selling the services of the factors of production — land, labour, capital and enterprise — to firms and they spend all their incomes on purchasing goods and services produced by firms. Firms sell all their goods and services to households and receive money in return. All of the money received by firms is in turn paid out to the households. This is called the circular flow of income. Macroeconomics is concerned with explaining various aspects of this flow of income between firms and households and discuss about the determinants of this flow. It also explains the causes of its expansion or contraction. The circular flow gives an idea of the general economic activity of the economy. When the size of the circular flow increases, the level of income and employment also increases. Similarly, when the size of the flow decreases, the level of income and employment also decreases. Since modern macroeconomics is concerned with policy issues, debates on economic policies, viz, monetary and fiscal policies, and also exchange rate policies in open economics, have enriched the development of macroeconomic analysis.

Importance of Macroeconomics

Macroeconomics has become an important branch of economics because of the following reasons :

Firstly, it provides us with tools to judge the performance of the economy as a whole. The performance of the economy is judged by the *Gross Domestic Product (GDP)*[1] of the economy and this aggregative concept is discussed in macroeconomics. Again, the economic growth is determined by the size of the per capita real income. Thus, to know the economy is working, an elementary knowledge of macroeconomics is essential.

Secondly, macroeconomics is also useful to the government for formulating appropriate policies. In a modern economy, the government interferes in economic activity. For this the government adopts different policies such

[1]More about GDP in later chapter.

as *fiscal and monetary policies* and so on. Such macroeconomic policies influence the entire economy. What policies — fiscal or monetary — would be undertaken by the government depends on the phase of the trade cycle or business cycle. If the economic activity is increasing (i.e. the economy is in boom), government policy will be different from its policy when the economic activity is decreasing (i.e the economy is moving to depression). To know the nature of the trade cycle and to make forecasts about business cycle, a knowledge of macroeconomics is necessary. Hence macroeconomics helps the government to take an appropriate policy.

Thirdly, for any business firm, the knowledge of macroeconomics is necessary, because the demand for many firm products is a function of income. The demand increases or decreases along with the increase or decrease in the level of the economic activity. Thus, to make a forecast about the demand for its product, the firm must be able to make an estimate about the level of the economic activity which requires the knowledge of macroeconomics.

Fourthly, we know that economy suffers from many problems such as unemployment, inflation etc. Why do such problems arise in the economy? Can such problems be automatically corrected? Is there any automatic mechanism within the economic system to solve these problems? These are some of the theoretical problems which require the knowledge of macroeconomics to understand and deal with them.

From the above analysis, it is clear that the study of macroeconomics is useful. Though macroeconomics is useful, it is not without limitations : *Firstly*, many propositions which are true for individuals may not be true for the economy as a whole. For example, an individual can borrow from another individual during a period of time, but the community as a whole cannot borrow from itself. There are many other examples which could be true for an individual, but may not be necessarily true for the community as a whole. Thus, it is difficult to generalise in macroeconomic theory.

Secondly, in macroeconomics, we deal with aggregates and these aggregates are taken as homogeneous entities. But this is not true.

Thirdly, all aggregates are not useful. Only those aggregates which can be functionally related happen to be useful.

Fourthly, the major part of the macro theory is applicable for a developed capitalist economy. It is not suitable for less developed economies. The problems of the developing economies are not same as those of the developed economies. Hence, the macroeconomic models built for the developed economies are unlikely to be suitable for the developing economies.

Development of Macroeconomics

Modern macroeconomics started with the major concern for unemployment that dominated thinking in the developed industrial world in the 1920s and 1930s. The theoretical breakthrough was attributed to Keynes and is often called the Keynesian revolution. While there is no doubt that there was a Keynesian revolution and that Keynes was the leading economist of his generation, it is worth knowing that he was not alone in contributing to our understanding of the subject. Many economists in the 1930s had important contributions to make on the subject.

The origin of macroeconomics can be traced back to the mercantalist writers who were concerned with the problem of economic growth of a country. Though they wrongly thought that the greater the gold and silver possessed by a country, the richer it could be. They also thought that the country could have economic prosperity only if it had a favourable balance of trade. But the first theoretical macroeconomic model can be seen in the writings of *Physiocrats*. The Tableau Economique developed by Quesnay in 18th century France gave a circular flow model of total product among three classes of people. Quesnay's tableau gave the idea of circular flow product and income which was later emphasised by Keynes. The Physiocrats thought that the economic growth depended on the net product produced by the agricultural sector. According to the Physiocrats, the agricultural sector was the only productive sector in the economy capable of producing a surplus. They thought that industry and trade are unproductive, incapable of generating a surplus.

The next step in the development of macroeconomics was taken by *classical economists* such as Adam Smith, David Ricardo, Robert Malthus, J. B. Say etc. The classical economists investigated the real relations of production in bourgeois society. Classical economists also believed in the Say's law of markets. The idea of classical economists are summarised in the *classical model of income and employment.* They believed that in a free enterprise economy, each economic unit would try to maximise its own interest and there was a harmony of individual interests. A basic result of the classical economics is that, given the flexibility of wages and prices, a competitive market would automatically operate at full employment level of output and employment. That is, the economic forces would always be generated to ensure that the demand for labour would always equal its supply. So long as there is unemployment, money wages and prices would fall, output would increase and the additional supply of output creates its own demand (Say's law) and there can be no overproduction. In this way, full employment would be automatically reached and there could be no involuntary unemployment. The economy could temporarily deviate from full employment level but market forces would operate to restore the full employment equilibrium.

The Great Depression of the 1930s in all the capitalist countries of the world rudely shattered the belief of the self-correcting mechanism of the capitalist economic system as propounded by the classical economists. In his book, "The General Theory of Employment, Interest and Money" published in 1936, Keynes vehemently criticised the postulates of the classical theory and provided a new theory of employment and income. Modern macroeconomic theory is largely based on the idea of Keynes work.

The main result of the Keynesian theory is that the level of real national income and, therefore, employment, is determined largely by the level of aggregate demand. This is very different from the classical theory where supply creates its own demand. In the Keynesian theory, it is the demand which determines how much is to be supplied. He argued that if firms find that they are producing more than is being demanded, they will observe an involuntary increase in their inventories of unsold goods and will so rectify this by cutting back on production and laying-off workers. National income will then fall until the value of what is produced is equal to the value of aggregate demand. If firms find that they are not producing enough to satisfy demand, they will experience an unwanted fall in their inventories and so will attempt to increase production and hire more workers.

There will be one level of national income at which the aggregate demand is equal to the total value of production. This is called the equilibrium level of income. An important point to remember is that, in the Keynesian theory, the equilibrium level of income is not necessarily a full employment income. Even in equilibrium, some amount of involuntary unemployment may be present in the economy. This is the reason he called his theory a general theory and he regarded the classical theory as a 'special case' where the equilibrium and full employment level of income coincide. Another contribution of Keynes is to break the classical dichotomy and to integrate the price theory with the monetary theory. He showed how all the variables — real and monetary — were simultaneously determined in an economic system in which the money was used both as a medium of exchange and as a store of value.

Keynes's theory has policy implications which are different from the classical theory. Classical economists do not like government intervention in the economy and they think that the government is likely to make things worse by intervening. Thus, they favour monetary policy. On the other hand, Keynes was not in favour of monetary policy. He saw an useful role for the government and recommended the use of fiscal policy for full employment and economic stability.

The influence of Keynes in the development of modern macroeconomics is really profound. Much of the modern macroeconomics is based on Keynes' work and has been developed by post-Keynesian economists such as Hicks, Hansen, Modigliani, Tobin etc. Post-Keynesian economists have refined and developed some of the ideas introduced by Keynes.

In the *post-Keynesian* period, macroeconomics have developed in two directions. One school of thought believes that markets work best if left to itself; the other believes that government intervention can significantly improve the performance of the economy. In the 1960s, the debate on these questions involved monetarists on the one side and Keynesians on the other. In the 1970s, the debate on the same issues brought to the fore a new group — the new classical macroeconomists who, by and large, replaced the monetarists in keeping up the argument against active government intervention to improve economic performance. The new classical macroeconomics remains influential even today. On the other side, the new Keynesians — mostly trained in the Keynesian tradition — are moving beyond it. They do not believe that markets clear all the time but seek to understand and explain why markets may fail.

However, in this book we shall be mainly concerned with the Keynesian macroeconomics. We shall use the classical or the post-Keynesian as and when required.

2 BASIC CONCEPTS

ECONOMIC MODELS

Models are theories that summarise the relationship among economic variables. Models are useful because they help us to dispense with irrelevant details and to focus on important economic relations more clearly. A model is a description of reality with some simplification. To simplify analysis each model makes some assumptions which must be explicitly stated when a model is formulated.

A model may be expressed in terms of equations or diagrams. Of course, a model can also be expressed verbally. However, diagrams and equations are the most convenient method of expressing relationship among economic variables.

Models have two kinds of variables : *exogenous* and *endogenous variables* Exogenous Variables come from outside the model — they are inputs into the model. Endogenous variables come from inside the model — they are the output of the model. In other words, exogenous variables are fixed at the moment they enter the model, whereas endogenous variables are determined within the model. The purpose of a model is to show how the exogenous variables affect the endogenous variables.

For example, let us see how we can develop a model for bread. We assume that the quantity of bread demanded, Q^d, depends on the price of bread, P_b, and on aggregate income Y. This relationship is expressed in the equation

$Q^d = D\ (P_b,\ Y)$ where D denotes the demand function.

Similarly, we assume that the quantity of bread supplied, Q^s, depends on the price of bread, P_b, and on the price of flour, P_f, since flour is used to make bread. The relationship is expressed as $Q^s = S\ (P_b,\ P_f)$, whereas S denotes the supply function. Finally, we assume that the price of bread adjusts to equilibrate demand and supply : $Q^d = Q^s$. These three equations compose a model of the market for bread. Economic relationships involved in a model may be of different types.

Firstly, the relations could be behavioural. For example, consider the saving function $S = S(Y)$, which states that saving (S) is a function of income (Y).

Secondly, relationship between the variables could be technical. The technical relationships follow from technological considerations. For example, consider the production function $Y = F(K, L)$ which states that total output (Y) produced is a function of total capital employed (K) and total labour employed (L). This relationship is determined by the technological considerations underlying the production process. Hence it is a technical relationship.

Thirdly, the relationship may be definitional. Such relationships follow from the very definitions of the variables. For example, if Y_m represent money income, Y_r represents real income and P represents price level, then $Y_m = Y_r \times P$ represents a definitional equation.

A model must be complete. Mathematically, this means that number of equations should be equal to the number of Variables. For example, in our demand and supply model for bread, we have three unknowns and three equations. Hence the model is determinate. In the Simple Keynesian Model of income determination we have three equations : (i) $C = C(Y)$ (Consumption function); (ii) $I = I$ (Investment function); (iii) $Y = C + I$ (Equilibrium condition) we have three equations. Hence the model is determinate. We need to distinguish between variables and parameters in a model. The parameters are constants in relation to the variables in a model. For example, in a simple linear consumption function : $C = a + bY$, C and Y are variables while a and b are parameters. When any of the parameters changes the consumption function shifts its position.

Flexible versus Sticky Prices

One crucial assumption of macroeconomic models are the adjustment of wages and prices. Economists normally presume that the price of a good adjusts to equilibrate demand and supply, they assume that, at the going price, suppliers have sold all they want and demanders have bought all they want. This assumption is called market clearing. For answering most questions, economists use market-clearing models. But the assumption of continuous market clearing is not entirely realistic. For markets to clear continuously, prices must adjust instantly to changes in demand and supply. However, many wages and prices adjust sluggishly. Many labour contracts often set wages for longer years. Many firms leave their product prices unchanged for long periods of time. Although market clearing models assume that all prices and wages are flexible, in real world, we know, prices and wages are not so flexible.

The apparent stickiness of prices does not make market-clearing models useless. They might not describe the economy at every instant, but they do describe the equilibrium toward which the economy slowly moves. Thus most macroeconomists believe that market-clearing models are a good approximation to reality, especially in dealing with long-period issues. Prices and wages are flexible in the long-run.

However, for studying short-run issues, the assumption of price flexibility is less useful. Over short periods, many prices are fixed. Thus, many economists believe that price stickiness is a better assumption for studying short-run issues.

MONETARIST AND KEYNESIAN

The Keynesian view

Keynesian macroeconomists are those who advocate detailed intervention to 'fine tune' the economy in the neighbourhood of full employment and low inflation. They seek to control inflation by direct controls of wages and prices and to reduce unemployment by stimulating aggregate demand, using monetary and fiscal policy. They would use discretion to stimulate the economy in a depression or to hold the economy in a boom. They are not in favour of announcing policy change beforehand, so as to deter speculation. They modify their policy in the light of current and best-available forecasts. The intellectual leaders of this group are F. Modigliani, J. Tobin and many others in British universities.

The Monetarist View

Monetarists prefer the government to have policies towards a limited number of macroeconomic variables such as money supply, government expenditure, taxes, etc. They advocate the adoption of fixed rules for the behaviours of these variables. For example, a widely advocated rule is that the money supply should grow at a certain fixed per centage rate per year. Another rule widely advocated by them is that the government budget should be balanced over a period of four to five years. In any event, all policy inter-ventions which do occur should be announced as far ahead as possible so as to enable people to take account of them in planning their own economic affairs.

The intellectual leader of this school is M. Friedman, R. Lucas and many others in the American universities.

We should not form the impression that the Keynesian/Monetarists division is one that follows neat political boundaries. Although there is some tendency for there to be an association between monetarism and Conservatism, and between Keynesianism and liberalism/socialism, that association is far from perfect. Monetarists range all the way from diehard libertarians to orthodox Marxists. Keynesians do not go quite so far to the right, but they do go a long way in that direction.

Okun's Law

A relationship between real growth and changes in unemployment rate is known as Okun's law. Okun's law says that the unemployment rate declines when the growth is above the trend rate of *2.25* per cent. Specifically, for every per centage point of growth is real *GDP* above the trend rate that is sustained for a year, the unemployment rate declines by one-half per centage point. This relationship is stated in equation; $\Delta u = -0.5\ (y - 2.25)$ where Δu denotes the change in the unemployment rate, y is the growth rate of output. The use of the formula can be seen as: Suppose growth rate in a given year is *4.25* per cent. That would imply a reduction of unemployment rate of *1.0* per cent *[= 0.5 (4.25 – 2.25)]*.

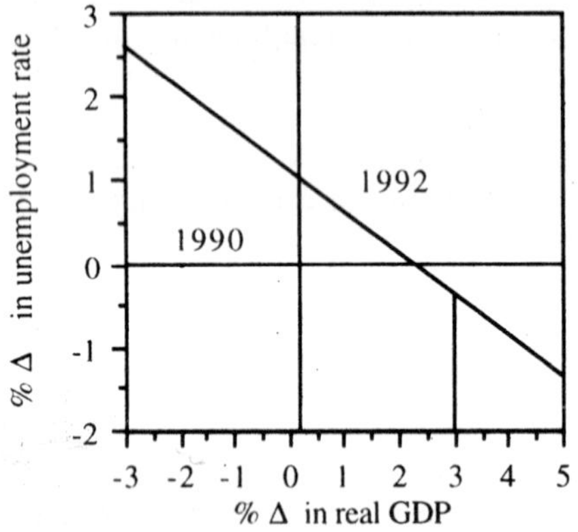

Fig. 2.1 : Okun's Law

Fig. 2.1 shows the change *(Δu)* in unemployment rate on the vertical axis and the % Δ in real *GDP* on the horizontal axis. Each point represents one year.

Ex-post and Ex-ante

An economic concept can be defined either in ex-post or ex-ante sense. Ex-ante magnitudes refer to as planned or intended or desired magnitudes. They are determined by the decisions taken by different economic units. For example, in any year, different economic units plan to save some amount. The sum total of such planned savings is the total ex-ante saving of the economy.

Ex-post concepts refer to actual magnitudes. Thus, ex-post national income refers to the actual national income of a country. Similarly, ex-post saving refers to the actual saving. Ex-post magnitudes can be measured only after they have occurred. There is, however, no guarantee that the ex-ante value of a variable will be necessarily equal to ex-post value. Thus, ex-ante saving may not be equal to ex-post saving, people may not be able to save what they plan or desire to save. If individuals succeed in realising their saving plans, i.e. when each individual saves an amount which is equal to plan saving, their ex-ante total saving will be equal to ex-post total saving. Similarly, ex-ante total investment will be equal to ex-post total investment if all the investment plans are realised. Ex-ante values are relevant for determining equilibrium values of different variables. For example, the equality of ex-ante savings and ex-ante investments determines the equilibrium level of income in the Keynesian model of income determination. Similarly, equilibrium price is determined by the equality of ex-ante demand and ex-ante supply and so on.

Equality and Identity

An equation represents a relationship between several variables which is true for some specific values of the variables but not true for all values. For example, let us consider the relation $y = 2x + 5$. It is not true for all possible values of x and y. But it is true for certain values of x and y only. An equation is characterised by "=" sign while an identity is denoted by "≡" sign. We can solve an equation and can determine the value of the variables for which the equation is satisfied. An equation represents a functional relationship. For example, suppose it is assumed that aggregate consumption depends on the level of Y of the economy. Then assume that the consumption is a linear function of income (Y). This equation can be written as $C = a + bY$ where a and b are parameters. It represents an equation and not an identity. It can be tested. But an identity cannot be tested. It is always true by definition. Hypothesis about economic behaviours can be represented by an equation. But identities cannot represent a behavioural relationship.

However, an identity is a relation between several variables which is true for all possible values. For example, when it is said that $(x - y)^2 \equiv x^2 - 2xy + y^2$ it is true for all possible values of x and y. Hence it is an identity. An identity is denoted by "≡" notation. An identity is always true by definition. An identity cannot be solved for determining the values of the variables since it is satisfied for all values of the variables. An example of an identity can be given from macroeconomics. Income be either consumed or saved. Hence total income will always be equal to the sum of total consumption and total saving. It is true for all levels of income. Thus, it is an identity. We can write identity as $Y \equiv C + S$ where Y is total income, C is total consumption and S is total savings. We cannot use this identity to determine the equilibrium level of income. An accounting relationship such as the equality between actual saving and actual investment represents an identity. An identity is a mere tautology and it explains nothing.

Static and Dynamic Analysis

When the variables involved refer to the same point in time (or period of time), then this analysis is known as static analysis. On the other hand, if the variables involved refer to different points of time (or periods of time) then this analysis is called dynamic analysis. When we say that the quantity demanded during a period of time depends on price in that period of time, then this represents a static relationship. For example, if savings of the economy during a period of time depends on the level of income of that period, then this represents a static relationship. On the other hand, if it is said that planned supply in any period depends on the price of the previous period, i.e. $x_t = F(P_{t-1})$ where x_t is planned supply in period t and P_{t-1} is the price in the previous period, then this represents a dynamic relationship.

Suppose, we are considering a *Simple Keynesian Model* of income determination, in which there are three equations : consumption is a function of income, $C = C(Y)$, then the investment function $I = \bar{I}_0$ and the equilibrium condition where Expenditure equals income : $Y = C + I$. Solving these three equations give us equilibrium values of all these variables. This analysis is a static analysis, all the variables refer to the same period of time. Further, the time element is not considered in the determination of equilibrium values of the variables. Similarly, the determination of equilibrium price by the equality of supply and demand is another example of static analysis.

Static analysis is concerned with the determination of equilibrium. However, it does not concern itself with the time it takes to reach an equilibrium or with the path to follow to reach the equilibrium. This is the concern of dynamic analysis.

The useful static analysis is known as *comparative statics*. In comparative static analysis one equilibrium position is compared with another equilibrium position. In static analysis there are several parameters which are assumed to be constant at a particular level. If any of these changes the equilibrium position will also change. When we compare one equilibrium position with another corresponding to different values of the same parameter, we call it comparative static analysis. The Keynesian multiplier analysis is an example of comparative static analysis.

In the comparative static analysis one equilibrium position is compared with another equilibrium position without analysing the process of movement. Such a process of analysis is unnecessary if the speed of adjustment is very quick. However, when the speed of adjustment is slow, we need dynamic analysis to get a complete picture of the movement from one equilibrium to another.

Dynamic analysis is necessary for the following reasons. First, dynamic analysis is necessary to consider the stability of the system. An equilibrium is known as stable if any disturbance from the equilibrium brings the system back to equilibrium again. For example, if we start from a disequilibrium position and then want to know whether the system moves towards equilibrium or not we require to analyse the time path of the relevant variable. This is known as dynamic analysis. Second, since adjustment of one variable takes time to cause a change in another variable, there are lags in many functions. The presence of these lags requires dynamic analysis. Third, there are certain variables which depend on the rate of growth of other variables. Such problems require dynamic analysis.

Stocks and Flows

Stock and flow variables are an important distinction in macroeconomics. A flow variable has a time dimension. It is always measured over a period of time. A stock variable has no time dimension. It is measured at a given point in time. The stock variable is just a number, not a rate flow of so much per period. For example, the concepts like total money supply, total bank deposits, etc. are stock concepts whereas the concepts like national income, national output, total consumptions, etc. are flow concepts. When we measure the national income we consider a period of time, namely one year. Thus national income is measured as a flow per year. Similarly, total investment, total saving, total consumption etc. are expressed as amount per year — so they are flow concepts. But the total supply of money is a stock concept which is measured on a particular point in time. Thus, flow variable must specify the period of time to which this flow refers. If we talk about the income of an individual we must mention the time period of this income flow. If we say that the individual has an income of £10,000, it is meaningless because we have not mentioned the time period. If the time period is one month, it means something — that the individual is earning £10,000 per month or £1,20,000 per year. Thus, the time period of a flow variable is very important. However, the stock variable is measured without any reference to time period. In economics we use both flow variables and stock variables and it takes a little practice to master these concepts. The main test is whether a time dimension is needed to give the variable meaning.

The distinction between stock and flow variables can be explained with the help of an example. The bathtub is a classic example used to illustrate stocks and flows. The amount of water in the tub is a stock : it is the quantity of water in the tub at a given point in time. The amount of water coming out of the tap is a flow : it is the quantity of water added to the tub per unit of time. But the units with which we measure stocks and flows differ. We say that the bathtub contains 100 gallons of water, but that water is coming out of the tub through the tap at a rate of 5 gallons per minute.

Stocks and flows are often related. In the bathtub example, these relations are clear. The stock of water in the tub represents accumulated water, and the flow of water represents the change in the stock. When developing theories to explain economic variables, it is often useful to think about whether the variables are stocks or flows and the relationships between them.

Here are more *examples of stocks and flows* that we study in macroeconomics :

1) A consumer's wealth is a stock; his income and expenditure are flows.

2) The amount of capital in an economy is a stock; the amount of investment is a flow. For example, if K_0 is the stock of capital at the beginning of a year and if K_1 is the stock of capital at the end of the year then $(K_1 - K_0) = I_0$ is the flow of investment during the year.

3) The number of unemployed people in a given year is a stock; the number gaining their employment is a flow.

4) The government debt is a stock; the budget deficit is a flow. The ratio of two flow magnitudes having the same time dimension is a pure number without any time dimension. For example, $APC = \frac{c}{y}$ is the ratio of consumption flow to income flow and is also a pure number without any time dimension. Again, the derivative of a flow with respect to another flow is also a pure

number without any time dimension. Thus, the marginal propensity to save, $MPS = \frac{\Delta S}{\Delta Y}$ has no time dimension and is a pure number.

Concept of Equilibrium

Equilibrium is a concept borrowed from mechanics where we get the idea of equilibrium system of forces. In mechanics a system of forces is said to be in equilibrium if two forces making to move the body in opposite directions are counter-balanced. Thus, an equilibrium situation is a state of rest. In economics we use the tern to mean that a single price for a product is established in a market and when no economic forces are being set up to change that price. In other words, in equilibrium, the price and quantity of a commodity match both consumers' and producers' expectations and thus there is no discrepancy between the actual and desired prices and quantities. Consequently, market is cleared and there are no involuntary holdings of unsold stocks. The equilibrium behaviours of consumers and producers — whether in a single market or in the economy as a whole — is characterised by the fact that there exists no feeling of urgency on the part of the buyers and sellers to change their behaviour.

In contrast, disequilibrium situation is one in which some buyers and sellers feel compelled to change their behaviour because forces are at work that change their circumstances. By changing their behaviour, however, they change the circumstances of other producers and consumers who may initially have been in equilibrium. A disequilibrium sets in motion a chain of adjustment and readjustment processes; for example, on the stock market, buyers and sellers change their behaviour daily in response to changing circumstances.

The economy as a whole would be in equilibrium when the planned demand for output is equal to planned supply of output. The whole economy would be in equilibrium when aggregate demand equals aggregate supply.

Equilibrium analyses are of two types: *partial equilibrium* and *general equilibrium*. In partial equilibrium analysis equilibrium is reached in one market assuming that all other things remain unchanged. However, in general equilibrium analysis, different markets of the economy are interdependent. In microeconomics, partial equilibrium analysis is generally used. But, in macroeconomics, general equilibrium analysis is usually used as in the classical or the Keynesian macroeconomic systems.

An equilibrium is a state of rest in which no economic forces are being generated to change the situation. In a market for a good, such a state of rest can be said to exist when there is neither excess demand for nor excess supply of the good.

An equilibrium is said to be a *stable equilibrium* when economic forces tend to push the market towards it, or any divergence from the equilibrium position generates forces which tend to restore the equilibrium. However, the equilibrium could be unstable when a small change in equilibrium price sends the system further and further away from equilibrium.

Production Possibility Frontier with Constant Opportunity Cost

A production possibility frontier joins together the different combinations of goods and services which a country can produce using all available resources and the most efficient techniques of production. Let us assume that a country produces only two goods: food and cloth. Fig. 2.2 shows the different combinations of these commodities which may be produced. The horizontal axis measures the quantity of cloth in metres and the vertical axis measures the quantity of food in tonnes. The line *AB* is the production possibility frontier which shows that when all resources are efficiently employed in the production of food, *OA* tonnes can be produced and when all resources are employed in the production of cloth, *OB* metre can be produced. All points over the production possibility frontier represents combination of cloth and food which can be produced when all resources are efficiently employed. All points inside the line, such as *C*, represent combinations which can be produced using less than the available resources or by using them less efficiently. Points outside the line, such as *D*, represent combinations which are unattainable.

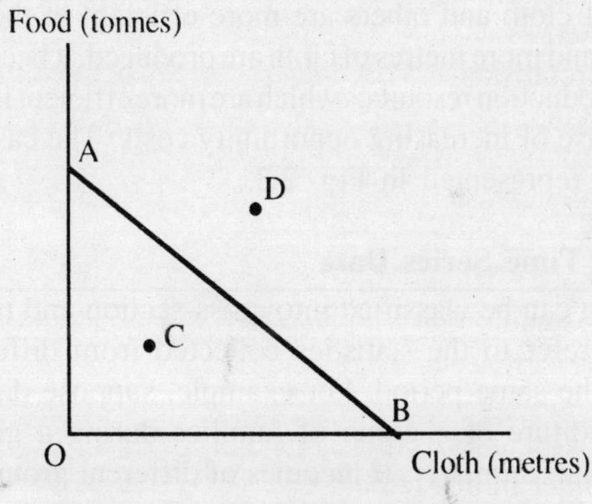

Fig. 2.2 : Production Possibility Frontier with Constant Opportunity Cost

The slope of the production possibility frontier *(OA/OB)* measures the *opportunity cost* in terms of food of producing extra 1 metre of cloth. Similarly, the slope *(OB/OA)*, measures the opportunity cost in terms of cloth of producing extra 1 tonne of food. This means that every additional metre of cloth produced requires OA/OB tonnes of food be forgone and vice versa. The slope of the production possibility curve is also known as the *marginal rate of transformation.* When the production possibility frontier is drawn as a straight line, the opportunity cost and the marginal rate of transformation remain unchanged no matter how much cloth is produced. This is called constant opportunity costs which is unrealistic. It means that all factors of production can be used equally efficiently in either the production of food or the production of cloth. It is more realistic to assume that some factors are more efficient

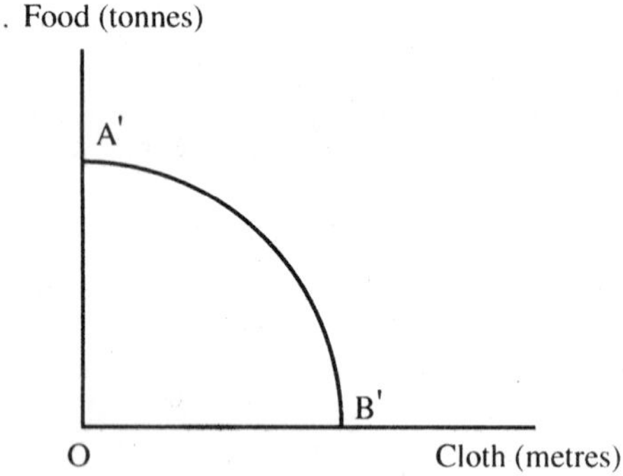

Fig. 2.3 : Production Possibility Frontier with Increasing Opportunity Cost

in the production of cloth and others are more efficient in the production of food. Thus, as more and more metres of cloth are produced, it becomes necessary to move into cloth production resources which are more efficient in the production of food. This is a case of increasing opportunity costs. The case of increasing opportunity cost is represented in Fig. 2.3.

Cross-section and Time Series Data

Economic data can be classified into cross-section and time series data. Cross-section data refer to the statistics collected from different groups of population during the same period. For example, suppose data collected on consumption expenditure of a group of families during a given year. This is a cross-section data. Similarly, if incomes of different groups are collected during a year, this will give us cross-section data. Cross-section data are useful in order to verify different functional relationships which are supposed to be invariant over time.

On the other hand, time series data is recorded with reference to time periods. The businessman is perhaps more interested in using time series data as an aid to business forecasting, particularly in areas of sales, so that in an appropriate time budget allocations may be made for investment and advertising for the year ahead. When we collect national income figures of a country for different years it represent time series data. If we are to plot a time series data in a graph we plot time(t) on the horizontal axis and the value of the variable on the vertical axis. Time series data are necessary when we are interested in the analysis of seasonal or cyclical variations. Cross-section data are more useful in order to verify functional relationships which are supposed to be invariant over time. Both types of data are useful in the study of macroeconomics. For example, consumption function hypothesis may be tested either with reference to cross-section or time-series data.

Aggregate Demand and Supply

The key concepts in macroeconomics are aggregate demand and aggregate supply. Here we provide a brief preview of these concepts and their interaction. The level of output and the price level are determined by the interaction of aggregate demand and aggregate supply. Under some conditions, employment depends only on total spending or aggregate demand. At other time, supply limitations are an important part of the policy problem and have to receive important attention.

From 1930s to the 1960s macroeconomics was very much demand determined. But in recent years the emphasis has been shifted, and aggregate supply and supply side economics have gained in importance. This shift of emphasis and interest are fostered by the slow growth and high inflation experienced in the 1970s.

What are the relationships between aggregate demand and supply, output and employment, and prices? Aggregate demand is the relationship between spending on commodities and the level of prices. When unemployment is high, increased spending — or an increase in aggregate demand — will raise output and employment with little effect on prices. For example, during the Great Depression of the 1930s, it would certainly be appropriate to use expansionary aggregate demand policies.

But if the economy is close to full employment, increased aggregate demand will be inflationary. The aggregate supply side of the economy has to be introduced. The aggregate supply curve specifies the relationship between the amount of output firms produce and the price level. The supply side not only tells us how successful demand expansions will be in raising output and employment, but it also has a role of its own. Supply shocks can reduce output and raise prices, as was the case in the 1970s when the price of oil increased sharply. Conversely, policies that increase productivity — and hence aggregate supply — can help reduce inflationary pressure.

The Unemployment Rate

One aspect of economic performance is how well an economy uses its resources. Since an economy's workers are its chief resource, keeping workers employed is a concern of policy-makers. The unemployment rate is the statistic that measures the percentage of those people who want to work but could not find any job.

Unfortunately, unemployment has been a recurring feature of Western capitalist economy and its eradication has become one of the major policy objectives.

The labour force is defined as the sum of the employed and unemployed, and the unemployment rate is defined as the per centage of the labour force unemployed.

Labour Force = Number of Employed + Number of Unemployed.

$$\text{Unemployment Rate} = \frac{\text{Number of Workers Unemployed}}{\text{Total Labour Force}} \times 100$$

A related statistic is the labour-force participation rate, the percentage of the adult population in the labour force:

$$\text{Labour-Force Participation Rate} = \frac{\text{Labour Force}}{\text{Adult Population}} \times 100$$

Natural Unemployment

Natural unemployment is defined as that which exists even when the overall demand for labour is equal to its supply at the prevailing level of real wages. Or, it is that unemployment which exists when the labour market is in equilibrium. Such unemployment persists because of frictions in the economy which prevent some workers from taking up the available jobs. Natural unemployment may be illustrated in Fig. 2.4 where DD_L is the demand curve for labour and SS_L is the supply curve of labour. The curve *EE* shows the actual number employed at different wage rates and, because of frictions in

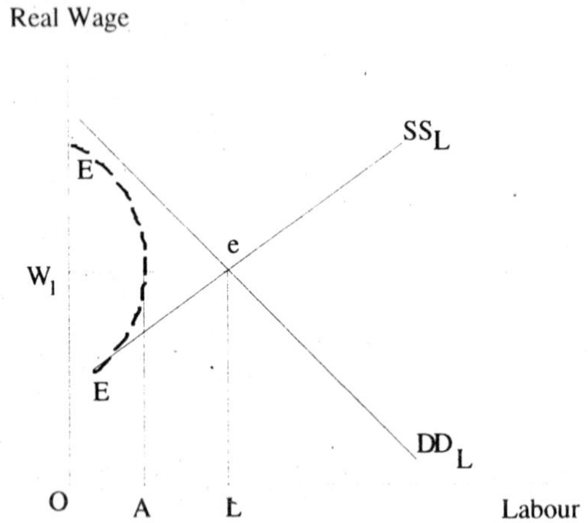

Fig. 2.4 : Natural Rate of Unemployment

the economy, actual employment always falls short of the demand for and supply of labour. At the real wage rate OW_1, the demand and supply of labour are just equal at *OL*, but actual employment is only *OA*, thus *AL* is the 'natural' unemployment.

3 NATIONAL INCOME ACCOUNTING

Definition of National Income

National income of a country means the sum total of incomes earned by the citizens of that country during a given period, say a year. It should be noted that national income is not the sum of all incomes earned by all citizens, but only those incomes which accrue due to participation in the production process.

Individuals participate in the production process by supplying factors of production which they possess. There are four *factors of production* : natural resources or land; human resources or labour; produced means of production or capital; and entrepreneurs or organisation. The payment for the use of land is called rent. Payment for the use of labour is known as wages and payment for the use of capital is known as interest. The factors of production — land, labour and capital are primary factors of production and their contractual payments are called factor incomes. The surplus — what is left after the payment of these primary factors — is called the profit. This residual income is paid to the organiser of production as profit. Thus, income for the participation in the production process may take four forms : rent, wages, interest and profit. By national income we mean the sum-total of all rent, wages, interest and profit earned in the production process during a given period by all the citizens, which is known as the factor payments total.

From this definition of national income, we exclude two types of personal income. The first is *transfer payments* and the second is *capital gains*. When a citizen receives a certain sum of money without participating in the production process it is called transfer payments. For example, the unemployment benefit, income of a beggar, etc. are personal incomes but not national income because they provide no services against their receipts. Again, when we sell out assets which has appreciated in value, and realise a gain it is known as capital gain which is excluded from the calculation of national income because it renders no productive service for reaping this gain.

Measurement Problems of National Income

Problems arise in aggregation largely because of the difficulty of finding an appropriate unit of measurement. In adding up the total output of a country, there is no single physical unit of measurement that can be used : the millions of different types of goods and services are all measured in different units, for example, steel is measured in tonnes and cloth is measured in metres and it is, of course, impossible to add tonnes to metres! The problem is partially overcome by using money as the unit of measurement—this greatly simplifies the adding up, but it gives rise to the problem of distinguishing between *real* and *nominal values*, which will be discussed in details later.

In addition, there are many problems of measuring national income of an economy. These problems may be stated as follows : *Firstly*, there is the problem of which goods and services should be included. We know that *gross domestic product (GDP)* is the money value of all goods and services currently produced within an economy involving economic activity which means transforming scarce resources to satisfy human wants. We normally include those activities which generate goods and services to be sold in the market for money. Thus, we exclude from national income accounting all personal and household services which do not pass through the market. This way of measuring is not correct because this excludes all goods that are not sold in the market. In a developing economy a substantial part of the national income (or output) is not marketed and, hence, these products are not included in the national income account.

The *second* problem is to exclude *transfer payments* and *capital gains* from national income accounts. Receipts from illegal activities should also be excluded from the national income calculation.

The *third* problem is associated with the *valuation of inventories*. The general rule is that when a firm increases its inventory of goods, this investment in inventory is counted both as past expenditure and as part of income. Thus, production of inventory increases GDP just as production for final sale does. There are mainly two methods of valuation of inventories : *the market price method* and *the cost price method*. In the market price method imputed profits are included which are unlikely to be realised in the same year. However, the cost price method does not include imputed profit. Another problem of inventory valuation is that the total quantity may remain the same, but this may not mean that each individual item remains unchanged during the year. Now, if prices are rising, the value of the new items are likely to rise faster than the value of the old items. Similarly, if prices are falling, the value of the new items are likely to fall less than that of the old items. Moreover, even if the size of the inventories remains unchanged its value is likely to change, an adjustment may be necessary to take account of the effect of price change. The adjustment is called the inventory valuation adjustment.

The *fourth* problem is imputed values of the *non-market goods, and services*. Although most goods and services are valued at their market prices when computing GDP, some are not sold in the marketplace and, therefore, do not have market prices. If GDP is to include the value of these goods and services, we must use an estimate of their value. Such an estimate is called an imputed value. One in which imputations are important is housing.

A person who rents a house is buying housing services and is providing income for the landlord; the rent is part of GDP, both as expenditure by the renter and as income of the landlord. However, many people live in their own homes. Although they do not pay rent to a landlord, they are enjoying housing services similar to those of renters. To take account of the housing services enjoyed by homeowners, GDP includes the rent that these homeowners pay to themselves. Of course, homeowners do not in fact pay themselves this rent but the market rent for a house could be imputed to be included in GDP. This imputed rent is included both in the houseowner's expenditure and in the homeowner's income.

Another area in which imputations arise is in valuing the services provided by the government. For example, law and order, fire fighters, defence, etc. provide services to the public. Measuring the value of these services is difficult because they are not sold in the marketplace and, therefore, do not have a market price. GDP includes these services by valuing them at their cost. Thus, the wages of these public servants are used as a measure of the value of their output.

In many circumstances, an imputation is called for in principle but is not made in practice. Since GDP includes the imputed rent on owner-occupied houses, one might expect it also to include the imputed rent on car, jewellery, and other durable goods owned by households. Yet the value of these services is left out of GDP. In addition, some of the output of the economy is produced and consumed at home and never enters the marketplace. For example, meals cooked at home are similar to meals cooked at a restaurant, yet the value-added in meals at home is left out of GDP.

Finally, no imputation is made for the value of goods and services sold in the underground economy. The *underground* economy is that part of the economy that people hide from the government either because they wish to evade taxation or because the activity is illegal. Since the imputations necessary for computing GDP are only approximations, and since the value of many goods and services is left out altogether, GDP is an imperfect measure of economic activity. These imperfections are most problematic when comparing standards of living across countries. The size of underground or black economy varies from country to country. So long as the magnitude of these imperfections remains fairly constant over time, GDP is useful for comparing economic activity from year to year.

Total Output, National Product, National Income and National Expenditure

The value of the economy's total output can be measured in three ways which can be seen by examining Fig. 3.1. The figure shows the flows of income and expenditure in this simple model. The two main economic agents are households and firms. The households are the owners of factors of production,

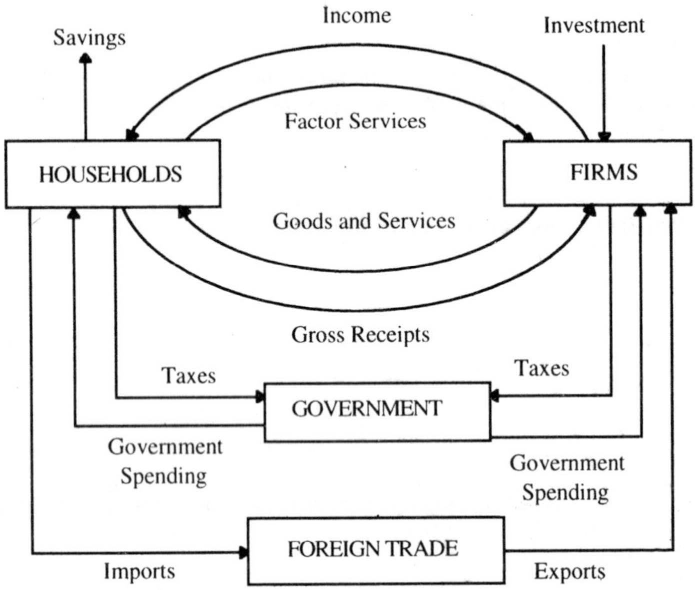

Fig. 3.1 : Extended Circular Flow

the services of which they sell to firms in exchange for income (such as rent + wages + interest + profit). We assume for simplicity that all profits to be distributed to households and not retained by the firms. The firms use the factors of production to produce many different goods and services which they sell to households, foreigners, the government and other firms and receive in return the values of goods and services they produced. The figure also shows that the part of household income which is not spent on consumption is either saved, spent on imports or is taken in taxes by the government.

The government itself uses its tax revenue (as well as money from other sources) to finance government spending, including transfer payments (such as pension, unemployment benefit and student grants and loans). Before proceeding further we want to define the terms consumption (C), investment (I) and savings (S).

Definition : *Consumption* (C): It is regarded as total expenditure by households on goods and services which yield utility in the current period.

Savings (S) are that part of the disposable income which is not spent in the current period. It follows that disposable income ($Y - T$) minus saving equals consumption.

Investment (I) is the production of or expenditure by firms on goods and services which are not for current consumption : that is, real capital goods, like factors-machines, bridges and motorways, all goods which yield a flow of consumer goods and services in future period.

There are three ways of measuring the annual value of total output in an economy — are by calculating its national product, national expenditure and national income.

National Product

This is found by adding up the value of all final goods and services produced by firms during the year. It is to be noted that all final goods and services produced must be included, whether they are to be sold to consumers or to the government, whether they are to be sold to foreigners as exports, or whether they are capital goods to be sold to other firms. It is important to include only final goods and services : all *intermediate goods* must be excluded so that *double-counting* is avoided. For example; in production of a woollen coat, only the value of the final cost should be counted. The value of the raw wool and woollen cloth are included in the value of the coat. If we were to count them as well we should be guilty of double-counting. If all intermediate goods were included in the calculation of the national product, we would seriously overestimate the value of the country's total output.

National Expenditure

This is found by adding up all the spending on the final goods and services produced by firms. Such an aggregate will only equal the value of total output if those goods which are produced but not sold are also included — this item, which is called 'net changes in stocks and work in progress', is normally counted as part of firms' investment spending. National expenditure is the sum of consumption of domestically produced goods, investment, government expenditure and exports $(C + I + G + X)$. It must be noted that, in order to avoid double-counting, only spending on final goods and services is included.

National Income

It is because goods and services are produced by factors of production that income is created in the economy, so another way of calculating the value of total output is to add up all the incomes paid out to the owners of the factors of production. Moreover, it comes to the same thing to add the values-added by all firms at the different stages of production. This may be illustrated by a simple example in which production of woollen coat involves the following three stages of production :

(a) A sheep farmer produces raw wool and sells it to a mill for *£100*. This represents an income of *£100.00* for the farmer. Value-added = *£100.00*.

(b) The mill uses the raw wool to produce cloth which it sells to a coat factory for *£210*. This represents income of *£110* for the mill — remember that *£100.00* has had to be paid for the raw wool. Value-added = *£110.00*.

(c) The coat factory produces the coat and sells it for *£400*. This includes *£210* to cover the cost of cloth and *£190* to pay incomes including profits. Value-added = *£190*.

The total *value-added* in this example *(£400.00)* is just equal to the value of the final coat; it is also equal to the sum of all incomes paid at each stage of production. The value of a country's total output can be found either by adding the values-added by all firms or by adding up the incomes (that is, wages + rents + interest + profits) of all factors of production, those producing intermediate goods as well as those producing final goods. In either case, double-counting will be avoided. It is important to exclude all transfer payments as these represent nothing more than a redistribution of income from taxpayers to the transfer recipients, including them would involve double counting.

Assuming : (a) that all measures are calculated accurately; (b) that only final goods and services are counted in the national expenditure and national product figures; (c) that any change in unsold stocks are included in the national income figures; (d) that all incomes (including profits but excluding transfer payments) are counted in the national income figures, then it must follow that all three measures will provide an identical figure for the value of national income and output. That is

National Income ≡ National Expenditure ≡ National Product

In principle, these three aggregates simply represent different ways of measuring the flow of output or income being created in an economy over a period of time.

Components of Expenditure

Economists and policymakers care not only about the economy's total output of goods and services but also about the allocation of this output among alternative uses. National income accounts allocate GDP among four broad categories : Consumption (C), Investment (I), Government expenditure (G), and Net exports $(X - M)$ or (NX).

Thus, let Y stand for *GDP*. $Y = C + I + G + X - M$ or $Y = C + I + G + NX$. Each pound of GDP is placed in one of these categories. This equations is an identity. It is called the *national income accounts identity*.

We have already defined almost all of the components of GDP except *NX*, net exports, that is, trade with other countries in an open economy. Here we will give the definition of *NX* and explain in detail about open economy later on. Net exports are the value of goods and services exported to other countries minus the value of goods and services imported from other countries. It represents the net expenditure from abroad for our goods and services, which provides income for domestic producers.

GDP versus GNP

Gross domestic product (GDP) measures the total income of everyone in the economy. But who exactly is included in this everyone? Citizens of a country working abroad? Foreigners working in the country?

To answer these questions, we should compare gross domestic product with gross national product. Distinction between them are presented below :

Gross domestic product (GDP) is the total income earned domestically. It includes income earned by foreigners domestically, but it does not include incomes earned by residents abroad.

Gross national income (GNP) is the total income earned by nationals. It includes the income that nationals earn abroad, but it does not include the income earned within a country by foreigners.

These two measures of income differ because a person can earn income and reside in different countries.

Several examples given below will explain the difference between GDP and GNP. Suppose an Indian resident comes temporarily to U.K. to work. The income he earned in U.K. is part of U.K. GDP because it is earned in U.K. But the income is not part of U.K. GNP because the worker is not a U.K. national. Similarly, if a U.K. resident works in India, his income is part of U.K. GNP, but it is not part of U.K. GDP.

For example, suppose Japanese resident owns an apartment in London. The rent he earns is part of U.K. GDP because this income is earned in U.K. But the rent is not part of U.K. GDP because the landlord is not a U.K. national. Similarly, if a U.K. resident owns a factory in India, the profit he makes is part of U.K. GNP, but it is not part of U.K. GDP.

For most purposes, the distinction between GDP and GNP is not crucial, because most people earn most of their income in their home country, GDP and GNP move closely together. U.K. policymakers have used both GNP and GDP as the primary measure of the country's income.

Other Measures of Income

The national income accounts include other measures of income that differ slightly from GDP and GNP. It is important to be aware of various measures because economists and the press often refer to them.

We like to see how the alternative measures of income relate to one another by starting with GNP and subtracting various quantities. To get net national product (NNP), we subtract the *depreciation of capital* — the amount of capital depreciates during the year : NNP = GNP − Depreciation.

Depreciation is called the consumption of fixed capital. It is about 10 per cent of GNP in many economies. Since the depreciation of capital is a cost of producing the output of the economy, subtracting depreciation shows the net result of economic activity. For this reason, some economists believe that NNP is a better measure of economic well-being.

Market Price and Factor Cost

The next adjustment in the national income accounts is for indirect taxes. Market prices are very often distorted by *indirect taxes* and *subsidies* : indirect taxes have the effect of raising the prices of goods above its costs, while subsidies lower such prices. National income and national product are both measured at *'factor costs'*. To ensure that national expenditure is also the same as the national income and national product, it is necessary to convert market prices to factor cost by adding subsidies and subtracting indirect taxes. Thus, we get national expenditure at market price, minus indirect taxes plus subsidies ≡ Net National Expenditure at factor cost.

It is preferable to measure the value of total output at factor cost rather than in Market prices so as to remove the influence of indirect taxes and subsidies.

Stock Appreciation

We know that all three measures of total output include the value of the net change in stocks of unsold goods. If prices are rising, the value of firms' stocks well rise too. To take account of this so-called 'stock appreciation', it is necessary to subtract that amount in computing the national income.

The national income accounts further divide national income into five components, depending on the way income is earned. The five categories of national income are : *Compensation of employees* — the wages and fringe benefits earned by workers. *Proprietors' income*—the income of noncorporate business, such as small firms. *Rental income* — the income that landlords receive, including the imputed rent that homeowners 'pay' to themselves, less expenses, such as depreciation. *Corporate profits*—the income of corporations after payments to their workers and creditors. *Net interest* — the interest domestic business pay minus the interest they receive, plus interest earned from foreigners. A series of adjustments takes us from national income to personal income, the amount that households and noncorporate business receive. Three of these adjustments are important. First, we reduce national income by the amount corporations earn but do not pay out, either because corporations are retaining earnings or because they are paying taxes to the government. This adjustment is made by subtracting corporate profits and adding back dividends. Second, we increase the national income by the net amount the government pays out in transfer payments. This adjustment equals government transfers to individuals minus social insurance contributions paid to the government. Third, we adjust national income to include the interest that households earn rather than the interest the businesses pay. This adjustment is made by adding *personal interest income* and subtracting *net interest*. Thus, personal income is : Personal Income = National Income – Corporate Profits – Net Interest + Dividends + Government transfers to Individuals + Personal Interest Income – Social Insurance contributions.

If we subtract personal tax payments and certain non-tax payments to the government (such as parking tickets), we obtain disposable personal income.

Personal Disposable Income = Personal Income – Personal Tax and Non-tax payments. Personal disposable income is the amount households and noncorporate business have available to spend after satisfying their tax obligations to the government.

Nominal GDP versus Real GDP

We have examined some of the rules used in constructing GDP, let us return to the question of whether GDP is a good measure of economic well-being. Consider the economy that produces only apples and oranges. In this simple economy GDP is the sum of the value of all the apples and the value of all the oranges produced. That is,

GDP = (Price of apples × Quantity of apples)
+ (Price of oranges × Quantity of oranges).

GDP can increase either because prices rise or quantities rise.

GDP computed in this way is not a good measure of economic well-being. That is, it does not accurately reflect how well the economy can satisfy the demands of households, firms and the government. If all prices double without any change in quantities, GDP would double. Yet it would be misleading to say that the economy's ability to satisfy demands has doubled, because the quantity of every good produced remains unchanged. We call the value of goods and services measured at current prices *nominal GDP*.

A better measure of economic well-being would be the economy's output of goods and services that would not be influenced by changes in prices. For this purpose, economists use *real GDP*, which is the value of goods and services measured at constant prices. To compute real GDP, a base year is chosen —say, 1992. Goods and services are then added up using 1992 prices to value the different goods. In our two-goods economy, real GDP for 1996 would be

Real GDP = (1992 prices of apples × 1996 Quantity of apples)
+ (1992 prices of oranges × 1996 Quantity of oranges).

Similarly, real GDP in 1997 would be

Real GDP = (1992 prices of apples × 1997 Quantity of apples)
+ (1992 prices of oranges × 1997 Quantity of oranges).

Because the prices are held constant, real GDP varies from year to year only if the quantities vary. Thus, real GDP summarises the output of the economy measured in base-year (1992). Because the ability of the society to provide satisfaction for its members depends on the quantities of goods and services produced, real GDP provides a better measure of economic well-being than nominal GDP.

GDP Deflator

From nominal GDP and real GDP we can compute the GDP deflator. The GDP deflator is defined as : $GDP\ deflator = \dfrac{Nominal\ GDP}{Real\ GDP}$. The GDP deflator is the ratio of nominal GDP to real GDP.

To understand better nominal GDP, real GDP, and the GDP deflator, consider an economy with only one good, bread. In any year, nominal GDP is the amount of sterling spent on bread in that year. Real GDP is the number of loaves of bread produced in that year times the price of bread in some base year. The GDP deflator is the price of bread in that year relative to the price of bread in the base year.

Actual economies produce many goods. Nominal GDP, Real GDP, and the GDP deflator aggregate the many different prices and quantities. For simplicity, consider an economy with two goods — apples and oranges. Let P denote the price of a good, Q the quantity, and a superscript "92" the base year 1992; then the GDP deflator would be :

$$GDP\ deflator = \frac{\left(P_{apples} \times Q_{apples}\right) + \left(P_{oranges} \times Q_{oranges}\right)}{\left(P^{92}_{apples} \times Q_{apples}\right) + \left(P^{92}_{oranges} \times Q_{oranges}\right)}$$

The numerator is nominal GDP, and the denominator is real GDP. Both nominal GDP and real GDP can be viewed as the price of a basket of goods; in this case, the basket consists of the quantities of apples and oranges. The GDP deflator compares the current price of this basket to the price of the same basket in the base year.

The definition of the GDP deflator allows us to separate nominal GDP in two parts : one part measures quantities and the other measures prices.

That is, Nominal GDP = Real GDP × GDP Deflator.

Nominal GDP measures the pound value of the output of the economy. Real GDP measures the amount of output — that is, output valued at constant (base-year) prices. The GDP deflator measures the price of the typical unit of output relative to its price in the base year.

Comparing Nominal National Income and Real National Income per capita

	1992	1996
Nominal National Income (N.I.)	£*12* million	£*24* million
Price Index	*100*	*120*
Real National Income (1992 price)	£*12* million	£*20* million $\left(\frac{100}{120} \times 24\right)$
Population	*3,000*	*4,000*
Real Per capita N.I.	*4,000*	*5,000*

The first step in our analysis is to calculate national income at constant (1992) prices or to deflate by GDP deflator to eliminate the effect of prices. As 1992 is the base year, the nominal and real national incomes are the same in that year. In 1996, though, the price index is *120* — which means part of the increase in national income is a result of the rise in prices and another part is a result of the rise in physical output. The rise in prices is eliminated by dividing nominal national income by the GDP deflator which is known as deflating the nominal national income to get the real national income. We can see from the deflated figures that real national income (or GDP) has increased by $66\frac{2}{3}$ per cent during the period and not by 100 per cent as the nominal income shows. The next step is to consider the increased size of population because, although real national income has risen, it has to be shared out among increasing population. Dividing the real national income by population, we get *'real per capita national income'* of £*4,000* in 1992 and £*5,000* in 1996, an increase of *25* per cent. In this example, we see, although nominal national income rose by *100* per cent, real national income per capita rose by only *25* per cent. We can conclude that an increase in nominal national income will be equivalent to an increase in real national income per capita if both prices and population do not change. Since prices and populations do change over time, it is important to compare real national income per capita rather than nominal national income, before concluding about whether or not economy is growing and economic welfare is changing with it.

Measuring the Cost of Living : Consumer Price Index

A pound today does not buy as much as it did 20 years ago. The cost of almost everything has gone up. This increase in the overall level of prices is called inflation. In later chapters we examine in detail the causes and effects of inflation. Here we discuss how economists measure changes in the *cost of living.*

Consumer Price Index (C.P.I.)

The most commonly used measure of the level of prices is the *consumer price index (CPI).* The Department of Employment has the job of computing the CPI or *Retail Price Index* (RPI). It begins lay collecting the prices of thousands of goods and services. Just as GDP turns the quantities of many goods and services into a single number measuring the value of production, the CPI or RPI turns the prices of many goods and services into a single index measuring the overall level of prices.

How should we aggregate the many prices in the economy into a single index that reliably measures the price level? We could compute an average of all prices. Yet this approach would treat all goods and services equally. Since people consume more bread then chicken, the price of bread should have a greater weight in the CPI or RPI than the price of chicken. The Department of Employment Statistics weighs different items by computing the price of a basket of goods and services purchased by a typical consumer. The CPI or RPI is the price of this basket of goods and services relative to the price of the same basket in some base year.

For example, suppose that the typical consumer buys 5 apples and 2 oranges every month. That is, the basket of goods consists of 5 apples and 2 oranges. The CPI or RPI is :

$$CPI\ \ or\ RPI = \frac{(5 \times Current\ Price\ of\ apples) + (2 \times Current\ Price\ of\ oranges)}{(5 \times 1992\ Price\ of\ apples) + (2 \times 1992\ Price\ of\ oranges)}$$

In this CPI or RPI, 1992 is the base year. The index tells us how much it costs now to buy 5 apples and 2 oranges relative to how much it cost to buy the same basket in 1992.

The CPI or RPI is the most closely watched index of prices, but it is not the only index. Another is the producer price index, which measures the price of a typical basket of goods bought by firms rather than consumers. In addition to these overall price indexes, the Department of Employment computes price indexes for specific types of goods, such as food, housing and energy.

CPI or RPI and the GDP Deflator

We have already discussed another measure of prices — the implicit price deflator for GDP, which is the ratio of nominal GDP to real GDP. The GDP deflator and the CPI give somewhat different information about the overall level of prices in the economy. There are three key differences between the two measures :

The first difference is that the GDP deflator measures the prices of all goods and services produced, whereas the CPI or RPI measures the prices of only the goods and services bought by consumers. Thus, an increase in the price of goods bought by firms or the government will show up in the GDP deflator but not in the CPI or RPI.

The second difference is that the GDP deflator includes only those goods produced domestically. Imported goods are not part of GDP and do not show up in the GDP deflator. For example, an increase in the price of Toyota made in Japan and sold in the U.K. affects the CPI or RPI, because the Toyota is bought by consumers in the U.K., but it does not affect the GDP deflator.

The third difference concerns how the two measures aggregate the many prices in the economy. The CPI or RPI assigns fixed weights to the prices of different goods, whereas the GDP deflator assigns changing weights. In other words, the CPI or RPI is computed using a fixed basket of goods, whereas the GDP deflator allows the basket of goods to change over time as the composition of GDP changes. To see how this works, consider an economy that produces and consumes only apples and oranges.

The GDP deflator is :

$$GDP\ deflator = \frac{Nominal\ GDP}{Real\ GDP}$$

$$= \frac{\left(P_{apples} \times Q_{apples}\right) + \left(P_{oranges} \times Q_{oranges}\right)}{\left(P^{92}_{apples} \times Q_{apples}\right) + \left(P^{92}_{oranges} \times Q_{oranges}\right)}$$

$$The\ CPI\ or\ RPI\ is: \quad \frac{CPI}{RPI} = \frac{\left(P_{apples} \times Q^{92}_{apples}\right) + \left(P_{oranges} \times Q^{92}_{oranges}\right)}{\left(P^{92}_{apples} \times Q^{92}_{apples}\right) + \left(P^{92}_{oranges} \times Q^{92}_{oranges}\right)}$$

These equations show that both the CPI and the GDP deflator compare the cost of a basket of goods today with the cost of that same basket in the base year. The difference between the two measures is whether the basket changes over time. The CPI uses a fixed basket, whereas the GDP deflator uses a changing basket. The following example shows how these approaches differ. Suppose that major frosts destroy the nation's orange crop : the quantity of oranges produced falls to zero, and the price of the few oranges that remain is driven sky-high. Because oranges are no longer part of GDP, the increase in the price of oranges does not show up in the GDP deflator. But the CPI is computed with a fixed basket of goods that includes oranges, so the increases in the price of oranges causes a substantial rise in the CPI. A price index with a fixed basket of goods is called a *Laspeyres index* and a price index with a changing basket is called *Paasche index.* Economists have studied the properties of these different types of price indexes to determine which is better. The answer is that neither is clearly superior.

The purpose of any price index is to measure the cost of living — that is, how much it costs to maintain a given standard of living. When prices of different goods are changing by different amounts, a Laspeyres index tends to overstate the increase in the cost of living, whereas a Paasche index tends to understate it. A Laspeyres index uses a fixed basket and thus does not consider that consumers have the opportunity to substitute less expensive goods for more expensive ones. Conversely, a Paasche index accounts for the substitution of alternative goods, but it does not reflect the reduction in consumers' welfares that may result from such substitutions.

For example, the CPI is a Laspeyres index, it overstates the impact of the increase in orange prices on consumers : by using a fixed basket of goods, it ignores consumers' ability to substitute apples for oranges. By contrast, the GDP deflator is a Paasche index, it understates the impact on consumers : the GDP deflator shows no rise in prices, yet surely the high price of orange makes consumers worse off.

Estimation of National Income in the Presence of Government Activities

The government undertakes several economic activities in a mixed economy. The government is engaged in mainly four types of economic activities which should be constituted while calculating the national income of a country. *Firstly*, the government may be engaged in the production of goods and services which are sold in a market like private firms. For example, transport, utility services, etc.

Secondly, the government provides certain services free of charge to the public which are not sold in the market. For example, law and order, defence, education, etc.

Thirdly, the government imposes *taxes* and grants *subsidies*. The taxes may be *direct taxes* and *indirect taxes*. Direct taxes are those taxes which are imposed on personal and corporate incomes. On the other hand, indirect taxes are taxes imposed on commodities.

Fourthly, the government also makes transfer payments to the public and grants subsidies to firms. Transfer payments are those payments against which no services are rendered. For example, pensions, unemployment benefit, child benefit, etc.

Let us now examine how these activities can be incorporated in the national income account. The first type of activity poses no problem because the public sector firms can be treated as a private firm. The ownership of an enterprise is irrelevant when considering its contribution to the national product. Thus, a public enterprise could be treated in the same way as a private enterprise. Therefore, the final product produced by public enterprises or the values-added by them should be included in the national product. Or, factor incomes generated in public sector undertakings should be included in the national income total.

The second type of activity by the government creates two problems when calculating national income accounting. One problem is the conceptual problem regarding whether or not these services should be treated as final products or as intermediate products. The other problem is the problem of valuation — since these services are not sold in the market, they have no market price.

The conceptual problem can be dealt with as follows : Now the question is whether these services — the maintenance of law and order and defence — are to be regarded as services which satisfy the wants of the consumers directly, or are they to be regarded as facilitating the production of other goods and services? If we accept the first proposition then it becomes a final product and should be included in the national production. On the other hand, if we accept the second proposition then it becomes an intermediate goods and should not be included in the national product to avoid double counting. Now there are reasons to believe that such services are to be regarded as partly satisfying one and partly the other. It is true that part of the services provided by the government are directed to protect the life and liberty of individuals while

part of them are directed towards the protection of the productive process. However, it is impossible to make a dividing line between these two and, hence, the entire common services are to be treated as final products. Thus, the value of these services should be included in the national product.
How can the value of such services be determined? This brings us to the valuation problem. These services are not offered for sale in the market. Therefore, there is no market price for such services. Hence, such services cannot be valued on the basis of market prices. To solve the valuation problem of such services, we must take into account the cost of providing these services and include items in the national product. Alternatively, the factor incomes paid to the persons who provide these services should be included in the national income total. The value of the government services can be obtained by subtracting transfer payments from the total government expenditure.

Thus taking into consideration the government activity we get the following identities :

GDP ≡ Gross value of output of the private sector + Gross value added by private enterprises + value of public sector's common services.

GDE ≡ Consumption expenditure on domestically produced good + investment expenditure + public sector expenditure on common services.

GDI ≡ (wage bill of public and private sectors) + (rents paid by public sector and private sector) + (gross profit of private enterprises and gross profit of public sector enterprises) + (interest received by both sectors).

Let us examine other two items and the problems arise as a result of transfer payments and imposition of taxes. Taxes are of two types : *direct taxes* and *indirect taxes*. Direct taxes are imposed on personal and corporate incomes while indirect taxes are imposed on commodities. In the case of transfer payments people receive income from the government without rendering any service. Again, direct taxes are paid by people to the government without receiving any service in return. Thus, direct taxes and transfer payments are similar in nature and transfer payments can be regarded as negative direct taxes. Both these items do not affect the computation of national income.

However, transfer payments and direct taxes cause personal incomes and personal disposable incomes to differ from national income : Personal income ≡ national income + transfer receipts while personal disposable income ≡ personal income – direct taxes ≡ national income + transfer receipts – direct taxes.

However, indirect taxes and subsidies do pose some problems. Indirect taxes and subsidies given on commodities create distortion on market price and cost price. Thus, we get the following relations : Market price ≡ factor cost + (indirect taxes – subsidies) ≡ factor cost + net indirect taxes.

The government also *borrows money* from the public by issuing bonds and the government makes interest payments to the bond-holders. Interest on public debt is considered as a transfer payment and, hence, is not included in national income total.

National Income Estimate in an open Economy

As in a closed economy, in an open economy also we can look at the national income from three sides — the production side, the income side and the expenditure side. Let us first consider the expenditure side of the national income account. Gross National Expenditure (GNE) at market prices ≡ Consumption (C) + Gross Investment + government expenditure on goods and services ≡ $C + I + G$. Now expenditure on home produced goods and services by foreigners must also be included in gross national expenditure. If X stands for exports, then the value of X must be added to $C + I + G$. Again, some part of $C + I + G$ is not spent on domestically produced goods and services but on goods and services produced by foreigners. Such expenditure is equal to the value of imports (M).

Hence the value of imports must be deducted from $C + I + G$. If M stands for the value of imports then we have $GNE \equiv C + I + G + X - M$ or $C + I + G + NX$ where NX means net exports. Now let us consider the output side of the national income. On the output side the value of the national product is equal to the sum total of values added by all the productive units of the economy. We know that production takes place only in firms. For a single firm, value added = total sales (including exports) minus purchases from other firms (including imports). If we take the sum of the value added by all firms we get total value added by all firms ≡ sales to households + sales to enterprises + sales to government + sales to foreigners – purchase from foreigners. Thus we get $GNP \equiv C + I + G + X - M$.

Let us now consider the income side. By income we mean income originated as a result of participation in the production process. Now in an open economy foreigners participate in the domestic production process. Foreign capital is also employed in the domestic production process. Similarly, domestic residents may participate in the production process outside the country and domestic capital may be employed in the foreign production process. In this way a part of the income produced within the economy is earned by foreigners and a part of the income produced outside the country is earned by domestic residents. Taking these two items we get net income from abroad. Thus, net income from abroad ≡ income receipts from abroad – income paid to foreigners. This is a part of the national income, though this part does not arise out of production within the domestic economy.

In an open economy a distinction is made between gross domestic product and gross national product. In a close economy, gross domestic product (GDP) is equal to gross national product (GNP). But in an open economy some adjustments are necessary for conversion of the gross domestic product into gross national product. In an open economy, gross national product (GNP) is equal to gross domestic product (GDP) plus net income from abroad. Moreover, in an open economy net domestic product is equal to gross domestic product minus depreciation. Net national income in an open economy is equal to net domestic produces plus net income from abroad.

GNP ≡ GNI ≡ GNE. These identity between them is preserved even in an open economy.

National Income Identities

It can be seen from national income accounting that actual saving *(S)* of an economy is equal to actual investment *(I)* during a give period of time. This is called the *accounting identity* between saving *(S)* and investment *(I)*.

We denote the value of output (GDP) in a simple economy, without a government and foreign trade, by Y. Consumption expenditure is denoted by C and investment spending as I. The first key identity is that output produced and output sold. Output sold can be written as the sum of consumption and investment spending. Thus, we can write the identity of output produced and output sold : $Y \equiv C + I$........ (1)

It is an identity because all output produced is either consumed or invested including the accumulation of inventories as part of investment.

The next step is to find a relation among saving, consumption and output. All output produced in the economy will go to private individuals as income, Y. This income will either be spent on consumption or saved. Thus we can write : $Y \equiv C + S$ .... (2) when S is private saving. Identity (2) tells us that the whole income is allocated to read : $C + I \equiv Y \equiv C + S$..........(3) where the left hand side shows the components of demand, and the right-hand side shows the allocation of income. This identity shows that output produced is equal to output sold. The value of output produced is equal to income received which is spent on goods or saved. Identity (3) can be slightly reformulated to let it look like saving and investment relation. $I \equiv Y - C \equiv S$ .... (4). This gives the simple economy identity between saving and investment and that some of the investment might well be inventory investment. We now complicate the economy by introducing government and foreign trade. In such an economy, the $GNP \equiv Y \equiv C + I + G + X - M$..............(5). Again, from the $GNI \equiv C + S + T + T_R$ ....(6), where T_R is transfer payments and T is tax payment. Since $GNP \equiv GNI$ .....(7). From identity (7) we get $C + I + G + NX \equiv C + S + T + T_R$ .... (8)

or, $I + G + NX \equiv S + T + T_R$

The left-hand side of the identity (8) represents total output not going to consumption expenditure while the right-hand side gives the total income that is not spent. If we identify non-consumed output as investment and income not going to consumption as saving, then the above identity can be regarded as a *saving-investment identity*.

If we assume that it is a closed economy, then *(X – M)* or *NX* is dropped and the above identity can then be written as : $I + G \equiv S + T + T_R$ ....(9)

or, $I \equiv S + (T - G + T_R)$ .... (10)

This represents another version of saving-investment identity. The left-hand side of identity (10) represents private investment. The first term on the right hand side of identity (10) represents private saving and the second term, $(T - G + T_R)$ is government saving.

Finally, if there is no government activity then the term $(T - G + T_R)$ will disappear and the above identity becomes $I \equiv S$. This represents saving-investment identity of the simple one sector model of the economy.

It would be noted that saving-investment identity is a definitional identity which follows from the definition of saving and investment. This identity has nothing to do with the equilibrium in the economy. Whether the level of income is in equilibrium or not, aggregate actual investment is always identically equal to aggregate actual saving.

National Income and Economic Welfare

The GNP are generally used for two purposes : one is to indicate the level of economic well-being of the people and the other is to measure the level of economic activities of the nation. When GNP (or the output of final goods and services by the country in a year) of a country is taken as an index of economic well-being of the people, it is suggested that the market price of the product should be used as a measure of the benefit derived by the people from the consumption of the product. If GNP is supposed to indicate the level of utilisation of scarce resources, the cost price should be the basis of evaluation. In a competitive equilibrium, the two evaluations are identical, since the market price happens to be equal to the cost price. In the presence of a monopolistic control over the market, the market price is higher than the cost price. The GNP measurement for the purpose of evaluating the welfare level should be done at the market price, while an evaluation of the level of economic activity should be done at the cost price. However, there are several reasons for which the GNP cannot be considered as good index of economic welfare.

Firstly, the GNP considers only market transactions, whereas welfare depends on both *market and non-market transactions*. In less-developed economies, non-market transactions occupy a substantial part, thus, the GNP fails to give a true indicator of the welfare of the people in these countries.

Secondly, the GNP does not consider the *social cost* associated with production. Some negative externalities are likely to arise as output expands and these factors will tend to offset the effects of any increase in average income. So, although consumers may on average be better-off so far as their spending power is concerned, they may be worse-off overall when environmental factors are taken into consideration. For example, consider the building of a large chemical factory in the heart of the countryside, the extra production may increase real output per capita, but the factory will pollute the air and water and cause severe visual pollution in an area of natural beauty. If these external costs offset the increase in real output per capita, then any overall improvement in economic welfare would only be apparent and not real.

The some argument applies if output has been increased only through the work-force taking fewer hours of leisure and putting more hours of work. Again, the improvement in welfare resulting from increased spending power may be offset by a reduction in welfare resulting from loss of leisure. Overall, there may be no real improvement in welfare.

Thirdly, if the rise in real output per capita is caused by an expansion of investment goods industries and public sector expenditure on civil servants, while at the same time there is a decline in consumer goods industries, the current economic welfare may fall rather than rise. The simple reason for this is that economic welfare stems from the consumption activity.

Fourthly, the GNP does not include *unpaid services* rendered by the members of the household but such unpaid services also increase the level of welfare.

Fifthly, welfare also depends on the *distribution of income*. The Pareto condition of welfare states that economic welfares will increase if at least one consumer is made better-off without at the same time any other being made worse-off. Adopting this condition, we can interpret an increase in real output per capita as an actual improvement in economic welfare if no distributional changes occur which may make any individuals or groups worse-off.

Unfortunately, increases in real output per capita often do leave some people or groups of individuals in society worse off. For example, suppose that there were a big new discovery of a fuel, like oil, whose production will increase a country's real national income. An unfavourable side-effect of this may be a reduction in demand for some other fuel, like coal. Some coal-workers may lose their jobs or be put on short-time. These people will have been made worse-off by the oil discovery which, on average, increased real output per capita, making many other people better-off. By applying the P*areto condition*, we cannot say that the oil discovery improves actual economic welfare. In cases like this we can apply Hicks-Kaldor condition for a potential improvement. According to the *Hicks-Kaldor criterion*, if any change occurs which redistributes income in such a way that the gainers can potentially compensate the losers and still be better-off than they were before, then we can say that potential economic welfare has increased. However, we can interpret the situation as actual improvement if full compensation were actually paid.

From the above analysis it is clear that the GNP cannot be used as an index of actual economic welfare. The GNP should, however, be used to measure changes in the level of economic activity. It should not be used to judge the quality of life or the level of welfare.

Other Uses of National Income Account

We can conclude from the analysis of the previous section that a change in national income can only be used as an indicator, and not as an accurate measure, of a change in economic welfare. There are other uses of the national income statistics that we wish to mention.

Making International Comparisons

Care must be taken in using real output per capita figures to compare different countrys' standard of living. First, a further adjustment is necessary to convert the figures to the same currency using the rate of exchange. This poses problems because the market rate of exchange is not necessarily the ideal measure of the relative values of the goods and services consumed in each country. Secondly, different countries have different needs and tastes which cannot be easily taken into account in making comparisons.

Government Planning

There is a close connection, at least in the short-run, between real national income and the level of employment in the economy. A rise in the national income with a fairly constant *Capital Stock* will generally be associated with a fall in unemployment. Since governments have "*full employment*" as one of their major policy objectives, it is important for them to have an accurate national income statistics. A rising national income in the long-run is called economic growth and this is another important policy objective of governments. We can, therefore, conclude that the national income figures play an important role in the planning of both *short run and long run government policies.*

The Equilibrium Level of National Income

In the microeconomics market for a single good, an equilibrium is said to exist when the demand for the goods is equal to the supply of it. Similarly, in macroeconomics, the *equilibrium level* of national income has been reached when there are no economic forces operating to change the level of national income. This occurs when the total demand (aggregate demand) is equal to total supply (aggregate supply). That is, for equilibrium level of income to be achieved, we require that :

(AD) Aggregate Demand = Aggregate Supply (AS)

Only when this condition is satisfied we can say that the total value of goods and services that households and the other economic agents want to buy is equal to the total value that firms want to produce. It may, however, be noted that AS cannot strictly be regarded as being the same as national income. National income is the value of the actual amount produced and is equal to the national product and expenditure. AS is the amount that firms want to produce given the general level of wages and prices. The two will only be equal : (a) if wages and prices are such that firms plan to product what is currently being produced; and (b) if firms are able to implement their production plans successfully.

Conclusion

Here we introduce the notion of national income accounting and the equivalent of national product, expenditure and product demonstrated. We highlighted the problems of using national income as an indicator of economic welfare. Finally, we considered the meaning of an equilibrium in macroeconomics.

The determination of the equilibrium level of national income is of crucial importance in macroeconomic analysis because it is this which determines to a large extent the level of employment in the economy. It is the debate about the forces which determine this equilibrium which fundamentally separates the various schools of thought in macroeconomics.

Exercise

1. The following data show the GNP figures, price indices and population for an hypothetical economy in 1988 and 1991:

	1988	1991
GNI	£ 5,000 m	£ 10,000 m
Price Index (1985 = 100)	120	160
Population	10 m	12 m

   (a) Calculate real national income in both years.
   (b) Find real national income per capita in both years.
   (c) Comment on the change in potential economic welfare. What other data would be useful in determining the change in economic welfare?

2. Use the following data to compute national income (that is, NNP at factor cost) :

Value of physical increase in stocks and work-in-progress	£ 500 m
Imports of goods and services	£ 30,000 m
Government expenditure on goods and services	£ 20,000 m
Gross domestic fixed capital formation	£ 16,000 m
Exports of goods and services	£ 28,000 m
Depreciation	£ 10,000 m
Taxes on expenditure	£ 15,000 m
Net property income from abroad	£ 1,000 m
Consumer expenditure	£ 70,000 m
Subsidies	£ 300 m

3. A country used to export 80 million tonnes of pig iron per annum at the rate of £ 1,000 per tonne and to import 50 million tonnes of steel per annum at the rate of £ 2,000 per tonne. The setting up of the steel

industry in the country under protection leads to a decrease in export of pig iron by 40 million tonnes per annum whereby steel import could be reduced to 30 million tonnes per annum. The international prices of both commodities remain unchanged. Estimate the amount of value-added per annum by the domestic steel industry.

4. The following discussion deals with GNP, GDP and NDP :
   (a) In 1993, U.K. GDP was £657 billion; GNP was £650 billion. Why is there a difference?
   (b) In 1993, U.K. GDP was £657 billion; NDP was £505 billion. What accounts for the difference?

5. The following information is taken from the national income accounts for a hypothetical economy :

GDP	£ 600 billion
Gross investment	£ 80 billion
Net investment	£ 20 billion
Consumption	£ 400 billion
Government purchases on goods and services	£ 110 billion
Government budget surplus	£ 10 billion

What is: (a) NDP
(b) Net exports
(c) Government tax revenue
(d) Personal saving
(e) Disposable income?

4 EQUILIBRIUM IN THE GOODS SECTOR

Equilibrium Condition for Income Determination

Equilibrium is the state of rest of a thing. In Economics we use the term to mean the 'state of no change' of economic variables which are determined by opposite forces of social behaviour. As, output (or *GNP*) takes an equilibrium value when the quantity of output produced is equal to the quantity demanded. The value of the *GNP* is the aggregate output which is supplied into the market by all producers taken together. How much output is to be produced dependeds on the aggregate demand for output. If the *GNP* exceeds the aggregate demand, all producers cannot sell their output; unsold stock accumulates, and, as a consequence, production is curtailed to bring the aggregate supply down to the level of the aggregate demand. Conversely, if the output falls short of

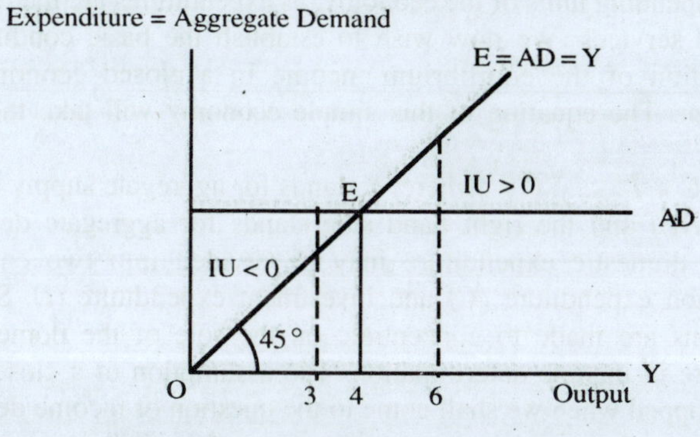

Fig. 4.1 : Equilibrium in the economy

the aggregate demand, stocks would be exhausted; as a result more output would be produced to push the value of the output to the level of the aggregate demand. So, it is the aggregate demand that determines the equilibrium output in the economy. Fig. 4.1 illustrates the equilibrium in an economy. In Fig. 4.1, we show the level of output on the horizontal axis and aggregate demand (or expenditure) on the vertical axis. The 45° line shows the equality between the level of aggregate demand and output *(Y)*. At point *E*, both aggregate demand and output are equal to 4 billion. Point *E* is thus the point of equilibrium output, at which the quantity of output produced is exactly equal to the quantity demanded. If firms were producing more than 4 units, say 6 units, then output would exceed demand. Firms would not be able to sell all they produced. They would then cut their output. Similarly, if output were less than 4 units, say 3 units, there would be shortage of output. They would, therefore, increase output. Thus, the point E is the equilibrium point, firms are selling all they are producing, people are buying all they want to buy, and there is no tendency for the level of output to change. At any other level of output pressure would be generated to change the level of output. The disequilibrium can be eliminated either if output changes or if people's demand for output changes or by a combination of the two. For the moment we shall assume that a disequilibrium will result in a change in output. This assumption implies the existence of unemployed resources in the economy and ignores the whole question of how the excess supply or demand is translated into a change in output. If no mechanism exists even then output can change, given the constraints facing the economy. It will not change if there is a lack of a signalling device and incentive to induce producers to change their behaviour. With this assumption the disequilibrium will result in an increase in output when there is an excess demand, and a decrease in output when there is an excess supply.

The value of the aggregate demand is nothing but aggregate expenditure (E) of all spending units of the economy, as expenditures are made for buying goods and services. We now wish to establish the basic condition for the determination of the equilibrium income in a closed economy without government. The equation of this simple economy will take the following form :

$Y = C + I$ .... (1) where, Y stands for aggregate supply of domestic output *(GNP)* and the right hand side stands for aggregate demand. This aggregate domestic expenditure may be divided into two categories — consumption expenditure (C) and investment expenditure (I). Such simple assumptions are made to concentrate on the role of the domestic private expenditure in income determination. The assumption of a closed economy will be dropped when we shall come to the question of income determination in an open economy, and the government expenditure will be introduced when we shall examine the role of the government budget in income determination.

In this chapter, we deal with a closed economy without government, and, thus, we use the simple equation, $Y = C + I$, as the basic equilibrium condition in our analysis. Alternatively, we can state the simple equilibrium condition with the help of Aggregate Saving (S) Concept, defined as the difference between income (Y) and consumption expenditure (i.e., $S = Y - C$). Equilibrium condition may be written as : $S = I$ .... (2)

Equations (1) and (2) can be written as : $Y = C + I$ or, $Y = C + S$

i.e., $C + I = C + S$. If we deduct C from both sides of the equation,

$$C + I - C = C + S - C \qquad \therefore \; I = S$$

Thus, we get equation (2) from equation (1). The supply of new capital, S, and the demand for new capital, I, are equal.

In interpreting equation (2) as an equilibrium condition, we must distinguish it from the saving-investment identity that always holds good for any period. The amount of saving that has already been made in any period which is identically equal to amount of investment that has actually been made in the same period. The reason being that investment includes inventory accumulation. Any discrepancy between consumption and production automatically leads to a change in the accumulation of inventory. The saving-investment identity denotes realised saving and realised investment. The equilibrium condition is the equality between planned saving and planned investment. Equation (2) requires the conformity between plan saving and plan investment made independently of each other by different groups of people on the basis of two separate sets of factors.

Income Determination in the Simple Keynesian Model

In the simple closed economy model without government, the aggregate demand for output, derived from aggregate expenditure, has two parts — the consumption expenditure and the investment expenditure. We assume that the consumption expenditure is a linear function of income and investment expenditure is given autonomously. The model is represented by the following two equations : (3) $C = a + bY$ and (4) $\bar{I} = A$, a positive constant. The consumption function is such that the marginal propensity to consume *(mpc)* is given by $\frac{\Delta C}{\Delta Y} = b$, *where* b is a positive function lying between *0* and *1*. The aggregate demand as a function of income is given by $a + b(Y) + \bar{I}$. Income attains the equilibrium value, when the following condition is satisfied :

(5) $Y = a + b\,(Y) + \bar{I}$

Alternatively, we can derive the saving function from the consumption function and use the *equation* $S = I$ as the condition for equilibrium. The model may be written as :

(6) $S = S(Y)$ or, $S = -a + (1 - b)Y$

(7) $I =$ a positive constant

(8) $S(Y) = \bar{I}$ or, $-a + (1 - b)Y = \bar{I}$

The saving function is derived from the consumption function in the following way :

$S = Y - C = Y - (a + bY)$ $\therefore$ $S = -a + (1 - b)Y$, where the marginal propensity to save : $\frac{\Delta S}{\Delta Y} = (1 - mpc) = (1 - b)$

Solving either equation (5) or equation (8) for Y, we get the value of equilibrium income. For a graphic solution of equation (5) the consumption function is at first plotted in the graph and then the constant amount of investment expenditure is added to it to produce the aggregate demand curve.

In Fig. 4.2, the $a + bY$ is the consumption function and $a + bY + \bar{I}$ curve is the aggregate demand function. The $a + bY + \bar{I}$ curve is parallel to the consumption function, as the vertical distance between the two curves stands for the constant amount of the autonomously given investment expenditure. Then, a 45° line is drawn from the origin as OE which gives the equality between income (Y) and the aggregate expenditure. The point of intersection

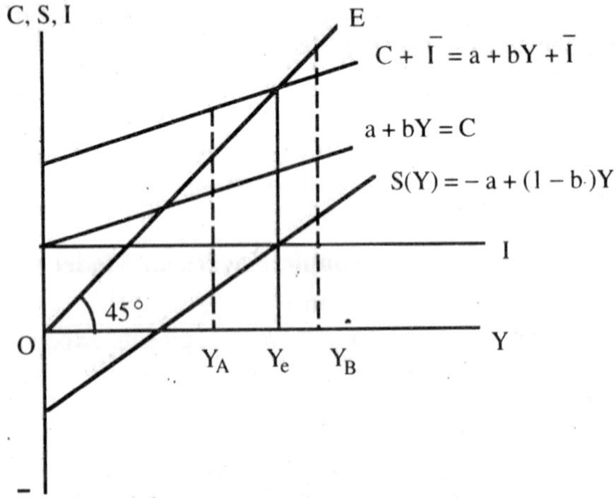

Fig. 4.2 : Income Determination in a Simple Keynesian Model

between $a + bY + \bar{I}$ curve and the 45° line gives the solution of equilibrium for Y. Here Y_e is the equilibrium income. For a graphic solution of equation (8) the saving function is plotted on the graph, and then, the horizontal investment function is drawn. The intersection between the saving function and investment function gives the solution of equation (8) for Y. In the same figure (Fig. 4.2) this solution produces the same equilibrium income, Y_e.

The algebraic solution is given below :

$$Y = C + I.$$

If $C = a + bY$ is the consumption function and $I = A$ is the investment function, the equilibrium income $Y_e = a + bY + \bar{I} = \frac{1}{1-b}(a + A)$.

We can get the same solution by employing the saving function, $S = I$ or where $S = -a + (1-b)Y$

$$-a + (1-b)Y = A \qquad \therefore \; Y_e = \frac{1}{1-b}(a + A)$$

For a specific consumption function, $C = 100 + 0.8Y$ and a constant amount of investment expenditure $I = 100$, find the equilibrium income :

$$Y_e = \frac{1}{1-0.8}(100 + 100) = \frac{1}{0.2}(200) = 1{,}000.$$

The same equilibrium income can be obtained from the saving function; when consumption function is $C = 100 + 0.8Y$, $S = -100 + (1 - 0.8)Y$ and $I = 100$,

$$S = \bar{I} \quad \text{or,} \; -100 + 0.2Y = 100 \quad \therefore Y_e = \frac{1}{0.2}(100 + 100) = 1{,}000$$

The reason why income is settled at the equilibrium level is this : If income lies below Y_e, say at Y_A, aggregate expenditure $(C + I)$ exceeds Y (or I exceeds S), implying that there is an excess demand for output, which leads to an increase in Y; conversely, if income is above Y_e, say at Y_B, aggregate expenditure $(C + I)$ falls short of Y_e(or I is less than S), implying that there is excess supply which leads to a fall in Y. This shows that whenever income is not in equilibrium, it automatically moves towards equilibrium. This movement also ensures the attainment of equilibrium, if it is a stable equilibrium. The stability condition requires that *mpc* in this model must be less than one. Thus, we can determine the equilibrium income with the help of a consumption function and an autonomously given investment function by solving the equation, $Y = a + bY + I$, for Y, only if $mpc = \frac{\Delta C}{\Delta Y}$ is less than 1. Herein lies the importance of the assumption that $0 < mpc < 1$. Without this assumption the equilibrium condition becomes useless, as the equilibrating condition does not work. Thus $mpc < 1$, is the stability condition and where $mpc = 1$, multiplier is ∞, it is unstable condition.

The equilibrium condition discussed above has to be supplemented by the following adjustment hypothesis :

$$(9) \qquad \frac{dY}{dt} = \lambda\,(a + bY) + I - Y = \lambda\,[I - a + (1 - b)Y],$$

where λ is a positive adjustment factor.

The positive value of the dynamic adjustment coefficient λ can be justified in two ways. First, if prices are rigid, the excess demand (supply) will give signal to the producers to increase (decrease) production through (an increase) a decrease in inventories. Second, in a system of flexible prices, the signal will come from the increase (decrease) in prices in the presence of excess demand (supply).

The excess demand function can be linearised by taking the first two terms of Taylor's series expansion around the equilibrium value, Y_e. Then equation (9) becomes a first order linear differential equation, the solution of which will give us the same dynamic stability condition, viz, $mpc < 1$, as we derived earlier with the help of the static analysis.

The simple Keynesian model has two parameters : the *mpc* and the autonomous investment function. A change in any one of the parameters will lead to a change in equilibrium income. An increase in the *mpc* will make both consumption function and aggregate expenditure function steeper in Fig. 4.2; and, then, equilibrium income will go up. An increase in autonomous investment expenditure will produce a parallel upward shift in the aggregate expenditure (aggregate demand) function in Fig. 4.2 which will also increase equilibrium income.

The Multiplier

The effect of a change in autonomous investment on equilibrium income is known as investment multiplier. The multiplier is the rate of change of the equilibrium income when autonomous investment expenditure changes. It can be derived from the equilibrium condition written earlier : $Y = a + bY + I$, where $(a + I)$ are autonomous demand. If we differentiate Y with respect to I we get :

$$(10) \quad \frac{dY}{dI} = \frac{1}{1-b} = \frac{1}{1-mpc} = \frac{1}{mps}$$

It follows from equation (10) that an increase in autonomous investment by ΔI will lead to an increase in equilibrium income by $\Delta Y = \frac{1}{mps}\Delta I$; since $0 < mpc < 1$ (and also, $0 < mps < 1$), the investment multiplier is greater than one. The multiplier relationships are illustrated in Fig. 4.3 below. When there is an increase in autonomous investment, the aggregate demand schedule shifts up to AD'. The equilibrium moves from E to E'. As we know, in equilibrium, aggregate demand equals income. From one equilibrium to another,

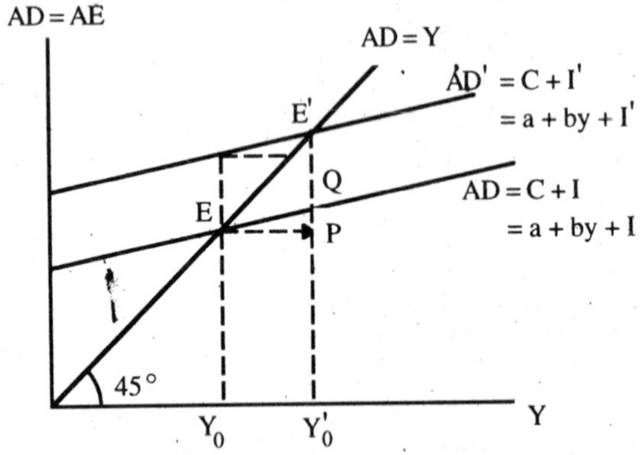

Fig. 4.3 : Multiplier Relationship

it must also be true that the change in income, ΔY_0, is equal to the change in aggregate demand, ΔAD. Next, we split the change in aggregate demand into the change in autonomous spending, $(\Delta \bar{A} = a + \bar{I})$, and the change in expenditure induced by the consequent change in income, that is $b\Delta Y_0$:

$$\Delta Y_0 = \Delta \bar{A} + b\Delta Y_0 \qquad \text{or,} \quad \Delta Y_0 = \frac{1}{1-b}\,\Delta \bar{A}.$$

In terms of the diagram, this increase in income $(Y_0' - Y_0)$, which equals $PE = PE'$, exceeds the increase in autonomous spending, $E'Q$. The excess is a result of the AD curve's having a positiv slope rather than a horizontal slope. The multiplier is greater than one because consumption demand increases with output — any increase in output produces further increase in demand.

Income Determination with both Consumption and Investment as Functions of Income

Now we consider that both consumption and investment as rising functions of income. When both the consumption and investment expenditures are increasing functions of income, the model would be similar to the one developed earlier. The only difference is that, instead of a constant amount of the investment expenditure, we now have a rising function of income. The set of equations of the model is as below :

(11) $C = a + bY$

$I = cY$

$Y = a + bY + cY$ where the marginal propensity to invest *(mpi)* is positive.

(12) $S = -a + (1 - b)Y$

$I = cY$

thus, $S(Y) = I(Y)$ or, $-a + (1 - b)Y = cY$

The saving-investment equality is used as the condition of equilibrium in equation (12).

Solving the equation, $Y = a + bY + cY$, we get the value of the equilibrium income. The graphical method of the solution is also the same as that in the last section. The consumption and investment functions are vertically added to produce the aggregate demand curve as before. This is given in Fig. 4.4.

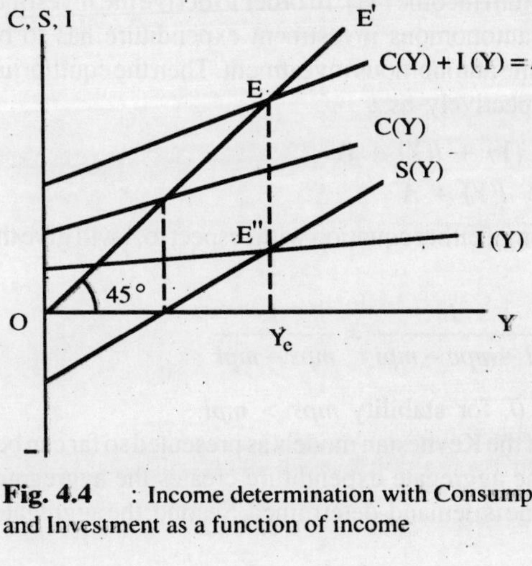

Fig. 4.4 : Income determination with Consumption and Investment as a function of income

The $C(Y) + I(Y)$ curve is the aggregate demand curve. The vertical distance between the aggregate demand curve and the consumption function is now a rising function of income. The equilibrium solution is given at the point of intersection between the aggregate demand and the 45° line. The solution of equation (12) is also plotted on the same graph. Now both the curves are positively sloped. The intersection between $S(Y)$ and $I(Y)$ gives the solution for the equilibrium income. Both solutions give the same equilibrium income, Y_e , as before.

However, the stability condition will now be different from that in the last section. The stability condition now implies that $mpc + mpi < 1$. In other words, the sum of the marginal propensities to spend must be less than one. Alternatively, the stability condition also implies that the *mpi* must be less than the *mps*. Referring to Fig. 4.4 we note that the stability condition must be interpreted to mean that the investment function must be flatter than the saving function and the aggregate demand curve than the 45° line. Since the marginal propensity to spend must be less than one it also means that *mpc* must be less then one since *mpi* is positive. Once again we see the importance of the assumption that the *mpc* is less than one.

The dynamic stability condition may be derived in the same way as before by introducing the same adjustment mechanism, viz :

$$(13)\quad \frac{dY}{dt} = \lambda[C(Y) + I(Y) - Y] = \lambda[I(Y) - S(Y)]$$

Again, a linear approximation of the excess demand function by Taylor's series expansion around Y_e will yield the same stability condition as in the static analysis.

In this model, there are three parameters : the *mpc* (or the *mps*), the *mpi* and the autonomous investment; a change in any one of them will produce a change in equilibrium income (Y_e). In order to derive the investment multiplier in this model, the autonomous investment expenditure has to be introduced explicitly. Let *A* be the autonomous investment. Then the equilibrium conditions can be written respectively as :

$$(14)\quad Y = C(Y) + I(Y) + A$$

$$(15)\quad S(Y) = I(Y) + A$$

Differentiation of either equation with respect to *A* will give the investment multiplier as :

$$(16)\quad \frac{dY}{dA} = \frac{1}{1 - mpc - mpi} = \frac{1}{mps - mpi}$$

Since $mpi > 0$, for stability $mps > mpi$.

The essence of the Keynesian models as presented so far can be summarised as follows: First, the aggregate expenditure creates the aggregate demand for output and the income is demand-determined. Second, the aggregate expenditure has two parts : one part is a rising function of income and the other part is exogenously given. Third, the equilibrium income is determined by the equality of income and expenditure. For this reason, the Keynesian model is known as the income-expenditure theory. Fourth, for the stability of the equilibrium the marginal propensity to consume *(mpc)* has to be less than one and greater than zero. Fifth, because of the stability condition, any change in autonomous expenditure will have a multiplier effect on equilibrium income.

The model can be mathematically stated with the help of the following equations :

(17) $E = E(Y) + A$, where E is the aggregate expenditure

(18) $Y = E(Y) + A$, where Y is income

(19) $\frac{dY}{dt} = \lambda[E(Y) + A - Y]$

The dynamic stability is ensured if $0 < \frac{dE}{dY} < 1$, and the multiplier is given by $\frac{1}{(1 - dE/dY)}$

Dynamics of Income Determination

If income is not in equilibrium in any period, the forces of excess demand brings about changes in the subsequent periods. The income determination analysis made so far does not enable us to find out the values of income in different periods of time. For determination of income in each period of time and for drawing the path of income over time, we need dynamics of income determination. If time is treated as a descrete variable, we enter into a period analysis in which income in any period of time is determined. If, on the other hand, time is treated as a continuous variable, we take resort to a continuous analysis in which income at any period of time is known.

In the dynamic income determination analysis, each macro-variable is treated as a function of time. The value of a variable in one period determines its value in the subsequent period or periods. The macro-functional relations may have lagged adjustments in the sense that the values of a variable in one period may depend on the value of another variable in another period. To develop a simple theory of the dynamics of income determination, we introduce two lag models — the production lag and the consumption lag. A production lag exists when production in one period is made on the basis of the demand in the preceding period. As to the basis of the production lag, we assume that the production in a particular period is equal to the demand in the preceding period. Similarly, when the consumption expenditure in any period depends on the income of the preceding period, there is a consumption lag in the system.

The un-lagged consumption function is $C_t = f(Y_t)$, where the

$mpc = \frac{dc_t}{dY_t}$; whereas, the lagged consumption function takes the form : $C_t = f\ (Y_{t-1})$, where the $mpc = \frac{dc_t}{dY_{t-1}}$. When there is a production lag, $Y_t = E_{t-1}$, and when there is no production lag, $Y_t = E_t$. The aggregate expenditure in any period is $E_t = C_t + I_t$.

If we assume a linear consumption function and autonomous investment expenditure, which is repeated in each period, then the lagged consumption function may be written as $C_t = a + bY_{t-1}$ and the autonomous investment expenditure be 'A'. When there is no production lag,

$$Y_t = E_t = C_t + I_t = bY_{t-1} + (a + A).$$

Again, the linear unlagged consumption function is $C_t = a + bY_t$. If there is a production lag, $Y_t = E_{t-1} = C_{t-1} + I_{t-1} = bY_{t-1} + (a+A)$.

Thus, in either case, we have the equation $Y_t = bY_{t-1} + (a + A)$, which determines income in any period in terms of the income in the preceding period and the parameters, a, b, and A. The equilibrium income

$$Y_e = \frac{1}{1-b}(a + A) \quad \text{because in equilibrium } Y_t = Y_{t-1} = Y_e$$

If Y_0 is the income in period 0 and it is not in equilibrium, incomes in subsequent periods will be

$$Y_1 = bY_0 + (a+A)$$
$$Y_2 = bY_1 + (a+A) = b^2Y_0 + (1-b)(a+A)$$
$$Y_3 = b^3Y_0 + \left(1+b+b^2\right)(a+A)$$

....

$$Y_t = b^tY_0 + \left(1+b+b^2+.....+b^{t-1}\right)(a+A)$$
$$= b^tY_0 + \frac{1-b^t}{1-b}(a+A) = b^t\left(Y_0 - Y_e\right) + Y_e$$

We may use the last result to get the value of income of any period. We get the values of Y_t in the last expression. Taking the successive value of Y_t for $t = 1, 2,........, n$, and plotting them on a graph, we get the path of income over time. If the mpc is a fraction lying between zero and one, i.e., $0 < b < 1, b^t \to 0$ as $t \to \infty$. Thus, we come to the conclusion that $Y_t \to Y_e = \frac{1}{1-b}(a+A)$ the equilibrium value, as $t \to \infty$. In

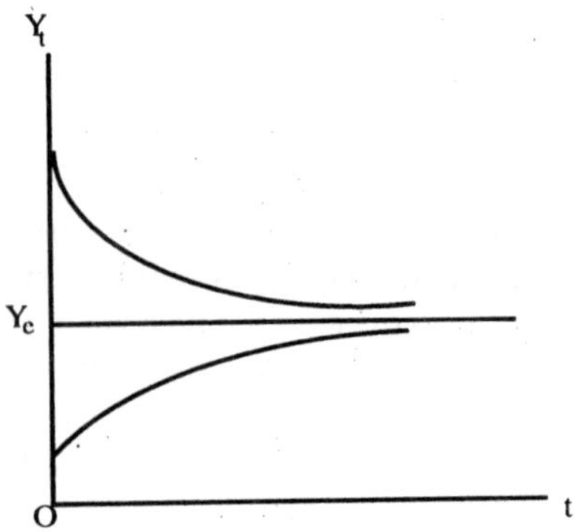

Fig. 4.5 : Actual Path of Income

other words, the straight line drawn at the height of Y_e in Fig. 4.5 is an asymptote to the actual path of income. If income in period 0 is less than Y_e, it rises in the subsequent periods and approaches the equilibrium value. Conversely, if income in period 0 is greater than Y_e, it falls in the subsequent periods and approaches the equilibrium value. When $b > 1$, there is an explosive growth or an indefinite fall of income; the path of income will then diverge from the equilibrium value.

In the continuous case, we do not use the time subscript and write the consumption function as $C = a + bY$, where C and Y are continuous functions of t. Then the dynamic adjustment mechanism is used. $\frac{dY}{dt} = \alpha[(a + A) + bY - Y]$, where α is positive adjustment parameter. The adjustment equation can be written as $\frac{dY}{dt} + \alpha(1 - b)Y = \alpha(a + A)$; which is a first order linear, non-homogeneous differential equation. The homogeneous part of the equation is $\frac{dY}{dt} + \alpha(1 - b)Y = 0$, which has a complementary function. Let the solution for the homogeneous part be $Y = \beta e^{\lambda t}$, where β and λ are arbitrary constants to be determined and e is the base of natural logarithm.

Then $\frac{dY}{dt} = \lambda Be^{\lambda t}$ and, thus, $\frac{dY}{dt} + \alpha(1 - b)Y = \lambda Be^{\lambda t} + \alpha(1 - b)Be^{\lambda t}$, from which it follows that $[\lambda + \alpha(1 - b)]Be^{\lambda t} = 0$; where $[\lambda + \alpha(1 - b)] = 0$ and so $\lambda = -\alpha(1 - b)$. Thus, the complementary function is given by $Y_C = Be^{-\alpha(1-b)t}$, where B has to be determined from the initial condition.

Let the particular function be $Y = K$, a constant. Then $\frac{dY}{dt} = 0$ and so $0 + \alpha(1 - b)Y = \alpha(a + A)$, from which it follows that the particular function is $Y_p = \frac{a + A}{1 - b} = Y_e$. Now the general solution is $Y = Y_e + Y_p = Y_e + Be^{-\alpha(1-b)t}$. To obtain the particular solution, the constant B has to be determined from the initial condition. Let $Y = Y_0$ when $t = 0$. Then $Y_0 = Y_e + B$ and so, $B = Y_0 - Y_e$. Now the definite solution is $Y = Y_e + (Y_0 - Y_e)e^{-\alpha(1-b)t}$ which describes the path of income overtime. If $1 - b > 0$, i.e. $mps > 0$ or $mpc < 1$, $Y \rightarrow Y_e$ as $t \rightarrow \infty$, since $\alpha > 0$.

The dynamic income determination is useful in finding out the multiplier effect of a change in investment. The implication of the multiplier theory, as we have already seen, is that an increase in autonomous investment (or any expenditure) produces an expansionary effect on income which is much greater than the original increase in expenditure.

In order to make the theory meaningful and operationally valid, we should investigate the process through which the multiplier works. When the autonomous investment is increased, there is an effect first on the aggregate demand, and, then, on income. In the first place, the increase in investment expenditure produces a rise in the aggregate demand just by the amount of the increment in investment. Then, the resultant increase in income leads to an increase in the consumption expenditure. This increase in the consumption expenditure leads to a further increase in the aggregate demand, which produces a further increase in income. In this way the process continues, until the effect is exhausted. It is the successive increases in consumption expenditure which produce the multiplier effect on income until it reaches its limit.. The dynamic analysis helps us to derive the full course of the multiplier process. We then have different values of the increment in income in different periods. We write ΔY_1, ΔY_2, ...ΔY_n to denote increments in income in periods *1, 2, ...n* over the income in period *0*. The increment in investment, ΔI, takes place in period *1*, and the sequence of increments in income goes on as follows :

$$\Delta Y_1 = \Delta I$$
$$\Delta Y_2 = \Delta I + mpc.\,\Delta Y_1 = (1 + mpc).\,\Delta I$$
$$\Delta Y_3 = \Delta I + mpc.\,\Delta Y_2 = (1 + mpc + mpc^2).\,\Delta I$$
$$\cdots\cdots\cdots\cdots\cdots\cdots\cdots\cdots\cdots\cdots$$
$$\Delta Y_n = (1 + mpc + mpc^2 + \ldots\ldots + mpc^{n-1}).\,\Delta I$$
$$= \frac{(1 - mpc^n)}{(1 - mpc)}.\,\Delta I$$

The multiplier takes the values *1*, *1 + mpc*, *1 + mpc + mpc*^{2} + ..., $(1-mpc^n)/(1-mpc)$ successively in periods *1, 2, 3 ....n*. If the *mpc* lies between *0* and *1*, $\Delta Y_n \to \frac{1}{(1-mpc)}\Delta I$, as $n \to \infty$. That is, the simple Keynesian multiplier is the limiting value of the period multiplier, as the time approaches infinity. A major part of the final increment in income is realised within the first few periods, as shown in Fig. 4.5, the simple Keynesian multiplier gives good approximations for practical purposes, if the period of time is very small. The time period involved in the multipliers process depends on lags in the economic system.

The multiplier process works in this way : investment expenditure goes as factor income, which is spent by the people to purchase consumption goods; the consumption expenditure creates a demand for goods, and so on the process continues. Thus, a complete round of income creation may have the following lags : (a) Payment lag, (b) Consumption lag, and (c) Production lag. Incomes are not paid in the period in which they are earned. Expenditure to create demand cannot be made until the payment lag is over. The length of the payment lag depends on the institutional factor in the country. In creased consumption expenditure does not take place in the period in which income is earned because of a lagged effect of an increase in income and the consumption expenditure. Until the consumption lag is over, demand is not increased. An increase in demand is not immediately translated into an increase in production, until the production lag is over. The length of a period in the multiplier process is the sum of these three lags. These lags have the effect of delaying the realisation of the multiplier effect.

In an actual multiplier process there are some leakages. A part of the additional income is taken away by the government as taxes and the income that is left after the payment of taxes is called disposable income on which consumption expenditure is based. The tax leakage reduces consumption expenditure, if it is not compensated by an increase in government expenditure. The net effect is to reduce the value of the multiplier. Another leakage comes from expenditure on imported goods which has the effect of reducing the value of the multiplier. A counter-effect is produced by an increase in income through exports. Of course, the entire amount originally leaked out may not come back and hence the multiplier effect may be reduced.

Even if we retain our assumption of a closed economy without the government, we encounter some leakages. The *mpc* may decline progressively with the rise income. This may be because the consumption function itself has diminishing *mpc* or because there may be redistribution of income from those who have a higher *mpc* to those who have a lower *mpc*.

If an investment expenditure is a negative function of the rate of interest, the value of the multiplier is further reduced by the rise in interest rate. With the rise in income, money required for transaction purposes rises. If the quantity of money supplied remains unchanged, less money would be available for speculative purposes. Then, there is a rise in the rate of interest, which reduces investment expenditure. Thus, the multiplier effect is reduced through the money supply restriction.

Equilibrium Condition : re-examined

To concentrate on the understanding of the concepts used in our analysis so far, we shall first subdivide total desired expenditures into only two categories, Consumption and Investment. With this subdivision of total expenditures the equilibrium condition for the goods sector is : $Y = C + I$ ....(20).

As before, it is useful to note that the equilibrium condition can be restated in another way. From (20), $Y - C = I$ ....(21). If we define saving *(S)* as the difference between total income and desired consumption, i.e., $S \equiv Y - C$, then equation (21) can be restated as : $S = I$ .... (22).

Equation (22) is just a different way of saying the same thing as equation (20). It shows a situation in which desired expenditures are equal to output. By definition, *S* is the difference between the total quality of goods and services produced per time period *(Y)* and the quantity of goods and services people want to use for consumption *(C)*. Thus, *S* measures the quantity of goods and services produced but not wanted for consumption and, thus, all the goods and services left over for other uses. With our subdivision of total expenditures, the only other use for goods is investment. Thus, the condition for equilibrium, $S = I$, is identical to the one $Y = C + I$.

Consumption

For simplicity we assume that consumption (C) is a function of current real income, i.e., $C = f(Y)$. This is obviously an over-simplification and we shall examine a more sophisticated version later on. For the purpose of keeping the discussion simple, it is also assumed, as before, that consumption is a linear function of real income. Thus, $C = a + bY$........(23).

We also know that the $mpc = \frac{dC}{dY} = b$. The average propensity to consume is $\frac{C}{Y} = \frac{a}{Y} + b$. For the moment we also assume, as before, that desired investment is autonomously given, $I = A$ .... (24).

Substituting (23) and (24) into the equilibrium condition, we obtain : $Y = a + bY + A$ .... (25) and solving for Y_e, the equilibrium income, we have : $Y(1-b) = a + A \quad \therefore Y_e = \frac{1}{1-b}(a + A)$ ....(26).

If investment now changes by ΔI to A_1, we get new equilibrium income. Using the same procedure as above, it is, $Y_1 = \frac{1}{1-b}(a + A_1)$ ....(27). The change in income (ΔY) resulting from the change in investment ΔI is $\Delta Y = \frac{1}{1-b}\Delta I$.............(28). Again, the multiplier is $\frac{1}{1-b}$. This is identical to what we did in more general terms above.

Investment

The second major component of desired expenditure is investment, current expenditure on goods and services for satisfying future wants. To formulate some useful hypothesis about the determinant of desired investment, we must examine the behaviour of those groups making investment decisions.

The reason why a firm undertakes an investment in an income-yielding real asset, for example, a machine, is because it expects an income stream in the future. To acquire the asset, the firm can either borrow funds or use its own funds. In either case the cost to the firm of acquiring assets can be represented by the interest rate. If the firm borrows funds, the interest rate measures what it has to pay for the funds and, thus, what it has to pay for the income stream it acquires. If the firm invests its own funds, the interest rate measures the opportunity cost of acquiring the income stream from the assets.

Assume the price of a machine is *£400* and the interest-rate is *10* per cent. Suppose the machine has a known life of only two years and is expected to yield *£240* each year. The decision facing the firm is whether such investment is profitable. To give an answer to this question we will have to calculate

Net Present Value of the investment and to compare that with the *Present Cost*. If the *Net Present Value* is greater than the *Present Cost*, that investment can be considered worthwhile.

Net Present Value can be calculated as follows :

$$NPV = \frac{240}{(1+r)} + \frac{240}{(1+r)^2} = \frac{240}{(1.1)} + \frac{240}{(1.1)^2} = \frac{240}{1.1} + \frac{240}{1.21} = £\ 416.5$$

$NPV > PC = 416.5 > 400$, thus, the investment is profitable at *10* per cent interest rate. If, however, the interest rate is *20* per cent, $NPV < PC$, $367 < 400$, the investment is not profitable. Thus, higher the interest rate, the higher must be the expected income stream from the investment to make it worthwhile. At lower interest rate, lower-yielding investments will be undertaken.

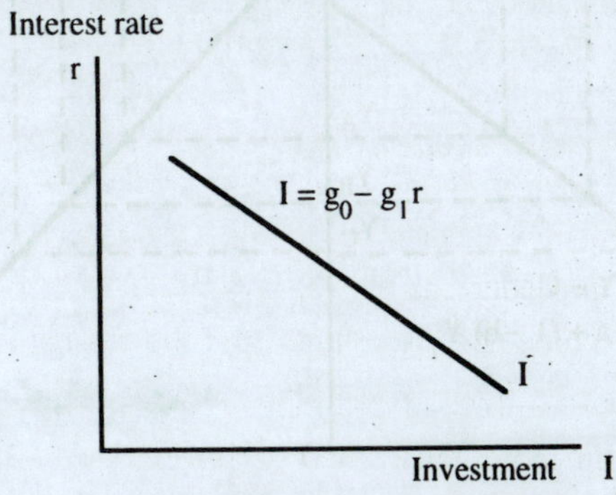

Fig. 4.6 : Investment Function

Following the above discussion, our first approximation of the behaviour of desired investment is that it is a function of the interest rate, i.e., $I = g(r)$. For simplicity we again assume a linear relationship $I = g_0 - g_1(r)$ ....(29). In Fig. 4.6, the real investment is measured on the horizontal axis and the interest rate on the vertical axis. The *I* curve represents the demand curve for real investment shown by equation (29).

Equilibrium Condition and the Derivation of IS-curve

We have simplified model for two compents of expenditures into which we have subdivided total desired expenditures—consumption and investment. Substituting these hypotheses into the condition for equilibrium in the goods sector, $Y = C + I$, we have, $Y = a + bY + g_0 - g_1 r$ ....(30)

Solving for *Y* we get $Y = \frac{1}{1-b}[a + g_0 - g_1 r]$ ....(31)

The equation (30) is a relationship between two variables *Y* and *r* (all the other elements are behavioural constants). It shows the combinations of *Y* and *r* for which the equilibrium condition in the goods sector is satisfied;

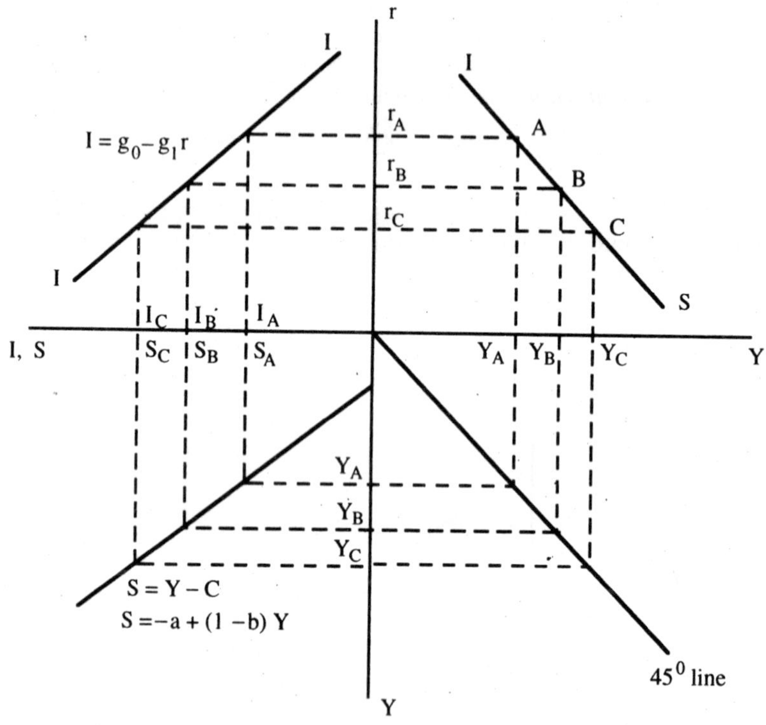

Fig. 4.7 : Derivation of IS curve

or for which $S = I$. It may be noted here that we cannot solve equation (31) for Y to determine the equilibrium income, until we know the interest rate, r. If we do not know the rate of interest, we cannot find out the investment expenditure. When the investment expenditure is known, the equilibrium income can be determined by solving equation (31) for Y, as is known from the investment function. With a given rate of interest the model becomes the same as before. The behavioural relationships and the equilibrium condition are shown in the above diagram (Fig. 4.6).

In the four-quadrant diagram (Fig. 4.7), the real income per unit time is measured on the right horizontal and bottom vertical axes. Along the top vertical axis we measure the interest rate. Along the left horizontal axis we measure both saving and investment per unit time (this is done because both saving and investment are measured in the same unit). The quadrant 2 represents the investment function $I = g_0 - g_1 r$. The third quadrant represents the assumption about consumption, $C = a + bY$, combined with the definition of savings, $S = Y - C$; thus it gives the relationship between savings and income, i.e., $S = -a + (1 - b)Y$. The fourth quadrant has a $45°$ line which represents the identity $Y \equiv Y$ (it allows the transcription of income from the vertical to the horizontal axes). In the first quadrant we derive the curve representing the equilibrium condition in the goods sector [equation (31) above] — the combination of income and the interest rate for which $Y = C + I$ or for which $S = I$. It is derived as follows. At the interest rate, r_A for example, desired investment is equal to I_A. The saving function shows that saving will be equal to that investment at income Y_A. Transcribing that income to horizontal axis via $45°$ line we get point *A*, i.e., (r_A, Y_A) at which $S_A = Y_A$. We can do this for all points, e.g. *B*, *C* etc. By joining all such points we get *IS* curve which gives the goods market equilibrium schedule.

Fig. 4.7 shows that the *IS* curve is negatively sloped, which summarizes the assumptions about consumption and investment (because we use these to construct the curve) and the condition for equilibrium in the goods sector. However, as we assumed that equilibrium in the goods sector is attainable and then when we say that the *IS* curve represents equilibrium, we do not just mean that it shows all the combinations of income *(Y)* and the interest rate *(r)* for which $S = I$ because we measured them and plotted them in that way. What we mean is that, given our assumptions about the goods sector, it will be true that saving will equal investment, because, if saving is not equal to investment (i.e., at some points off the *IS* curve), something will change — and continue to change — until equilibrium is achieved. This proposition about the equilibrium properties of *IS* curve can best be seen in Fig. 4.8. The three points *A, B, C* all represent the same income Y_0 but different interest rates. Given the assumption that consumption, and, therefore, saving, only depend on income, saving is the same at the three points *A*, *B*, and *C*. Let us say S_0. From the *IS* curve, point *B*, which is on the curve, represents a combination of income and interest rate at which $S = I$. At the interest rate, r_B, desired investment I_B is equal to S_0. At point *A*, desired investment as shown by the investment function is I_A which is less than I_B. However, as *A* represents the same income as *B* (and *C*) saving is the same as at *B*,

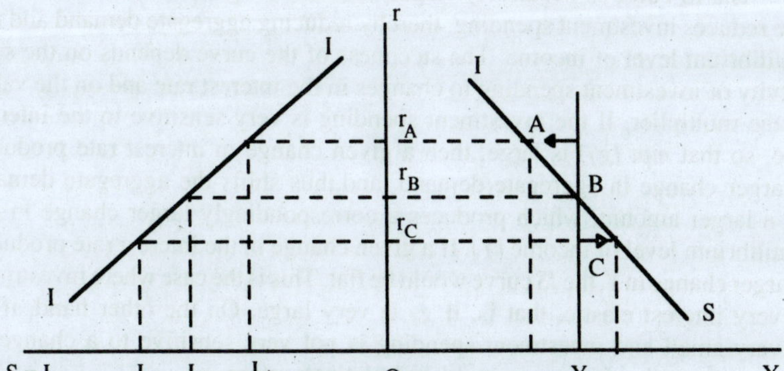

Fig. 4.8 : Saving-Investment equality and Equilibrium Properties of IS curve

i.e., S_0. Thus, at A, $S_0 > I_A$, which means that output is greater than desired expenditures. With the assumptions we made about the reaction of output and, thus, real income to a disequilibrium, output will fall until equilibrium is reached. Similarly, at point C, desired investment is equal to I_c but saving is equal to S_0, thus $I_c > S_0$, which implies that desired expenditures are greater than output. Again, given our assumption that output will rise until equilibrium is reached again, represented by some point on the *IS* curve, we may summarise by concluding that the *IS* curve shows the combination of income and the interest rate at which the goods sector will be in equilibrium because we have assumed some specific economic relationships and an equilibrium process (though yet unsatisfactory) which leads to this conclusion.

Using equation (31), we get the slope of the *IS* curve :

$$\frac{dY}{dr} = -g_I \frac{1}{1-b} \quad \text{............ (32)}$$

This $(-g_I)$ is the slope of the investment function. It measures the change in investment arising from a change in the interest rate. If we multiply this change in investment by the multiplier $\frac{1}{1-b}$, we get the change in desired expenditures arising from the change in the interest rate. Thus the responsiveness of aggregate demand to changes in the interest rate depends on two factors. The first is the responsiveness of investment to changes in the interest rate. The second is the size of the multiplier. These considerations will be important when we will consider the effectiveness of government policies.

From the *IS* curve we can gain further understanding of its economics by asking the following questions : (I) What determines the slope of the *IS* curve? (II) What determines the position of the *IS* curve and what causes its shifts?

Slope of the *IS* curve

The *IS* curve is negatively sloped because a higher level of the interest rate reduces investment spending, thereby reducing aggregate demand and the equilibrium level of income. The steepness of the curve depends on the sensitivity of investment spending to changes in the interest rate and on the value of the multiplier. If the investment spending is very sensitive to the interest rate, so that *mpi* (g_I) is large, then a given change in interest rate produces a larger change in aggregate demand, and,thus shifts the aggregate demand by a larger amount, which produces a correspondingly larger change in the equilibrium level of income (Y). If a given change in the interest rate produces a larger change in Y, the *IS* curve would be flat. This is the case where investment is very interest elastic, that is, if g_I is very large. On the other hand, if g_I is very small and investment spending is not very sensitive to a change in interest rate, the *IS* curve would be relatively steep.

Role of the Multiplier and Steepness of the *IS* curve

We now consider the effect of the multiplier on the steepness of the *IS* curve. The larger the multiplier, the greater is the rise in income, the flatter the *IS* curve. Similarly, the larger the multiplier, the larger the change in income produced by a given change in interest rate.

We have seen, the smaller the sensitivity of investment spending to the interest rate and the smaller the multiplier, the steeper is the *IS* curve. Given that the slope of the *IS* curve depends on the value of the multiplier, the fiscal policy can affect that slope. The multiplier is affected by the tax rate: an increase in the tax rate reduces the multiplier. Thus, the higher the tax rate, the steeper is the *IS* curve.

Position of the *IS* curve

A shift of the *IS* curve is caused by a change in autonomous spending. An increase in aggregate demand due to higher autonomous spending shifts the aggregate demand curve raising equilibrium level of output at interest rate r_1. The *IS* curve shifts as a result. At each level of interest rate, the equilibrium income is now higher. The horizontal shift of the *IS* curve is equal to the multiplier times the increase in autonomous spending as given by Fig. 4.9. Thus, an increase in government spending $(G + T_R)$ will shift the *IS* curve to the right, with the extent of the shift depending on the size of the multiplier. A reduction in government spending shifts the *IS* curve to the left.

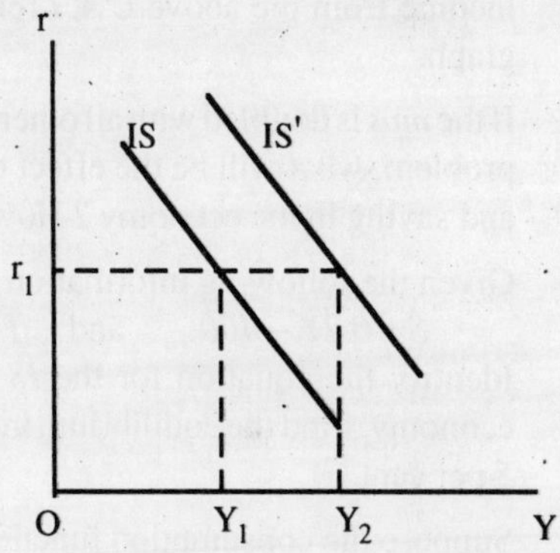

Fig. 4.9 : A Shift of the IS curve

Goods Sector and the Price Level

Although the price level is not very relevant in the discussion of the condition for equilibrium in the goods sector — which is specified in terms of the quantity of goods and services — it may, however, be relevant to the specification of the behavioural relationships determining desired expenditures. Whether a change in the price level will or will not affect desired expenditures depends on the behavioural relationships determining the various elements of the aggregate demand — consumption which was assumed to be a function of income. The question is, whether this relationship is function of real income or money income. It is reasonable to assume that consumption is a function of real income. The same question may be asked about the second element of desired expenditures — investment. Are the decisions about investments made in real terms or not? Again, we shall assume that people desire the same quantity of real investment.

Thus, we assume that both the elements of desired expenditures are not affected by changes in the price level. Therefore, the *IS* curve, which is derived from these elements, is also unaffected by changes in the price level.

Exercise

1. The consumption and investment functions are $C = 200 + 0.8Y$ and $I = 300 + 0.20Y$, respectively. Write down the equilibrium condition for income determination and the dynamic adjustment equation, derive the dynamic path of income, examine the stability condition and determine the equilibrium income.

2. Write down the equations relating consumption and savings to national income from the above $C + I$ relations and plot these relationships on a graph.

3. If the *mps* is doubled with all other things remaining same as in the previous problem, what will be the effect on the equilibrium level of consumption and saving in the economy ? How would you account for these changes ?

4. Given the following information for an economy :

   $S = 0.2Y - 400$ and $I = 400 - 6{,}000\, r$

   Identify the equation for the *IS* curve and derive the *IS* curve for this economy. Find the equilibrium income for interest rates of *10* per cent and *5* per cent.

5. Suppose the consumption function in an economy is given by

   $C = 100 + 0.6Y$ while investment is given by $I = 200$.

   (a) What is the equilibrium level of income in this economy ?

   (b) What is the level of saving in this economy when income is £2,000 ?

   (c) If output were at the level of *1,500*, what would the level of involuntary inventory accumulation be? How can you find the equilibrium again ?

   (d) What is the value of the simple Keynesian multiplier here ?

   (e) If *I* were to rise to *400*, what would be the equilibrium income ?

6. If the *mpc* is *c* and the *mps* is *s*, write the multiplier in terms of *s*.

5 EQUILIBRIUM IN THE MONEY SECTOR

In the last chapter, we examined the decisions of the goods sector — the flow of output and desired expenditure (AE). In this chapter, we examine the decisions involving the allocation of wealth among different assets. Thus, decision-making in this sector is called the money sector, because we concentrate on the allocation of wealth between money and all other assets — here we shall represent by bonds. We make this particular subdivision of the wealth sector because money represents command over resources; each individual can exchange it for goods and services, even though the economy as a whole cannot. Money does not refer to all wealth but to one type of wealth. Money is the stock of assets that can be readily used to make transactions.

The functions of money: Money has three functions. It is a medium of exchange, an unit of account and a store of value.

As a medium of exchange, money is what we use to buy goods and services. 'It is a legal tender for all debt' is printed on the U.K. pounds. When we walk into stores, we are confident that the shopkeeper will accept our money in exchange of the goods they are selling. To understand this function of money, try to imagine an economy without it; a barter economy. In such a world, trade requires the double coincidence of wants. A barter economy permits only simple transactions.

As an unit of account, money provides the terms in which the prices are quoted and debts recorded.

As a store of value function of money, it is a way to transfer purchasing power from the present to the future. If I earn today £100, I can hold the money and spend it tomorrow, next week, or next month. Of course, money is an imperfect store of value: if prices are rising, the real value of money is falling. Even so, people hold money because they can trade the money for goods and services at sometime in the future.

Types Of Money

Money that has no intrinsic value is called fiat money, since it is established as money by government decree. Although today fiat money is the norm in most economies, historically most societies used for money a commodity with intrinsic value. This type of money is called commodity money. Gold is the most widespread example of commodity money. An economy in which gold used as money is called gold standard. Gold is a type of commodity money because it can be used for many other purposes apart from transactions. The gold standard was common during the late 19th century.

From Commodity Money To Fiat Money

It is not surprising that some form of commodity money arises to facilitate exchange; people are willing to accept a commodity money because of its intrinsic value. The development of fiat money is more perplexing. What would make people begin to value something that is intrinsically useless ?

To understand how it evolved from commodity money to fiat money, imagine an economy in which people carry around bags of gold. When purchase is made, the buyer measures out the appropriate amount of gold. If the seller is convinced about the weight and purity of gold, the buyer and seller make the exchange.

The government first intervenes to reduce transaction cost — time it takes to verify the purity and to measure the correct quantity of gold. To help reduce these costs, the government mints gold coins of known purity and weight. The coins are easier to use than gold bullion because their values are widely recognised. The next step for the government is to issue gold certificate — pieces of paper that can be redeemed for a certain quantity of gold. These bills are just as valuable as the gold itself. In addition, because the bills are lighter than the gold,they are easier to use in transactions. Eventually, these gold-backed government bills, instead of gold, became the monetary standard. Finally, the gold backing becomes unnecessary. As long as everyone continues to accept the bills in exchange, they will have value and serve as money. Thus, the system of commodity money evolves into a system of fiat money.

How Money Is Controlled

The quantity of money available is called the money supply. In an economy that uses fiat money, the government controls the money supply. Just as the level of taxation and the level of government purchases are policy instruments of the government, so is the supply of money. The control of money supply, in all countries is delegated to an institution called the Central Bank. The control of money supply is called monetary policy. The primary way in which the Central Bank controls the money supply is through open-market operations — the purchase and sale of government bonds. The purchase increases the quality of money supply, whereas, the sale decreases its supply.

How The Quantity Of Money Is Measured

Let us examine how economists measure the quantity of money. Because money is the stock of assets used for transactions, the quantity of money is the quantity of those assets. The most obvious asset to include in the quantity of money is currency, the sum of fiat money — paper money and coins. Most day-to-day transactions use currency as the medium of exchange.

A second type of asset used for transactions is Current Account or Checking Accounts. If most sellers accept personal checks, assets in a Checking Account or Current Account are almost as convenient as currency. In both cases, the assets are in a form that is ready to facilitate a transaction. Thus, Current Account deposits are added to currency when measuring the quantity of money. Once we admit the logic of including Current Account in the measured money stock, many other assets become candidates for inclusion. Funds in Savings Accounts, for example, can be easily transferred into Checking Accounts; these assets are almost as convenient for transactions.

Since it is unclear exactly which assets should be included in the money stock, various measures are available. Table 1 presents several measures of the money stock which are regarded as money especially in the U.K.

Table 1

M_0 : This is notes and coins, plus commercial bank deposits held with the Bank of England (Central Bank). M_0 is also called high-powered money or the monetary base.

M_1 : This is notes and coins, plus sight deposits (Current Account) against which cheques can be issued.

M_2 : This is M_1, plus deposits with Building Societies.

M_3 : This is M_1, plus Sterling time deposits, plus holdings of bank certificate of deposit.

M_{3C} : This is M_3, plus deposits of U.K. residents held in other currencies.

M_4 : This is M_3, plus private-sector holdings of building society shares, deposits and Sterling certificates of deposit, less building society holdings of bank deposits and bank certificates of deposit and notes and coins.

M_5 : This is M_4, plus holdings by the private sector of bank bills, treasury and local authority deposits, certificates of tax deposit and national saving instruments.

The Quantity Theory Of Money

Having defined what money is and examined how it is controlled and measured, we can now analyse how the quantity of money affects the economy. For this we need to see how the quantity of money is related to other economic variables.

People hold money to buy goods and services. The more money they need for transactions, the more money they hold — thus, the quantity of money is closely related to number of transactions.

The link between transactions and money expressed in the following quantity equation : $MV = PT$, where T represents the total number of transactions during some period of time, say, a year; P is the price of a typical transaction. The product of the price of a transaction and the number of transactions, PT, equals the number of money exchanged in a year.

M is the quantity of money and V is called the transaction velocity of money and measures the rate at which money circulates in the economy. For example, suppose that *60* loaves of bread are sold in an economy in a given year at a price of *£0.50* per loaf. Then $T = 60$ loaves per year, and $P = £0.50$ per loaf. $PT = £0.50 \times 60 = £30$. Thus, the right-hand side of the quantity equation equals *£30* per year, which is the money value of all transactions.

Suppose further that the quantity of money in the economy is *£10*. Then $V = PT/M = 30/10 = 3$ times per year. The quantity equation is an identity; the definitions of the four variables make it true. The equation is useful because it shows that if one of the variables changes, one or more of the others must also change to maintain the equality. For example, if the quantity of money increases and the velocity of money remains unchanged, then either the price or the number of transactions must rise.

From Transactions To Income

Economists use a slightly different version of the quantity equation. The problem with the previous equation is that it is difficult to measure the number of transactions T. Thus, the number of transactions T is replaced by the total output of the economy Y. If Y denotes the amount of output and P is the price of one unit of output, then the money value of output is PY. In other words, Y is real *GDP*, P is the *GDP* deflator, and PY nominal *GDP*. The quantity equation becomes $MV = PY$. Because Y is total income, V is called the income velocity of money. This version is the most common and is useful for economic analysis.

Money Demand Function And The Quantity Equation

The demand for money is a demand for real balances. In other words, people hold money for its purchasing power, for the amount of goods they can buy with it. This amount is M/P and is called real money balances. People are not concerned with their nominal money holdings.

An individual is free from money illusion if a change in the level of prices, holding all real variables constant, leave the person's real behaviour, including real money demand unchanged. By contrast, an individual whose real behaviour is affected by a change in the price level, all real variables remaining unchanged, is said to suffer from money illusion.

A money demand function is an equation that shows what determines the quantity of real money balances people wish to hold for transaction purposes. A money demand function is $(M/P)^D = kY$, where k is a constant. This equation states that the quantity of real balances demanded is proportional to real Y. Holding money makes it easier to make transactions. So higher Y leads to a great demand for money balances (M/P).

The quantity equation can be derived from this money demand function. To do so we add the condition that $(M/P)^d$ must equal the (M/P) supply. Thus, $(M/P)^d = (M/P) = kY$. Rearranging the terms we can write: $M(1/k) = PY$, where $V = 1/k$. We can write this as $MV = PY$.

Hence, when we use quantity equation, we assume that the supply of real money balances equals the demand which is proportional to income.

The quantity equation can be transformed into useful theory—the quantity theory of money — by making additional assumption that velocity is constant. This assumption of constant velocity provides a good approximation to reality. Let us see what this assumption implies about the effects of the money supply on the economy. Once the assumption of constant velocity is accepted, the quantity equation can be seen as a theory of nominal *GDP*. The quantity equation says $M\overline{V} = PY$, where $\overline{V}$ means fixed velocity. Therefore, a change in the quantity of money (M) must cause a proportional change in nominal *GDP* (PY). That is, the quantity of money determines the money value of the economy's output.

The Demand For Money

People hold money though it is not costless. Money, unlike other assets, does not yield an explicit rate of return. It is thus a relevant question to ask what money gives which makes individuals willing to pay the price to hold it. There are three motives for holding money : the transactions motives, the speculative motive, and the precautionary motive. The transactions motive arises from the function of money as a medium of exchange. Most economic activity involves exchange and barter is an inconvenient and expensive way of making exchanges. Money is an asset which is generally acceptable as a medium of exchange and can be easily exchangeable for goods and other assets. One of the reasons for holding wealth in the form of money is that it allows us to make transactions without undergoing the costs and inconveniences of converting some other assets into money. For this particular motive, it seems reasonable that the two variables which would be important in determining how much money people want to hold are the volume of transactions, and the cost of holding wealth in the form of money. The first of these variables can be represented by real income (Y), because the higher is Y the greater will be the volume of transactions. The cost of holding money is forgone interest rate, which shows what could be earned if wealth were held in the form of interest-bearing assets, rather than in the form of money. People decide how much money to hold on the basis of costs and benefits.

Transaction theories explain the money demand function which is known as the Baumol-Tobin model and it remains a leading theory of money demand today.

Keynesian analysis assumes that transactions demand for money is a function of income and it is not dependent on the level of income.

The Baumol-Tobin Model of Cash–Management

The Baumol-Tobin model analyses the costs and benefits of holding money. The benefit of holding money is the convenience of making transactions. The cost of this convenience is the forgone interest.

To see how people trade off these benefits and costs, consider a person who plans to spend £*Y* gradually over the course of a year. How much should he hold in the process of spending this amount ? That is, what is the optimal size of average cash balances ?

Suppose we withdraw £*Y* at the beginning of the year and gradually spend the money. Fig. 5.1(a) shows our money holdings over the course of the year. Money holding begins at *Y* and ends the year at zero, averaging *Y/2* over the year.

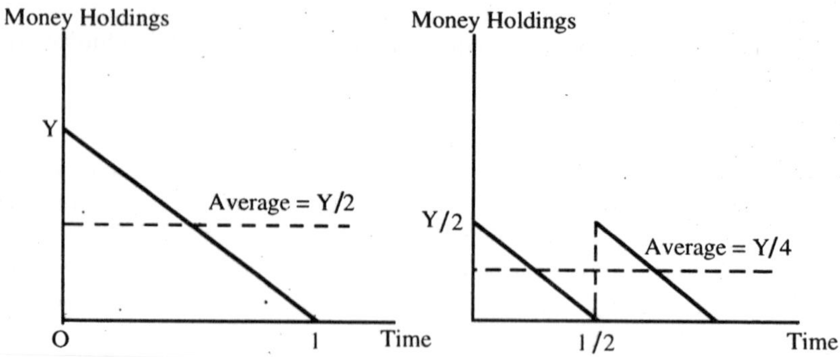

(a) Money holdings with one withdrawal a year

(b) Money holdings with two withdrawals a year

Fig. 5.1 Average Money Holdings

A second plan is to make two possible withdrawals. In this case, we withdraw £*Y/2* at the beginning of the year, gradually spend this amount over the first half of the year, and then make another withdrawal of £*Y/2* for the second half of the year. Fig. 5.1(b) shows that money holdings over the year vary between Y/2 and zero, averaging *Y/4*. This plan has the advantage that less money is held on average, so less interest is forgone, but it has the disadvantage of requiring two withdrawals rather than one.

More generally, suppose the individual makes *N* withdrawals over the course of the year. Each time we withdraw £*Y/N* we then spend the money gradually over the following *1/N* th of the year.

The question is, what is the optimal choice of *N*? The greater *N* is, the less money is held on average and the less interest is forgone. But as N increases, so is the inconvenience of making frequent withdrawals.

Suppose the cost of going to the bank is some fixed amount F which includes the time spent in travelling to and from the bank and waiting in line to make withdrawals. For example, if a trip to the bank takes *20* minutes and a person's wage is *£9* per hour, then F is *£3*. Also, let r denote the interest rate and thus r measures the opportunity cost of holding money.

Now we can analyse the optimal choice N which determines money demand. For any N, the average amount of money held is $Y/(2N)$, so the interest forgone is $rY/(2N)$. Since F is the cost per trip to the bank, the total cost of making trips is FN. The total cost is the sum of forgone interest and the cost of trips to the bank.

$$\textit{Total Cost} = \textit{Forgone Interest} + \textit{Cost of Trips} = \frac{rY}{2n} + FN$$

$\frac{dC}{dN} = -\frac{rYN^{-2}}{2} + F$, where $\frac{dC}{dN} = 0$, which yields the formula for optimal $N = N^*$. The larger the number of withdrawals N, the smaller the interest forgone, and the larger the cost of travelling to the bank.

Fig. 5.2 shows how total cost depends on N. There is a value of N that minimises total cost. The optimal value of N, is $N^* = \sqrt{\frac{rY}{2F}}$. Average money holding $= \frac{Y}{2N^*} = \sqrt{\frac{YF}{2r}}$

(N^* minimises total cost).

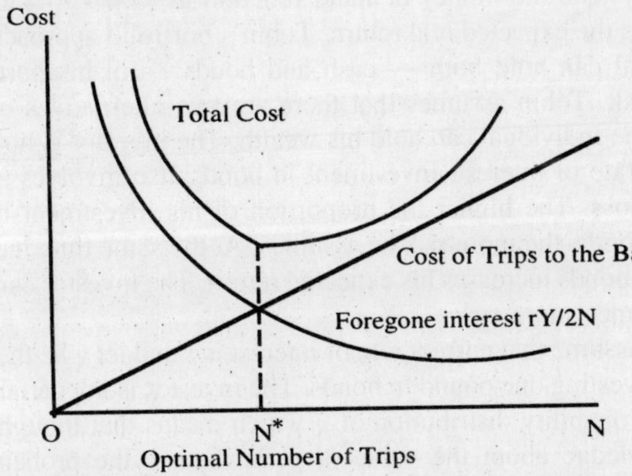

Fig. 5.2 Average Money Holding which minimises Total Cost

This expression shows that the individual holds money if the fixed cost of withdrawal F is higher, if expenditure Y is higher or if the interest rate r is lower.

So far, we have been interpreting the Baumol-Tobin model as a model of the demand for currency. But one can interpret the model more broadly. Suppose a person holds a portfolio of monetary assets and non-monetary assets. Let r be the difference in the return between monetary and non-monetary assets, and let F be the cost of transferring non-monetary assets into monetary assets, such as brokerage fee. The decision about how often to pay a brokerage fee is analogous to the decision about how often to withdraw money from bank. Thus, the Baumol-Tobin model describes this person's demand for monetary assets. By showing that money demand depends positively on Y and negatively on r, the model provides a micro-economic justification for the money demand function, $L(r, Y)$.

The Speculative Motive Or Portfolio Theories of Money Demand

Theories of money demand that emphasise the role of money as a store of value are called portfolio theories. These theories stress that people hold money as part of their portfolio of assets. Money offers a different combination of return and risk compared to the assets. The prices of stocks and bonds may rise or fall, whereas money offers a safe return. Thus, households choose to hold money as part of their optimal portfolio. One of the best models of the demand for money as an asset is James Tobin's "Liquidity Preference as Behaviour towards Risk." The demand for money depends on the risk and return offered by money and by various assets households can hold instead of money. Moreover, money demand should depend on total wealth. For example, we can write the money demand function as : $(M/P)^d = L(r_s, r_d, \pi_e, w)$, where r_s is the expected real return. Tobin's portfolio approach shows how an individual can hold both — cash and bonds — in his portfolio in order to avoid risk. Tobin assumes that there are two alternatives cash and bonds in which the individual can hold his wealth. The investor is not certain about the future rate of interest. Investment in bonds also involves a risk of capital gains or loss. The higher the proportion of his investment balances that he holds in bonds, the more risk he assumes. At the same time increasing his investment in bonds increases his expected return. The investor can expect return if he assumes more risk.

Now let us assume that current rate of interest is r and let g be the capital gain or loss by investing one pound in bonds. The investor is not certain about g, but he has a probability distribution of g which means that though he has no definite knowledge about the value of g, he knows the probability of occurrence of different values of g. It is assumed that this probability distribution has an expected value of zero and is independent of the current rate on bonds.

A portfolio consists of A_1 of cash and A_2 of bonds, where $A_1 + A_2 = 1$. The return on a portfolio is given by

$$R = A_2(r + g), \quad 0 \leq A_2 \leq 1 \quad \text{.....................(1)}$$

$\therefore E(R) = A_2(r + g) = A_2E(r) + A_2E(g)$. But the current rate of interest is constant so that $E(r) = r$ and by assumption $E(g) = 0$. Thus, $E(R) = A_2 r$. Let the expected value of R be denoted by μ_R. Then we get

$$E(R) = \mu_R = A_2 r \quad \text{..........................(2)}$$

The risk attached to a portfolio is to be measured by the standard deviation of R, denoted by σ_R. A high standard deviation means high probability of large deviations from mean value μ_R both positive and negative. Thus, a high value of σ_R implies the chance of large capital gains or chances of large capital losses. Similarly, a low σ_R means a low capital gains or losses. Thus, σ_R. measures the risk of portfolio.

The standard deviation of R can be written as follows, since $R = A_2(r + g)$ and $E(R) = A_2(r)$, $\therefore R - E(R) = A_2 g$

$$\therefore \{R - E(R)\}^2 = A_2^2 g^2 \quad \therefore E\{R - E(R)\}^2 = A_2^2 E\{g - E(g)\}^2 \quad [\because E(g) = 0]$$

$$\therefore \sigma_R{}^2 = A_2{}^2 \sigma_g{}^2 \qquad \therefore \sigma_R = A_2 \sigma_g \quad \text{..........................(3)}$$

This shows that the standard deviation of R depends on the standard deviation of g and on the proportion invested in bonds. From equations (2) and (3), it can be seen that the proportion invested in bonds A_2 determines both $E(R) = \mu_R$ and the risk σ_R of the portfolio.

From equation (2), we get $A_2 = \mu_R / r$ and from equation (3), we get $A_2 = \sigma_R / \sigma_g$. $\therefore \mu_R / r = \sigma_R / \sigma_g$, or $\mu_R = (r/\sigma_g)\sigma_R$ ....(4)
Since $0 \leq A_2 \leq 1$, therefore, $0 \leq (\sigma_R / \sigma_g) \leq 1$, i.e., $0 \leq \sigma_R \leq \sigma_g$.

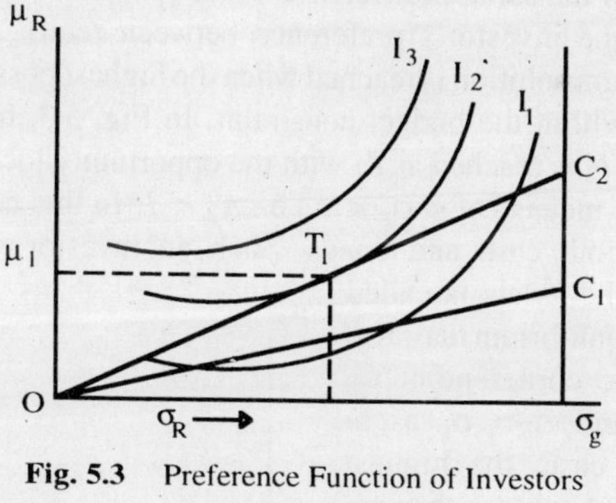

Fig. 5.3 Preference Function of Investors

Equation (4) gives us a relation between μ_R and σ_R. This is the opportunity locus of the investor which shows the terms on which the investor can get higher expected return at the expense of assuming more risk. If we plot σ_R on the horizontal axis and μ_R on the vertical axis, we can get a straight line through the origin with slope (r/σ_g). In Fig. 5.3, the line OC_1 represents the opportunity locus when the current rate of interest is r_1. The slope of OC_1 is (r_1/σ_g). If the rate of interest is r_2, the opportunity locus becomes OC_2 which is steeper than C_1 when $r_2 > r_1$. Since $\sigma_R \leq \sigma_g$, the lines OC_1 and

OC_2 terminate at σg. Given the current rate of interest the opportunity locus is fixed. The opportunity locus gives the different opportunities open to an investor and which one he is going to select depends on the preference pattern

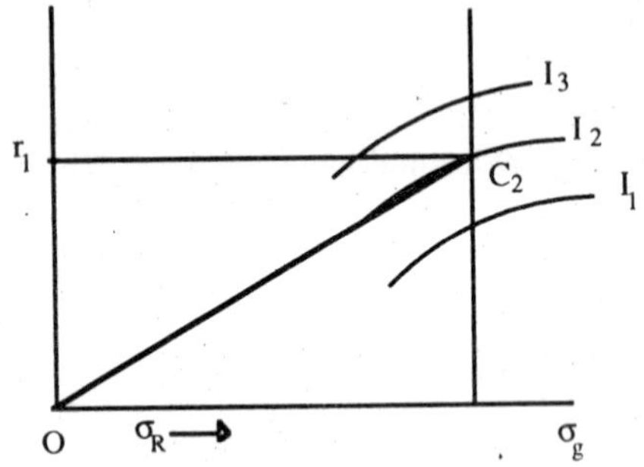

Fig. 5.4 Equilibrium Solution of Highest Risk-taker

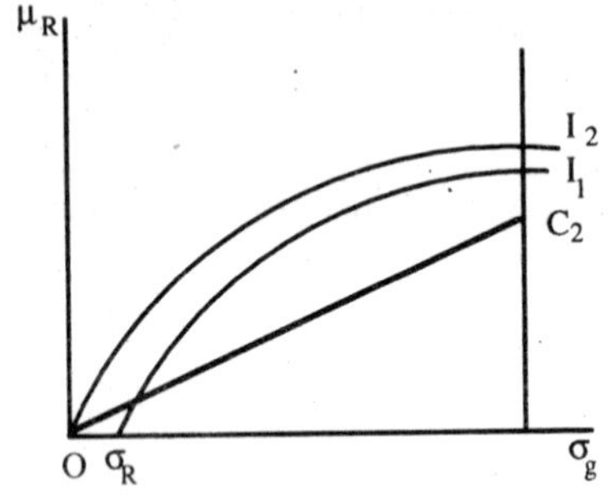

Fig. 5.5 Equilibrium Solution of Investor who takes No-Risk

of the investor. The preference pattern or utility function is represented by an indifference map. Let us assume that utility received by the investor, U, is a function of μ_R and σ_R, i.e., $U = U(\mu_R, \sigma_R)$. Indifference curves measure the level of utilities. The greater the utility level, the higher will be the indifference curve. The investor is indifferent between all combinations of (σ_R, μ_R) that lie on the same indifference curve (I). The slope of IC depends on the nature of the investor's preference between return and risk.

The equilibrium solution is reached when the highest possible indifference curve is attained within the budget constraint. In Fig. 5.3, highest attainable indifference curve I_2 is reached at T_1 with the opportunity locus OC_2. At point T, $\sigma_R < \sigma_g$, which means $\sigma_R < \sigma_g < 1$ i.e., $A_2 < 1$. In this equilibrium point, individual holds both cash and bonds. Such an investor who holds some amounts of both the assets is called a diversifier. The equilibrium may also be achieved at the corner point C_2 where $\mu_R = r_1$ and $\sigma_R = \sigma_g$ as in Fig. 5.4. In this case, the highest indifference curve I_2 passes through the point C_2 . At this point (C_2), $\sigma_R = \sigma_g$, $\sigma_R/\sigma_g = 1$ or $A_2 = 1$. In this case, the entire amount of wealth is held in the form of bonds.

Similarly, a corner equilibrium can also take place at O where $\sigma_R = 0$, i.e., $A_2 = 0$ and $A_1 = 1$. In this case, the entire balance is held in cash. Such a solution can be shown

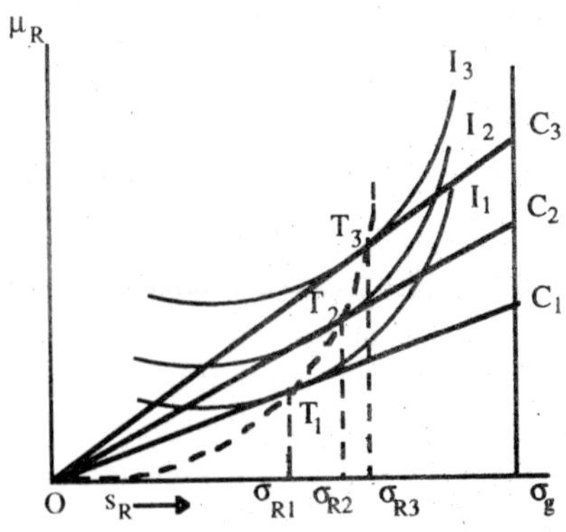

Fig. 5.6 Equilibrium of a Standard Investors at Different Interest Rates

in Fig. 5.5. The highest indifference curve is I_2 which passes through O and as this is in equilibrium the investor holds all cash and no bond. These corner solutions indicate that investors are non-diversifiers.

Empirically, we find that most of the investors in the real world are diversifiers. Thus, the situation depicted in Fig. 5.3 may be taken as the standard case. Now let us see how in the standard case, the portfolio equilibrium changes with change in the current rate of interest. This is shown in Fig. 5.6. Suppose the current rate of interest is r_1. At r_1 the opportunity locus is OC_1 and it is tangent at T_1 with indifference curve I_1. Now suppose the rate of interest increases to r_2. At r_2, the opportunity locus is C_2 and the point of tangency between I_2 and C_2 is at T_2 and so on. The locus of the successive points of tangency between *ICs* and opportunity loci is called the optimum portfolio curve. From the opportunity portfolio curve, we can see that as the interest rate increases, σ_R also increases where $\sigma_{R1} < \sigma_{R2} < \sigma_{R3}$. It follows from constant σ_g that $\frac{\sigma_{R1}}{\sigma_g} < \frac{\sigma_{R2}}{\sigma_g} < \frac{\sigma_{R3}}{\sigma_g}$. This means that as the rate of interest increases, so also the portfolio of bonds held increases. As A_2 increases, A_1 decreases. Thus, as the interest rate increases so the proportion of wealth held in the form of cash decreases. This gives us an inverse relationship between the rate of interest and the demand for cash. So the portfolio balance approach can explain the downward sloping liquidity preference function.

It is also possible to have an optimum portfolio curve downward sloping which means that as the interest rate goes up, the proportion invested in bonds decreases. This is shown in Fig. 5.7 where $\sigma_{R2} < \sigma_{R1}$, so that $\frac{\sigma_{R2}}{\sigma_g} < \frac{\sigma_{R1}}{\sigma_g}$. This means that A_2 decreases as the interest rate increases. Here A_1 increases as A_2 decreases. Thus, we get a direct relationship between the rate of interest and the demand for cash. This ambiguity can be explained with the help of income and substitution effects of a change in the rate of interest. The optimum portfolio curve is similar to price consumption curve. When we move along the price consumption curve, a price effect takes place which is the result of income and substitution effects. Similarly, the rate of interest can produce two such effects. For example, an increase in the rate of interest provides incentive to take more risk due to substitution effect which tends to increase A_2. At

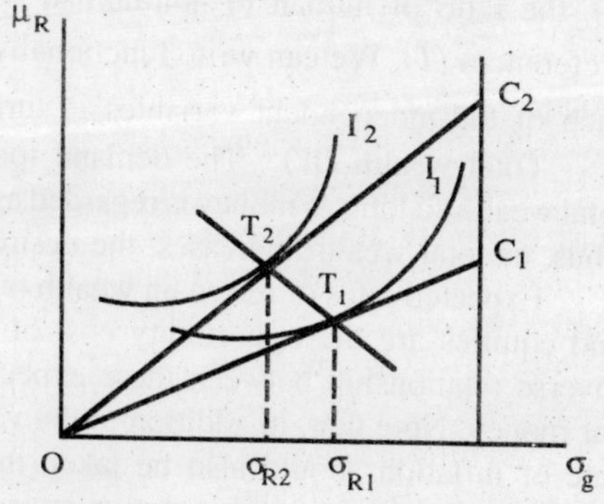

Fig. 5.7 Equilibrium at Different Rates of Interest

the same time a higher interest rate increases the real income of the investor and gives him more security. This income effect will tend to reduce A_2. Thus, the income effect and substitution effect work in opposite directions. The net effect will depend on the relative strengths of these two effects. If the income effect is stronger than the substitution effect, we shall get a direct relationship between the rate of interest and the demand for cash, as shown in Fig. 5.7. On the other hand, if the substitution effect is stronger than the income effect, we shall get an inverse relationship between the rate of interest and the demand for cash, as shown in Fig. 5.6.

The portfolio balance approach has the great merit that it can explain the inverse relationship between the demand for cash and the rate of interest without assuming inelasticity of expectations of future rates of interest. It also provides an explanation of why rational individuals hold diversified portfolios containing both cash and bonds. This approach provides a logically more satisfactory foundation for the Keynesian liquidity preference theory. It is not difficult to extend this theory where there are more than two assets.

The Modern Quantity Theory

Milton Friedman restated the quantity theory as a theory of the demand for money, and this 'Modern Quantity Theory' has become the basis of view put forward by monetarists. In this theory, money is seen as just one of a number of ways in which wealth can be held, along with all other human and non-human wealth.

Since money is seen as just one of the ways in which wealth can be held, Friedman sees the real demand for money (M_D / P) as depending on total wealth (W), the expected rates of return on the various forms of wealth (r), the ratio of human to non-human wealth (ω) and society's tastes and preferences (T). We can write functionally as $\frac{M_D}{P} = f(W, r, \omega, T)$. Consider each of the independent variables in turn.

Total wealth (W) : The demand for money will be directly related to total wealth so long as money is regarded as a 'normal good' by wealth-holders. Thus, as total wealth increases, the desire to hold money will also increase.

Expected rates of return on wealth (r) : Since the rates of return on bonds and equities are the opportunity cost of holding money, we can expect an inverse relationship between these expected rates of return and the demand for money. Note that, in addition to the various rates of interest, the expected rate of inflation should also be taken into account. The higher the rate of inflation, the greater is the negative return from holding money and the more attractive are the interest-bearing assets. Thus, there is also an inverse relationship between the rate of inflation and the real demand for money.

The ratio of human wealth to non-human wealth (ω) : This variable is included by Friedman because human wealth is very illiquid. It cannot be sold and individuals have a limited ability to transfer non-human wealth into human wealth. The higher the ω ratio, the greater will be the demand for money in order to compensate for the limited marketability of such wealth.

Tastes and preferences *(T)* : Friedman argues that the demand for money is also a function of a number factors which are likely to influence wealth holders' tastes and preferences for money.

The fundamental problem with this demand for money function is to find a method of measuring total wealth. According to Friedman, the permanent income (Y_ρ) may provide a proxy variable. This is a long-run measure of income which can be thought of as the present value of the expected flow of income from the stock of human and non-human wealth over a long period of time. It is normally estimated as an average of past, present and expected future incomes. Incorporating this into the function, and assuming that T and ω are constant especially in the short-run, we can write as : $\frac{M_D}{P} = f(Y_\rho, r)$ which is not very different from Keynesian liquidity-preference function, $L = f(Y, r)$. There are, however, two crucial differences. First, in the Keynesian function — where money is a close substitute for bonds only — the demand for money is interest-elastic, because if the rate of return from holding bonds changes, wealth holders are unlikely to react in any other way than changing their money holdings; but in Friedman's money demand function money is likely to exhibit low interest-elasticity. Secondly, the Keynesian function includes current (Y) income only, whereas Friedman uses permanent income (Y_ρ) as a proxy variable for total wealth.

The precautionary motive is just as important as a motive for holding money as the other. In transaction demand for money, we focussed on transaction costs and ignored uncertainty. Here we concentrate on the demand for money that arises from uncertainty about the payments they might have to make. Suppose that people do not know precisely what payments they will be receiving in the next few weeks and what they will have to make. The person might need to take a cab in the rain, or have to pay for a prescription. If they do not have to pay, they will incur a loss. Let us denote the loss incurred for a shortage of cash by *£q*.

The more money people hold, the less likely they are to incur the costs of illiquidity. But the more money people hold, the more interest they will have to forgo. We are back to a trade-off situation similar to that examined in relation to the transactions demand. Somewhere between holding so little cash that one will have to forgo some purchase and holding lots of money so that there is little chance of not being able to make any payment, there must thus be an optimal amount of precautionary balances to hold.

To determine the optimal amount of money to hold, we compare the marginal cost (M_C) of increasing money holding by *£1* with the expected marginal benefit (M_B) of doing so. The (M_C) is the interest forgone or r which is shown in Fig. 5.8. The M_B of increasing money holding arises from the lower expected costs of illiquidity. Increased precautionary balances from zero has a large M_B, since that takes care of small, unexpected disbursements that are likely to occur. As we increase cash balances further, we continue to reduce the probability of illiquidity at a decreasing rate. Thus, the M_B of additional cash is a decreasing function of cash holdings, as shown by the M_B curve in Fig. 5.8.

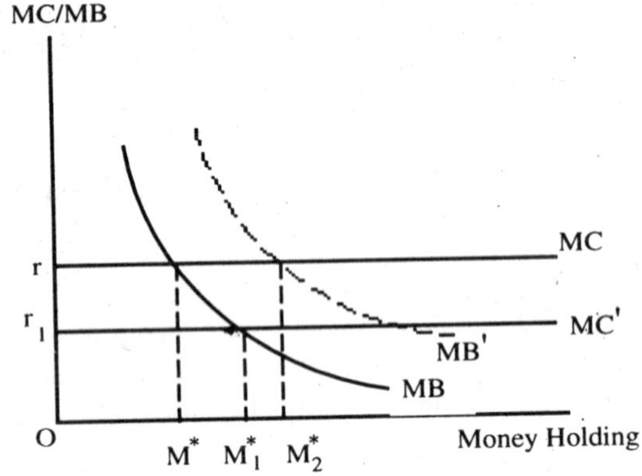

Fig. 5.8 Optimal Money Holding

The optimal.level of precautionary demand is reached at M^* where $M_C = M_B$. It is clear from Fig. 5.8 that precautionary balances will be larger when the interest rate is lower. A reduction in the interest rate to r_1 shifts the MC to $M_{C'}$ and increases M^* to M_1^*. The lower cost of holding money makes it profitable to insure more heavily against the costs of illiquidity. An increase in uncertainty leads to increase in money holdings because it shifts up the M_B to M_B' and M^* to M_2^*. Finally, the lower the costs of illiquidity, q, the lower the money demand.

The precautionary demand depends on : the alternative costs in terms of interest forgone, the cost of illiquidity, and the degree of uncertainty that determines the probability of illiquidity.

The Supply Of Money

Here we see that the banking system plays a key role in determining the money supply, and in most countries the only supplier of currency is some central authority, for example, the Issue Department of the Bank of England. We discuss various instruments that the Central Bank can use to alter the money supply. We can thus treat the supply of currency as being exogenous, possibly affecting the economic system but not being affected by it, except so far as the central authority decides it wants to be affected. We defined the quantity of money as the amount of money held by the public, and we assumed that the Central Bank also controls the money supply by increasing or decreasing the quantity of money in circulation through open-market operations. Although this explanation is acceptable as a first approximation, it is not complete because it omits the role of the banking system in determining money supply.

Thus, the money supply is determined not only by the Central Bank, but also by the behaviour of households which hold money and of banks in which money is held. The money supply includes both currency in the hands of the public and the deposits of banks that households can use on demand for transactions. That is, if *M* denotes the money supply, *C* currency, and *D* demand deposits, we can write :

Money Supply (M) = Currency (C) + Demand Deposits (D)

To understand the money supply, we must understand the interaction between currency and demand deposits and how Central Bank influences these two components of the money supply.

100-Percent Reserve Banking

Suppose that banks accept deposits but do not make loans. The only purpose of the banks is to provide a safe place for depositors to keep their money. The deposits that banks receive but do not lent out are called Reserve. In this simple economy, all deposits are held as Reserves : banks accept deposits, place the money in reserve until the depositor makes a withdrawal. This system is called 100-Percent Reserve Banking.

A Balance Sheet of a bank under 100-Percent Reserve Banking looks like Fig. 1. A bank's Balance Sheet shows its assets and liabilities. Under this system, banks hold deposits as reserves. If the bank holds 100% of deposits in reserve, the banking system does not affect the supply of money.

Fig. 1. Bank's Balance Sheet for a Deposit of £1,000

Assets	*Liabilities*
Reserves £1,000.00	Deposits £1,000.00

Fractional-Reserve Banking

In most countries, the banking system operates on a partial reserve basis which means banks use some of their deposits to give loans. The banks keep some fraction of their deposits on hand so that reserves are available whenever depositors want to make withdrawals. The banks have a legal requirement to hold some fraction of their deposits in the form of some particular assets, known as Reserve Assets. This system is known as Fractional-Reserve Banking.

Fig. 2 shows the Balance Sheet of Fractional-Reserve Banking System. This Balance Sheet shows the maximum amount of deposits that the banks can create depends on reserve-deposit ratio — the fraction of deposits kept in reserve. We assume that the banks are required to keep *20%* of their deposits as reserve ratio. Firstbank keeps *£200* of the *£1,000* in deposits in reserve and lends out the remaining *£800.*

Figure 2. (a) Firstbank's Balance Sheet

Assets		*Liabilities*
Reserves	£200.00	Deposits £1,000.00
Loans	£800	

(b) Secondbank's Balance Sheet

Assets		*Liabilities*
Reserves	£160.00	Deposits £800.00
Loans	£640	

Thus, we can see that Firstbank increases the supply of money by *£800* when it makes this loan. Before the loan is made, the money supply is *£1,000*. After the loan is made, the money supply is *£1,800* , the depositor still has a demand deposit of *£1,000*, but now the borrower holds *£800* in currency. Thus, under a fractional-reserve system, banks create money.

The creation of money does not stop with Firstbank. If the borrower deposits the *£800* in another bank, the process of money creation continues. Fig. 2(b) shows the Balance Sheet of Secondbank. Secondbank receives the *£800* in deposits, keeps *20%* or *£160*, in reserve, and then lends out *£640*, and so on, with each deposit and loan, more money is created.

Although this process of money circulation can continue, it does not create an infinite amount of money. Let r denotes the reserve-deposit ratio, then the amount of money that the original *£1,000* creates is :

$$\text{Original Deposit} = £1{,}000$$

$$\text{Firstbank Lending} = (1 - r) \times £1{,}000$$

$$\text{Secondbank Lending} = (1 - r)^2 \times £1{,}000$$

$$\text{Total Money Supply} = [\ 1 + (1 - r) + (1 - r)^2 + \ldots\ ] \times £1{,}000$$

$$= (1/R) \times £1{,}000$$

If $R = 0.2$, then the original *£1,000* generates *£5,000* money.

The banking system's ability to create money is the primary difference between banks and other financial institutions. Financial markets have the important function of transferring the economy's resources from those households that wish to save some of their income for the future of those households and firms that wish to borrow to buy investment goods to be used in future production. This process is called financial intermediation. Many institutions in the economy act as financial intermediaries ; the most important examples are the stock market, the bond market, and the banking system. Yet, of these institutions, only banks have the legal authority to create assets that are of the money supply, such as Current Accounts. Thus, banks are the only financial institutions that directly influences money supply. It may also be noted that although the system of fractional-reserve banking creates money or liquidity, it does not create wealth.

A Model Of The Money Supply

We have seen how banks create money. Here we present a model of the money supply under fractional-reserve banking. The model has three exogenous variables : 1) The monetary base B is the total amount of money held by the public as currency C and by the banks as Reserves R. It is directly controlled by the Central Bank. 2) The reserve-deposit ratio r is the fraction of deposits that banks hold in reserve. It is determined by the laws regulating banks. 3) The currency-deposit ratio C_r expresses the preferences of the public about how much money to hold in the form of demand deposits D and how much to hold in the form of currency C. The model shows how the money supply depends on the monetary base, the reserve-deposit ratio, and the currency-deposit ratio. It allows us to examine how the policy of the monetary authority and the choices of banks and households influence the money supply.

We begin with the definitions of money supply and the monetary base : $M = C + D$; $B = C + R$

The first equation states that the money supply is the sum of currency and demand deposits. The second equation states that the monetary base is the sum of currency and bank reserves. Now divide the first equation by the second to obtain : $\frac{M}{B} = \frac{C+D}{C+R}$. Then divide the numerator and denominator by D, $\frac{M}{B} = \frac{\frac{C}{D}+1}{\frac{C}{D}+\frac{R}{D}}$.

We already know that C/D is the currency-deposit ratio C_r, and the R/D is the reserve-deposit ratio r. Substituting these and bringing B from the left to the right side of the equation, we get $M = \frac{Cr+1}{Cr+r} \times B$. This equation shows how the money supply depends on three exogenous variables.

Thus, the money supply is proportional to the monetary base. The factor of proportionality, $(C_r + 1)/(C_r + r) = m$ and is called the money multiplier. We can write : $M = m \times B$.

Each pound of the monetary base produces m pounds of money. Because the monetary base has a multiplier effect on the money supply, the monetary base is sometimes called high-powered money. For example, in the US economy the monetary base is *\$300* billion, the reserve-deposit ratio r is 0.1 and the currency-deposit ratio, C_r, is *0.4*. In this case, the money multiplier is $m = \frac{0.4+1}{0.4+0.1} = 2.8$ and the money supply is $M = 2.8 \times 300 = 840$.

Each dollar of the monetary base generates *2.8* dollars of money, so that the total money supply is *$840* billion.

We can now see how changes in three exogenous variables — B, r, and C_r — causes money supply to change:

1) The money supply is proportional to the monetary base. Thus, an increase in the monetary base increases the money supply by the same percentage.
2) The lower the reserve-deposit ratio, the more money loans banks can make and more money they can create. Thus, a decrease in the reserve-deposit ratio raises the money multiplier and the money supply.
3) The lower the currency-deposit ratio, the more money banks can create. Thus, a decrease in the currency-deposit ratio raises the money multiplier and the money supply.

The Three Instruments Of Monetary Policy

The monetary authority controls the money supply directly and/or indirectly by altering either the monetary base or the reserve-deposit ratio. To do this, the monetary authority has at its disposal three main instruments of monetary policy : open-market operations, reserve requirements and the discount rate.

Open-market Operations are the purchases or sales of government bonds by the Central Bank/monetary authority. When it buys bonds from the public, the money it pays for bonds increases the monetary base and thereby increases money supply. When it sells bonds to the public, the money it receives reduces the monetary base and thus decreases the money supply. Open-market operations are the most-often used policy instrument of the Central Bank .

Reserve Requirements are Central Bank regulations that impose on banks a minimum reserve-deposit ratio. An increase in reserve requirement raises the reserve-deposit ratio and thus lowers the money multiplier and the money supply. This is the least-frequently used instrument.

The *discount rate* is the interest rate that the Central Bank *(BOE)* charges when it makes loans to banks. Banks borrow from the Central Bank *(CB)* when they find themselves with too few reserves to meet reserve requirements. The lower the discount rate, the cheaper are borrowed reserves and the more banks borrow at the *CB's* discount window. Hence, a reduction in the discount rate raises the monetary base and the money supply.

Although these instruments give the *CB* substantial power to influence the money supply, the *CB* cannot control money supply perfectly. Bank discretion in conducting business can cause the money supply to change in ways the *CB* did not anticipate.

Money Market Equilibrium

If investment is assumed to be a function of the rate of interest then we need to know the rate of interest to determine the equilibrium level of income. From the equality of saving and investment we can derive the equilibrium income, provided we know the interest rate. For this reason, we consider the determination of the interest rate in the Keynesian theory which is also known as liquidity preference theory.

According to Keynes, the interest rate is a monetary phenomenon. It depends on the supply of and the demand for money. Money is the most liquid asset. Liquidity is an important attribute of an asset. The more quickly an asset can be converted into cash without incurring any loss, the more liquid the asset is. Obviously money is the most liquid asset. The interest is the price paid for lending money or for partying the liquidity. Thus, the price of money or the rate of interest is determined by the equality of demand and supply of money.

The demand for money depends on three factors which Keynes called the 'motives' or 'reasons' for holding money. These motives are : 1) The Transaction Motive, 2) The Precautionary Motive and 3) The Speculative Motive. Let us now discuss these motives in more details.

1) **The Transaction Motive** : The transaction motive arises from the function of money as a medium of exchange. An individual earns income after an interval of time, say a week, or a month, etc. During any two income-receiving periods, the individual will have to make transactions. In other words, the payments and receipts are not synchronised. While the payments are made throughout the period, the income is received after a period of time. To carry out transaction during the period of time, an individual must hold a part of his income in the form of cash. Thus, the demand for money comes from its functions. Money acts as a means of payments or medium of exchange. It also acts as a form of asset. Money balances kept by the people may be divided into two parts — active balance and idle balance. Active balance is held for the function of money as a means of payment, and idle money is held for its function as a form of asset.

Active balance is also called 'transaction' and 'precautionary' balances. In short, we call it transaction balance (M_t) which is assumed to be proportional to income. So, the transaction balance of the economy will depend on the national income of the economy and can be written as : $M_t = kY$ ....*(1)*, such that $dM_t/dY > 0$, where k is a positive constant. Economists like Baumol, Tobin and others hold the view that the transaction balance of the economy depends not only on the level of income, but also on the rate of interest. If the rate of interest is higher, people will economise the use of cash, thereby reducing the average transaction balance of the economy.

2) **Precautionary Motive** : Precautionary motive for holding cash arises from the desire of the individual to hold some cash for meeting unforeseen

events like, sickness, accident etc. To meet uncertain future obligations each individual will hold a part of his income in the form of money. Such cash balances are known as precautionary balances. The difference between transaction demand and precautionary demand is that in the former case no uncertainty is involved. People hold money because payments and receipts are separated. But uncertainty is the source of precautionary demand. People hold precautionary balances to meet uncertain circumstances. It also depends on the level of income. Thus, the precautionary balance is a function of national income (Y), *i.e.*, $M_p = M_p(Y)$, such that $dM_p / DY > 0$, where M_p is the amount of precautionary balance and Y is income.

3) **Speculative Motive** : It is the speculative motive for holding cash that makes the Keynesian theory of demand for money different from classical theory. Keynes considered the asset demand for money as idle balances. Keynes also assumed that there are two ways in which wealth can be held : money and bonds. If an individual holds money, he gets no interest income, on the other hand, if he holds bonds instead, he can get interest income. He can also make capital gains or losses by selling bonds at some future date. Now the question is why should people hold money instead of bonds ? The answer is that if he holds bonds he gets interest income. But he can also make capital gain or loss. Now if the sum of interest income and capital gain (loss) is positive, he will hold bonds. However, if the sum of interest income and capital loss is negative, he will hold only cash. Such idle balances which an individual holds rather than bonds is known as speculative balance or speculative demand for money.

Whether an individual holds money or bond depends on his expectations. Expectations are formed on the basis of his experience. If the current rate of interest is normal, people will expect it to prevail in the future. If the current rate is lower than the normal rate, the rate of interest will be expected to rise in the future and bond prices will fall. On the other hand, if the current rate is lower than the normal, the rate of interest will fall in the future and bond prices will rise. However, expectations differ among individuals. The higher the current rate of interest above the normal rate, the greater is the percentage of people expecting the current rate to fall and vice versa. As the divergence between the current rate and the normal rate rises the percentage of people expecting the current rate to rise or fall also increases.

There are three assumptions regarding this function : a) there is a maximum rate of interest (r_{max}) at which speculative demand for money is zero, b) there is a minimum rate of interest (r_{min}) at which speculative demand is infinity — (r_{min} is called the floor rate below which the rate of interest cannot fall), and (c) between these two extreme rates, the speculative demand for money is inversely related with the interest rate. Thus, we can write the speculative demand for money as : $M_s = L(r)$.......(2) where $L'(r) = \infty$ for $r = r_{min}$, $L'(r) = 0$ for $r = r_{max}$ and $L'(r) < 0$ for $r_{min} < r < r_{max}$.

In Fig. 5.9, we draw the graph of equation (1) by measuring income horizontally and the transaction demand for money vertically. In Fig. 5.10, we plot the graph of equation (2) by measuring speculative demand for money horizontally and the rate of interest vertically. The total demand for money (M_d) is the sum of the transaction balance and the speculative balance. Thus, the demand for money can be written as : $M_d = M_t + M_s = kY + L(r)$.......(3) In its general form, the function can be written as : $M_d = L\ (Y, r)$ where $LY = k > 0$, and L_r obeys the same restrictions as those on $L'(r)$.

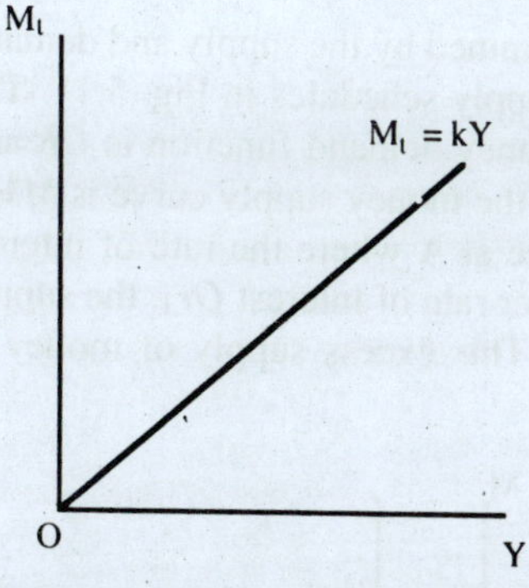

Fig. 5.9 Demand for Active Balances

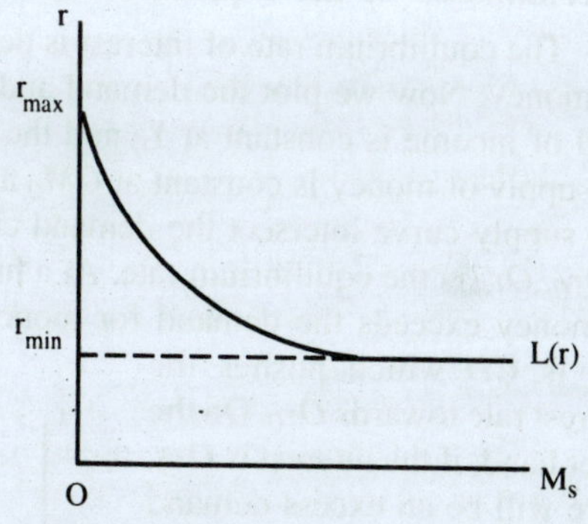

Fig. 5.10 Demand for Idle Balances

Total demand for money will depend on the demand for active balances and on the demand for idle balances. Demand for active balances (M_t) is a function of the level of income while the demand for idle balances (M_s) is a function of the rate of interest. Total demand for money (M_d), is thus the sum of M_t and M_s; *i.e.*, $M_d = M_t + M_s = kY + L_2(r) = L\ (Y,r)$ ....(4)

Thus, the total demand for money (M_d) is a function of both the level of income and the rate of interest. This is known as the demand function of money or the liquidity preference function.

This function is such that $\partial L / \partial y > 0,\ \partial L / \partial r < 0$. This means that if the level of income remains the same, the demand for money varies with the rate of interest, or, if the rate of interest remains the same, the demand for money varies directly with the level of income.

The money market is in equilibrium, when the demand for money is equal to the given supply of money. When the demand for money exceeds the supply of money, some people will find that their demand for money is not satisfied. They will sell bonds to acquire money. As a result, bond prices will fall and hence interest rate will rise. Alternatively, when the supply of money is greater than demand, some people will hold too much money. They will try to get rid of excess money by buying bonds. As a consequence, bond prices will rise and thus interest rate will fall. Thus, to have equilibrium in the money market, the demand for money must equal its supply.

$M_s = kY + L(r) = L(Y,r)$ ....(5),

where M_s is the institutionally given quantity of money or given money supply in the economy.

In the Keynesian theory, it is assumed that the supply of money is given by the monetary authority. Total supply of money is independent of the rate of interest. The supply schedule can be represented by a vertical straight line.

Determination of the Equilibrium Rate of Interest

The equilibrium rate of interest is determined by the supply and demand for money. Now we plot the demand and supply schedules in Fig. 5.11. The level of income is constant at Y_0 and the money demand function is CE and the supply of money is constant at OM_0 and the money supply curve is MM_0. The supply curve intersect the demand curve at A where the rate of interest is Or_0. Or_0 is the equilibrium rate. At a higher rate of interest Or_1, the supply of money exceeds the demand for money. This excess supply of money at Or_1 is CD which pushes the interest rate towards Or_0. On the other hand, if the interest is Or_2, there will be an excess demand for money. The excess demand in the money market will push the interest rate towards Or_0. This adjustment process can be expressed in terms of the following equation : $dr/dt = f(M_d - M_s)$, such that $dr/dt >$ or $=$ or < 0, according as $(M_d - M_s) >$ or $=$ or < 0, where M_d is the demand for money and M_s is the supply of money. In other words, it means that the rate of interest will decrease when there is excess supply of money, it will increase when there is an excess demand for money and will remain constant when there is no excess demand or supply $(M_d = M_s)$.

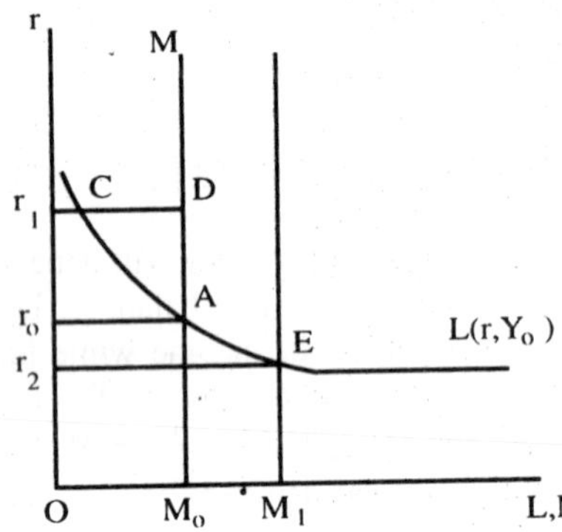

Fig. 5.11 Determination of the Equilibrium Rate of Interest

Now let us consider the effect of an increase in the supply of money and its effect on the equilibrium rate of interest. As the supply of money increases, the money supply schedule shifts to the right. Suppose the supply of money increases from M_0 to M_1. The new equilibrium interest rate is $Or_2 < Or_0$. Thus, when the money supply increases, the equilibrium rate of interest decreases. The reason is that since the level of income remains unchanged, the demand for active balance will also remain constant. The additional supply of money can be absorbed if the demand for idle balances (L) increases. Now

L will increase only when the interest rate falls. In other words, the additional supply of money will be diverted in the bond market thereby raising the demand and prices of bonds. This will mean a fall in the rate of interest. Thus, the supply of money reduces the equilibrium rate of interest.

Liquidity Trap

If, however, the supply of money schedule intersects the demand schedule at the latter's horizontal part, a further increase in money supply will not reduce the market rate of interest. In this situation, everyone will prefer cash to bonds and hence the additional supply of money will not increase bond prices and the rate of interest will not fall. In this situation, monetary policy will be ineffective. For example, during a period of deep depression, when the rate of interest is very low and the liquidity preference schedule is completely interest-elastic, any increase in money supply will have no effect on the interest rate, income and employment. In this situation, monetary policy is said to be trapped and that is the reason why horizontal part of the money demand schedule is known as the liquidity trap. It sets a floor below which the interest rate cannot fall.

Criticism of the Keynesian Theory of Interest Rate

Keynesian theory of interest rate determination has been criticised on the following counts : First, in the Keynesian theory, the rate of interest cannot be determined unless the level of income is known. For one level of income, we shall get one equilibrium interest rate. If the level of income changes, the equilibrium interest rate also changes. Equilibrium rate of interest is, therefore, indeterminate in the Keynesian theory of interest rate determination.

In the money market, we have the following three equations and four unknowns: r, Y, M, L.

1) $M_d = M_t + M_s = kY + L(r)$........................ Money Demand Function

2) $M = M_0$............. ....Money Supply Function

3) $M_d = M$ ....Equilibrium Condition

The system is indeterminate. The equilibrium condition can be written as : $kY + L(r) = M_0$, where we get one equation and two unknowns r, Y. Thus, we get different combinations of Y and r for which the above equation is satisfied. The locus of all combinations of r and Y gives us the *LM* curve. The *LM* curve gives us the money market equilibrium.

Secondly, Keynes ignores the influence of the real factors, such as, saving and investment in determining interest rate as he assumes it to be a monetary phenomenon. This seems unrealistic.

Thirdly, the Keynesian theory is a short-run theory. Only in the short run, an increase in the supply of money leads to a decrease in interest rate. However, if the supply of money generates inflationary expectations, then increase in the supply of money tends to raise rather than lower the interest rate.

Fourthly, in the Keynesian theory, an individual can hold either bonds or money but not both. But in the real world, individuals hold both. The Keynesian theory cannot explain this phenomenon.

Derivation of LM Curve

In the money market, we get one money supply and money demand function and one equilibrium condition. The money demand function is written as : $M_d = M_t + M_s = kY + L(r)$, where M_d is the total demand for money, kY is the demand for active balances or transaction balances and L is the demand for passive balances or speculative balances. The demand for active balances (M_t) depends on the level of income, while the idle balances (M_s) depends on the interest rate. M_t is the constant fraction of money national income : $M_t = kPY$, where Y is the real national income, P is the price level and k is the fraction of income people want to hold in the form of cash.

The M_s or $L(r)$ is normally a downward-sloping function with two exceptions. There is a very high rate of interest at which M_s is zero and a low rate of interest at which M_s is infinitely interest-elastic. We also assume that the price level is constant at P_0 and M_t is an increasing function of income. Hence the equilibrium condition in the money market can be written as : $M_0 = kP_0Y + L(r)$. This is a single equation with two unknowns r and Y. From this equation, we can get different combinations of r and Y for which demand for money is equal to the supply of money. The locus of all such combinations gives us the LM curve as given in Fig. 5.12. From the given level of income, we know how much money will be kept for transaction balances $(M_t = kP_0Y)$. Then the rest of the money supply, $M - M_t$, is available for speculative balances $[M_s = L(r)]$ to determine the rate of interest which gives equilibrium in the money market. Thus, corresponding to each level Y, there is a rate of interest (r) which produces equilibrium in the money market. With a given quantity of money, we get a relation between Y and r which gives us the *LM* curve. The relationship is this — a rise in Y leads to an increase in the money required in the transaction balance, and thus, money available for speculative balance (M_s) is reduced ; to get money released for transaction balance the rate of interest has to be increased. Then, a rise in Y leads to an increase in the rate of interest at which the money market is in equilibrium.

If the entire money supply is absorbed for transaction purposes, no money can be released from the speculative balance which has come down to zero. With a given quantity of money, income has a maximum limit above which it cannot rise. At this Y, the rate of interest would be maximum, Y_{max} , at which speculative demand is zero. Conversely, a fall in income will reduce the transaction demand for money, and thus, money available for speculation will increase and the rate of interest will be reduced. If the rate of interest has already reached the floor, it cannot fall further. Then the extra money will be absorbed in the speculative balance without a further fall in interest rate. Then, we have three phases of the *LM* curve: a vertical phase where the speculative demand for money is interest-inelastic and the income has reached its highest attainable level and the rate of interest is r_{max} ; a horizontal phase where speculative demand for money is interest-elastic for low levels of income where the interest rate stays at the floor level, Y_{min} ; and, a positively sloped phase in between the two extremes.

A method of deriving the *LM* curve is given in Fig. 5.12. In the first quadrant, we can find the *LM* curve which shows the relationship between *Y* and *r*. In the second quadrant, we derive the speculative function, taking

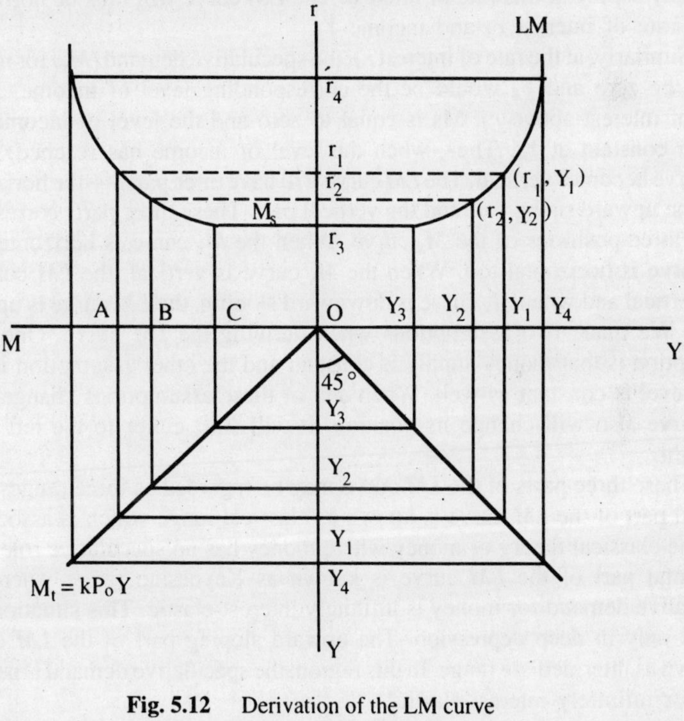

Fig. 5.12 Derivation of the LM curve

M as the origin. Any point on *OM* divides the total money between speculative balance (M_s) and the transaction balance (M_t). The *45°* line is drawn in the fourth quadrant to equate *Y* measured in two axes. In the third quadrant, we have plotted the M_t curve which is a straight line through the origin. Now we start from the interest rate r_1. At this rate of interest the demand for idle balances is *MA* and the money available for active balances is *OA*. From quadrant three, we know that *OA* amount of active balance will be able to support Y_1 amount of income. Thus, we can say that when the interest rate is r_1 and the level of income Y_1, the money market is in equilibrium (i.e., the total demand for money is equal to the total supply of money). (Y_1,r_1) is a point on the *LM* curve and this point is shown in the first quadrant. Now, we consider a lower interest rate r_2 where M_s is *MB* and M_t is *OB*. At M_t of *OB*, income is equal to Y_2. Thus, we get another point (r_2,Y_2) on *LM*. Other points on the *LM* curve can be obtained in the same way.

It can be noted that as *r* increases, *Y* also increases; thus, we can say that *LM* curve is upward rising. Now if we take the interest rate of r_3, the income level is Y_3. At this rate of interest idle balance, M_s, is at horizontal part and the rate of interest has reached the floor level, so it cannot fall further. Whatever may be the level of income below Y_3, money demand will be equal to money supply at this rate of interest. The LM curve will thus be horizontal at the rate of interest r_3 and income Y_3.

Similarly, at the rate of interest r_4, the speculative demand (M_s) for money would be zero and Y_4 would be the corresponding level of income. At all rates of interest above r_4, Ms is equal to zero and the level of income will remain constant at Y_4. Thus, when the level of income has reached Y_4, the *LM* curve becomes vertical. The *LM* curve will have three parts—the horizontal part, the upward rising part and the vertical part. These three parts correspond to the three positions of the M_s curve. When the M_s curve is horizontal, the *LM* curve is horizontal too. When the M_s curve is vertical, the *LM* curve is also vertical and when M_s curve is downward sloping, the *LM* curve is upward rising. We made two assumptions when deriving the *LM* curve. One such assumption is that money supply is constant and the other assumption is that price level is constant as well. When any of these assumptions changes, the *LM* curve also will change its position. It will shift either to the left or to the right.

These three parts of the *LM* curve may be regarded as three ranges. The vertical part of the *LM* curve is known as classical range which is associated with the classical theory of money where money has no speculative role. The horizontal part of the *LM* curve is known as Keynesian range where the speculative demand for money is infinitely interest-elastic. This situation can prevail only in deep depression. The upward sloping part of the *LM* curve is known as intermediate range. In this region, the speculative demand is neither zero nor infinitely interest-elastic.

The Slope of the *LM* Curve

The equation of the *LM* curve is given by $M_D = kP_0Y + L(r)$. Differentiating both sides with respect to *Y* we get,

$0 = kP_0 + L'(r)\frac{dr}{dy}$ or, $L'(r)\frac{dr}{dy} = -kP_0$ $\therefore$ $\frac{dr}{dy} = -\frac{kP_0}{L'(r)} > 0$. When

$L'(r) < 0$, so that $\frac{dr}{dy} > 0$, the *LM* curve is upward rising. It is horizontal when $L'(r) = \infty \ \therefore \frac{dr}{dy} = 0$. It is vertical when $L'(r) = 0 \ \therefore \frac{dr}{dy} = \infty$.

Shift of the *LM* Curve

If the real quantity of money is increased (reduced), the *LM* curve will shift to the right (left). This is shown in Fig. 5.13. In Fig. 5.13(b), we draw the demand for real money balances for a given level of income Y_1. With the initial money supply, $\overline{M}/\overline{P}$, the equilibrium is at point E_1, with interest rate at r_1. The corresponding point on the *LM* curve is E_1.

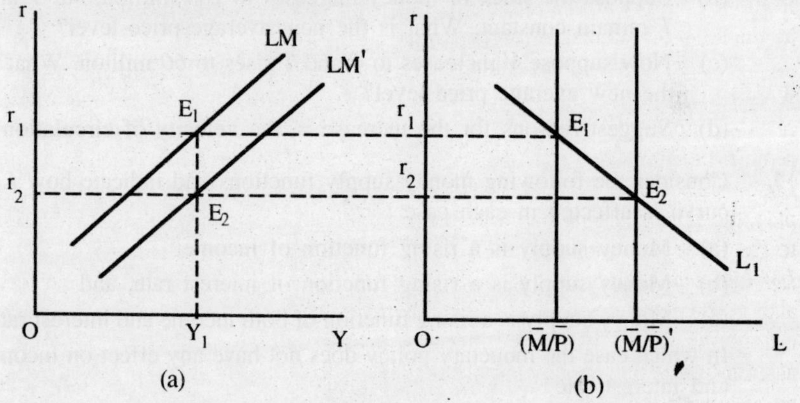

Fig. 5.13 Shift of the LM curve

Now the real money supply increases from $(\overline{M}/\overline{P})$ to $(\overline{M}/\overline{P})'$, which is represented by a rightward shift of the money supply schedule. To restore equilibrium in the money market at income level Y_1, the interest rate has to decline to r_2. The new equilibrium is at E_2. This shows that in Fig. 5.13(a), the *LM* curve has shifted to *LM'*. At Y_1, the equilibrium interest rate has to be lowered to induce people to hold more money. Alternatively, income has to be increased to raise the transaction demand for money and thus to absorb the real money supply. Similarly, if the real money supply is reduced, the *LM* curve will shift to the left.

Exercise

1. A worker's average earnings are *£100* per week, all of which he spends at an even rate throughout each period. What are his average monthly holdings if he is paid: (a) weekly; (b) monthly? Suppose his income increases by *25* per cent. How are the answers to (a) and (b) affected?

2. Consider the following information about a hypothetical economy:
   Stock of money = *£60* million;
   Each pound changes on average *5* times per year;
   The number of transactions is *50* million per year.
   (a) Find the average price level.
   (b) Suppose the stock of money increases to *£80* million, but V and T remain constant. What is the new average price level?
   (c) Now suppose V increases to *6* and T rises to *60* million. What is the new average price level?
   (d) Suggest reasons for the increase in the velocity of circulation.

3. Consider the following money supply functions and indicate how *LM* curve is affected in each case :
   (a) Money supply is a rising function of income;
   (b) Money supply is a rising function of interest rate, and
   (c) Money supply is a rising function of both income and interest rate.
   In which case the monetary policy does not have any effect on income and interest rate?

4. Show how the Cambridge Cash Balance equation can be made equivalent to Fisher's Version of the quantity theory. What are the points of difference between them?

5. A wealth-holder distributes his total wealth between money and bonds. There occurs a ceteris paribus increase in the dispersion of a symmetrical distribution of capital gains or losses. Show the effect of this change on the wealth-holder's demand for money. Make a careful distinction between substitution and income effect.

6 THE GOODS AND MONEY SECTORS TOGETHER

In the last few chapters, we separately analysed two sectors involving two types of economic decision-making — decision about allocation of the flow of output and of wealth. However, these sectors are interrelated. Desired investment is assumed to be a function of interest rate, which is also the equilibrating variable in the money sector. The demand for money is assumed to be a function of real income, which is determined in the goods sector. Thus, the interest rate and income are linking variables transmitting changes from the monetary sector to the goods sector and from the goods sector to the money sector. We now examine this relationship in more detail and analyse the concept of general equilibrium in the whole economy, consisting of the goods and money sectors.

Fig. 6.1 is a summary of equilibrium in the two sectors. The *IS* and *LM* curves represent the conditions that have to be satisfied in order for the goods and money sectors, respectively, to be in equilibrium. Now our task is to determine how these markets are brought into simultaneous equilibrium. For simultaneous equilibrium, interest rates and income levels have to be such that both goods market and money market are in equilibrium. That condition is satisfied at the point E in Fig. 6.1 which is the point of general equilibrium. This occurs at one combination of real income and the interest rate r_e and Y_e and with this combination of income and interest rate there is no tendency for anything to change; individuals are in equilibrium in their allocation of wealth among different assets, and in their allocation of output among different uses.

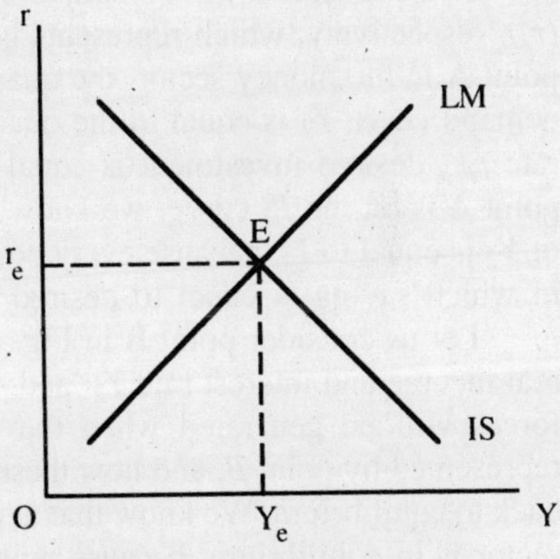

Fig. 6.1 General Equilibrium

Even though we are not concerned with the problem of economic dynamics, it is nevertheless important to understand the economic forces generated in this equilibrium, which tend to bring the system back to equilibrium.

Fig. 6.2(b) represents the equilibrium conditions for the goods and money sectors. Fig. 6.2(c) shows the money sector from which the *LM* curve in Fig.6.2(b) is derived and Fig 6.2(a) shows the desired investment schedule which together with the consumption function (not shown here) was used to derive the *IS* curve in Fig 6.2(b).

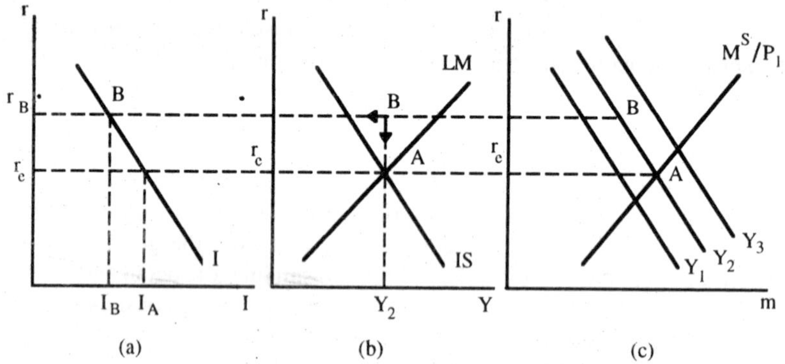

Fig. 6.2 Derivation of General Equilibrium Condition

Point *A* shows the combination of real income (Y_2) and interest rate (r_e), respectively, which represents general equilibrium for the economy. At point A in the money sector, the quantity of money demanded shown by the demand curve Y_2 is equal to the quantity of money supplied. At the interest rate r_e , desired investment is equal to I_A; this is shown in Fig. 6.2(a). As point *A* is on the *IS* curve, we know that saving generated by a real income of Y_2 is equal to I_A, because every point on the *IS* curve represents a situation in which saving is equal to desired investment.

Let us consider point B in Fig. 6.2(b) which shows the combination of real income and interest rate Y_2 and r_B, respectively. We want to know what forces will be generated when the economy found itself in the situation represented by point *B*, and how these forces will work to bring the economy back to equilibrium. We know that at point *B* neither the goods nor the money sector is in equilibrium, because point *B*, is off both the *IS* and *LM* curves. Thus, something will have to change in both sectors. In the money sector 6.2(c), we can see that at the combination of income and interest rate represented by point *B*, the quantity of money demanded is less than the quantity of money supplied. Individuals will try to re-allocate their wealth from money to bonds, thus pushing interest rate down. The arrow pointing down at *B* represents this tendency. At panel 6.2(a), we see that at the interest rate r_B, desired investment is I_B . However, at real income Y_2, saving is equal to I_A, because we assume that *S* is a function of real income only ; thus at point *B*, $S > I_B$. Hence in the goods sector, point *B* represents a situation in which $AD < Y$. Given our present assumption about the effects of a disequilibrium in the goods sector, $S >$ *(desired)* I will tend to reduce output (real income). The arrow pointing to the left at B represents this tendency. (According to our assumptions about the goods sector disequilibrium, this only affects output, not the price level and as such it does not affect the *LM* curve).

The initial forces generated in disequilibrium have further repercussions on the whole economic system. The fall in the interest rate generated by excess supply of money will affect desired $I = f(r)$. The fall in real income Y generated by $S > I$*(desired)* in the goods sector will affect the demand for money, which is a function of real Y only. As the interest rate falls, desired I rises, reducing $S > I$*(desired)*. As real Y falls, the demand for money and the interest rate fall, strengthening the effects mentioned above. All of this will continue until point A is reached — equilibrium point, in Fig. 6.2.

Disequilibrium and Dynamics in the Goods and Money Market

Equilibrium is said to be a stable one when economic forces tend to push the market towards it. Fig. 6.3 shows that the general equilibrium described here is indeed a stable one. To show this, we consider all the points to the left of the *IS* curve, like point A where interest rate r_1 and the level of Y_1 are too low for equilibrium to be achieved in the real sector. This means that the total value of output is less than the demand. In this situation, businesses find their inventories run down involuntarily and so act to increase output which pushes up Y. For all points to the left of the *IS* curve, there is an excess demand for goods and thus there is pressure on income to rise. Similarly, for all points to the right of the *IS* curve, there is excess supply of goods and there is pressure on Y to fall.

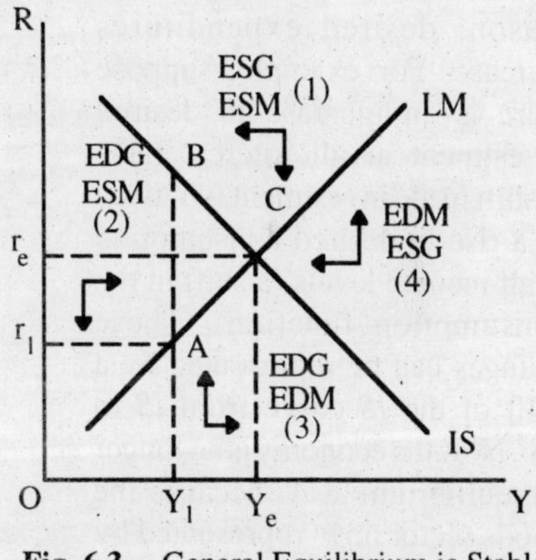

Fig. 6.3 General Equilibrium is Stable one

Now we consider points above the *LM* curve, like point B. At this point, with the level of Y, OY_1, the interest rate is too high for money market equilibrium to be achieved. This means that the supply of money exceeds the demand for money and so downward pressure is exerted on the interest rate. This is true for all points above the *LM* curve, as shown in Fig. 6.3 and it is also true that upward pressure will be exerted on interest rates at all points below the *LM* curve as there is excess demand for money.

The direction of the pressure being exerted on incomes and interest rates in the four quadrants are indicated by arrows in Fig. 6.3. At any disequilibrium point, such as *C*, economic forces will be pushing the market towards the general equilibrium position.

Shifting the *IS* and *LM* Curves

Having analysed equilibrium in the two sectors, it is useful to examine how changes in behaviour will affect the two variables in which we are interested at present—real income and interest rate. There are four behavioural functions that determine equilibrium in the two sectors: the investment function and consumption function and the supply of money function and the demand for money function. These functions were used to derive the *IS* and the *LM* curves and thus the behaviour represented by these functions is held constant along the *IS* and *LM* curves. A change is behaviour can be represented by a shift in these functions. Such shifts will result in the shift of the *IS* or *LM* curves, or, both.

Let us start from a situation of general equilibrium as shown by point *A* in Fig. 6.4. This is an equilibrium for that set of behavioural functions which underlies the derivation of the *IS* and *LM* curves intersecting at *A*. We now assume that for some reason, desired expenditures increase. For example, suppose there is an increase in desired investment at all interest rates (a shift in the investment function) or a rise in desired consumption at all income levels (a shift in the consumption function). These changes can be represented by a shift of the *IS* curve from *IS* to *I'S'*. Now the economy is no longer in equilibrium at *A* because the goods sector now represented by *I'S'* is no longer in equilibrium.

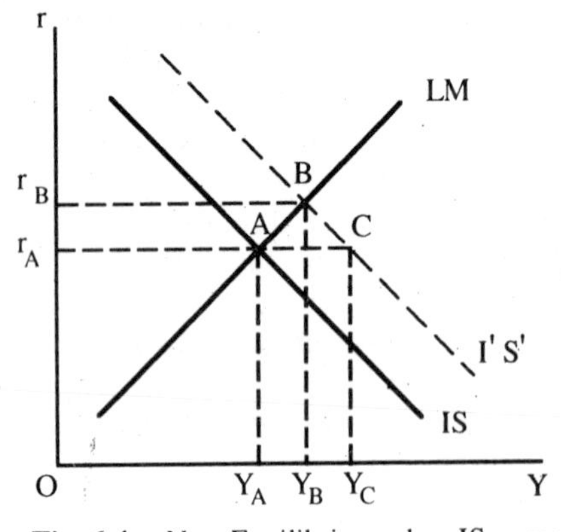

Fig. 6.4 New Equilibrium when IS curve shifts

However, the money sector is still in equilibrium as there is no change in the behaviour of the functions which affect money sector. We know that with the new *IS* curve, point A represents a situation in which desired expenditures are greater than total output (or $I > S$). This will lead to an increase in *Y*. As real *Y* rises, point *A* no longer represents equilibrium in the money sector either, because the increase in real *Y* affects the quantity of money demanded and thus equilibrium in the money sector will also change, though has been no behavioural change in the money sector (and hence the *LM* curve does not shift; there is a movement along the curve). The rise in the interest rate will have effects on desired *I* and on real *Y*.

This process will continue until a new equilibrium is reached at *B* with interest rate at r_B and real income at Y_B. At B, both the money and goods sectors are in equilibrium. It may be pointed out here that if the shift in desired expenditures or *AD* had not affected the interest rate, real income would have changed from Y_A to Y_C, which is equal to the initial change in *AD × the multiplier*. This would be true if the *LM* curve is horizontal. Real *Y* only rises to Y_B because some of the initial increase in *AD* is offset by the effect of the rise in the interest rate on desired *I*, called the 'crowding-out effect'.

A shift of the *LM* curve can occur because of a change in the demand for money or in the supply of money. An increase in the supply of money or a decrease in the demand for money, can be represented by a shift of the *LM* curve to the right. To examine the effect of such changes, let us again start from a position of equilibrium at point A in Fig. 6.5. Assume there is an increase in the supply of money brought about by an open-market operation by the monetary authority. With the new money supply, equilibrium in the money sector can be represented by *L'M'* curve in Fig. 6.5. At *A*, the goods sector is still in equilibrium, since nothing has happened to change the *IS* curve. However at *A*, the quantity of money supplied is greater than the quantity of money demanded as the situation in the money sector represented by the *L'M'* curve. Individuals will be attempting to reallocate their wealth from money into bonds, thus driving the interest down. The fall in interest rate also affects the goods sector via its effect on desired *I*; thus point *A* will not remain an equilibrium point for the goods sector either. The changes in the goods sector thus generated will have repercussions on the money sector. The process will continue until a new equilibrium is reached at point *B*, at which both sectors are in equilibrium again.

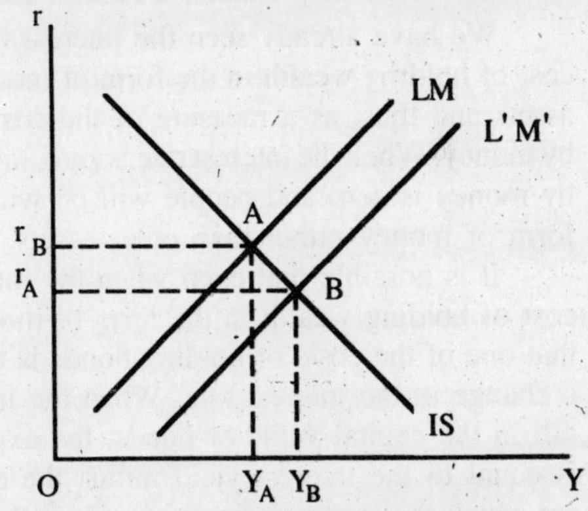

Fig. 6.5 New Equilibrium when LM curve shifts

The above discussion shows how changes in one sector of the economy are transmitted to the other sectors, and how the final equilibrium of the whole system is reached. It is obvious that changes occurring in one sector can only be transmitted to another sector if there exist variables linking the two sectors, and if these changes affect these linking variables. In our model, the linking variables are the interest rate and real *Y*. The interest rate is an effective linking variable, transmitting changes of behaviour occurring in the money sector to the goods sector, because the change in the money sector had an effect on the interest rate and the interest rate enters in the goods sector through investment decisions. Real Y is an effective linking variable, transmitting changes of behaviour in the goods sector to the money sector, because changes of behaviour in the goods sector has an effect on real income Y and real Y enters into decision in the money sector through changes in the demand for money. To get a better idea about these linking variables, we examine the following cases: (i) the demand for money is perfectly elastic with respect to the interest rate; (ii) the supply of money is perfectly elastic with respect to the interest rate; (iii) the desired investment function is perfectly inelastic with respect to the interest rate; and (iv) the real balance effect.

i) The Perfectly Elastic Demand for Money or the Liquidity Trap

We have already seen the interest rate as a measure of the alternative cost of holding wealth in the form of money rather than in the form of other assets and thus, as a measure of the cost of acquiring the services yielded by money. When the interest rate is zero, the cost of acquiring services provided by money is zero and people will be willing to hold all their wealth in the form of money rather than other assets.

It is possible that even when the interest rate is positive, the expected cost of holding wealth in the form of money is zero. We have already seen that one of the costs of holding bonds is the risk of capital loss arising from a change in the interest rate. When the interest rate rises, there would be a fall in the capital value of bonds; the expected return from holding a bond is equal to the interest yield minus the expected capital loss. If these two are equal, the expected final return is still zero, even though the interest yield is positive. Assume for the moment that the interest rate is considered to be normal, say, r_n. If the interest rate falls below r_n, individuals expect it to return to r_n and thus they expect to suffer a capital loss if they hold bonds. Let $r_L < r_n$ be the interest rate which would cause capital loss if the interest

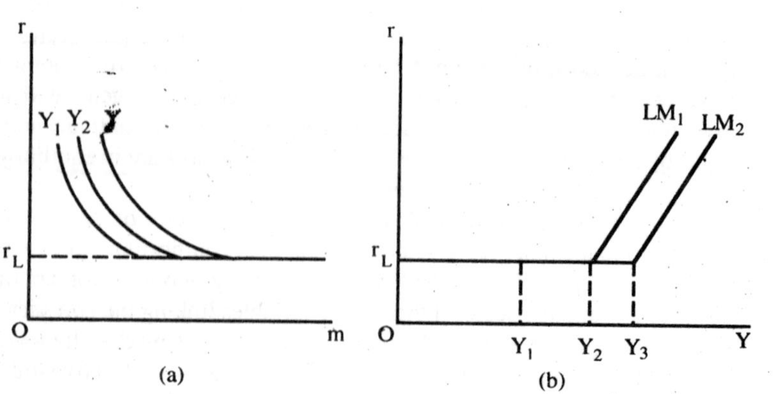

Fig. 6.6 Perfectly Elastic Demand For Money or the Liquidity Trap Situation

rate rises from r_L to the expected rate r_n which exactly offsets the return represented by r_L. In this case, at the interest rate r_L, the expected return from holding a bond is zero. At the interest rate above r_L, it is positive, and at an interest rate below r_L, it is negative. This case is represented by a demand curve for money which becomes perfectly elastic at the interest rate r_L in Fig. 6.6.

Fig. 6.6 (a) shows 3 demand curves for money for three different incomes, where $Y_1 < Y_2 < Y_3$, having the property that at the interest rate r_L they become perfectly elastic — at this interest rate people are willing to hold all their wealth in the form of money. M^{s_1} and M^{s_2} are two different supply curves of money. In Fig. 6.6 (b), the *LM* curves are derived to represent this situation. They are perfectly elastic at the interest rate r_L for incomes up to Y_2 for LM_1 and up to Y_3 for LM_2. The increase in money supply from M^{s_1} to M^{s_2} only affects the elastic part of the *LM* curve, because an increase in the supply of money along the perfectly elastic part of the demand curve for money has no effect on the interest rate. Individuals are willing to hold more money, rather than bonds at r_L, where the cost of holding money is zero and individuals are indifferent between money and bonds.

Fig. 6.7 represents a general equilibrium situation for a goods sector represented by *IS* curve and a money sector exhibiting the properties above, represented by *LM*, with equilibrium for both sectors on the horizontal part of the *LM* curve at Y_e and r_L, respectively. Assume there is an increase in the supply of money shown by a shift of the *LM* curve from LM_1 to LM_2. This has no effect on the equilibrium value of real *Y* or the interest rate because the part of the *LM* curve affected by this change is not relevant to the determination of equilibrium.

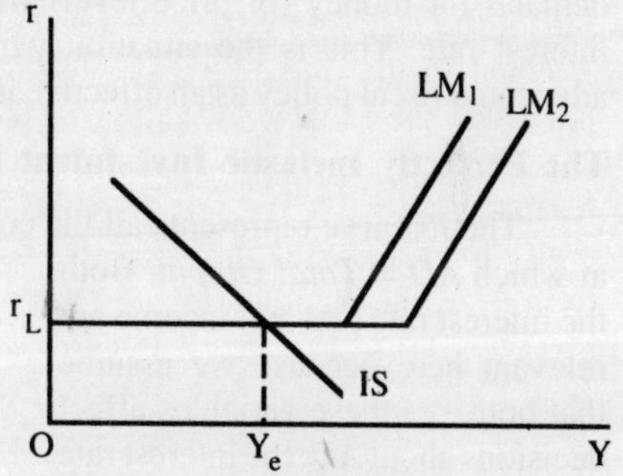

Fig. 6.7 General Equilibrium at the Liquidity Trap Situation

The Supply of Money is Perfectly Elastic

This happens when the monetary authority decides to fix the interest rate at some given level. To do this, they will have to supply whatever quantity of money is demanded at that rate, otherwise the interest rate would be affected by the excess demand or supply of money and would not be maintained at the desired level. This is shown in Fig. 6.8(a) which shows a supply curve that is perfectly elastic at the interest rate r_f and three demand curves for three incomes. In Fig. 6.8(b), we derive the *LM* curve for this situation. It is perfectly elastic at the interest rate r_f. We can see that any changes in the demand for money (or price level) will have no effect on the *LM* curve.

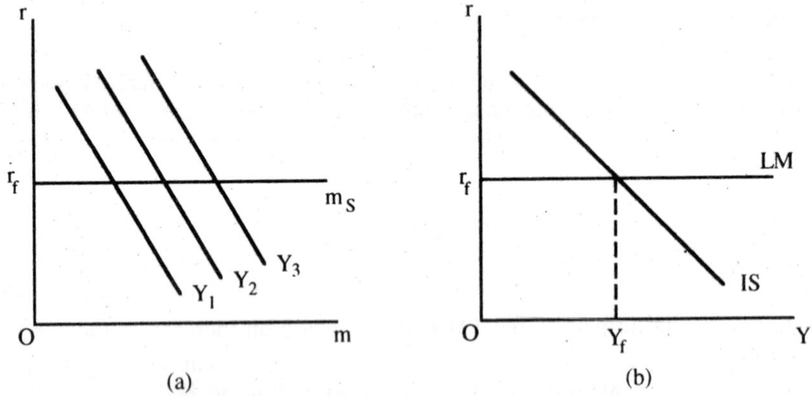

Fig. 6.8 Perfectly Elastic Money Supply

If we draw the *IS* curve on the *LM* curve of Fig. 6.8(b), we have the same general equilibrium situation as the one in Fig. 6.7. Again changes in the demand for money (or price level) will have no effect on equilibrium *Y* or interest rate. This is the situation which Keynes experienced and thus, he advocated fiscal policy as an effective instrument for influencing the economy.

The Perfectly Inelastic Investment Function

The *IS* curve represents all the combinations of income and interest rate at which *AD* = *Total Output*. Both the interest rate and real income are relevant here because we assume that both these variables affect decisions about *AD*; the interest rate affects desired investment and real income affects desired consumption. If we now drop the assumption that desired investment depends on the interest rate, real *Y* becomes the only variable that affects *AD*, and the *IS* curve in such a situation will be perfectly inelastic. Fig. 6.9 shows such an *IS* curve with two *LM* curves representing two different conditions in the money sector (two different supply functions). With both *LM* curves, general equilibrium in the two sectors

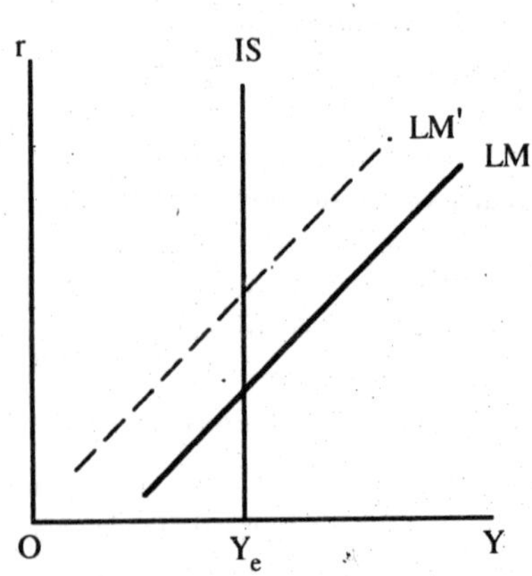

Fig. 6.9 The Perfectly Inelastic Investment Function

occurs at the same real income but at different interest rates. Thus any changes in the money sector (shifts in the *LM* curve) only affect the interest rate, but leave real *Y* unchanged. However, changes in the goods sector (shift of the *IS*) affect both real *Y* and the interest rate.

The Real Balance Effect

The Neo-Classical economists, mainly Prof. Pigou, produced an argument against the Keynesian liquidity trap case in the shape of real balance effect. According to this, with a constant nominal money supply, a general deflation of wages and prices tend to increase the real value of people's holdings of money above their desired levels. Consequently, people will reduce their savings and increase their consumption in an attempt to reduce their real balances. In a situation of unemployment, as wages and prices fall and the *LM* curve shifts to the right, the *IS* curve will also shift to the right as consumption increases. With both curves now shifting to the right, the equilibrium levels of income and hence employment must increase (even in the liquidity trap and with interest-inelastic investment) and there is now nothing to stop full employment from being reached, This is illustrated in Fig. 6.10.

Theoretically, then, the neo-classical economists appear to have the stronger case. Only when it came to policy-making, did the Keynesians have the upper hand, given the recognised inflexibility of wages and prices downward.

The cases examined here are important in showing, how, by changing assumptions about behaviour, the inter-relationship between the two sectors is changed. In the first two cases, we still assume that there is a linking variable between the goods and money sectors; desired investment is assumed to be a function of the interest rate. However, the assumptions about the money sector are such that any changes in this sector do not affect the linking variable (the interest rate) and thus such changes are not transmitted in the goods sector. In the case of the assumption about a perfectly inelastic investment function, the goods sector is totally independent of the money sector — no behaviour in the goods sector is affected by the money sector. Even if changes in the money sector affect the interest rate, it is unlikely to affect the goods sector so long as the interest rate plays no role in any behaviour relevant to that sector. (If consumption is a function of interest rate, this would reintroduce a link between the goods and the money sectors even though desired

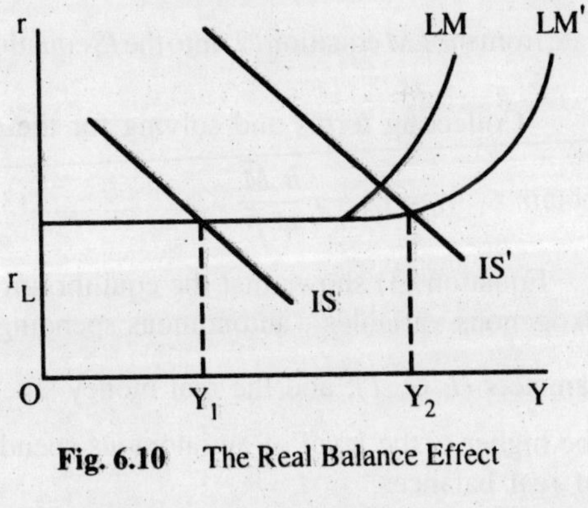

Fig. 6.10 The Real Balance Effect

investment is not a function of the interest rate). However, changes in the goods sector do affect the money sector, because the variable linking the two — real income — is effective as long as the demand for money is a function of real income which may change because of the real balance effective.

A Formal Treatment of the *IS-LM* Model

Equilibrium Income and the Interest Rate

The intersection of the *IS* and *LM* curves determines equilibrium income and interest rate. We derive expressions for these values by using the equations of *IS* and *LM* curves.

IS curve : $Y = \alpha_G(\overline{A} - br)$ ....(1) where $\alpha_G = \dfrac{1}{1-b(1-t)}$

and $\overline{A} = \overline{I} + \overline{G}$;

and the equation describing money market equilibrium as

LM curve : $r = \dfrac{1}{h}\left(kY - \dfrac{\overline{M}}{\overline{P}}\right)$ ....(2)

The intersection of the *IS* and *LM* curves in the diagrams corresponds to a situation in which both the *IS* and *LM* equations hold — the same income levels and interest rate assure equilibrium in both the goods and the money market. In terms of the equations, this means we can substitute the interest rate from the *LM* equation (2) into the *IS* equation (1) : $Y = \alpha_G\left[\overline{A} - \dfrac{b}{h}\left(kY - \dfrac{\overline{M}}{\overline{P}}\right)\right]$

Collecting terms and solving for the equilibrium level of income, we obtain : $Y_0 = r\overline{A} + r\dfrac{b}{h}\dfrac{\overline{M}}{\overline{P}}$ ....(3), where $r = \dfrac{\alpha_G}{(1 + k\alpha_G b/h)}$

Equation (3) shows that the equilibrium level of income depends on two exogenous variables : autonomous spending, $\overline{A}$, including fiscal policy parameters *(I, G, T)*; and the real money stock, $\dfrac{\overline{M}}{\overline{P}}$. If equilibrium *Y* is higher, the higher is the level of autonomous spending, $\overline{A}$, and the higher the stock of real balances.

The equilibrium rate of interest, r_0, is obtained by substituting the equilibrium level of Y_0 from equation (3) into the equation of the *LM* curve (2)

$$r_0 = \frac{k}{h} Y_0\overline{A} - \frac{1}{h + kbQ_G} \cdot \frac{\overline{M}}{\overline{P}} \quad ....(4)$$

Equation (3) shows that the equilibrium interest rate depends on the parameters of fiscal policy $\overline{A}$, and on the real money stock. A higher real stock of money implies a lower equilibrium rate of interest.

7 MACROECONOMIC SYSTEM

Classical Theory of Full-employment

Karl Marx gave the name 'Classical Economics' to the writings of Adam Smith, David Ricardo and their followers who investigated relations of production in bourgeois society. Subsequent economists, like Marshall, Edgeworth, Pigou and their followers who believe in Say's law of markets, are also called classical economists. Say's law states that the supply creates its own demand and there is no possibility of general over-production. The classical economists believe that in a competitive capitalist economy there exists an automatic mechanism which brings about full employment. This automatic mechanism is known as 'invisible hand' and impersonal market forces emanating from individual behaviour patterns are governed by self-interest.

The classical model of income and employment determination is divided into four markets: the money market, the commodity market, the bond market and the labour market. However, following Walrasian law, the commodity market is dropped and the equilibrium conditions in three markets — the labour market, the money market and the bond market — are considered. In each market, there exists a demand function, a supply function and equilibrium condition. Thus, the classical model can be represented with the help of certain equations.

We start our analysis with the labour market of the economy. It is assumed that there exists an aggregate production function, the demand function for labour and the supply function of labour. The aggregate production function describes the relationship between real income *(Y)* and the level of employment *(N)*, given the capital stock $Y = f(N, K_0)$................(1) where Y is output, N is employment and K_0 is the given capital stock. We assume that the marginal productivity of labour is positive but follows a diminishing marginal product of labour i.e $\frac{dY}{dN} > 0$ and $\frac{d^2Y}{dN^2} < 0$. Profit-maximisation under perfect competition leads to production of output at the point of equality between the real wage rate and the marginal product of labour. The quantity of output to be produced determines the number of people to be employed. Alternatively, given the money wage rate, profit-maximising employment is directly determined at the point of equality between the money wage rate and the value of the marginal product, provided that it is falling at the level of employment. The value of marginal product is the marginal product multiplied by the price of the product. The profit-maximising condition can be written as $W = P.\frac{dY}{dN}$ where W is the money wage rate and P is the price level or $\frac{W}{P} = \frac{dY}{dN}$ ....(2) that is, the real wage rate should be equal to the marginal physical product of labour *(MPP of L)*. If we plot the level of employment on the horizontal axis and the real wage rate on the vertical axis, the marginal product of labour curve will give us the labour demand curve. It gives us the amount of labour demand at different real wage rates. Thus, we get the inverse relationship between the real wage rate and the demand for labour. Now we consider the supply curve of labour. It is assumed by the classical economists that money wages and prices are flexible both in the upward and in the downward directions. The supply of labour is assumed to be a direct function of the real wage rate which means that the real wage rate increases so the supply of labour also increases. The classical labour supply function can be written as : $N = N(W/P)$.............(3) such that $\frac{dN}{d(W/P)} > 0$.

Thus we get the following three equations for the labour market:

1) $Y = f(N, K_0)$

2) $\frac{dY}{dN} = \frac{W}{P}$

3) $N = N\ (W/P)$

From these three equations, we can solve for three unknowns: Y, N and W/P, i.e the level of income, level of employment and real wage rate can be determined from the above three equations. Now consider Fig. 7.1 where the upper graph shows the aggregate labour market at a real wage rate of (W/P) and the level of employment equals to ON_f. At the intersection of the downward sloping labour demand curve and the upward sloping labour supply curve, the equilibrium real wage rate and the equilibrium level of employment is determined. Once we know the equilibrium level of employment, it is easy to get the equilibrium level of income from the aggregate production function in the lower graph in Fig. 7.1. The equilibrium level of employment N_f, the equilibrium real wage rate (W/P) and the equilibrium level of output Y_f are given in Fig. 7.1. The classical economists called this equilibrium the 'full employment' level. According to them, any unemployment that existed at the wage rate $\left(\frac{W}{P}\right)_f$ must be due to frictions or restrictive practices in the economy or must be voluntary. At the real wage rate $\left(\frac{W}{P}\right)_f$, those who are

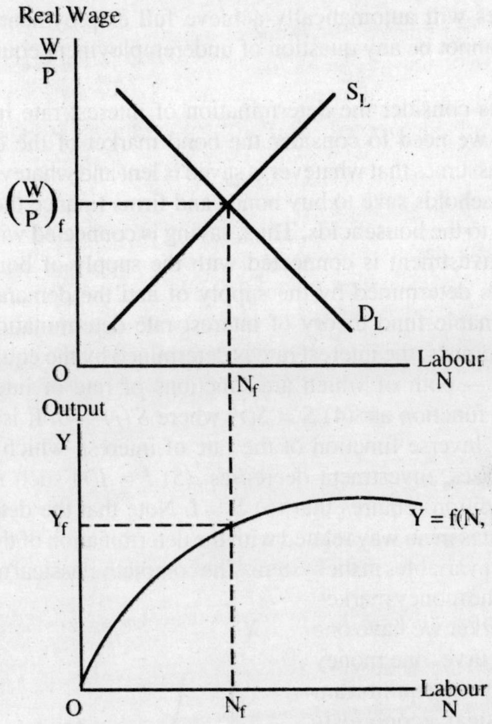

Fig. 7.1 Full-employment Equilibrium

willing to work at the going wage rate would find jobs. If the real wage rate is greater than $\left(\frac{W}{P}\right)_f$ labour supply will be greater than labour demand and unemployment will prevail. There is no problem in the classical model where money wages are flexible. If there is unemployment, money wages will fall because of competition among workers. As money wages fall, the employment of more labour becomes profitable. More workers will be demanded and more employment will be created. As a consequence, the supply of output will also increase. The additional output can only be disposed off if the price level falls. Thus, if the price level decreases in the same proportion, the real wage rate will remain unchanged and the incentive to employ more workers will not be present. Hence it is necessary that the classical model requires that the price level must fall in lower proportion than money wage rate. In other words, so long as there is unemployment in the economy, the real wage rate will fall, the supply of labour will decrease and the demand for labour will increase until full employment is reached. Thus, perfect flexibility of money wages and prices will automatically achieve full employment in the labour market. There cannot be any question of underemployment equilibrium in the classical model.

Now, let us consider the determination of interest rate in the classical model. For this we need to consider the bond market of the economy. The classical model assumes that whatever is saved is lent and whatever is borrowed is invested. Households save to buy bonds and firms finance their investment by selling bonds to the households. Thus, saving is connected with the demand for bonds and investment is connected with the supply of bonds. Since the rate of interest is determined by the supply of and the demand for loans, it is known as loanable fund theory of interest rate determination. According to classical economists, the interest rate is determined by the equality of saving and investment — both of which are functions of rate of interest. We can write the saving function as: (4) $S = S(r)$ where $S'(r) > 0$. It is assumed that investment is an inverse function of the rate of interest, which means as the rate of interest rises, investment decreases. (5) $I = I(r)$ such that $I'(r) < 0$. Equilibrium condition requires that (6) $S = I$. Note that the determination of the rate of interest is in no way related with the determination of the equilibrium values of the other variables in the system. The complete classical model requires the equations of the money market.

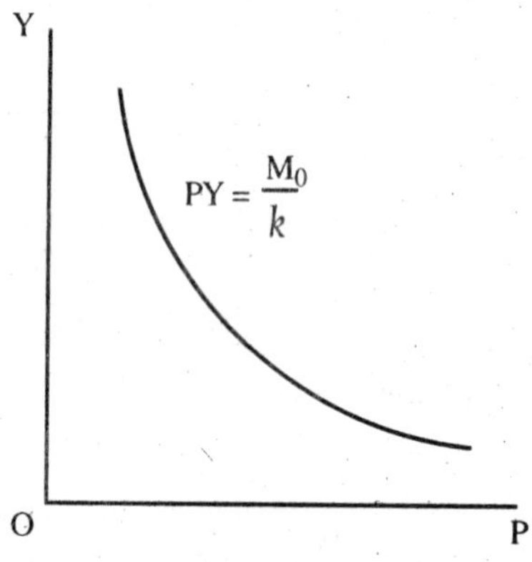

Fig. 7.2 Inverse Relationship Between Y and P

In the money market we have one money demand curve, one money supply curve and one equilibrium condition. Classical economists only considered the transactions demand for money. The demand for money is thus a function of the level of income only and not a function of the rate of interest. It can be assumed that the demand for money is a constant fraction of the money national income, i.e. (7) $M_d = kPY$, where M_d is the demand for money, Y is the real output, P is the price level and k is a constant fraction. On the supply side it is assumed that the supply of money is exogenously given, M_0 i.e. (8) $M_s = M_0$. Equilibrium condition requires $M_d = M_s$. The money market equilibrium condition can be written as (9) $M_0 = kPY$. But we already know Y from equations (1) to (3). Thus we can find P from the equilibrium condition of the money market i.e. from equation (9). We have already known the equilibrium value of W/P. If we know P we can determine W. Therefore, the money wage rate can also be determined. Since M_0 and k are constants, equation (9) can be written as $PY = \frac{M_0}{k}$ = *constant.*

This shows that as Y increases P must decrease since PY is a constant. The equation $PY = \frac{M_0}{k}$ is presented in Fig. 7.2.

The complete classical model contains the following 9 equations:

1) $Y = f(N, K_0)$ 2) $\frac{dY}{dN} = \frac{W}{P}$

3) $N = N(W/P)$ 4) $S = S(r)$

5) $I = I(r)$ 6) $S = I$

7) $M_d = kPY$ 8) $M_s = M_0$

9) $M_d = M_s$

There are also 9 variables in the model : $Y, N, W, P, M_d, M_s, S, I, r$. Thus, the system is determinate. It may also be noted that the system is decomposable. We can solve equations (1) to (3) for 3 variables: $Y, N, W/P$. Once Y is known the equations (7) to (9) determine P. Equations (4) to (6) determine the rate of interest independently. Graphically the complete classical model can be represented in Fig. 7.3. In part I, we have drawn the labour demand curve and the labour supply curve. In part II, we determine the equilibrium level of output. In part III, we have drawn the rectangular hyperbola and, in part IV, we have drawn a straight line through the origin with the slope $(W/P)_f$. The equilibrium level of employment and the equilibrium real wage rate is determined in part I of the Fig. 7.3. Part II determines the equilibrium level of output. Given the level of output in part II, part III determines the equilibrium price level and the part IV determines the equilibrium money wage rate. In part V, equilibrium rate of interest is determined. Note that parts I to IV are linked with one another but part V is not connected with them. This shows that the determination of the equilibrium rate of interest is not connected with the determination of the equilibrium values of other variables. This means that any change in the savings or investment function will affect only the interest rate and not the other variables. For example, if the investment function shifts in the downward direction and the saving function remains unchanged, then only the equilibrium rate of interest will fall to r'. But it will have no impact on employment, money wage rate, price level and real income.

In the classical system, there are two parts — the real part of the system and the monetary part. The real variables such as the real wage rate, the level of output and employment are determined in the real sector while the monetary variables such as the price level and money wage rate are determined in the monetary part.

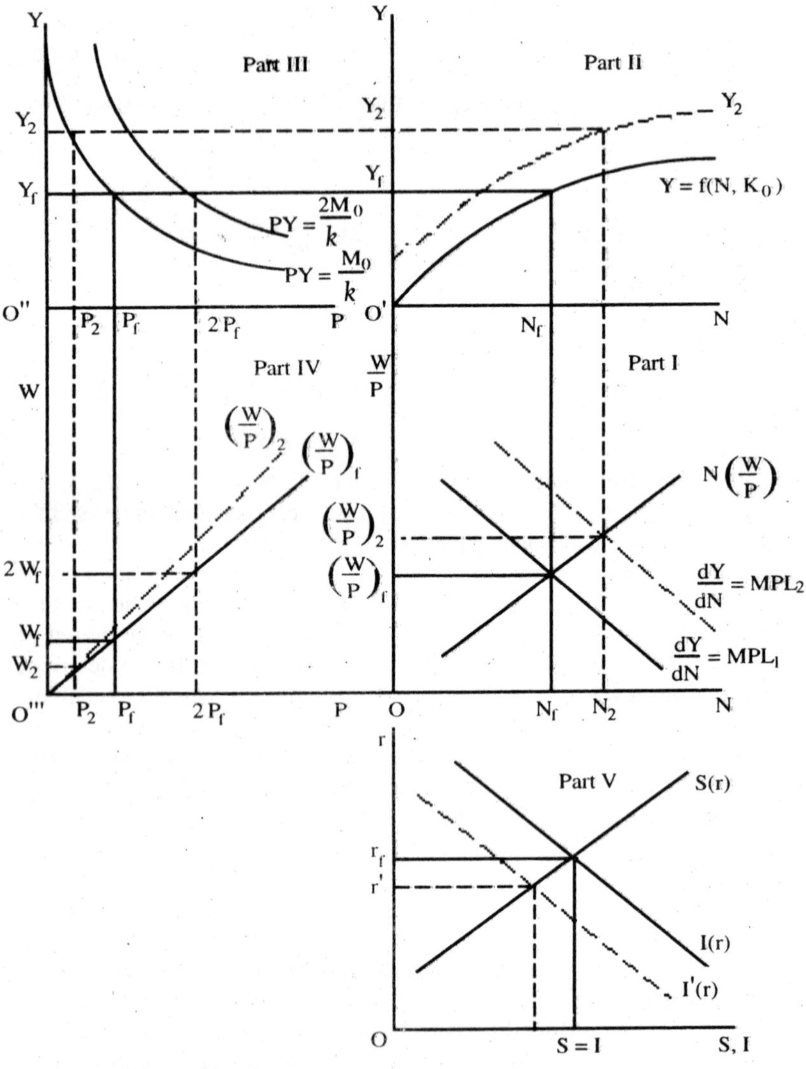

Fig. 7.3 Graphic Presentation of the Complete Classical Model

Effect of a Change in Money Supply

An important feature of the classical model is that employment, real wage rate, real income and the interest rate are independent of the quantity of money. If the quantity of money is changed by the monetary authority, disequilibrium will be created in the money market only. In terms of the system of equations we can write that equation (1) - (3) will remain unchanged when money supply changes. Thus, the level of income, the level of employment and the real wage rate will not be affected when money supply changes. The equilibrium rate of interest as determined by equations (4) - (6) will also remain unchanged. Equation (7) - (9) will only be affected when money supply changes. Equations (7) - (9) can be written as a single equation $M_0 = kPY$, where k and Y remain constant. Hence, to maintain equilibrium in the classical system P must increase when money supply (M_0) increases. P will increase in the same proportion in which money supply increases. Since the real wage rate remains unaffected, it means money wage rate must increase in the same proportion in which the price level increases. Thus, when the supply of money changes the real variables in the system will remain unchanged while monetary variables will change proportionately. In this sense, money is said to be neutral in the classical model.

Suppose the money supply is doubled from M_0 to $2M_0$. Then, in Fig 7.3, the rectangular hyperbola of part III will shift to the right to $\frac{2M_0}{k} = PY$.

The equilibrium remains unchanged at Y_f but the equilibrium price level is doubled to $2P_f$. Since the real wage rate in part I remains unaffected, the real wage line in part IV remains at the same level. From this line we get the money wage rate given the price level which is now $2P_f$ and the money wage rate becomes $2W_f$. Thus, an increase in the quantity of money affected only parts III and IV of the Fig. 7.3. But it has no impact on parts I, II and V in Fig. 7.3. Similarly, if money supply decreases, price and money wages will be reduced in the same proportion. Thus, in the classical model money is a "veil" which leaves real variable of the system unaffected when money supply is changed.

Effect of a Shift of the Production Function

We can see the effect of an upward shift of the production function in the classical model. The upward shift implies an increase in the marginal product of labour. As the marginal product of labour increases, the labour demand curve shifts to the right as in part I in Fig. 7.3. In part II of Fig. 7.3, the production function shifts from Y to Y_2, we get a new marginal product curve MPL_2 in part I. The equilibrium real wage rate increases from $\left(\frac{W}{P}\right)_f$ to $\left(\frac{W}{P}\right)_2$ and the equilibrium employment increases from N_f to N_2. Output increases from Y_f to Y_2 both because of higher productivity and larger employment. When money supply remains unchanged, the price level falls from P_f to P_2 in part III. Since the real wage rises the real wage line rotates from $\left(\frac{W}{P}\right)_f$ to $\left(\frac{W}{P}\right)_2$. As can be seen from the Fig. 7.3, when the price level falls money wage rate also falls from W_f to W_2. However, depending on the slopes of the various functions, the new money wage might also be higher than the old. The real wage rate will definitely be higher as well.

Shift of Labour Supply Curve

We can see the effects of a rightward shift of the labour supply curve in the classical model. We assume that the money supply remains unchanged when labour supply curve shifts upward. The effects can be analysed with the help of the Fig. 7.4.

In part I of Fig. 7.4, the labour supply curve has shifted from $N_1\left(\frac{W}{P}\right)$ to $N_2\left(\frac{W}{P}\right)$. This has the effect of increasing the equilibrium level of employment from N_1 to N_2 and reducing the equilibrium real wage rate from $\left(\frac{W}{P}\right)_1$ to $\left(\frac{W}{P}\right)_2$. In part II, we can see that when the level of employment has increased from N_1 to N_2, the level of output has also increased from Y_1 to Y_2. In part

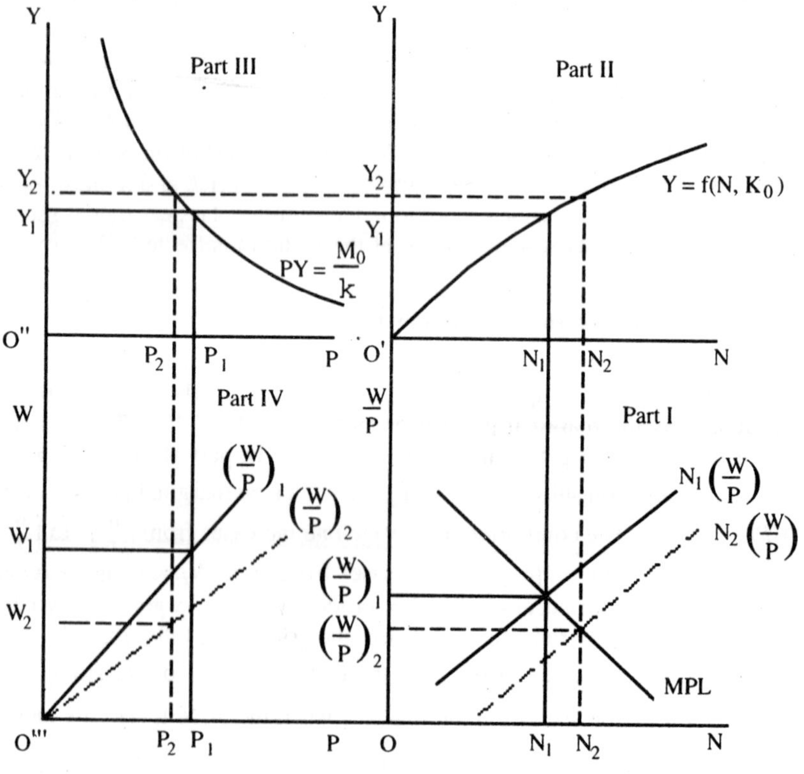

Fig. 7.4 Effects of a Rightward shift of the Labour Supply Curve

III, we can see that as the level of output increases from Y_1 to Y_2 the equilibrium price level decreases from P_1 to P_2 . As the real wage rate has decreased from $\left(\frac{W}{P}\right)_1$ to $\left(\frac{W}{P}\right)_2$ the real wage line $\left(\frac{W}{P}\right)_2$ has lower slope than the real wage line $\left(\frac{W}{P}\right)_1$. From the real wage line $\left(\frac{W}{P}\right)_2$ it can be seen that the money wage rate is lower at W_2, when the price level has come down to P_2. Thus, the effect of an increase in the supply of labour can be summarised as below : a lower real wage, a larger employment, a larger output, a lower money wage rate and the lower price level. The rate of interest will remain unaffected. It is interesting to note that a change in the real variable affects the money variable as well.

A Generalised Classical Model of Income and Employment

Let us now consider a classical model which is different from simple classical model in many respects. In the simple model we assumed that the determination of interest rate is independent of the determination of the level of income. The interest rate is determined by saving and investment which are functions of the rate of interest. Now, suppose that saving and investment depend not only on the rate of interest but also on the level of income. We have the following general saving and investment functions: $S = S(r, Y)$ such that $\frac{\delta S}{\delta r} > 0$, $\frac{\delta S}{\delta Y} > 0$. $I = I(r, Y)$ where $\frac{\delta I}{\delta r} < 0$ and $\frac{\delta I}{\delta Y} > 0$. And $S = I$ is the equilibrium condition. In this general model the determination of the interest rate is not independent of the level of income since the level of income enters in the model as a variable in the saving and investment functions.

Again, in the simple classical model, it is assumed that the demand for money is a function of income only. It is independent of the rate of interest. Now, we take into consideration the speculative demand for holding money which is also a function of the rate of interest. Thus, we modify our analysis by assuming that the demand for money is a function not only of the level of income but also a function of interest rate. We now introduce the speculative demand for money into the classical model. The money demand function may be written as follows : $\frac{M_d}{P} = L(r, Y)$, where $\frac{M_d}{P}$ is the demand for real money balances. This is the same as the liquidity preference function of Keynes which states that the demand for money is a function of both the level of income and the rate of interest. This means that the demand for real money balances is inversely related with the rate of interest and directly related to the level of income which means that $\frac{\delta(M_d/P)}{\delta Y} > 0$ and $\frac{\delta(M_d/P)}{\delta r} < 0$.

We now assume that the money wages and prices are perfectly flexible and the perfect competition prevails in the economy. Entrepreneurs try to maximise their profit. Total capital stock is constant. The volume of output depends on the level of employment, given the capital stock. The aggregate production function can be written as : $Y = f(N, K_0)$ where N is employment, K_0 is a given stock of capital. We also assume that the demand for labour is the value marginal product of labour and the supply of labour is a positive function of real wage rate. The generalised classical model can be written as

1) $Y = f(N, K_0)$

2) $\frac{dY}{dN} = \frac{W}{P}$

3) $N = N\left(\frac{W}{P}\right)$

4) $\frac{M_d}{P} = L(r, Y)$

5) $M_s = M_0$

6) $M_d = M_s$

7) $S = S(r, Y)$

8) $I = I(r, Y)$

9) $S = I$

In this model, there are 9 equations and 9 unknowns: $Y, N, W, P, M_d, M_s, S, I, r$. Hence the system is deterministic. Now, let us consider the nature of the system. Equations (1) - (3) determine the values of Y, N and W/P, three unknowns. This is a full employment equilibrium because of the assumption of perfect flexibility of money wages and prices. Thus, full employment level of income is automatically achieved. In the last three equations (7) - (9), we consider first the saving functions $S = S(r, Y)$ which has three unknowns, we can get relationship between S and r assuming that Y is constant at a certain level. Similarly, we can get one investment function relating investment and interest rates for one level of income. Thus, we get the saving and investment functions corresponding to the level of income Y_f. At this point of intersection between the saving and investment functions the equilibrium rate of interest is determined. This is illustrated in Fig. 7.5. In Fig. 7.5, the investment function is $I(r, Y_f)$ which corresponds to the full employment level of income, Y_f and the saving function is $S(r, Y_f)$ which also corresponds to the full employment level of income Y_f. They intersect at the point E which gives us the equilibrium

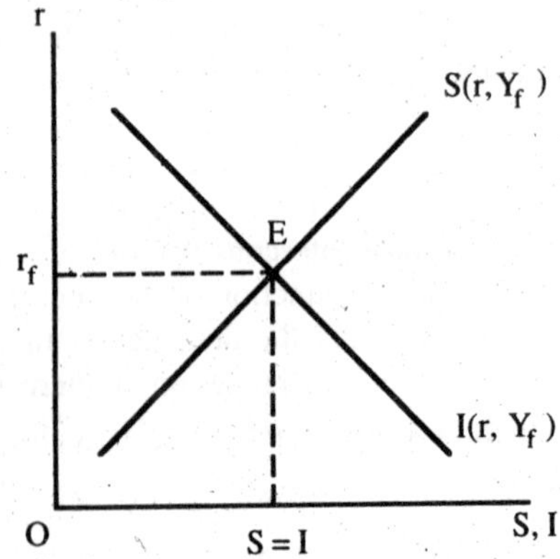

Fig. 7.5 Equilibrium Rate of Interest

level of the rate of interest r_f. At this rate of interest, saving equals investment at full employment level of income and employment.

Let us now consider the money market equations (4) to (6). These equations can be written as $\frac{M_0}{P} = L(r, Y)$. or $M_0 = PL(r, Y)$..................................(10).

It is a single equation with only one unknown, since r and Y are already known. It is possible to determine the equilibrium P level from the demand for money function even if it is a function of interest rate. The price level is determined from the equilibrium condition of the money market so long as money wages and prices are assumed to be perfectly flexible. In other words, when the money wages and prices are flexible, liquidity preference function determines the price level.

This is still a classical model since its conclusions are the same as those of the simple classical model. Like the simple classical model, full employment equilibrium is automatically achieved in the labour market. Underemployment equilibrium is not possible in this system. Moreover, like the classical model, the rate of interest is also determined by the saving and investment functions and the price level is determined from the equilibrium of the money market where money demand function is dependent on the rate of interest. Consider the effects of a change in money supply in this model. Equations (1) to (3) will remain unaffected when money supply increases which means equilibrium levels of employment and income will remain unchanged when money supply increases. As a result, the saving and investment functions and, hence, the equilibrium rate of interest will remain unaffected. Only the equilibrium condition of the money market will be affected as the supply of money increases. The equilibrium condition of the money market can be written as $M_0 = PL(r, Y)$. In this equation r and Y will remain unaffected and thus the only variable that will be affected when the money supply changes is the price level. The price level will increase in the same proportion as increase in money supply. This result is not different from the simple classical model. Thus, money is also neutral in this model. It is clear from this analysis that even if we introduce a few modifications in the simple classical model the properties of the classical model remain unchanged as long as equations (1) - (3) are retained i.e. we assume perfectly flexibility of wages and prices. These equations (1) - (3) may be called the heart of the classical model. So long as they remain intact the classical conclusion will not change.

However, in this modified version, there are two exceptions where full employment will not be achieved even if money wages and prices are perfectly flexible.

Two Exceptional Cases

First, we consider the situation where the saving and investment functions are such that there is no positive intersection between them as in Fig. 7.6 to achieve full employment.

The saving function at full employment intersects the investment function at full employment to produce a negative rate of interest r_f. That is, a negative rate of interest is required to maintain the equality between saving and investment at full employment. Since the rate of interest cannot be negative, the full employment cannot be achieved under this circumstances. Here, at all positive rate of interest, saving is greater than investment at full employment. The shapes of saving and investment functions are such that they prevent full employment being achieved in this situation. In other words, the interest-inelasticity of investment and saving functions cannot give full employment in this case. The second situation is where the speculative demand function for money may act as an obstacle to achieve full employment. We know that there is a lower limit below which interest rate may not fall. This lower limit is set by the liquidity trap where the speculative demand for money becomes horizontal. Now, if the rate of interest required to achieve full employment is less than the rate of interest permitted by the

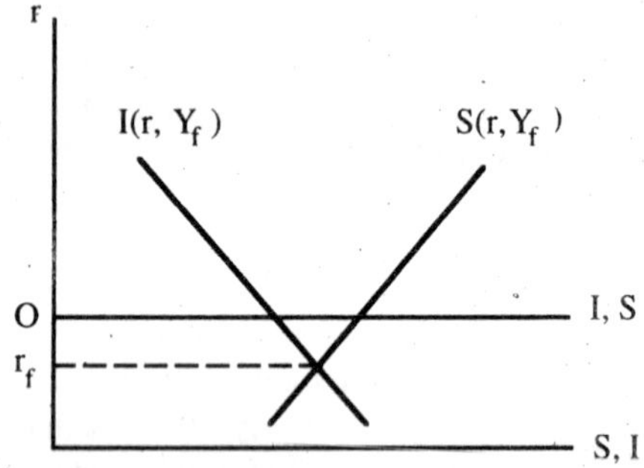

Fig. 7.6 No Positive intersection between Savings and Investment Functions

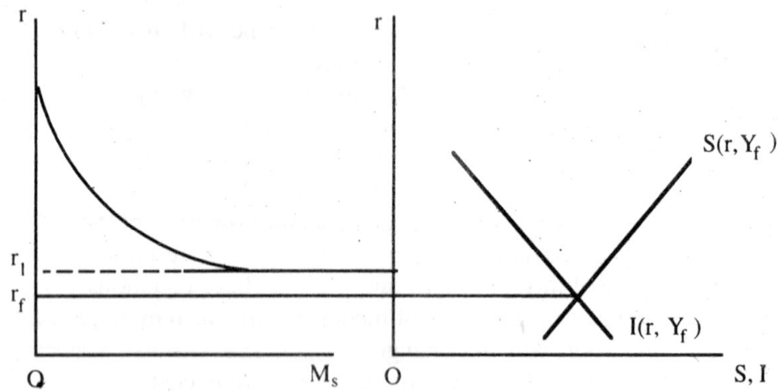

Fig. 7.7 Liquidity Trap prevents Full-employment

liquidity trap situation, then full employment may not be achieved, as the Fig. 7.7 shows. The rate of interest required to achieve full employment is r_f. But the minimum rate of interest permitted by the liquidity trap situation is r_l. To achieve full employment, we require the rate of interest r_f, but the liquidity trap situation does not allow the rate of interest to fall below r_l. In this case, the speculative demand for money function prevents the economy to achieve full employment. Apart from these two special cases, full employment will be automatically achieved in this modified classical model as in simple classical model. Hence, this model may also be described as a classical model.

Summary of the Classical Theory of Full-employment

1) A basic result of the classical economics was that, given flexible wages and prices, a competitive market economy would operate at full employment, which means that economic forces would always be generated to ensure that the demand for their labour would always equal its supply.

2) The equilibrium levels of income and employment were believed to be determined mainly in the labour market. The demand curve for labour (=*MPL* in a competitive economy) shows the relationship between real wage and the employer's demand for labour. This relationship is inverse: the lower the real wage, the more workers will be employed. The supply curve for labour shows a direct relationship between the real wage and supply of labour by households; the higher the real wage, the greater the supply of labour.

3) Suppose that the wage rate is flexible and that the economy is sufficiently competitive to ensure that labour market equilibrium. Can we be sure that aggregate demand will be sufficient to take up the full-employment output produced ? The classical economists answer is yes—whatever the full employment level of output, the income generated in producing it will necessarily lead to spending which will be just sufficient to purchase the entire output produced. The supply will create its own demand and there can be no overproduction. This is the famous Say's law which shows that households receive income equal to the value of goods and services produced. Part of this income they spend and part they save. Consumption demand falls short of the total value of production by the amount of savings. This shortfall is made up by the investment demand and so long as investment and saving are equal, aggregate demand will equal the total value of goods and services produced. The classical economists argued that, given a flexible rate of interest and competitive market for loanable funds, savings and investment would always be made equal by changes in interest rates. For example, if savings exceeded investment, interest rates would fall, causing investment to rise and savings to be reduced. Similarly, if investment exceeded savings, the demand for loanable funds would exceed their supply and this would push interest rate upwards, bringing forth more saving and reducing investment until they are equal again.

Thus, we can say that the classical system depends upon: (a) the dependence of investment and savings on the rate of interest, (b) the flexibility of wages, prices and interest rates, (c) the existence of competitive forces in the economy. Given these conditions, there could be no overproduction and full employment would be assumed. Keynes criticised the classical theory on the following grounds —

a) Savings depend mainly on the level of national income and are not much affected by changes in interest rates. Investment may be influenced by interest rates, but also depends on business expectations. Given this, it is unlikely that the rate of interest would ensure equality between planned savings and planned investment and thus Say's law will no longer hold.

b) He argued that, because of monopoly power in both the goods and labour markets, wages and prices will tend to be inflexible, at least in the downward direction. This means that in a situation where saving exceeds investment so that aggregate demand is less than the total value of production, firms will reduce output and lay off workers. It is in this way that demand deficient unemployment is created.

c) He also argued that even if wages and prices are flexible, aggregate demand may not be sufficient to ensure full employment.

In the Keynesian theory, the level of real national income and employment is determined largely by the level of aggregate demand. This is really very different from the classical model where supply creates its own demand and in the Keynesian model, as we will analyse below, it is demand which determines how much is supplied. The argument is that if firms find that they are producing more than is being demanded, they will observe an involuntary increase in inventories of unsold goods and so will rectify this by cutting production and laying off workers. National income will fall until the value of production is equal to the value of aggregate demand. If, however, firms find that they are producing less than what is demanded, they will experience an unwanted fall in inventories and so this time will try to increase output and hire more workers.

There will be one level of national income at which aggregate demand is equal to the total value of production, which is called the equilibrium level of income. An important point to remember is that, in the Keynesian model, the equilibrium level of income is not necessarily the same as the full employment level of income. This is the reason Keynes called his theory a general theory — he regarded the classical theory as no more than the 'special case' whose equilibrium and full employment level of income coincided. In the next chapter, we will discuss Keynesian model.

8 THE COMPLETE KEYNESIAN MODEL

The Keynesian System

The theoretical scheme of the classical/neo-classical economists describes the self-equilibrating character of competitive capitalism, but failed to explain the long depression of the 1930s. Economists and policy-makers became sceptical about the classical postulates. As a result, a new macroeconomic system was developed in the publication of the General Theory of Employment, Interest and Money by J. M. Keynes which is known as the Keynesian Macroeconomics. Thus, Keynesian system is the core of modern macroeconomic theory.

The Keynesian system gives an alternative set of postulates and establishes the case of an under-employment equilibrium. In the Keynesian system, involuntary unemployment can exist if part of work-force do not get jobs even when they are willing to work at the existing money wage rate because of the absence of job opportunities. The existence of involuntary unemployment makes the economy attain equilibrium before full employment is reached. It is the theoretical possibility of the under-employment equilibrium which is the most striking departure of the Keynesian system from the classical system. Another feature of the Keynesian system which makes it different from the classical system is the interdependence among all macroeconomic variables. In this system, real income, rate of interest, price level, employment and real wages are all determined simultaneously.

As we have seen, in the simple Keynesian model of income determination, the equilibrium level of income is determined by the equality of planned saving and planned investment (or by the equality of aggregate demand and aggregate supply). Saving is a function of income and investment is a function of interest rate. Thus, in the market for commodities, we write the following three equations:

1) $S = S(Y)$ — Saving function
2) $I = I(r)$ — Investment function
3) $S = I$ — Equilibrium condition

The system is indeterminate because this model has three equations and four unknown variables (S, I, r and Y). Since investment is a function of the rate of interest, we cannot determine the equilibrium level of income from the equations of the commodity market. Unless we know the equilibrium rate of interest we cannot know the equilibrium level of income. From the equilibrium condition in the commodity market we can get the different combinations of r and Y for which saving will be equal to investment. All these combinations of Y and r give the *IS* curve. To determine the interest rate we turn to the liquidity preference theory of interest rate determination. In this theory also, there are three money market equations which are given below:

(4) $M_D = M_t + L(r) = KPY + L(r) \rightarrow$ money demand function

(5) $M = M_0 \rightarrow$ money supply function

(6) $M_D = M \rightarrow$ equilibrium condition

In the money market also there are three equations and four unknowns: L, M, r and Y. Hence we can only determine the value of r when we know the value of Y. From the equilibrium condition in the money market, we can find different combinations of r and Y. The locus of all such points gives the *LM* curve.

We have seen that we cannot determine the equilibrium level of income from equations of the commodity market alone. Similarly, it is also not possible to determine the rate of interest from the equations of the money market alone. Equilibrium level of income depends on the interest rate and the equilibrium rate of interest also depends on the level of income. One cannot be determined without the other. There is interdependence between the commodity market and the money market. Thus, equilibrium income and interest rate are determined simultaneously. Since the equilibrium in both the markets have to be achieved simultaneously, we can get general equilibrium.

In order to develop the Keynesian system, we need to bring together the six functional relations. The consumption function (or the saving function), the investment function, the demand for money function, the aggregate production, the demand and the supply function of labour. Of these six functional relations, three are the same as in the classical system and the other three are significantly different from the classical forms. The investment function, the aggregate production function and the demand function for labour are based on the same postulates in the Keynesian and classical system. But the other three functions, the saving function — the demand function for money and the supply function for labour — are significantly different from the classical system. We discuss first the commodity and the money market relations to determine the equilibrium level of income and the equilibrium interest rate simultaneously. In the system so far developed, there are six equations and six unknown variables. Thus, the system of equations can be solved. The equations (1) - (3) can be written as a single equation:

(3') $S(Y) = I(Y)$ — Equation of the *IS* curve

Similarly, equations (4) - (6) can be expressed as a single equation:
The equation of the *LM* curve: (6') $M_0 = KPY + L(Y)$

The system of six equations can be transformed into a system of two equations and two unknowns: r and Y. Equations (3') and (6') are simultaneous equations which can be solved to get the equilibrium values of r and Y.

The *IS* curve gives us different combinations of *r* and *Y* for (*S* will be equal to *I*) which the commodity market would be in equilibrium. This curve is normally downward sloping. The *LM* curve will give us different combinations of *r* and *Y* for which the money market would be in equilibrium ($M_D = M_0$). The *LM* curve as before will have horizontal range upward rising and vertical range.

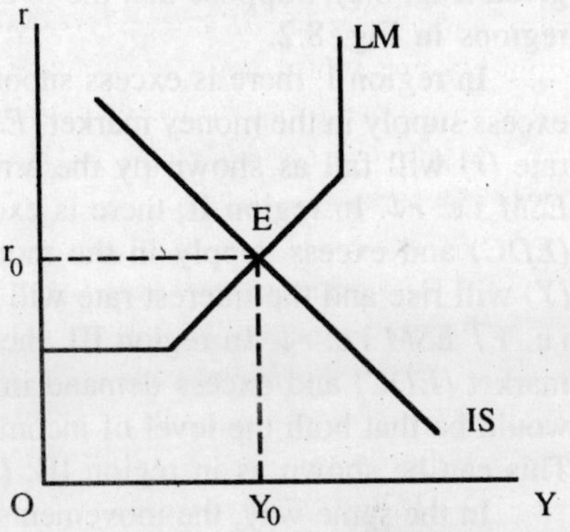

Fig. 8.1 General Equilibrium

We bring the *IS* and *LM* curves in a single diagram (Fig. 8.1). These two curves intersect at *E* where both the equilibrium conditions are fulfilled (i.e., *IS* = *LM*). At point *E*, the equilibrium level of income Y_0 and the equilibrium rate of interest r_0 are achieved. When *IS* curve is downward sloping and the *LM* curve is upward rising they can intersect once only. Hence the equilibrium is unique.

Stability Condition of the Equilibrium

If the slope of *IS* curve minus the slope of the *LM* curve is negative, then the equilibrium can be said to be stable. Since the *IS* curve is normally negatively sloped and the *LM* curve is positively sloped the stability condition is automatically fulfilled. However, if the *IS* curve is positively sloped, then the stability condition can only be satisfied if its slope is less than the *LM* curve. This requires the *IS* curve to cut the *LM* curve from above. Otherwise the equilibrium would be unstable.

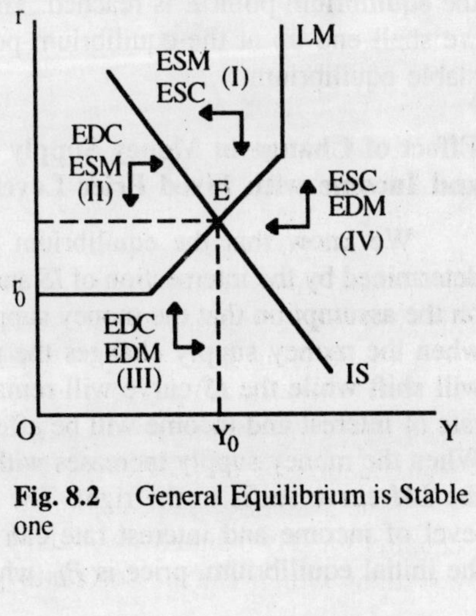

Fig. 8.2 General Equilibrium is Stable one

Alternatively, the stability condition can be analysed by assuming the dynamic adjustment in commodity and money markets work in such a way that whenever there is an excess demand or excess supply, the rate of interest and the level of income will change. Or if we assume that the rate of interest will decrease (increase) if there is an excess supply (demand) in the money market and the level of income will increase (decrease) if there is an excess demand (supply) in the commodity market. The stability can be proved with the help of the diagram given (Fig. 8.2). Suppose that the *IS* and *LM* curves intersect to produce four regions in Fig. 8.2.

In region I, there is excess supply in the commodity market *(ESC)* and excess supply in the money market *(ESM)*. Thus, both income *(Y)* and interest rate *(r)* will fall as shown by the arrows. In region I: there is *ESC* i.e. $Y\downarrow$ *ESM* i.e. $r\downarrow$. In region II, there is excess demand in the commodity market *(EDC)* and excess supply in the money *(ESM)*. Thus, the level of income *(Y)* will rise and the interest rate will as the arrows show. In region II: *EDC* i.e. $Y\uparrow$ *ESM* i.e. $r\downarrow$. In region III, there is excess demand in the commodity market *(EDC)* and excess demand in the money market *(EDM)*. The result would be that both the level of income and the rate of interest will increase. This can be shown as in region III: *(EDC)* i.e. $Y\uparrow$ and also (EDM) i.e. $r\uparrow$.

In the same way, the movements of r and Y in region IV can be shown as follows:

In region IV: *(ESC)* i.e. $Y\downarrow$ and (EDM) i.e. $r\uparrow$. It can now be shown that if we start from any other point than the point of intersection between the *IS* and the *LM* curves the market forces will work to bring the level of income and the rate of interest to the point of intersection of the *IS* and the *LM* curves at *E*. The different market forces affecting *r* and *Y* in different regions are shown by the direction of arrows in Fig. 8.2. For example, in region I, arrows indicate that both *r* and *Y* will fall because there is excess supply in both the commodity and money markets. As a result of their fall, we can either directly approach the equilibrium point *E* or can enter the region where market forces will again be generated to push *r* and *Y* either towards *E* or to region III and so on. The market forces will continue to work until the equilibrium point *E* is reached. Thus, from whatever point we start with, we shall end up at the equilibrium point *E*. Therefore, the equilibrium is a stable equilibrium.

Effect of Change in Money Supply on the Equilibrium Rate of Interest and Income with Fixed Price Level

We know that the equilibrium level of income and interest rate are determined by the intersection of *IS* and *LM* curves. We derived the *LM* curve on the assumption that the money supply and the price level are given. Thus, when the money supply changes the price level being given, the *LM* curve will shift while the *IS* curve will remain unaffected. Hence, the equilibrium rate of interest and income will be affected when the money supply changes. When the money supply increases with the price level remaining unchanged, the *LM* curve shifts to the right. The effect of this shift on the equilibrium level of income and interest rate can be seen in Fig. 8.3. Suppose that, at the initial equilibrium, price is P_0, where the level of income is Y_0, and the

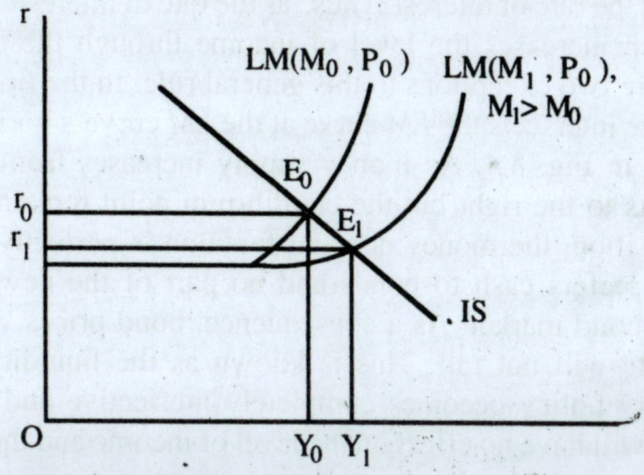

Fig. 8.3 Effect of change in Money Supply on Equilibrium

interest rate is r_0. Now, money supply increases from M_0 to M_1, the *LM* curve shifts to the right and the new equilibrium point moves from E_0 to E_1 — where income is Y_1 and the rate of interest is r_1. Since $r_1 < r_0$ and $Y_1 > Y_0$, we can say that the effect of an increase in money supply is to increase the equilibrium level of income (from Y_0 to Y_1) and to reduce the interest rate (from r_0 to r_1).

Now we wish to discuss the mechanism through which these changes take place. As the supply of money increases, the demand for money remaining unchanged, a situation of excess supply is created in the money market which

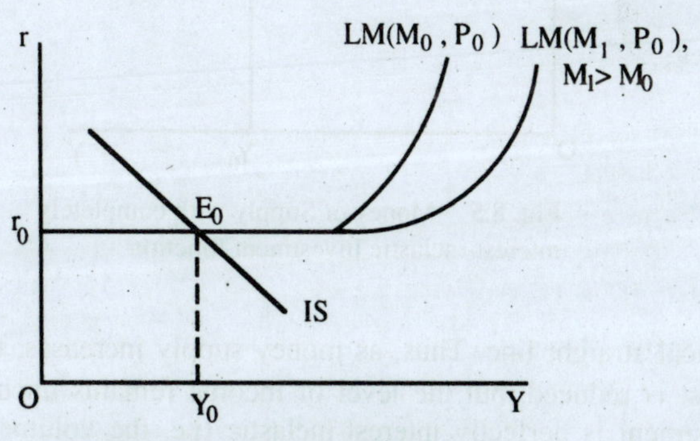

Fig. 8.4 No change of Equilibrium

leads to a fall in the market rate of interest. Alternatively, it can be said that, as money supply increases, a part of the additional money entered into the bond market increases the demand for bond leading to an upward movement in the price of bonds. An increase in the price of bonds means a fall in the interest rate. We also know that there is an inverse relationship between investment and the rate of interest. Thus, as the rate of interest falls, investment increases which increases the level of income through the usual multiplier effect. There are two exceptions to this general rule. In the first case, suppose that the *IS* curve intersects the *LM* curve at the *LM* curve's horizontal position. This is shown in Fig. 8.4. As money supply increases from M_0 to M_1, the *LM* curve shifts to the right but the equilibrium point remains unchanged at E_0. In this situation, the money demand function is perfectly interest-elastic and everyone prefers cash to bonds and no part of the new money supply will reach the bond market. As a consequence, bond prices will not rise and the interest rate will not fall. This is known as the liquidity trap situation where monetary policy becomes completely ineffective and the changes in money supply will have no effect on the level of income and the rate of interest as discussed earlier.

The second case arises when the investment function is completely interest-inelastic. In this case $I'(r) = 0$ and $\frac{dr}{dY} = \infty$. This means that *IS* curve

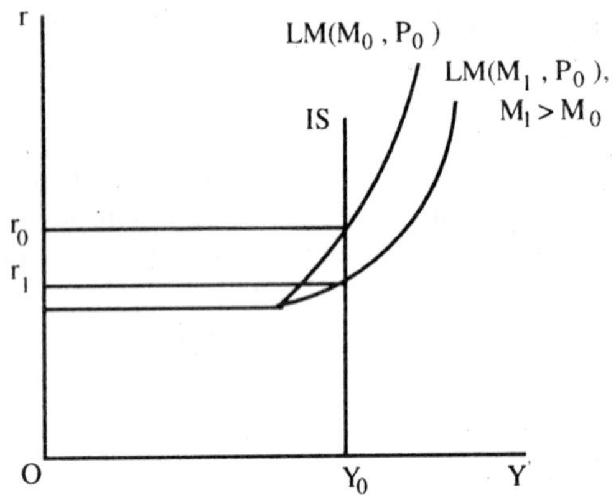

Fig. 8.5 Money of Supply with completely interest-inelastic Investment function

is a vertical straight line. Thus, as money supply increases, the market rate of interest is reduced, but the level of income remains unchanged because the investment is perfectly interest-inelastic (i.e. the volume of investment do not change in response to change in the rate of interest). As investment remains unchanged the level of income also remains the same as shown in Fig. 8.5. The effect of change of money supply can be mathematically analysed as follows.

Two equilibrium conditions are given below :

(7) $S(Y) = I(r)$ and (8) $M_0 = KPY + L(r)$.

By differentiating the two equations with respect to M_0, we can see the effect of change in money supply on Y and r.

$$S'(Y)\frac{dY}{dM_0} = I'(r)\frac{dr}{dM_0} \quad or, \ S'(Y)\frac{dY}{dM_0} - I'(r)\frac{dr}{dM_0} = 0 \quad ....(9)$$

$$\text{and } 1 = KP\cdot\frac{dY}{dM_0} + L'(r)\frac{dr}{dM_0} \quad or, \ KP\frac{dY}{dM_0} + L'(r)\frac{dr}{dM_0} = 1 \quad ......(10)$$

Solving equations (9) and (10) with the help of Cramer's rule, we get

$$\frac{dY}{dM_0} = \frac{\begin{vmatrix} 0 & -I'(r) \\ 1 & L'(r) \end{vmatrix}}{\begin{vmatrix} S'(Y) & -I'(r) \\ KP & -L'(r) \end{vmatrix}} \quad \text{and} \quad \frac{dr}{dM_0} = \frac{\begin{vmatrix} S'(Y) & 0 \\ KP & 1 \end{vmatrix}}{\begin{vmatrix} S'(Y) & -I'(r) \\ KP & L'(r) \end{vmatrix}}$$

$$\text{or,} \quad \frac{dY}{dM_0} = \frac{I'(r)}{S'(Y)L'(r) + I'(r)\cdot KP}$$

By assumption $I'(r) < 0$, $S'(r) > 0$, $L'(r) < 0$, $KP > 0$. $\therefore \frac{dY}{dM} > 0$.

This means that M_0 and Y are directly related. The two special cases can be easily obtained. When $I'(r) = 0$, $\frac{dY}{dM_0} = 0$, i.e. Y remains unchanged as money supply increases. This is the case of perfect interest-inelasticity of investment function. When $L'(r) = \infty$, $\frac{dY}{dM_0} = 0$, the speculative demand for money is completely interest-elastic and the level of income remains unchanged even if money supply increases. This is the case of liquidity trap.

Again $\frac{dr}{dM_0} = \frac{S'(Y)}{S'(Y)L'(r) + KPL'(r)} < 0$. Since $\frac{dr}{dM_0} < 0$, the interest rate decreases as money supply increases and the liquidity trap situation is $L'(r) = \infty$ and $\frac{dr}{dM_0} = 0$. In the case of perfectly interest-inelastic investment, function $I'(r) = 0$ and $\frac{dr}{dM_0} = \frac{1}{L'(r)} < 0$. The rate of interest decreases with the increased supply of money.

Investment Multiplier in the *IS-LM* Model

Suppose the investment function is now written as : $I = I(r) + \bar{A}$ where $\bar{A}$ represents autonomous investment. Thus, a change in $\bar{A}$ means a change in autonomous or exogenous investment expenditure. Now let us examine how the equilibrium level of income is affected when $\bar{A}$ changes in the *IS-LM* model. There are two equations in the model:

(1) $S(Y) = I(r) + \bar{A}$ and (2) $M_0 = KPY + L(r)$

From the solution of these two simultaneous equations, we get the equilibrium values of Y and r. When $\overline{A}$ changes the equilibrium value of Y and r will also change which can be obtained by differentiating equations (1) and (2) with respect to $\overline{A}$ and solving for $\frac{dY}{d\overline{A}}$ and $\frac{dr}{d\overline{A}}$.

By differentiating, we get the following result :

$$S'(Y) = I'(r)\frac{dr}{d\overline{A}} + 1 \quad \text{and} \quad 0 = KP\frac{dY}{d\overline{A}} + L'(r)\frac{dr}{d\overline{A}}$$

or, $S'(Y)\frac{dY}{d\overline{A}} - I'(r)\frac{dr}{d\overline{A}} = 1$ ....(3) and $KP\frac{dY}{d\overline{A}} + L'(r)\frac{dr}{d\overline{A}} = 0$.......(4)

Cramer's rule gives us the following solution :

$$\frac{dY}{d\overline{A}} = \frac{\begin{vmatrix} 1 & I'(r) \\ 0 & L'(r) \end{vmatrix}}{\begin{vmatrix} S'(Y) & -I'(r) \\ KP & L'(r) \end{vmatrix}} \quad \text{and} \quad \frac{dr}{d\overline{A}} = \frac{\begin{vmatrix} S'(Y) & 1 \\ KP & 0 \end{vmatrix}}{\begin{vmatrix} S'(Y) & -I'(r) \\ KP & L'(r) \end{vmatrix}}$$

From these we get, $dY = \dfrac{L'(r)}{S'(Y)L'(r) + KPI'(r)} d\overline{A}$

$$or, \quad dY = \frac{1}{S'(Y) + KP\dfrac{I'(r)}{L'(r)}} d\overline{A} \quad \text{.......................(5)}$$

Thus, we get the income multiplier in the *IS-LM* model as

$$\frac{1}{S'(Y) + KP\dfrac{I'(r)}{L'(r)}}$$

From our assumption that $S'(Y) > 0$, $I'(r) < 0$ *and* $L'(r) < 0$, the multiplier is positive which means that as $\overline{A}$ increases the equilibrium level of income also increases. Thus, the multiplier in the *IS-LM* model is smaller than the multiplier in the simple Keynesian model as given below :

$$\frac{1}{S'(Y) + KP\dfrac{I'(r)}{L'(r)}} < \frac{1}{S'(Y)}.$$

This is so because the investment in the IS-LM model is not completely autonomous. One part of the investment is a function of the rate of interest and the other part is autonomous. When the autonomous investment increases the equilibrium level of income and the rate of interest also increases. An increase in the rate of interest decreases induced investment. Thus, the net increase in income is lower in this case when investment is also a function of the rate of interest.

However, there are two exceptional cases when the multiplier in the *IS-LM* model will be equal to the simple Keynesian multiplier $\frac{1}{S'(Y)}$. First, where the investment function is completely interest inelastic, the full multiplier effect is obtained i.e. the multiplier becomes $\frac{1}{S'(Y)}$ when $I'(r) = 0$. Second, if the money demand function is absolutely interest elastic, then also full-multiplier effect can be obtained. When $L'(r) \to \infty$, from $\frac{dr}{dA} = \frac{-KP}{S'(Y)L'(r) + KPI'(r)}$ we get $\frac{dr}{dA} = 0$. This means that the rate of interest does not rise when autonomous investment increases and induced investment also does not fall. Thus, the full multiplier effect is obtained.

This can be explained with the help of Fig. 8.6. As autonomous investment increases the *IS* curve shifts to the right. Now the effect on the equilibrium level of income depends on where the *IS* curve intersects the *LM* curve. We can have three situations as the Fig. 8.6 shows. First, suppose the *IS* curve intersects the *LM* curve at its horizontal part before and after the shift. When the *IS* shifts to IS_1', the level of income increases from Y_1 to Y_1', but the interest rate remains unchanged at $r_1 = r_1'$. In this range, $L'(r) \Rightarrow \infty$ and the multiplier

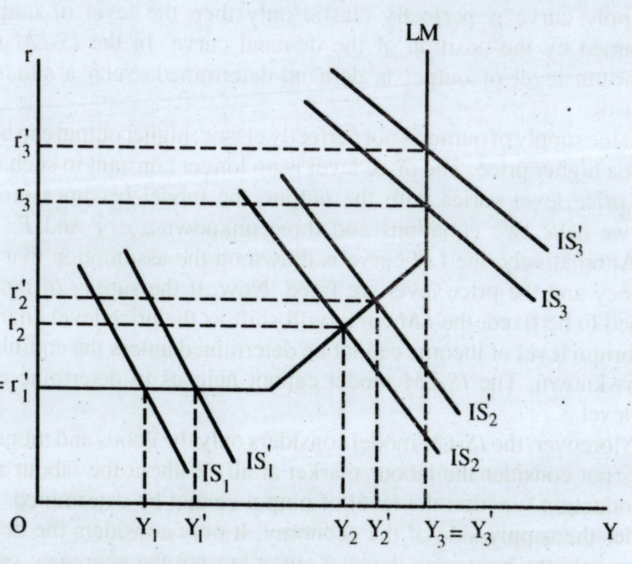

Fig. 8.6 Effect of a change in Autonomous Investment on the Equilibrium level of Income and Interest Rate

is equal to $\frac{1}{S'(Y)}$. Second, suppose the IS_2 curve shifts from IS_2 to IS_2' and intersects the LM curve at its rising part. Here the equilibrium level of income increases from Y_2 to Y_2' and the interest rate increases from r_2 to r_2'. In this range, the multiplier is equal to $\frac{1}{S'(Y)+KP\frac{I'(r)}{L'(r)}}$. Third, now suppose that the IS curve intersects the LM curve at its vertical part both before and after the change. When IS curve shifts from IS_3 to IS_3', the equilibrium level of income remains the same and only the interest rate increases from r_3 to r_3' where $L'(r) = 0$, $\frac{dY}{d\bar{A}} = 0$, which means Y remains the same. From equation (5), we get $\frac{dr}{d\bar{A}} = -\frac{1}{I'(r)} > 0$, which means that the interest rate increases.

Limitation of the *IS-LM* Model

The assumption behind the *IS-LM* model is that the price level is given as constant and the level of income is demand determined. The assumption of fixed price implies that the aggregate supply curve is perfectly elastic (a horizontal straight line). This is true only if there is excess capacity in the economy so that extra output can be produced at constant marginal cost. If the supply curve is perfectly elastic only then the level of output can be determined by the position of the demand curve. In the *IS-LM* model, the equilibrium level of output is demand-determined. Such a situation seems unrealistic.

If the supply of output is not perfectly elastic, higher output can be produced only at a higher price. The price level is no longer constant in such a situation. If the price level varies with the output, the model becomes indeterminate since we have two equations and three unknowns: r, Y and P.

Alternatively, the *LM* curve is drawn on the assumption that the supply of money and the price level are fixed. Now, if the supply of money is still assumed to be fixed, the *LM* curve will shift as the price level changes. Thus, equilibrium level of income cannot be determined unless the equilibrium price level is known. The *IS-LM* model cannot help us to determine equilibrium price level.

Moreover, the *IS-LM* model considers only the goods and money markets. It does not consider the labour market at all. Without the labour market and the production function the level of output cannot be determined. It does not consider the supply side of the economy. It only considers the demand side. It gives only the aggregate demand curve but not the aggregate supply curve without which the equilibrium price level cannot be determined.

The Labour Market

Unless the equilibrium price level is determined, we cannot find out the equilibrium level of income and interest rate. Let us see how the equilibrium price level is determined in the economy. In the labour market, we derive the labour demand and the labour supply functions. The labour demand function is derived from the aggregate production function as in the classical system. The aggregate production function gives us aggregate output as a function of the volume of employment, given the capital stock (K_0), which is constant in the short-run, and the level of output, which will increase as employment increases. The aggregate production function may be written as $Y = f(N, K_0)$, where K_0 is a given capital stock and N is the volume of employment in the economy. It is assumed that $\frac{dY}{dN} > 0$ and $\frac{d^2Y}{dN^2} < 0$ i.e. the marginal productivity of labour increases at a decreasing rate as more labour is employed. The total product curve is given in Fig. 8.7. The slope of the production function at any point gives the marginal productivity of labour and the shape of the curve reflects the assumption of the diminishing marginal productivity of labour.

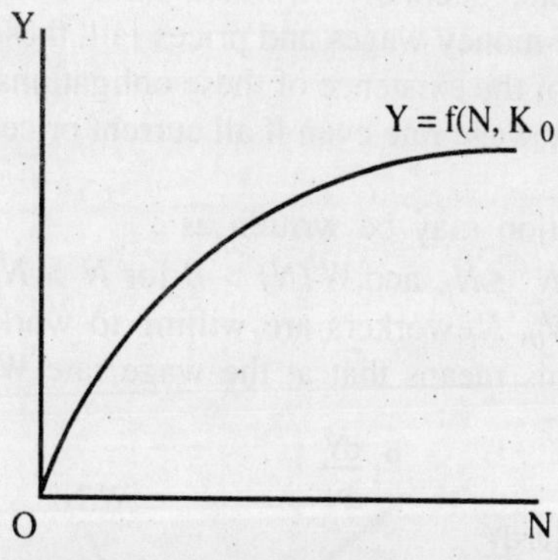

Fig. 8.7 The Total Product Curve

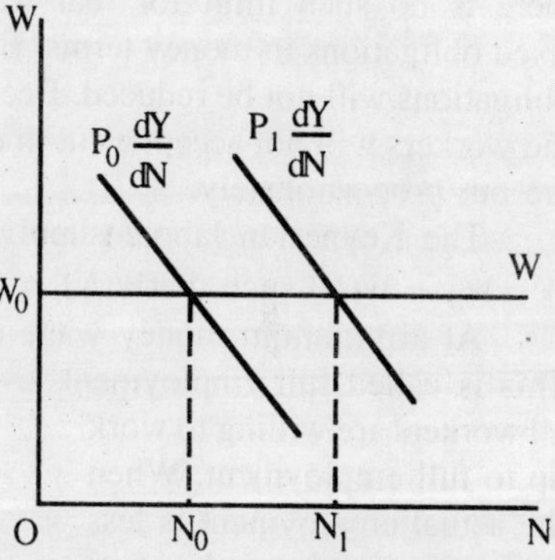

Fig. 8.8 Demand and Supply curves of Labour

The assumptions of perfect competition and profit maximisation will give us the demand curve for labour where the value of marginal product is equal to the money wage rate. If W is the money wage rate and P is the price level, the condition of profit maximisation can be written as $W = P\frac{dY}{dN}$. The demand curve for labour is determined from the aggregate production function. The labour demand curve is downward sloping as we have seen in the case of labour demand curve under classical system. For each price level we shall get one labour demand curve. For example, if the price level is P_0, the labour demand curve is $P_0\frac{dY}{dN}$ where $\frac{dY}{dN} = MPP$ of labour. Similarly, if the price level is P_1, the labour demand curve is $P_1 \frac{dY}{dN}$ where $P_0 < P_1$. As the price level increases, labour demand curve shifts to the right as Fig. 8.8 shows.

The supply function of labour in the Keynesian system is totally different from that in the classical system. Keynes assumes that at the existing money wage rate W_0, there is a number of workers (N_f) who are willing to work, irrespective of price level. The money wage rate is assumed to remain fixed at the existing level, until full employment is reached. When the full employment is achieved, money wage rate rises to induce an increase in the supply of labour. Keynes assumes that money illusion exists in the supply of labour function. When an individual is concerned not with the real value of money but only with the nominal value of money, the individual is said to be suffering from money illusion. This means that the supply of labour is a function of money wage rate. There are several reasons for assuming that labourers suffer from money illusion. Firstly, Keynes thought that due to the growth of the trade unions, the workers will not accept a low money wage whatever the real wage rate may be. In other words, the money wage rate is rigid — at least in downward direction — and cannot fall below a certain level, though there is no such limit for real wage rate. Secondly, workers have some fixed obligations in money terms. Even if money wages and prices fall, these obligations will not be reduced. Because of the existence of these obligations, the workers will not accept a cut in money wage rate even if all current prices are cut proportionately.

The Keynesian labour supply function may be written as :

$W = W_0 + W(N)$ such that $W(N) = 0$ for $N \leq N_f$, and, $W'(N) > 0$ for $N > N_f$.

At a minimum money wage rate W_0, N_f workers are willing to work. This is called full employment level. This means that at the wage rate W_0 all workers are willing to work up to full employment. When the actual employment is less than or equal to the full employment level the money wage rate is constant. But if the volume of employment is greater than the full employment level, the wage rate will increase as employment increases which is shown in Fig. 8.9. In the vertical axis we plot the money wage rate and in the horizontal axis the volume of employment is measured. The money wage rate is constant at W_0 up to full employment level, N_f, thereafter it increases as employment increases. If N represents the

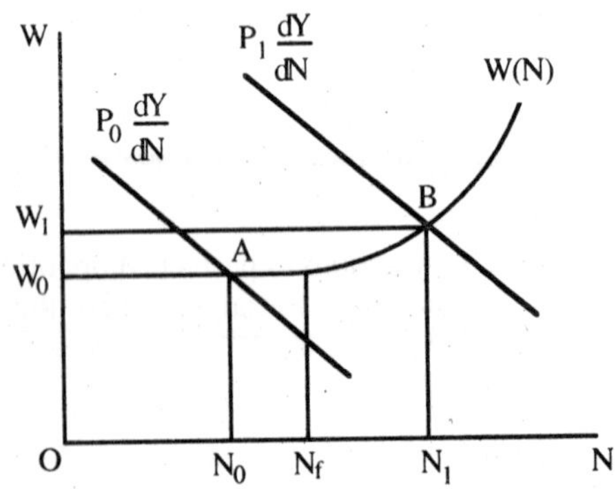

Fig. 8.9 Volume of Employment and Wage Rate

supply of labour and W represents the money wage rate then the labour supply can be written as $N = N(W)$. In inverse form the Keynesian labour supply function is written as: $W = W(N)$.

Equilibrium in the labour market will be achieved where demand and supply of labour are equal which is shown in Fig. 8.9. If the price level is assumed constant at P_1, the labour demand curve $P_1 \frac{dY}{dN}$ cuts the supply curve at its upward rising point B where the equilibrium money wage rate is W_1 and employment is N_1. This is a full employment situation (as all willing to work at this wage rate (W_1) are employed). However, if the labour demand function intersects the labour supply function at its horizontal part at point A, the equilibrium wage rate is W_0 and the equilibrium employment is N_0. At this situation, there is unemployment of N_0N_f. At the wage rate of W_0, ON_f workers are willing to work, but ON_0 workers are getting jobs. Thus, N_0N_f workers are involuntarily unemployed. This is a condition of under-employment equilibrium which exists because of the shape of the labour supply function. This involuntary unemployment cannot be solved by reducing the money wage rate because it cannot fall any more.

The equilibrium position in the labour market will depend on the labour demand curve which depends on the price level. As price level changes, the labour demand curve also changes and hence the equilibrium level of un-employment. Unless we know the equilibrium price level, we cannot determine the equilibrium level of employment.

There is no guarantee that full employment will be automatically achieved in the labour market. If the labour demand curve intersects the labour supply at the latter's horizontal part then full employment may not be achieved at all and involuntary unemployment may prevail. Thus, there is no automatic mechanism to achieve full employment in the labour market.

From the labour market, we shall get labour demand corresponding to price level. Given the supply of labour, the equilibrium level of employment can be determined. From the aggregate production function we know that as the level of employment increases so the level of output also increases. Thus, from the equilibrium in the labour market we can get different combinations of P and Y for which the demand for labour is equal to the supply of labour. The aggregate supply curve will be upward rising. The aggregate supply *(AS)* curve shows the amount of output supplied at different prices. It is determined from the labour market which represents those combinations of P and Y for which the demand for labour is equal to the supply of labour. The labour market will always be in equilibrium at any point on the AS curve.

Mathematically, the AS curve can be derived as follows: we have 3 equations for the labour market: $Y = \phi(N, K_0)$, $W = P\frac{dY}{dN}$ and $W = W_0 + W(N)$. Since we have 3 equations and 4 unknowns, we cannot solve for these 4 unknowns. So, we eliminate N and W and get a relation between Y and P which represents upward sloping AS curve for the economy.

From the equilibrium conditions in the commodity and money market, we can derive the aggregate demand curve. Suppose we derive *LM* curve for constant money supply M_0 and constant price level P_0 which represents those combinations of *r* and *Y* for which the demand for money is equal to the supply of money. We can also derive an *IS* curve which represents those combinations of *r* and *Y* for which investment equals saving. The equilibrium level of income and interest rates are simultaneously determined by the intersection of *IS* and *LM* curves. Now, we assume that the supply of money remains constant at M_0 but the price level changes. As a result, the *LM* curve will shift and we shall get a new equilibrium position and a new equilibrium level of income. This is shown in Fig. 8.10. For one price level we get one *LM* curve and one equilibrium level of income determined by the intersection of *IS* and *LM* curves. When the price level is P_0 and the money supply is M_0, we get one *LM* curve $LM(M_0, P_0)$ and the equilibrium level of income Y_0 as in Fig. 8.10.

Now, suppose that the price level increases to P_1 and *LM* curve shifts to $LM(M_0, P_1)$ and the equilibrium level of income to Y_1. If, however, the price level decreases to P_2, the equilibrium level of income increases to Y_2 and *LM* curve shifts to $LM(P_2, M_0)$. By plotting the points (P_0, Y_0), (P_1, Y_1) and (P_2, Y_2) we get a downward sloping aggregate demand curve as shown in Fig. 8.11. From equilibrium conditions of the commodity and money market we get : $S(Y) = I(r)$ and $M_0 = kYP + L_2(r)$. In these two equations, we have three unknowns *r*, *Y* and *P* and, hence, we cannot solve for these unknowns. Thus, we eliminate r from these two equations and get a downward sloping relation between *P* and *Y* which gives us the aggregate demand curve for the economy.

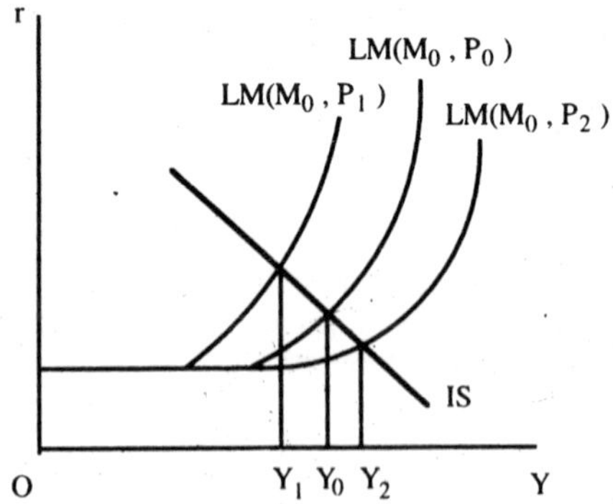

Fig. 8.10 Change in Price level produces New Equilibrium

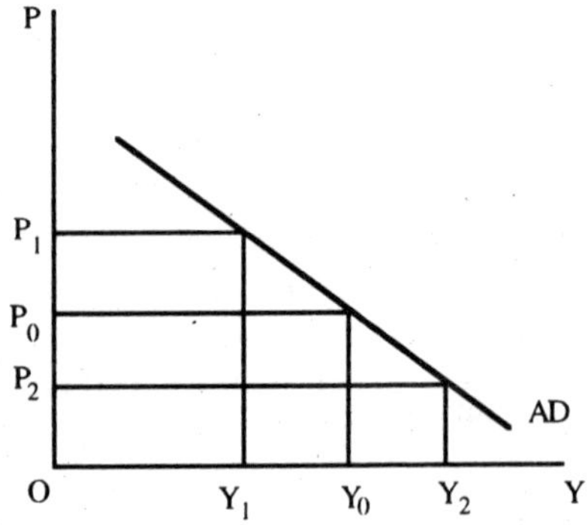

Fig. 8.11 Downward sloping Aggregate Demand Curve

Thus, we derive from the labour market different combinations of *P* and *Y* for which the labour market is in equilibrium. Again, from the money and commodity markets we get combinations of P and Y for which the money and commodity markets will be in equilibrium. The first relation is known as the aggregate supply curve which is upward sloping and the second relation is known as the aggregate demand curve which is downward sloping. If we plot them together in a single diagram as in Fig. 8.12, the two curves intersect at point A which satisfies the equilibrium conditions in all three markets. More about AD and AS later on.

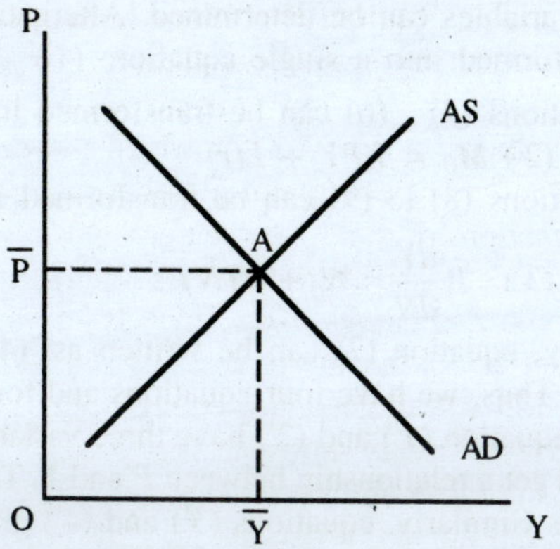

Fig. 8.12 Downward sloping Aggregate Demand Curve and Upward sloping Aggregate Supply Curve

In the complete Keynesian model, economy is divided into four markets: the commodity market, the money market, the bond market and the labour market. It is the general equilibrium system where the equilibrium of the entire economy is considered. From the general equilibrium theory we know that if three out of four markets are in equilibrium the fourth market must also be in equilibrium. This is the Walras law. According to Walrasian law, Keynes dropped the bond market from his analysis and considered equilibrium conditions in other three markets. If these three markets are in equilibrium then the bond market must also be in equilibrium. In each market there are three equations.

The complete Keynesian model will be described by the following equations. The commodity market has the following three equations:

(1) $S = S(Y)$ Saving function

(2) $I = I(r)$ Investment function

(3) $S = I$ Equilibrium condition.

In the money market, we have three equations:

(4) $M_D = KPY + L(r)$ Money demand function

(5) $M = M_0$ Money supply function

(6) $M_D = M_0$ Equilibrium condition

The labour market has 3 equations:

(7) $Y = f(N, K_0)$ Aggregate production function

(8) $W = P\dfrac{dY}{dN}$ Labour demand function

(9) $W = W_0 + W(N)$ Labour supply function

Thus, we have nine equations and nine variables: $S, I, r, Y, L, M, P, N, W$. The system can be solved and the unique equilibrium values of all the variables can be determined. Alternatively, equations (1) to (3) can be transformed into a single equation: (1') $S(Y) = I(r)$.

Equations (4) - (6) can be transformed into a single equation:

(2') $M_0 = KPY + L(r)$

Equations (8) to (9) can be transformed into

$$(3') \quad P\frac{dY}{dN} = W_0 + W(N)$$

Lastly, equation (7) can be written as: (4') $Y = f(N, K_0)$.

Thus, we have four equations and four unknowns: Y, r, P and N. Note that equation (1') and (2') have three variables: Y, r and P. We can eliminate r and get a relationship between P and Y. This gives us the aggregate demand curve. Similarly, equations (3') and (4') give us the aggregate supply curve. At the intersection point of the aggregate demand and supply curves all four equations (1') - (4') are satisfied. Here the price level P acts as the linking variable between (1') - (2') and (3') - (4').

Alternatively, we can write the system of equations with employment (N) as the linking variable. Let us rewrite the equations where we replace $f(N,K_0)$ for Y. Equation (1') can then be written as $S\{f(N, K_0)\} = I(r)$......(1")
Equation (2') can be written as: $M_0 = KPf(N, K_0) + L(r)$ ....(2")
Equation (3') is written as, $Pf(N, K_0) = W_0 + W(N)$.............................(3")
Thus, we have three equations and three unknowns: N, r and P. Now we consider first equations (1") and (3"). Here we have three variables r, P and N. These can be solved for r and P in terms of N. By substituting the values of P and r in (2"), we get just one equation in one unknown: N and we can determine N from (2"). Once N is known r can be found from (1") and P can also be found from (3"). In this way, the system can be solved. Thus, the Keynesian system is deterministic, but the full employment is not guaranteed.

Graphical Exposition of the Complete Keynesian Model

The complete Keynesian model can also be represented graphically by bringing together all the markets. We can identify from the diagram the equilibrium values of all the variables of the system. The Fig. 8.13 depicts the complete Keynesian model.

The figure shows the aggregate demand and aggregate supply (AS) curves. The aggregate demand curve is drawn on the assumption of a constant money supply M_0. The aggregate supply curve, AS, intersects the AD to produce equilibrium price level $\overline{P}$ and the equilibrium output level $\overline{Y}$, when the level of output is known, the corresponding level of employment $\overline{N}$ can be obtained from the aggregate production function $\{r = f(N, K_0)\}$. The labour demand and supply curves are drawn on the left hand side of the aggregate production function. The labour demand curve is drawn for the price level $\overline{P}$. The labour demand curve intersects the labour supply curve to give us equilibrium employment

$\overline{N}$. Since the labour demand curve intersects the labour supply curve at the latter's horizontal part, there is invoIuntary unemployment of $N_f - \overline{N}$. The equilibrium money wage rate is W_0. We have drawn the *IS* and *LM* curves above the *AD* and *AS* curves. The *LM* curve corresponds to the money supply M_0 and the equilibrium price level $\overline{P}$. At the intersection of *IS* and *LM* curves the equilibrium rate of interest $\overline{r}$ is determined. From this diagram (Fig. 8.13), we can determine all important variables of the system.

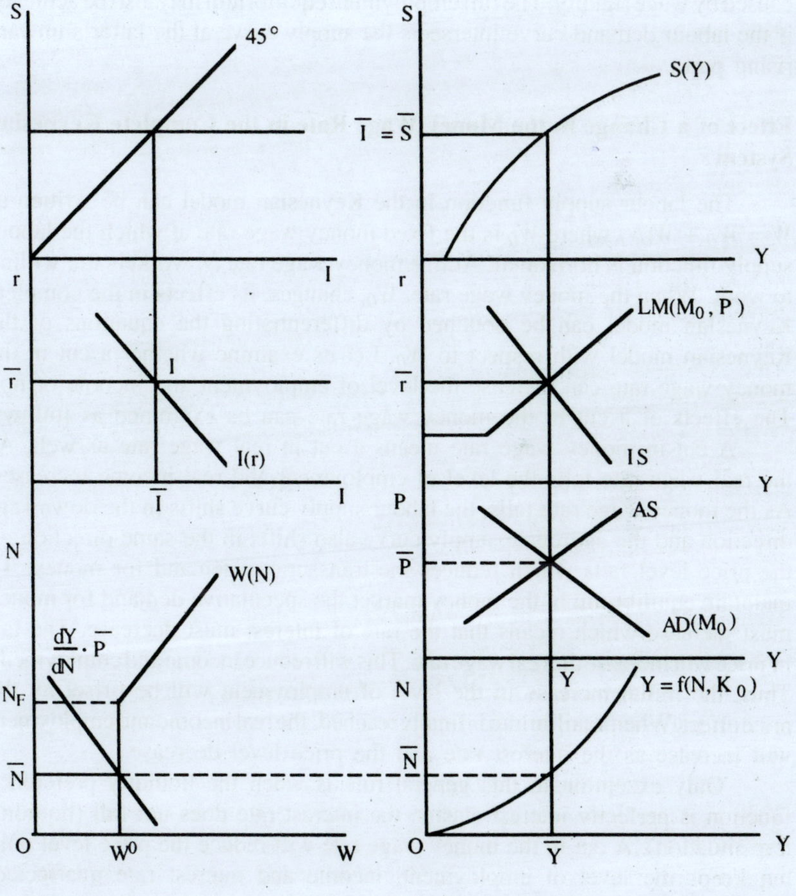

Fig. 8.13 Complete Keynesian Model

Again, when *Y* is known, *S* can be determined from the saving function *S(Y)* which we have drawn above the *IS-LM* curves. When the equilibrium level of income is $\overline{Y}$, the saving is $\overline{S}$. The equality between saving and investment is shown through 45° line. When the equilibrium rate of interest is known, the level of investment can be known from the diagram below the 45° line and to the left hand side of the *IS-LM* curves which give the equilibrium rate of interest. By extending the diagram, it is possible to show the transactions and the speculative demand for money separately which is avoided here.

In this way, all the equations of Keynesian model may be represented. The equilibrium system represented here is an underemployment equilibrium because there exists involuntary unemployment of $N_f - \overline{N}$ which has been caused by wage rigidity. The full employment equilibrium may also be achieved if the labour demand curve intersects the supply curve at the latter's upward rising part.

Effect of a Change in the Money Wage Rate in the Complete Keynesian System

The labour supply function in the Keynesian model can be written as $W = W_0 + W(N)$ where W_0 is the fixed money wage rate at which the labour supply function is horizontal. At this money wage rate N_f workers are willing to work. When the money wage rate, W_0, changes, its effects in the complete Keynesian model can be obtained by differentiating the equations of the Keynesian model with respect to W_0. Let us examine whether a cut in the money wage rate can increase the level of employment and income or not. The effects of a cut in the money wage rate can be examined as follows.

A cut in money wage rate means a cut in real wage rate as well. As the real wage rate falls the level of employment and real income increases. As the money wage rate falls, the labour supply curve shifts in the downward direction and the aggregate supply curve also shifts in the same direction — the price level falls which reduces the transactions demand for money. To maintain equilibrium in the money market the speculative demand for money must increase which means that the rate of interest must decrease. The fall in price will increase the real wage rate. This will reduce income and employment. Thus, the initial increase in the level of employment will be offset by the price effect. When equilibrium is finally reached, the real income and employment will increase as the interest rate and the price level decrease.

Only exception to this general rule is when the liquidity preference function is perfectly interest-elastic, the interest rate does not fall (liquidity trap situation). A cut in the money wage rate will reduce the price level only but keeps the level of employment, income and interest rate unaffected. Mathematically, its effect can be derived as follows : we consider three equations of the complete Keynesian system:

(1) $S\{f(N)\}$ (2) $KPY + L(r) = M_0$ (3) $P\dfrac{dY}{dN} = W_0 + W(N)$

Differentiating these three equations with respect to W_0 and rearranging we get the following:

$$\begin{bmatrix} S'\dfrac{dY}{dN} & -I' & 0 \\ KP\dfrac{dY}{dN} & L' & KY \\ P''\dfrac{d^2Y}{dN^2}-W' & 0 & \dfrac{dY}{dN} \end{bmatrix} \begin{bmatrix} \dfrac{dN}{dW_0} \\ \dfrac{dr}{dW_0} \\ \dfrac{dP}{dW_0} \end{bmatrix} \begin{bmatrix} 0 \\ 0 \\ 1 \end{bmatrix}$$

Let D denote the determinant formed by the coefficients of three variables $\frac{dN}{dW_0}, \frac{dr}{dW_0}, \frac{dP}{dW_0}$ and solving these equations with Cramer's rule we get

$$\frac{dN}{dW_0} = \frac{-I'KY}{D} < 0, \quad \frac{dr}{dW_0} = \frac{-S'\dfrac{dY}{dN}KY}{D} > 0, \quad \frac{dP}{dW_0} = \frac{-S'\dfrac{dY}{dN}L' + KP\dfrac{dY}{dN}I'}{D} > 0.$$

This shows that, as W_0 falls, N and Y increase but r and P fall. In the case of perfectly interest-elastic liquidity preference function $L' = \infty$, it can be seen that $\frac{dN}{dW_0} = 0$, $\frac{dr}{dW_0} = 0$ and $\frac{dP}{dW_0} = \frac{1}{\frac{dY}{dN}} > 0$.

It means that in the case of liquidity trap situation a fall in the money wage rate has no effect on the level of employment, income and the rate of interest. It leads to a fall in the price level only.

Effect of Change in Money Supply in the Complete Keynesian Model where the Price Level is Flexible

In the Keynesian system, the equilibrium price level is determined by the intersection of aggregate demand and aggregate supply curves. When the aggregate demand curve is drawn, money supply is assumed to be constant. Thus, when the money supply increases the aggregate demand curve shifts to the right. The aggregate supply curve will not be affected by money supply as it does not enter into the determination of the aggregate supply curve.

Let us now see how the *AD* curve will be affected when the money supply increases. In Fig. 8.14, we can see that, as the supply of money increases, the *LM* curve shifts to the right at each price level and, hence, the level of income will increase at each price level. When the price level is P_0 and the money supply is M_0, the equilibrium income is Y_0. When the supply of money increases to M_1, the equilibrium level of income will increase to Y_0', the price level remaining unchanged. Similarly, when the price level is P_1 and money supply is M_0, the equilibrium income is Y_1. Now if the money

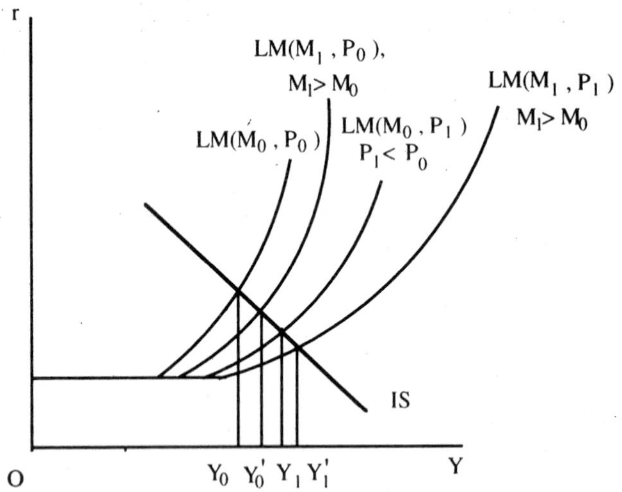

Fig. 8.14 Change in Money Supply with Flexible Prices

supply increases to M_1, the equilibrium level of income increases to Y_1'. Thus, we see that, as the money supply increases, at each price level a higher level of income will be required, to have equilibrium in commodity and money markets. This means that the *AD* curve will shift to the right as in Fig. 8.15.

When the aggregate demand curve shifts to the right, the equilibrium price level increases from P_0 to P_1 and the equilibrium income also increases from Y_0 to Y as in Fig. 8.16.

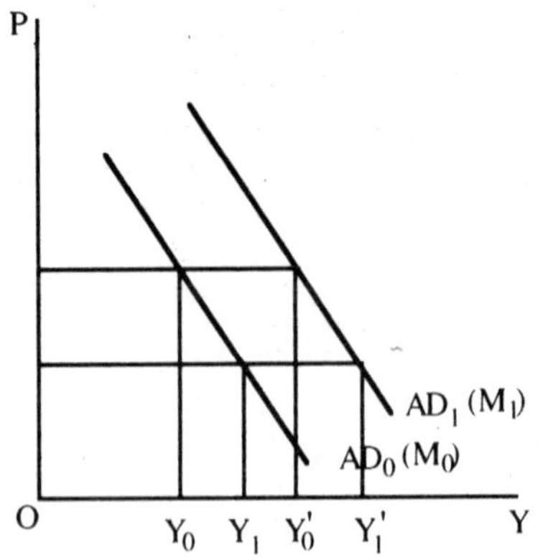

Fig. 8.15 Money Supply and AD Curve

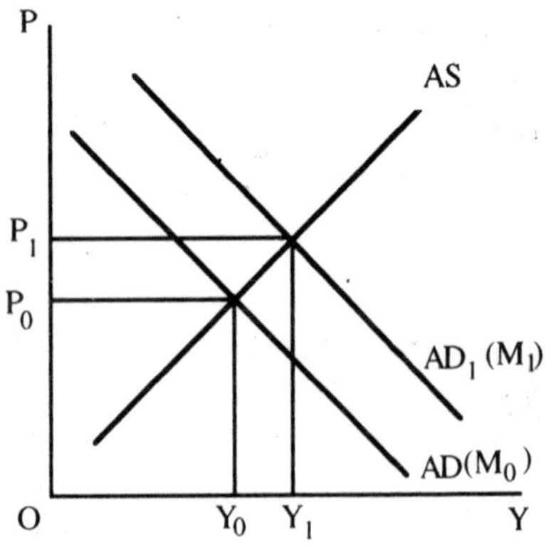

Fig. 8.16 AD curve has its effect on equilibrium Price level and Income

As the level of income increases, the rate of interest falls. Moreover, the value of employment will increase as total output increases. The price level increases and the labour demand curve shifts in the upward direction. If the labour demand curve intersects the labour supply curve at the latter's rising part then the money wage rate will increase. Otherwise, it will remain unchanged. Since employment can increase if the real wage rate falls, it must fall when the money supply increases. This means that the price level must increase rapidly than the money wage rate if the real wage rate is to fall. Mathematical derivation of the result is given in the Appendix(1).

Effect of Change in Autonomous Investment in the Keynesian Model

Here we will consider the effect of change in autonomous investment on the equilibrium values of the variables in the Keynesian model. Suppose autonomous investment increases which will shift the investment function in the upward direction. So the *AD* curve shifts in the upward direction as well. However, the aggregate supply curve remaining the same when the *AD* curve shifts in the upward direction, the equilibrium price and income increase. As real income increases, the level of employment also increases. Furthermore, when the price level increases, the demand for transaction balances increases and the money market equilibrium requires that the speculative balances should decrease. This means that the interest rate should increase which will reduce induced investment and also the aggregate demand. This process continues until a new equilibrium is established. Thus, the effects of an increase in autonomous investment can be summarised as follows: a higher level of employment and income, a higher interest rate and price level and a lower real wage rate.

There are two limiting cases in which this result will not follow. Firstly, if the liquidity preference function is perfectly elastic and, secondly, if the speculative demand for money is zero. Mathematical derivation of the result is given in the Appendix (2).

Limitation of the Keynesian Theory

After the World War II, Keynesian demand-management policies were used by the governments of most Western developed economies in an attempt to keep down unemployment which was the main economic problem. Generally, these policies were successful in preventing unemployment like that experienced in the 1930s, but, unfortunately, they tended to give rise to the phenomenon known as stop-go. That is, in a period of high unemployment, the government used to expand aggregate demand; which would reduce unemployment but at the same time give rise to inflationary situation so that the government eventually would have to reduce aggregate demand. Thus, all go periods used to be followed by stop period and it became difficult to achieve long-run economic growth. This is mainly because the Keynesian model is a short-term one and in the short-run the management of the economy may become very erratic.

A second limitation of the model as we have pointed out in this chapter is that it fails to take into account the problem of inflation. Indeed, the basic model assumes that prices and wages are fixed and the only time they were allowed to rise is after the attainment of full employment. Experience in 1970s has shown us that high rates of inflation can co-exist with high rates of unemployment and no explanation is provided in the Keynesian theory. Furthermore, the coincidence of inflation and unemployment makes the Keynesian policy recommendations questionable.

A further criticism that has been levelled against the Keynesian model is that it tends to understate the influence of money on the real variables in the economy. We have already seen that a change in the money supply in this model affects national income through its effect on the rate of interest; it is because of this that Keynesians put more faith in fiscal rather than monetary policy.

Monetarists have been mainly concerned with these three criticisms of the Keynesian theory. They also make the following points: (a) that short-term demand may do more harm than good; (b) that there is a close relationship between changes in the money supply and changes in money national income in the long-run.; (c) that without government interference the economy will tend towards natural rate of unemployment.

Some Special Criticisms of the Keynesian Model

There are two general criticism of the Keynesian model. Firstly, the Keynesian model is "too aggregative". Secondly, this model is too static. It means that the model does not consider the short-run dynamics of income change and that it is unsuitable to the analysis of long-term economic growth. The model is a short run model in that it assumes a given capital stock. Keynes was interested in the short run as he said, "in the long run we are all dead".

The Keynesian model can be dynamised at least in two directions. Firstly, it is possible to introduce time lags in different functions and analysis of the time path to achieve different equilibrium values. Secondly, it may be possible to consider the effect of an increase in the capital stock on the equilibrium values of different variables. The model is "too static" for the analysis of either the problems of economic growth or the business cycle.

Apart from these general criticisms, we can advance some criticisms devoted to the specific parts of the Keynesian model.

Firstly, the Keynesian liquidity preference function has been criticised mainly on the ground that he considered only two assets — money and bonds. This is an over-simplification. In the real world, there are different types of monetary and non-monetary assets. All these are considered in the modern portfolio approach to the demand for money. Keynes' division of the demand for money into three parts — transaction demand, precautionary demand and speculative demand — has also been criticised. It has been argued that it is difficult to separate between units of money held for speculative and transaction purposes. The same unit of money may be used for either purpose.

Secondly, the Keynesian investment theory has been criticised and new theories have been offered as an alternative to the Keynesian theory which have been discussed later in this book.

Thirdly, the Keynesian consumption function has been criticised and several alternative hypothesis has been developed which we consider later on.

Fourthly, the hypothesis that firms maximise profits has been criticised. Recent developments of the theory of firms show that the objective of the modern firms is not only the maximisation of profits. There are alternative objectives such as sales revenue maximisation and managerial utility maximisation and so on.

Fifthly, the theory of money wage determination in the model is inadequate.

Sixthly, Keynes did not consider the " Real balance effect" or the Pigou effect of the flexibility of the price level in the face of unemployment.

Lastly, unemployment is today's problem. But the greatest problems in the modern world are associated with inflation and economic growth. The Keynesian analysis is incapable of dealing with these twin problems. Keynes was mainly concerned with unemployment in the short run. He did not consider the problem of economic growth or inflation. He was mainly concerned with the problem of depression. However, attempts have been made in recent years to extend the Keynesian analysis to the problems of inflation and economic growth.

Appendix 1

Money Supply in Complete Keynesian Model

Mathematically, the effects of an increase in the supply of money is given as follows. The complete Keynesian model is represented in the following equations:

(1) $S\{F(N)\} = I(r)$

(2) $KPF(N) + L(r) = M_0$

(3) $PF'(N) = W_0 + W(N)$

These three equations have three unknowns: N, r and P. Solving these three equations, we obtain the equilibrium values of three variables. In these three equations, money supply is a parameter. When money supply changes the equilibrium values of these 3 variables also change. The effects of change in M on the equilibrium values of the three variables can be determined by differentiating equations (1) - (3) with respect to M_0. We get the following:

$$S'F'\frac{dN}{dM_0} - I'\frac{dr}{dM_0} + 0.\frac{dP}{dM_0} = 0 \quad \text{.........................(4)}$$

$$KPF'\frac{dN}{dM_0} + L'\frac{dr}{dM_0} + KY\frac{dP}{dM_0} = 1 \quad \text{.....................(5)}$$

$$(PF''-W')\frac{dN}{dM_0} + 0\frac{dr}{dM_0} + F'\frac{dP}{dM_0} = 0 \quad \text{...........(6)}$$

In matrix form, equations (4) - (6) can be written as:

$$\begin{bmatrix} S'F' & -I' & 0 \\ KPF' & L' & KY \\ (PF''-W') & 0 & F' \end{bmatrix} \begin{bmatrix} dN/dM_0 \\ dr/dM_0 \\ dP/dM_0 \end{bmatrix} = \begin{bmatrix} 0 \\ 1 \\ 0 \end{bmatrix}$$

These three equations can be solved for three unknowns dN/dM_0, dr/dM_0, dP/dM_0. Solving for dN/dM_0 with the help of Cramer's rule, we get

$$\frac{dN}{dM_0} = \frac{\begin{vmatrix} 0 & -I' & 0 \\ 1 & L' & KY \\ 0 & 0 & F' \end{vmatrix}}{\begin{bmatrix} S'F' & -I' & 0 \\ KPF' & L' & KY \\ (PF''-W') & 0 & F' \end{bmatrix}} = \frac{I'F'}{D}$$ where D stands for the determinant.

Expanding the determinant D, we get $D = S'L'(F')^2 + I'KP(F')^2 - I'KY(PF''-W')$.

From the assumptions regarding the nature of different functions of the Keynesian model it is seen that $D < 0$. Again since $I' < 0$ *and* $F' > 0$, we have $dN/dM_0 > 0$. This means that as M_0 increases the equilibrium value of N also increases. Again since $Y = F(N)$, $\frac{dY}{dM_0} = F' \cdot \frac{dN}{dM_0} = \frac{I'(F')^2}{D} > 0$.

This means that as M_0 increases the equilibrium value of Y also increases. Again solving equations (4) - (6) for dr/dM_0 by Cramer's rule, we get:

$$\frac{dr}{dM_0} = \frac{\begin{vmatrix} S'F' & 0 & 0 \\ KPF' & 1 & KY \\ (PF''-W') & 0 & F' \end{vmatrix}}{D} = \frac{S'(F')^2}{D} < 0$$

Since $S' > 0$, $(F')^2 > 0$ and $D < 0$, it shows that $dr/dM_0 < 0$, this means that as M_0 increases the equilibrium value of r decreases. Finally, solving for dP/dM_0 with the help of Cramer's rule, we get

$$\frac{dP}{dM_0} = \frac{\begin{vmatrix} S'F' & I' & 0 \\ KPF' & L' & 1 \\ (PF''-W') & 0 & 0 \end{vmatrix}}{D} = \frac{-I'(PF''-W')}{D} > 0$$

This shows that, as M_0 increases the equilibrium value of P also increases. Again, the money wage rate is given by $W = W_0 + W(N)$. If $N \leq N_f$, then $W(N) = 0$ and $\frac{dW}{dM_0} = 0$. If, on the other hand, $N > N_f$, $W'(N) > 0$. In that case $\frac{dW}{dM_0} = W'\frac{dN}{dM_0} > 0$. Thus, as M_0 increases, the equilibrium value of W either increases or remains the same, since $\frac{dW}{dM_0} \geq 0$.

Again, $\frac{W}{P} = F'(N)$, $\therefore \frac{d(W/P)}{dM_0} = F''(N)\frac{dN}{dM_0}$.

Since $F'' < 0$, and $\frac{dN}{dM_0} > 0$ thus, $\frac{d(W/P)}{dM_0} < 0$.

We thus get the following results from our analysis :

$$\frac{dN}{dM_0} > 0,\ \frac{dY}{dM_0} > 0,\ \frac{dr}{dM_0} < 0,\ \frac{dP}{dM_0} > 0,\ \frac{dW}{dM_0} \geq 0 \text{ and } \frac{d(W/P)}{dM_0} < 0.$$

The effect of an increase in money supply can be summarised as follows: A higher level of income, a higher level of employment and a higher price level is associated with a lower real wage rate, a lower interest rate and a higher money wage rate.

In this context, it can be said that money is not neutral in the Keynesian model because it is seen that, in this model, increased money supply affects the real variables of the system like the level of income and employment.

However, we can consider two special cases. First, if $L' = \infty$, then $\frac{dN}{dM_0} = 0$. Accordingly, $\frac{dr}{dM_0} = 0$, $\frac{d(W/P)}{dM_0} = 0$, $\frac{dY}{dM_0} = 0$. The change in the supply of money will have no impact on the equilibrium values of other variables in the system. In the liquidity trap situation, monetary policy is completely useless. Secondly, if $I' = 0$, i.e. interest inelasticity of investment function, we get $\frac{dN}{dM_0} = 0$, $\frac{dP}{dM_0} = 0$, $\frac{dr}{dM_0} = \frac{1}{L'} < 0$, $\frac{dY}{dM_0} = 0$. Thus, a change in the quantity of money will have no impact on the level of income and employment if the liquidity preference function is perfectly interest-elastic or if the investment function is absolutely interest inelastic.

Appendix 2

Mathematical Derivation of the Effect of Change in Autonomous Investment

The complete Keynesian model is expressed as follows:

(1) $SF(N) = I(r) + \alpha$

(2) $KPF(N) + L(r) = M_0$

(3) $PF'(N) = W_0 + W(N)$

Here α represents the shift factor in the investment function. An increase in α means an increase in the autonomous component of investment. Differentiating equations (1) - (3) with respect to α and rearranging, we get the following:

$$(4)\quad S'F'\frac{dN}{d\alpha} - I'\frac{dr}{d\alpha} + 0\frac{dP}{d\alpha} = 1$$

$$(5)\quad KPF'\frac{dN}{d\alpha} + L'\frac{dr}{d\alpha} + KY\frac{dP}{d\alpha} = 0$$

$$(6)\quad (PF'' - W')\frac{dN}{d\alpha} + 0\frac{dr}{d\alpha} + F'\frac{dP}{d\alpha} = 0$$

In matrix form, these equations may be expressed as:

$$\begin{bmatrix} S'F' & -I' & 0 \\ KPF' & L' & KY \\ (PF''-W') & 0 & F' \end{bmatrix}\begin{bmatrix} dN/d\alpha \\ dr/d\alpha \\ dP/d\alpha \end{bmatrix} = \begin{bmatrix} 1 \\ 0 \\ 0 \end{bmatrix}$$

In these three equations, there are three unknowns $dN/d\alpha$, $dr/d\alpha$ and $dP/d\alpha$.

Let D be the determinant formed by the coefficients of these three unknowns.

Now solving these three equations with the help of Cramer's rule, we get:

$$\frac{dN}{d\alpha} = \frac{L'}{D},\quad \frac{dr}{d\alpha} = \frac{-KP(F')^2 + KY(PF''-W')}{D},\quad \frac{dP}{d\alpha} = \frac{-L'(PF''-W')}{D}$$

Moreover, $\dfrac{dY}{d\alpha} = \dfrac{dN}{d\alpha}\cdot\dfrac{dY}{dN} = F'\dfrac{dN}{d\alpha} = \dfrac{L'(F')^2}{D}$

From the signs of the relevant functions

$$D < 0 \text{ and } \frac{dN}{d\alpha} > 0, \ \frac{dr}{d\alpha} > 0, \ \frac{dP}{d\alpha} > 0, \ \frac{dY}{d\alpha} > 0.$$

Further that $\frac{W}{P} = F'$, $\frac{d(W/P)}{d\alpha} = F''.\frac{dN}{d\alpha} < 0.$

This shows that, if α increases i.e. if autonomous investment increases, the equilibrium values of N, Y, r and P will increase while the equilibrium value of W/P will decrease. The two limiting cases can also be deduced from this analysis. Firstly, if $L' = \infty$ then $\frac{dY}{d\alpha} = \frac{1}{S'}$ and $\frac{dr}{d\alpha} = 0.$

Secondly, when $L' = 0$, $\frac{dY}{d\alpha} = 0$ but $\frac{dr}{d\alpha} > 0.$

9 KEYNES VERSUS THE CLASSICISTS

Comparison Between the Classical and the Keynesian Model

We have already discussed the Keynesian and the classical models separately. Now it would be proper to compare these models together. The comparison between the two models might be simple and clear if we write the equations of the models side by side.

We write the equations of the simple classical model and the complete Keynesian model below:

Classical Model | **Keynesian Model**

(1) $Y = f(N, K_0)$ (I) $Y = f(N, K_0)$

These equations give us aggregate production of the two systems which are similar.

(2) $\frac{dY}{dN} = \frac{W}{P}$ (II) $\frac{dY}{dN} = \frac{W}{P}$

The labour demand functions of the two systems are exactly the same.

(3) $N = N\left(\frac{W}{P}\right)$ (III) $W = W_0 + W(N)$ such that $W(N) = 0$ for $N \leq N_F$ and $W'(N) > 0$ for $N > N_F$.

The equation (3) is the classical labour supply function which is significantly different from (iii) which is the Keynesian labour supply function.

(4) $M_0 = kPY$ (IV) $M_0 = kPY + L(r)$

The equation (4) is the classical money demand function which has an additional element, $L(r)$, with the classical money demand function. This is known as the liquidity preference function or the speculative demand for money function in the Keynesian system.

(5) $S = S(r)$ (V) $S = S(Y)$

The equation (5) is the classical saving function. Saving is a function of interest rate in the classical model. But in equation (V) we have Keynesian function where saving is a function of income (Y). The saving function in the two systems are completely different.

(6) $I = I(r)$ (VI) $I = I(r)$

These equations show investment function in the two systems which is a function of rate of interest in both the classical and Keynesian models.

(7) $S = I$ (VII) $S = I$

The equations (7) and (VII) are equilibrium conditions which cannot be different.

Thus, saving and investment equality give us equilibrium condition in both the systems.

We have seven equations amd seven unknowns in both the models. The system is determinate in both the models. As it can be seen, the classical model differs from the Keynesian model in three respects. The difference is in the labour supply functions in equations (3) and (III). The second difference is in the money demand function in equations (4) and (IV). Lastly, there is a difference in the saving function in equations (5) and (V).

In the classical model the supply of labour is assumed to be a function of real wage rate and the money wage rate is assumed to be flexible in both directions. On the other hand, in the Keynesian model the supply of labour is assumed to be a function of the money wage rate which is inflexible at least in downward direction. The money wage cannot fall below W_0. In the classical Model money demand is assumed to be a function of the level of income only. They considered only the transactions — precautionary demand for money — money is considered to be a function of medium of exchange only. However, in the Keynesian Model, money demand is assumed to be a function of both the level of income — medium of exchange of money — and the rate of interest — store of value function of money. The speculative demand for money is Keynesian innovation. Lastly, Keynes assumed that income is the main determinant of saving and not the interest rate as the classicists assumed.

The conclusions are also different in the two models. In the classical model, full-emloyment equilibrium is automatically reached. But in the Keynesian model there is no such automatic mechanism. The equilibrium may be one of full-employment or underemployment. While the classical economists denied the possibility of underemployment equilibrium, Keynes argued that there is no difficulty of getting an underemployment equilibrium.

The "Classical Economists" maintained two propositions about the equilibrium properties of an economy — flexible wages and prices. First, that the equilibrium is one with full employment of labour. Second, that the nominal quantity of money in the economy only determines the equilibrium price level, but has no effect on the equilibrium value of any real variable. A real variable is one which has an effect on the allocation of resources over time or at a point of time. For example, the relative prices of commodities affect the quantities of commodities produced and consumed at a point in time; the interest rate affects the quantities of commodities consumed over time.

In the present context, real variables are real income, the interest rate and the real wage rate. According to the second proposition, none of these variables are determined by the nominal quantity of money. Their equilibrium values depend on the real factors — technology, tastes and the quantity of resources in the economy.

In the classical model, money is neutral. An increase in the supply of money affects only the price level and the money wage rate, keeping the real variables unaffected. But, in the Keynesian model, money is not neutral. A change in the quantity of money affects both the real and monetary variables.

Let us now examine which is the crucial difference between the classical model and the Keynesian model. Some economists think that it is difference in the labour supply function, others think that it is the difference in the money demand function, others say it is the difference in the saving function, while still others say that it is none of these but something else which is implicit in the formal structure. The crucial difference in conclusion is the possibility of underemployment equilibrium in the Keynesian model and full employment in the classical model.

We want to see which differences cause underemployment equilibrium. Let us introduce in the classical model the Keynesian money demand function. The classical model will look like the following:

(1) $Y = f(N, K_0)$ (2) $P.\frac{dY}{dN} = W$ (3) $N = N\left(\frac{W}{P}\right)$

Now (4) $M_0 = kPY + L(r)$ (5) $S = S(r)$ (6) $I = I(r)$ and (7) $S = I$

Here we will obtain automatic full-employment from equations (1) to (3). Equations (5)to (7) will determine the interest rate and the equation (4) will determine the price level. The resulting model would have classical character and full employment would be automatically achieved due to the assumption of wage-price flexibility. Thus, the addition of the speculative demand for money into the classical model will not generate underemployment equilibrium and, hence, it is not a crucial difference.

Similarly, we can see that the saving function will not make crucial difference either. If we replace the classical saving function by the Keynesian saving function, the resulting model will have the following system of equations:

(1) $Y = f(N, K_0)$ (2) $\frac{dY}{dN} = \left(\frac{W}{P}\right)$ (3) $N = N\left(\frac{W}{P}\right)$

(4) $M_0 = kPY$ (5) $S = S(Y)$ (6) $I = I(r)$ (7) $S = I$

In this case also, full employment will be automatically achieved from equations (1) to (3). The difference here is that a shift of the production function or a shift of the labour supply function will affect the interest rate which will change income and saving relative to investment. Hence the difference in the saving function is not a crucial difference between the models.

Instead of changing the money demand function and saving function separately, we change them at the same time. Here also full employment is automatically achieved because of wage-price flexibility. This model is also classical in character because, like the classical model, full employment is automatically achieved in the labour market, the rate of interest is determined from saving and investment functions and the money market determines the price level. Thus, it is seen that the difference in the saving and money demand functions together cannot explain the difference in conclusion.

From the above analysis, it is clear that the crucial difference between the classical and Keynesian money models is the labour supply function i.e. the equation three. If we replace equation(3) of the classical (labour supply function) model by the equation (iii) of the Keynesian model — keeping other equations unchanged — then automatic achievement of full employment will be prevented. Thus, we can say that the assumption of inflexibility of wages — especially in the downward direction — is the crucial difference between the Keynesian and the classical model. Underemployment equilibrium in the Keynesian model is caused by the assumption of wage rigidity — which is the crucial assumption of Keynes. In fact, it was the only possible cause of unemployment.

We have seen in the previous analysis that wage flexibility results in full-employment equilibrium in the labour market and price flexibility results in full-employment equilibrium in the output market. It is also true, in this model, that the nominal quantity of money cannot affect the interest rate. All real variables in the economy are also determined by tastes, technology and the quantity of resources. The nominal quantity of money determines the price level. To understand the debate concerning the two classical propositions, it is necessary to understand how price flexibility results in full employment equilibrium and what role the nominal quantity of money plays in the process. The crucial assumption in the model is not price flexibility, as such, but interest-rate flexibility. With a given quantity of nominal money, price flexibility is the means by which the interst rate changes to its equilibrium value.

In Fig. 9.1, we start from full employment equilibrium of $Y_F r_F$ for some price level P_0. r_F is the interest rate at which full employment saving is equal to investment. Now, suppose that everybody wants to save more than previously — which shifts the *IS* curve to *IS*$'$. The new equilibrium interest rate is r_F' at which new equilibrium saving is equal to investment at full employment.

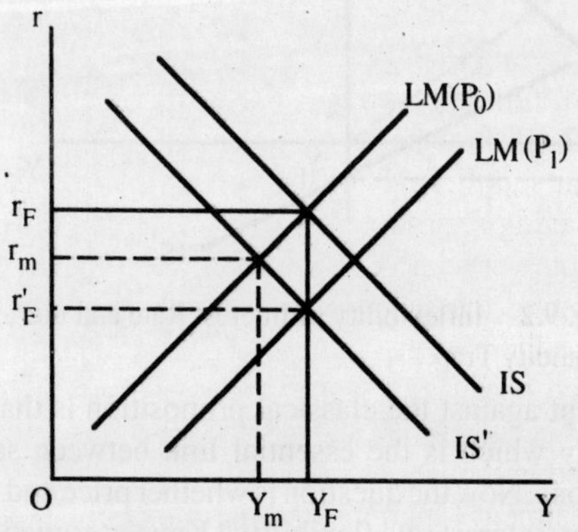

Fig. 9.1 Full Employment and Price Flexibility

If there is no change in the price level, the interest rate will be r_m and the aggregate deamnd will be Y_m, less than, full employment output Y_F.

To attain full employment equilibrium again, the interest rate must fall and investment must rise. The reason is not far to seek. People wish to save more than before, they desire more future consumption relative to current consumption. So investment must increase. A change in the interest rate is the signalling device transmitting information about the change in tastes and producing the incentive to increase investment on this information. However, this direct effect of the change in saving is on the price level and also on interest rate. With a given nominal quantity of money the fall in the price level leads to an increase in the real quantity of money and, thus, a fall in the interest rate. As long as there is an excess of saving over investment and an excess supply of goods, the price level and, thus, interest rate, will continue falling. If the interest rate reaches r_F' with the price level P_1, full employment saving will equal investment again. Therefore, what is crucial to the first classical proposition is the interest rate flexibility without which price flexibility will not be enough to attain full employment.

In the above model, the second classical proposition also holds. A change in the nominal quantity of money, without any change in real factor, will affect price level only. Any initial effect on the interest rate will be offset by the change in the price level.

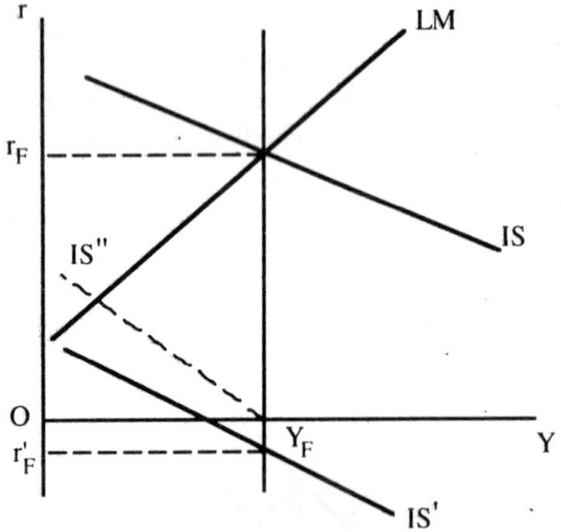

Fig. 9.2 Inflexibility of Interest Rate and the Liquidity Trap

Keynes' argument against the classical proposition is that it requires the interest rate flexibility which is the essential link between saving decisions and investment decisions. Now the question is whether price and wage flexibility guarnatee the necessary interest rate flexibility? Keynes argued that in a money economy there is inherent inflexibility in the interest rate because the interest rate in such an economy could never fall below zero (the liquidity trap situation). In Fig. 9.2, we start with a full-employment equilibrium at Y_F and r_F. Assume now that because of a change in tastes people want to save more at every level of income, shown by the shift of the *IS* curve to *IS*′. The equilibrium interest rate now is r_F' at which full-employment saving is equal to investment which is negative and is an unacceptable rate in a money economy. Thus, in Fig. 9.2, there is an excess of full-employment saving over investment, which will lead to a fall in the price level, but will not result in a fall in the interest rate to the required level. Flexibility of prices does not imply the necessary flexibility of the interest rate as we can have the liquidity trap at a positive or zero rate of interest.

Here comes Pigou who criticises Keynes on this point which is known as 'Pigou effect' in the economic literature. He gave a solution to the problem raised by Keynes. Let us first look at the mechanism of the solution.

Any discrepancy between full-employment saving and investment can be eliminated either by a change in investment or in saving. Price flexibility can achieve a change in investment by a correct amount as long as it can affect a change in interest rate by a correct amount. Keynes' point is that there is likely to be a situation where price flexibility may not do the trick; the interest rate cannot fall by the required amount and, thus, investment cannot rise by the required amount. However, another way out may be a change in saving. Again, the question is whether price flexibility can do this?

If consumption is solely a function of income, then a fall in the price level has no effect on consumption and thus on saving. One has to rely on investment effects to solve the discrepancy between investment and saving. If, however, consumption also depends on wealth, then a change in price can eliminate the discrepancy between saving and investment by affecting saving. There exists a category of wealth which is affected by a change in the price level, namely the real quantity of money. For a given quantity of nominal money, the fall in the price level raises the real quantity of money and, thus, the percieved wealth of the community. Thus, the new function can be written as $C = F\left(Y, \frac{M}{P}\right)$ a fall in the price level even if it has no effect on the interest rate (the Keynesian case) will still be effective in achieving full-employment by increasing consumption (reducing saving) and not by increasing investment (via a change in the interest rate). In Fig. 9.2, the change in the price level will shift the *IS* curve to *IS*″.

In the Keynesian case, we have a situation in which people want to save even at a zero rate of interest, they are not saving for the purpose of acquiring future income streams. They are then saving for the purpose of acquiring wealth for its own sake (positive time preference). They are willing to give up current consumption for the sake of accumulating wealth and, therefore, must be deriving some amenity value from it. The Keynesian case can only arise if wealth is in the consumption function and we also have — via the "Pigou effect"— a solution to the Keynesian problem. The 'Pigou effect' is based on the idea that changes in the real quantity of money will affect consumption. A change in the real quantity of money may be achieved either by a change in the price level for a given quantity of nominal money or a change in the nominal quantity of money for a given price level. 'Pigou Effect' will be discussed in detail here.

Pigou Effect and Full-employment

The basic difference between the Classical and the Keynesian economics is that, in the Classical Model, full-employment is automatically achieved, whereas, in the Keynesian model, no such automatic mechanism exists. In the simple Keynesian model of income determination, the equilibrium level of income is determined by the equality of planned saving and investment, the equilibrium level of income thus determined may or may not be full-employment equilibirum as given in Fig. 9.3.

If investment is I_1 , the equilibrium level of income is Y_1. If investment is I_2, the equilibrium level of income is Y_2 and so on. Suppose the full employment level of income is Y_2 as determined from the labour market. The full-employment will be achieved only if the investment schedule is I_2. There is no reason to believe that the investment schedule will always be at I_2. Thus, there is no automatic machinery to ensure full employment. Against the Keynesian argument the classical economists argue that saving and investment are functions of both the rate of interest and the level of income:

$$S = S(r,Y) \quad \text{and} \quad I = I(r,Y).$$

According to them, if saving at full employment is not equal to investment, the rate of interest will change and the flexibility of the interest rate will ensure

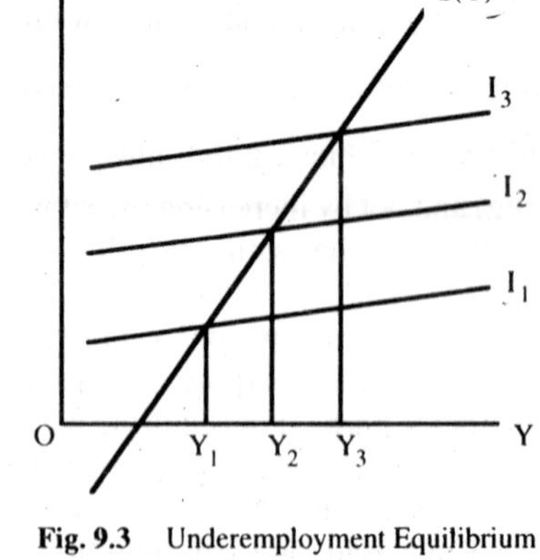

Fig. 9.3 Underemployment Equilibrium

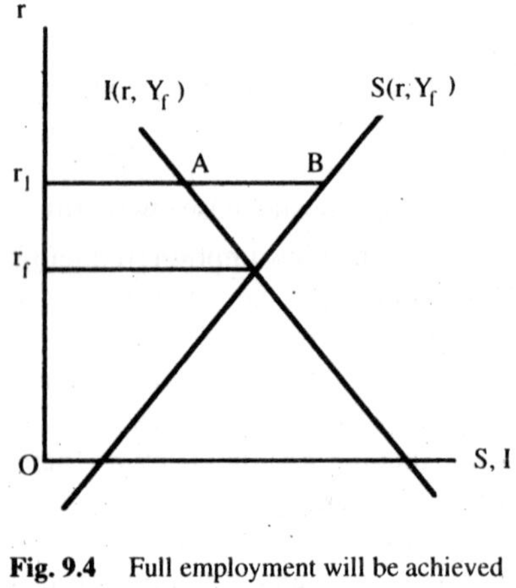

Fig. 9.4 Full employment will be achieved by the Interest Rate Flexibility

the equality between investment and saving at full employment. We can see this in Fig. 9.4.

Suppose that investment and saving schedules are at full employment level of income. If the rate of interest is r_1, investment at full employment will be less than saving at full employment by the amount *AB*. Assuming that the rate of interest is flexible, the rate of interest will fall until saving becomes equal to investment at full employment. It is through flexibility of the interest rate that full employment is automatically achieved. If the investment function is I_1, then saving at full employment will exceeed investment. As a consequence the interest rate will fall. As the interest rate falls, the investment function shifts upwards until I_2 is reached. Thus, even if investment function is I_1 or I_3, it will eventually reach I_2 through the interest rate flexibility.

To this the Keynesian economists argue that, at times the saving and investment schedules are such that the rate of interest required to maintain full employment becomes zero or negative as shown in Fig 9.5. In Fig. 9.5, the saving and investment schedules intersect to produce a negative rate of interest at full employment. In such a situation, full employment cannot be achieved because a negative rate of interest is not feasible in a money economy. Whether the system will generate full employment depends on whether or not full employment saving and investment intersect at a positive rate of interest. However, there is no automatic mechanism to ensure that the investment and saving functions will always intersect at a positive rate of interest.

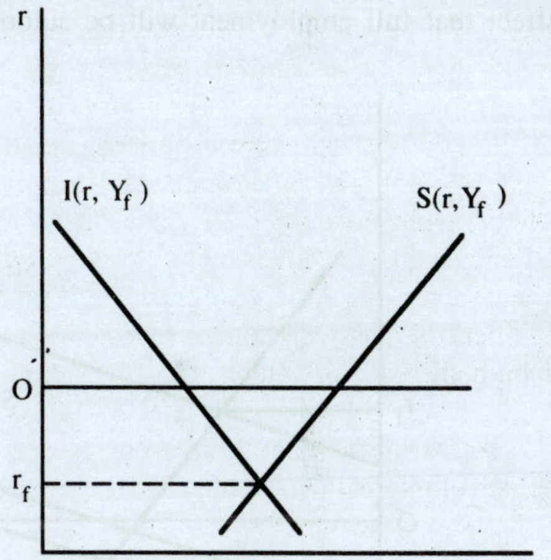

Fig. 9.5 Full Employment is prevented by Negative Interest Rates

Against this negative argument of Keynes, Pigou, Patinkin etc. have given replies. They introduced another variable into the saving function. The saving function can now be written as $S = S\left\{r, Y, \frac{M_0}{P}\right\}$ where $\frac{M_0}{P}$ is the real value of cash balances. They argue that as the real value of cash balances goes up $\left(\frac{\partial s}{\partial\left[\frac{M_0}{P}\right]}\right)$, saving decreases.

The argument of Pigou is that if people save only to earn interest then saving would be zero when the rate of interest is zero or negative. In that case, saving and investment would always intersect at a positive rate of interest. If people save even at a negative rate of interest, it means that they save for other reasons. The extent of such saving out of current income is inversely related to the real value of cash balances. If this is sufficiently large, all the secondary desires for saving will be fulfilled. At this point, the only reason for saving is to earn future income. If the real value of cash balances is large enough, saving becomes zero at a positive rate of interest — irrespective of the income level. The dependence of the saving function on the real value of the cash balances is known as Pigou Effect or Real Balance Effect. In short, Pigou Effect states that the aggregate consumption expenditure is directly related to the volume of wealth and saving is inversely related to the volume of wealth.

According to Pigou it is through the 'Pigou Effect' or the Real Balance Effect that full employment will be automatically achieved. The argument

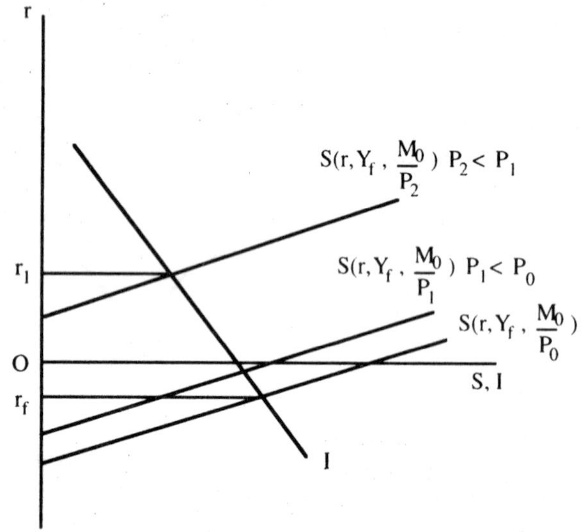

Fig. 9.6 Pigou Effect and Full Employment

of negative rate is invalid, if we accept complete flexibility of prices. Suppose that at a given price level, the rate of interest needed to achieve full employment is negative. If full employment investment is less than saving, national income starts falling, and unemployment results. If workers accept the reduction of money wages then the price level will begin to fall which increases the real value of the given money supply. As a consequence, the saving function shifts to the left until it intersects the investment function at a positive rate of interest as shown in Fig. 9.6.

Assume that the initial price level is P_o, the investment function at full employment intersects the saving function at r_f, a negative rate of interest. As a result, the price level falls to P_1 and the real value of given money supply rises, i.e. $\frac{M_0}{P_1} > \frac{M_0}{P_0}$. Thus, the saving function shifts to the left to a new position $S\left[r, Y_f, \frac{M_0}{P_1}\right]$.

If the new saving function does not intersect the investment function at a positive rate of interest, the price level will fall further and the saving function will shift to the left until a positive rate of interest is achieved at full employment. Thus, the negative rate of interest will be avoided through the Pigou Effect. Thus, Pigou Effect ensures an automatic mechanism to full employment through the price flexibility.

The Pigou effect does not guarantee that full employment will always be achieved. Suppose that the strength of the Pigou effect is very small, so that a successive fall in the price level cannot produce a sufficient shift in the saving function to generate a positive interest rate. In such a situation the falling price level would fail to bring about full employment. To achieve full employment we need an additional assumption, that the intensity of the Pigou effect is such that it would produce a sufficient shift in the saving function to intersect the investment function at a positive rate of interest.

10 AGGREGATE DEMAND

Aggregate demand is the relationship between then quantity of output and the aggregate price level. Alternatively, the aggregate demand curve tells us the quantity of goods and services people will buy for any level of prices. Now aggregate demand would be examined thoroughly. First we use the quantity theory of money to provide a simple derivation of the aggregate demand curve. Second, we use *IS -LM* Model to derive the aggregate demand curve.

The Quantity Equation as Aggregate Demand

The quantity theory tells us that, $MV = PY$, where M is the money supply, V is the velocity of money (which is assumed constant), P is the price level, and Y is the amount of total output. This equation states that the money supply determines the nominal value of output which is PY.

We know that the quantity equation can be written in terms of the demand for and the supply of real money balances:

$$\left(\frac{M}{P}\right)^s = \left(\frac{M}{P}\right)^d = kY \text{ where } k = \frac{1}{V}.$$

Now the quantity equation states that the supply of real balances $\left(\frac{M}{P}\right)^s$ equals the demand $\left(\frac{M}{P}\right)^d$ and that the demand is proportional to the amount of output, Y.

For any fixed money supply, the quantity equation shows a negative relationship between the price level P and output Y as in Fig. 10.1. This is called the Aggregate Demand Curve *(ADC)* .

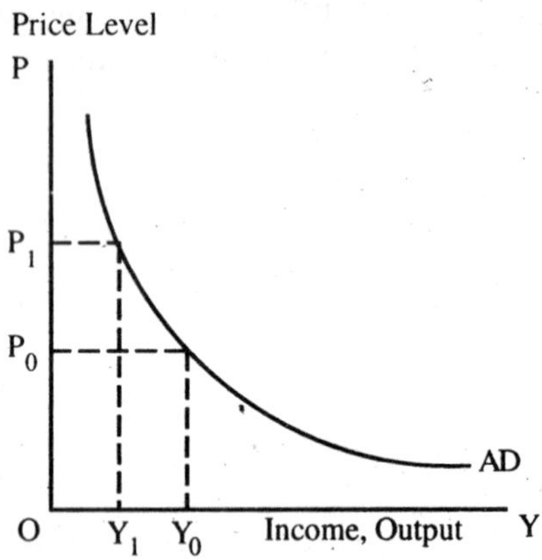

Fig. 10.1 Downward Sloping Aggregate Demand Curve

Why Aggregate Demand Curve slopes downward

The aggregate demand curve slopes downward because for any fixed money supply, the quantity equation fixes the nominal value of output PY. Thus, if the price level goes down, output must go up and vice versa.

Better way to understand negative relationship between P and Y is to consider the link between money and transactions. Since we have assumed that V is constant, the money supply determines the money value of all transactions in the economy. If the price level falls, so that each transaction requires less money, the quantity of transactions and, thus, the quantity of goods and services purchased, must rise.

We could also look at the demand and supply of real balances. If Y is higher, people engage in more transactions and need higher real balances M/P. For a fixed money supply M, higher real balances imply a lower price level. Conversely, if the price level is lower, real money balances are higher; the higher real balances allow a greater volume of transactions and, thus, a higher level of Y.

Shifts in the ADC (Aggregate Demand Curve)

The *ADC* is drawn on the assumption of fixed money supply. In other words, it tells us the possible combinations of P and Y for a given value of money supply (M^S). If the money supply changes, the possible combinations of P and Y change — that is, the *ADC* shifts. Let us examine the situations in which a shift may occur.

First, consider what happens when monetary authority increases the money supply. The quantity equation, $MV = PY$, tells us that there is an increase in PY. For any given output, the price level is higher, for any given price level, the output is higher.Fig. 10.2 shows the *ADC* shifts outward to *AD'*.

Next, consider what happens when the monetary authority reduces the money supply. The quantity equation, $MV = PY$, tells us that the reduction in the money supply leads to a proportionate reduction in the nominal value of output, PY. For any price level, the amount of output is lower, and for any given output, the P level is lower. Fig. 10.2 shows the *ADC* curve shifts inward to *AD"*.

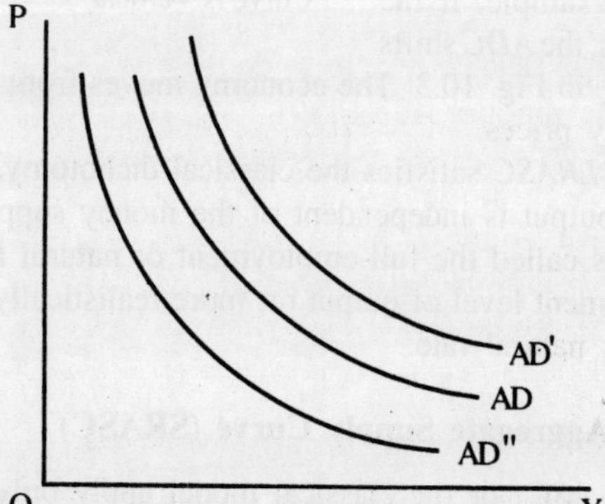

Fig. 10.2 Changes in Money Supply Shifts the Aggregate Demand Curve

Aggregate Supply Curve (ASC)

The *ADC*, by itself, does not tell us about the price or output; it merely gives a relationship between these two variables. We need another relationship between P and Y that accompany *ADC* — an *ASC*. The *ADC* and the *ASC* together give us the equilibrium price level and output.

Aggregate Supply is the relationship between the quantity of goods and services supplied and the price level. Because prices are flexible in the long run and fixed in the short run, we need to discuss two different AS curves, the long run *ASC (LRASC)* and the short run *ASC (SRASC)* and the transition from the Short Run to the Long Run Aggregate Supply Curve.

The Vertical ASC in the Long Run

We derive the long run ASC from the classical model. We know that the amount of output produced depends on the amounts of Capital and Labour and on the available technology. To show this, we write :

$$Y = F(\overline{K}_0, L) = \overline{Y}$$

According to the classical model, output does not depend on the price level. Thus, the *LRASC* is vertical as in Fig. 10.3. The intersection of the *ADC* with this vertical *LRASC* determines the price level.

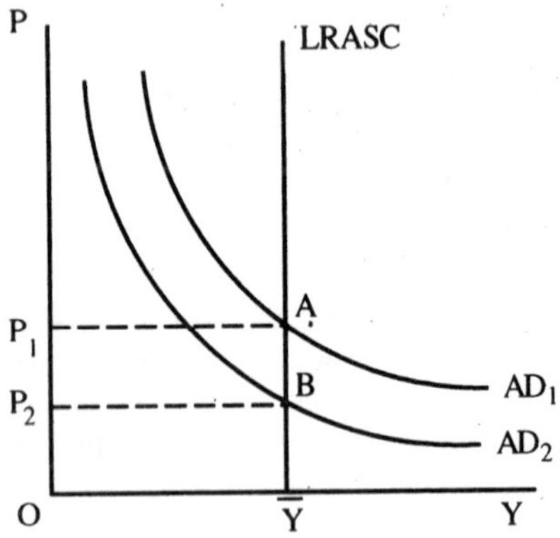

Fig. 10.3 Long-run Aggregate Supply Curve is Vertical

If the *LRASC* is vertical, then changes in *ADC* affect prices but not output. For example, if the money supply falls, the *ADC* shifts downward, as AD_2'in Fig. 10.3. The economy moves from *A* to *B*. This shift in *AD* affects only prices.

The vertical *LRASC* satisfies the classical dichotomy, since it implies that the level of output is independent of the money supply. This long-run output level, $\overline{Y}$, is called the full-employment or natural level of output. It is the full-employment level of output or, more realistically, at which unemployment is at its natural rate.

The Short Run Aggregate Supply Curvé (SRASC)

The vertical *ASC* or the classical model apply only in the long run. In the short run, some prices are sticky and, thus, do not adjust to changes in demand. This price stickiness implies that the *SRASC* is not vertical.

As an extreme case, all prices are fixed at predetermined levels. At these prices, firms are willing to sell as much as they could, and they hire just enough labour to produce the amount demanded. Since the price level is fixed, we represent this situation in Fig.10.4 with a horizontal *ASC*.

The short-run equilibrium of the economy is the intersection of the *ADC* and this horizontal *SRASC*. In this case, changes in *AD* do affect the level of output. For example, if the monetary authority suddenly increases the money supply, the *ADC* shifts outward as in Fig. 10.4. The economy moves from the old intersection of *AD* and *AS* at point *A*, to the new intersection at *B*. Since the price level is fixed, the shift in *AD* causes output to rise as in Fig. 10.4. A rise in *AD* increases output in the short-run because prices do not adjust instantly. After a sudden rise in *AD*, firms are stuck with prices that are too low. With demand high and prices low, firms sell more of their product, which causes them to increase employment and production.

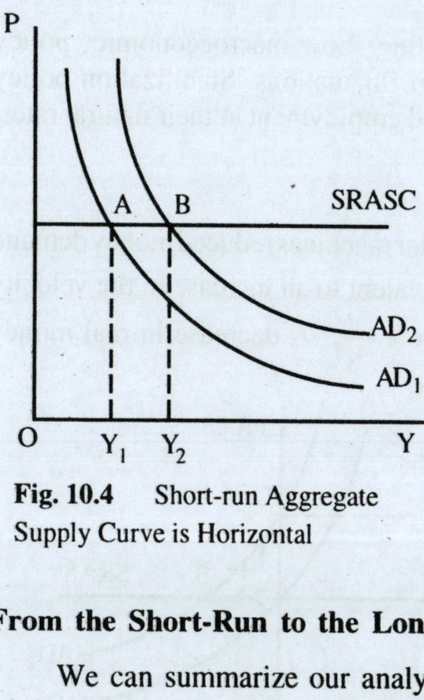

Fig. 10.4 Short-run Aggregate Supply Curve is Horizontal

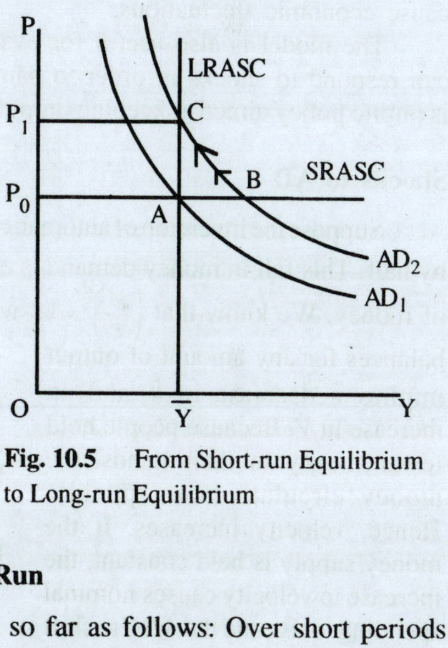

Fig. 10.5 From Short-run Equilibrium to Long-run Equilibrium

From the Short-Run to the Long Run

We can summarize our analysis so far as follows: Over short periods of time, prices are sticky, the *SRASC* is flat, and changes in *AD* affect the output of the economy over the long period of time, prices are flexible, the LRASC is vertical, and changes in *AD* affect only the price level. Thus, changes in *AD* have different effects over different time period.

Let us trace the effects over time of a rise in *AD*. Suppose the economy begins in long-run equilibrium, as shown in Fig. 10.5 where there are three curves: the *ADC*, the *LRASC* , and the *SRASC*. The long-run equilibrium is at the point where *ADC* cuts the *LRASC*. Prices have adjusted to reach this equilibrium. Thus, when the economy is in its long-run equilibrium, the *SRASC* must cross at this point as well.

Now, suppose that the monetary authority increases the money supply. In the short-run, prices are sticky, so the economy move from point *A* to *B*. Output and employment increases above their natural levels, which means the economy is in boom. Over time, in response to the high demand, wages and prices rise. The gradual increase in the price level moves the economy upward along the *ADC* to point *C*, which is the new long-run equilibrium. In the new equilibrium (*C*), output and employment are back again to their natural levels, but prices are now higher — (P_1) than the (P_0), old price level long-run equilibrium point *A*.

Shocks and Instability

Shocks disrupt economic well-being by pushing output and employment away from their natural rates. The model of *AD* and *AS* shows how shocks cause economic fluctuations.

The model is also useful for evaluating how macroeconomic policy can respond to shocks in order to dampen fluctuations. Stabilization policy is public policy aimed at keeping output and employment at their natural rates.

Shocks to AD

Suppose the invention of automatic teller machines reduced money demand by half. This fall in money demand is equivalent to an increase in the velocity of money. We know that $\left(\frac{M}{P}\right)^d = kY$ where $k = \frac{1}{V}$. A decrease in real money balances for any amount of output implies a decrease in *k* and an increase in *V*. Because people hold fewer money in their hands, the money circulate more quickly. Hence, velocity increases. If the money supply is held constant, the increase in velocity causes nominal spending to rise and the *ADC* to shift upward, as in Fig. 10.6. In the short-run, the increase in demand raises the output — thus, it causes an economic boom. At the existing prices, firms sell more. The economy begins in long-run equilibrium, at *A*. An increase in *AD* — due to an increase in the velocity of money — moves the economy from *A* to *B*, where output is above the natural (potential) level.

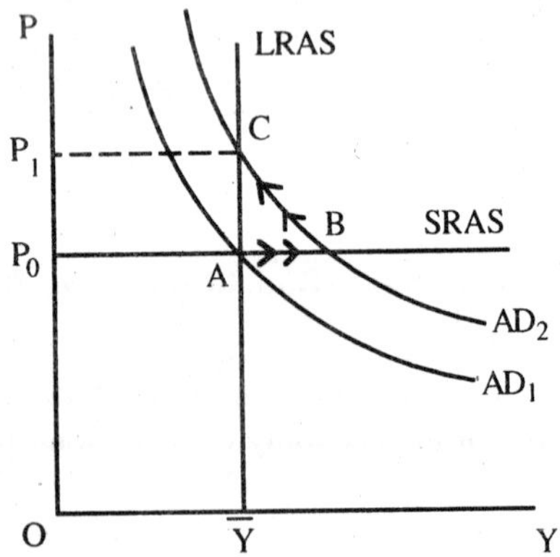

Fig. 10.6 Shift of Aggregate Demand Curve

Over time, the higher level of *AD* increases wages and prices. As the price level rises, the quantity of output demanded declines, and the economy gradually approaches the natural rate of production, and the economy moves from *B* to *C*. But during the transaction, the economy's output is higher than the natural rate.

What can the monetary authority do to dampen this boom? It might reduce the money supply to offset the increase in velocity which would stabilize *AD′*. Thus, the monetary authority can reduce or even eliminate the impact of demand shocks if it can control the money supply.

Shocks to AS

A supply shock is a shock to the economy that alters the cost of production and, as a result, the prices that firms charge. Supply shocks have a direct impact on the price level, they are also called price shocks. Examples are (1) A drought that destroys crops, (2) A new environment protection law, (3) the *OPEC* cartel and (4) An increase in Union aggressiveness.

All these are adverse supply shocks; they push up costs and prices. A favourable supply shock reduces costs and prices.

Fig. 10.7 shows how an adverse supply shock push up costs and prices. The *SRASC* shifts upward. If *AD* is held constant, the economy moves from *A* to *B*, leading to a combination of increasing prices and falling output below the natural rate. An experience like this called stagflation, because it combines stagnation with inflation. Eventually, as prices fall, the economy returns to the natural rate at *A*. But the cost of this process is a painful recession.

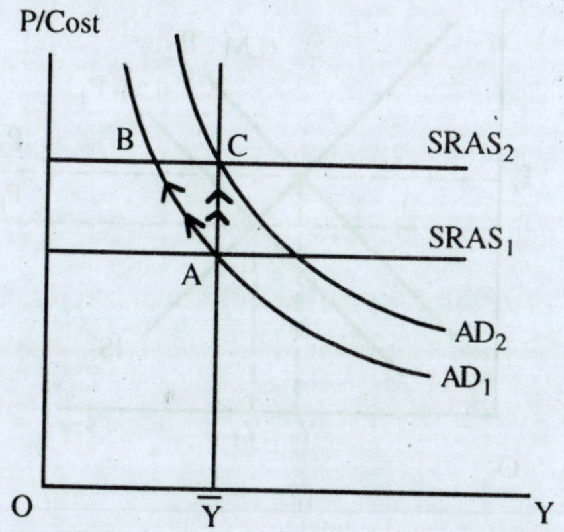

Fig. 10.7 Adverse Supply Shock Push up costs and prices

In response to an adverse supply shock, the policy maker can increase *AD* to prevent a reduction in output. If the increase in *AD* coincides with the shock to *AS*, the economy moves immediately from point *A* to *C* as in Fig. 10.7. In this case, the monetary authority is said to have accommodated the supply shock. The cost of this policy is permanently higher level of prices. There is no way to adjust *AD* — both to maintain full employment and to keep the price level stable.

The IS-LM Model and the Theory of Aggregate Demand Curve

We used the *IS-LM* model to explain national income in the short-run when the price level is fixed. To see how the *IS-LM* Model fits into the model of *AD* and *AS* developed above, we now examine what happens in the *IS-LM* model as the price level changes. The *IS-LM* model provides a theory to explain the position and slope of the *ADC*.

As we have seen, the *ADC* is a relationship between the price level and the level of national income. We derived this relationship from the quantity theory of money. For a given money supply, a higher price level implies a lower level of income (*Y*). Increase in the money supply shift the *ADC* outward, and decrease in the money supply shift the *ADC* inward.

We now use the *IS-LM* model to derive the *ADC*. First, we use the *IS-LM* model to show that national income falls as the price level rises; the downward sloping *ADC* expresses this relationship. Second, we examine what causes the *ADC* to shift.

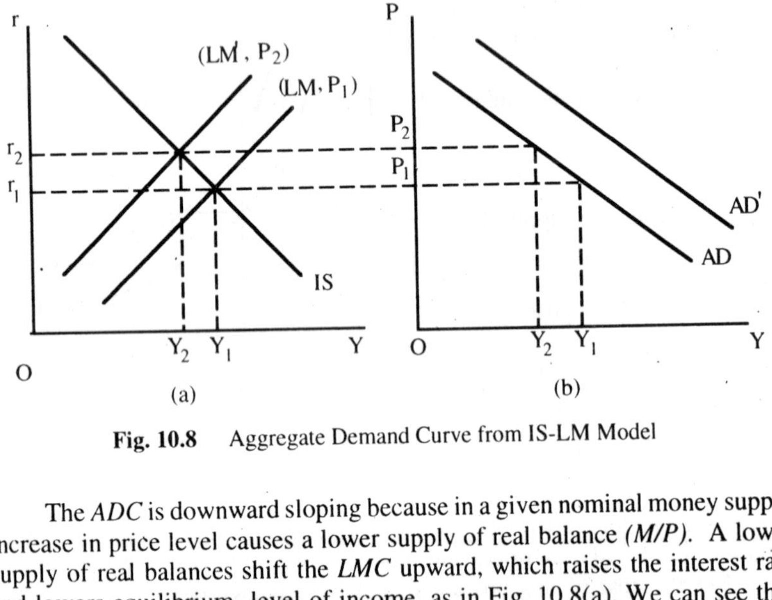

Fig. 10.8 Aggregate Demand Curve from IS-LM Model

The *ADC* is downward sloping because in a given nominal money supply increase in price level causes a lower supply of real balance (*M/P*). A lower supply of real balances shift the *LMC* upward, which raises the interest rate and lowers equilibrium level of income, as in Fig. 10.8(a). We can see that when the price level rises from P_1 to P_2, national income falls from Y_1 to Y_2. The *ADC* in Fig.10.8(b) plots the negative relationship between national income and the price level that arises from *IS-LM* model.

What causes the *ADC* to shift?

Because the *ADC* summarizes the results of the *IS-LM* Model, shocks that shifts the *ISC* or the *LMC* cause the *ADC* to shift. Expansionary fiscal or monetary policy raises income in the *IS-LM* model and thus shifts the *ADC* outward as in Fig. 10.8(b). Similarly, contractionary fiscal or monetary policy lowers income and thus shifts the *ADC* inward.

To sum up, a change in income in the *IS-LM* model resulting from a change in the price level represents a movement along the *ADC*. A change in income in the *IS-LM* model resulting from a change in fiscal or monetary policy for a fixed price level it represents a shift in the *ADC*.

Monetary and Fiscal Policy Change Shift the *ADC* : Monetary Policy Change

Fig. 10.9(a) shows a monetary policy change. For any given price level, an increase in the money supply raises real money balances, shifts the *LMC* downwards and raises *Y* ; and a decrease in the money supply decreases real money balances, shifts the *LMC* upward, and lowers income. Thus, an increase

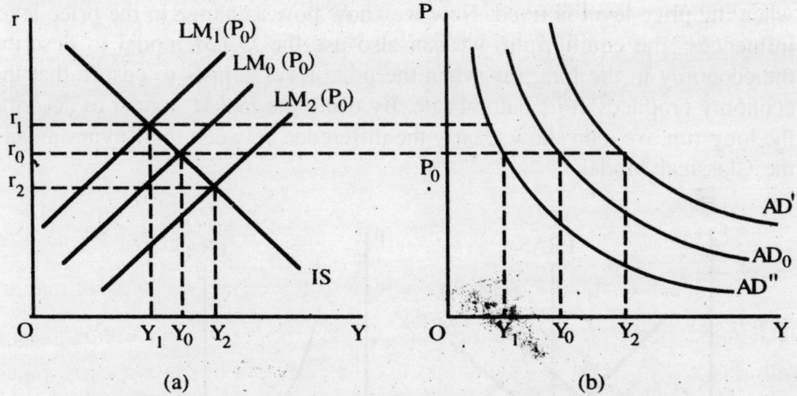

Fig. 10.9 Monetary Policy and Shift of Aggregate Demand

in money supply shifts the *ADC* to the right to *AD'* and a decrease in money supply shifts it to the left to *AD"* from AD_0 as Fig 10.9(b) shows.

Fiscal Policy Change

Fig 10.10(a) shows a fiscal policy change — a fiscal expansion, such as an increase in government expenditure or a decrease in taxes; a fiscal

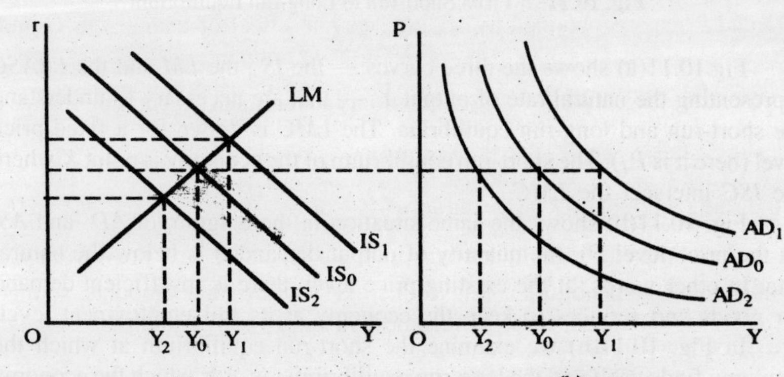

Fig. 10.10 Fiscal Policy and Shift of Aggregate Demand

contraction, such as decrease in government expenditure or an increase in taxes. The fiscal expansion shifts the *ISC* outward or fiscal contraction shifts *ISC* inward and, for any given price level, raises or reduces income. Hence a fiscal expansion shifts the *ADC* outward from *AD* to AD_1 or a fiscal contraction shifts the *ADC* inward from AD_0 to AD_2 as Fig.10.10(b) shows.

The *IS-LM* Model in the Short-Run and Long-Run

The *IS-LM* model is designed to explain the economy in the short-run when the price level is fixed. Now we know how a change in the price level influences the equilibrium, we can also use the *IS-LM* model to describe the economy in the long run when the price level adjusts to ensure that the economy produces at its natural rate. By using the *IS-LM* model to describe the long-run, we can show clearly the difference between the Keynesian and the Classical Model.

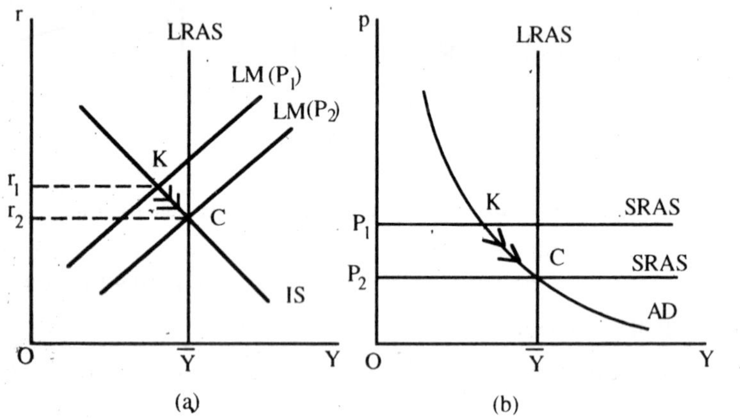

Fig. 10.11 From Short-run to Long-run Equilibrium

Fig.10.11(a) shows the three curves — the *IS* , the *LM* and the *LRASC* representing the natural rate of output $\overline{Y}$ — that are necessary to understand the short-run and long-run equilibriua. The *LMC* is drawn for a fixed price level (here it is P_1). The short-run equilibrium of the economy is point *K*, where the *ISC* intersect the *LMC*.

Fig. 10.11(b) shows the same situation in the diagram of *AD* and *AS*. At the price level P_1, the quantity of output demanded is below the natural rate. In other words, at the existing price level, there is insufficient demand for goods and services to keep the economy at its full employment level.

In Fig. 10.11(b) we examine the short-run equilibrium at which the economy finds itself and the long-run equilibrium towards which the economy moves. Point *K* describes the short-run equilibrium, where it is assumed that price level is fixed (P_1). Eventually, the low demand for output causes the price to fall, which moves the economy back towards its full employment level (natural rate). When the price level reaches P_2, the economy is at point C, which is the long-run equilibrium. In Fig. 10.11(b), $AD = AS$ at point C, and the quantity of commodity demanded equals the natural rate of output $\overline{Y}$. This long-run equilibrium is reached in Fig. 10.11(a) in the *IS-LM* Model by a shift in the *LMC*. The fall in price level (P_1 to P_2) increases real money balances and thus shifts the *LMC* to the right to intersect with the *ISC* at C.

We can now see the difference between Keynesian and Classical approaches to the determination of national income and employment. The Keynesian assumption is that the prices and wages are fixed at point *K*. Depending on monetary, fiscal and other determinants of *AD*, output and employment may deviate from the natural rate. The classical assumption is that prices and wages are flexible and eventually reached at point *C*. The prices and wages adjust to ensure that national income and employment are always at the natural or full employment level.

In other words, we can think of the economy as being described by three equations. The first two are the *IS* and *LM* equations,

(1) $Y = S(Y) + I(r)$ *(IS)*

(2) $M = L(r,Y) = kPY + L(r)$ *(LM)*

These two equations — *IS* and *LM* — contain three variables : *Y, r* and *P*. The classical approach is to complete the model with the assumption that output reaches the natural rate, so the third equation is (3) $Y = \overline{Y}$. This assumption implies that *r* and *P* must adjust to satisfy the *IS* and *LM* equations.

The Keynesian approach is to complete the model with the assumption of fixed prices, so the third equation is (3') $P = P_1$. This assumption implies that, *r* and *Y* must adjust to satisfy the *IS* and *LM* equation.

What assumption is most appropriate? The answer depends on the time horizon. The classical assumption best describes the long run. The Keynesian assumption best describes the short-run.

General Equilibrium with Flexible Wages

In Fig. 10.12 the *IS* and *LM* curves summarize the conditions of equilibrium in the goods and money sectors, respectively. The Y_F line shows the one level of output at which the labour market is in equilibrium — the quantity of labour demanded is equal to the quantity of labour supplied. It is derived from the production function and the labour market in the previous chapter (P...). The Y_F is vertical because, on our present assumptions, the interest rate plays no role in the determination of equilibrium in the employment sector. Any point off the Y_F line implies an excess demand or an excess supply of labour, which will lead to change in the real wage rate, employment and output. For the entire economy to be in equilibrium we must have equilibrium in all sectors. If any sector is not in equilibrium, some variables in that sector must change and this is likely to affect the combination of real income and interest rate at which all three sectors are in equilibrium — *AD* is equal to total output;

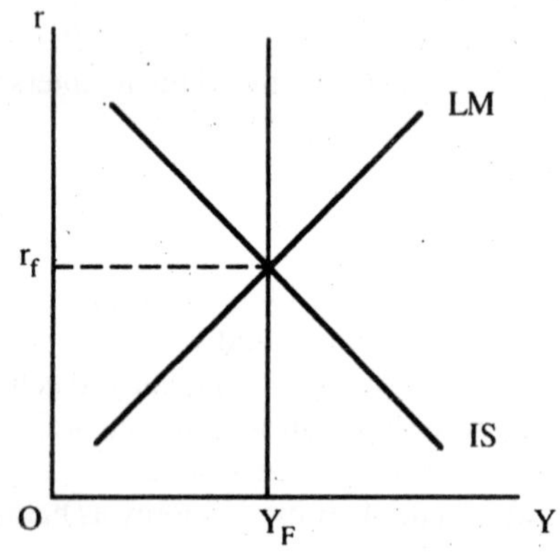

Fig. 10.12 General Equilibrium with Flexible Wages

the quantity of money demanded is equal to quantity of money supplied and the quantity of labour demanded is equal to the quantity of labour supplied.

To have a better understanding about the equilibrium, we will examine the forces generated in the system in disequilibrium, and how these forces operate to bring the economy back to equilibrium. In Fig. 10.13 two possible disequilibria are shown. With the *IS* curve and *LM'* curve, the money and goods sectors are in equilibrium at point *A* where the *AD* is at Y_A. However,

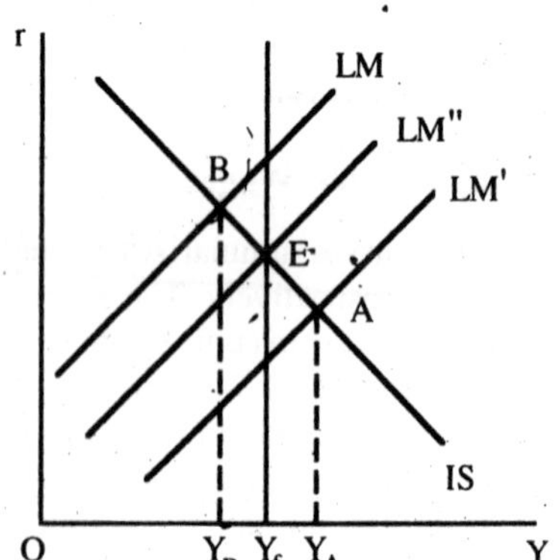

Fig. 10.13 Disequilibrium and adjustment in the economy

given the condition in the employment sector, and the production function, actual output is Y_f. There is thus excess demand for goods and services equal to Y_A-Y_f. Given our present assumptions about the effects of this discrepancy, the disequilibrium at point *A* will lead to a rise in prices. We can now use our analysis to see how this rise in prices will affect some or all of the variables entering the determination of equilibrium in the goods and money sectors, and whether the price rise will tend to eliminate the disequilibrium.

We have seen that changes in the price level have no effect on any of the variables used in the construction of *IS* curve. We assumed that the behaviour represented by the *IS* curve $(C + I)$ is not affected by the price level — it is all expressed in real terms. However, we know that changes in the price level do affect equilibrium in the money sector, though the demand for money is specified in real terms, the supply of money is given in nominal terms. Thus, the rise in the price level generated by the excess of desired expenditure over output will lead to a leftward shift of *LM* curve. The rise in prices will continue as long as there is an excess of *AD* over output $(Y_A > Y_f)$,which means as long as the *IS* and *LM* curves intersect to the right of *E*. When the real quantity of money is such that LM' coincides with LM'' curve, all the sectors would be in equilibrium again. The change in the price level eliminates the discrepancy between desired expenditure and Y_F $(Y_A \neq Y_F)$ by changing *AD*. However, this does not occur directly. The change in the price level has a direct effect on the real quantity of money. The change in *AD* occurs because of the link between the real quantity of money and the interest rate and also because of the link between the interest rate and investment. These links are implicit in the *IS* and *LM* model.

It should however be noted that the change in the price level has no effect on Y_f curve, which shows equilibrium in the employment sector, because all the behavioural variables in that sector were specified in real terms. It is true that, given any money wage rate, a change in the price level will affect the real wage rate, but on our present assumptions any change in the real wage, due to a change in the price level, will be offset by a change in the money wage rate, as we have seen before. Only at the real wage rate the labour market is in equilibrium.

Let us now examine the disequilibrium at point *B* in Fig.10.13. At point *B*, $AD = Y_B$. If the employment sector is in equilibrium, output is equal to Y_f, and at point *B* output is greater than *AD* $(Y_f > Y_B)$. This will reduce prices and increase the real quantity of money (*LM* curve shifts towards LM''), which will result in a fall in the interest rate and, thus, a rise in desired investment. This process will continue so long as output is greater than *AD* and a new equilibrium is reached at *E*.

Another possibility is that at point *B* the goods sector is in equilibrium, $AD = Y_B$ output, but the employment sector is not. There is, thus, no pressure on the price level. However, if the employment sector is not in equilibrium, something must change there. What sort of disequilibrium is implied by this situation? It might be an equilibrium at less than full-employment output, this situation implies an excess supply of labour. But this is not correct. All we know is that, at *B*, employment is less than the full-employment. This may be either because the real wage rate is too high and there is an excess supply of labour or because the real wage rate is too low and there is an excess demand for labour. The employment sector is such that the wage rate will fall if there is an excess supply of labour and rise if there is an excess demand for labour. In both cases, employment and output will rise. However, as output increases, a discrepancy would appear between *AD* and output; prices will start falling, the real quantity of money will start rising and *AD* will start rising, too. This process will continue until we have equilibrium in all sectors at *E*.

In Fig. 10.14 we can see the two possibilities just discussed and thus implications for the forces generated in the system. The top right quadrant gives all the sectors of the economy — the *IS*, *LM* and Y_F curves. The bottom right quadrant shows the production function relating output to employment, and the bottom left quadrant represents the labour market. The two possible

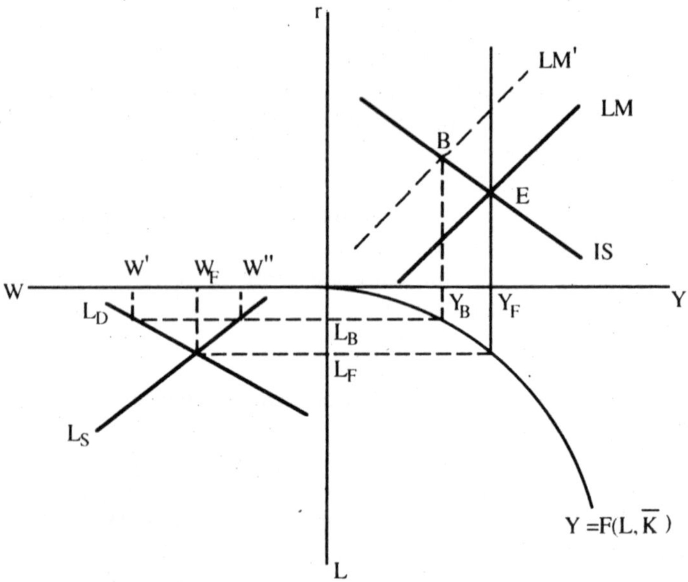

Fig. 10.14 Disequilibrium and its implications

types of disequilibria represented by point *B* depends on whether employment at *B* is L_B or L_F. If employment is L_F the labour market is in equilibrium and output is Y_F. This means that — in the goods market — $AD < Y_F$. All prices fall, given the nominal stock of money, the real quantity of money rises, thus leading to a fall in the interest rate and rise in desired investment. This will shift the *LM* curve to the right and ultimately equilibrium will reach again in *E*. Real wages do not change— money wages change in the same proportion as the change in prices.

On the other hand, if employment is L_B and output would be Y_B, the point *B* represents equilibrium in the goods market → $AD = Y_B$ — but dis-equilibrium in the labour market. Either the real wage rate is too high (W') and there is an excess supply of labour, or it is too low (W'') and there is an excess demand for labour. In the former case, the money wage rate will fall (and also real wage rate falls), and in the latter case it will rise. In both the cases employment and output will increase which will mean that equilibrium in the goods market no longer exists. Output $(Y_F) >$ than *AD* and this leads to a fall in prices and an increase in *AD*. This process will continue until point *E* is reached where the economy will be in equilibrium again. Real wages change to equilibrate the labour market.

Thus, we can see that the variables play a crucial role in equilibrating the whole system; the price level and the wage rate. Changes in the price level produce equilibrium in the goods sector, changes in the wage rate produce

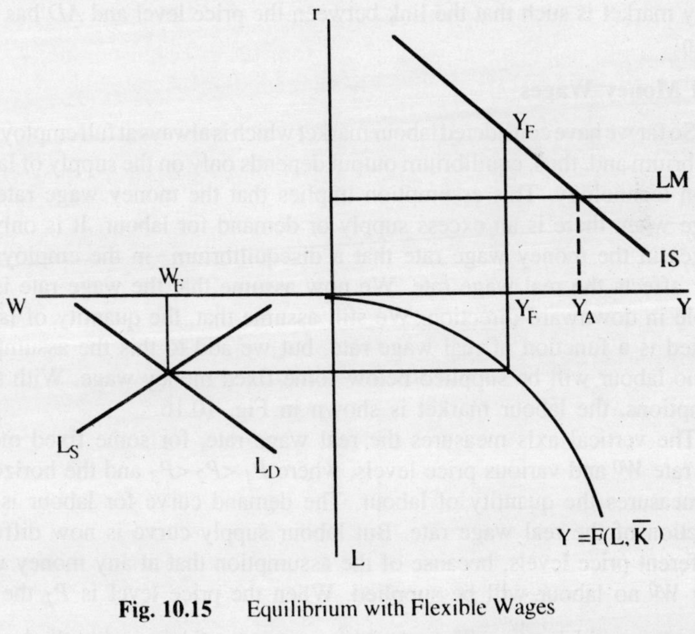

Fig. 10.15 Equilibrium with Flexible Wages

equilibrium in the employment sector. It is clear from the above analysis that wages and prices have to be flexible to be effective in equilibrating the system. They have to react to disequilibrium — prices in the goods market, and wages in the labour market. Moreover, the links by which changes in these two variables affect output *(Y)* and *AD* have to be operative. For example, if disequilibrium in the goods market affects the price level but condition in the money market is such that changes in the price level do not have any effect on the interest rate — and, thus, have no effect on desired investment — then the price level does not have any effect on output and *AD*. This situation will prevail where we assume that the supply of money is perfectly elastic and, thus, the *LMC* is perfectly elastic too as Fig. 10.15 shows.

With flexible wages, total output will always be Y_F, otherwise the wage rate will change. This situation can be seen in Fig. 10.15, where $AD(Y_A)$ is greater than output (Y_F), therefore, prices will start rising as before. However, the rise in prices would not be able to eliminate disequilibrium because the price rise has no effect on the employment sector as the employment sector is in equilibrium and money wages change in the same proportion as the price level, and, thus, real wages remain unchanged and, therefore, output and employment remain unchanged. The rise in prices has no effect on *AD*; the *LMC* and the interest rate remain unchanged. Thus we see that even though the disequilibrium in the goods market results in changes in the price level, these changes cannot remove the disequilibrium because the condition in the money market is such that the link between the price level and *AD* has been broken.

Fixed Money Wages

So far we have considered labour market which is always at full employment equilibrium and, thus, equilibrium output depends only on the supply of labour and on technology. This assumption implies that the money wage rate can change when there is an excess supply or demand for labour. It is only via changes in the money wage rate that a disequilibrium in the employment sector affects the real wage rate. We now assume that the wage rate is not flexible in downward direction. We still assume that, the quantity of labour supplied is a function of real wage rate, but we add to this the assumption that, no labour will be supplied below some fixed money wage. With these assumptions, the labour market is shown in Fig. 10.16.

The vertical axis measures the real wage rate, for some fixed money wage rate W^0 and various price levels, where $P_1 < P_2 < P_3$ and the horizontal axis measures the quantity of labour. The demand curve for labour is still a function of the real wage rate. But labour supply curve is now different at different price levels, because of the assumption that at any money wage below W^0 no labour will be supplied. When the price level is P_1 the real wage rate would be $\frac{W^0}{P_1}$. The maximum amount of labour supplied at the real wage $\frac{W^0}{P_1}$ is L_1^S. However, our assumption is that at any money wage below W^0 no labour will be supplied. Given the price level P_1, this assumption means that at any real wage below $\frac{W^0}{P_1}$ no labour will be supplied and the supply curve is now $O\frac{W^0}{P_1}CL^S$. Now, if the price level is $P_2 > P_1$, the maximum quantity of labour supplied will be L_2^S at the same money wage rate W^0. However, for the price level P_2, the supply curve of labour is $O\frac{W^0}{P_2}BL^S$ because of our assumption that no labour will be supplied at a real wage rate below $\frac{W^0}{P_2}$.

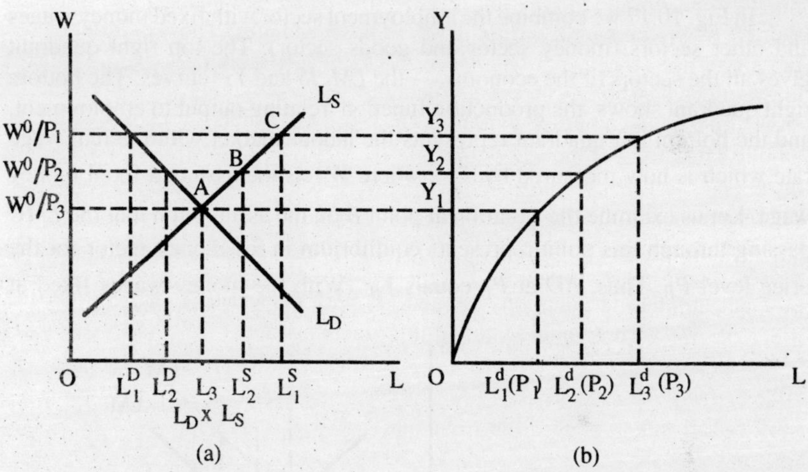

Fig. 10.16 Fixed Money Wage and Disequilibrium

Similarly for other price levels and different minimum money wage rate, say W^0.

Let us now define equilibrium in a labour market in which the money wage rate is fixed. In Fig. 10.16(a), the real wage rate is $\frac{W^0}{P_1}$ where W^0 is the fixed money wage and the price level is P_1. At this real wage the quantity of labour demanded is L_1^D, the maximum quantity of labour supplied is L_1^S. There is, thus, an excess supply of labour. However, given the assumption that the money wage is inflexible downwards, this excess supply of labour has no effect on the wage and, therefore, employment. For the given money wage W^0 and price level P_1, the labour market is in equilibrium at L_1^D. Similarly, for the given money wage W^0 and price level P_2, the labour market is in equilibrium at L_2^D. We can see that once a fixed money wage is introduced, employment becomes a function of the fixed money wage and the price level.

Fig 10.16(b) shows a production function relating output to employment for various price levels and the given fixed money wage W^0. For example, when the price level is P_1, equilibrium employment is L_1^d, and the corresponding output is Y_1. Similarly for the other price levels. Now there is no longer a single quantity of output corresponding to equilibrium in the labour market, but different outputs depending on the price level. The crucial difference between the previous model and the fixed wage model is that now the price level affects equilibrium employment and output.

General Equilibrium with a Fixed Money Wage

In Fig. 10.17 we combine the employment sector with fixed money wages and other sectors (money sector and goods sector). The top right quadrant gives all the sectors of the economy — the *LM, IS* and Y_F curves. The bottom right quadrant shows the production function relating output to employment, and the bottom left quadrant represents the labour market with the real wage rate which is now measured by $\frac{W^0}{P}$, where W^0 is the assumed fixed money wage. Let us examine the situation at point *B* on the assumption that the *LMC* passing through this point represents equilibrium in the money sector for the price level P_B. Thus, *AD* at P_B equals Y_B. With the money wages fixed at

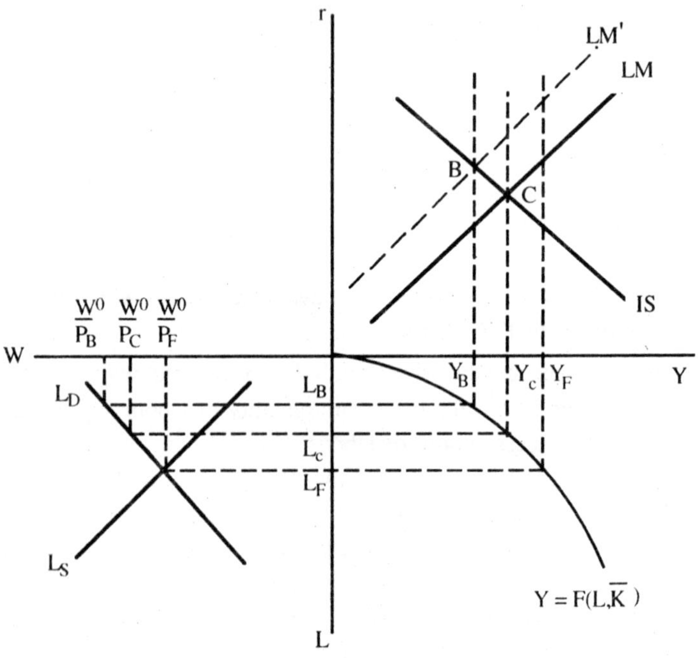

Fig. 10.17 General Equilibrium with a Fixed Money Wage

W^0 and the price level P_B, the real wage rate is equal to $\frac{W^0}{P_B}$, and output and employment are equal to Y_B and L_B, respectively. Output is equal to *AD* and both the employment sector and the goods sector are in equilibrium; the excess supply of labour has no effect on employment and output and thus on the equilibrium.

Now we assume that the *LMC* passing through point *B* represents equilibrium in the money sector for the price level P_F and the fixed money wage W^0. At the real wage rate of $\frac{W^0}{P_F}$, employment is L_F and output is Y_F. The output is greater than *AD*. This discrepancy will lead to a fall in prices, and an increase in the real quantity of money, a fall in the interest rate and thus an increase in *AD* (this will shift the *LMC* to the right). However, the fall in prices also raises the real wage rate, and, thus, employment and output fall. This process will continue as long as $Y > AD$; until point C is reached with the price level P_c. At this point, *AD* equals output at point Y_c, and all the sectors are again in equilibrium. The main difference between the effects of the disequilibrium examined above and the identical disequilibrium examined under a flexible wage is that, there changes in prices were accompanied by changes in money wages, keeping the real wage rate and, thus, output, constant at the level associated with equilibrium in the labour market.

The Price Level

The introduction of the employment sector into the model shows the importance of the price level in achieving overall equilibrium in the economy because of its effect on the *AD* and output (in flexible money wage it effects the *AD* only). Thus, it is important to understand exactly how the price level is determined, and what real variables are affected by it. Here we want to summarize the results.

Fig. 10.18(a) shows various equilibria in the goods sector for a given *IS* curve, and a given quantity of nominal money M^0 at various price levels $P_1 > P_2 > P_3$. We can see the relationship between the price level and *AD*. In the bottom half of Fig. 10.18(b) the relationship between the price level and *AD* is shown. This curve is drawn for the assumed conditions in the goods and the money sectors shown in Fig. 10.18(a). A shift in the *IS* curve or the supply curve of nominal money will shift the *AD* curve. The *IS* curve from Fig. 10.18(a) and *LM* curve for the price level P_3 are shown in the top half of Fig.10.18(b).

We now turn to the relationship between the price level and aggregate supply (*AS*). We know already that whether *AS* depends on the price level or not, it depends on the conditions in the labour market, i.e. on whether the wage rate is flexible or not. If the wage rate is flexible, employment is determined independently of the price level and thus *AS* is independent of the price level

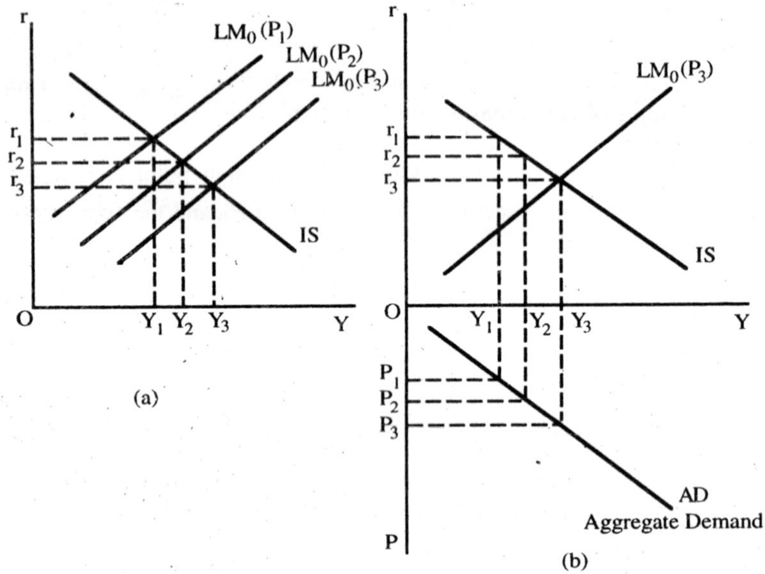

Fig. 10.18 Price level and Aggregate Demand (AD)

as well. If, however, the money wage is fixed, output and employment become a function of the price level. Fig. 10.19 shows these relationships.

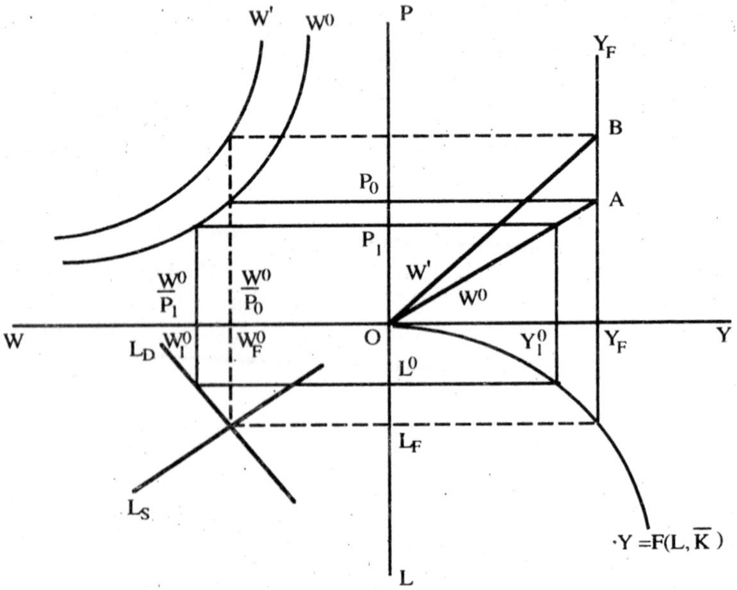

Fig. 10.19 Price level and Aggregate Supply (AS)

Fig. 10.19 represents the labour market (left quadrant) and the production function (right quadrant) in bottom two quadrants and the top left quadrant shows the relationship between the real wage rate (W^0) and the price level (P) for some given money wage. Thus, W^0 curve shows the relationship between the price level and the real wage $(W = \frac{W^0}{P})$ when the money wage is fixed at W^0. Similarly, W' curve, represents a money wage greater than W^0. We derive the relationship between AS and the price level in the top right quadrant. If the money wage is flexible we can ignore the top left quadrant, because, in that case, the equilibrium real wage, employment and output are W_f, L_f and Y_f, respectively, whatever be the price level. With flexible money wages, AS is independent of the price level and is represented by $Y_F Y_F$. Assume, however, that the money wage is fixed at W^0. If the price level is P_0, the real wage rate is $\frac{W^0}{P_0} \leq W_F$, employment is L_F and output is Y_F. If the price level is P_1, the real wage rate $\frac{W^0}{P_1} = W_1^0$, employment is L^0, and output is Y_1^0. If we do this for all price levels we get the curve W^0AY_F showing the relationship between output and the price level. If the money wage is fixed at $W' > W^0$, the relationship between output and the price level is shown by the curve $W'BY_F$.

We can combine the AD curve from Fig.10.18(b) and the AS curve of Fig. 10.19 to see the interaction between AD and output (AS). This is done in Fig. 10.20, for flexible wages and Fig. 10.21 for fixed wages. If wages are flexible the AS is represented by the Y_FY_F curve and Aggregate Demand by the AD curve, for the IS curve shown and a quantity of nominal money M^0. Equilibrium in the economy is at Y_F and P_F and r_F. At any price level above P_F, output (AS) will be greater than AD, driving prices down; at any price level below P_F it will be $AD > AS$ (output), driving prices up.

If the quantity of money changes to $M' > M^0$, AD shifts to AD', the new equilibrium will be at Y_F, r_F and P'. The only effect of the change in the quantity of money is to change the equilibrium price level; nothing else is affected. The equilibrium interest rate and Y are determined independently of what happened in the money sector. For any given behaviour with respect to consumption and investment (i.e., for any given IS curve) the money sector (given by the LMC) only affects the price level. The result seems strange, because when we analysed the money sector we saw that the interest rate was the equilibrating variable, reacting to any excess demand or supply of money, yet, when we put together the money sector with the rest of the economy, we find that the equilibrium interest rate is not affected by what happens in the money sector.

This seeming paradox is not hard to explain. Once we introduce an independent determinant of output, an employment sector with flexible wages, and assume that prices are flexible, the price level will always react to a

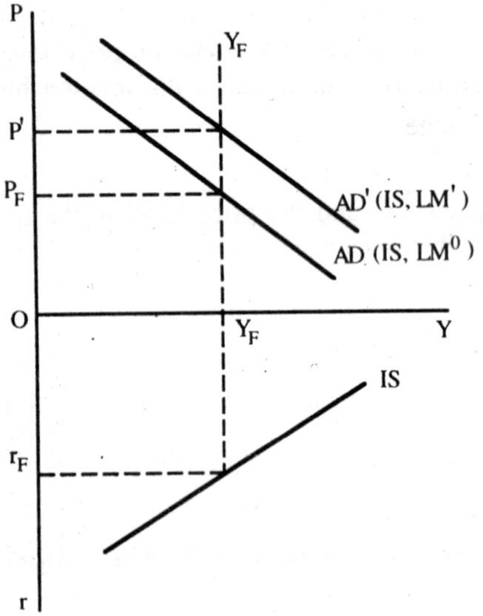

Fig. 10.20 Flexible Wages and Interaction between Aggregate Demand and Aggregate Supply

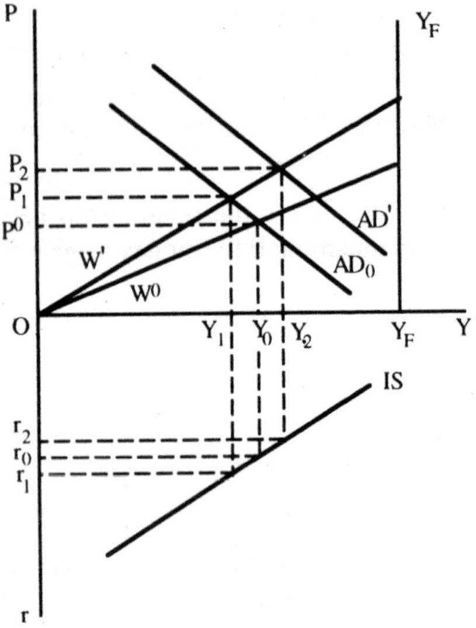

Fig. 10.21 Fixed Wages and Aggregate Demand and Aggregate Supply

disequilibrium between *AD* and *AS* (output) via its effects on the real quantity of money, thus, on the interest and on *AD*. If the interest rate is not at that level which equates *AD* and output*(AS)* , then price level will change, thus changing the interest rate. Only one interest rate (r_F) is compatible with equilibrium between *AD* and the given level of output and this interest rate will be achieved by changes in the price level. Thus, starting from equilibrium, for example, Y_F , r_F and P_F, any change in the money sector will initially affect the interest rate as before, but this will have repercussions on the price level via the effect of the interest rate on *AD*, and this will offset the initial effect on the interest rate.

Thus far we have seen the price level in a situation in which wages are flexible and, therefore, output *(AS)* is independent of the price level. If money wage is fixed at W^0, as in Fig. 10.21, the *(AS)* output curve is W^0Y_F. With the *AD* curve AD_0, general equilibrium will be Y_0, P_0 and r_0. At any price level above P_0, output *(AS)* will be greater than *AD* and prices will fall, increasing *AD* via its effect on the interest rate, and decreasing output *(AS)* via the effect on the wage rate; the opposite will occur at any price level below P_0. If the fixed money wage is W', the new equilibrium will be one with a lower real income, a higher price level and a higher interest rate (Y_1, P_1, r_1). Thus, all the factors that were relevant in determining the price level, we now have a new factor—the fixed money wage which affects output and the price level by interaction between output *(AS)* and *AD*. A change in the money sector, for example, an increase in the quantity of money from M^0 to M' will shift the ADC from AD^0 to AD^I. The effect of this will be to raise income to Y_2 the price level to P_2, and to lower the interest rate to r_2 Thus, change in the money sector do affect the interest rate and the price level. The difference between the present case fixed money wage and the previous one with flexible wages is that the initial effect of the change in the money sector of increased *AD*, and, thus, the price level, is accompanied by a change in output. Thus, the disequilibrium created between output *(Y)* and *AD* is eliminated both by a decrease in *AD* and increase in output *(Y)* due to rise in prices; in the previous case only the former occurred.

The Extreme Cases

The above analysis can be used to examine the effects on equilibrium when the links between the monetary sector and the goods sector are broken, either because the *LM* curve is perfectly elastic or because the *IS* curve is perfectly inelastic. Both of these would lead to a perfectly inelastic *ADC* . Figure 10.22 shows a situation in which the money sector is characterised by a perfectly elastic *LMC*. This is the top part of Fig. 10.21. First, let us assume that the employment sector is one with flexible wages, therefore, the Y_FY_F curve is the one representing the output sector. With the aggregate

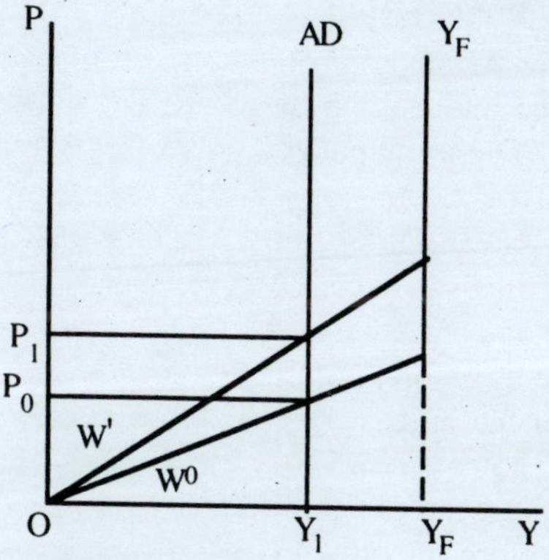

Fig. 10.22 Equilibrium when the link between sectors are broken

demand curve as *AD*, we see that *AD* at any price level are Y_I and output at any price level is Y_F. Because $Y_F > AD$, prices will fall but with our present assumptions this has no effect on any of the variables in the system. There is no way to achieve equilibrium in the system. If the *AD* curve cuts the *Y* axis to the right of Y_FY_F curve, prices would start rising and continue to do so without any effect on the system.

If the employment sector is characterised by the fixed money wage W^0, the *AS* is shown by the curve W^0Y_F. With the aggregate demand curve, *AD*, equilibrium would be at price OP_0. At any price level above P^0 output is greater than *AD* and prices fall, raising real wages and thus reducing employment and output. A rise of the fixed money wage to W' would raise the price level to P_1 leaving the real wage rate, output and employment unchanged. This is the situation in which the price level can still operate to equilibrate the economy, even though it has no effect on *AD*. If the *AD* curve intersects the *Y* axis to the right of the Y_FY_F curve we would have the same situation as in the case of flexible wages.

The price level would continue to rise indefinitely.

EXERCISE
From Chapter 6 to 10

1. Construct an *IS-LM* model in which you assume that investment does not depend on the interest rate, and the demand for money does not depend on income. In that model what determines real income? What determines the interest rate?

2. Somebody tells us that the value of the multiplier $\frac{1}{1-mpc}$ is 5, and asks us to predict the effect on real income of an increase in desired expenditure of 100. What other information would we need? How would we use them?

3. Assume an economy with a fixed money wage is in equilibrium at less than full employment. What are the effects on real income, the interest rate and the price level of (a) a cut in money wages (b) an increase in the quantity of money and (c) a cut in taxes?

4. Assume an economy with flexible wages and prices. Examine the effects on the real wage, real income, the interest rate and the price level of
   (a) A technology innovation which makes it possible to get a higher level of output with the same quantity of inputs, but leaves the marginal product of labour unchanged.
   (b) A technological innovation as in (a) but one which also increases the marginal product of labour.
   (c) A change in tastes such that people now prefer more leisure relative to goods.

5. Answer question (5) assuming an economy with a fixed money wage at less than full-employment equilibrium.

6. Consider a model in which the money demand function is $M_d = kPY$, while all other functional relations are the same as in the Keynesian system. Derive the *IS* and *LM* curves; and show diagrammatically the equilibrium position in the model. Then examine the effects of (a) an increase in the quantity of money, (b) an increase in the money wage rate, and (c) an increase in autonomous investment, on real income, price level, employment and rate of interest.

7. A macroeconomic model contains the following functional relations :

   1) $S = S(r)$: Saving function

2) $I = I(r)$: Investment function

3) $M_d = L(r, Y, P)$: Money Demand function

4) $Y = f(N)$ = Aggregate Production function

5) $\frac{dY}{dN} = \frac{W}{P}$, Labour Demand function

6) $\frac{W}{P} = \frac{W_0}{P} + \frac{W(N)}{P}$, Supply function for Labour.

Derive the *IS* and *LM* curves and show the equilibrium position. What will be the effect of an increase in the quantity of money on employment, price level, interest rate and on real income.

8. Construct a macroeconomic model by incorporating the Keynesian Money Demand Function and Saving Function in an otherwise Classical System and derive the *IS* and *LM* curves. Show the equilibrium position. What will be the effect of an increase in money supply and autonomous investment on employment, real income, interest rate and the price level.

9. Assume a pure quantity adjustment model in which both the money wage and prices are fixed. What is the effect on real income of a rise in money wages assuming (a) the marginal propensity to consume out of wage income is greater than profit income; (b) the marginal propensity to consume out of profit income is zero?

10. Consider a closed economy with no government. The following equations represent the savings and investment functions respectively :

$I = 20 - 2r$ *and* $S = 0.5Y$

where r is the rate of interest and Y is the level of national income. Find the equation of the *IS* curve and plot in a graph. If the equation of the *LM* curve is $Y = 4 + 2r$

(a) Find the equilibrium level of income and interest rate;

(b) Calculate the effect on the level of income and the rate of interest of an autonomous fall in investment of 100;

(c) Explain why the fall in income is less than that predicted by the multiplier.

11. Discuss the view that completely flexible wages and prices would ensure the automatic attainment of full employment in an economy.

11 INCOME DETERMINATION WITH GOVERNMENT SECTOR

Simple Keynesian Model With Government

In the simple Keynesian model of income determination we assumed that there is no government activity in the economy. Let us relax this assumption to see how the equilibrium level of income can be determined in the presence of economic activity of the government. The government collects money from the economy and spends money into the economy. Government expenditures and receipts have an important effect on the economy.

Government budget has two sides — the expenditure side and the receipt side. Money inflows in the receipt side of the budget are of three types — taxation, public borrowing and sales of goods and services; while money outflow in the expenditure side of the budget are also of three types — purchase of goods and services *(G)*, transfer payment (T_r) and repayment of debts. Taxation is a compulsory contribution made by the people to the government against which no direct payments are made by the government. A taxpayer becomes poorer by the amount of taxes. Hence, the income available in the hands of the people is reduced by the amount of taxes paid. Public borrowing is made through the sale of new Government Bonds, which people voluntarily purchase. Neither their income nor their wealth is reduced thereby. They simply alter the form and composition of wealth in the private sector. An increase in the net indebtedness of the government to the central bank takes place through the creation of new money by the central bank.

Money outflows from the government are of three types — transfer payments (T_r), government expenditure on goods and services *(G)* and debt repayments. Transfer payments are made by the government to the people against which no services are rendered. For example, government subsidy to the public sector, unemployment benefit and similar payments belong to the category of transfer payments. A transfer payment increases the disposable income of the people. Debt repayment does not make people richer, but it simply changes the composition of assets. The former bond holders have now money instead of bonds. Government expenditure on goods and services is made directly by the government which increases aggregate demand in the economy.

Let us now examine how the equilibrium level of income can be determined when the government activity in the economy is taken into account. When there are government activities in the economy, aggregate demand will have three components: Consumption Expenditure *(C)*, Investment Expenditure *(I)* and Government Expenditure on goods and services *(G)*. Thus, the aggregate demand $= C + I + G$. Let us assume again that investment expenditure and government expenditure are autonomously given. Consumption expenditure is assumed to be a function of disposable income (Y_d) which is defined as $(Y - T + T_r)$ where Y is income earned, T is taxes paid by the public and T_r is transfer payments received by the public from the government. It is assumed that taxes and transfer payments are independent of the level of income. The equilibrium condition of income determination can be written as:

$$Y = C + \bar{I} + \bar{G} \quad \text{or,} \quad Y = C\left(Y - \bar{T} + \bar{T}_r\right) + \bar{I} + \bar{G}$$

In this equation, $\bar{T}$, $\bar{T}_r$, $\bar{I}$ and $\bar{G}$ are autonomous components. There is one unknown, *Y*, which can be determined from this equation. The level of *Y*, which is satisfied by the above equation, is called the equilibrium level of income. The government expenditures have to be treated separately because they are not determined by the same variables as private expenditures. The government expenditures are policy-determined and not uniquely related to any other variables in the model. The only change now would be in the specific equation of the *IS* curve, which shows equilibrium in the goods sector, would have to contain an additional term *G*, an exogenously determined term. It should be remembered that government activity is not confined to the acquisition of goods and services only, it also uses its power of transaction to acquire claims on resources from the private sector. The equilibrium condition can be restated as :

$$Y - C = I + G \quad or, \quad S + T = \bar{I} + G$$

Equilibrium condition without a government was $Y = C + I$ or, $Y - C = \bar{I}$ *or,* $S = \bar{I}$; which now should subdivide the claims to output into two parts — the claims to output of the private sector $(Y - T)$ and the claims to output of the government sector *T*. Thus, we have $S + T = \bar{I} + G$, which is the alternative way of expressing $Y = C + \bar{I} + \bar{G}$. $S + T = \bar{I} + G$ and can also be written as $S + (T - G) = \bar{I}$.

The term $(T - G)$ may be called government savings while *S* refers to private savings. $S + (T - G)$ is total saving (both public and private) and $\bar{I}$ represents total investment. We, thus, get a new version of familiar saving-investment relation.

We know that the equilibrium level of income is determined where $W = J$, where *W* is withdrawal and *J* is injection. The withdrawal $W = S + \bar{T}$ while the injection $J = \bar{I} + \bar{G}$. When they are equal, the size of the circular flow remains unchanged and the level of income is said to be in equilibrium. Now, we assume that decisions about how much to consume are made on the basis of individual's real income *(Y)*. The introduction of the government sector changes the relevant income variable of the private sector decision-making from Y to $(Y - T) = Y_d$, disposable income. Using linear approximation, the consumption function becomes $C = a + b\,(Y - T)$, where T represents the taxes collected by the government. In most tax systems T is not exogenous but depends on Y, when Y changes, the amount of tax revenue collected by the government also changes, and, thus, disposable income (Y_d) changes. Let us assume for simplicity a linear approximation for the relationship between taxes and income, such that $T = t_0 + tY$, where t_0 is the amount of taxes which is independent of income (Y) and t is the marginal rate of taxes. $Y - T$ is disposable income (Y_d) where T is the amount of tax revenue collected by the government. Since the government also makes transfer payments, then T should be the net taxes collected, the difference between total taxes and total transfer payments, like taxes they affect the economy via their effects on disposable income (Y_d). They should not be confused with government expenditures on goods and services.

Substituting the tax relationship into the consumption function, we have:

$$C = a + b\,(Y - t_0 - tY) = a + b\,[Y\,(1-t) - t_0] \quad \text{................(1)}$$

Equation (1) represents the consumption function on the assumption that desired consumption depends on Y_d, and taxes depend on total income (Y). We assume that the introduction of the government sector does not change the investment function. Substituting the new consumption function from above and the old investment function $(I = g_0 - g_r)$ into the new equilibrium condition for the goods sector, $Y = C + \bar{I} + \overline{G}$, we get :

$$Y = a + b[Y(1 - t) - t_0] + g_0 - g_r + \overline{G}$$

$$or,\ Y\,(1 - b)\,(1 - t) = a - bt_0 + g_0 - g_r + \overline{G}$$

$$\therefore Y = \frac{1}{1 - b(1-t)}\left(a - bt_0 + g_0 - g_r + \overline{G}\right) \text{....................(2)}$$

Thus, equation *(2)* is an equation with two variables, Y and r, the other elements in this equation are either government determined constants; t, t_0 and G, or behaviourally determined constants a, g_0 and g. This is the *IS* equation with multiplier $\frac{1}{1-b(1-t)}$. The equation summarises the equilibrium condition for a goods sector, which now includes a government, and a relationship between two variables Y and r. This is similar to the equilibrium condition for a goods sector without a government. The multiplier and constant terms are different, but the meaning of the equation, new *IS* curve, is the same. We recall that the whole analysis of the interrelationships in the economy for which we used the *IS* curve did not depend on any particular value of the multiplier, or the other parameters of the *IS* curve. Thus, we conclude that the introduction of the government sector into this model does not change any of our previous conclusions about the equilibrium conditions for the economy and the forces generated in the disequilibrium. However, we now have three added variables under government control which can be used to affect the equilibrium values of income, employment, the price level and the interest rate, when these are not at a level consistent with some policy goal.

Different Budget Multipliers with Lumpsum taxes

In the simple Keynesian model we know that when autonomous expenditure changes, there will be a multiplier effect and the equilibrium income will change. Let us see how the equilibrium income changes when there are government activities.

We make the following assumption : *(i)* The price level is fixed and money wages are rigid in the downward direction. Increase in expenditures is assumed to be reflected in increased output. *(ii)* Aggregate real consumption expenditure is a function of real disposable income, *(iii)* All taxes are lumpsum taxes which are independent of income and *(iv)* The consumption function is linear. Suppose $C = a + b(Y - T)$ is the consumption function where $0 < b < 1$ and $a > 0$. The equilibrium condition can be written as $Y = C + \bar{I} + \bar{G}$ or, $Y = a + b(Y - T) + \bar{I} + \bar{G}$. Differentiating both sides with respect to G and assuming that T and I remain constant, we get

$$\frac{dY}{dG} = b\frac{dY}{G} + 1 \quad \text{or,} \quad \frac{dY}{dG}(1-b) = 1 \quad \text{or,} \quad \frac{dY}{dG} = \frac{1}{1-b} \quad \therefore\ dY = \frac{1}{1-b}dG$$

The government expenditure multiplier is $\frac{1}{(1-b)}$ which is positive and greater than unity on the assumption that $0 < b < 1$. Since b is the *MPC*, $1 - b$ is the *MPS*. Thus, the government expenditure multiplier is equal to the reciprocal of the *MPS*. Now we consider the effect of a change in taxes, assuming that government expenditure remaining unchanged. The multiplier effect of a change in T can be written as follows and the equilibrium condition may be given as $Y = a + b(Y - T) + \bar{I} + \bar{G}$. Differentiating both sides with respect to T, we get

$$\frac{dY}{dT} = b\left(\frac{dY}{dT} - 1\right) \quad \text{or,} \quad \frac{dY}{dT}(1-b) = -b \quad \therefore \quad \frac{dY}{dT} = -\frac{b}{(1-b)} \quad \text{or,} \ dY = -\frac{b}{(1-b)}dT$$

Taxation multiplier is $-\frac{b}{(1-b)}$. The balanced budget multiplier shows that if the government expenditure and taxes increase by the same amount, so that the budget is balanced, the level of income will increase by the amount of the increase in government expenditure. The balance budget multiplier is equal to unity and this redistributes income towards the government. The government's marginal propensity to spend is equal to one, while that of the private sector is less than one. Let b be the *MPC* of the private sector and when tax increases *(dT)* by the amount *dG*, the level of income decreases by the amount $-\frac{b}{(1-b)}dT$. On the other hand, when the government spends this sum in purchasing goods and services, the level of income increases by the amount $\frac{1}{(1-b)}dG$. Hence, the balanced budget increase in income from the increase in government expenditure and taxes is given by $dY = \frac{1}{(1-b)}dG + \frac{-b}{(1-b)}dT = \frac{1-b}{1-b} = 1$.

Balanced Budget Multiplier is Unity. We can also decrease the government expenditure and taxes. The decrease in government expenditure will reduce the level of income while the decrease in taxes will increase the level of income. The net impact will be expansionary if $|dG| < b.|dT|$.

When both G and T are variable, we get the equilibrium condition from the total differential $dY = b\,(dY - dT) + dG$ or $(1 - b)dY = -bdT + dG$

or, $dY = \frac{1}{(1-b)}(dG - bdT)$.

When both $\overline{G}$ and $\overline{T}$ change by the same amount, we have $dG = dT$.

$$\therefore dY = \frac{1}{(1-b)}(dG - bdG) \quad \text{or, } dY = \frac{(1-b)dG}{(1-b)} = dG.$$

When $dG = dT$, we have $dY = dG = dT$.

This is our famous balanced budget multiplier.

Budget Adjustment with Income-Tax

Now we assume that, income-tax is not autonomously given as above but is a function of income. We consider a linear proportional tax function $T = t.Y$ where t represents the marginal rate of tax.

The disposable income is now equal to $Y - T = Y - tY = Y(1 - t)$. We assume, as before, a linear consumption function : $C = a + b(1 - t)\,Y$. The slope of the consumption function is now $(1 - t)$. Note that in the case of lumpsum tax, the slope of the consumption function does not change, but only the vertical intercept changes. But, in the case of income-tax, slope of the consumption function changes, while the intercepts remain the same. Assuming linear consumption function, as before, and lumpsum taxes, $\overline{T}$, we get the consumption function as :

$C = a + b(Y - T)$ or $C = (a - bT) + bY$ which shows that, when the lumpsum tax is imposed the intercept of the consumption function is reduced to $(a - bT)$ but the slope remains unchanged. In the case of the linear and proportional tax function $T = t.Y$, the consumption function becomes $C = a + b\,(1 - t)Y$ which shows that as a result of the imposition of the tax the intercept of the consumption function remains constant at 'a' but the slope decreases to $b\,(1 - t)$ and the consumption function becomes flatter.

The equilibrium condition in the commodity market is :

$$Y = C + \overline{I} + \overline{G} \quad \text{or, } Y = a + b(1-t)Y + \overline{I} + \overline{G}$$

It is assumed that the investment expenditure and government expenditure are autonomously given. We can now consider the effect of budget adjustments on the equilibrium level of income. Consider the effect of ΔG with the tax yield remaining constant. Since the tax yield is unaffected, there is no difference between lumpsum tax and an income-tax. The level of income will increase and the multiplier effects can be shown as :

$dY = \frac{1}{1-b} dG$. The multiplier is greater than one. It is the same as we obtained in the case of lumpsum taxes. However, with the increase in income, the tax yield may remain constant if the rate of tax decreases.

We now consider the effect of change in G with the tax rate remaining constant. In this case,

$$\frac{dY}{dG} = b(1-t)\frac{dY}{dG} + 1 \quad \text{or,} \quad \frac{dY}{dG}[1-b(1-t)] = 1 \quad \text{or,} \quad dY = \frac{1}{1-b(1-t)} dG.$$

The multiplier is now equal to $\frac{1}{1-b(1-t)}$ which is smaller than the multiplier $\frac{1}{1-b}$, because here the tax yield T increases with income and does not remain unchanged. In the case of a lumpsum tax when the level of income increases with increase in G, the tax yield does not increase. But in the case of income-tax as the level of income increases the tax yield increases as well. Hence, the multiplier effect is higher in the case of lumpsum tax than in the case of income-tax.

If we now consider the effect of change in tax yield holding G unchanged, then we get : $\frac{dY}{dT} = -\frac{b}{1-b}$ or, $dY = -\frac{b}{1-b} dT$. This means that as the tax yield increases, the level of income decreases and vice versa. The balanced budget case is one where we make equal changes in G and T. The effect of change in G and T can bc obtained by adding separate effect of changes in G and T.

We have seen that $dY = \frac{1}{1-b} dG$, when only government expenditure changes and $dY = -\frac{b}{1-b} dT$ when only the tax changes. When both G and T change by the same amount, $dG = dT$ and $dY = \frac{1}{(1-b)} dG + \frac{-b}{(1-b)} dG$. $\therefore dY = dG = dT$. This is the balanced budget multiplier which is unity, as we have proved before. If government expenditure and taxes increase by the same amounts, so that the budget is balanced, level of income will increase by the amount of the government expenditure.

We consider the effect of change in t with G remains unchanged on the equilibrium level of income. The equilibrium condition can be written as : $Y = a + b(1-t)Y + \bar{I} + \overline{G}$ or, $Y = a + bY - btY + \bar{I} + \overline{G}$

Differentiating both sides with respect to t, we get:

$$\frac{dY}{dt} = b\frac{dY}{dt} - b.Y - bt\frac{dY}{dt}$$

$$\text{or, } \frac{dY}{dt}(1-b+bt) = -bY \quad \text{or, } \frac{dY}{dt} = \frac{-bY}{1-b+bt} \quad \text{or, } dY = \frac{-bY}{1-b+bt}dt$$

The multiplier now depends on the initial level of income and tax rate The lower the initial rate of tax, the greater will be the rate of increase in income. Thus, when the tax rate is changed, its effect in the level of income depends on the initial tax rate and the level of income.

During a period of depression we require the same type of budget adjustment, whether we use lumpsum tax or income-tax. The level of income can be increased either by a decrease in taxes, government expenditure remaining the same or, by increasing government expenditure, the tax yield remaining unchanged or, by a change in tax rate, government expenditure remaining unchanged.

Balanced Budget Multiplier : Diagrammatic Presentation

The budget is said to be balanced when the tax yield is equal to government expenditure. If $G = T$ and then $\Delta G = \Delta T$ in any period then the budget will continue to be in balance. The multiplier effect of equal change in T and G is known as balanced budget multiplier. Our assumptions here is the same as in previous section. The equilibrium condition can be written as : $Y = C + \bar{I} + \overline{G}$ where consumption function $C = a + b(Y - T)$, the balanced budget multiplier can be obtained as follows : $Y = a + b(Y - T) + \bar{I} + \overline{G}$. When G changes and T remains unchanged we get $\frac{dY}{dG} = \frac{1}{1-b}$ or, $dY = \frac{1}{(1-b)}dG$.

Again, when T changes and G remains unchanged, we get :

$$\frac{dY}{dT} = \frac{-b}{1-b} \text{ or, } dY = \frac{-b}{1-b}dT.$$

When both G and T change at the same time we get $dY = \frac{1}{(1-b)}dG + \frac{-b}{(1-b)}dT$.

In this case of equal change in G and T, we get $dG = dT$, where $dY = \frac{(1-b)}{(1-b)}dG$.

Thus, when $dG = dT$, we have $dY = dG = dT$.

This is the famous balanced budget multiplier.

The balanced budget multiplier can also be represented in Fig. 11.1. In the case of lumpsum tax, the slope of the consumption function remains unchanged, while the vertical intercept changes. The consumption function, before tax, can be written as $C = a + bY$ and, after tax, it becomes $C = a + b(Y - T) = (a - bT) + bY$. Here the slope remains the same but

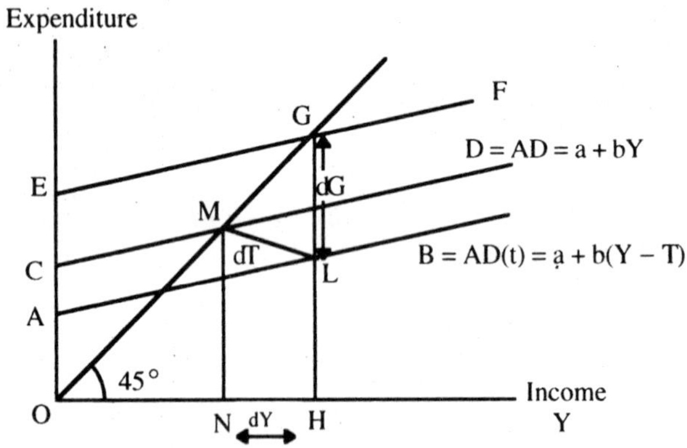

Fig. 11.1 Balanced Budget Multiplier

the intercept changes. In Fig. 11.1 income is measured on the horizontal axis and expenditure on the vertical axis CD = aggregate demand = $C+\bar{I}+\bar{G}$ prior to tax and ON is the initial equilibrium level of income. Now a tax is imposed by the amount ML and the vertical impact of the consumption is reduced to OA and the aggregate demand is now AB. Expenditure of GL is made equal to tax yield ML. Thus, the aggregate demand curve shifts to the position EF with the level of income OH. Consumption expenditure is at HL and the increase in income $NH = ML = GL$. Thus, the balanced budget multiplier holds good for $1:1$ expansion in income.

To obtain the balanced budget multiplier for income-tax, we assume that the tax yield, T, depends on income. For simplicity's sake we assume linear proportional tax function : $T = t.Y$, where t is the rate of tax. The disposable income is given by $Y - tY = (1-t)Y$. The consumption function is assumed to be linear : $C = a + b(1-t)Y$. In the case of the income-tax the slope of the consumption function is changed but the intercept remains unchanged. The equilibrium condition can be written as :

$$Y = C+\bar{I}+\bar{G} \quad \text{or,} \quad Y = a+b(1-t)Y+\bar{I}+\bar{G}.$$

We now consider the effect of change in G, assuming that the tax yield remains unchanged. When the tax yield remains constant, there is no difference between the income-tax and the lumpsum tax. The equilibrium condition can be written as $Y = a+b(Y-T)+\bar{I}+\bar{G}$. Differentiating both sides with respect to G, and rearranging, we get $dY = \frac{1}{1-b}dG$.

Now, G remains unchanged and the tax yield changes. This can be obtained as : $Y = a+b(Y-T)+\bar{I}+\bar{G}$.

Differentiating both sides with respect to T, and rearranging, we get, $dY = -\frac{b}{(1-b)}dT$. The effect of change in both T and G can be obtained by adding the separate effects of change in G and T, i.e.

$$\frac{dY}{dG} + \frac{dY}{dT} = \frac{1}{1-b} + \frac{-b}{(1-b)} \qquad \text{or, } dY = \frac{(1-b)}{(1-b)}dG = dT$$

Thus, the balanced budget multiplier in the case of income-tax is also unity. The balanced budget multiplier of income-tax can be represented in Fig. 11.2.

Let the aggregate demand curve be $A'C'$ before tax. After the income-tax is imposed the slope of the consumption function is reduced though the

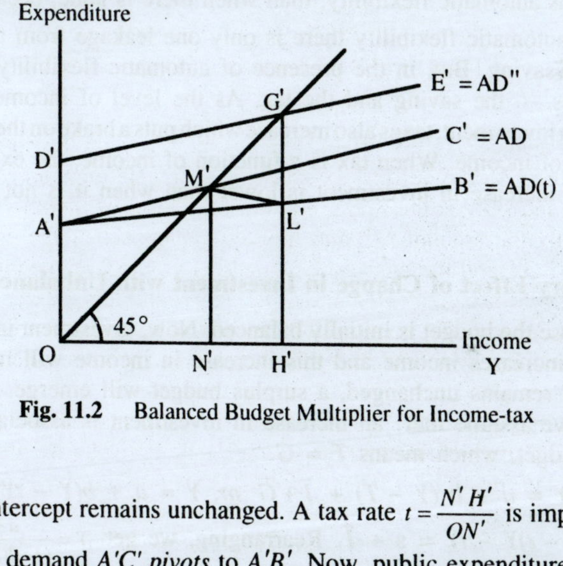

Fig. 11.2 Balanced Budget Multiplier for Income-tax

vertical intercept remains unchanged. A tax rate $t = \frac{N'H'}{ON'}$ is imposed and the aggregate demand $A'C'$ *pivots* to $A'B'$. Now, public expenditure is increased by $L'G'$ which is equal to $M'L'$ which shifts the aggregate demand function to $D'E'$ though the consumption expenditure initially remains unchanged at $M'N' = L'H'$. Thus, the increase in income, $N'H'$, is equal to the increase in government expenditure, $L'G'$, which is equal to increase in tax yield, $M'L'$. Thus, the balanced budget multiplier for income-tax is also obtained.

Stabilization and Balanced Budget

We know the effect of change in investment expenditure on the equilibrium level of income. If we now assume that all taxes are lumpsum taxes and T is autonomous, the investment multiplier is equal to $\frac{1}{1-b}$.

Since $Y = a + b(Y - T) + \bar{I} + \bar{G}$ $\therefore$ $\Delta Y = b\Delta Y + \Delta I$ $\therefore \Delta Y = \frac{1}{(1-b)}\Delta I$.

Now we assume that, taxes vary with income $T = T(Y)$ and it is a linear function of income $T = tY$, where t is a marginal tax rate.

Hence $Y = a + b(Y - tY) + \bar{I} + \bar{G}$ or, $Y = a + b(1 - t)Y + \bar{I} + \bar{G}$

$\therefore$ $\Delta Y = b(1 - t)\Delta Y + \Delta I$ $\therefore$ $\Delta Y = \frac{1}{1 - b(1-t)}\Delta I$

The investment multiplier is equal to $\frac{1}{1-b(1-t)}$ which is less than $\frac{1}{1-b}$. This means that the multiplier effect of a change in investments is lower when there is automatic flexibility, than when there is none, because, in the absence of automatic flexibility there is only one leakage from the circular flow — the saving. But, in the presence of automatic flexibility, there are two leakages — the saving and the tax. As the level of income rises due to increase in investment, taxes also increase which puts a brake on the expansion in the level of income. When tax is a function of income, the expansionary effect of an increase in investment is lower than when it is not a function of income.

Expansionary Effect of Change in Investment with Unbalanced Budget

Suppose the budget is initially balanced. Now, investment increases — which also increases income and this increase in income will increase tax yield. As G remains unchanged, a surplus budget will emerge.

Now we assume that an increase in investment is associated with a balanced budget, which means $T = G$.

Then $Y = a + b(Y - T) + \bar{I} + \bar{G}$ or, $Y = a + b(Y - tY) + \bar{I} + tY$ or $Y - b(1 - t)Y - tY = a + \bar{I}$. Rearranging, we get $Y = \frac{a + \bar{I}}{(1-b)(1-t)}$.

$\therefore \Delta Y = \frac{1}{(1-b)(1-t)}\Delta I$. The multiplier associated with the change in investment is $\frac{1}{(1-b)(1-t)}$ and this is greater than the previous multiplier $\frac{1}{1-b(1-t)}$. This means that, when private investment increases and taxes also vary with income, the level of income will increase more when the budget is balanced than when it is unbalanced (deficit). Similarly, in the case of decrease in investment, the decrease in income will be larger when the budget is balanced than when it is not balanced. Thus, the balanced budget reinforces expansionary or contractionary tendencies. This implies that, the aim of income stabilization is not compatible with the requirement of the balanced budget. Furthermore, the balanced budget policy of the government may aggravate these fluctuations, rather than eliminate it. The balanced budget policy is, therefore, not a sound policy from the point of view of stabilization. Our advice to the government in this respect is to produce a surplus budget in a period of economic prosperity and a deficit budget in a period of severe recession.

A Deficit Budget and Multiplier

It is commonly believed that a deficit budget is always expansionary. It is not always true. Budget deficit may not be expansionary and there is no unique deficit multiplier. Let us start with a balanced budget situation and then consider the effect of deficit budget.

We now assume that the government expenditure is increased by ΔG with taxes remaining unchanged. There is then a budget deficit by ΔG. Income increases by ΔY such that $\Delta Y = \frac{1}{(1-b)}\Delta G$. Here the multiplier is $\frac{1}{(1-b)}$.

Now, suppose that the government reduces taxation by the amount ΔT, with G remaining unchanged. There is a budget deficit of ΔT and the level of income increases by $\Delta Y = \frac{-b}{(1-b)}\Delta T$. The multiplier here is $\frac{-b}{(1-b)}$. Again assume that, the government now increases transfer payments by ΔT_r, which is larger than ΔT, whereas G remains the same. The budget deficit is equal to $\Delta T_r - \Delta T$. Let us see how it effects the equilibrium level of income. Since $Y = a + b\,(Y - T + T_r) + \bar{I} + \bar{G}$

$$\therefore\ \Delta Y = b(\Delta Y - \Delta T + \Delta T_r) = \frac{-b}{(1-b)}(\Delta T_r - \Delta T)$$

In this case also the multiplier is equal to $\frac{-b}{(1-b)}$.

Suppose, that the government expenditure is increased by ΔG which is greater than the increase in ΔT, transfer payments do not change. The budget deficit is now $\Delta G - \Delta T$. Consider its effect on the level of income.

Since $Y = a + b(Y - T + T_r) + \bar{I} + \bar{G}$

$$\therefore\ \Delta Y = b(\Delta Y - \Delta T) + \Delta G \text{ or } \Delta Y(1 - b) = \Delta G - b\Delta T$$

$$\therefore \Delta Y = \frac{1}{(1-b)}(\Delta G - b\Delta T)$$

We know that $\Delta G > \Delta T$ and the budget deficit is expansionary. But $\frac{1}{(1-b)}$ is not the multiplier in this case as the deficit here is $(\Delta G - \Delta T)$ and not $(\Delta G - b\Delta T)$.

Lastly, suppose that this time the government reduces taxation by an amount $\Delta T \times G$, transfer payments remain the same. The budget deficit is $\Delta T - \Delta G$. Hence, the change in income may be given by $\Delta Y = \frac{1}{(1-b)}(\Delta G - b\Delta T)$.

Note that, ΔY may be negative or positive. It will be negative when $|\Delta G| > |b\Delta T|$, even when there is a deficit in the budget and the level of income will fall. It will be positive only when $|\Delta G| < |b.\Delta T|$. When $|\Delta G| = |b\Delta T|$, $\Delta Y = 0$ and the level of income remains unchanged. This analysis shows that the budget deficit is not always expansionary. It could be contractionary or even neutral.

Built-in-Stability of the Tax-System

We have seen in a simple economy without government the investment multiplier is given by $dY = \frac{1}{(1-b)} dI$ where b is the $mpc(\ 0 < b < 1)$. This shows that fluctuations in autonomous investment leads to fluctuations in the level of income. Now, the question is whether this fluctuations in the level of income can be controlled by the government's activity in the economy. If the government's budget contain a mechanism to control that fluctuations then it is said that a built-in-flexibility exists in the budget.

We take the following assumptions to see how the existence of a built-in-flexibility leads to smaller fluctuations: (1) Taxes depend on the level of income, such that, as the level of income increases, total tax yields also increase. The tax is a linear and proportional function of income, i.e. $T = tY$, where t is marginal tax rate. (2) Government's expenditure is autonomously given. (3) The consumption is a linear function of disposable income : $C = a + b\ (Y - tY)$. (4) Investment is autonomously given. (5) The economy is a closed economy.

The equilibrium condition of income determination can be written as

$$Y = C + \bar{I} + \bar{G} \quad \text{or,} \quad Y = a + b(1-t)Y + \bar{I} + \bar{G}$$

Now, differentiating both sides with respect to I and rearranging, we get $dY = \frac{1}{1-b(1-t)} dI$. The investment multiplier is equal to $\frac{1}{1-b(1-t)}$ whereas the investment multiplier without government, or when taxes are autonomously given, can be written as $\frac{1}{(1-b)}$. It is clear that, $\frac{1}{(1-b)} > \frac{1}{1-b(1-t)}$. This means that, the multiplier effect of a change in autonomous investment will be lower when taxes are a function of income than when they are not. Thus, it can be said that when taxes vary directly with the level of income, there is built-in-flexibility in the budget which regulates fluctuations in the economy. The mechanism works as follows : Suppose investment expenditure increases and, as a result, the level of income also increases. If taxes are a function of income then, as income increases, the tax collection also increases. As tax revenue increases, the level of income decreases. Thus, the original increase in income is dampened and, hence, the level of income is reduced when there is built-in-flexibility in the budget.

Now the question is : how can we measure the effectiveness of built-in-flexibility? Following Musgrave, we can suggest a measure of the effectiveness of built-in-flexibility as follows : Let dY_A is the change in the absence of built-in-flexibility and let dY is the change in income in the presence of built-in-flexibility. Then $dY_A = \frac{1}{(1-b)} dI$ and $dY = \frac{1}{1-b(1-t)} dI$. Then $g = 1 - \frac{dY}{dY_A}$ may be taken as a measure of the effectiveness of built-in-flexibility, where $0 < g < 1$. When $g = 0$, $dY = dY_A$, the change in the level of income will be the same both in the absence and in the presence of built-in-flexibility. So, the built-in-flexibility is ineffective. If $g = 1$, $dY = 0$, the level of income remains constant and does not change at all even if investment changes. This means the built-in-flexibility is completely effective. The greater the value of g the greater will be the effectiveness and vice versa:

$$g = 1 - \frac{dY}{dY_A} = 1 - \frac{\frac{1}{1-b(1-t)} dI}{\frac{1}{1-b} dI} \quad or, \; g = 1 - \frac{1-b}{1-b(1-t)} = \frac{bt}{1-b(1-t)}$$

This means that the effectiveness of built-in-flexibility depends on two factors : the $mpc = (b)$ and $Mtr = t$. Apart from the mpc, g depends on the elasticity of the tax function. For example, if $t = 1$, then entire increase in income is taken away in the form of tax collection, which means that the marginal rate of tax (Mrt) is 100%. In this case, when $t - 1$, $g = b$ and since $mpc < 1$, it follows that $g < 1$. This means that so long as the mpc is less than unity built-in-flexibility cannot be perfect to keep the level of income perfectly stable.

Government Budget in the *IS-LM* Model

So far we have been discussing government activities on the simple Keynesian model of income determination. Now we wish to incorporate government activities in the *IS-LM* Model. The equilibrium condition in the commodity and money market can be written, respectively, as :

(1) $S(Y_d) + T = S(Y - T) + T = I(r) + G$

(2) $M = L\,(r,Y)$, where $\frac{\partial L}{\partial r} < 0$, $\frac{\delta L}{\delta Y} > 0$ and T, G and M are autonomously given.

Hence, in the above two equations, we have only two unknowns: r and Y. Thus, solving these two equations simultaneously we can determine equilibrium income and interest rate. Equation (1) gives us the *IS* curve and Equation (2) gives the *LM* curve. The *IS* curve represents the combinations of r and Y for which $S + T = I + G$ is satisfied; whereas the *LM* curve represents the combinations of r and Y for which the demand for money is equal to the supply of money or $M = L\,(r, Y)$. It should, however, be noted that when the government activities are introduced the equation of the IS curve is affected, whereas the equation of the LM curve remains unchanged. The introduction of the government activities do not change the slope of the IS curve, so long all taxes are lumpsum taxes and government expenditure is autonomously given, the equation of the IS curve becomes :

$$S(Y - T) + T = I(r) + G.$$

By differentiating both sides we get

$S'dY = I'dr$ or $\frac{dr}{dY} = \frac{S'}{I'}$ which is the same as when the government activities are not introduced. Thus, the IS curve shifts parallel when G and T are autonomous. Since G and T enter the equation of the IS curve, the position of the IS curve will shift if G and T changes. Thus, if T decreases (increases), the IS curve shifts to the right (to the left), G remaining unchanged; on the other hand, if G increases (decreases), T remaining the same, the IS curve shifts to the right (to the left). Thus, in our model, the tax-expenditure policy of the government will change the equilibrium level of income and the interest rate by affecting the IS curve only.

We can obtain the effect of ΔG or ΔT by differentiating equations (1) and (2) with respect to G or T and solving for $\frac{dY}{dT}$ and $\frac{dr}{dT}$ (or $\frac{dY}{dG}$ and $\frac{dr}{dG}$).

Differentiating equations (1) and (2) with respect to T, we can get the effect of ΔT, with G and M remaining unchanged.

$S'\left(\frac{dY}{dT} - 1\right) + 1 = I'\frac{dr}{dT}$ and $0 = L_r\frac{dr}{dT} + L_Y\frac{dY}{dT}$ where $L_r = \frac{\partial L}{\partial r}$ and $L_Y = \frac{\partial L}{\partial Y}$

or, $S'\frac{dY}{dT} - I'\frac{dr}{dT} = -(1 - S')$ and $L_Y\frac{dY}{dT} + L_r\frac{dr}{dT} = 0.$

Solving by Cramer's rule we get

$$\frac{dY}{dT} = \frac{\begin{vmatrix} -(1-S') & -I' \\ 0 & L_r \end{vmatrix}}{\begin{vmatrix} S' & -I' \\ L_Y & L_r \end{vmatrix}} = \frac{-L_r(1-S')}{S'L_r + L_Y I'}$$

$$\text{and, } \frac{dr}{dT} = \frac{\begin{vmatrix} S' & -(1-S') \\ L_Y & 0 \end{vmatrix}}{\begin{vmatrix} S' & -I' \\ L_Y & L_r \end{vmatrix}} = \frac{(1-S')L_Y}{S'L_r + L_Y I'}$$

On the assumption that $0 < S' < 1$, $L_Y > 0$, $L_r < 0$ and $I' < 0$, it follows that $\frac{dr}{dT} < 0$ and $\frac{dY}{dT} < 0$. This means that when T increases (decreases), G remaining the same, the equilibrium level of income decreases (increases), and the rate of interest also decreases (increases). Geometrically, this can be shown in the Fig. 11.3, when G remains unchanged and T increases, the IS curve shifts to the left from IS_0 to IS_1, the LM curve remains the same. As a result the equilibrium income and interest rate decreases from Y_0 to Y_1 and r_0 to r_1, respectively as in Fig. 11.3. Similarly, when T decreases, G remains unchanged, the IS curve shifts to the right from IS_0 to IS_2 and Y and r will increase from Y_0 to Y_2 and r_0 to r_2.

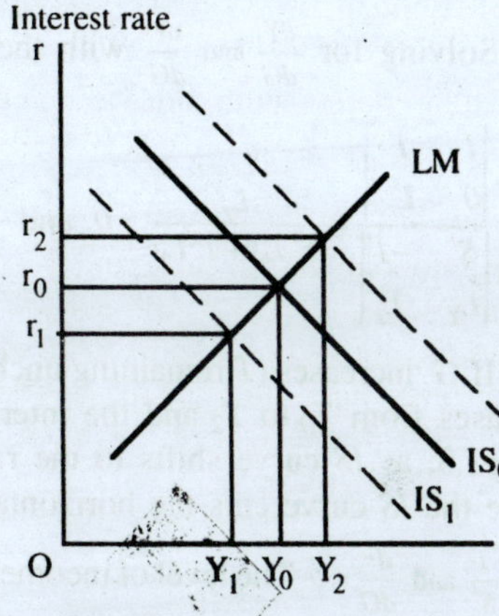

Fig. 11.3 Government Budget in the IS-LM Model

However, in a limiting case of the liquidity trap situation where

$L_r \to$, $\dfrac{dY}{dT} = \dfrac{-(1-S')}{S'} < 0$ and $\dfrac{dr}{dT} = 0$;

In this situation, if T increases, Y decreases but r remains the same.

Diagrammatically, this can be represented in Fig. 11.4, when $L_r \to \infty$, the LM curve is horizontal (liquidity trap situation). Now, if the IS curve cuts the horizontal part of the LM curve and the IS curve shifts to the left, then it is obvious that the level of income falls, but the interest rate remains unchanged. We can now consider the effect of change in G, T remaining unchanged. Differentiating equations (1)

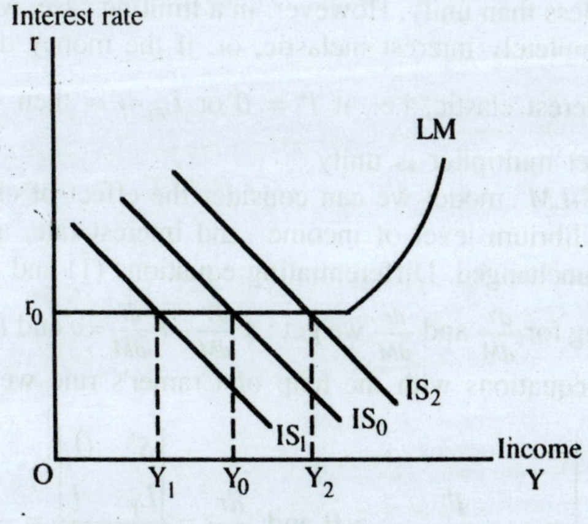

Fig. 11.4 Government Budget in the Liquidity Trap situation

and (2) with respect to G we get

$$S'\frac{dY}{dG} - I'\frac{dr}{dG} = 1 \text{ and } L_Y\frac{dY}{dG} + L_r\frac{dr}{dG} = 0.$$

Solving for $\frac{dY}{dG}$ and $\frac{dr}{dG}$ with the help of Cramer's rule we now get

$$\frac{dY}{dG} = \frac{\begin{vmatrix} 1 & -I' \\ 0 & L_r \end{vmatrix}}{\begin{vmatrix} S' & -I' \\ L_Y & L_r \end{vmatrix}} = \frac{L_r}{S'L_r + I'L_Y} > 0 \text{ and } \frac{dr}{dG} = \frac{\begin{vmatrix} S' & 1 \\ L_Y & 0 \end{vmatrix}}{S'L_r + I'L_Y} = \frac{-L_Y}{S'L_r + I'L_Y} > 0$$

If G increases (T remaining unchanged) the equilibrium level of income increases from Y_0 to Y_2 and the interest rate will increase from r_0 to r_2, in Fig. 11.3, as *IS* curve shifts to the right from IS_0 to IS_2. In a special case, where the *IS* curve cuts the horizontal part of the *LM* curve, $L_r \to \infty$ and $\frac{dY}{dG} = \frac{1}{S'}$ and $\frac{dr}{dG} = 0$. The level of income increases but the rate of interest remains the same.

Now we consider the balanced budget multiplier when both G and T change by equal amounts their combined effect on income can be obtained by taking the sum of their individual effects. Thus,

$$\frac{dY}{dT} + \frac{dY}{dG} = \frac{-L_r(1-S')}{S'L_r + I'L_Y} + \frac{L_r}{S'L_r + I'L_Y} = \frac{1}{1 + \frac{I'L_Y}{S'L_r}}.$$

So long as $I' < 0$, $S' > 0$, $L_Y > 0$ and $L_r < 0$ the balanced budget multiplier is positive but less than unity. However, in a limiting case, where investment function is completely interest inelastic, or, if the money demand function is perfectly interest elastic, i.e., if $I' = 0$ or $L_r \to \infty$ then $\frac{dY}{dG} + \frac{dY}{dT} = 1$, the balanced budget multiplier is unity.

In the *IS-LM* model we can consider the effect of change in money supply on equilibrium level of income and interest rate, assuming that G and T remain unchanged. Differentiating equations (1) and (2) with respect to M and solving for $\frac{dY}{dM}$ and $\frac{dr}{dM}$ we get : $S'\frac{dY}{dM} - I'\frac{dr}{dM} = 0$ and $L_Y\frac{dY}{dM} + L_r\frac{dr}{dM} = 1$. Solving these equations with the help of Cramer's rule we get

$$\frac{dY}{dM} = \frac{\begin{vmatrix} 0 & -I' \\ 1 & L_r \end{vmatrix}}{\begin{vmatrix} S' & I' \\ L_Y & L_r \end{vmatrix}} = \frac{I'}{S'L_r + I'L_Y} > 0 \text{ and } \frac{dr}{dM} = \frac{\begin{vmatrix} S' & 0 \\ L_Y & 1 \end{vmatrix}}{\begin{vmatrix} S' & -I' \\ L_Y & L_r \end{vmatrix}} = \frac{S'}{S'L_r + I'L_Y} < 0.$$

This shows that, if money supply increases the equilibrium level of income increases but the interest rate decreases. If money supply increases the *LM* curve shifts to the right, assuming that the *IS* curve remain unchanged. However, if $L_r \rightarrow$, $\frac{dY}{dM} = 0$ and $\frac{dr}{dM} = 0$. In this liquidity trap situation, monetary policy become completely ineffective. Lastly, consider the combined effect of equal change in *G* and *M* on income when *T* remains unchanged. This is given by $\frac{dY}{dG} + \frac{dY}{dM} = \frac{L_r + I'}{S' L_r + I' L_Y} > 0$. In this case, we can make a comparison between the effects of tax-financed increase in *G* and financing increase in *G* by money creation. In the former case we get $\frac{dY}{dG} + \frac{dY}{dT} = \frac{S' L_r}{S' L_r + I' L_Y}$ and in the latter case we get $\frac{dY}{dG} + \frac{dY}{dM} = \frac{L_r + I'}{S' L_r + I' L_Y}$. Now, by mathematical manipulation we get, $= \frac{(1 - S') L_r + I'}{S' L_r + I' L_Y} > 0$. This means that, $\frac{dY}{dG} + \frac{dY}{dM} > \frac{dY}{dG} + \frac{dY}{dT}$ which means that, the expansionary effect of an increase in *G* financed by an equal increase in *M* will be higher than the expansionary effect of an increase in *G* financed by an equal increase in *T*. This can be shown in Fig. 11.5 where both the *IS* and *LM* curves shift to the right; in the first case, where income increases from Y_0 to Y_1 and r_0 remains unchanged. But in the second case, only the *IS* curve shifts to the right by a small amount when the *LM* curve remains unchanged. Thus, *Y* increases by Y_0 to Y_1 *and* *r* increases from r_0 to r_1.

So far, our assumption was that all taxes are lumpsum and autonomous. We now introduce an income-tax instead of lumpsum tax. Let $T = tY$ be the tax function where *t* is the marginal (and also average) tax rate. When the

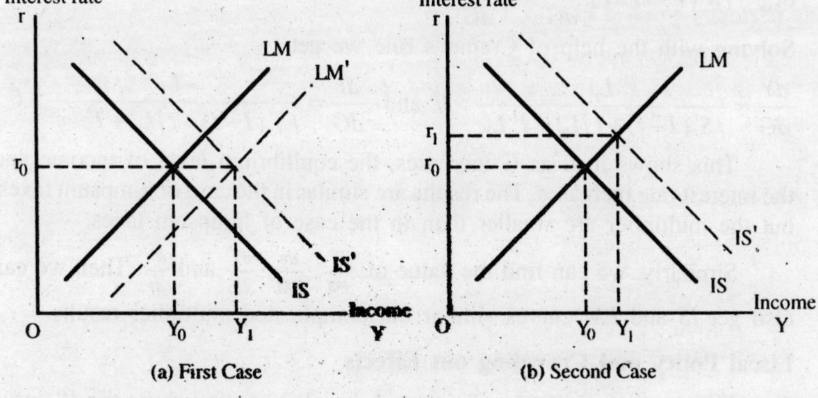

Fig. 11.5 Expansionary Effect of Government Budget

tax function is $T = tY$, the slope of the *IS* curve is now affected. This is shown as follows:

The equation of the *IS* curve can be written as : $S(Y_d) + T = I(r) + G$ where $Y_d = Y - T$ and $T = tY$. Thus, $Y_d = Y - tY = (1 - t)Y$. Therefore, $\frac{dY_d}{dY} = (1-t)$, $\therefore S(Y_d) + tY = I(r) + G$. Differentiating both sides with respect to Y we get : $S'\frac{dY_d}{dY} + t = I'\frac{dr}{dY}$ or $S'(1-t) + t = I'\frac{dr}{dY}$.

$$\therefore \frac{dr}{dY} = \frac{S'(1-t)+t}{I'}.$$

This is the slope of the *IS* curve which depends on the tax rate (t).

In the absence of proportional income-tax the slope of the *IS* curve is $\frac{S'}{I'}$ and in the presence of proportional income-tax the slope of the *IS* curve is $\frac{S'(1-t)+t}{I'} = \frac{S'+t(1-S')}{I'}$.

Since $t > 0$ and $0 < S' < 1$, it is obvious that $\frac{S'+t(1-S')}{I'} > \frac{S'}{I'}$ which means that slope of the *IS* curve increases when the tax function is assumed to be linear and proportional. The *IS* curve become steeper than before.

Now the equation of the *IS* curve is $S(Y_d) + tY = I(r) + G$ and that of the *LM* curve is $L(r, Y) = M$. Differentiating both these equations with respect to G and solving for $\frac{dY}{dG}$ and $\frac{dr}{dG}$ we can get the effects of change in G on the equilibrium level of income and the interest rate. We then have

$$S'\frac{dY_d}{dY}\cdot\frac{dY}{dG} + t\cdot\frac{dY}{dG} = I'\frac{dr}{dG} + 1 \text{ and } L_Y\frac{dY}{dG} + L_r\frac{dr}{dG} = 0$$

or, $$[S'(1-t)+t].\frac{dY}{dG} - I'\frac{dr}{dG} = 1.$$

Solving with the help of Cramer's rule we get

$$\frac{dY}{dG} = \frac{L_r}{[S'(1-t)+t]L_r + I'L_Y} > 0 \text{ and } \frac{dr}{dG} = \frac{-L_Y}{[S'(1-t)+t]L_r + I'L_Y} > 0.$$

This shows that, as G increases, the equilibrium level of income and the interest rate increases. The results are similar in the case of lumpsum taxes, but the multiplier are smaller than in the case of lumpsum taxes.

Similarly, we can find the value of $\frac{dY}{dM}$, $\frac{dr}{dM}$, $\frac{dY}{dt}$ and $\frac{dr}{dt}$. Then we can also get *IS* and *LM* curves similar but complicated multiplier results.

Fiscal Policy and Crowding out Effects

Fiscal policy shifts the *IS* curve. A fiscal expansion shifts the *IS* curve to the right and a fiscal contraction shifts it to the left.

The multiplier, in the commodity market, associated with the change in G is the reciprocal of the MPS, assuming lumpsum taxes. That is, $\frac{dY}{dG}=\frac{l}{S'}$ where S' is the MPS. The multiplier in the IS-LM model with lumpsum taxes is : $\frac{dY}{dG}=\frac{L_r}{S'\,L_r+I'\,L_Y}=\frac{l}{S'+I'\,L_Y}$ and $\frac{dr}{dG}=\frac{-L_Y}{S'\,L_r+I'\,L_Y}$. We can see that the multiplier in the IS-LM model is smaller than in the simple Keynesian model. That is $\frac{l}{S'+I'\,L_Y}<\frac{l}{S'}$.

This result can be explained as follows:

When G increases the level of income and interest rate increases. At unchanged rate of interest, increase G increases the level of aggregate demand. To meet the increased demand, output must rise as shown by the shift in the IS schedule. At each rate of interest, equilibrium income must rise by multiplier times G. If the economy is initially in equilibrium at point E as in Fig. 11.6, and G rises, we would move to point E'' with unchanged interest rate. At E'' goods market is in equilibrium where planned spending equals output. But the asset market is not in equilibrium. Income has increased and, thus, the quantity of money demanded is higher. Since there is excess demand

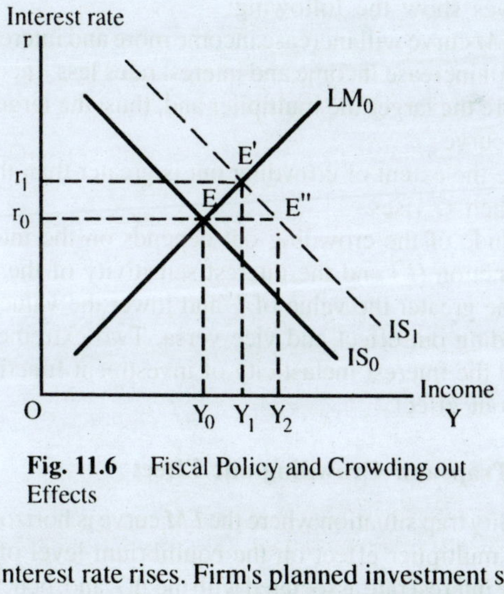

Fig. 11.6 Fiscal Policy and Crowding out Effects

for money, the interest rate rises. Firm's planned investment spending declines at higher interest ratés, and, thus, aggregate demand decreases.

The new equilibrium is at point E'. The increase in income $(Y_1 - Y_0)$ is less than the amount indicated by the simple multiplier $(Y_2 - Y_0)$ because, higher interest rate crowd-out some investment spending.

We assume that the money market clears quickly and continuously, while output adjust only slowly. This implies that, as government spending increases, we stay initially at point E, as there is no disturbance in the money market. The excess demand for goods leads firms to increase output, and that increase in output and income raises demand for real balances. The resulting excess demand for money, causes interest rate to rise, and we proceed up along the *LM* curve with rising output and rising interest rates, until we reach the new equilibrium at E'.

Crowding-out and the Different Shape of the LM Curve

Comparing E' to initial equilibrium at E, we see that increased G raises both income and interest rate. But another comparison is between E' and E'', the equilibrium in the commodity market with unchanged interest rates. Comparing E'' and E' it becomes clear that the adjustment of interest rates and their impact on aggregate demand dampen the expansionary effect of increased G. Income increases to Y_1 rather than to Y_2 because the rise in the interest rate from r_0 to r_1 reduces the level of investment spending. Thus, we can say that, increase in G crowds out private investment. Crowding out occurs when expansionary fiscal policy causes interest rates to rise, thereby reducing private investment spending.

What factors determine how much crowding out takes place? The different *IS* and *LM* curves show the following:

The flatter *LM* curve will increase income more and interest rates less. The flatter *IS* curve will increase income and interest rates less. Income and interest rates increase more the larger the multiplier and, thus, the larger the horizontal shift of the *IS* curve.

In each case the extent of crowding out is greater than the more interest rate increases when G rises.

The magnitude of the crowding out depends on the interest sensitivity of investment function (I') and the interest sensitivity of the money demand function (L_r). The greater the value of I' and lower the value L_r, the greater will be the crowding out effect and vice versa. Two extreme cases are : the liquidity trap and the interest inelasticity of investment function. where there is no crowding out effect.

The Liquidity Trap and Crowding out Effect

In the liquidity trap situation where the *LM* curve is horizontal, an increase in G has its full multiplier effect on the equilibrium level of income. There is no change in the interest rate associated with the ΔG, and, hence, no investment spending is crowded out. This can be shown in Fig. 11.7(a) below where *LM* curve is horizontal, monetary policy has no impact on the economy and fiscal policy has a full effect. If the demand for money is very sensitive to the interest rate, so that the *LM* curve is horizontal, fiscal policy is effective and monetary policy is ineffective as Fig. 11.7(a) shows as *IS* shifts from

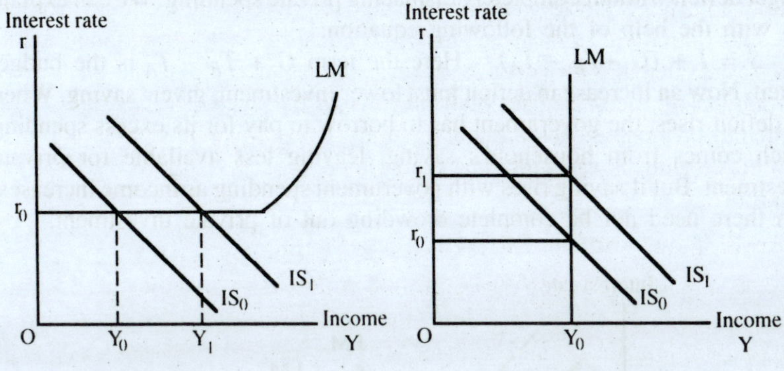

(a) Liquidity trap situation (b) Classical case

Fig. 11.7 Crowding out in Two Extreme cases

IS_0 to IS_1. If the *LM* curve is vertical, then increase in *G* has no effect on the equilibrium level of income and it increases the interest rate only. In this case an increase in *G* shifts the *IS* curve to *IS*$'$ but has no effect on income. If the demand for money is not related to interest rate, as a vertical *LM* curve implies, then there is a unique level of income at which the money market is in equilibrium as Fig.11.7(b) shows.

Crowding out and the Classical Case

When the *LM* curve is vertical an increase in *G* cannot change the equilibrium level of income and only raises the equilibrium interest rate which will offset private spending. In this case, the increase in interest rates crowds out an amount of private spending equal to an increase in government spending. Thus, there is a full crowding out if the *LM* curve is vertical. In Fig.11. 7(b), we show complete crowding out.

Is Crowding Out a possibility

To consider the possibility of crowding out three points must be made. The first point is that, if we consider an economy below full-employment and given prices, then fiscal expansion will increase output. But when we talk about fully employed economy, crowding out becomes a possibility because output cannot then be increased. In such situations an increase in demand will increase the price level rather than an increase in output.

Second point is that, in an economy with unemployed resources there will not be full crowding out because the *LM* curve cannot be vertical. A fiscal expansion will raise interest rates and income. Crowding out is, thus, a matter of degree. The increase in aggregate demand raises income which raises the level of saving which again makes it possible to finance a larger budget deficit without completely displacing private spending. We can explain this with the help of the following equation:

$S = I + (G + T_R - T_A)$. Here the term $G + T_R - T_A$ is the budget deficit. Now an increase in deficit must lower investment, given saving. When the deficit rises, the government has to borrow to pay for its excess spending which comes from household's saving, leaving less available for private investment. But if saving rises with government spending as income increases, then there need not be complete crowding out of private investment.

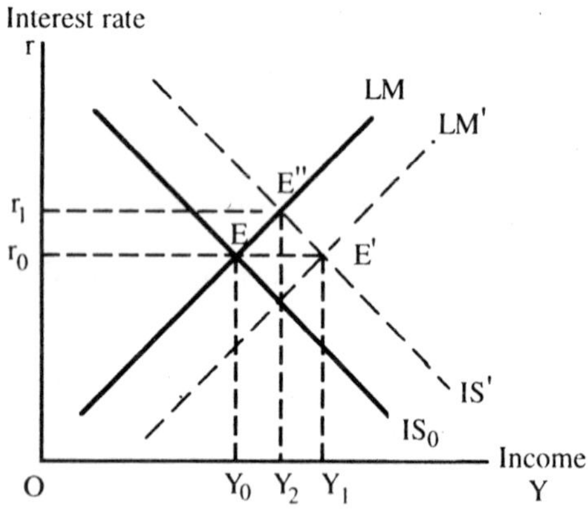

Fig. 11.8 Fiscal Expansion without Crowding out Effect

The third point is that, with unemployment, interest rates may not rise at all when the fiscal expansion is accommodated by the monetary authority by increasing money supply. Monetary policy is accommodating fiscal expansion when the money supply is increased to prevent interest rates from increasing. This accommodation policy of the central bank is also referred to as monetizing budget deficits which shifts the *IS* and *LM* curves to the right, as in Fig. 11.8. Income will definitely increase, but interest rates remain unchanged and, thus, private investment will not be adversely effected.

Effectiveness of Monetary and Fiscal Policy

We can compare the relative effectiveness of fiscal and monetary policy with the help of a simple model. By monetary policy we mean the changing of the supply of money by the monetary authority without directly altering current income stream. Monetary policy will affect the position of the *LM* curve through changes in money supply, as shown in Fig 11.9. An increase in the real money stock shifts the *LM* curve to the right to LM_1 and the asset markets adjust immediately through decline in interest rate between points

E and E_1. The lower interest rates stimulate investment and other expenditures and increase income until a new equilibrium is reached at E_2. This shows that a rise in real money stock increases equilibrium income and lowers equilibrium interest rates as Fig. 11.9 shows.

By fiscal policy we mean the change in government expenditure *(ΔG)* and taxation. We assume that ΔG without any change in money supply with the public. A tax-financed expenditure or a deficit financed by a sale of bonds

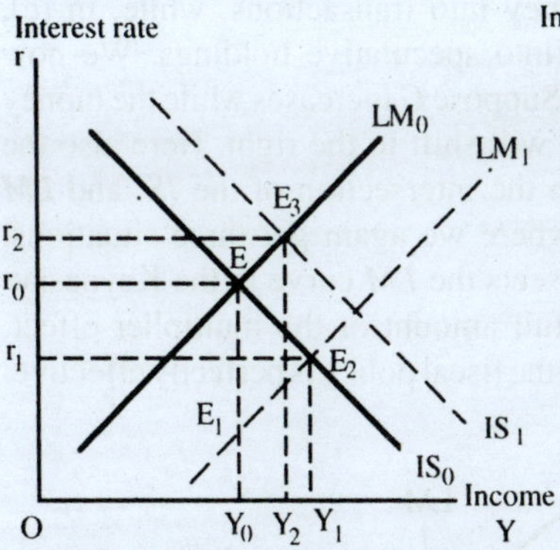

Fig. 11.9 Effectiveness of Monetary Policy

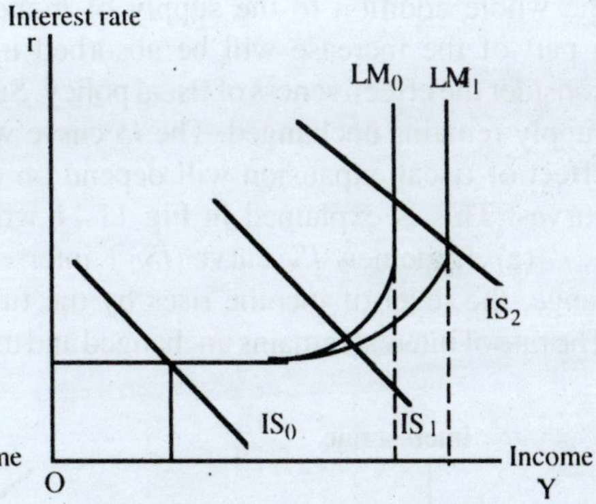

Fig. 11.10 Effectiveness of Fiscal Policy

to the public may be used as an example of fiscal policy. In short, pure fiscal policy operates through ΔG and, thereby, affecting the *IS* with no effect on the LM curve, as the Fig. 11.9 shows, when IS_0 shifts IS_1 and LM_0 remains unchanged and both income and interest rates increase to Y_2 and r_2, respectively.

Now we examine the effectiveness of monetary policy with the different shape of the *LM* curve. The horizontal portion (perfectly interest-elastic demand for money) is called the Keynesian range while the vertical portion is called the Classical range. The upward rising portion is the Intermediate range.

Suppose the money supply increases and the *LM* curve shifts to the right. The effect of monetary expansion will depend on the point of intersection of the *IS* curve with the different range of the *LM* curve as shown in Fig. 11.10.

(a) If the *IS* curve *(IS_0)* intersects the *LM* curve at the latter's horizontal portion, then the change in money supply will have no effect on income and interest rate. In the Keynesian range, in the liquidity trap situation, the monetary policy is completely ineffective.

(b) The intersection of the *IS* curve *(IS_2)* with the *LM* curve at the latter's vertical portion — the classical range — where the speculative demand for money is zero. The entire increase in money supply will be absorbed by the transaction demand for money. This will happen when money income increases either due to increase in price level or increase in real income. The interest rate falls because the increase in money supply will induce people to use this extra money to buy bonds. This will increase bond prices which means a fall in the rate of interest.

(c) If the IS curve *(IS_1)* cuts the *LM* curve in its intermediate range, an increase in money supply will increase the level of income and decrease the rate of interest. The rate of interest will fall and the level of income will rise less than in (b) because, in (b), the rate of interest falls enough to absorb the whole addition to the supply of money into transactions, while, in (c), a part of the increase will be absorbed into speculative holdings. We now consider the effectiveness of fiscal policy. Suppose *G* increases while the money supply remains unchanged. The *IS* curve will shift to the right. Here also the effect of fiscal expansion will depend on the intersection of the *IS* and *LM* curves. This is explained in Fig 11.11 where we again get three situations.

(a) If the new IS_0 curve (IS_0') intersects the *LM* curve in the Keynesian range, the level of income rises by the full amount of the multiplier effect. The rate of interest remains unchanged and the fiscal policy is perfectly effective.

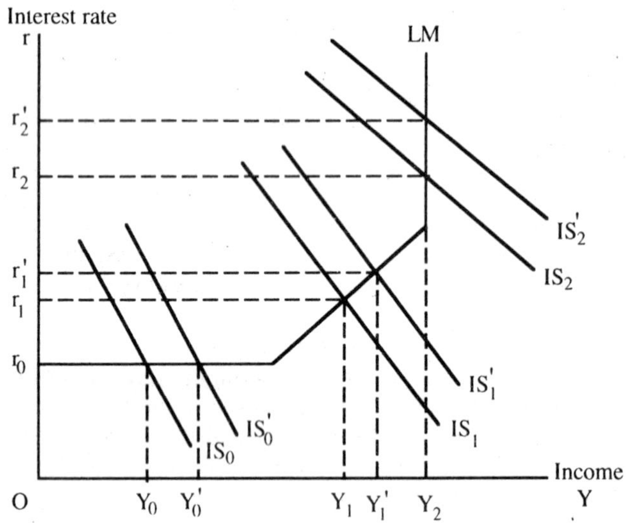

Fig. 11.11 Effectiveness of Fiscal Policy at Different stages of the LM curvre

(b) In the classical range where *IS* curve shifts from IS_2 to IS_2' the level of income remains constant at Y_2 and the rate of interest rises from r_2 to r_2'. In this range fiscal policy is not effective at all.

(c) If the *IS* curve cuts the *LM* curve in the intermediate range and the IS curve shifts from IS_1 to IS_1', the level of income rises from Y_1 to Y_1'

and the rate of interest also rises from r_1 to r_1'. The increase in the level of income is not as high as in the Keynesian range. Similarly, the increase in the rate of interest is not as great as in the classical range. The effectiveness of fiscal policy is in between the two extreme cases. The relative effectiveness of fiscal and monetary policy is mathematically derived in the Appendix of the Chapter.

Policy Debate

Some economists view the economy as inherently unstable and argue that the economy experiences frequent shocks to aggregate demand and aggregate supply. Unless policymakers use fiscal and monetary policy to stabilize the economy, these shocks will lead to unnecessary fluctuations in output, employment and price level. According to the popular saying, macroeconomic policy should stimulate the economy when it is depressed and slowing the economy when it is overheated.

Other economists consider the economy as naturally stable and blame bad economic policies for the large fluctuations of the economy. They argue that economic policy should not try to "fine tune" the economy. Instead, policymakers should recognise their limitations and be satisfied if they do no harm.

This debate has continued for many years and the fundamental issue now is how policymakers should use the theory of economic fluctuations. We now ask two questions that have arisen in this debate: First, should monetary and fiscal policy take an active role to stabilize the economy, or should policy remain passive? Second, should policymakers be free to use their discretion in responding to changing economic conditions or should they be committed to following a fixed rule?

Should Policy be Active or Passive

Economic policymakers consider stabilisation as one of their primary responsibilities. When government is considering a major change in fiscal or monetary policy, foremost in the discussion amongst the policymakers are whether the change will influence inflation and unemployment and whether aggregate demand needs to be stimulated or depressed.

Although the government has long conducted monetary and fiscal policy, the view that it should try to stabilize the economy is more recent. To many economists the case for active government policy is clear and simple. The model of aggregate demand and aggregate supply shows how shocks to the economy cause recession. It also shows how monetary and fiscal policy can prevent recessions by responding to these shocks. These economists consider it wasteful not to use these policy instruments to stabilize the economy. Other economists are critical of the government's attempts to stabilize the economy and argue that the government should take a "hands off" approach to macroeconomic policy. At first, this view might seem surprising. To find out, why these critics want the government to refrain from using monetary and fiscal policy to stabilize the economy, let's consider some of their arguments.

Lags in Implementation and Effect of Policies

Economic stabilization would be easy if the effects of policy were immediate. Making policy would be like driving a car, policymakers would simply adjust their instruments to keep the economy on the desired path. Driving a car changes direction almost immediately after the steering wheel is turned.

But economic policymakers face a problem similar to that of a pilot of a large ship because a ship changes course long after the pilot adjusts the rudder. Like a ship's pilot, economic policymakers face the problem of long lags. Indeed, the problem for policymakers is even more difficult, because the lengths of the time lags are hard to predict. These lags greatly complicate the conduct of the government policy.

Economists distinguish between two lags in the conduct of Stabilization Policy : the inside lag and the outside lag. The inside lag is the time between a shock and the policy action that responds to that shock. This lag arises because it takes time for policymakers first to recognise the shock and then to put appropriate policies into effect. The outside lag is the time between a policy action and its influence on the economy. This lag arises because policies do not immediately influence income, spending and employment. Fiscal policy has a long inside lag because, changes in spending or taxes require legislation and the legislative process is often slow and cumbersome. These delays make fiscal policy an imprecise tool for stabilizing the economy.

Monetary policy, on the other hand has a long outside lag. It works through interest rates, which in turn influence investments. But many firms make investment plans far in advance. Thus, a change in monetary policy is thought not to affect economic activity until about six months after it is made.

The long and variable lags associated with fiscal and monetary policy make stabilising the economy difficult. Advocates of passive policy argue that, because of these lags, successful stabilisation policy becomes an impossible task. Indeed, attempts to stabilise the economy are too often destabilizing. Suppose the economy's condition changes between the time when action is taken and the time when it affects the economy. Thus, active policy may end up stimulating the economy when it is overheated or depressing the economy when it is cooling off. Advocates of active policy admit that, such lags do require policymakers to be cautious. However, they argue, these lags do not necessarily imply that policy should be completely passive, especially in the face of severe economic downturn.

Automatic stabilisers are designed to reduce the lags associated with the stabilisation policy. Automatic stabilisers are policies that stimulate or depress the economy when necessary without any deliberate policy change. For example, as we have already seen, the system of income-tax automatically reduces tax revenue when the economy goes into a recession, without any change in the tax laws, because individuals and corporations pay less tax when their incomes fall. Similarly, the unemployment benefits and other welfare payments automatically raise transfer payments when the economy move into a recession. We can view these automatic stabilisers as fiscal policy without any inside lag.

Economic Forecasting

Since policy influences the economy after a substantial lag, successful stabilisation policy requires the ability to predict accurately future economic conditions. If we cannot predict correctly what will happen in six months or a year, we cannot decide whether monetary or fiscal policy should be used to expand or contract aggregate demand. Unfortunately, economic developments are unpredictable, at least with our given understanding of the economy.

One way forecasters try to look ahead is with the index of leading indicators. A large fall in the leading indicators signals that a recession is likely. Another way of forecasting is with the models of the economy. These models are made up of many equations, each representing a part of the economy. After making assumptions about the path of the exogenous variables, such as monetary policy, fiscal policy, etc., these models make predictions about unemployment, inflation and other endogenous variables. One must not forget, however, that the validity of these predictions is only as good as the model and the assumptions about the exogenous variables.

Role of Expectation in Policy-making

Economics is a young science, and there is still much that, we do not know which suggests that economists should be cautious when advising policymakers. Economists are not completely confident when they make assessments about the effects of alternative policies.

Although there are many topics about which knowledge of economists is limited, Lucas has emphasized the question of how people from expectations of the future. Expectations play a crucial role in the economy because they influence the behaviour of consumers, investors, and other economic actors. Expectations depends on many things, including the economic policies been pursued by the government. Thus, estimating the effect of a policy change requires knowing how people's expectations will respond to policy change. Lucas has criticised the traditional methods of policy evaluation for not properly taking into consideration this impact of policy on expectation which is known as the Lucas critique.

Active or Passive Role in the Economy

If the economy has experienced many large shocks to aggregate supply and aggregate demand, and if government policy has successfully insulated the economy from these shocks, then the case for active policy would be clear. Conversely, if the economy has experienced few large shocks, and if the fluctuations we have observed can be traced to inept economic policy, then the case for passive policy would be clear. Alternatively, our view of stabilization policy should be influenced by whether policy has been historically stabilising or destabilising. Thus, the debate over macroeconomic policy frequently turns into a debate over macroeconomic history.

Exercise

1. The economy is at full employment. Now the government wants the investment expenditure to rise without allowing aggregate demand to go beyond full-employment. What policy rise is required? Use the *IS-LM* diagram to show your policy proposals.

2. Use the IS-LM model to show the impact of the income-tax cut under two assumptions: one, the government keeps interest rates constant through an accommodating monetary policy, two, the money stock remains unchanged. Explain the difference in results.

3. In a closed economy, the consumption function is given by $C = 200 + 0.8Y_d$ where C is the consumption expenditure and Y_d is the disposable income. The investment expenditure is fixed at 200. Consider each of the following cases and obtain the effect on the equilibrium income :
(i) the government imposes a lumpsum tax to meet its expenditure amounting to 100, (ii) the government exempts 500 of income from taxation, collects 10 per cent of the rest as income-tax and spends the whole amount on the purchase of goods and services, and (iii) keeping the exemption limit unchanged, the tax rate increased to 20 per cent and the entire amount is spent.
If the equilibrium income is desired to be raised to 3,000 with the help of a balanced budget, what will be the required tax rate when the exemption limit remains unchanged?

4. In a proportional tax regime, there is a ceteris paribus reduction in the tax rate. Diagrammatically show the crowding out effects in the short-run and in the long-run.

5. An increase in government expenditure is financed by money creation. Show diagrammatically the short-run and long-run crowding out effects.

Appendix

Mathematical Appendix of the Effectiveness of Monetary and Fiscal Policy :

Equilibrium conditions of commodity and Money Markets :

(1) $Y = C(Y) + I(r) + G$ and

(2) $M = kP_0Y = L(r)$

The effect of an increase in money supply can be obtained by differentiating the equations (1) and (2) with respect to M. We get:

$$(3) \quad \frac{dY}{dM} = C'(Y)\frac{dY}{dM} + I'(r)\frac{dr}{dM}$$

$$(4) \quad I = kP_0\frac{dY}{dM} + L'(r)\frac{dr}{dM}$$

Solving (3) and (4) we get :

$$\frac{dY}{dM} = \frac{I'(r)}{S'(Y)L'(r) + I'(r)kP_0} \text{ and } \frac{dr}{dM} = \frac{S'(Y)}{S'(Y)L'(r) + I'(r)kP_0}.$$

In the intermediate range $\frac{dY}{dM} > 0$ and $\frac{dr}{dM} < 0$.

In the Keynesian range $L'(r) = \infty$, so that $\frac{dY}{dM} = 0$ and $\frac{dr}{dM} = 0$.

In the classical range, $L'(r) = 0$, so that $\frac{dY}{dM} = \frac{1}{kP_0}$ and $\frac{dr}{dM} = \frac{S'(Y)}{I'(r)kP_0}$.

In the classical range the change in the interest rate depends on the slope of the saving function, investment demand function and the transaction demand for money function.

The effect of an increase in government expenditure can be obtained by differentiating equations (1) and (2) with respect to G, we get :

$$\frac{dY}{dG} = C'(Y)\frac{dY}{dG} + I'(r)\frac{dr}{dG} + 1$$

$$kP_0\frac{dY}{dG} + L'(r)\frac{dr}{dG} = 0$$

$$\therefore S'(Y)\frac{dY}{dG} - I'(r)\frac{dr}{dG} = 1 \text{............} (5)$$

$$kP_0\frac{dY}{dG} + L'(r)\frac{dr}{dG} = 0 \text{.............} (6)$$

Solving (5) and (6) by Cramer's rule we get

$$\frac{dY}{dG} = \frac{L'(r)}{S'(Y)L'(r) + I'(r)kP_0} \text{ and } \frac{dr}{dG} = \frac{-kP_0}{S'(Y)L'(r) + I'(r)kP_0}$$

In the Keynesian range, $L'(r) = \infty$ so that $\frac{dY}{dG} = \frac{1}{S'(Y)}$ and $\frac{dr}{dG} = 0$.

In the Classical range, $L'(r) = 0$ so that $\frac{dY}{dG} = 0$ and $\frac{dr}{dG} = -\frac{1}{I'(r)} > 0.$

In the intermediate range, $\frac{dY}{dG} > 0$ and $\frac{dr}{dG} > 0$.

12 THE CONSUMPTION FUNCTION

The consumption function states that aggregate real consumption expenditure of an economy is a function of real national income. This is called the Keynesian Consumption Function. The classical economists used to argue that consumption was a function of the rate of interest such that as the rate of interest increased the consumption expenditure decreased and vice versa. Keynes stated that the rate of interest may have some influence on consumption but the real income was the important determinant of consumption. It should be remembered that in the consumption function consumption expenditure refers to intended or ex-ante consumption and not actual consumption. Similarly, income refers to anticipated income and not actual income. Therefore, the consumption function shows what consumption expenditure would be at different levels of income. The aggregate consumption in the economy can be found out from the consumption expenditure of different individuals purchasing commodities. The quantity of the commodities are $q_1, q_2......q_n$ and the prices of these commodities are $P_1, P_2......P_n$. Hence, the total consumption expenditure of all the individuals in the economy will be equal to $\sum_{i=1}^{n} P_i q_i$. But from the consumer's utility maximisation analysis we know that, the amount of any commodity consumed is a function of all prices and the level of income of the consumer *i.e.* $q_i = q_i(P_1, P_2 ....., P_n, Y)$ where i = 1, 2, ... n and y is the income of the consumer. Let C_j is the total consumption expenditure of *j*th individual. Then $C_j = \sum_{i=1}^{n} P_i q_i = \sum_{i=1}^{n} P_i q_i (P_1, P_2, ..., P_n, Yj)$ and C_j is also a function of $(P_1, P_2, ..., P_n, Y_j)$. Since $q_i(P_1, P_2, ..., P_n, Y_j)$ are homogeneous functions of degree zero, it follows the $C_j(P_1, P_2, ..., P_n, Y_j)$ will be homogeneous of degree one. This means that, when all prices and the level of income change in the same proportion, the consumption expenditure will also change in the same proportion. If we write all prices as P and all money incomes as Y_m, then we can write that $C_m = C_m(Y_m, P)$ where C_m is the aggregate consumption expenditure in money terms. This function will also be homogeneous of degree one in Y_m and P. Thus, the aggregate consumption function states that real consumption is a function of real income and then the consumption function can be written as $C = C(Y)$ where C is real consumption expenditure and

Y is real national income. This is the Keynesian Consumption Function. The straight line consumption function has a constant slope at all points. The *(MPC)* marginal propensity to consume decreases as income increases.

According to Keynes the consumption function must posses the following characteristics :

(1) Aggregate real consumption expenditure is a stable function of real income.

(2) The marginal propensity to consume *(MPC)* or the slope of the consumption function defined as $\frac{dc}{dY}$ must lie between zero and one, *i.e.* $0 < MPC < 1$.

(3) The average propensity to consume *(APC)* or the proportion of income spent on consumption defined as $\frac{C}{Y}$ should be decreasing as income increases. From the relation between marginal and average we know that, when average falls, marginal is below average. Thus, when the average propensity to consume *(APC)* falls, the marginal propensity to consume *(MPC)* must be lower than the *APC*.

(4) The marginal propensity to consume *(MPC)* itself probably decreases or remains constant as income increases.

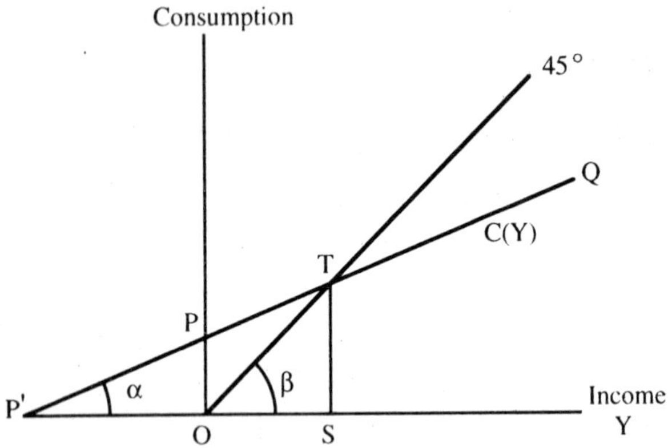

Fig. 12.1 Simple Consumption Function

These four characteristics specify the shape of the consumption function. It can be seen clearly that, if we draw a straight line consumption function with a positive intercept with the vertical axis, and intersecting the 45° line from above, it will satisfy all the four characteristics. In Fig. 12.1 we draw Y on the horizontal axis and C on the vertical axis. The consumption function, PQ, is a straight line and OT is a straight line passing through the origin making an angle of 45° which intersect the consumption function from below at point *T*. This consumption function *PQ* satisfies all the four characteristics. (i) It represents a stable relationship between *C* and *Y*. (ii) The slope of the line *PQ* represents the marginal propensity to consume *(MPC)* which has a positive slope. Again the consumption function cuts the 45° line from above. This means consumption function (*PQ*)is flatter than the 45° line and its slope is less than 45° line. The slope of $PQ = MPC$ and the slope of the 45° line = tan 45° = 1. Thus, it satisfies the second characteristic that $0 < MPC < 1$. (iii) But the average propensity to consume will be different at different points of the consumption function. For example, at point *P*, $C = OP$ and $Y = 0$, so that, $APC = \frac{C}{Y} = \frac{OP}{O} = \infty$. It means at point *P*, the *APC* is infinity (∞). Again consider the point *T* where consumption is *TS* and income is *OS*, so that, $APC = \frac{TS}{OS}$ = slope of $OT = 1$. Thus, *APC* at point T is one. The APC at any point on the consumption function is slope of the line joining that point with the origin. To the left of *T*, the *APC* is greater than one and to the right of *T*, *APC* is less than one. It means, to the left of the point T consumption is greater than income *i.e.*, $C > Y$, so that, $APC = \frac{C}{Y} > 1$. On the other hand, to the right of the point *T*, consumption is less than income, i.e. $C < Y$, so that, $APC = \frac{C}{Y} < 1$. Thus, the *APC* decreases as we move along the consumption function from left to right. Since the average propensity to consume *(APC)* decreases as income increases the marginal propensity to consume *(MPC)* must be less than the average propensity to consume. Thus, the third characteristic is also fulfilled by this straight line consumption function.

Fourthly, if the consumption function is a straight line the slope of the consumption function is constant at all points, i.e. the constant *MPC* satisfies the fourth characteristic. If the *MPC* is to decrease as income increases the consumption function has to be non-linear. It will be concave to the horizontal axis. In other words, the equation of a straight line linear consumption function can be written as $C = a + bY$, where *a* and *b* are constants. Let us also assume that $a > 0$ and $0 < b < 1$ and $\frac{dc}{dY} = b = MPC$. Since $b > 0$, the function is upward rising. Again the $APC = \frac{C}{Y} = \frac{a}{Y} + b$. In this case, $\frac{C}{Y}$ will decrease as *Y* increases. So the $APC = \frac{C}{Y} = \frac{a}{Y} + \frac{dc}{dY} = MPC + x$. $\therefore APC > MPC$.

These four characteristics of the consumption function mentioned by Keynes were not derived from theoretical analysis or empirical evidence. He derived these proportions from intuition. Keynes called it a "fundamental psychological law" that people do not spend the entire amount of the increase in income and save a part of it. This means that, marginal propensity to consume *(MPC)* is positive but less than one. The consumption income ratio falls as income increases which means that there is a non-proportional relationship between consumption and income.

Subjective and Objective Factors affecting Consumption Expenditure

According to Keynes, aggregate real consumption expenditure depends on aggregate real national income, other things remaining constant. The factors other than the level of income that affect consumption can be divided into three groups : (a) Subjective, (b) Objective and (c) Structural. Subjective factors are psychological ones that cannot be quantitatively measured. Objective factors are considered to be economic variables that can be measured quantitatively. Structural factors include aspects particularly relevant for the problem of aggregation. Let us first consider the subjective or psychological factors affecting consumption. The subjective factors consist of basic values, states of mind, attitudes, etc., which cannot be measured in quantitative terms. Keynes discuss the various motives for saving, such as, precaution, foresight, ... enterprise, pride and avarice; and also the motives for consumption, such as, "enjoyment, short-sightedness, generosity, miscalculation, ostentation and extravagance." He called them subjective factors that are unlikely to change significantly in the short-run.

Psychological factors, such as, expectations and attitudes do influence consumption. Rational behaviour suggests that a consumer who expects an increase in income or in price level would consume more than one who expects no such changes. Keynes accepted this logic but felt that expectations can be ignored because different people in an economy will have different expectations, and such expectations will probably cancel out each other in the aggregate analysis.

Now, let us consider the objective factors. The first objective factor after income is the interest rate. A rise in the interest rate may affect aggregate consumption expenditure in various ways. For example, a rise in the rate of interest will reduce bond prices, thereby discouraging the consumption propensities of the bondholders. It may also have the effect of substituting one type of asset for another. Classical economists used to believe that, consumption or saving was primarily a function of the rate of interest. However, Keynes did not consider the interest rate to be an important factor in influencing consumption or saving.

The second factor influencing consumption expenditure is the volume of wealth. The argument is that, everything being equal, the more savings a man has, the less would be his desire to accumulate more. For example, if two persons have identical needs, tastes and incomes, but one has acquired a large fortune, his incentive to accumulate more will be less than the other person's desire to accumulate wealth. This means that if a person has already a great volume of wealth his propensity to consume will be high. This is also true for the whole economy. The greater the volume of wealth in the economy the greater will be the consumption expenditure. This is known as the Pigou effect.

A part of wealth is also held in the form of money. Any change in money holdings without an equivalent change in other wealth would be regarded as wealth effect. More money means more spending. It should be remembered that consumption expenditure depends on the real quantity of money and not on nominal quantity of money. Thus, if the nominal quantity of money remain the same but the price level changes, there will be a change in the real quantity of money, which will change consumption expenditure. This is known as real balance effect. The third factor affecting consumption expenditure is the terms of consumer credit which have been considered to have significant affect on purchases of consumer durables. The less restricted the terms of credit, the greater will be the demand for consumer durables. However, the impact of consumer credit on the volume of consumption expenditure is difficult to measure.

The last but not the least, the sales effort of the producers would affect consumption expenditure. The sales effort through advertisement has a significant effect on the consumption expenditure. Other things remaining the same, the greater the volume of advertising expenditure greater will be the consumption expenditure.

Now, we wish to consider the structural factors affecting consumption. The first important structural factor is income distribution. We know that the marginal propensity to consume of low income people is substantially higher than the marginal propensity to consume of high income people. Hence, when there is redistribution of income from rich income groups to poor income groups, this will increase consumption expenditure in an economy even if the level of income remains unchanged. This is because the loss of consumption of the rich people will be over-compensated by the gain of consumption of the poor since the marginal propensity of the poor is higher than the rich. Since the distribution of income changes slowly, it is unlikely to have a short-run impact in the economy at all.

When considering cross-section studies of consumption expenditure we find that at any given income level there are significant differences between the consumption spending of different families. These differences can be explained at least partly, by demographic factors, such as family size, place of residence, home ownership, stage in the family life cycle and so on. Other things remaining the same, spending of big families must be greater than that of smaller families. Rural families spend less than urban families. Families with young children are likely to spend more than without small children. These demographic factors are unlikely to change in the short-run and hence can be ignored in the short-run analysis. The fiscal policy can also influence the aggregate consumption expenditure. If the government raises more money through taxation, it will reduce the disposable income and hence the consumption expenditure will fall. Similarly, if the government reduces taxes or make more transfer payments, the disposable income will increase and hence the consumption expenditure will also increase. Even if the national income remains unchanged, disposable income may change because of the fiscal operation of the government and, thereby, may change consumption expenditure as well.

The financial policies of the large corporations may also change the aggregate consumption expenditures. The dividend policies of large joint stock companies may increase or decrease income and thereby may change the consumption expenditure. Corporate savings may reduce disposable income of consumers and hence consumption expenditure at any level of national income. Alternatively, if the corporations keep a large fraction of their income in the form of undistributed profits, this may discourage consumption expenditure, or if the corporations give away a large fraction of their incomes in the form of dividend the consumption expenditure may increase.

We can conclude by saying that, there are many subjective, objective and structural factors which may influence consumption expenditure, but most of these factors remain unchanged in the short-run, and hence the short-run aggregate consumption expenditure may be regarded as a function of income. When any of these factors that are assumed to remain constant change, the consumption function will shift as well.

Empirical Support for the Consumption Function

The Keynesian consumption function hypothesis was based neither on any theoretical foundation nor on any statistical study. It is mainly based on intuition. Two types of data may be used to test the validity of Keynesian hypothesis. One is budget studies data and the other is time series data. In the budget studies data we have information on consumption and income of families of different income groups within a year. In the time series data we have information on total consumption and total income for a number of years. Keynes consumption function hypothesis has received support from the different budget studies and time series data. The earlier studies indicated that, the Keynesian consumption function is a good approximation of how consumers behave.

The cross-section budget studies involve taking a sample of households and classifying them according to their income groups. Divide the average level of consumption spending for each income group by the corresponding average level of income give each group's average propensity to consume *(APC)*. It has been found that the *APC* has a marked tendency to fall as we move from lower to higher income groups; also, the *APC* is greater than the *MPC* (Marginal Propensity to Consume) in every case. This is a typical result and supports the 'absolute income' hypothesis.

The study also reveals that households with higher income consume more,which implies that the marginal propensity to consume *(MPC)* is positive. These studies also found that households with higher income save more, which implies that *MPC* < *1*. These data supported Keynes's prediction that, the *MPC* lies between zero and one. In addition, studies also found that, higher-income households save a larger fraction of their income, which confirmed Keynes's proposition that the *APC* falls as income rises.

Other studies examined aggregate time series data on consumption and income for the period between the two World Wars. These datas also supported some of the propositions of Keynesian consumption function. During these years income was usually low and thus, consumption and saving were low, indicating that, the *MPC* lies between zero and one. In addition, during those years of low income, the ratio of consumption to income was high, thus confirming Keynes's second proposition. Finally because the correlation between income and consumption was so high that no other variables appeared to be important for explaining consumption and thus, income appears to be the primary determinant of consumption. Thus, the Keynesian consumption function has been supported by time-series data as well.

Simon Kuznets : The Consumption Puzzle

Short-run time series studies and household data found a relationship between consumption and income similar to the one proposed by Keynes. But studies of long-run time series found that the *APC* did not vary systematically with income. This long-run consumption function has a constant A*PC*, whereas the short-run consumption function has a falling *APC*. The results of this study do not support the 'absolute income' hypothesis as outlined above. Further, the long-run consumption function is found to be proportional as shown in Fig. 12.3.

The 'absolute income' hypothesis appears to explain the cross-section and short-run time series data well, but fails to explain the long-run time series data. One objective of the more recent theories has been to try and reconcile this apparent conflict in the different sets of statistical results.

The Consumption Ratchet

According to Dussenberry, the consumption function is irreversible with respect to the fall in income. This means that the consumption function applicable to the rise in income but inapplicable to the fall in income because, when income rises people become used to the high level of consumption and it becomes difficult to reduce consumption when income falls. For example, suppose that as income of an individual increases by £200, consumption increases by only £140. This phenomenon is known as the "Consumption Ratchet".

The ratchet idea can be explained as follows : During the long-term growth of income, the consumption function shifts in the upward direction. This upward shift normally occur during periods of relatively high income. Such shifts are irreversible during subsequent declines of income. Each shift "takes-off" from a platform provided by the previous peak. This gives the source of the ratchet effect.

The Saving Function

The saving function can be deduced from the consumption function. Saving (S) is defined as the difference between income and consumption, i.e. $S = Y - C = Y - C(Y)$. It means that saving (S) is a function of income, i.e. $S = S(Y)$. The saving function can be known from the consumption function. The average propensity to consume is $\frac{S}{Y}$ and the marginal propensity to consume is $\frac{ds}{dY}$, change in saving when income changes. The saving function has the following characteristics :

(1) Saving is directly related to income, i.e. $\frac{ds}{dY} > 0$. Further, the Marginal Propensity Save (MPS) lies between 0 and 1, i.e. $0 < \frac{ds}{dY} < 1$.

(2) Average Propensity to Save (APS) increases as income increases. This means that MPS is greater than APS. If consumption is a linear function of income, the saving function will also be a linear function of income. If the consumption has a positive intercept with the vertical axis the saving function will have a negative intercept with the vertical axis.

The saving function has four characteristics as the consumption function has four characteristics. The four characteristics of saving functions are given as follows :

(1) Saving is a stable function of income,

(2) The marginal propensity to save lies between zero and one,

(3) The average propensity to save is directly related to income,

(4) The marginal propensity to save remains constant or increases as income increases. The consumption function and the saving function are both linear or non-linear. However, if the consumption function is concave from below, the saving function is convex from below.

By taking the vertical differences between the 45° line and the consumption function we get the saving function as in Fig. 12.2, when $Y = 0$, consumption expenditure is equal to OP, which means that saving is equal to $OP'(-OP)$. When the level of income (Y) is OB, consumption equals income and, hence, the saving is nil. To the left of B saving is negative as income is less than consumption and, to the right of B, income is greater than consumption and, therefore, saving is positive. Thus, we get the saving function $P'Q'$ from the consumption function PQ. The slope of the saving function is the MPS like

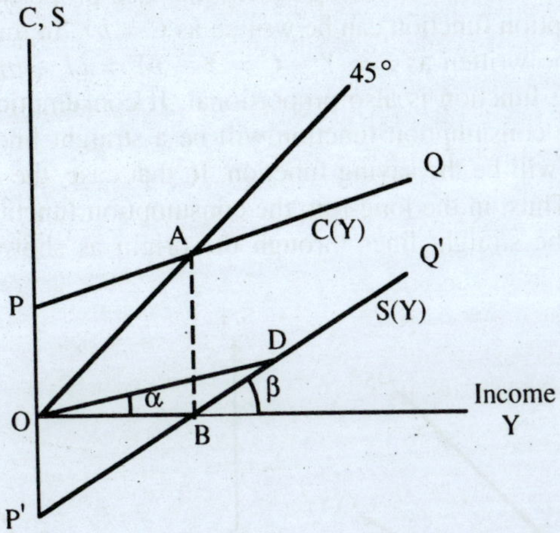

Fig. 12.2 Consumption (C) and Saving (S) Functions together

the slope of the consumption function which is the *MPC*. If the saving function is a straight line, its slope will be the same at all points. The average propensity to save at any point with the origin, for example at point *D* on the saving function, the *APS* is equal to the slope of the line $OD = \tan \alpha$, whereas the *MPS* is equal to $\tan \beta$. Since β is greater than α, $\tan \beta$ is also greater than $\tan \alpha$, i.e. $MPS > APS$. This means that *APS* increases as income increases. When the consumption function is a straight line, its equation can be written as $C = a + bY$, where *a* and *b* are parameters.

Now, $S = Y - C = Y - a - bY = -a + (1 - b)Y$ which means that the saving function is also a straight line with a negative intercept with the vertical axis $-a$ and a slope is equal to $(1 - b)$ which lies between 0 and 1, i.e. $0 < 1 - b < 1$.

Further, that $\frac{ds}{dY} = 1 - b$ and $\frac{S}{Y} = -\frac{a}{Y} + (1 - b)$

$\therefore APS = -\frac{a}{Y} + MPS$; this shows $APS < MPS$

The sum of the *APC* and *APS* is equal to one and also the sum of *MPC* and *MPS* is equal to one. This can be given as follows:

Since, $Y = C + S$, dividing both sides by Y, $1 = \frac{C}{Y} + \frac{S}{Y}$, that is, $APC + APS = 1$. Again, differentiating both sides with respect to Y, we get, $1 = \frac{dc}{dY} + \frac{ds}{dY}$ or $MPC + MPS = 1$.

Thus, if we know one we can get the other. Again, if the consumption function is proportional the saving function is also proportional. The proportional consumption function can be written as $C = bY$. In this case, the saving function can be written as $S = Y - C = Y - bY = (1 - b)Y$. It can be seen that the saving function is also proportional. If consumption is proportional to income, the consumption function will be a straight line passing through the origin. So will be the saving function. In that case, the $APC = MPC$ and $APS = MPS$. Thus, in the long-run, the consumption function and the saving function will be straight lines through the origin as shown in Fig. 12.3.

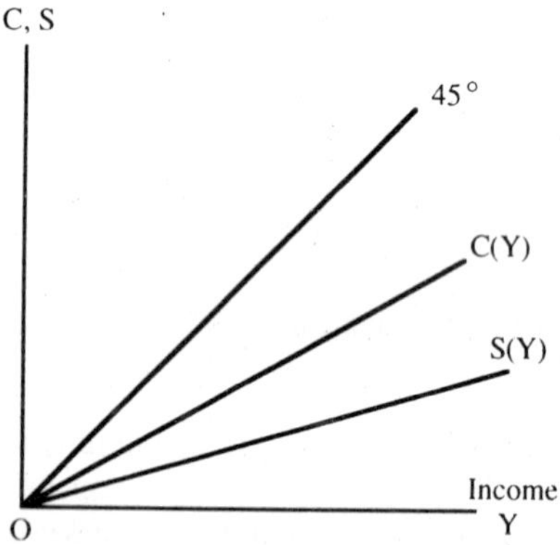

Fig. 12.3 The long-run Consumption and Saving Functions

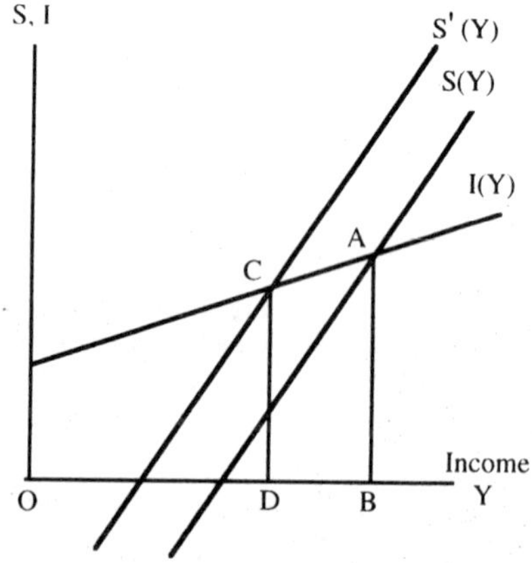

Fig. 12.4 Paradox of Thrift

Paradox of Thrift

The simple prediction that equilibrium national income is decreased when the desire to save rises and increased when the desire to save falls, has been called the paradox of thrift. It is no paradox at all. It is really a simple prediction of a model in which national income is demand-determined. More saving means less spending and, thus, reduces the aggregate demand. Less saving means more spending and this means an increase in aggregate demand.

Let us assume that both investment and saving are functions of income and that the *MPS* is greater than the marginal propensity to invest. The investment function will then intersect the saving function from above. Now we assume that the saving habits have changed and people become more thrifty than before. The result will be more saving at each level of income which means that the saving function will shift to the left and the effect of such a shift on the equilibrium level of income and on the volume of saving can be shown in the figure. In Fig. 12.4, as the saving function shifts to the left from *S(Y)* to *S'(Y)* the volume of saving is reduced from *AB* to *CD*. Thus we get the paradoxical result which can be explained as follows.

Firstly, it can be explained from the logical point of view that, what is true for each individual taken in isolation may not be true for all individuals taken together. To argue that what is true for individual must also be true for the aggregate is fallacious and is known as the fallacy of composition. Thus, it could be true that, when each individual saves a higher percentage of income, total saving may be less.

Secondly, we can also explain the paradox from the economic point of view. We know that the saving is a function of income. We also know that the equilibrium level of income is reduced when there is a leftward shift of the saving function. Thus, when the propensity to save increases, it reduces the level of income from *OB* to *OD*. Since the level of income is reduced, the volume of saving also comes down automatically. Hence, the lower aggregate saving is the result of decrease in income, which is the result of the higher saving propensity.

For example, suppose originally the saving propensity of the people was 0.2 and the equilibrium level of income was 200. The total saving was 40. Now suppose the propensity to save has increased to 0.3. This means that the saving function shifts to the left and the equilibrium level of income fall to 100. At this level of income (100) total saving is 30. Thus, even if the saving propensity increases, total saving decreases — due to the fall in the level of income.

The paradox of thrift is an important factor to consider in an economy. In the Keynesian model we see that, as the saving propensity increases, the equilibrium level of income decreases. It points out that saving is an undesirable element as it lowers the level of income. If saving is undesirable how can we ask the developing countries to save more? Is the paradox of thrift applicable to the developing countries? In the Keynesian model of income determination we assume that the economy is an advanced capitalist economy in depression where substantial unemployment exists, because of lack of effective demand. In such an economy there are idle capital goods which can be used if the effective demand can be increased. The increase in effective demand will increase income and employment. Supply of output in such an economy is highly elastic and demand-determined. But the situation is different in a developing economy. In a developing economy, unemployment is not caused by a deficiency in effective demand. It is a result of the low quantity of capital goods to work with. Employment cannot be increased because of lack of capital goods. Unlike unemployment in a developing economy which cannot be reduced by increasing total spending. Since supply of output is inelastic in a developing economy an increase in spending will only lead to an increase in the price level. In a developing economy, more capital goods should be employed to increase income and employment.

More capital goods can be obtained only through capital formation in a developing economy. Thus, it is only through saving that the level of income and employment can be increased in such an economy. It is clear from this analysis that the same prescriptions are not applicable in different economies where objective conditions are different. While a capital formation approach is needed in a developing economy, a spending approach may be applicable in an advanced economy. This analysis also shows that, the Keynesian theory is inapplicable in a developing economy. Conclusions derived from the Keynesian theory are relevant for a developed economy and not applicable in a developing economy.

It needed to explain how these two consumption functions could be consistent with each other. Franco Modigliani and Milton Friedman each proposed explanations of these seemingly contradictory findings. But before we see how Modigliani and Friedman tried to solve the consumption puzzle, we need to discuss Irving Fisher's contribution to consumption theory. Both Modigliani's life-cycle hypothesis and Friedman's permanent income hypothesis rely on the theory of consumer behaviour proposed by Fisher.

Irving Fisher and Intertemporal Choice

When people decide how much to consume and save, they must consider both the present and the future. The more consumption they enjoy today, the less they will be able to enjoy tomorrow. In making this tradeoff, households must look ahead of their expected future income and to the consumption of goods and services they could afford.

Fisher developed the model with which economists analyze how rational, forward-looking consumers make intertemporal choices — that is, choices

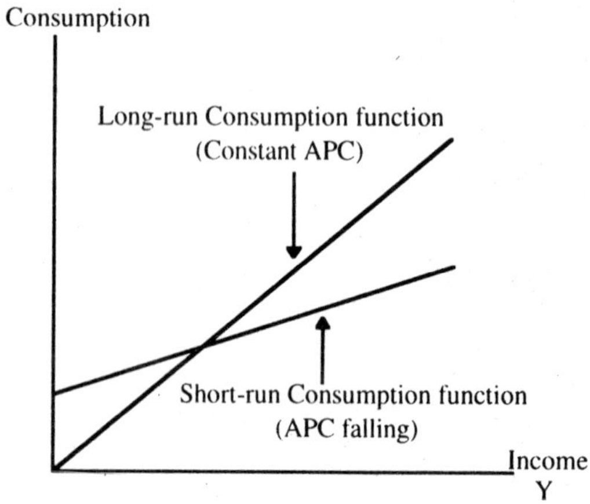

Fig. 12.5 Short-run and Long-run Consumption Function

involving different periods of time as Fig. 12.5 shows. Fisher's model shows the constraints consumers face and how they choose consumption and saving.

The Intertemporal Budget Constraint

Everyone would prefer to increase the quantity of goods they consume. The reason they consume less than they desire is that their consumption is constrained by their income, which is called budget constraint. When they are deciding how much to consume today and how much to consume tomorrow, they face an intertemporal budget constraint. To understand how people decide their level of consumption, we need to examine this constraint.

We examine the decision facing a consumer who lives for two periods. Period one represents the consumer's youth and period two represents the consumer's old age. The consumer earns income of Y_1 and consume C_1 in period one, and earns income of Y_2 and consumes C_2 in period two. Because the consumer has the opportunity to borrow and save, C in any one period can be either greater or less than Y in that period. Consider how the consumer's Y in the two periods constraints C in the two periods.

In period 1, $S_1 = Y_1 - C_1$, where S is saving. In period 2, C equals the accumulated S, including the interest earned on the S, plus period II's Y. That is, $C_2 = (1 + r)S + Y_2$ where r is the interest rate. For example, if $r = 5\%$, then for every pound of S in period 1, the consumer enjoys an extra £1.05 of consumption in period 2. In this two period model, the consumer does not save in the second period.

Two equations still apply if the consumer is borrowing rather than saving in period 1. S represents both S and borrowing. If first period $C_1 < Y_1$, the consumer is saving, and $S > 0$. *If* $C_1 > Y_1$, the consumer is borrowing, and $S < 0$, let us assume that the interest rate for borrowing is the same as the interest rate for saving.

To derive the consumer's budget constraint, combine the equations. Substituting the first equation for S into the second equation we obtain

$$C_2 = (1 + r)(Y_1 - C_1) + Y_2$$

Rearranging the terms we get : $(1 + r)C_1 + C_2 = (1 + r)\,Y_1 + Y_2$.

Now, divide the both sides by $(1 + r)$ we get: $C_1 + \dfrac{C_2}{(1+r)} = Y_1 + \dfrac{Y_2}{(1+r)}$.

This equation relates C in the two periods to Y in the two periods.

The consumer's budget constraint is interpreted easily. If $r = 0$, the budget constraint says that total $C = C_1 + C_2 =$ total $Y = Y_1 + Y_2$. If $r > 0$, future C and future Y are discounted by $(1 + r)$. This discounting arises from the interest earned on savings. Since the consumer earns interest on current Y that is saved, the future Y is worth less than current Y. Similarly, because future C is paid for out of S that have earned interest, future C costs less than current C. The factor $\dfrac{1}{(1+r)}$ is the price of second period C measured in terms of first period C : it is the amount of first period C that the consumer must forgo to obtain one unit of second period C.

The Consumer's Budget Constraint

Fig. 12.6 shows the combinations of first-period and second-period consumption that the consumer can choose. If he chooses points between *A* and *B*, he consumes less than his *Y* in the first-period and saves the rest for the second-period. If he chooses points between *A* and *C*, he consumes more than his *Y* in the first-period and borrows to make up the difference.

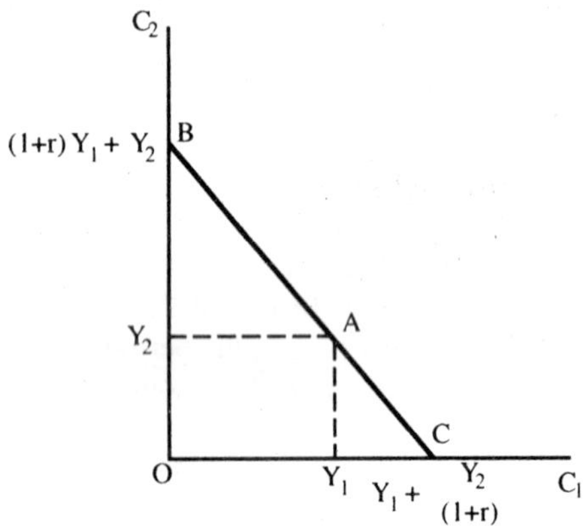

Fig. 12.6 Budget Constraint

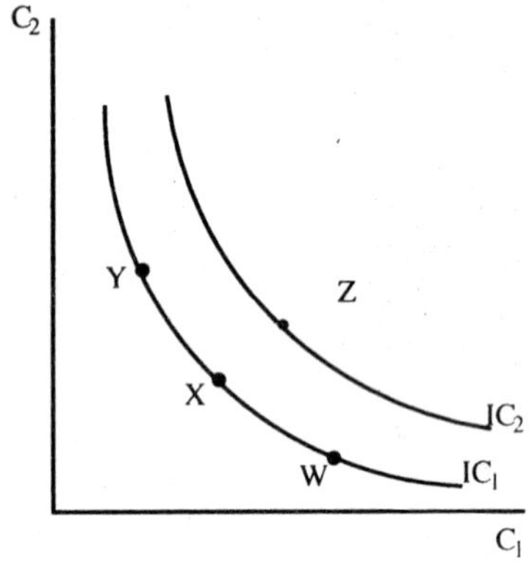

Fig. 12.7 Consumer Preferences

Consumer Preferences

Consumer's preferences regarding consumption in the two periods can be represented by indifference curve *(IC)*. An *IC* shows the combination of two consumptions in the two periods that make the consumer equally happy. Higher *ICs* are preferred to lower ones. Fig.12.7 shows two of many *ICs*. The consumer is equally happy at points *W, X, Y,* but prefers point *Z* to *W, X* or *Y* because *Z* is on a higher *IC*.

Optimisation

Having discussed the consumer's budget constraint and preferences, we can consider the decision about how much to consume. The consumer would like to end up with the best possible combination of consumption in the two periods — that is, on the highest possible *IC*. But the budget

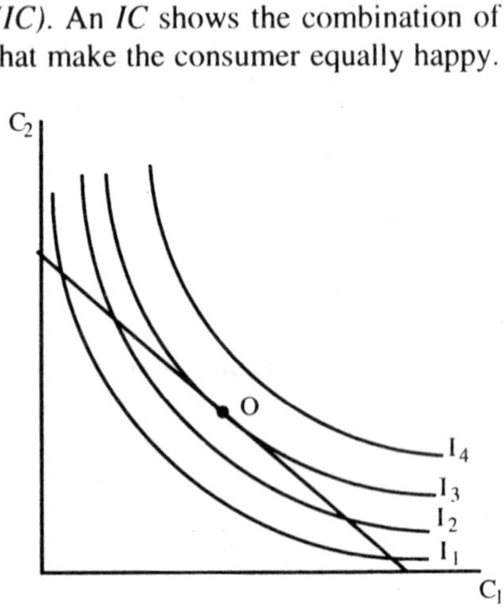

Fig. 12.8 Optimisation of Consumption

constraint requires that the consumer also ends up on or below the budget line, because the budget line measures the total resources available to him.

Fig. 12.8 shows that the consumer achieves the highest level of satisfaction by choosing the point on the budget constraint that is on the highest *IC* (I_3 in Fig. 12.8). At the optimum, *IC* is tangent to the budget constraint where the slope of the *IC* (is the *MRS)* is equal to the slope of the budget line (is $1 + r$). We conclude that, at point *O*, $MRS = 1 + r$. The consumer chooses consumption in the two periods, so that, the $MRS = 1 + r$.

Changes in Income Effect on Consumption

In Fig. 12.9 we see an increase in incime in both periods which shift the budget constraint outward. If consumption in period one and two are both normal goods, this increase in income raises consumption in both periods.

In contrast to Keynes's consumption function, Fisher model says that consumption does not depend primarily on current income. Instead, consumption depends on the resources the consumer expects over his or her lifetime.

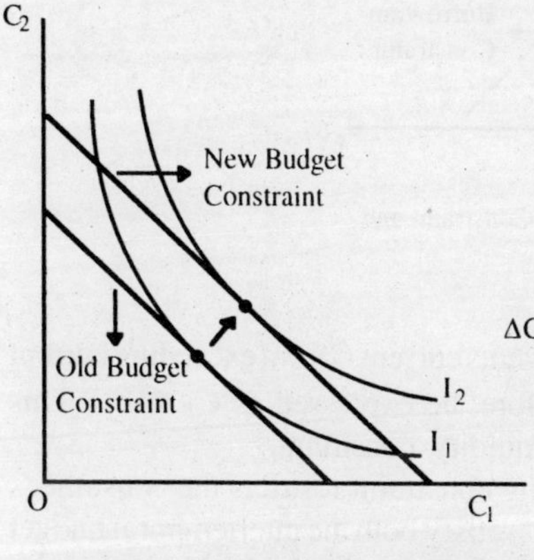

Fig. 12.9 Changes in Income Effect on Consumption

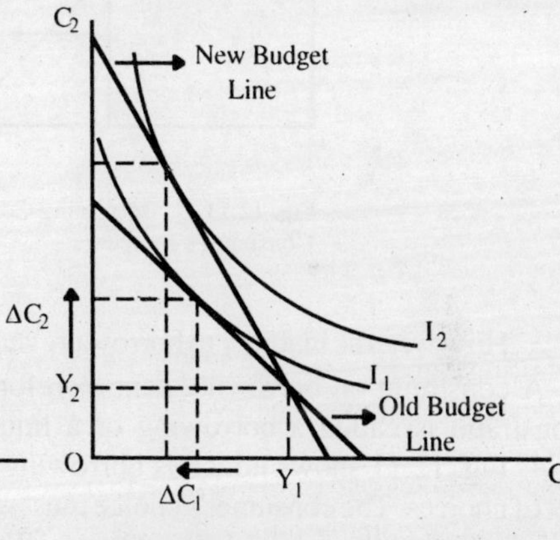

Fig. 12.10 Interest Rate Effect on Consumption

Changes in Real Interest Rate after Consumption

An increase in the interest rate tilts the budget constraint around the point (Y_1, Y_2). In Fig. 12.10 the higher interest rate reduces first-period consumption and raises second-period consumption because of two effects — income effect and substitution effect.

The income effect is the change in consumption that results from the movement to a higher *IC*. The income effect tends to make the consumer choose more consumption in both periods.

The substitution effect means the change in consumption that results from the change in the relative price of consumption in the two periods. Now consumption in period two becomes less expensive relative to consumption in period one when interest rate rises.

Constraints on Borrowing

Fisher's model assumes that the consumer can borrow as well as save. The ability to borrow allows current consumption to exceed current income which means he consumes some of his future income today.

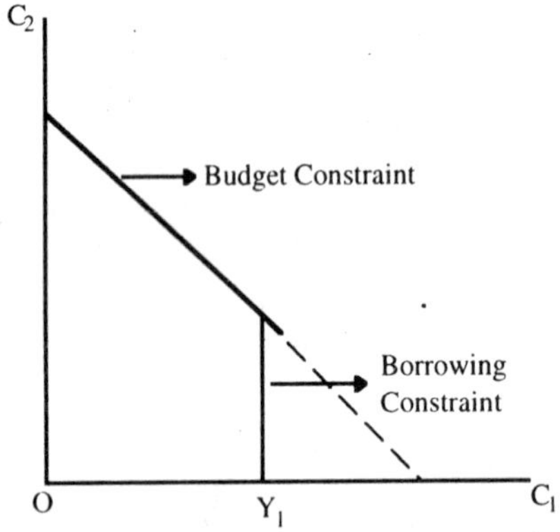

Fig. 12.11 Borrowing Constraint and Consumer's choice

However, the inability to borrow prevents current *C* from exceeding current *Y*. A constraint on borrowing can, therefore, be expressed as $C_I \leq Y_I$. This constraint is called a borrowing or a liquidity constraint.

Fig. 12.11 shows how this borrowing constraint restricts the consumer's set of choices. The consumer's choice must satisfy both the intertemporal budget constraint and the borrowing constraint. The area under the budget constraint represents the combinations of first-period consumption and second-period consumption. That satisfies both constraints.

The Consumer's Optimum with a Borrowing Constraint

When the consumer faces a borrowing constraint, there are two possible situations. In Fig. 12.12(a), the consumer chooses first-period consumption to be less than first-period income, so the borrowing constraint is not binding and does not affect consumption.

In Fig.12(b), the borrowing constraint is binding. The consumer would like to borrow more and chose point *D*. But because borrowing is not allowed, the best available choice is Point *E*. When the borrowing constraint is binding, $C_I = Y_I$. Hence, for those consumers who would like to borrow but cannot,

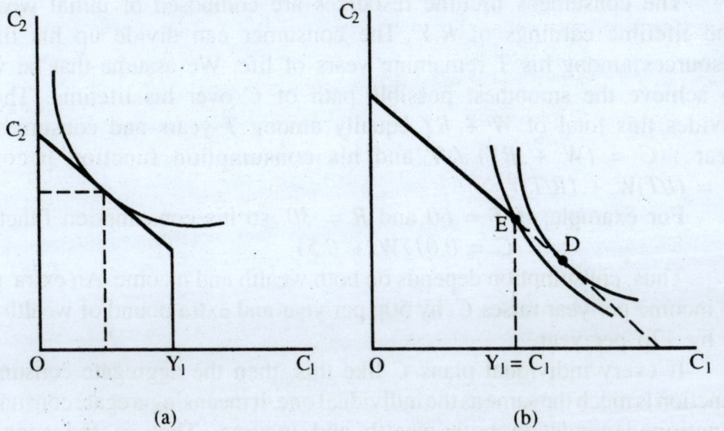

Fig. 12.12 Consumer's optimum with a Borrowing Constraint

consumption depends only on current Y_1. This analysis leads us to absolute income hypothesis, which may be criticised on grounds: (1) for not providing adequate explanation of the different sets of income-consumption data and (2) for not taking into account the influence of wealth and the rate of interest on consumption and so far not being consistent with the micro-economic analysis of consumer behaviour.

Franco Modigliani and the Life-cycle Hypothesis

F. Modigliani and his colaborators Albert Ando and Richard Brumberg wanted to solve the consumption puzzle — that is, to explain the opportunity conflicting pieces of evidence that came to light when Keynes's consumption function was tested. According to Fisher's model, consumption depends on a person's lifetime income. Modigliani emphasized that Y varies systematically over people's lives and that saving allows consumers to move Y from those times in life when Y is high to those times when it is low. This interpretation of consumer behaviour formed the basis for his life-cycle hypothesis.

The Hypothesis

One reason that income varies over a person's life is retirement at about 60, and they expect their incomes to fall when they retire. Yet they do not want a large drop in their standard of living, as measured by consumption. They can maintain consumption provided they save during their working life. Let us see what this motive for saving implies for the consumption function.

Consider a consumer who expects to live another T years, has wealth W, and expects to earn income Y until he retires R years from now. What level of C will the consumer choose if he wishes to maintain a smooth level of C over his life?

The consumer's lifetime resources are composed of initial wealth W and lifetime earnings of $R.Y$. The consumer can divide up his lifetime resources among his T remaining years of life. We assume that he wishes to achieve the smoothest possible path of C over his lifetime. Thus, he divides this total of $W + RY$ equally among T years and consumes each year : $C = (W + RY) / T$ and his consumption function becomes : $C = (I/T)W + (R/T)Y$

For example, if $T = 60$ and $R = 30$, so his consumption function is

$$C = 0.017W + 0.5Y$$

Thus, consumption depends on both wealth and income. An extra pound of income per year raises C by 50p per year and extra pound of wealth raises C by 17p per year.

If every individual plans C like this, then the aggregate consumption function is much the same as the individual one. It means, aggregate consumption function depends on both wealth and income. That is, the economy's consumption function is : $C = \alpha W + \beta Y$, when $\alpha = MPC$ out of wealth and $\beta = mpc$ out of income.

The Life-cycle Consumption Function

The life-cycle model says that, consumption depends on wealth as well as Y. In other words, the intercept of the C Function depends on wealth as Fig. 12.13 shows. This model of consumer behaviour can solve the consumption puzzle. The life-cycle consumption function implies that the average propensity to consume is : $\frac{C}{Y} = \alpha\left(\frac{W}{Y}\right) + \beta$

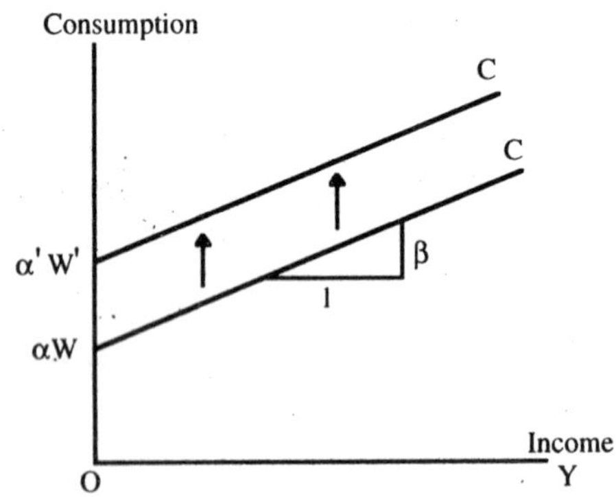

Fig. 12.13 The Life-cycle Consumption Function

We should find that high Y implies a low average propensity to consume *(APC)* when looking over short periods of time. But, over the long period, wealth and income grow together, which implies a constant ratio W/Y and, thus, a constant *APC*. Fig. 12.13 shows, for any given level of wealth, the life-cycle Consumption function looks like the one Keynes suggested. This function holds only in the short-run when wealth is constant. In the long-run, as wealth increases, the Consumption function shifts upward as in Fig. 12.13. This upward shift prevents the *APC* from falling as income increases. Thus, Modigliani reconciled the apparently conflicting studies of the Consumption function.

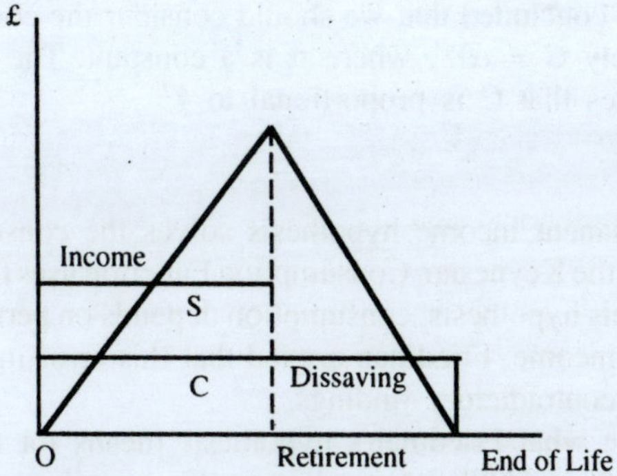

Fig. 12.14 The Life-cycle Model to Predict Saving Behaviour

The life-cycle model makes many other predictions as well. It implies that saving varies over a person's life in a predictable way. If the consumer smooths *C* over his life, he will save and accumulate wealth during his working years and then dis-save and run down his wealth during retirement as Fig. 12.14 shows.

Permanent Income Hypothesis — M. Friedman

Friedman's permanent income hypothesis complements Modigliani's life-cycle hypothesis: both use Fisher's theory of the consumer to argue that *C* should not depend on current *Y* alone. But, unlike the life-cycle hypothesis, which emphasizes that income follows a regular pattern over a person's lifetime, the permanent income hypothesis emphasizes that people experiences random and temporary changes in their income from year to year.

The Hypothesis

Friedman suggested that, current income *Y* as the sum of two components, permanent income Y^P and transitory income Y^T. That is, $Y = Y^P + Y^T$. Permanent income is that income which persists into the future. Transitory income is that, *Y* which does not persist. Alternatively, permanent income is average *Y*, and transitory *Y* is the random deviation from that average.

According to Friedman, consumption should primarily depend on Y^P, because consumers use saving and borrowing to smooth consumption in response to transitory changes in *Y*. For example, if a person received a permanent rise of £10,000, his consumption would rise by about as much. Yet if a person won £10,000 in a lottery, he would not consume it all in one year. Instead, he would spread the extra *C* over the rest of his life. Assuming an interest rate of zero and a remaining lifespan of 50 years, *C* would rise by only £200 per year in response to the £10,000 lottery. Thus, consumers spend their permanent *Y*, but they save most of their transitory *Y*.

Friedman concluded that we should consider the consumption function as approximately $C = \alpha Y^P$, where α is a constant. The permanent income hypothesis states that C is proportional to Y^P.

Implications

The permanent income hypothesis solves the consumption puzzle by suggesting that the Keynesian Consumption Function uses the wrong variables. According to this hypothesis, consumption depends on permanent income and not on current income. Friedman argued that this error-in-variables explains the seemingly contradictory findings.

Let us see what Friedman's hypothesis means for the *APC*.

$APC = C/Y = \alpha Y^P/Y$. According to this hypothesis, the *APC* depends on the ratio of permanent income to current income. When current *Y* temporarily rises above permanent *Y*, the *APC* temporarily falls; when current *Y* temporarily falls below Y^P, the *APC* temporarily rises.

Friedman also argued that the household data reflect a combination of permanent and transitory income. Households with high permanent income would have proportionately higher *C*. If all variables in current income came from the permanent component, one would not observe differences in the *APC* across households. If, however, some of the variation in income comes from the transitory component, households with high transitory *Y* would not have higher consumption. Thus, researchers would find that high-income households have, on average, lower *APC*.

Similarly, consider the time-series studies. Friedman reasoned that year-to-year fluctuations in *Y* are dominated by transitory *Y*. Thus, years of high *Y* should be years of low *APC*. But, over long periods of time, the variation in *Y* comes from the permanent components. Hence, in the long time-series, one should observe a constant *APC*.

Rational Expectation and Consumption

The permanent income hypothesis is based on Fisher's model which builds on the idea that, forward-looking consumers base their consumption decisions not only on their current income but also on the future expected income. Thus, the permanent income hypothesis highlights that consumption depends on people's expectations.

Recent studies have combined this view with the assumption of rational expectations which states that people use all available information to make optimal forecasts about the future. We know that this assumption has potentially profound implications for the costs of stopping inflation and also have profound implications for consumption.

Robert Hall was the first economist to derive the implications of rational expectations for consumption. He demonstrated that, if the permanent income hypothesis is correct, and if consumers have rational expectations, then changes in consumption over time would be unpredictable. When changes in a variable are unpredictable, the variable is said to follow a random walk. According to Hall, the combination of the permanent income hypothesis and rational expectations implies that consumption follows a random walk.

Hall argued as follows. According to the permanent income hypothesis, consumers face fluctuating income and try to smooth their consumption over time. At a particular moment, consumers choose *C* based on their current expectations of their lifetime incomes. Over time, they change their consumption because they receive information which causes them to review their expectations. For example, changes in consumption reflect "surprises" about lifetime income. If consumers are optimally using all available information, then these surprises should be unpredictable. Thus, changes in their consumption should be unpredictable as well.

The evidence shows that the random-walk theorem does not describe the real world situation exactly. That is, changes in aggregate *C* are somewhat predictable. Yet, because the degree of predictability is small, some economists consider the random-walk theorem as a good approximation to reality.

The rational expectations approach to consumption has an implication not only for forecasting but also for the analysis of economic policies. If consumers obey the permanent income hypothesis and have rational expectations, then only unexpected policy changes influence consumption. These policy changes take effect when they change expectations.

If the consumers have rational expectations, policy-makers influence the economy not only through their actions but also through the public's expectation of their actions. However, expectations cannot be observed directly. Thus, it is difficult to know how and when changes in fiscal policy alter *AD*.

Conclusion

In the work of Keynes, Fisher, Modigliani and Friedman, we have seen a progression of views on consumer behaviours. Keynes proposed that *C* depends largely on current *Y*. Since then, economists have argued that consumers face an intertemporal decision. Consumers look ahead to their future resources and needs, implying a more complex Consumption function, than the one proposed by Keynes. Keynes suggested a Consumption function of the form : $C = f\ (current\ \ Y)$.

Recent work suggests instead that $C = f$ *(Current Y, Wealth, Expected Future Y, Interest Rates).*

Alternatively, current Y is only one determinant of aggregate C.

Economists continue to debate the relative importance of these determinants of C. There remains disagreement on the effect of interest rates and the prevalence of borrowing constraints. One reason economists sometimes disagree about the effects of economic policy is that they are assuming different Consumption functions.

Exercise

1. Explain why the long-run marginal propensity to consume is less than the short-run one.
2. How can you test the hypothesis that marginal propensity to consume is equal to the average propensity to consume?
3. Table 1 shows the results of a Cross-Section Budget Study :

Income Group £ Per Week	Average Income £ Per Week	Consumption £ Per Week
Under 10	7.89	9.73
10 - 19.99	14.97	16.46
20 - 29.99	25.01	23.96
30 - 39.99	34.97	29.82
40 - 49.99	44.97	35.90
50 - 59.99	54.69	42.12
60 - 79.99	68.14	48.31
80 and over	112.26	70.92

Calculate the average and marginal propensity to consume for each income group and comment on the significance of your results for the theories of consumption outlined in this chapter.

4. Consider the view that the link between aggregate consumption and current measured income is a tenuous one.
5. Derive the consumption function of an individual who inherits wealth from his parents and bequeaths some wealth for his children. Write down his utility function and budget constraint explicitly and indicate the nature of the derived consumption function.
6. How can we statistically test the hypothesis that $MPC = APC$?

13 INVESTMENT DEMAND

We study investment to better understand fluctuations in the economy's output. We have seen simple investment function relating investment to the real interest rate: $I = I(r)$. That function states that, an increase in the real interest rate reduces investment. We now want to see more closely the theory behind this investment function.

There are three types of investment spending. Business fixed investment includes the plant and machine that business buy to use in production. Inventory investment includes those goods that businesses put aside in stores, including inputs, finished goods and work-in-progress. Residential investment includes the new housing that people buy to live in and that landlords buy to rent out.

Here we build models of each type of investment to explain these fluctuations. As we develop the models, it is useful to keep in mind the following questions :

Why is investment negatively related to the interest rate?

What causes the investment function to shift?

Why does investment rise during booms and fall during recessions?

At the end of our discussion, we return to these questions and summarize the answers that the model offer.

Business Fixed Investment

The standard model is called the neo-classical model of investment. This model examines the benefits and costs to forms of owing capital goods. The model shows how the level of investments — the addition to capital stock — is related to the marginal product of capital *(MP_K)*, the interest rate, and the tax rules affecting firms.

Let us imagine that, there are two kinds of firms in the economy. Production firms produce goods and services using capital that they rent. Rental firms make all the investments in the economy; they buy capital and rent it out to the production firms. However, most firms in an economy perform both functions : they produce goods and services and they invest in capital for future production. For analytical purpose, it is instructive to separate these two activities by imagining that they take place in different firms.

The Rental Price of Capital

Let us first consider the typical production firm which decides how much capital to rent by comparing the cost and benefit of each unit of capital. The firm rents capital at a rental rate R and sells its output at a price P; the real cost of a unit of capital to the production firm is R/P. The real benefit of a unit of capital is the MP_K. The MP_K declines as the amount of capital rises: the more capital the firm has, the less an additional unit of capital will add to its production. To maximize profit, the firm rent capital until the MP_K falls to equal the real rental price.

Fig. 13.1 shows the equilibrium in the rental market for capital. Thus, the MP_K determines the demand curve. The demand curve slopes downward

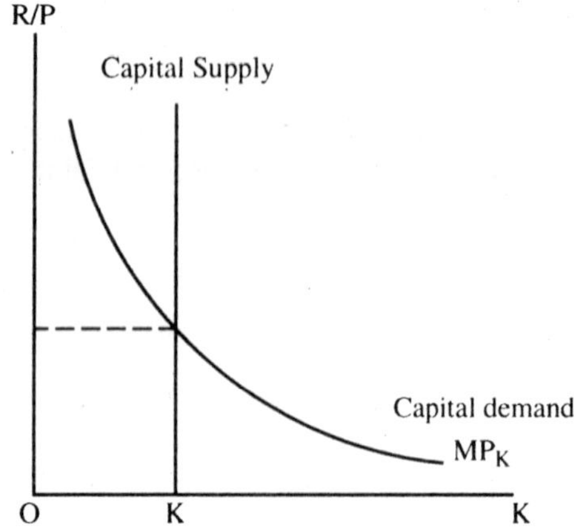

Fig. 13.1 The Equilibrium Price of Capital

because the MP_K is low when the level of capital is high. At a particular point, the amount of capital in the economy is fixed, so the supply curve is vertical. The real rental price of capital adjusts to equilibrate supply and demand.

To see what variables influence the equilibrium rental price, we need to consider a particular production function. We consider the Cobb-Douglas Production Function. A Cobb-Douglas Production Function is

$Y = AK^{\alpha}L^{1-\alpha}$. where Y is output, K capital, L labour, A a parameter measuring the level of technology, and α a parameter between zero and one that measures capital's share of output. The MP_K for the Cobb-Douglas Production Function is $MP_K = \alpha A\ (L/K)^{1-\alpha}$.

This equation identifies the variables that determine the real rental price. It shows the following:

(1) The lower the stock of capital, the higher the real rental price of capital.

(2) The greater the amount of labour employed, the higher the real rental price of capital.

(3) The better the technology, the higher the real rental price of capital. Events that reduce the capital stock, or raise employment or improve the technology raise the equilibrium real rental price of capital.

The Cost of Capital

Let us consider the rental firms. These firms buy capital goods and rent them out. Since we want to explain the investments made by the rental firms, we begin by considering the cost and benefit of owning capital.

The benefit of owning capital is the revenue from renting it to the production firms. It receives the real rental price of capital, R/P, for each unit of capital it owns and rents out.

The cost of owning capital is $iP_k - \Delta P_K + \delta P_K = P_K (i - \Delta P_K/P_K + \delta)$ The cost of capital depends on the price of capital, the interest rate, the rate at which capital prices are changing, and the depression rate.

For example, consider the cost of capital to a car-rental company. The company buys cars at £10,000 each and rents them out to other businesses. The company faces an interest $i = 10\%$ per year, so the interest cost is £1,000(iP_K) per year for each car. Car prices are rising at 6% per year, so the firm gets a capital gain ΔP_K = £600 per year. Cars depreciate at 20% per year, so the loss due to wear and tear δP_K = £2,000 per year. Thus, the company's cost of capital is : Cost of Capital = £1,000 – £600 + £2,000 = £2,400.

The cost of the car-rental company of keeping a car in its capital stock is £2,400 per year.

We assume that, the price of capital goods rises with the prices of other goods. In this case, $\Delta P_K/P_K$ equals the over all rate of inflation Π. Because, $i - \Pi = r$, we can write the cost of capital as :

Cost of Capital = $P_K\ (r + \delta)$

This equation states that, the cost of capital depends on the price of capital, the real interest rate, and the depreciation rate.

Finally, we wish to express the cost of capital relative to other goods in the economy. The real cost of capital is

Real Cost of Capital = $(P_k/P)(r + \delta)$

This equation states that, the real cost of capital depends on the relative price of a capital good P_k/P , the real interest rate r, and the depreciation rate δ.

The Determinants of Investment

Now to consider a firm's decision about capital stock. For each unit of capital, it earns real revenue R/P and bears the real cost $(P_k/P)(r + \delta)$. The real profit per unit of capital is = Revenue – Cost = $R/P - (P_k/P)(r + \delta)$. Since the real rental price in equilibrium equals the MP_K, we can write the profit rate as :

$$\text{Profit Rate} = MP_K - (P_k/P)(r + \delta).$$

The firm makes a profit if the $MP_K >$ Capital Cost. It incurs a loss if the $MP_K <$ Capital Cost.

Let us see the economic incentive that lie behind the firm's investment decision. The firm's decision regarding its capital stock depends on whether owning capital is profitable. The change in the stock of capital (net investment) depends on the difference between the MP_K and the cost of capital. If the $MP_K >$ the cost of capital, firms find it profitable to add to their capital stock. If the MP_K < the cost of capital, they allow their capital to depreciate.

We can also see that, the separation of economic activity between production and rental firms is not necessary for our conclusion regarding investment. The production firm adds to the capital stock if the $MP_K >$ the Capital stock. Thus, we can write $\therefore$ $\Delta K = I_n[MP_K - (P_k/P)(r + \delta)]$ where I_n is the function showing how much net investment responds to the incentive to invest.

We can now derive the investment function. Total investment is the sum of net investment and the replacement investment. The investment function is : $I = I_n\ [MP_K - (P_K/P)(r + \delta)] + \delta_K$. Fixed investment depends on the MP_K, the cost of capital, and the amount of depreciation.

This model shows why investment depends on the interest rate. An increase in the real interest rate raises the cost of capital and reduces the amount of profit from owing capital and incentive to accumulate more capital and vice versa. Thus, the investment schedule relating investment to interest rate slopes downward, as in Fig. 13.2. The model also shows what causes the investment schedule to shift. Any event that increases the MP_K raises the profitability of investment and causes the investment schedule to shift outward as in Fig. 13.2 from $I_1(r)$ to $I_2(r)$. For example, a technological innovation that increases the production function parameter A raises the MP_K and, for any given interest rate, raises the accumulation of capital.

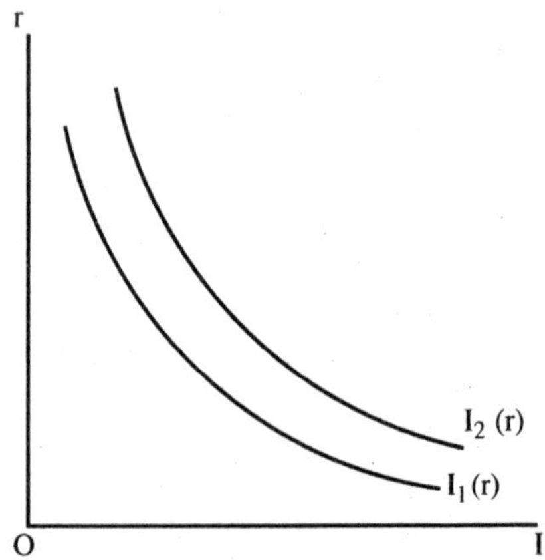

Fig. 13.2 Investment is a Function of Interest Rate

Finally, consider what happens as this adjustment of the capital stock continues over time. If the $MP_K >$ the cost of capital, the capital stock will rise and the MP_K will fall. If the $MP_K <$ the cost of capital, the capital stock will fall and the MP_K will rise. Eventually, as the capital stock adjusts, the MP_K approaches the cost of capital. When the capital stock reaches a steady-state level, we can write $MP_K = (P_K/P)(r + \delta)$. Thus, in the long-run, the MP_K = the cost of capital. The speed of adjustment towards the steady-state depends on how quickly firms adjust their capital stock, which in turn depends on how costly it is to build, deliver and instal new capital.

Taxes and Investment

The tax laws influence firm's incentives to accumulate capital. Sometimes policymakers change the tax laws in order to shift the investment function and influence *AD*. Here we consider some of the most important provisions of corporate taxation.

The corporate income-tax is a tax on corporate profits. Its effect on investment depends on how the law defines "profit" for the purpose of taxation. Suppose, first, that the law defined profit as we did above – *R/P* of capital minus the cost of capital. In this case, even though firms would be sharing a fraction of their profits with the government, it would be rational for them to invest if the R/*P* > the cost of capital, and to disinvest if the *R/P* < the cost of capital. A tax on profit, measured in this way,would not alter investment incentives.

Yet the corporate income-tax does affect investment decisions. There are many differences between the law's definition of profit and our difinition. One major difference is the treatment of depreciation. Our definition of profit deducts the current value of depreciation as a cost which considers depreciation on how much it would cost today to replace worn out capital. By contrast, under the corporate tax laws, firms deduce depreciation using historical cost. That is, the depreciation deduction is based on the price of the capital when it was originally purchased. In periods of inflation, replacement cost is greater than historical cost, so the corporate tax tends to understate the cost of depreciation and overstate profit. As a result, the tax law sees a profit and levies a tax even when economic profit is zero, which makes owning capital less attractive. Thus, economists believe that, the corporate income-tax discourages investment.

The investment tax credit is a tax provision that encourages the accumulation of capital. This tax credit reduces a firm's taxes by a certain amount for each pound spend on capital goods which reduces the effective purchase price of a unit of capital P_K. Thus, the investment tax credit reduces the cost of capital and increases investment and, therefore, stimulate investment.

The Stock Market and Tobin's *q*

There is a link between fluctuations in investment and fluctuations in the stock market. The stock market is the market in which shares are traded. Stock prices reflect the incentives to invest.

James Tobin proposed that, firms base their investment decisions on the following ratio, which is called Tobin's q :

$$q = \frac{\textit{Market Value of Installed Capital}}{\textit{Replacement Cost of Installed Capital}}$$

The numerator is the value of the economy's capital as determined by the stock market. The denominator is the price of the capital if it were purchased today.

Tobin argued that, net investment should depend on the value of q. If $q > 1$, then the stock market values installed capital at more than its replacement cost. In this case, managers can raise the market value of their firm's stock by buying more capital. Conversely, if $q < 1$, the stock market values capital at less than its replacement cost and hence managers will not replace capital.

The neoclassical model and q theory of investment are closely related. Since Tobin's q depends on current and future expected profits from installed capital. If the $MP_K >$ the cost of capital, then installed capital is earning profits. These profits make the rental firms desirable to own, which raises the market value of these firm's stock, implying a high value of q. Similarly, if the $MP_K <$ the cost of capital, then installed capital is incurring losses, implying a low market value and a low value of q.

The advantage of Tobin's q as a measure of the incentive to invest is that it reflects the current profitability and the expected future profitability. Tobin's q theory of investment emphasizes that, investment decisions depend not only on current economic policies, but also on policies expected to prevail in the future.

Tobin's q theory provides a way to interpret the role of the stock market in the economy. Suppose we observe a fall in stock prices. Since the replacement cost of capital is fairly stable, a fall in the stock market usually implies a fall in Tobin's q . A fall in q reflects investors' pessimism about the current or future profitability and hence a fall in investment, which could lower *AD*. Thus, q theory gives a reason to expect fluctuations in the stock market to be closely lied to fluctuations in output and employment.

Financing Constraints

When a firm wants to invest in new capital, it often raises the necessary funds in financial markets. This financing may take several forms—obtaining loans from banks, selling bonds to the public or selling shares on the stock market. The neoclassical model assumes that, if a firm is willing to pay the cost of capital, the financial market will make the funds available.

Yet firms face financial constraints which can prevent firms from undertaking profitable investments. Financial constraints influence the investment behaviour of firms just as borrowing constraints influence the consumption behaviour of households. Borrowing constraints cause households to determine their consumption on the basis of current rather than permanent Y, financing constraints cause firms to determine their investment on the basis of their current cash flow rather than expected profitability.

Residential Investment

We consider here the determinants of residential investment. We begin by presenting a simple model of the household market.

The Stock Equilibrium and the Flow Supply

There are two aspects of the model. First, the market for the existing stock of houses determines the equilibrium housing price. Second, the price of houses determines the flow of residential investment.

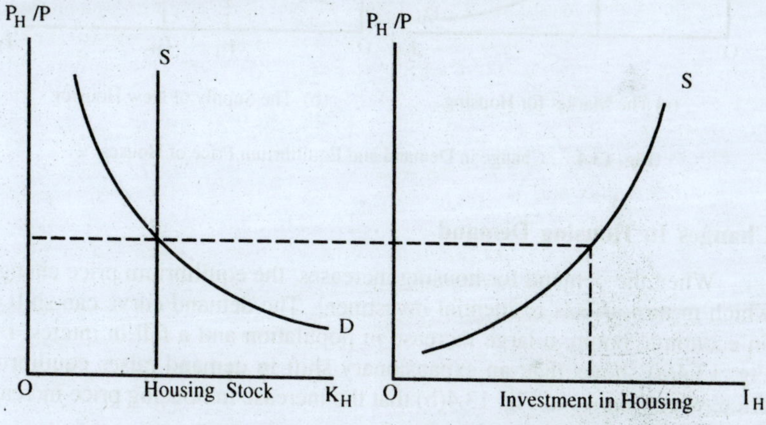

(a) The Market for Housing (b) The Supply of New Housing

Fig. 13.3 The Stock Equilibrium and Supply of Houses

Fig. 13.3(a) shows the relative price of housing P_H/P is determined by the demand and supply of the existing stock of houses. The relative price then determines the flow of new housing that firms build.

At any point of time, the supply of houses is fixed as in Fig. 13.3(a). This is shown by a vertical supply curve. The demand curve for houses slopes downward. The price of housing adjusts to equilibrate supply and demand.

Fig. 13.3(b) shows that, the relative price of housing determines the supply of new houses. The costs depend on the overall price level P, and their revenue depends on the price of houses P_H. The higher the relative price of housing, the greater the incentive to build houses, and the more houses are built. Thus, the flow of houses depends on the equilibrium price set in the market for existing houses. The relative price play the same role for residential investment as Tobin's q does for business fixed investment.

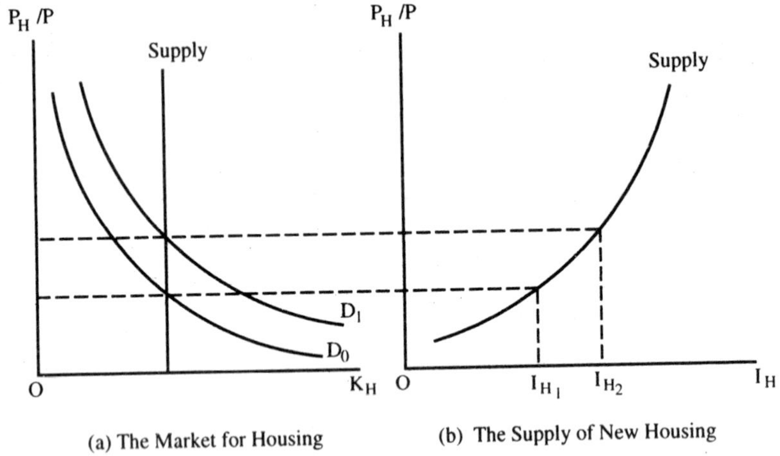

Fig. 13.4 Change in Demand and Equilibrium Price of Houses

Changes In Housing Demand

When the demand for housing increases, the equilibrium price changes, which in turn affects residential investment. The demand curve can shift for an economic boom, a large increase in population and a fall in interest rate. Fig. 13.4(a) shows that, an expansionary shift in demand raises equilibrium price, which shows in Fig. 13.4(b) that the increase in housing price increases residential investment.

The Tax Treatment Of Housing

The tax laws affect the accumulation of fixed business investment, so do they affect the accumulation of residential investment. However, their effects are opposite. Instead of discouraging investment, as the corporate income tax does for business, the personal incom- tax encourages households to invest in housing.

A house-owner is a landlord with a special tax treatment. He does not require to pay tax on the imputed rent, yet he is allowed to deduct mortgage interest up to a certain amount of mortgage (£50,000).

The size of this subsidy to house-ownership depends on the rate of inflation. The reason is that, the tax law allows house-owners to deduct their nominal interest payments. Since the nominal interest rate on mortgage rises when inflation rises, the value of the subsidy is higher at higher rate of inflation.

Some economists have criticized the tax treatment of house-ownership, because of this, they believe that, there are too much investment in housing.

Inventory Investment

Inventory investment is one of the smallest components of spending, yet its remarkable volatility makes it important.

Reasons for Holding Inventories

Before presenting a model to explain fluctuations in inventory investment, we must discuss the motives for holding inventories.

One motive for holding inventories is to smooth the level of production over time. Consider a firm that experiences temporary booms and busts in sales. Rather than adjusting production to match the fluctuations in sales, it may be cheaper to produce goods at a steady rate, when sales are low, inventory accumulates, when sales are high, inventory decumulates. This motive for holding inventories is called 'production smoothing'.

A second motive for holding inventories is that they allow a firm to operate more efficiently. For example, retail firms can sell merchandise more efficiently if they have goods on hand to show to customers. Manufacturing firms keep inventories of spare parts in order to reduce the time that, the assembly line is shut-down when a machine breaks. Thus, we can view inventories as a factor of production: the larger the stock of inventories a firm holds, the more output it can produce.

The third reason for holding inventories is to avoid running out of goods when sales are unexpectedly high. Firms often have to make production decisions before knowing how much customers demand would be. If demand exceeds production and there are no inventories, the goods will be out of stock for a period, and the firm will lose sales and profit. Inventories can prevent this from happening. This motive for holding inventories is called stock-out avoidance.

Lastly, inventories are often dictated by the production process. Many goods require a number of steps in production and, thus, take time to produce. When a product is only partly completed, its components are counted as part of a firm's inventory. These inventories are called 'work-in-progress'.

The Acceleration Model of Inventories

There are many motives for holding inventories, and there are many models of inventory investment. One simple model that, explains the data well is the accelerator model which is applied to all types of investment. Here we apply it to the type for which it works best i.e.inventory investment.

Third model assumes that firms hold a stock of inventories, that is proportional to the firm's level of output. There are various reasons for this assumption, when output is high, firms need more material and supplies on hand, and they have more goods in the process of production; when the economy is booming, retail firms want to have more merchandise on the shelves to show customers. This assumption means if N is the stock of inventories and

Y output, then

$N = \beta Y$ where β is a parameter reflecting how much inventory firms wish to hold as a portion of output.

Inventory investment I is the change in the stock of inventories ΔN. Thus, $I = \Delta N = \beta \Delta Y$.

The accelerator model predicts that, inventory will be proportional to the change in output. When output rises, firms want to hold more inventories, so they invest in them. When output falls, firms want to hold less inventories, so they allow their inventories to run down.

How the model earned its name? Since the variable Y is the rate at which firms are producing goods, ΔY is the acceleration of production. The model tells that, inventory investment depends on whether the economy is speeding up or slowing down.

Inventories and the Real Interest Rate

Inventory investment also depends on the real interest rate. When a firm holds a good in inventory and sells it tomorrow it gives up the interest it could have earned between today and tomorrow. Thus, the real interest rate measures the opportunity cost of holding inventories.

When the real interest rate rises, holding inventories becomes more expensive, so firms try to reduce their stock. Thus, an increase in the real interest rate depresses inventory investment.

Conclusion

The purpose here has been to examine the determinants of investment. Out of the various models of investment, three themes arise.

First, we have seen that, investment spending are inversely related to the real interest rate. A higher interest rate rises the cost of capital to firms, raises the cost of borrowing to home buyers and also raises the cost of holding inventories. Thus, the models developed here justify the investment function discussed.

Second, we have seen what causes the investment function to shift. An improvement in technology raises the MP_K and thus, raises business fixed investment. An increase in the population raises the demand for housing and thus residential investment. Importantly, various economic policies, such as, changes in the investment tax credit and the corporate incom- tax, alter the incentives to invest and thus, shift the investment function.

Third, we have seen why investment is so volatile over the business cycle : investment spending depends on the output of the economy and on the interest rate. In the neoclassical model of business fixed investment, high employment increases the MP_K and the incentive to invest. Higher Y also raises the demand for houses, which increases house prices and residential investment. Higher output raises the stock of inventories firms wish to hold, stimulating inventory investment. The models predict that, an economic boom should stimulate investment, and a recession should depress it. Now we wish to discuss other theories of investment demand.

Investment Demand

Investment spending is a very important topic in macroeconomics for two reasons. First, changes in investment accounts for fluctuation of *GDP* movement in the business cycle. Second, it determines the rate at which the economy adds to its stock of capital, and thus, helps to determine the economy's long-run growth and productivity. Faster growing economies generally invest a higher proportion of their GDPs than slower growing economies.

Investment often refers to buying financial and physical assets. In macroeconomics, investment is a flow of spending that adds to the physical stock of capital. Investment spending may be disaggregated into three categories. The first is business fixed investment. The second category is residential investment. And the third is inventory investment.

Investment may be either induced a autonomous. Investment that is induced by changes in the level of income or changes in the interest rate is known as induced investment. Autonomous investment is that type of investment, which is independent of changes in the level of income or the interest rate. Shift in autonomous investment is influenced by factors other than rate of interest or level of income, such as, innovation, public policy, size and composition of population, etc. In the simple Keynesian model, investment is assumed to be autonomous.

Induced investment takes place either due to change in the level of income or due to change in the rate of interest. If investment is a function of the level of income then it can bewritten as $I = I(Y)$. The ratio I/Y will be called the average propensity to invest and dI/dY is called the marginal propensity to invest. We can combine autonomous and induced investment in a single function. If investment function is written as $I = g + hY$ where g and h are constants. Here g represents autonomous investment hY is induced investment. Here g is independent of the level of income, for even when $Y = 0$, $I = g$. The part hY depends on income and, hence, it is induced investment.

Marginal Efficiency of Capital

In the Keynesian theory, investment expenditure is assumed to be a function of interest rate. The Keynesian theory of investment is known as the marginal efficiency of investment theory *(MEI)*. Before considering the marginal efficiency of investment theory, let us consider first the relation between the stock of capital and the flow of investment in an economy. Investment is an addition to the stock of capital which is measured at any point of time while investment is measured over a period of time. For example, if the capital stock in the beginning of a year is K_1 and if it is equal to K_2

at the end of the year, then $(K_2 - K_1)$ is the volume of investment during this year. If capital stock remains unchanged there is zero investment, if it increases, there will be positive investment and if decreases there will be dis-investment, whether an investment is taking place or not depends on the growth of capital stock. The capital stock can grow, if net investment takes place. Since capital is a factor of production, it will be employed in such a manner as to maximise profit.

There is an optimum amount of capital stock that maximises profit. For example, if the actual capital stock of a firm is less than the optimum, the firm is not in equilibrium with respect to its stock of capital. In such a situation, firm can increase profit by adding to its capital stock, so that, actual capital becomes equal to its optimum capital. In this case investment will take place. Similarly, there will be disinvestment if the actual capital is greater than the optimum capital. Thus, it is clear that investment will take place only when the firm is not in equilibrium. If the actual stock of capital is equal to the optimum stock of capital the firm is in equilibrium and there will be no further investment. This analysis can be generalised for the whole economy. For the economy as a whole we can get the volume of actual and an optimum stock of capital. Investment will take place if the actual stock of capital is less than the optimum stock of the economy. The optimum stock of capital is that stock which maximises total profit. To maximise profit, a firm employs any factor up to the point where marginal cost is equal to the marginal revenue product or marginal revenue product is equal to the price of that factor. However, it is difficult to apply this rule for any durable capital assets which remains productive for a number of periods and provides a series of yields over its life time. Hence it is difficult to determine the marginal productivity of the durable capital asset. Even if we can determine the marginal productivity of capital, another problem remains: whether we should take the market rate of interest as the price of capital or the supply price of capital as the price of capital. These problems can be resolved with the help of the marginal efficiency of capital theory, which helps to determine the optimum capital stock. The marginal efficiency of capital is the value of i for which the following equation is satisfied, $C = \frac{Y_1}{(1+i)} + \frac{Y_2}{(1+i)^2} + \ldots\ldots\ldots + \frac{Y_n}{(1+i)^n}$, where $Y_1, Y_2 \ldots\ldots Y_n$ are yield of capital in various years and C is the supply price of the machine. The marginal efficiency of capital is defined as that rate of discount for which the present value of the series of returns obtainaible from the machine during its lifetime is equal to its supply price. The prospective yields $Y_1, Y_2 \ldots\ldots Y_n$ and the supply price C are taken as given. Thus, we have only one equation and one unknown , i , which can be determined from the above equation.

We have one problem in solving the above equation. The equation has n roots as it is an *nth*degree equation. We can thus get n values of i, which one should be taken as the marginal efficiency of capital ? Moreover, what is the guarantee that, there will be at least one real value of i ? However, we can show that, if we assume (a) $Y_1, Y_2 ......Y_n$, $C \geq 0$ and (b) $i \geq -1$, then there exists at least one real value of i . This can be given as follows:

Let, $V = \frac{Y_1}{(1+i)} + \frac{Y_2}{(1+i)^2} + ... + \frac{Y_n}{(1+i)^n}$ where $Y_1, Y_2 ......Y_n$ are given and constants.

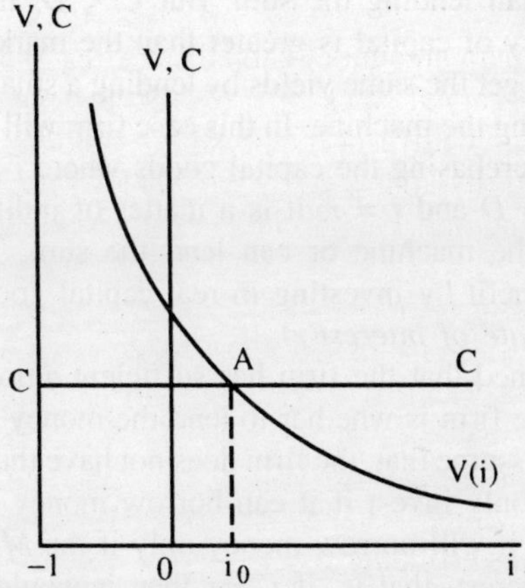

Fig. 13.5 Marginal Efficiency of Capital

Hence the value of V will depend on the value of i, *i.e.*, $V = V(i)$. Further, if $i \rightarrow$, $V \rightarrow 0$ or if, $i \rightarrow -1$, $V \rightarrow \infty$. Thus, V varies inversely with i. As i increases V decreases and vice versa. Therefore, the $V(i)$ function will be downward sloping. This is shown in Fig. 13.5.

$V(i)$ function is asymptotic. Since C is given and independent of i it is represented by a horizontal straight line. At point A, where $V = C$, the *MEC* is determined. Thus, we can get at least one real value of i for which $V = C$. The equation

$$C = \frac{Y_1}{(1+i)} + \frac{Y_2}{(1+i)^2} + ... + \frac{Y_n}{(1+i)^n} \quad \text{or,} \quad \frac{Y_1}{(1+i)} + \frac{Y_2}{(1+i)^2} + ... + \frac{Y_n}{(1+i)^n} - C = 0.$$

If we assume that, $C, Y_1....Y_n \geq 0$ and $i \geq -1$, then in this equation we have one change of sign. It can be said that there is one positive real root for which the above equation is satisfied. Investment could be conventional or non-conventional. The conventional investment is one where all the yields are non-negative. The non-conventional investment is one where some of the yields are negative.

Now, let us find out how the MEC determines the optimum stock of capital. Let 'r' be the market rate of interest. If the firm wants to get the same yields $Y_1, Y_2 ......Y_n$ by lending money at market rate of interest it will have to lend an amount of money, D, which is given by the following equation : $D = \frac{Y_1}{(1+r)} + \frac{Y_2}{(1+r)^2} + ... + \frac{Y_n}{(1+r)^n}$ where D is the capitalised value of an income producing assets. The firm can get the same yields $Y_1, Y_2 ...... Y_n$ etc., either by purchasing the capital goods at a cost of C or by lending the sum of money, D. If $D > C$, it will be profitable for the firm to purchase the machine rather than lending the sum. But $C < D$, if $i > r$, i.e., when the marginal efficiency of capital is greater than the market rate of interest. If $C > D$, the firm can get the same yields by lending a smaller sum compared to the cost of purchasing the machine. In this case firm will benefit by lending the sum rather than purchasing the capital goods where $i < r$, *i.e.,* when the $MEC < r$. When $C = D$ and $i = r$, it is a matter of indifference. The firm can either purchase the machine or can lend the sum. Thus, we can say that, the firm will benefit by investing in real capital goods only when the *MEC > the market rate of interest(r).*

So far, we assumed that the firm has sufficient amount of money and the problem before the firm is whether to lend the money or to purchase the machine. Let us now assume that, the firm does not have the sufficient amount of money and it can only invest if it can borrow money at the market rate 'r', which means that it will borrow money only if the *MEC* is greater than the market rate of interest, that is, if $i > r$ then it would be profitable for firm to borrow funds to purchase the machine. If, however, $i < r$ or *MEC < the market rate of interest*, such borrowing will not be profitable.

Marginal Efficiency of Capital *(MEC)* is the proportional rate of return over cost from investment in real capital goods. It depends on two factors : the supply price and the series of prospective yields. For any single firm the supply price of capital may be taken as given which means that the capital market is perfectly competitive. But the yields from the capital goods will not remain the same. If more and more capital goods are employed in the production process other factors remaining unchanged, the marginal productivity of new capital goods will diminish. Thus, if the firm employs more units of capital, the yields from successive units will diminish which means the law of diminishing marginal productivity will operate. Hence we can say that, the *MEC* will diminish as more capital goods are employed in the production process.

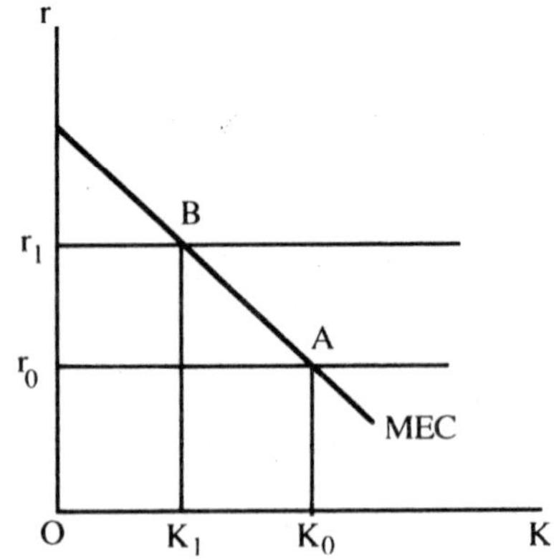

Fig. 13.6 Profitmaximising Employment of Capital

If, as in Fig. 13.6, the units of capital goods are measured in the horizontal axis and the *MEC* on the vertical axis, we can get a downward slopping relationship between the *MEC* and the units of capital goods which is known as *MEC* schedule. With the *MEC* schedule we can determine the optimum stock of capital.

If the market rate of interest is r_0, the firm would be able to maximise profit by employing K_0 units of capital goods, where the *MEC* is equal to the market rate of interest. If the employment of capital is less than K_0, when the market rate of interest is r_0, the $MEC > r_0$, so that it will be profitable to employ more capital goods. This process will stop when K_0 units of capital will be employed where the *MEC* is equal to r_0. Similarly, when the rate of interest is r_1, the point *B* will be the point of maximum profit where the *MEC* is equal to the rate of interest and the capital stock is equal to K_1 as shown in Fig. 13.6. Thus, we can say that the optimum stock of capital is K_0, when the rate of interest is r_0 and equals K_1, if the rate of interest is r_1 and so on. The *MEC* can give us the optimum stock of capital. Proceeding in this way we can get the *MEC* schedule for the whole economy which will be downward sloping as well. It will give us the optimum stock of capital for the economy at different rates of interest.

Determinants of the MEC

As we have seen above, the *MEC* is that value of *i* for which the following equations is satisfied: $C = \frac{Y_1}{(1+i)} + \frac{Y_2}{(1+i)^2} + ... + \frac{Y_n}{(1+i)^n}$.

From this equation it can be seen that, the *MEC* directly depends on two factors : (1) the prospective yields and (2) the supply price of capital. Other things remaining the same the *MEC* varies directly with the perspective yields and inversely with the supply price. This means that if the yields diminish and the supply price increases, the *MEC* will fall.

The expected yields are obtained by subtracting operating cost from the total revenue. Moreover, these yields are prospective and, thus, they may change when the expectations change. The higher the operating costs, the lower will be the yields and lower will be the *MEC*. Thus, if the raw materials become more expensive or if the wage rate increases, the *MEC* will fall. If the price of output increases, other things remaining the same, the *MEC* will rise. On the other hand, if the price of output falls, other things remaining unchanged, the *MEC* will also fall. The expected yields may also change due to changes in the expectations of the entrepreneurs. If the entrepreneurs are more optimistic about the future, they will expect higher yields to prevail. If, on the other hand, they are pessimistic about the future, they may expect lower yield. Thus, in a period of boom, they will have a bright outlook for the future and the *MEC* will be higher. Alternatively, in a period of slump, the *MEC* will be lower. Apart from the above factors, the *MEC* may also depend upon the following exogenous factors, such as size of population, size of the market, changes in the methods of production, etc. Other things remaining the same, the bigger the size of the market or the greater the size of the population, the greater will be the *MEC*. Similarly, if a new technology is invented which reduces the cost per unit of output, the yields will increase and the *MEC* will rise.

The *MEC* schedule is downward sloping because it is assumed that, the yields diminishe as more capital goods are used. Furthermore, it may be assumed that larger output can be sold at lower prices, other things remaining the same. For this reason, the *MEC* falls. However, when other factors change, the *MEC* schedule shifts its position.

MEI and the MEC

The optimum stock of capital is determined by the *MEC* at different rate of interest. If the actual capital stock is not equal to the optimum capital stock then capital stock must be adjusted to make it equal to the optimum level. The problem is to determine how the rate at which the actual stock proceeds towards the optimum stock. We have actually two problems : (1) is to determine the optimum stock and (2) is to determine the rate of growth of the actual capital stock for the flow of investment. The first problem is solved by the *MEC* theory. The second problem require the *MEI* theory.

Before, we discuss the *MEI* theory it is necessary to distinguish between gross and net investment. Gross investment is the addition to the stock of capital during a period of time. Net investment is equal to the difference between gross investment and depreciation. Thus, in any period of time if gross investment is equal to zero, net investment is equal to depreciation and will be negative. Net investment will be zero if the gross investment is equal to the amount of depreciation. If the rate of gross investment is equal to the amount of

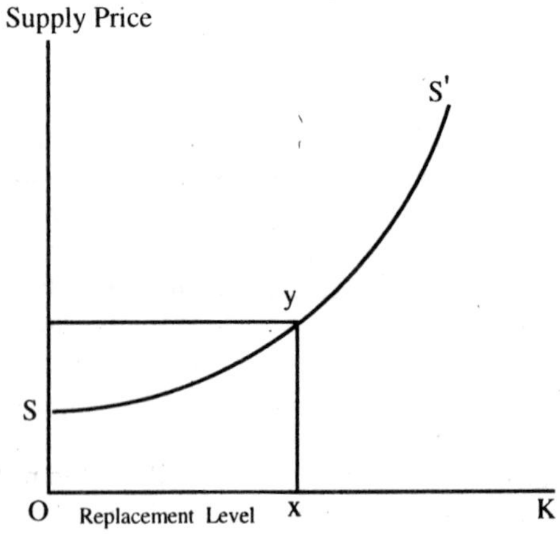

Fig. 13.7 Supply Price of Capital is determined by the replacement level of Investment

depreciation, it is called the replacement investment, which is necessary to keep the stock of capital intact.

In calculating the *MEC* we assume that, the supply price of capital is constant and it is determined by the replacement level of investment. In Fig. 13.7, *SS'* is the supply curve of capital. Let *Ox* be the amount of capital required for replacement. *xy* is the supply price for this level of capital stock. This supply price, *xy*, is taken into account in calculating the *MEC*. Thus, the schedule of *MEC* corresponds to a supply price where net investment is zero. If net investment is positive the amount of capital stock required is greater than *Ox* and, hence, the supply price is greater than *xy*. Further, the supply price would be different for different level of investment. However, the expected yields of the *MEI* (marginal efficiency of investment) is calculated on the assumption that the supply price of capital is increasing. Thus, the *MEC* is calculated on the assumption of a constant supply price of capital whereas the *MEI* is calculated on the assumption of variable supply price. The *MEI* will be different for different levels of investment. As the rate of investment increases, supply price increases and the *MEI* decreases. So, we can get one *MEI* schedule like the *MEC* schedule. While the *MEC* schedule refers to the stock of capital but the *MEI* schedule refers to flow of investment. The relation between the two are given in Fig. 13.8.

Suppose the market rate of interest is Or_2 and from the *MEC* schedule we can find out that the optimum stock of capital is OK_m. Now, suppose that the actual stock of capital is OK_0 which is less than the optimum capital stock. Thus, there is scope for more investment. Now, we need to determine the rate at which investment will take place when the rate of interest is Or_2. If the rate of interest is Or_0 then the actual capital stock is K_0, which is equal

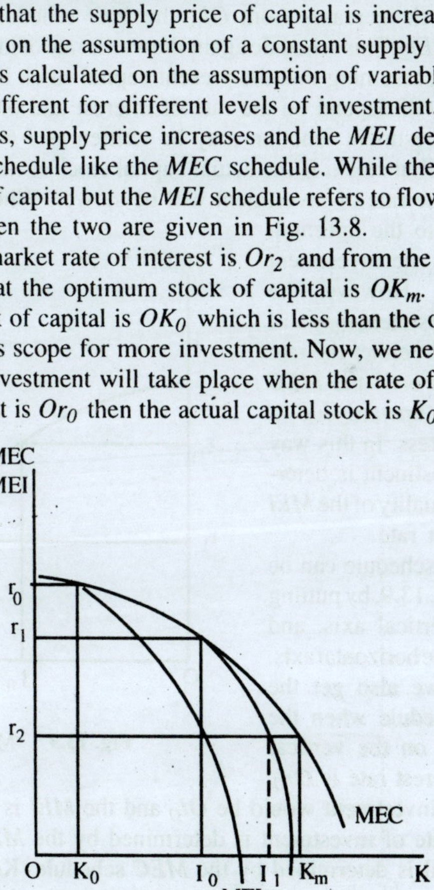

Fig. 13.8 Relationship between MEC and MEI

to the optimum stock of capital and the zero net investment. As capital stock increases above K_0, there is positive net investment and the supply price of capital goods will increase. The supply price increases as the rate of investment increases. The *MEI* is calculated on the basis of an increase in supply prices and, hence, will be below the *MEC*. We can get the *MEI* schedule for different rates of investment. As the rate of investment increases the *MEI* decreases which will depend on the rate of the supply schedule of capital goods. Thus, the *MEI* schedule is regarded as a mirror image of the supply schedule of capital goods.Given the rate of interest of Or_2, the rate of investment will be equal to K_0I_0, where the *MEI* is equal to the rate of interest. K_0I_0 is the short-run rate of investment and the *MEI* is the investment schedule when we start from the interest rate r_0 and original capital stock of K_0 and, when the capital stock increases from OI_0, the *MEI* schedule shifts its position from MEI_1 to MEI_2. This schedule again shows the rate of investment at different rates of interest assuming that the present capital stock is OI_0. Thus, the rate of investment will depend on the rate of interest and on the initial stock of capital. The investment function may be written as $I = I(r, K_0)$ where K_0 is the initial capital stock. If the actual capital stock is nearer to the optimum capital stock, the rate of investment will be slower. When the actual capital stock is equal to the optimum capital stock, net investment will be zero. However, the net positive investment may still be possible if either the rate of interest falls or if the *MEC* schedule shifts upward due to technical prog-ress. In this way the rate of investment is determined by the equality of the *MEI* and the interest rate.

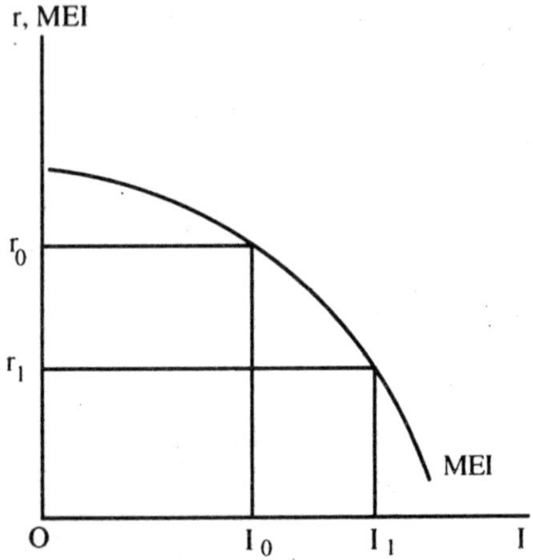

Fig. 13.9 MEI Schedule

The *MEI* schedule can be drawn, as in Fig. 13.9, by putting *MEI* on the vertical axis, and investment on the horizontal axis. In Fig. 13.9, we also get the investment schedule when the interest rate is on the vertical axis. If the interest rate is Or_0, the volume of investment would be OI_0 and the *MEI* is equal to the rate of interest. The rate of investment is determined by the *MEI* schedule and the optimum capital is determined by the *MEC* schedule. Keynes was confused between these two concepts. What he termed as the *MEC* is actually the *MEI* schedule. This confusion was first cleared by Prof. Lerner.

The Present Value Criterion for Investment

Present value criterion is an alternative to the *MEC* criterion for evaluating an investment project. According to the *MEC* criterion, we know that, any capital goods is worth purchasing if its *MEC* is greater than the rate of interest. But the *MEC* criterion suffers from important limitation. It is difficult to determine the *MEC*, to avoid this difficulty one can use the present value criterion.

According to the present value criterion, the firm determines the present value by discounting the series of yields to be obtained from the capital goods. From this discounted present value the cost of capital goods is taken away. This gives us the net present value *(NPV)* of the capital goods. Suppose *C* is the cost of capital and the capital goods will produce for n years yielding $Y_1, Y_2 ...... Y_n$ during its life. Let *r* denote the market rate of interest. Then the *NPV* of the capital goods is given by the formula :

$$NPV = \frac{Y_1}{(1+r)} + \frac{Y_2}{(1+r)^2} + ... + \frac{Y_n}{(1+r)^n} - C$$

The yields and the cost of capital goods are taken as given. Hence, given the rate of discount or interest, we can determine the *NPV* from the above formula.

Fig. 13.10 Net Present Value criterion of Investment

On the basis of this criterion a project will be acceptable if its *NPV* is positive. If the *NPV* of a project is negative, it would be rejected. The firm can rank projects on the basis of their *NPV*. If the supply of capital is unlimited the firm will invest in all projects having a positive *NPV*. However, if the investment capital is limited the firm will invest in the projects having the highest *NPV* until its funds are exhausted. In Fig. 13.10 we plot *NPV* on the vertical axis and real investment on the horizontal axis. Now let us suppose the rate of interest is constant at r_0. At this rate of interest the *NPV* of different units of capital are calculated and have been ranked in descending value of *NPV*. The *NPV* curve is $V_0 I_0$ when the rate of interest is r_0. If the firm has enough funds it will invest up to I_0 where the *NPV* of the marginal project is zero. Hence we can say that, investment will be OI_0 when the rate of interest is r_0. If the rate of interest increases to r_1, the *NPV* for each project will be lower than before, provided the supply price and yields remain unchanged. This means that the *NPV* curve will shift downward when the interest rate increases and the *NPV* curve becomes $V_1 I_1$. This shows that at a higher rate of interest investment will be lower and hence there is an inverse relationship between the rate of interest and the level of investment. The investment function can thus be written as $I = I(r)$ such that $I'(r) < 0$.

Comparison between the MEC and the NPV Methods

There are two methods for the appraisal of investment projects the *MEC* method and the *NPV* method. In the *MEC* method any project is accepted if its *MEC* is higher than the rate of interest and not otherwise. On the other hand, in the *NPV* method, any project is accepted if its *NPV is* positive not otherwise.

Now let us compare these two methods, first for conventional investments which means that, the entire capital investment occurs at the beginning of the project while yields are produced throughout the life of the project. In the case of non-conventional investment capital expenditure occurs not only at the beginning of the project but during the entire life of the project.

In the case of conventional investments *MEC* and the *NPV* methods give the same accept-reject decisions. In the *MEC* criterion any project is accepted if its *MEC* is greater than the rate of interest and rejected if its *MEC* is less than the rate of interest. Similarly, in the case of the *NPV* criterion, any project will be accepted if it has a positive *NPV* and any project having a negative *NPV* will be rejected.

If the *MEC* is less than the rate of interest, the *NPV* is negative and the project is rejected on both criteria. Again, if the *MEC* is greater than the rate of interest the *NPV* is positive and the project is accepted according to both the criteria.

Thus, it is clear that, both the criteria give identical results in the matter of accept-reject decisions for conventional investment.

However, a conflict may arise between the two methods when ranking mutually exclusive projects. This can be explained with the help of Fig. 13.11. Suppose, the two mutually exclusive projects *x* and *y* have their *NPV* of VV' and WW', respectively. Given the yields and the capital cost of the project, the *NPV* of any project is a function of the interest rate. For different interest rates we can have different *NPVs* which give us the different *NPV* curves.

The *NPV* curves are downward sloping for conventional investments. The discount rates *OP* and *OQ* will give the *NPV*s of zero for*X* and*Y* projects and also the *MEC* for these projects, respectively. Now assume that the rate of interest *OC* and the *NPV* of the Project *X* is *AC* and that of the Project

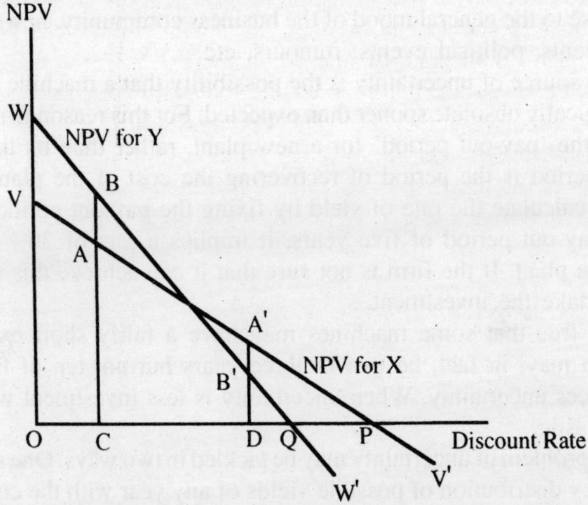

Fig. 13.11 Comparison Between the MEC and the NPV Methods

Y is BC. Since *AC* < *BC*, the project *Y* has a higher *NPV* than the project *X*. Thus, according to the *NPV* criterion, the project *Y* is to be preferred to Project *X* at a discount rate of *OC* which gives conflicting result by the two methods. However, if the rate of discount is *OD*, then both methods give identical results because the *NPV* of *X* is higher than the *NPV* of *Y*.

We can generalise the result thus obtained as follows : If the rate of interest is greater *(OC)* than the rate at which the *NPVs* of mutually exclusive projects are equal, both methods will give consistent results which means the project with the higher *NPV* will also have the higher *MEC*. If, however, the rate of interest is less than *(OD)*—the rate at which mutually exclusive projects have equal *NPVs*—the two methods will give conflicting results which means, the project with the higher M*EC* will have the lower *NPV*, and vice versa.

In the case of non-conventional investments, a conflict between the two methods (*MEC* and *NPV)* may arise even in a situation of accept-reject decisions.

Expectations

The *MEC* is calculated on the basis of yields which can be obtained from the life-time of the machine. These yields are expected but not actual. These expected yields require the expected variable costs which are associated with the production of this output and the expected future price levels. Thus, expectations enter into the determination of the level of investment. But the expectations may or may not be fulfilled. There is no certainty that the expected yields required in the calculation of the *MEC* will materialise in practice. Expectations are uncertain and also volatile. They may change drastically in response to the general mood of the business community, news of technical developments, political events, rumours, etc.

One source of uncertainty is the possibility that a machine may become technologically obsolete sooner than expected. For this reason firms may often consider the 'pay-out period' for a new plant, rather than its life span. The pay-out period is the period of recovering the cost of the plant. The firms normally calculate the rate of yield by fixing the pay-out period. If the firm takes a pay-out period of five years, it implies a rate of 20% yield of the cost of the plant. If the firm is not sure that it can achieve this return it will not undertake the investment.

It is true that some machines may have a fairly short expectation of life which may, in fact, be two or three years but not ten of fifteen years. This reduces uncertainty. When uncertainty is less investment will be more interest-elastic.

The problem of uncertainty may be tackled in two ways. One is to consider a frequency distribution of possible yields of any year with the corresponding probabilities. The weighted arithmetical mean of these yields may be taken as the most probable yield of that year. Another way is to consider the "certainty equivalent" of uncertain values which is the objective value of the distribution, plus any premium or less any discount for uncertainty.

Capacity of the Capital Goods Sector

Gross investment means addition to the stock of capital. Investment takes place when firms are not in equilibrium or optimum. If a firm has less than optimum capital, and if the capital goods are available, then investment can take place very rapidly. However, if capital goods are in short supply, then the rate of investment will be determined by the production capacity of the capital goods industries. Now, suppose that a firm is in optimum capital stock. No investment will take place unless interest rate falls. If, however, the interest rate falls, the optimum stock of capital will increase and the rate of investment for a single firm will depend on the capacity of the Capital Goods Sector.

For the economy as a whole the gross investment will also depend on the production capacity of the Capital Goods Industry. Net investment will also depend on the capacity of capital goods industries less the annual rate of depreciation.

In the present analysis three rates of investment are possible. If the optimum stock of capital is greater than the actual stock, the firms demand more capital and the capital goods industries will operate at full capacity to meet gross investment need and net investment will be equal to gross investment minus depreciation. If the optimum stock of capital does not grow at the same rate as the actual stock, the actual stock will be equal to the optimum stock and net investment will be zero. The third rate of investment will occur when the optimum stock falls short of actual stock. In that case, net investment will be negative, at a rate determined by the rate of depreciation.

This analysis has an important implication in that the capital goods industries oscillate violently between conditions of feverish activity and stagnation. When the industry, in general, is short of capital, capital goods industries are operating at full capacity and it is trying to expand its own capacity. Thus, the capital goods industry's effort to add its capacity extends and intensifies the boom. In depression, capital goods industry itself had excess capacity and it will prolong depression. From this analysis we can conclude that, if we start from an equilibrium position and if the optimum stock increases, a boom of considerable consequence may follow. On the other hand, when the actual is greater than optimum, gross investment is zero, capital goods industry stops producing and depression spreads in the whole economy.

Accelerator Theory of Investment

Now we like to discuss the 'accelerator' theory of investment. According to this theory, the level of current net investment depends on past income changes. In its simplest form, this can be written as follows :

$I_t = v(Y_t - Y_{t-1})$, where I_t is net investment in current period, Y_t is the current national income, Y_{t-1} is national income in the previous period, v is an 'accelerator', a constant. Gross investment is equal to net investment plus any replacement investment. So we can write: $GI = v(Y_t - Y_{t-1}) + R_t$, where GI is current gross investment and R_t is current replacement investment.

For the accelerator theory to be valid, it is necessary that firms must demand additional capital to meet the increased demand for their product. Consider the following example.

Let us assume that, a single firm which initially has a stock of ten machines each of which is capable of producing 50 units of output per year. To keep the analysis simple, assume that, there is no depreciation so that, there is no need to think about replacement investment. Suppose initially the total demand for the firm's product is 500 units. This is shown for year 1 in Table 1 : note that, the desired capital stock to meet this demand is ten machines and since the firm already has ten machines, no net investment is necessary. So long as demand stay at 500 units, no net investment will be necessary. Now, suppose in year 2, demand increases to 1,000 units — the desired capital stock will rise to 20 machines and to achieve this, net investment of ten machines is necessary. In year 3, demand has risen to 1,500 units, so that, the desired capital stock goes up to 30 machines — since the firm has already 20 machines, another 10 need to be added. Note that, although demand has risen in year

3, net investment has remained the same. In year 4, demand continues to increase, by 250 units to 1,750 units : the desired capital stock goes up to 35 and so net investment of 5 machines is necessary. Since demand has risen by a small amount than previously, investment has actually fallen. In year 5, demand is still 1,750 units — the firm has already 35 machines necessary to meet this demand and so no new machine (investment) is required.

Table 1 : An example of the Accelerator Principle

Year(1)	Demand (D) (2)	Desired Capital (3) Stock	Net Investment(4) (No. of machines)
1	500	10	0
2	1,000	20	10
3	1,500	30	10
4	1,750	35	5
5	1,750	35	0

The example highlights the following points about the theory:

(a) To maintain net investment at a constant positive level, demand for the firm's product must rise at a steady rate.

(b) For net investment to increase, demand must be increasing at an increasing rate.

(c) If demand should level off and remain constant, net investment will fall to zero.

Note that, the relationship expressed in Table 1 can be written as follows : $NI = 1/50\ (D_t - D_{t-1})$ where NI is the net investment of the firm, D_t is the current demand for the firm's product and D_{t-1} is last year's demand for the firms product. If all firms behave in a similar way to this, then we can say that, the aggregate net investment in the economy will depend on changes in aggregate demand — they have to be measured in value terms and since the value of aggregate demand in equilibrium is the same as national income, we have $I_t = v(Y_t - Y_{t-1})$.

Two main *criticism* may be advanced against this theory:

(1) It assumes that, firms faced with increased demand for their products will immediately attempt to increase their capital stock. This means that there is no excess capacity. This is unrealistic — it is more likely that firms would be able to meet initial increase in demand by allowing excess capacity that it already there.

(2) It fails to take into consideration businessmen's expectation. If businessmen consider the increase in demand to be temporary, they would not respond to it at all : this is likely to be the case if they are generally pessimistic about the future. Alternatively, if they are generally optimistic and see the increase in demand as a signal for further increases, they may buy more machines than predicted by the theory.

In conclusion, we can say that, net investment in an economy will depend on the following factors (1) the rate of interest (r) ; (2) national income changes in the past; (3) the state of business expectation (B). We can write the function as : $I_t = f\ (r,\ Y_t - Y_{t-1},\ B)$.

However, since it takes time for firms to adjust their capital stock in response to changes in demand, it may be realistic to introduce a time lag into the function and write : $I_t = f(r, Y_{t-1} - Y_{t-2}, B)$. Only empirical analysis can tell which of the three variables is the most important.

Exercise

1. Suppose a firm which initially has a stock of 100 machines, each of which produces 50 units of output per time period. Assume that the 100 machines have been purchased at the rate of 10 per period for the last ten periods, so that, from now on, depreciation is equal to 10 machines per time period. The table below gives the demand for the firm's product over the time periods from 0 to 5.

Table : The demand for the firm's product overtime

Time Period	Demand
0	5,000
1	6,000
2	10,000
3	12,000
4	12,000
5	10,000

   (a) Calculate the firm's gross investment in time period 0 to 5.
   (b) Write down the equations of the relationship between gross investment and changes in demand.
   (c) Comment on the applicability of this model to the real world.

2. There are two investment projects A and B, yielding the same value of output at the end of 3 years. Project A costs £1 million in year 1 and £2.0 million in year 2 with no cost in year 3, while project B costs £2 million in year 1, nothing in year 2 and £1 million in year 3. Examine the relative projectability of the two projects and advice which project to accept at alternative rate of interest.

3. Explain why the housing market usually prospers when (real) mortgage rates are low.

4. Suppose an explicitly temporary tax credit is enacted at the rate of 10 per cent and lasts only 1 year.
   (a) What is the effect of this tax measure on investment in the long run?
   (b) What is the effect in the current year and in the following year?

14 THE INTERNATIONAL TRADE SECTOR

The additional important element introduced by international trade is that countries can use goods which they themselves could not produce—they can import those goods from other countries; and they can dispose of goods which they themselves do not want to use—they can export goods. The constraints facing individuals in an open economy would be different from those they face in a closed one. We relax our assumption of closed economy with which we started our analysis and instead assume that we are dealing with an open economy. In an open economy we consider imports and exports. The exports and imports of goods are not an act of charity. It involves an exchange of goods for goods, the constraint facing individuals is still total output. If it involves an exchange of goods for some form of wealth, it means that individuals can use more or less than they produce by reducing or increasing their claims to future goods. Let us now examine how the equilibrium level of income can be determined in an open economy. For this we make the following assumptions : (1) The economy is an open economy having foreign trade. (2) The exchange rate, the interest rate, the price level and the wage rate are constant. (3) Aggregate investment expenditure within the economy is autonomous : $I = I_0$ where I represents investment expenditure in real terms. (4) Aggregate consumption expenditure is a function of aggregate income : $C = f(Y)$ where Y represents income in real terms. For simplicity we take linear consumption function : $C = a + by$, where a and b are constants, $0 < b < 1$. (5) For the moment activities on the part of the government are excluded. (6) Exports are autonomously given while imports depend on the level of income, i.e., $X = X_0$ and $M = M(Y)$ where M is import and X is export. We can also take a linear imports function : $M = q + my$, where q, m are constants, $m > 0$. Hence $\frac{dM}{dY} = m$ is called a marginal propensity to imports *(mpm)*.

As in a closed economy, equilibrium level of income in an open economy will also be determined by the equality of aggregate demand and aggregate supply; but in an open economy we must add to this imports *(M)* and exports *(X)*. In an open economy aggregate demand is equal to $C + I + X$ and aggregate supply is : $Y + M$. The equilibrium condition in an open economy can be

written as : $Y + M = C + I + X$ *or,* $Y = C + I + (X - M)$.........*(1)* where the right hand side is the aggregate demand and the left hand side is the aggregate supply. But we know that *C* and *M* are functions of income *(Y)*, while *X* and *I* are autonomously given. In the above equation we have one unknown. We can determine the equilibrium income by solving this equation. If we write the equilibrium condition in linear form we get :
$Y = a + by + I_0 + X_0 - q - my$ *or,* $Y(1 - b + m) = a + I_0 + X_0 - q$

or $Y_0 = \dfrac{a + I_0 + X_0 - q}{(1 - b + m)}$ where Y_0 represents the equilibrium level of income.

which can be determined from this equation. This equilibrium income can also be obtained graphically as we have done in the Keynesian model for income determination in a closed economy. Now our aggregate demand curve is $C(Y) + I_0 + X_0 - m(Y)$ *or* $a + bY + I_0 + X_0 - mY$. This intersection between this aggregate demand curve and 45° line gives us the equilibrium level of income (Y_0). This is shown in Fig. 14.1—Y_0 is the equilibrium level of income. An alternative way of expressing the equilibrium condition is : $Y = C + I + X - M$ or $Y - C = I + X - M$ or $S = I + X - M$ where $S = Y - C$, or $S + M = I + X$ or $W = J$, where *W* is withdrawal and *J* is injection.

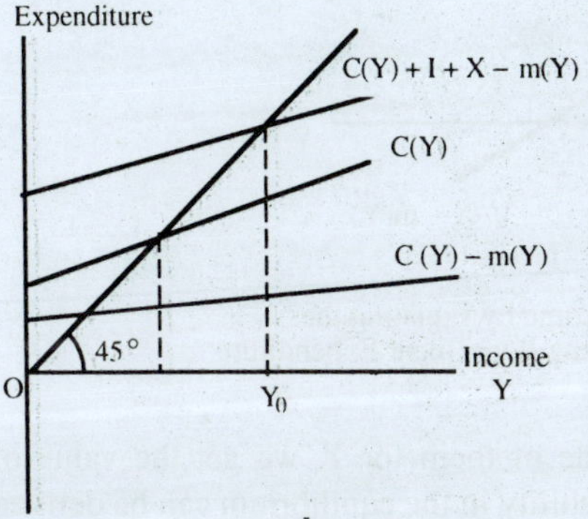

Fig. 14.1 The Equilibrium Level of Income

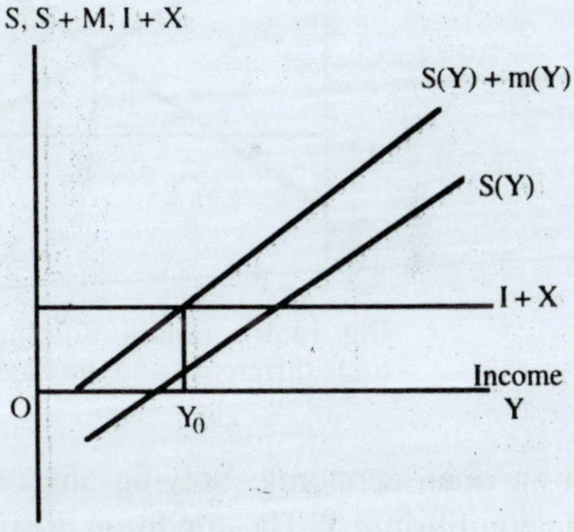

Fig.14.2 The Alternative way to Express the Equilibrium Income

We add the saving function to the import function to obtain $W = S + m$. The horizontal *I* curve will have to be replaced by an $J = I + X$ which will give the equilibrium solution. This is shown in Fig. 14.2, where Y_0 is the equilibrium income. Alternatively, we can say that there will be equilibrium in the commodity market of an open economy, if the excess of saving over investment is equal to the excess of exports over imports $S - I = X - M$. Note that, equilibrium in a closed economy requires the equality between *S* and *I*. But this is not necessary in an open economy. Even if $S \neq I$, there can be equilibrium in an open economy provided the excess of S over I equals the excess of X over M. Again even if $S = I$ there can be no equilibrium in an open economy, unless exports are also equal to imports $(X = M)$.

Another way of expressing the same equilibrium condition is by the equation of the balance of trade to the difference between the saving and the investment expenditure. The condition of equilibrium is:

$$X - m(Y) = S(Y) - I.$$

The left hand side of the equation is a falling function of Y and its right hand side is a rising function of Y. The intersection between the $X - m(Y)$ curve and the $S(Y) - I$ curve gives the solution of the equation, which is shown in Fig. 14. 3, where Y_0 is again the equilibrium income. Thus, there are three alternative ways to express the condition for equilibrium in the goods market

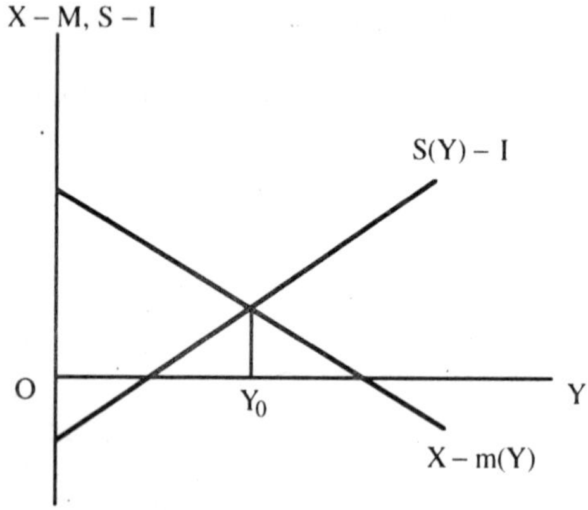

Fig. 14.3 Equilibrium Income by Equating the trade difference and the Saving Investment Expenditure

in an open economy. Solving any one of them for Y, we get the value of the equilibrium Y. The condition of stability in the equilibrium can be derived from the adjustment hypothesis :

$\frac{dY}{dt} = \lambda[C(Y) + I + X - m(Y) - Y]$ where λ is a positive adjustment factor. If the sum of the *mps* and *mpm* is positive, the stability condition is satisfied.

In order to evaluate the comparative static effect of a change in exports of the country, we differentiate the equation $X - m(Y) = S(Y) - I$ with respect to X and obtain $\frac{dY}{dX} = \frac{1}{(S' + m')}$ which is known as export multiplier. If exports are autonomously increased by ΔX, the equilibrium income will increase by

$\Delta Y = \frac{1}{(S'+m')}\Delta X$. The investment multiplier also happens to be equal to $\frac{1}{(S'+m')}$.
Then with the increase in income imports will increase by $\Delta M = m'\Delta Y = \frac{m'}{(S'+m')}\Delta X$ and saving will increase by $\Delta S = S'\Delta Y = \frac{S'}{(S'+m')}\Delta X$.

If the balance of trade is defined as $B = X - M$, the automatic increase in exports will produce the following change in the trade balance: $\Delta B = \Delta X - \Delta M = \frac{S'}{(S'+m')}\Delta X$, which happens to be equal to the change in saving given above.

If investment is a function of the interest rate, the condition for equilibrium in the goods market can be written as : $S(Y) + M(Y) = I(r) + X$, which can be represented in $Y - r$ plane by the *IS* curve for the open economy. The slope of the *IS* curve is given by $\left(\frac{dr}{dY}\right)_{IS} = \frac{S'+m'}{I'} < 0$, which means that, the *IS* curve in an open economy is steeper than that in a closed economy. An increase (a decrease) in exports will produce a rightward (leftward) shift of the *IS* curve.

Once the investment expenditure is treated as a function of the rate of interest, the money market needs to be introduced to complete the model. The condition of equilibrium in the money market is given by $M = L(r, y)$, money supply = money demand which is needed to produce the *LM* curve. To determine *Y* and *r* simultaneously we need equality between *IS* and *LM* as we have seen before.

In the open economy, the equation of equilibrium is closely connected with the equilibrium in the balance of trade. For an equilibrium in the balance of trade, the value of exports must be equal to the value of imports. If the value of export exceeds the value of imports, there will be surplus in the balance of trade. Alternatively, when the value of imports exceeds the value of exports, a deficit appears in the balance of trade. The question now is whether there can be any equilibrium in the output and money markets when there is either a deficit or a surplus in the balance of trade. Disequilibrium in the balance of trade $(X \neq m)$ is likely to produce changes in the economy. These changes may affect the aggregate demand. As a consequence, the level of income may change. When the amount of exports is less than the amount of imports, the people of the country would have to make payments to foreign countries, for which they will have to buy foreign currencies. The additional foreign currency must be obtained through the sacrifice of an equivalent amount of the domestic currency in the foreign exchange market. Under the flexible rate system, the additional demand for foreign currency leads to a rise in its price in terms of domestic currency. This is known as depreciation of exchange rate of the deficit country. When there is a surplus in the balance of trade, under the flexible rates system, it leads to an exchange rate appreciation. Thus, under the flexible exchange rates regime, the balance of trade disequilibrium leads to an appreciation or a depreciation of currency. As a result of this change the relative prices of imports and exports would change which are likely to affect the aggregate demand. However, under gold standard, the deficit country will experience outflow of gold and, hence, there will be a contraction of money supply in the country. On the contrary, if there is a surplus in the balance of trade, there will be inflow of gold into the country and money supply will increase thereby in the surplus country. So, under gold standard, the disequilibrium in the balance of trade produces a change in money supply in the domestic economy which will be followed by a change in the interest rate. This will change the aggregate demand in the economy as well. If there is disequilibrium in the balance of trade, there cannot be equilibrium in the goods and money markets. Thus, to have domestic equilibrium there must also be equilibrium in the balance of trade.

Hence, we can keep the domestic money supply independent of the trade balance in a fixed exchange rate regime through the 'Sterilization Policy' which means that, the monetary authority can reduce (increase) the domestic money supply by an equal amount when a surplus (deficit) in the balance of trade leads to an increase (decrease) in it. Then the following equations can be used to determine the equilibrium values of Y and r in the domestic economy: $S(Y) + m(Y) = I(r) + X$, and $L(Y, r) = M$. By differentiating these equations with respect to X, we can evaluate the effects of an autonomous increase in exports as given below :

$$\begin{bmatrix} S'+m' & -I' \\ L_Y & L_r \end{bmatrix} \begin{bmatrix} dY/dX \\ dr/dX \end{bmatrix} = \begin{bmatrix} 1 \\ 0 \end{bmatrix}$$

which can be solved for $\begin{bmatrix} dY/dX \\ dr/dX \end{bmatrix} = \begin{bmatrix} S'+m' & -I' \\ L_Y & L_r \end{bmatrix} \begin{bmatrix} 1 \\ 0 \end{bmatrix}$

From the last equation it can be seen that $\dfrac{dY}{dX} = \dfrac{L_r}{(S'+m')L_r + I' L_Y}$ and

$\dfrac{dr}{dX} = \dfrac{-L_Y}{(S'+m')L_r + I' L_Y}$, where $(S' + m') L_r + I'L_Y < 0$.

So long as $L_r \neq \infty$, $\dfrac{dY}{dX} > 0$ and $\dfrac{dr}{dX} > 0$.

This shows that monetary reaction makes the size of the export multiplier smaller.

The export multiplier is now: $\dfrac{1}{(S'+m')+I'\dfrac{L_Y}{L_r}} < \dfrac{1}{S'+m'}$.

However, if $I'=0$ or if $L_r \to \infty$, then the two multiplier's become equal.

The Balance of Payment and the Exchange Rate

The balance of payments surplus may be defined as the difference between exports and imports. We have assumed that exports are autonomously given and imports are function of income. This shows the relationship between income and balance of payments. We have not considered prices of exports and imports and also the exchange rate. Let us now assume at first that the rate of exchange has been fixed politically at a certain level which is now changed and prices remain unchanged. Let us see how a change in the exchange rate affects the balance of payments surplus. We assume that, prices of exports and imports are equal to unity. The following notations are used in the analysis : X = Value of exports in domestic currency. M = Value of imports in foreign currency. B = Balance of payments surplus in domestic currency. E = Exchange Rate of domestic currency per unit of foreign currency. e_x = Elasticity of demand for exports. e_m = Elasticity of demand for imports. Since the prices of exports and imports have been assumed to be constant, X and M denote the physical quantities of imports and exports as well. It is assumed that the demand for imports is a function of exchange rate, $M = M(E)$ such that, $\dfrac{dM}{dE} < 0$. As E increases this means that the domestic currency has been devalued. Imports are now more costly in terms of domestic currency and the demand for imports falls as E increases. The elasticity of demand for imports is given by $e_m = \dfrac{dM}{dE} \cdot \dfrac{E}{M}$.

Since $\dfrac{dM}{dE} < 0$, it is clear that $e_m < O$. Hence, $|e_M| = \dfrac{dM}{dE} \cdot \dfrac{E}{M}$. It is also assumed that, the demand for exports is a function of the reciprocal of the rate of exchange, thus, $X = \dfrac{X}{\left(\dfrac{1}{E}\right)}$ such that, $\dfrac{dX}{d(1/E)} < 0$, which implies that $\dfrac{dX}{dE} > 0$.

The elasticity of demand for exports is given by

$e_X = \dfrac{dX}{X} \cdot \dfrac{1/E}{d(1/E)} = \dfrac{dX}{EX} \cdot \dfrac{1}{-\dfrac{dE}{E^2}} = -\dfrac{E}{X} \cdot \dfrac{dX}{dE}$. Since $\dfrac{dX}{dE} > 0$, so $e_X < 0$ and the absolute value of $|e_X| = \dfrac{E}{X} \cdot \dfrac{dX}{dE}$. By definition $B = X - EM$. Since X and M are functions of E, it is clear that B is a function of E only. The effect of change in the rate of exchange (E) on the balance of payments can be obtained by differentiation B with respect to E.

We then get:

$$\frac{dB}{dE}=\frac{dX}{dE}-M-E\frac{dM}{dE}=\left\{\frac{dX}{dE}\cdot\frac{E}{X}\right\}\cdot\frac{X}{E}-M-\left\{\frac{E}{M}\cdot\frac{dM}{dE}\right\}\cdot M=M\left\{|e_X|\frac{X/E}{M}+|e_M|-1\right\}.$$

Now a devaluation improves the balance of payment surplus if $\frac{dB}{dE}>0$.

In this case the devaluation may be said to be successful $\frac{dB}{dE}>0$, if

$M\left\{|e_X|\frac{X/E}{M}+|e_M|-1\right\}>0$ or, if $|e_X|\frac{X/E}{M}+|e_M|-1>0$ or, if $|e_X|\frac{X/E}{M}+|e_M|>1$.

If it is assumed that trade is initially balanced to start with, then $B = X - EM = 0$, $X = EM$ or $X/E = M$ which means that, the condition for successful devaluation is $|e_x|+|e_m|>0$. This condition is known as the Marshall-Lerner Condition for the successful devaluation.

The Balance of Payments and Flow of Money

International flow of goods and services are important for equilibrium in the goods sector. However, what is important for balance of payments are financial flows associated with the transactions. In modern world, trade involves the exchange of goods for money, and money for goods. This is true both in the domestic as well as international trade. But, in international trade many currencies are involved. To buy foreign goods we must have foreign currency. Thus, international trade involves not only an exchange of goods for goods, but also an exchange of money for money. Money has a price like all other goods. This price is the exchange rate as we have discussed above. Given the exchange rate, we can convert the real balance of trade into the financial flows that it generates in terms of foreign currency. If X is the real quantity of exports and P is the domestic price of exports, then PX is the volume of exports in domestic currency. If E is the exchange rate, then EPX is the value of foreign currency generated by this amount of exports. If, on the other hand, M is the quantity of impofts and P_w is the foreign price of imports, then MP_w is the value of imports and thus, the outflow of foreign currency generated by imports. The net flow of foreign currency generated by international trade is given by : $EPX\left(\frac{EP}{P_w}\right)-MP_w\left(\frac{EP}{P_w}.Y\right)$.

Besides the financial flows arising from trade there are also financial flows arising from international transactions in assets. Such flows must also be taken into account when considering the balance of payments. International capital flows arise when residents of one country acquire assets of another country. Suppose, a British resident buys the US bonds, he will have to first exchange domestic currency into foreign currency, in this case for the US currency, and, hence, there will be a capital flow out of the U.K. Similarly, if an American firm wishes to buy a U.K. firm, it will have to exchange US currency for U.K. currency and there will be a capital flow into the U.K. Just as with international trade, so with international asset transactions require first an exchange of money for money. To acquire a US asset the British resident must buy US currency, and the same thing applies to US firm wishing to acquire the U.K. firm. Let *K* be the net flow of foreign currency generated by international capital transactions. Now the question is : what determines *K* ?

Individual acquire assets because they want a return to be generated in the future. Thus, when choosing among assets individual will compare the income streams and choose those assets which yield the highest rate of return. We, therefore, assume that international capital flows are a function of the difference of the interest rates in different countries. Thus, $K = K(r - r_w)$, where r is the domestic rate of interest and r_w is the world interest rate. If we assume that the r_w is given, we have a direct relationship between r and net capital inflows. The higher is the domestic interest rate, r, the larger will be capital inflows.

The balance of payments is defined as the total flow of currencies generated by both international trade and asset transactions. Using equation (as presented above) : $EPX\left(\frac{EP}{P_W}\right) - MP_W\left(\frac{EP}{P_W}.Y\right)$ and allowing B to stand for balance of payments in terms of foreign currency, we have $B = EPX\left(\frac{EP}{P_W}\right) - MP_W\left(\frac{EP}{P_W}.Y\right) + K(r - r_W)$ or in general terms $B = B(E, P, Y, r, r_w, P_w)$ ....(1).

Equation (1) states that, the *BOP* depends on variables, such as in the brackets. Any change in these variables will affect the *BOP*. If $B = 0$, the inflow of foreign currency is equal to the outflow. In this case the *BOP* is in equilibrium.

It is useful to understand why the introduction of international transactions complicate our analysis. We can see from equation (1) that, even if we take the P_w and r_w as fixed, *BOP* equilibrium depends on four variables : *E, P, Y* and *r*. If the *BOP* is to be in equilibrium we must have seen specific combination of these variables. We know that, at least three of these variables (*P, Y* and *r*) are determined by the interaction of the various behavioural functions and government policies. However, there is no guarantee that the equilibrium values of these variables will be exactly those required for *BOP* equilibrium. But any changes in these variables due to change in the economy will have *BOP* repercussions. As all fiscal and monetary policies attempt to change income, and will also affect the *r* and the price level, they will have *BOP* repercussions. Thus government policies will be constrained by *BOP* considerations.

We also have to examine what variables will be affected if the *BOP* is not in equilibrium and how these variables are related to the factors that determine domestic equilibrium. For example, if a *BOP* disequilibrium affects the exchange rate, as it would in the case of flexible exchange rate regime, we see that, such a disequilibrium will have repercussions on the domestic economy.

The interaction between domestic equilibrium and *BOP* equilibrium is different according to whether the exchange rate is fixed or flexible. As the problem is reasonably complicated, we consider it for both cases within the framework of the *IS-LM* model.

The Balance of Payments and the Domestic Economy : Fixed Exchange Rates

We start from an equilibrium in the *BOP (B = 0)*. The amount of foreign currency demanded by residents for the purchase of foreign goods and assets is equal to the amount of foreign currency sold by foreigners for their purchase of domestic goods and assets. Now, suppose, because of a change in tastes or income or domestic interest rate, residents want to buy more foreign goods and assets. To do so, they will have to purchase more foreign currency. But foreigners are not willing to sell any more foreign currency at the existing exchange rate. There is then an excess demand for foreign currency. If the exchange rate were not fixed, this excess demand would raise the price of foreign currency in terms of domestic currency — the exchange rate will fall. If the exchange rate is fixed, the monetary authority must supply the excess demand of foreign currency, if they want to maintain the fixed exchange rate. The monetary authority must supply the foreign currency from its reserves *(R)*.

What happens is that, the monetary authority sells foreign currency in exchange of domestic currency. Thus, the supply of domestic currency must fall. Thus, under a regime of fixed exchange rates any *BOP* disequilibrium affects the quantity of domestic money in the economy. This would thus create an important link between *BOP* equilibrium and domestic equilibrium. Moreover, it also implies that, the quantity of money itself is not under the total control of the monetary authority, an assumption which was important for our previous analysis, where we took the quantity of money as exogenously given.

Can the link between the *BOP* disequilibrium and the quantity of money be broken? Of course, the monetary authority can undertake open market operations to counteract the effects of the *BOP* disequilibrium on the money supply. When it sells foreign currency because of *BOP* deficit it must buy an equal amount of government bonds, and vice versa. The net effect of these operations on money supply would cancel out, as if residents were purchasing foreign currency from the central bank with their government bond holdings rather than with their money holdings. Such operations are known as sterilization. Whether such operations are possible or not depends on the degree of international capital mobility. If this is possible, we shall assume that, in the

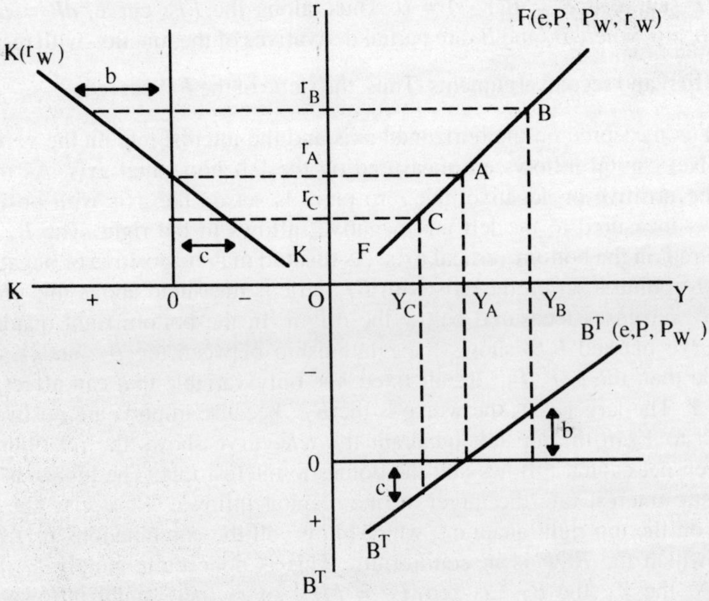

Fig. 14.4 Balance of Payments and the Domestic Economy

fixed-exchange regime, a *BOP* disequilibrium only affects the quantity of foreign currency reserves held by the central bank but leaves the nominal money supply unchanged.

From the *BOP* equation $B = B(e_p, Y, r, r_w, P_w)$, we can write *BOP* equation as $B = B(Y, r)$ on the assumption that variables e, P, r_w, P_w are constant. This relationship is derived in Fig. 14.4. In the top right quadrant although every point on the *FF* curve shows *BOP* equilibrium, there is a fundamental difference between Point *A* on the curve and all other points. At *A* the $B^T = 0$ and net capital flows are zero. Thus, at Point *A*, $X = M$, and there is no net wealth transfers among countries. At other points on *FF* curve, this is not so. At *B*, for example, there is a B^T deficit. The country is using more goods than it is producing. Foreigners are acquiring some domestic wealth, which are claims on future *Y*. Thus, residents are exchanging future *Y* for current imports — they are borrowing. Clearly this will have some effect on the constraints facing residents and, therefore, on their behaviour. We are ignoring this complication here as we are interested in the short-run.

The slope of the *FF* curve depends on the slope of the B^TB^T and the *KK* curves. The slope of the former measures the responsiveness of imports to changes in *Y*. The slope of the latter measures the responsiveness of

international capital flows to differences in interest rates. [The equation of the FF curve is $B = B(Y, r) = 0$. Thus, along the FF curve, $dB = B_1 dY + B_2 dr = 0$, where B_1 and B_2 are partial derivatives of the function with respect to the first and second arguments. Thus, the slope of the FF curve is $\frac{dY}{dr} = -\frac{B_2}{B_1}$].
Here Y is measured on the horizontal axis and the interest rate on the vertical axis. Net capital inflows are measured on the left horizontal axis. As these may be positive or negative, the zero point is set on the axis with positive inflows measured to the left and negative inflows to the right. The B_T is measured on the bottom vertical axis. As this too may be positive or negative, the zero point is set on the axis with B_T deficits measured above this origin and B_T surpluses measured below the origin. In the bottom right quadrant the curve marked $B'B'$ shows the relationship between the B_T and Y. We assume that, the e, P, P_W are all fixed, the only variable that can affect the B_T is Y. The larger is Y, the worse is the B_T because imports are positively related to Y. In the top left quadrant the KK curve shows the relationship between net capital inflows and the domestic interest rate. The higher is the domestic interest rate the larger are net capital inflows. We derive the FF curve on the top right quadrant, which shows all the combinations of Y and r for which the BOP is in equilibrium. This is done quite simply.

At the Y_A the B_T is zero $(X = M)$. At r_A, net capital inflows are equal to zero. Thus, point A represents BOP equilibrium. At Y_B there is a B_T deficit equal to b. We find the interest rate, r_B, for which net capital inflows are also equal to b. Thus, point B represents BOP equilibrium. Similarly, at Y_C, there is a B_T surplus equal to C. At an interest rate r_C net capital outflows are equal to C. Thus, point C also represents BOP equilibrium. We can do this for all Y and interest rate, and by joining such points we get the FF curve. Any point below and to the right of the FF curve the BOP is in deficit. Any point above and to the left of the FF curve the BOP is in surplus. The variables in brackets along each curve are those which we are assuming fixed. Any changes in these variables will shift the relevant curve.

Case 1: Fixed exchange rate with no international capital mobility (F_1F_1).

We have both domestic and balance-of-payments equilibrium at the combination of income and interest rate Y^* and r^*. The ISC shows equilibrium in the goods sector for an open economy as we have seen in the case of a closed economy. The LMC shows equilibrium in the money sector for some given nominal quantity of money. As usual the intersection of IS and LM curves determine equilibrium at Y^* and r^*. The situation depicted in Fig.14.5, where also we have balance-of-payment equilibrium, since F_1F_1 also passes through the same point. Vertical F_1F_1 (balance-of-payments equilibrium curve) means there is no international capital mobility with fixed exchange rate regime.

Assume that, now the government wants to undertake an expansionary fiscal policy to increase income to Y_P which is shown by the shift of the *ISC* to *IS'C*. This results in a balance-of-payment deficit. Any increase in income above *Y**, *equilibrium income,* will result in an increase in imports, because

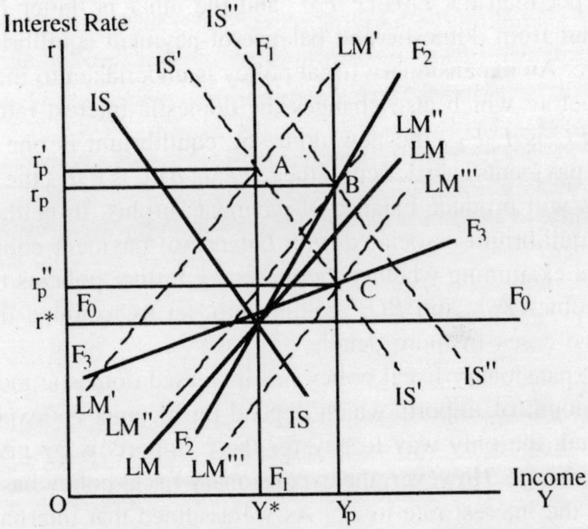

Fig. 14.5 Fixed Exchange Rate with or without some Capital Mobility

we assumed that, imports depend on income. There are only two ways for paying for the increased imports : either by giving up more domestic goods or by exchanging some wealth for them. However, in the present case, the increase in *Y* achieved by domestic policy has no effect on exports. Thus, foreigners do not want to accept more goods in payment for our imports. As there are no capital flows, the increased imports cannot be paid for by exchanging assets either. Thus, there is no way to pay for the extra imports induced by increased income, except with the stock of foreign-currency reserves available in the economy — namely by a balance-of-payment deficit financed from foreign currency reserves. Since the stock of foreign-currency reserves is unlikely to be unlimited, such a situation could only be maintained for a short period. Either the expansionary fiscal policy has to be reserved, or some other policy to reduce income to *Y** has to be undertaken. If the foreign currency flows are not stabilized, the deficit will cause outflow of foreign currency and an automatic fall in the quantity of domestic money. In this case the *LMC* will start shifting to the left until it intersects the *ISC* at point *A,* where we have again domestic and balance-of-payments equilibrium.

Case 2 : Fixed Exchange rate with some Capital Mobility.

We show the interaction between domestic and balance-of-payments equilibrium for the case of some capital mobility with an upward-sloping *FF* curve as F_2F_2 and F_3F_3 in Fig.14.5. Two *FF* curves are upward-sloping but one is steeper than the *LMC*(F_2F_2) and the other is flatter F_3F_3. Assume that, we start from domestic and balance-of-payment equilibrium at Y^* and r^* as before. An expansionary fiscal policy is undertaken to increase income to Y_P as before which also changes the domestic interest rate to r_P. If the relevant *BPC* is F_2F_2 , the new domestic equilibrium is one in which the balance-of-payments is in deficit. If the relevant *BPC* is F_3F_3, the new domestic equilibrium will produce balance-of-payment surplus. In neither case is the domestic equilibrium associated with balance-of-payment equilibrium.

Before examining whether there are any further policies to achieve the desired income (Y_P) and *BOP* equilibrium, let us examine the economies of these two cases in more detail.

The expansionary fiscal policy has increased domestic income and, via that, the amount of imports which depend on income. As exports have not been affected, the only way to pay for these imports is by giving up some assets in exchange. However, the expansionary fiscal policy has also resulted in a rise in the interest rate to r_p. As we assumed that international capital mobility depends on the interest rate, there will be an increase in capital inflows. Foreigners will purchase more assets, because the yield of domestic assets is now greater, while residents are purchasing more foreign goods, because their income is greater. If those were exactly to balance, the *BOP* would remain in equilibrium (when the slope of *FF* equals that of *LM*). However, with the F_2F_2 curve, the increase in the interest rate is not sufficient to induce foreigners to buy a sufficient amount of domestic assets to maintain *BOP* equilibrium. The required interest rate is r_p'. Thus, there is *BOP* deficit. With the F_3F_3 curve the increase in the interest rate due to fiscal expansion is larger than required to induce sufficient inflows to produce *BOP* surplus.

Both problems can be solved by a combination of domestic policies, such that, the domestic equilibrium is at *B* with F_2F_2 curve or at *C* with the F_3F_3 curve. To achieve domestic equilibrium at *B* all that is required is an expansionary fiscal policy and a contractionary monetary policy such that the resulting *IS* and *LM* curves interest at *B*. Similarly, to achieve a domestic equilibrium at *C* we need some contractionary fiscal policy and an expansionary monetary policy such that the resulting *IS* and *LM* curves intersect at *C*. In both cases what we have done is combine a set of policies to achieve just interest rate necessary to induce foreigners to purchase an amount of domestic assets to match the outflow of currency due to the increase in imports associated with the increase in income from Y^* to Y_P.

Case 3: Fixed Exchange Rate with Perfect Capital Mobility.

We start again, as in Fig. 14.5, from an initial domestic and *BOP* equilibrium at Y^* and r_w, with perfect capital mobility, r_w is the world interest rate and also domestic equlibrium interest rate. An expansionary fiscal policy is now carried out which shifts *IS* to *IS'*. The domestic interest rate is now above the world interest rate and we have massive capital inflows. To achieve *BOP* equilibrium at the higher income Y_P, the money supply will have to be increased until the $L'M'$ intersects $I'S'$ at r_w. This happens automatically because with

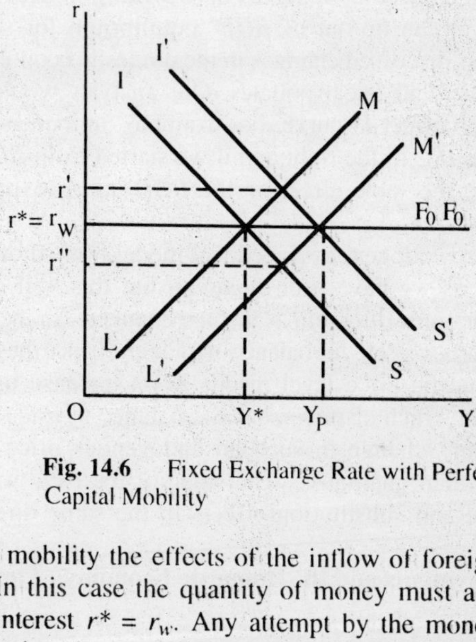

Fig. 14.6 Fixed Exchange Rate with Perfect Capital Mobility

perfect capital mobility the effects of the inflow of foreign currency cannot be sterilized. In this case the quantity of money must always be such that the domestic interest $r^* = r_w$. Any attempt by the monetary authorities to change the quantity of money without any associated changes in fiscal policies will result in capital outflows or inflows, which—via their effect on the money supply will—reverse the original change in the money supply. If we start from the initial equilibrium at Y^*, r_w as in Fig. 14.6 above, the monetary authorities increased the quantity of money shown by the shift of *LM* to $L'M'$ and fall in the interest rate from r_w to r'' there would be massive capital outflows which could not be sterilized and, thus, the money supply would fall back to its original level.

From these examples the general economic picture should be clear. With a fixed exchange rate the domestic economy is more or less constrained by the conditions of *BOP* equilibrium. How great this constraint is, and which variables are constrained, depends on the degree of capital mobility. In the case of no capital mobility *domestic income is fixed* by the *BOP* equilibrium condition. There is no policy or combinations of policies, which can change

Y while maintaining *BOP* equilibrium, of course, if a country has sufficient foreign-currency reserves it can for some time remain in *BOP* deficit.

If there is perfect capital mobility the domestic interest rate is constrained by the condition for *BOP* equilibrium. No policy or combination of policies can affect the domestic interest rate. Moreover, because of this constraint the domestic M_s has to adjust to keep the interest rate at the world level.

If there is some capital mobility, some combination of equilibrium Y and interest rate is required for *BOP* equilibrium, but such a combination can always be attained by a mixture of monetary and fiscal policies. If a country has sufficient foreign-currency reserves or is willing to accumulate foreign-currency reserves, it can be out of *BOP* equilibrium for some period.

We have so far discussed changes in the domestic economy arising from changes in monetary and fiscal policies. Our analysis would also apply to other changes which affect *IS* curve. For example, an increase in investment would also shift the *ISC* to the right and if we started from *BOP* equilibrium this would produce the same effect on the *BOP* as an expansionary fiscal policy.

If we introduce endogenous price level model instead of fixed domestic price level model, as we have been doing so far, this will cause price and *BOP* changes in the same direction as income changes. An increase in income via its effect on imports worsens the balance of trade and hence the *BOP*. Similarly, an increase in domestic price level results in an increase in imports and a decrease in exports, which also worsens the balance of trade and, hence, the *BOP*. Thus, the only change in such an endogenous price level model is quantitative rather than qualitative. The slope of the *FFC* would be steeper because of income and substitution effects in the same direction.

The Balance of Payments and the Domestic Economy : Flexible Exchange Rate

With flexible exchange rates any *BOP* disequilibrium will be solved by changes in the exchange rate. Any excess demand or for excess supply of foreign currency will affect the exchange rate. Thus, the *BOP* will always be in equilibrium but the exchange rate will change as exports, imports or capital flows vary $[e = B(P, Y, r, r_w, P_w)]$. However, such changes in the exchange rate impinge directly on equilibrium in the domestic economy because both imports and exports and, thus, aggregate demand, depend on the exchange rate. Thus, there is a direct link between *BOP* equilibrium and domestic equilibrium that is absent in the fixed exchange rate case. Of course, as in the case of fixed exchange rate, there are also the links from the domestic economy to the *BOP*, and, thus, to exchange rate via income, interest rates and the price level. There is, thus, two-way linkage between the *BOP* and domestic equilibrium. Any change in the domestic equilibrium will affect the *BOP*. And any change in the *BOP* will affect the exchange rate and, thus, have repercussions on the domestic equilibrium, we will examine this interaction in more detail.

As the linkage variable connecting domestic economy and *BOP* is the exchange rate, we first consider how changes in the exchange rate affect domestic equilibrium.

It is clear from an open economy *ISC* (derived previously) that, even if we hold both the domestic and foreign price level constant, equilibrium in the goods sector depends on the exchange rate as the Fig. 14.7(a) below demonstrates. We show three *IS* curves and a given *LMC*. Three *ISCs* shown are for three different exchange rates $e_0 > e_1 > e_2$. These *IS* curves summarize

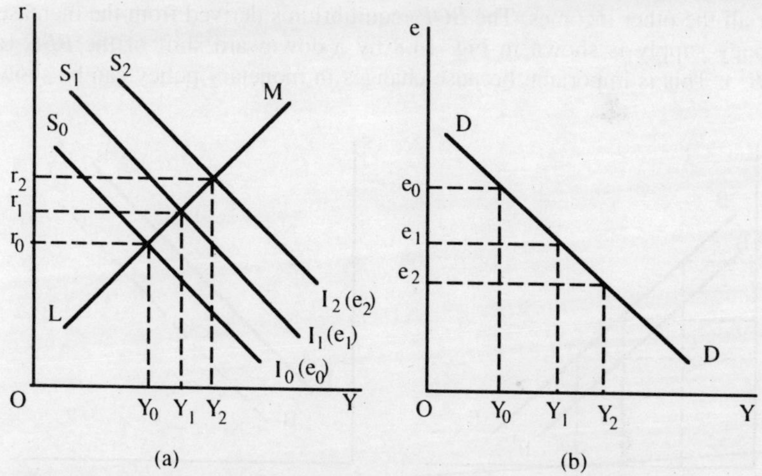

Fig. 14.7 The Balance of Payments and the Domestic Economy with Flexible Exchange Rate

IS equation. We can see clearly that the domestic equilibrium income and interest rate depends on the exchange rate. This relationship is shown in Fig. 14. 7(b), where income is measured on the horizontal axis and the exchange rate on the vertical axis. The *DD* curve plots all the points, such as (e_0, Y_0), (e_1, Y_1) and (e_2, Y_2). This *DD* curve shows the relationship between *AD* and the exchange rate(e). It is clear from the derivation of this curve that along this curve we hold constant all the variables which are held constant along the *IS* and the *LM* curves used to derive the *DD* curve. Thus, any change in the nominal quantity of money (increase or decrease), and any fiscal policy change (increase or decrease), will shift the curve outwards or inwards. Thus, policy change can be shown by shifts in the *DD* curve.

From the *FFC* of the fixed exchange we derive the *BB* curve (Fig.14.8) which shows the various combinations of income and exchange rates for which the *BOP* is in equilibrium. Any point above the curve is one in which the

BOP is in deficit and, therefore, exchange rate will fall. Any point below the curve a *BOP* is in surplus and the exchange rate rises.

When deriving the *BOP* equilibrium relationship (the *BB* curve) we made use of the money supply *(LMC)*. The reason for this is that the *BOP* depends on both trade and capital flows, which, for a given world interest rate, depends on the domestic interest rate. For any given equilibrium income, it is the money supply (the *LMC*) which tells us what the associated equilibrium interest rate is. This means that, any changes in the money supply will result in changes in the *BB* curve. If the money supply is increased (the *LMC* shifts to the right), at the previous exchange rate, the *BOP* is in deficit for all incomes and interest rates. Since the *BOP* is in deficit, exchange rate would fall. Similarly for all the other incomes. The *BOP* equilibriums derived from the increased money supply is shown in Fig. 14.8 by a downward shift of the *BBC* (as *B'B'*). This is important, because changes in monetary policy can be shown

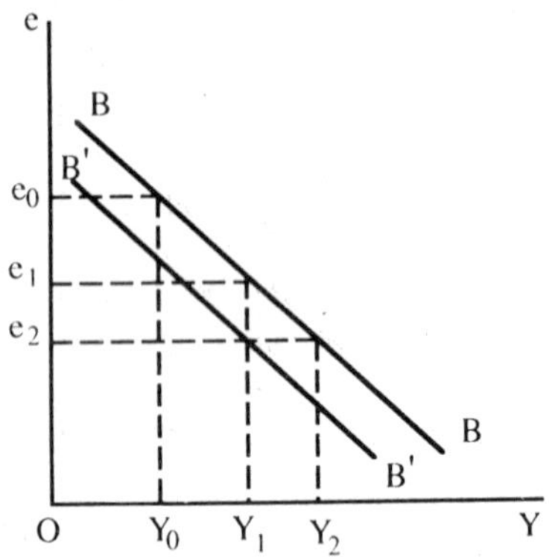

Fig. 14.8 The Balance of Payment Equilibrium and Money Supply

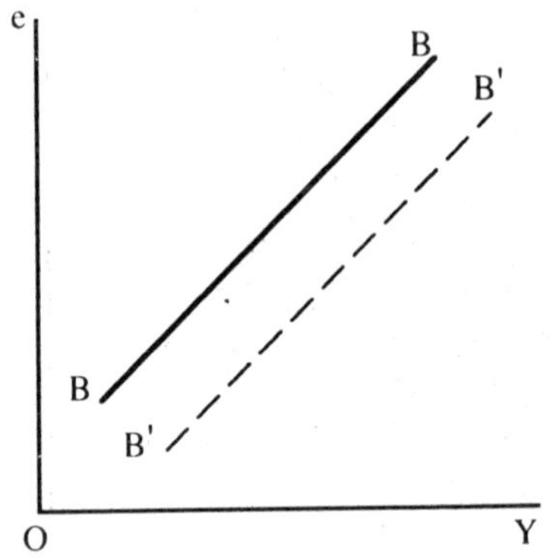

Fig. 14.9 The BB curve would be upward sloping if the FF curve is Flatter than LMC

by shifts in the *LMC* which will also shift the *BB* curve. We thus have to hold the quantity of money constant along the *BB* curve. All the variables held constant along the *BB* curve are quantity of money *(M)*, world interest rate (r_w), domestic price *(P)* and world price (P_w).

The *BOP* equilibrium curve *(BB)* was derived using the *FF* curve. However, we saw in our analysis of the fixed exchange rate case that the slope of the *FF* curve relative to *LMC* is important. We concluded there that an expansionary fiscal policy will result in a *BOP* surplus if the *FF* curve is flatter than the *LMC*, but a *BOP* deficit if it is steeper than the *LMC*. If the exchange rate is flexible, a *BOP* deficit will result in a fall in exchange rate, a *BOP* surplus will lead to a rise in the exchange rate. The *BB* curve would be downward sloping if the *FF* curves are steeper (as in Fig.14.8). The *BB* curve would be upward sloping, if the *FF* curves are flatter than *LMC*, as given in Fig.14.9. Again, it is obvious that an increase in the quantity of money will shift this curve downward, as in the previous case.

In the case of perfect capital mobility the *FF* curve is perfectly elastic. The *BB* curve for this case is perfectly inelastic as in Fig. 14.10. Again, increase in the money supply will shift the BB curve to the right as *B'B'*. In Figures 14.8 to 14.10 we draw the *BOP* equilibrium as a relationship between the exchange rate and income, and via this, of course, the associated domestic equilibrium interest rate. In Fig. 14.7 we derived the condition for domestic equilibrium as a relationship between domestic income and the exchange rate, and via this, of course, the domestic interest rate (the *DD* curve). To examine

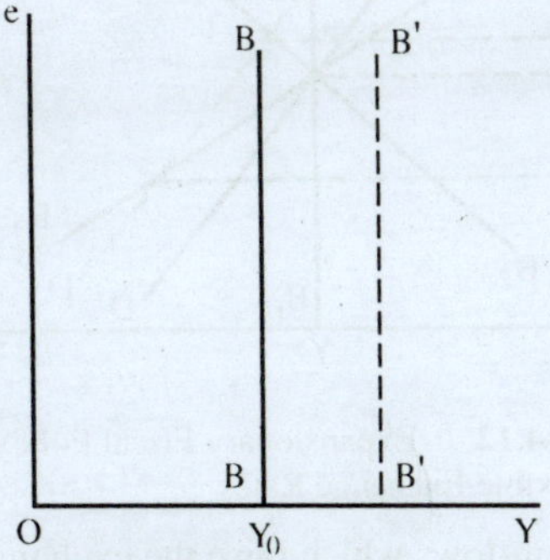

Fig. 14.10 The BB curve with Perfect Capital Mobility

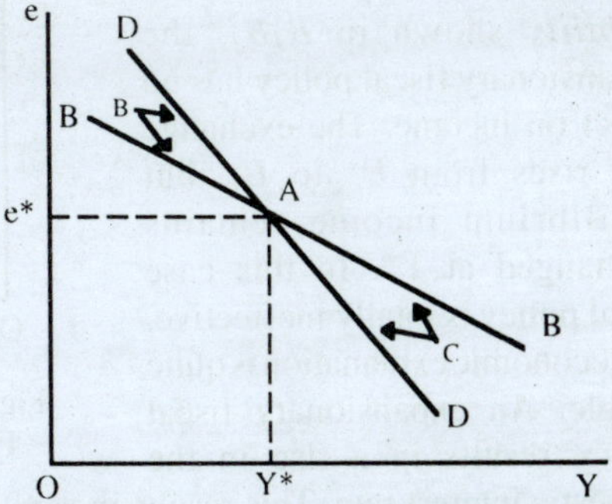

Fig. 14.11 Interactions between Domestic and BOP Equilibrium

domestic and *BOP* equilibrium and their interactions, we combine these two relationships in Fig. 14.11. We do this for the case of the downward-sloping *BB* curve leaving other cases to the reader.

At point *A* we have both domestic and *BOP* equilibrium with income *Y** and exchange rate *e**. Aggregate demand for commodities, including exports, is equal to the aggregate supply of commodities, including imports. The inflow of foreign currency—arising from exports and capital outflows, is equal to the outflows of foreign currency. Consider points *B* and *C*. At these points, both the *BOP* and the domestic economy is in disequilibrium. With the combination of *Y* and *e* shown by point *B*, aggregate demand is greater than aggregate supply. Thus, output will rise. Again, at *B*, the *BOP* is in deficit and the exchange rate will fall. The arrows at *B* show these tendencies. This is, of course, not the whole story. The fall in exchange rate via its effect on imports and exports will have further repercussion on aggregate demand. The rise in income via its effect on imports, and the associated changes in the interest rate via their effect on capital flows, will have further effects on the exchange rate. These intersections will continue until point *A* is reached where we have both *BOP* and domestic equilibrium. A similar story can be told about point *C*.

Government Policies : Flexible Exchange Rates

In Fig.14.12 we show an initial domestic and balance-of-payments equilibrium at income Y^* and an exchange rate E^* with aggregate demand curve *DD*. Three BB curves are shown for three cases examined in the last section. An expansionary fiscal policy will shift the *DD* curve to *D'D'*. We can now examine the effect of such a policy in the three cases.

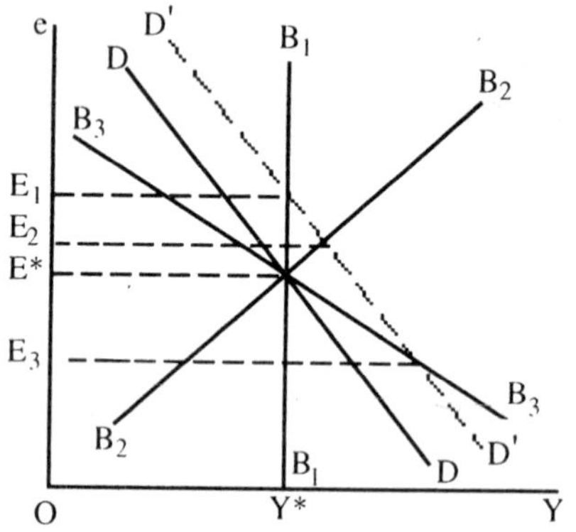

Fig. 14.12 Expansionary Fiscal Policy – Flexible Exchange Rates

In the case of *perfect capital mobility* shown in B_1B_1, the expansionary fiscal policy has no effect on income. The exchange rate rises from E^* to E_1, but equilibrium income remains unchanged at Y^*. In this case fiscal policy is totally ineffective. The economic explanation is quite simple. An expansionary fiscal policy results in a rise in the domestic interest rate. This results in capital inflows which raise the exchange rate, reducing exports and increasing imports, and thus, reducing aggregate demand. With perfect mobility this will continue as long as the domestic interest rate is above the world interest rate, which means as long as income is greater than initial income Y^*. When the exchange rate has risen sufficiently to reduce aggregate demand by the full fiscal policy amount, the *BOP* will again be in equilibrium.

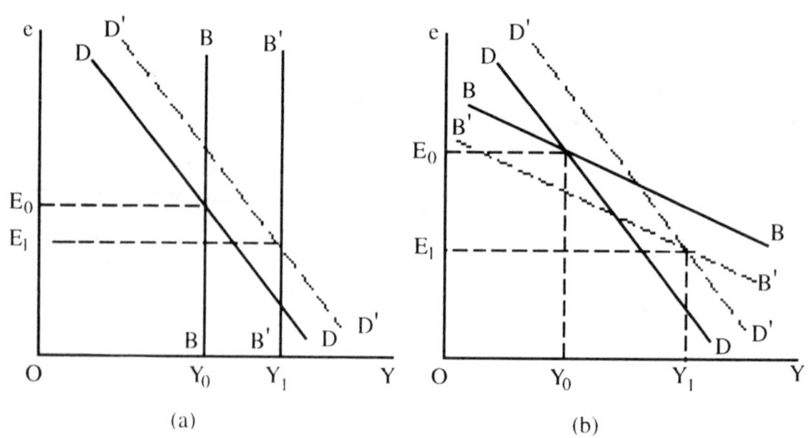

Fig. 14.13 Effect of Monetary Policy : Flexible Exchange Rates

With B_2B_2 *BOP* equilibrium curve, the expansionary fiscal policy results in an increase in *Y* with a rise in exchange rate (to E_2). With B_3B_3 curve there is an increase in *Y* with a fall in the exchange rate (to E_3). The different exchange rate effects arise because of the difference in the degree of capital mobility represented by the curves.

Again, it should be noted that, exactly the same results would occur if there was a shift of *DD* curve because of any exogenous increase in *AD*. Now we can see the effects of monetary policy for the case of *perfect capital mobility* in Fig. 14.13(a) and for the case of capital mobility (in the case of downward sloping *BB* curve) in Fig. 14.13(b). In both cases we start from an initial equilibrium at Y_0 and E_0. An expansionary monetary policy shifts the *DD* curve to $D'D'$ and the *BB* curve to $B'B'$. In both cases, expansionary monetary policy increases *Y* and reduces the *E*. Thus, even though in the case of perfect capital mobility fiscal policy is totally ineffective, monetary policy is effective in changing *Y*. An expansionary monetary policy reduces the domestic interest rate, and thus induces capital outflows. This leads to a fall in the exchange rate which increases exports and decreases imports, thus increases *AD*. This will continue until the increase in *AD* is sufficient to raise the domestic interest rate to the original level.

Exercise

1. Discuss the view that currency depreciation may be inflationary and, therefore, ineffective as a means of correcting a balance of payments deficit.
2. Under a regime of flexible exchange rates, do speculators have a stabilising or destabilising effect?
3. Identify the conditions under which the investment multiplier in an open economy in the *IS-LM* model is equal to the reciprocal of the sum of the *MPS* and *MPM*.
4. A country has a surplus in the trade balance and a deficit in the capital account of the balance of payments. Show diagrammatically how fiscal and monetary policies can be used to attain domestic and external equilibria simultaneously. How will our analysis be affected if the monetary authority is given the task of maintaining full employment income and the fiscal authority takes the task of the balance of payments equilibrium?
5. The saving function in an economy may be given $S = s - a + SY$, where *S* is saving, *Y* income and *s* and *a* the parameters of the function. If *v* is the optimum capital-output ratio, obtain the equilibrium patterns of capital-stock, investment and income.

6. The production function in an economy is $Y = K^{1/2}L^{1/2}$, where Y is income, K is the stock of capital and L is labour force. The saving function is $S = 0.2Y$, where S is saving. If the labour force grows at a constant proportional rate of 2 per cent, find the steady state values of per capita consumption and income. If the per capita consumption at the steady state is to be maximised, what should be your policy prescription for the government?

7. If 20 per cent of the income always goes to replacement of the depreciated capital stock in the conditions given in question (6) above, what would be the steady state values of per capita income and consumption?

8. The two countries, A and B, have an annual income of Rs. 40 millions andRs. 60 millions, respectively, at the end of the year 1985. Their propensity to save is 0.2 and the optimum capital-output ratio is 4. The government in country A wishes to catch up with the income level of country B by the end of the present century. By how much the propensity to save must be increased in A, if the capital-output ratio cannot be changed?

15 THE MUNDELL-FLEMING MODEL

In the last chapter, we discussed open economy model. Open economies export some of the goods and services they produce, and imports some of the goods and services they need but do not produce. Open economies can also borrow and lend in the world financial market.

Now we discuss how open economy behaves in the short-run. Our aim here is to understand how fiscal and monetary policies influence the aggregate income with the help of Mundell-Fleming Model, an open-economy version of the *IS-LM* Model. These models assume that the price level is fixed and then show what causes fluctuations in aggregate income. They also stress an intersection between the goods and money markets. The key difference is that the *IS-LM* Model assumes a closed economy, whereas the Mundell-Fleming Model assumes an open economy.

An important lesson of the Mundell-Fleming Model is that the behaviour of an economy depends on the exchange-rate system it has adopted. We examine first a floating exchange rate and then a fixed exchange rate, and in the end discuss the debate between floating and fixed exchange rates.

The Mundell-Fleming Model (1)[1]

We first discuss the Mundell-Fleming Model and then evaluate the various policies under floating and fixed exchange rates.

The Mundell-Fleming Model is made up of the following three equations:

$$IS : C(Y - T) + I(r) + G + NX(e)$$

$$LM : M/P = L(r,Y)$$

$$r = r^*$$

We review each of these equations before putting them together to make a short-run model of a small open economy.

The first equation describes the goods market. It is already familiar to us—the aggregate *Y* is the sum of consumption *C*, investment *I*, government expenditure *G*, and net exports *NX*. Consumption depends on disposable income *(Y – T)*. Investment is negatively related to interest rate*(r)*. Net exports depend

[1]See R .A. Mundell, International Economics, (New York, Macmillan, 1968) and also J. M. leming "Domestic Financial Policies under Fixed and under Floating Exchange Rates" IMF Staff Papers 9(Nov. 1962)369-379.

negatively on the real exchange rate(e). Since the Mundell-Fleming Model assumes that prices are fixed, changes in the real exchange rate are proportional to changes in the nominal exchange rate and when the nominal exchange rate rises, foreign goods become less expensive compared to domestic goods—which stimulates imports and depresses exports. The second equation is a familiar money market equation, which states that the supply of real money balances, M/P, equals the demand, $L(r, Y)$. The demand for money depends negatively on the interest rate and positively on income. The money supply is an exogenous variable controlled by the monetary authority. Like the *IS-LM* Model, the Mundell-Fleming Model takes the price level P as an exogenous variable. The third equation states that the world interest rate r^* determines the interest rate in the economy. This equation holds because we are examining a small open economy which is sufficiently small relative to the world economy wherefrom it can borrow or lend as much as it wishes without affecting the world interest rate.

These three equations fully describe the Mundell-Fleming Model. We will examine the implications of these equations for short-run fluctuations in an open economy.

The Model on a Y– E Graph

The most easy way to analyse the Mundell-Fleming Model is to draw the graph in which income is shown on the horizontal axis and the exchange rate is on the vertical axis as in Fig. 15.1. This graph is drawn holding the rate of interest constant at the world interest rate.

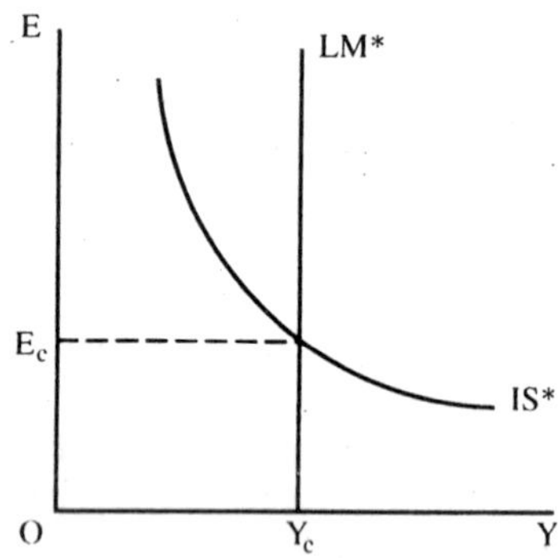

Fig. 15.1 The Mundell-Fleming model on a Y-E Graph

We label these curves *IS** and *LM** to remind us that, we are holding the interest rate constant at the world interest rate r^*. The equilibrium of the economy is found by the intersection of *IS** and *LM** curves. The intersection determines the level of income and the exchange rate.

The *LM** curve is vertical because the exchange rate does not enter into the *LM** equation. Given the world interest rate, the *LM** curve determines aggregate income, regardless of the exchange rate.

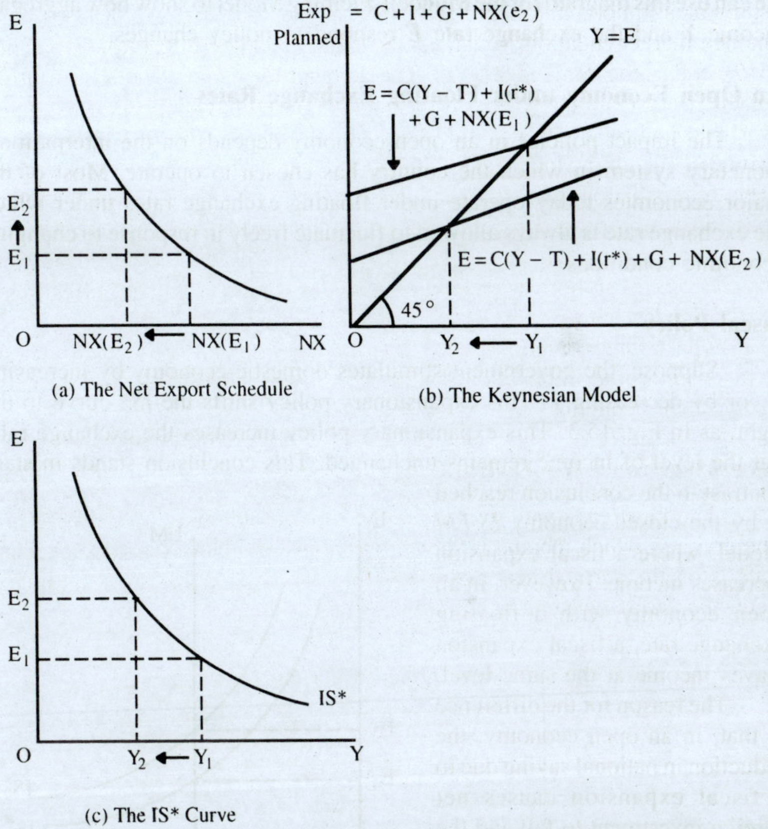

Fig. 15.2 Net Exports Schedule combined with Keynesian Model

The *IS** curve slopes downward because a higher exchange rate lowers net exports and, thus, lowers aggregate income. Fig. 15.2 shows how this works, where we combine net-exports schedule and Keynesian Model to derive the *IS** curve. An increase in exchange rate from E_1 to E_2 lowers net exports from $NX(e_1)$ to $NX(e_2)$. The reduction in net exports reduces planned expenditure and, thus, lowers income.

The *IS Curve:** The *IS** curve is derived from the net exports and the Keynesian Model. Fig. 15.2(a) shows the net-exports schedule: an increase in the exchange rate from E_1 to E_2 lowers net exports from $NX(E_1)$ to $NX(E_2)$.

Fig.15.2(b) shows the Keynesian Model: a decrease in net exports from $NX(E_1)$ to $NX(E_2)$ reduces income from Y_1 to Y_2. Fig. 15.2(c) shows the IS^* curve summarizing this inverse relationship between income and exchange rate. Now we can use this diagram for the Mundell-Fleming Model to show how aggregate income Y and the exchange rate E respond to policy changes.

An Open Economy under Floating Exchange Rates

The impact policies in an open economy depends on the international monetary system in which the country has chosen to operate. Most of the major economies today operate under floating exchange rates under which the exchange rate is always allowed to fluctuate freely in response to changing economic conditions.

Fiscal Policy

Suppose, the government stimulates domestic economy by increasing G or by decreasing T. This expansionary policy shifts the IS^* curve to the right, as in Fig. 15.3. This expansionary policy increases the exchange rate, but the level of income remains unchanged. This conclusion stands in stark contrast to the conclusion reached at by the closed-economy *IS-LM* Model, where a fiscal expansion increases income. However, in an open economy with a floating exchange rate, a fiscal expansion leaves income at the same level.

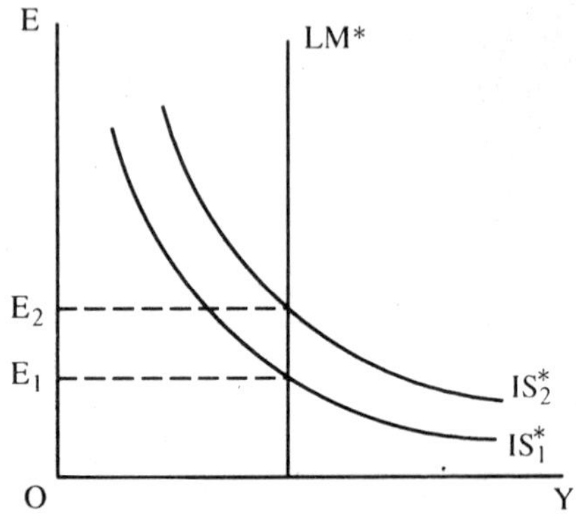

Fig. 15.3 Fiscal Policy in an Open Economy : Floating Exchange Rates

The reason for the difference is that, in an open economy, the reduction in national saving due to a fiscal expansion causes net foreign investment to fall and the exchange rate to appreciate—which reduces net exports, which offsets the expansion in the domestic economy.

To understand the difference better between the closed and open economies, consider the equation describing equilibrium in the money market: $M/P = L(r, Y)$, where the supply of real balances M/P is fixed, and the demand must always equal this fixed supply. In a closed economy, a fiscal expansion causes the interest rate to rise, and equilibrium income to rise. However, in an open economy, r is fixed at r^*, so there can only be one level of Y that may satisfy this equation. Thus, the appreciation of the exchange rate and the fall in net exports must be large enough to offset fully the expansionary impact of fiscal policy.

Monetary Policy

An increase in the money supply in a fixed price level increases real balances and, thus, shifts the LM^* curve to the right, as in Fig. 15.4. This raises income and lowers the exchange rate.

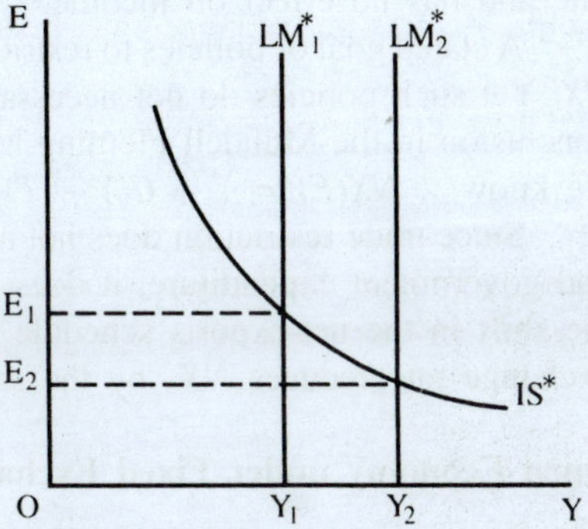

Fig. 15.4 Effect of Monetary Policy in an Open Economy

Although monetary policy increases income both in an open and in a closed economy, the monetary transaction mechanism is different. As we already know, in a closed economy an increase in money supply lowers the interest rate, which stimulates investment. However, in an open economy with a fixed interest rate, *($r = r^*$)*, an increase in money supply puts downward pressure on the domestic interest rate, capital flows out of the economy. This capital flow prevents the interest rate from falling, and it causes the exchange to go down. The fall in the exchange rate makes domestic goods inexpensive relative to foreign goods, which stimulates exports. Thus, in an open economy, monetary policy increases income by altering the exchange rate rather than the interest rate as in a closed economy.

Trade Policy

Suppose, the government wishes to reduce the demand for imports by imposing an import quota or a tariff. What would be its impact on income and the exchange rate?

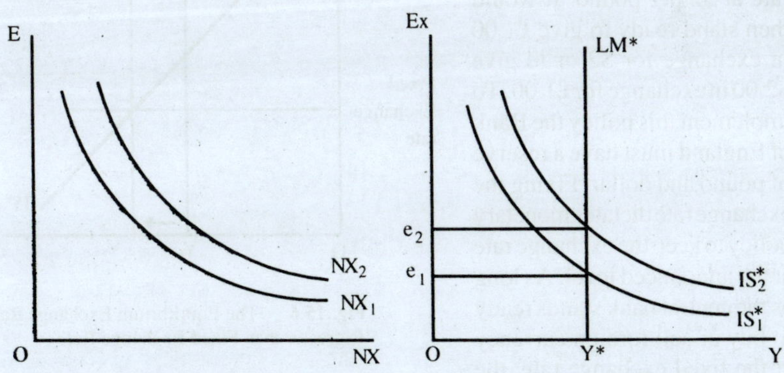

(a) The Shift in the Net Export Schedule (b) The Change in the Equilibrium

Fig. 15.5 Effect of Trade Policy on Income and Exchange Rate

Since net import equals exports minus imports, a reduction in imports will mean an increase in net exports, which shifts the net-exports schedule to the right, as in Fig.15.5(a). This shift in net-exports schedule moves the IS^* curve to the right as well. Thus, the trade restriction raises the exchange rate and has no effect on income.

A stated goal of policies to restrict trade is often to alter the trade balance *NX*. Yet such policies do not necessarily have that effect. We get the same conclusion in the Mundell-Fleming Model under flexible exchange rate. As we know : $NX(E) = Y - C(Y - T) - I(r) - G.$

Since trade restriction does not affect income, consumption, investment and government expenditure, it does not affect the trade balance. Although the shift in the net-exports schedule tends to raise *NX*, the increase in the exchange rate reduces *NX* by the same amount.

Open Economy under Fixed Exchange Rate

We now turn to the Fixed Exchange Rates System. In the 1950s and 1960s, most of the world economies were operating within the Bretton Woods System known as adjustable peg system. This system was abandoned in early 1970s, and exchange rates were allowed to float. In this section we discuss how such a system works, and examine the impact of economic policies on a fixed exchange rate.

How a Fixed-Exchange-Rate System Works

Under a system of fixed exchange rates, a central bank stands ready to purchase or sell the domestic currency for foreign currencies at a predetermined rate. Suppose, the central bank announced that it was going to fix the exchange rate at $2 per pound. It would then stand ready to give £1.00 in exchange for $2 or to give $2.00 in exchange for £1.00. To implement this policy the Bank of England must have a reserve of pound and dollar. Fixing the exchange rate dictates monetary policy to keep the exchange rate at the announced level. As long as the central bank stands ready to buy or sell foreign currency at the fixed exchange rate, the money supply adjusts automatically to the necessary level.

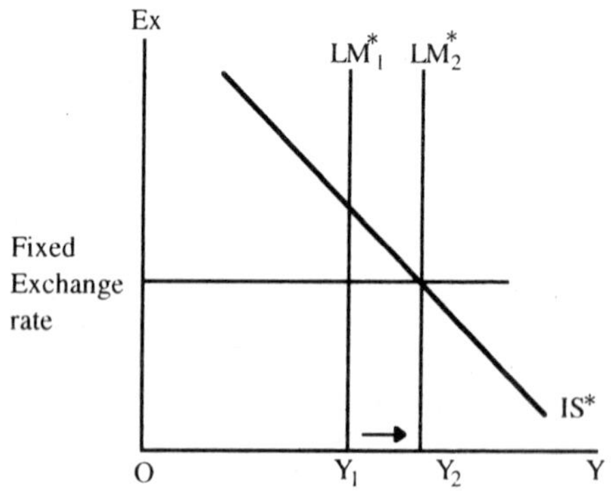

Fig. 15.6 The Equilibrium Exchange Rate is greater than Fixed Exchange Rate

We examine how fixing the exchange rate determines the money supply.

In Fig. 15.6, the equilibrium exchange rate exceeds the fixed exchange rate. Arbitrageurs will buy foreign currency in foreign-exchange markets and sell it to the central bank for a profit. This process automatically increases the money supply, shifting the *LM** curve to the right and lowering the exchange rate.

Fig.15.7 shows the equilibrium exchange rate is below the fixed exchange rate. Arbitrageurs will buy pounds in foreign-exchange markets and use them to buy foreign exchange from the central bank. This process automatically reduces the money supply, shifting the *LM** curve to the left and raising the exchange rate, as Fig. 15.7 shows.

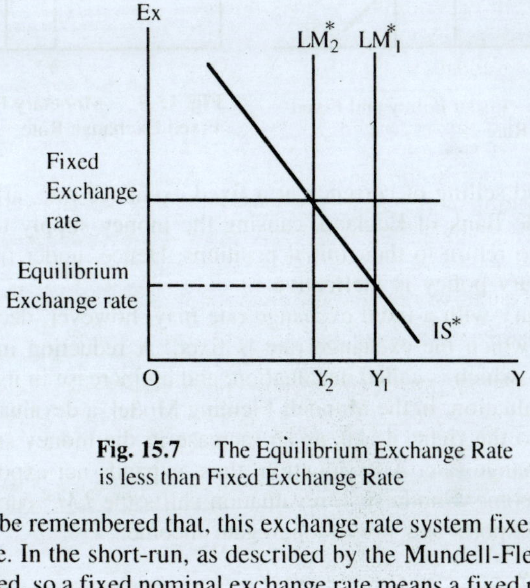

Fig. 15.7 The Equilibrium Exchange Rate is less than Fixed Exchange Rate

It must be remembered that, this exchange rate system fixes the nominal exchange rate. In the short-run, as described by the Mundell-Fleming Model, prices are fixed, so a fixed nominal exchange rate means a fixed real exchange rate as well.

Fiscal Policy

A fiscal expansion shifts the *IS** curve to the right as in Fig. 15.8. To maintain the fixed exchange rate, the central bank must increase the money supply and shift the *LM** curve to the right as well. Hence, in contrast to the case of floating exchange rates, under fixed exchange rates a fiscal expansion raises income. Hence, under fixed exchange rates, fiscal policy is effective.

Monetary Policy

If the central bank tries to increase the money supply — for example, by buying bonds from the public — it will shift the *LM** curve to the right, lowering the exchange rate , as in Fig. 15.9. Since, the central bank is committed

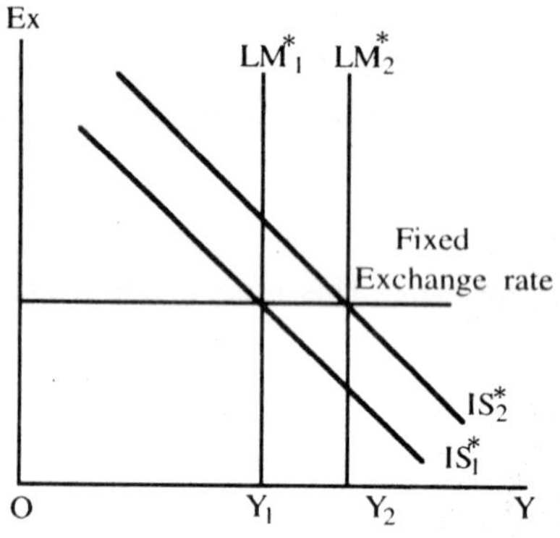

Fig. 15.8 Fiscal Policy and Fixed Exchange Rate

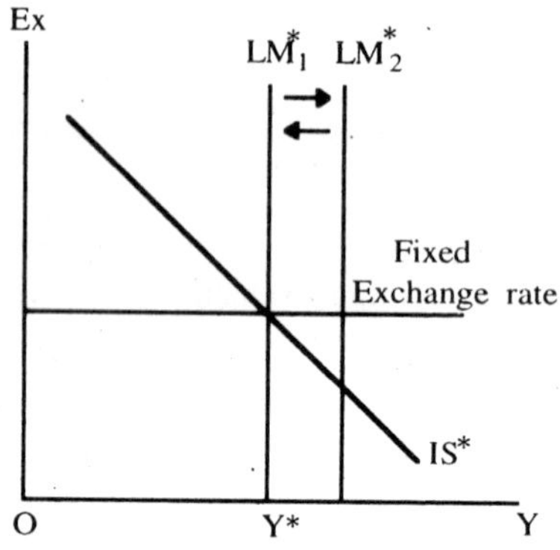

Fig. 15.9 Monetary Policy and Fixed Exchange Rate

to buying and selling of currency at a fixed exchange rate, arbitrageurs sell pounds to the Bank of England, causing the money supply to fall and the *LM** curve to return to their initial positions. Hence, under fixed exchange rates, monetary policy is ineffective.

A country with a fixed exchange rate may, however, decide to change the level at which the exchange rate is fixed. A reduction in the value of the currency, which is called devaluation, and an increase in its value, which is called revaluation. In the Mundell-Fleming Model, a devaluation shifts the *LM** curve to the right; it acts as an increase in the money supply under a floating exchange rate. A devaluation, thus, expands net exports and raises aggregate income. Similarly, a revaluation shifts the *LM** curve to the left, reduces net exports and lowers aggregate income.

Trade Policy

A tariff or an import quota reduces imports. This policy shifts the net exports schedule outward and thus shifts the *IS** curve to the right, as in Fig.15.10. The shift in the *IS** curve tends to raise the exchange rate. To keep the exchange rate at the fixed level, the money supply must rise, this shifts the *LM** curve to the right.

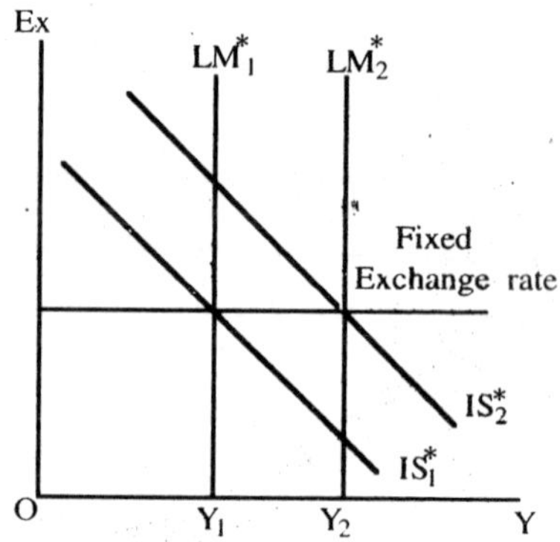

Fig. 15.10 Trade Policy under Fixed Exchange Rate

Under a fixed exchange rate, a trade restriction raises aggregate income. Further, the trade restriction also raises net exports NX. Since the exchange rate is fixed, an outward shift in the net export schedule implies an increase in net exports. To put it in another way, recall that, $NX = S - I$.

The expansion in income leads to an increase in saving, which implies an increase in net exports.

Summary of the Mundell-Fleming Model

The Mundell-Fleming Model shows that the power of monetary and fiscal policy to influence aggregate income depends on the exchange rate regime. Under floating exchange rates, only monetary policy is effective. Under fixed exchange rates, only fiscal policy is effective. The potency of the monetary policy is lost because the money supply is dedicated to maintaining the exchange rate at the pre-determined level.

Should Exchange Rate be Floating or Fixed?

Having examined how an economy works under fixed and floating exchange rates, we turn to the question of which exchange rate regime is desirable. The international monetary system is often a topic of heated debate among economists and policy-makers. Historically, many economists have favoured a system of floating exchange rates, but, in recent years, some have advocated a return of fixed exchange rates.

The main argument for a floating exchange rate is that it allows monetary policy to be used for other purposes. Under a fixed exchange rate, monetary policy is committed to a single goal of maintaining fixed exchange rate at a predetermined level. Yet the exchange is only one macroeconomic variable among many that monetary policy can influence. A floating exchange rate system allows monetary policy to pursue other goods, such as stabilisation policy.

Advocates of fixed exchange rates argue that, exchange rate uncertainty makes international trade more difficult. After abandoning the Bretton Woods System of fixed exchange rates in the early 1970s, exchange rates became more volatile. Some economists attributed this volatility to irrational speculation by the international investors. It is claimed by some economists that this volatility is harmful because it increases the uncertainty associated with the world trade. Despite this volatility, the amount of world trade has increased under floating exchange rates.

Advocates of fixed exchange rates sometimes argue that a fixed exchange rate is one way to discipline the monetary authority to prevent excessive growth in the money supply. Yet, there are many other policy rules to which the central bank could be committed. However, the fixed exchange rate has the advantage of being simpler to implement than some other policy rules, since the money supply adjusts automatically, but the policy may also leads to greater instability in income and employment. The choice between fixed and floating exchange rates is not as stark as it may seem at first. During periods of fixed exchange rates, countries can change the value of their currency, if it is necessary. During periods of floating exchange rates, countries can use targets for exchange rate when deciding whether to expand or contract the money supply. We hardly observe exchange rates that are completely fixed or floating. Instead, under both systems, stability of exchange rate is one among many of the central bank's objectives.

The Mundell-Fleming Model with a Change in Price Level

Now we want to see how the Mundell-Fleming Model operates with a change in price level. To examine price adjustment in an open economy, we must distinguish between the nominal exchange rate *E* and the real exchange rate $\mathcal{E}$, which equals *EP/P** . We can rewrite the Mundell-Fleming Model as :

$$Y = C(Y - T) + I(r^*) + G\ NX(E) \qquad IS^*$$
$$M/P = L(r^*, Y) \qquad LM^*$$

These are familiar *IS** curve and *LM** curve where net exports (*NX*) depend on the real exchange rate.

Fig.15.11 shows what happens when the price level falls. As lower price level implies a higher level of real balances, the *LM** curve shifts to the right, as in Fig. 15.11(a). The real exchange rate depreciates, and the equilibrium level of income rises.

The negative relationship between the price level and the level of income is shown in the aggregate demand curve as in Fig. 15.11(b). Thus, the aggregate demand curve implied by the Mundell-Fleming Model is similar to that implied by the *IS-LM* model. Policies that raise or lower income in the Mundell-Fleming Model shift the aggregate demand curve to right and the left, respectively.

We can extend our analysis to see how the short-run model discussed in this chapter is related to the long-run model discussed before. Fig. 15.12(a) shows the

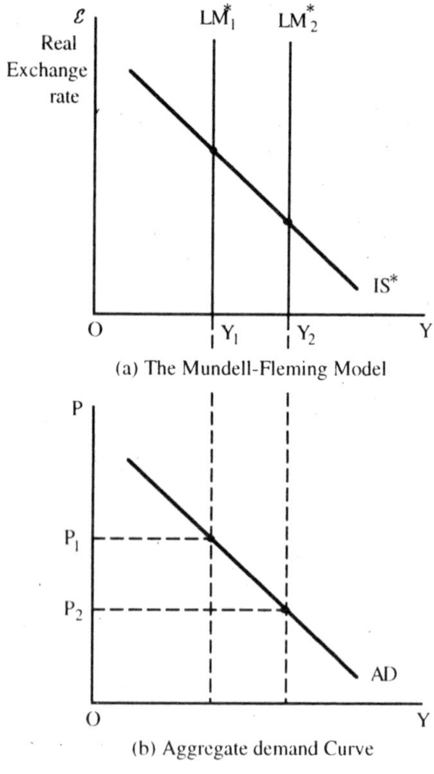

Fig. 15.11 The Mundell-Fleming Model with a change in Price Level

short-run and long-run equilibrium, IS^* and LM^* intersection at point K shows equilibrium under the Keynesian assumption that the price level is fixed at P_1. At this equilibrium, the demand for goods and services is too low to keep

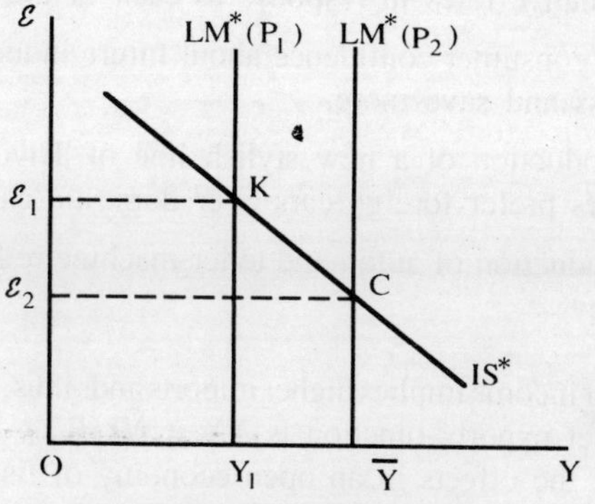

(a) The Mundell-Fleming Model

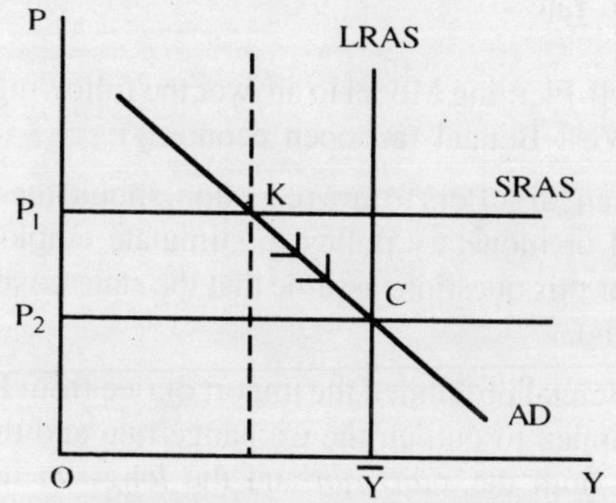

(b) The Model of Aggregate Demand and Aggregate Supply

Fig. 15.12 The Short-Run and Long-Run Equilibrium

the economy producing at its natural rate. The low demand causes the price to fall in the long-run. The fall in the price level increases real money balances, which shifts the LM^* curve to the right. The real exchange rate depreciates, which stimulates net exports.

The Mundell-Fleming as a Theory of Aggregate Demand

Eventually, the long-run equilibrium is achieved at point C under the classical assumption. The speed of transition from K to C depends on how quickly the price level adjusts to restore the economy to the natural rate, $\overline{Y}$.

Exercise

1. Use the Mundell-Fleming Model to predict what would happen to aggregate income, the exchange rate, and the trade balance under both floating and fixed exchange rates in response to each of the following:

   a) A fall in consumer confidence about future induces consumers to spend less and save more.

   b) The introduction of a new stylish line of Toyotas makes some consumers prefer foreign cars over domestic cars.

   c) The introduction of automatic teller machine reduces the demand for money.

2. Suppose higher income implies higher imports and, thus, lower net exports. That is, the net exports function is $NX = NX(E,Y)$.

   Examine the effects in an open economy of fiscal expansion on income and the trade balance under (a) a floating exchange rate, (b) a fixed exchange rate.

3. Use the Mundell-Fleming Model to answer the following questions about the State of West Bengal (an open economy):

   a) If West Bengal suffers from a recession, should the state government use fiscal or monetary policy to stimulate employment? Explain. (Note: For this question, assume that the state government can print rupee bills).

   b) If West Bengal prohibited the import of rice from Bangladesh, what would happen to output, the exchange rate and the trade balance? Consider both the *short-run* and the *long-run* impacts.

4. The Mundell-Fleming Model takes the world interest rate r^* as an exogenous variable. Let us consider what happens when this variable changes:

   a) What might cause the world interest rate to rise?

   b) In the Mundell-Fleming Model with floating and fixed exchange rates, what happens to aggregate income, the exchange rate, and the trade balance when r^* rises?

Appendix

A Short-run Model of the Large Open Economy

A large open economy differs from a small open economy, because its interest rate is not fixed by the world financial market. In a large open economy, it is necessary to consider the relationship between the net foreign investment and the interest rate. As the domestic interest rate falls, domestic investors find foreign lending more attractive, and foreign investors find lending less attractive. Thus, net foreign investment is negatively related to the interest rate. We add this relationship to the short-run model of national income. The equations of the model are :

$$(1) \quad Y = C(Y - T) + I(G) + G + NX(e)$$
$$(2) \quad M/P = L(r, Y)$$
$$(3) \quad NX(e) = NFI(r)$$

The first two equations are the same as the Mundell-Fleming Model. The third equation states that the trade balance $NX = NFI$ and that net foreign investment depends on domestic rate.

To see what this model means, substitute the third equation into the first, and thus, the model becomes:

$$Y = C(Y - T) + I(r) + G + NFI(r) \quad \text{... ....} \quad IS$$
$$M/P = L(r, Y) \quad \text{..........} \quad LM$$

These two equations differ from the close-economy *IS-LM* Model in that the expenditure now depends on the interest rate for two reasons. A higher interest rate implies lower investment, as before. But, now, it also implies lower net foreign investment and, thus, lower net exports.

The three graphs can be used to analyse this model. The Fig. 15.13(a) shows the *IS-LM* diagram where the interest rate r is on the vertical axis, Y is on the horizontal axis. The *IS-LM* curves determine the equilibrium level of income (Y_1) and interest rate (r_1).

The new term in the *IS* equation, $NFI(r)$, makes the *IS* curve flatter than it would be in a closed economy. The more responsive that $NFI(r)$, the flatter the *IS* curve is, where the small open economy represents the extreme case in which net foreign investment *(NFI)* is infinitely elastic at the world interest rate.

In this extreme case, the *IS* curve is completely flat.

Figs.15.13(b) and 15.13(c) show how the equilibrium from the *IS-LM* model determines net foreign investment, the trade balance, and the exchange rate. In 15.13(b) we can see the interest rate determines *NFI*. This curve is downward sloping because a higher interest rate discourages domestic investors from lending abroad and encourages foreign investors to lend here. In Fig. 15.13(c) we see that the exchange rate adjusts to ensure that net exports equal net foreign investment.

We can use this model to examine the impact of various policies. We assume that the economy has a floating exchange rate.

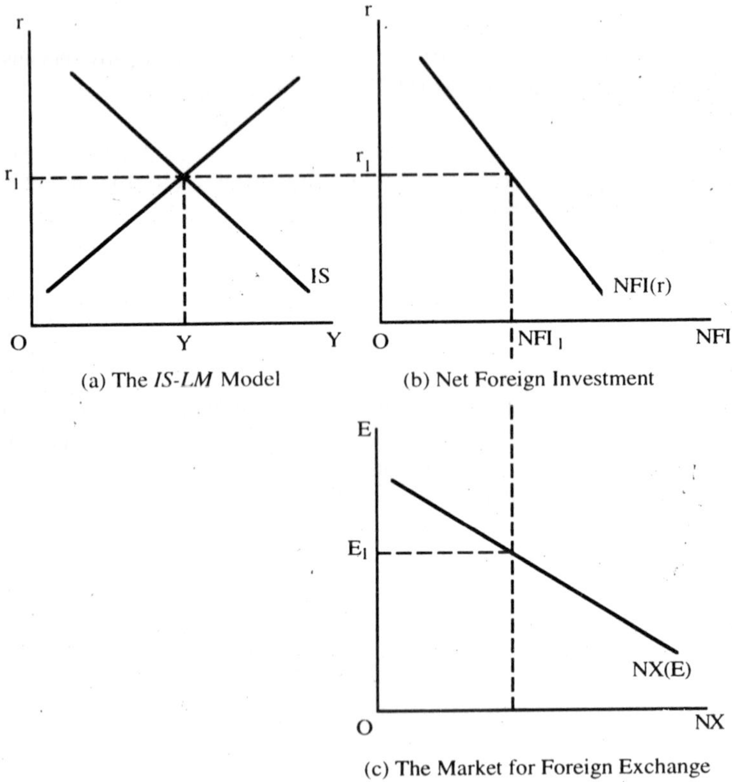

Fig. 15.13

Fiscal Policy : Impact of Fiscal Expansion

Fig. 15.14(a) shows that a fiscal expansion shifts the *IS* curve to the right. Income rises from Y_1 to Y_2, and the interest rate rises from r_1 to r_2. In Fig.15.14(b) we can see that the increase in interest rate causes net foreign investment to fall from NFI_1 to NFI_2 and Fig.15.14(c) shows that the fall in net foreign investment reduces the net supply of domestic currency, which causes the exchange rate to appreciate from E_1 to E_2.

Monetary Policy : The Impact of a Monetary Expansion

Fig. 15.15(a) shows that a monetary expansion shifts the *LM* curve to the right. Income rises from Y_1 to Y_2 and the interest rate falls from r_1 to r_2. These effects are similar to those in a closed economy. Fig. 15.15(b) shows

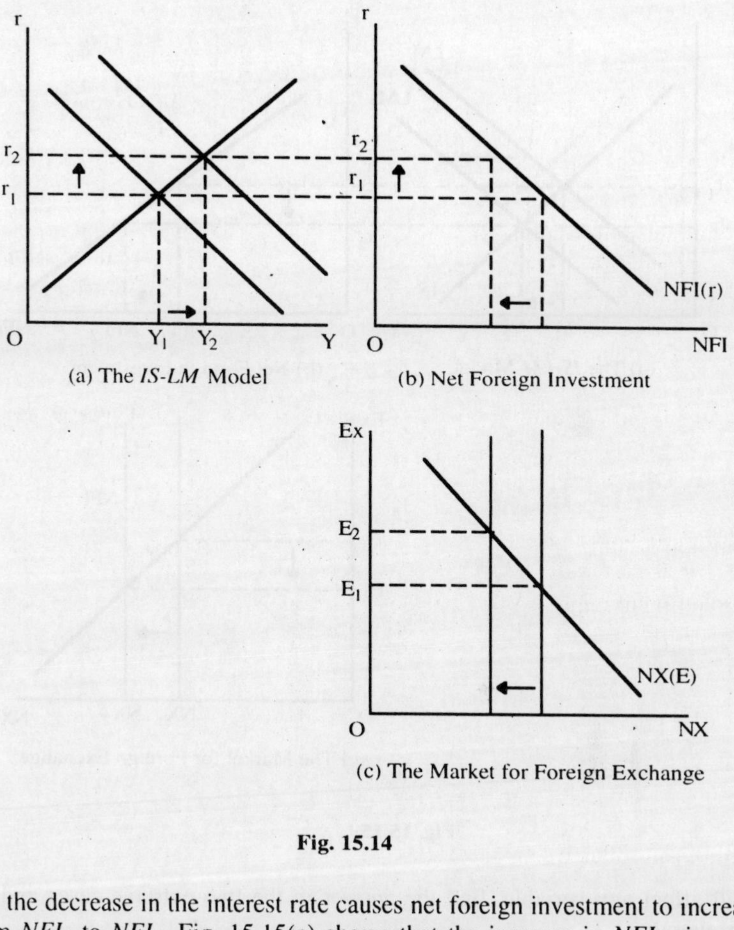

(a) The *IS-LM* Model

(b) Net Foreign Investment

(c) The Market for Foreign Exchange

Fig. 15.14

that the decrease in the interest rate causes net foreign investment to increase from NFI_1 to NFI_2. Fig. 15.15(c) shows that the increase in NFI raises the net supply of domestic currency, which causes the exchange rate to depreciate from E_1 to E_2. As domestic goods become cheaper relative to the foreign goods, net export rise.

The Rule of Thumb

The model of the large open economy is somewhat more complicated and cumbersome than the model of the closed economy and the model of the small open economy developed here. Fortunately, we can use the rule of thumb to help determine how policies influence a large open economy without remembering all the details of the model. The large open economy is an average of the closed economy and the small open economy. To find how any policy

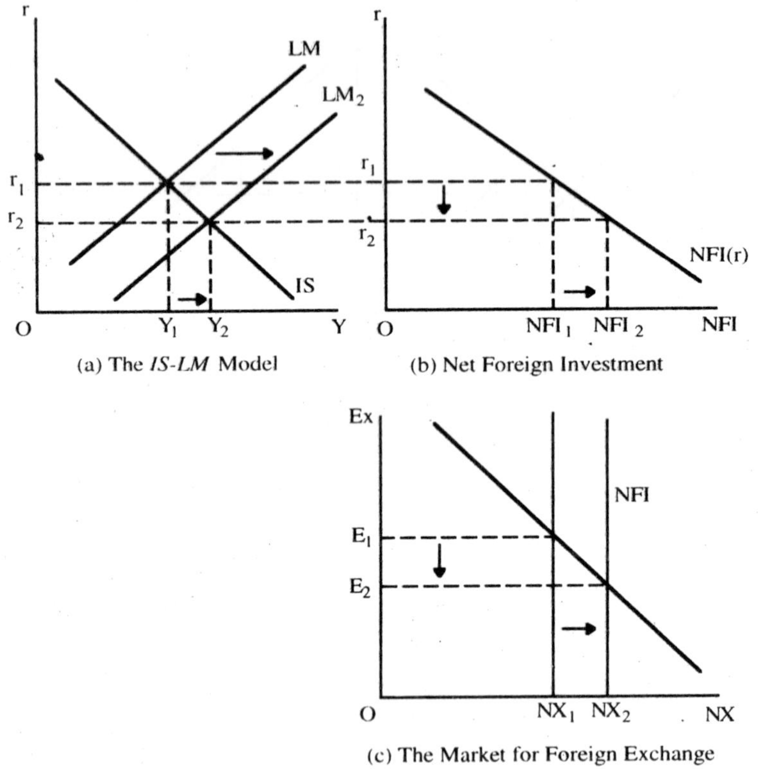

(a) The *IS-LM* Model

(b) Net Foreign Investment

(c) The Market for Foreign Exchange

Fig. 15.15

will affect any variable, find the answer in the two extreme cases and take an average.

For example, how does a monetary expansion affect the interest rate and investment in the short-run? In a closed economy, the interest rate falls and investment rises. In a small open economy, neither the interest rate nor investment changes. The effect in the large open economy is an average of these two cases; a monetary expansion reduces the interest rate and increases investment, but only slightly. The rise in net foreign investment offsets the fall in the interest rate and the rise in investment that would occur in a closed economy. But, unlike in a small open economy, the international flow of capital is not so strong as to negate fully these effects.

This rule of thumb makes the simple models all the more valuable. Although they do not describe perfectly the world in which we live, they do provide a useful guide to the effects of economic policy.

16 INFLATION AND UNEMPLOYMENT

Inflation is a situation of continuously rising prices. In the models presented —we cannot rationalize continuous change in price, unless there are continuous exogenous changes either in *AD* or *AS*. We first examine possible explanations of inflation within the comparative static framework presented. We then move on to more recent developments.

From *AS* to the Phillips Curve *(PC)*

A relationship between inflation and unemployment called the Phillips Curve (explained later) which shows the short-run trade-off between inflation and unemployment implied by the short-run *ASC*.

The *PC* is another way to express *AS*. The short-run *ASC* shows a positive relationship between the price level and output. Since inflation is the rate of change in the price level and since unemployment fluctuates inversely with output, the *ASC* implies a negative relationship between inflation and unemployment. The *PC* expresses this negative relationship.

The *PC* points out that the inflation rate — the % change in the price level — depends on three forces:

(1) Expected inflation

(2) The deviation of unemployment from the natural rate, called cyclical unemployment.

(3) Supply shocks.

These forces can be expressed in the following equation

$$n = n_e - \beta\ (u - u^n) + \varepsilon$$

Inflation = Expected inflation – β(cyclical unemployment) + Supply Shock. Where β is a parameter greater than zero. Notice that, there is a minus sign before β which means high unemployment tends to reduce inflation.

From ASC to the Phillips Curve

We can see that the *ASC* and Phillips curve express essentially the same relationship. The equation for the *ASC* is : $P = P^e + (1/\alpha)\ \left(Y - \overline{Y}\right)$........(1) We can derive the Phillips curve from the equation of the *ASC*.

First, subtract last year's price level P_{-1} from both sides of the equation to obtain: $(P - P_{-1}) = (P^e - P_{-1}) + (1/\alpha)\left(Y - \overline{Y}\right)$.

$(P - P_{-1})$ = Inflation π . $(P^e - P_{-1})$ = expected inflation, π^e. Thus, we can write the equation as $\pi = \pi^e + (1/\alpha)(Y - \overline{Y})$.

Application of Okun's law—which gives a relationship between output and unemployment—enables us to substitute $- \beta (u - u^n)$ for $(1/\alpha)(Y - \overline{Y})$ Thus, the equation becomes : $n - n^e - \beta (u - u^n)$. Here Okum's law states that, the deviation of output from its natural rate is inversely related to the deviation of unemployment from its natural rate; that is, when output is higher than the natural rate of output, unemployment is lower than the natural rate of unemployment.

Finally, if a supply shock ε is added to represent exogenous influence on prices, such as, a change in oil prices, a change in the minimum wage, etc., we get : $n = n^e - \beta (u - u^n) + \varepsilon$.

Thus, we obtain the Phillip's curve from the *AS* equation.

Now we can see that the *PC* retains the key feature of the short-run *ASC*; a link between real and normal variables that causes the classical dichotomy to fail. More precisely, the *PC* demonstrates the connection between real economic activity and unexpected changes in the price level. The *PC* is a convenient way to express and analyse *AS*.

Expectations and Inflation Inertia

To make the *PC* useful, we need to say what determines expected inflation. A simple and often plausible assumption is that, people form their expectations of inflation based on recently observed inflation. This assumption is called adaptive expectations. For example, suppose, people expect prices will rise this year at the same rate they did last year. Then $\pi^e = n_{-1}$.

Thus, we can write the *PC* as $\pi = n_{-1} - \beta(u - u^n) + \varepsilon$ which states that, inflation depends on past inflation, cyclical unemployment, and a supply shock.

The first term in this equation of the *PC*, n_{-1}, implies that inflation is inertial. If unemployment is at its natural rate and if there are no supply shocks, prices will continue to rise at the prevailing rate of inflation. This inertia arises because past inflation influences expectations of future inflation which influences wages and prices that people set.

In the model of *AS* and *AD*, inflation inertia is interpreted as persistent upward shifts in both the *ASC* and the *ADC*. Consider first *AS*. If prices have been rising quickly, people will expect them to continue to rise quickly. Since the position of the short-run *ASC* depends on the expected price level, the short-run *ASC* will shift upward over time. It will continue to shift upward until some event—such as a recession or a supply shock—changes inflation and, thus, expectations of inflation.

The *ADC* must also be shifting upward in order to confirm the expectations of inflation. Most often, the continued rise in *AD* is due to persistent growth in the money supply. If the central bank suddenly halted money growth, *AD* would stabilize, and the upward shift in *AS* would cause a recession. The high unemployment in the recession would reduce inflation and expected inflation, causing inflation inertia to subside.

The Two Causes of Rising and Falling Inflation

Two forces in the *PC* can generate the rate of inflation. The second term in the *PC*, $\beta(u - u^n)$, shows that cyclical unemployment — the deviation of unemployment from its natural rate — exerts upward or downward pressure on inflation. Low unemployment pulls the inflation rate up. This is called demand-pull inflation because high *AD* cause this type of inflation, whereas high unemployment pulls down the inflation rate and the parameter β measures the responsiveness of inflation.

The term, ε, shows that inflation may also be caused by supply shocks. An adverse supply shock — such as the rise in world oil prices — causes inflation to rise. This is called cost-push inflation because it is engineered by the increased cost of production.

The Short-Run Trade-off between Inflation and Unemployment

We consider the options the Phillips curve gives to a policymaker who can influence *AD* through monetary or fiscal policy. At any particular moment, expected inflation and supply shocks are not under the control of the policymaker; yet, by changing *AD*, the policymaker can alter inflation,

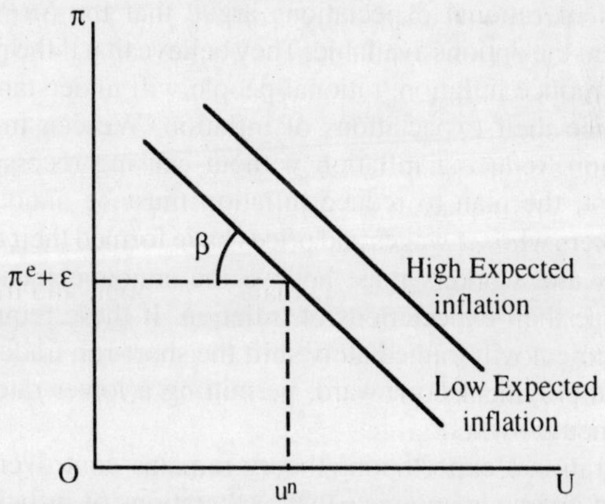

Fig. 16.1 Short-run Trade off between Inflation and Unemployment

output and unemployment. The policy-maker can expand *AD* to lower unemployment which will increase inflation or the policymaker can depress *AD* to increase unemployment and lower inflation.

Fig.16.1 shows the short-run trade-off between inflation and unemployment implied by the Phillips curve. The policymaker can manipulate *AD* to choose a combination of unemployment and inflation on this curve, called the short-run Phillips curve.

Notice that, the short-run Phillips curve depends on expected inflation. If expected inflation rises, the curve shifts upward, and the policymaker's trade-off becomes less favourable : inflation is higher for any level of unemployment. The curve is higher when expected inflation is higher.

Because people adjust their expectations of inflation over time, this tradeoff between inflation and unemployment holds only in the short-run.

Rational Expectations and Inflation

Because the expectation of inflation influences the short-run trade-off between inflation and unemployment, a crucial question is how people form expectations. Thus far, we have been assuming that expected inflation depends on recently observed inflation. This adaptive expectation is too simplistic to be applicable in all circumstances.

Rational expectations assume that people optimally use all the available information, including information about current policies, to forecast the future. Because monetary and fiscal policies influence inflation, expected inflation also depends on the monetary and fiscal policies. According to rational expectations theory, a change in monetary or fiscal policy will change expectations, and an evaluation of any policy change must incorporate this effect on expectations. This approach implies that inflation is less inertial than it first appears.

The advocates of rational expectations argue that the *SRPC* does not accurately represent the options available. They believe that if the policymakers are committed to reduce inflation, rational people will understand their commitment and reduce their expectations of inflation. We can imagine that a painless disinflation, reducing inflation without causing recession, has two requirements. First, the plan to reduce inflation must be announced before the firms and workers who set wages and prices have formed their expectations. Second, the firms and workers must believe the announcement; otherwise, they will not revise their expectations of inflation. If these requirements are met, the announcement will immediately shift the short-run trade-off between inflation and unemployment downward, permitting a lower rate of inflation without higher unemployment.

Although the rational expectations theory remains controversial, there is general agreement among economists that expectations of inflation influence the short-run trade-off between inflation and unemployment. Now we discuss how expectations influence inflation.

Inflation, Unemployment and the Phillips Curve

Two goals of economic policymakers are low inflation and low unemployment. Inflation is a situation of continuously rising prices, where there must be continuous exogenous changes either in *AD* or *AS*. We first examine possible explanations of inflation within the framework of the comparative static model presented previously. We then move on to examine a relationship between inflation and unemployment called the Phillips curve.

In Fig. 16.2 we start with an equilibrium of less than full employment arising from a fixed money wage W_0. The equilibrium price level and real income are P_0 and Y_0, respectively, and there are some level of unemployment associated with that real income. Assume now that the government has a policy of maintaining 'full employment'. To achieve this goal the government carried out expansionary fiscal or monetary policy. This is shown by the shift of the *AD* curve to AD'. If this was the end of the story, the result of the government policy would be to raise the price level to P', real income to Y' and to lower unemployment by some amount. However, given the fixed money wage and the rise in prices as a result of the government policy, there is a fall in real wage.

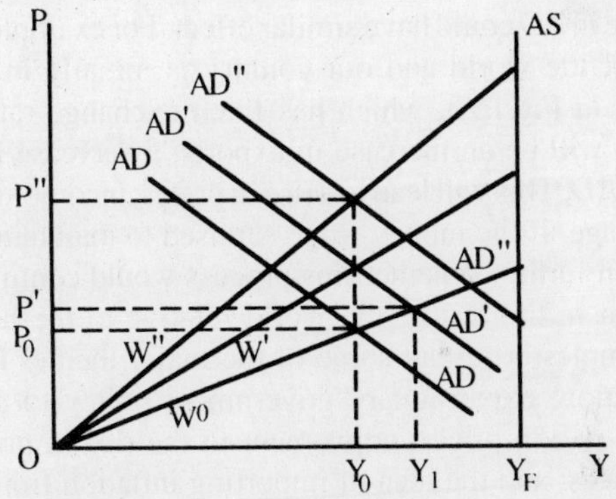

Fig. 16.2 Unemployment and Inflation

Now the question is: What will happen if workers wish to maintain their real wage? To do that, they raise the money wage to W'. The effect of this is to raise the price level to P'', income to Y_0 and unemployment at their previous level. Thus, the efforts to maintain the real wage have resulted in a rise of the money wage and the price level, with no effect whatsoever on employment or real income. What will happen if the government continues to maintain its 'full employment' policy and workers try to continue in their attempt to maintain their real wage? The *AD* curve will shift to AD'' and money wage to W'', again leaving employment, real income and the real wage unchanged, but raising the money wage and the price level. It may not take place immediately. There may be lags in the adjustment process. Thus, unemployment may fall for some time, and so the government policy may appear 'successful' until the adjustment in money wage—which may again raise the problem of excessive unemployment.

Let us take this analysis a little further. Assume that the process described above has continued for some time and people began to expect that prices will go on rising in the future. We also assume economy is at Y_0, P_0 and W_0 in Fig. 16.2. Now, suppose, the government undertakes an expansionary policy shown by the shift in the *AD* curve to *AD'* and the price level rises to P'. Now to compensate for the expected rise in prices in the future, the money wage rate is raised to W''. The adjustment in the money wage rate—to maintain real wage—is made on the basis of the expected price level rather than the current price level. In terms of the current price level this adjustment overcompensates for the rise in prices, so the real wage rises and income and employment fall. Now the government will have to undertake an expansionary policy just to maintain the original income Y_0. To increase income above Y_0 it would require an expansionary policy than before, and the effect on money wages and prices would be greater still.

In the above discussion the increases in *AD* occurred because of the expansionary government policy to raise income and employment. But any continuous increase in *AD* could have similar effect. For example, if an inflation starts in the rest of the world and our country is initially in equilibrium at P_0 ,Y_0 and W^0 as in Fig.16.3, which has fixed exchange rate with the rest of the world, there will be an increase in exports, a decrease in imports and, thus, an increase in *AD*. This will lead to a rise in prices, income and employment and a fall in real wage. If the money wage is raised to maintain the real wage, prices will rise even further.Whether this process would continue depends on the rate of inflation in the rest of the world relative to the home economy.

The above examples bring out some of the major themes in most current discussion of inflation; expansionary government policy to achieve certain goals, leading to a rise in prices, adjustment to the rise in prices and to the expected rise in prices; and the idea of importing inflation from abroad. Now the question is : Why do wages rise even though there is unemployment? What determines the formation of expectations? How fast do people adjust their expectation?

The first step to approach these questions is to pay more attention to the labour market than we have done so far. We have seen two possibilities in the labour market. In a flexible money wage, there is an unique full-employment equilibrium; in a rigid money wage, there would be some unemployment, depending on the money wage and the price level. In a world in which information, acquiring skills, and mobility were costless, the assumption of flexible money wages would lead to full-employment and no involuntary unemployment, *i.e.* anybody wanting to work at the going wage rate could do so. What happens if all these costs are not zero? Now we would find that, there is always some unemployment in a changing economy. It takes time to find the right job at the right wage; changing patterns of demand for goods in a changing technology require changing demands for particular skills, and it takes time to learn new skills. It is also costly to move and, therefore, sometimes worthwhile to wait in the expectation that mobility may not be necessary.

All the above imply that the concept of full-employment is a very ambiguous one, and not a very sensible one, if taken literally to mean that no one is unemployed.

In Fig. 16.3 we represent the labour markets with a demand and supply of labour as a function of real wages, which is measured by a money wage divided by a price level, which, for the moment we assume given. Assume

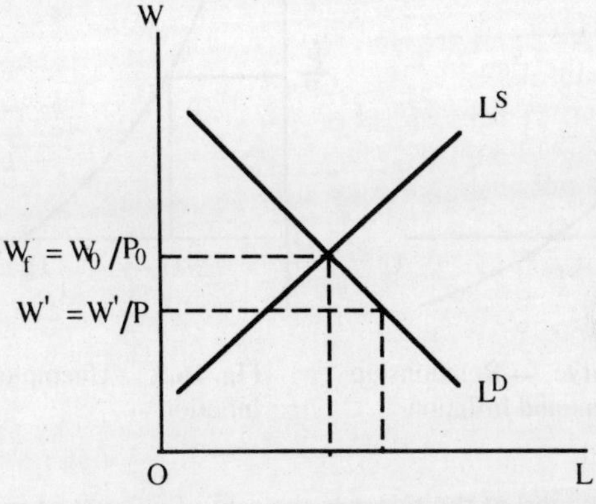

Fig. 16.3 Labour Market Equilibrium

we have flexible money wages. At the real wage $W_f = \frac{W_0}{P_0}$ we have full employment in the sense that there is no excess demand or supply of labour. However, this does not mean that there is no unemployment. Let us assume that, for a given structure of the labour market, unemployment is u_f as in Fig.16.4. If the real wage is $W' = \frac{W'}{P_0}$; what will happen? Because there is excess demand for labour, two things may happen. First, that the level of unemployment at this real wage is less than u_f. Second, that because of the excess demand the money wage will rise. The first proposition tells us that, if there is an excess demand for labour all the factors which led to unemployment at "full employment" would be mitigated. With an excess demand for labour a wider range of skills would be demanded and the employer would be willing to substitute available skills for unavailable ones. It is also likely that capital would move to areas where labour is available, thus reducing the cost of labour mobility, and information may also spread more quickly. We shall thus assume that there is an indirect relationship between the excess demand for labour and unemployment.

Given the excess demand for labour, money wages will rise, until the equilibrium wage rate is reached. Let us also assume that the rate at which money wages rise depends on the excess demand for labour; the greater the

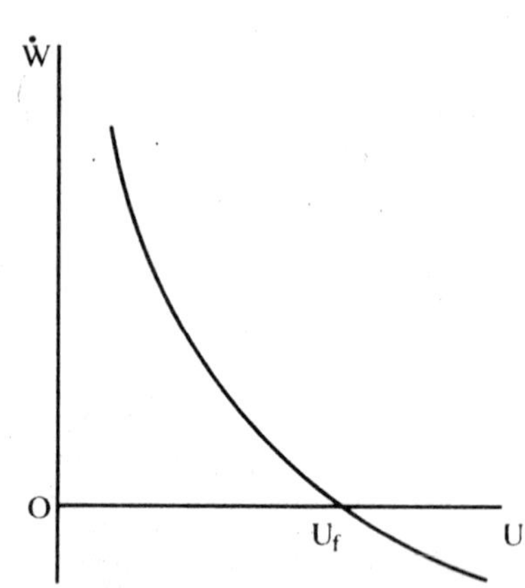

Fig. 16.4 Phillips curve — Relationship Between Unemployment and Inflation

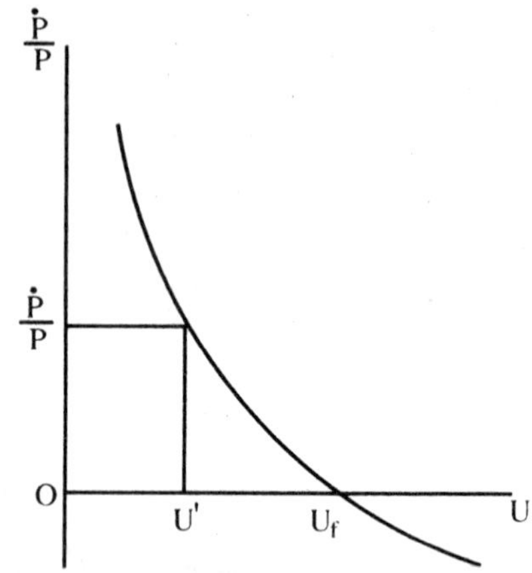

Fig. 16.5 Unemployment and Inflation

pressure in the labour market the faster is the rate of change of money wages. We thus have two relationships: first, a relationship between the excess demand for labour and unemployment; second, a relationship between the excess demand for labour and the rate of change of money wages. Combining these two we get a relationship between unemployment and inflation.

This relationship is shown in Fig. 16.4, where we measure on the vertical axis the percentage change in money wage rate per time period $(\dot{W})$ and on the horizontal axis unemployment (u). The full-employment is represented by u_f, where there is no tendency for money wages to change, even though there is some unemployment which is known as natural rate of unemployment. Any level of unemployment less than u_f implies that money wages will rise, because there is an excess demand for labour, and the rate at which they will rise depends on the excess demand for labour. At any unemployment greater than u_f there is an excess supply of labour and money wages are likely to fall, at a rate depending on the size of the excess supply. The relationship shown in Fig. 16.4 is called the Phillips Curve — called after Prof. A. W. Phillips who first discovered the empirical relationship between the change in wages and employment in the U.K. between 1861–1957 with approximately the shape shown in the Fig. 16.4.

So far we have been discussing the relationship between the change in wages and unemployment. To relate the above discussion to an analysis of inflation we have to postulate some relationship between a change in money wages and a change in prices. There have been various ways in which this has been done, such as, mark up theories of pricing or marginal productivity theory of wage determination. For our purpose it does not matter what is the exact relationship between the change in money wages and a change in prices. Let us assume that there is a positive relationship between the two. We can then translate Fig. 16.4 into Fig. 16.5, where we measure the rate of change of prices $(\dot{P})$ on the vertical axis and unemployment on the horizontal axis.

Assume that the government wishes to maintain unemployment at u', less than u_f. To do that, the government has to induce a rate of price change of $\dot{P}'$ which has been used in policy discussion to argue that the government has a choice between the two goals—inflation and unemployment. The government can have no inflation if it is willing to accept the level of unemployment of u_f. This is a more complex development of the first theme discussed above in terms of the comparative static model but it does not incorporate the second theme—expectations and adjustment to them.

Expectations and the Phillips Curve

To discuss expectations in the analysis of the Phillips Curve, and to sketch briefly some of the recent developments in this field we start with the labour market again. The real wage depends on two factors, the money wage and the price level. When there is inflation both the money wage and the price level are changing and both are expected to change to some extent. An individual selling his labour receives a money wage offer and he has to assess what is the real wage represented by this offer. To do this he has to think what the price level could be over the period for which he offered the money wage. For example, if an individual is offered a money wage W_0, the expected real wage is $\frac{W_0}{P_0}$ if the expected price level is P_0, and $\frac{W_0}{P_1}$ if the expected price level is P_1. The actual real wage is W_0 divided by whatever the price level is expected. We thus have a possibility that the actual real wage may be greater or smaller than the real wage expected by the suppliers of labour on which they base their decision about how much labour to supply. We shall call that wage the expected real wage, $w^e = \frac{\dot{W}^e}{P^e}$, the expected real wage is equal to the expected money wage divided by the expected price level.

We shall be interested in the rate of change of the variables and thus, $\dot{W}^e$ is the expected change of percentage in real wages. From the definition of expected real wages, $\dot{W}^e = \dot{W}^e - \dot{P}^e$ ....*(1)*. Equation (1) states that, the expected percentage change in real wages is equal to the expected percentage change in money wages minus the expected change in the price level. Now, assume that the expected change in money wages is equal to the actual change in money wages which is equal to the rate of inflation—the percentage change in prices. We are also assuming that there is an ongoing inflation in which prices and money wages change at the same rate. With this assumption, we have $\dot{W}^e = \dot{W} - \dot{P}$. By substituting this into equation (1) we have $\dot{W}^e = \dot{P} - \dot{P}^e$ ....(2). Equation (2) says that the expected change in the real wage depends on the difference between the actual rate of inflation and the expected rate of inflation. If the actual rate of inflation is greater than the expected rate, the expected real wage is increasing; if the actual inflation is equal to expected inflation, the expected real wage remains unchanged; and if the actual rate of inflation is less than the expected rate, the expected real wage is falling.

Fig. 16.6 shows the labour market. The supply curve shows the relationship between the quantity of labour supplied and the real wage. However, what is now important for the supply of labour is not the current real wage, but the expected real wage. Only if the expected change in the real wage is zero, is the current real wage the correct variable for the supply of labour. This is shown by the middle supply curve of labour where the expected rate of inflation is equal to the actual rate of inflation.

If the expected change in real wage is less, then, for each current real wage, labour supply would be reduced, because the current real wage is greater than the real wage as perceived by the suppliers of labour as shown by $L^s{}_1\left(\dot{W}^e < 0\right)$ supply curve shifts to the left of $L^s{}_0$ line. Again, from equation (2), this is the supply curve for which the expected rate of inflation is greater than the actual rate. Similarly, the supply curve $L^s{}_2\left(\dot{W}^e > 0\right)$ shows a situation for which the expected change in the real wage is positive, which will occur if the expected rate of inflation is less than the actual rate.

Consider now that an initial equilibrium in which the actual inflation rate is equal to the expected inflation rate and assume that both are zero (no inflation). The equilibrium in the labour market is at A where real wage is W_0 and employment is L_0. Associated with this full-employment there is some level of unemployment u_f, which is called the natural rate of unemployment. Assume that, now prices start rising, but at this level expectations about changes in the price level remain unchanged. Thus, the expected change in the price level is less than the actual change in the price level. The supply curve of labour moves to the right where real wage falls but the quantity of labour supplied rises to L_1 and unemployment falls. The greater is the rise in prices, the larger is the difference between the actual change in prices and the expected change in prices. The shift of the supply curve to the right is greater, employment is larger and unemployment is smaller.

Let us translate this into a Phillips curve. Fig. 16.7 measures the rate of change of prices on the vertical axis and unemployment on the horizontal axis. When the rate of change in prices is zero—and everyone expects it to continue to be zero—equilibrium in the labour market in Fig. 16.6 is at W_0.

L_0 with unemployment at u_f in Fig. 16.7. Assume that, now prices start rising at the rate $\dot{P}'$ though people still expect inflation to be at the old rate, namely, zero. The workers receive higher money wages and mistakenly belief that they are receiving higher real wages. Labour market equilibrium in Fig. 16.6 is now at $W_1 L_1$. Employment is greater and unemployment is smaller at u'

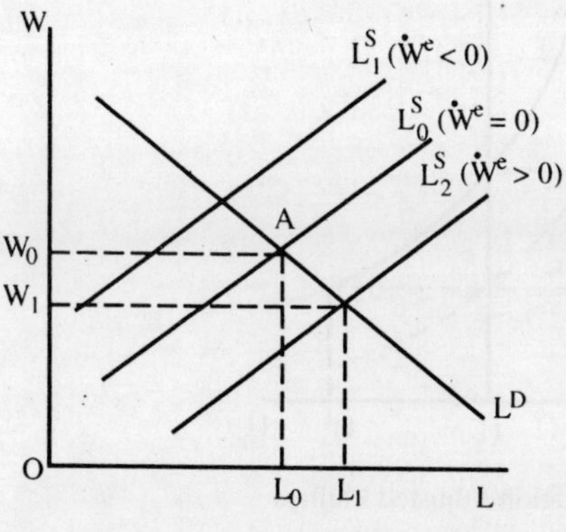

Fig. 16.6 Labour Market : Relationship Between the quantity of Labour Supplied and the Real Wage

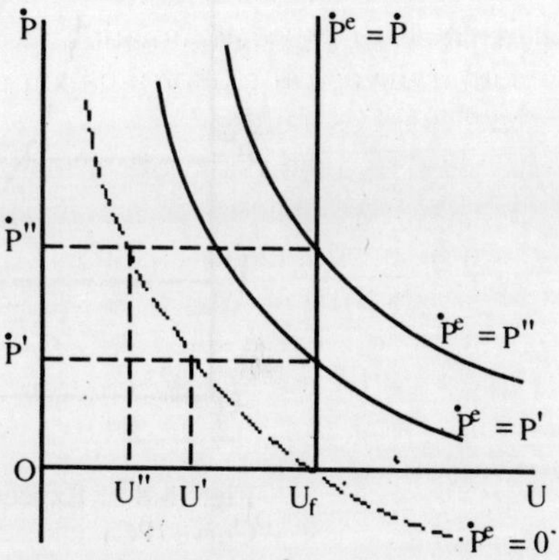

Fig. 16.7 Phillips Curve : Short-run and Long-run

on Fig. 16.7. If the change in prices and money wages is higher, say, $\dot{P}''$, the shift in the supply curve would be greater and unemployment smaller at u''. Thus, we get the downward sloping Phillips curve. However, it is clear that this Phillips curve was derived on the assumption that the expected change in prices is zero.

Now assume that, people begin to expect that the inflation will continue at some positive rate and the difference between the actual rate and expected rate of inflation will decrease and the supply curve of labour in Fig. 16.6 will start shifting back. Employment will start falling and unemployment rising. In Fig. 16.7 this can be shown by a shift of the Phillips curve to the right. Each of the Phillips curves in Fig. 16.7 is drawn for some specified expected rate of inflation. When that expected rate of inflation is equal to the actual rate of inflation, unemployment will be u_f. Thus, the vertical Phillips curve at u_f shows the relationship between inflation and unemployment when the expected rate of inflation is equal to the actual rate. Along this curve there is no relationship between the two, and unemployment cannot be changed by increasing the rate of inflation, which is known as the long-run Phillips curve.

The Phillips curve analysis which takes into account expectations gives some insight not only into the effect of inflation but also into the effects of reducing inflation. In Fig. 16.8 we assume that, there has been an ongoing inflation at the rate $\dot{P}''$ to which everyone has adjusted. Thus, we are on the said Phillips curve along which the expected rate of inflation is equal

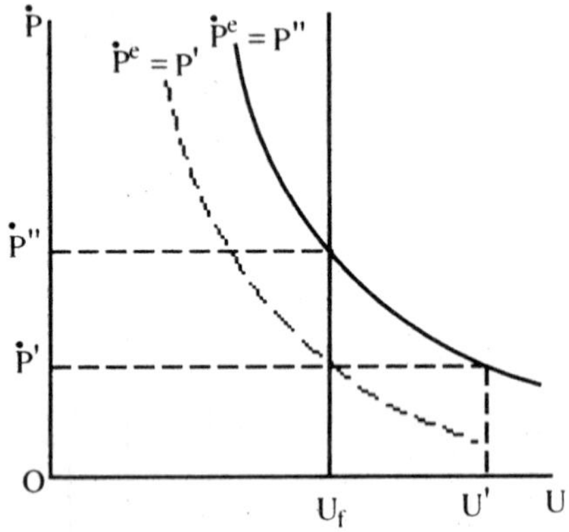

Fig. 16.8 Expectation Adjusted Phillips Curve (PC)

to $\dot{P}''$. Now assume that the rate of inflation is reduced to $\dot{P}'$. People still expect the rate of inflation to remain at the higher level, so we move along the solid Phillips curve. Unemployment, thus, rise to u'. Only after expectations become adjusted to the lower inflation rate does the Phillips curve starts shifting to the left, and unemployment starts falling. When full adjustment occurs, unemployment will be back at u_f and we will be on the dashed Phillips curve. Thus, once expectations about inflation have been built into the system it may be quite costly to reduce the rate of inflation.

Inflation and Interest Rates

Now we discuss the link between inflation and interest rates.

Two Interest Rates : *Real and Nominal* : Economists call the interest rate that the bank pays for our deposits the nominal interest rate and the increase in our purchasing power the real interest rate. If i denotes the nominal interest rate, r, the real interest rate, and π the rate of inflation, then the relationship among these three variables can be written as : $r = i - \pi$.

The real interest rate (r) is the difference between the nominal interest rate i and the rate of inflation.

The Fisher Effect

We can show that the nominal interest rate is the sum of the real interest rate and the inflation rate : $i = r + \pi$. This is called the Fisher Equation which shows that the nominal interest rate can change for two reasons : because the real interest rate changes or because the inflation rate changes.

The quantity theory shows that the rate of money growth determines the rate of inflation. The Fisher Equation tells us to add the real interest rate and the inflation rate to determine the nominal interest rate. Thus, the quantity theory and the Fisher Equation together tell us how money growth affects the nominal interest rate.

Two Real Interest Rates : Ex Ante and Ex Post

The real interest rate the borrower and lender expect when loan is made, is called the ex ante real interest rate, and the real interest rate actually realised, is called the ex post real interest rate.

Although borrowers and lenders cannot predict future inflation with certainty, they do have some expectation of the inflation rate. Let π denote actual future inflation and π^e the expectation of future inflation. The ex ante real interest is $i - \pi^e$, and the ex post real interest rate is $i - \pi$. The two rates differ when actual inflation π differs from expected inflation π^e.

How does this distinction between expected and actual inflation modify the Fisher effect? The nominal interest rate cannot adjust to actual inflation, because actual inflation is not known when the nominal interest rate is set. It can adjust to expected inflation only. The Fisher effect is more precisely written as : $i = r + \pi^e$.

The ex ante interest rate r is determined by equilibrium in the commodity market, whereas the nominal interest rate i moves with changes in expected inflation π^e.

The Social Costs of Inflation

So far our discussion about inflation does not tell us much about the social problem of inflation. We turn to these problems here.

It may appear surprising that, some economists argue that the costs of inflation are small especially when a country experience a moderate rate of inflation.

Expected Inflation

Consider first the case of expected inflation. One cost of expected high inflation is the distortion of the inflation tax on the amount of money people hold. A higher inflation rate leads to a higher nominal interest rate which, in turn, leads to lower real balances. If people are to hold lower money balances on average, they must make more frequent trips to the bank to withdraw money. The inconvenience of reducing money holding is called the shoe-leather cost of inflation.

A second cost of inflation arises because high inflation induces firms to change their prices more often. Changing prices is sometimes costly: for example, it may require printing and distribution of a new catalogue. These costs are called menu costs, because the higher the rate of inflation, the more often restaurants have to print new menus.

A third cost of inflation arises because firms facing menu costs change prices infrequently : thus, the higher the rate of inflation, the greater the variability in relative price. Since market economics rely on relative prices to allocate resources efficiently, inflation leads to microeconomic inefficiencies.

A fourth cost of inflation results from the tax laws. Many provisions of the tax code do not take into account the effects of inflation. Inflation can alter individual's tax liability, often in the ways that lawmakers did not intend.

A fifth cost of inflation is the inconvenience of living in a world with a changing price level. Money is the yardstick with which we measure economic transactions. When there is inflation, that yardstick is changing in length.

For example, a changing price level complicates personal financial planning. One important decision that all households face is how much of their income to consume today and how much to save for old age. A pound saved today and invested at a fixed nominal interest rate will yield a fixed sterling amount in the future. Yet the real value of that pound depends on the future price level. Deciding how much to save would be much simpler if one could count on the stable price level.

Unexpected Inflation

Unexpected inflation has an effect that is more pernicious than any of the cost discussed under anticipated inflation. It arbitrarily redistributes income and wealth among individuals. We can see how this works by examining long-term loans. Loan agreements specify a nominal interest rate, which is based on the expected rate of inflation. If actual inflation turns out differently from what was expected, the ex post real return that the debtor pays to the creditor differs from what both parties anticipated. If inflation is higher than expected, the debtor wins and the creditor loses because the debtor repays the loan with less valuable money. On the other hand, if inflation is lower than expected, the creditor wins and debtor loses because the repayment is worth more than anticipated.

Unanticipated inflation also hurts individuals on pension. Workers and firms often agree on a fixed nominal pension when the workers retires. Since pension is deferred earnings, the workers are essentially providing the firm a loan. Like any creditor, the worker is hurt when inflation is higher than anticipated. Like any debtor, the firm is hurt when inflation is lower than anticipated.

These situations provide a clear argument against highly variable inflation. The more variable the rate of inflation, the greater the uncertainty. Since most people are risk averse — they do not like uncertainty.

Given these effects of inflation uncertainty, it is surprising that nominal contracts are so prevalent. One might expect creditors and debtors to protect themselves from this uncertainty by writing contracts in real terms — that is, by indexing the price level. Indexation is often widespread with high and variable inflation.

Types and Causes of Inflation

Inflation is often defined as a state of rising prices. It is indicated by increase in the index number of prices over time. It reflects disequilibrium condition in the economy. Sometimes an inflationary situation may not exhibit itself by an increase in the price index because of price control and rationing practised by the government. In order to distinguish between the two situations we use the terms "open inflation" and "suppressed inflation". In an open inflation, the disequilibrium condition expresses itself through the rise in the price level, while in the case of a suppressed inflation the disequilibrium force is counteracted by the extra-market force. If extra-market forces are withdrawn, prices would rise and the inflation becomes open. Thus, to find out the causes of inflation, we must look into the conditions that are responsible for the existence of disequilibrium in the economy. Mere existence of price stability does not mean the absence of the inflationary situation. The price stability may be forced by the government intervention.[1]

The price level is in equilibrium so long there is equality between the aggregate demand and the aggregate supply. It may so happen that the overall aggregate demand is equal to overall aggregate supply, but some demands are greater than their respective supplies, while some other demands are less than their corresponding supplies. Had all prices been flexible, the result would be a change in the relative prices only; there would be no change in the general price level. When the prices are flexible only in the upward direction, an inflationary situation may arise, even when the aggregate supply is equal to the aggregate demand. Then prices are likely to be pushed up by the forces of excess demand where it exists, but they are not pulled down by the force of excess supply existing in the other markets. As a result, the level of prices increased. Thus, the downward inflexibility of prices in the face of excess supply—combined with the existence of excess demand in some markets—may be responsible for the emergence of an inflationary situation in the economy. This type of inflation is known as "structural inflation".

Though a structural inflation may be the consequence of the emergence of excess demand somewhere in the economy, it is basically caused by the rigidities in the inter-sectoral relations and also by the downward inflexibility of prices. The rigidities may exist either by technologically fixed input-output relations or by complimentarity among various commodities that are consumed by the people. Such a structural inflation is associated with structural unem-

[1] For detailed discussion of the suppressed inflation, see A. C. L. Day, 'Outline of Monetary Economics' (OUP, London,1958), and H. K. Charlesworth, 'The Economics of Repressed Inflation',(George Allen & Unwin Ltd, London,1956)

ployment. All productive agents must have a positive price. However, because of rigidities in the inter-commodity relations—both in the supply side and in the demand side—some productive agents may remain unemployed, while their prices may not come down to zero or negative. The downward inflexibility of prices may be caused by the emergence of monopolistic control over production.

In any case, because of the existence of downward inflexibility of prices, there is no spontaneous mobility of resources between sectors; and this together with the presence of some excess demands in some sectors of the economy may be responsible for the structural inflation.

The equilibrium in the price level may also be disturbed by some changes in the aggregate demand and supply. Given the aggregate demand for output, there may be an autonomous fall in the aggregate supply, thus resulting in excess demand in the output market, and this will lead to a rise in the level of price. Again, it may so happen that the fall in the aggregate supply is accompanied by a decline in the aggregate demand, but the fall in demand may be comparatively less than the supply. Thus, an excess demand appears in the output market to raise the price level. But this type of an inflationary situation is generated by an autonomous fall in the aggregate supply which means a leftward shift in the supply curve. The supply curve is given by the marginal cost curve. Thus, an autonomous increase in the cost of production leads to a leftward shift in the supply curve. When the rise in the cost of production affects almost all of the producers in the economy, the aggregate supply falls. This type of inflation is known as "the cost-push inflation". It is so called because the rise in the cost of production pushes the price up.

Again, given the aggregate supply, there may be an autonomous rise in the aggregate demand, when an excess demand appears in the economy to raise the price level. The rise in the aggregate demand may be combined with a less than proportionate rise in the aggregate supply. Whenever the autonomous rise in the aggregate demand is associated with an inelastic aggregate supply, an excess demand must arise in the market, and this leads to a rise in the price level. The ultimate responsibility for the price rise, then, lies in the autonomous increase in the aggregate demand, and this is the reason why it is called "the demand-pull inflation".

Though in economic theory prices are determined by the interaction between the forces of demand and supply, in practice price-formation is made through a different process in which the forces of demand and supply play an indirect role. The price of a product determines the income of the seller who frames the price in order to get his share in income. Price charged by the seller may or may not be accepted by the buyers. If the buyers refuse to pay the price asked by the sellers, he will have to revise the prices. But the sellers may also revise the prices on their own, if they want to increase their shares in income. The seller of a product fixes its price at such a level so as to get his expected share of income after covering all expenses. The same procedure may be adopted by the sellers of a factor of product. He may determine price in such a way as to realise his expected share in the product.

Prices framed in this way constitute the claims of different parties on the income that have been produced. When any party wants to improve its share in income, it may do so by an upward revision of its price. The initiative for the revision in their shares may be taken together by all parties at a time. The outcome of the struggle is that, the total claims are greater than the real income itself. In this case, prices are raised. Thus, an excess income-claim over the actual income may cause inflation. This type of inflation may be called "the income-demand inflation". One variety of the income-demand inflation is 'the cost inflation'. Another variety of it is called 'the profit inflation'.

In this way, we may think about a bewildering variety of inflation models. In fact, when inflation become a world-wide phenomenon, every writer on inflation puts forward his own theory. In this book it is impossible even to make a brief summary of the voluminous literature in this field. In the discussion that follows, we shall examine only those models that have become text book theories.

Demand-Pull Theory of Inflation

The earliest attempt was made by classical economists to explain inflation with the help of the quantity theory of money. According to this theory, the price level depends directly and proportionately on the quantity of money. Inflation occurs when the quantity of money increases. The rate of inflation depends on the rate of money supply. The quantity theory, however, could not explain the mechanism through which price level will rise as a result of the rise in money supply. It was Wicksell who analysed the mechanism by which an increase in money would lead to an increase in the price level. He pointed out that an increase in money supply increases the aggregate demand in the economy. Wicksell's theory states that, when money supply increases, the market rate of interest falls below the natural rate and this will induce investors and consumers to spend more in the economy. As a result, the aggregate demand will increase—which will increase the price level— assuming that aggregate supply will remain constant at full employment level. The price level will go on increasing, so long as the market rate of interest is below the natural rate. When money supply will stop increasing, the market rate of interest will rise and become equal to the natural rate and the inflationary pressure will be halted with it. Wicksell realised that the rise in the price level itself would not reduce aggregate demand, because, after a time lag, money incomes would rise in proportion to prices, leaving consumers and investors to compete for the limited supply of goods.

Keynesian theory of inflation is nothing more than a modification and generalisation of Wicksell's theory of inflation. Suppose, there is already full employment in the economy, and investment demand increases. This means that, total demand for goods and services is greater than the available supply. Thus, prices are bid up. Since consumer demand depends on real income which is not reduced by rising prices because the sale at higher prices creates an equivalent rise in money wages without eliminating excess demand. Thus, Keynes broke the close link between the quantity of money and the level of aggregate demand associated with classical economists. According to Keynes, there may be some inflation in the economy even with a constant money supply. In a situation of constant money supply, an increased price level would raise the transaction demand for money and, thus, push up interest rate, which would reduce investment demand. The decreased investment demand will moderate the inflationary pressure, but is unlikely to eliminate it. The reason is that the rise in interest rate will free some money from speculative demand to meet the added transaction demand. Only at zero speculative demand this would correspond to Wicksell's theory.

There is, thus, a significant difference between Wicksell's and Keynes' theory of inflation. For the former any increase in the supply of money is inflationary. For the latter, the rise in prices may occur even without any increase in the supply of money.

Again, an increase in the supply of money may not have any impact on prices in the Keynesian System, especially if the economy starts from a position of unemployment. Despite these differences, both the theories explain inflation as arising from an excess of aggregate demand over the full employment aggregate supply.

The Keynesian theory of inflation is normally explained with the help of "inflationary gap" which is defined as an excess of aggregate demand over aggregate supply at full employment.

Fig. 16.9 explains the condition of disequilibrium that exists in output market as a result of the emergence of the inflationary gap. In the vertical axis, we measure the total expenditure $(E = C + I + G + X - M)$ and in the horizontal

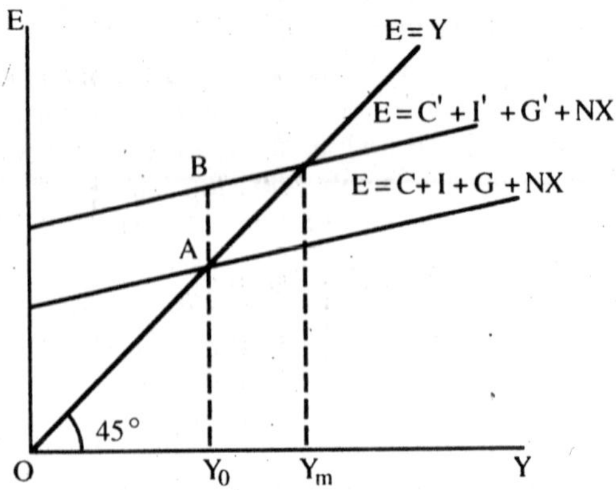

Fig. 16.9 The Inflationary Gap Analysis

axis, we measure real income. Let Y_0 be the value of the full employment output, which has been assumed to be a fixed quantity. If $C + I + G + NX$ is the aggregate demand curve, $Y_0 = C + I + G + NX$ at A and, then, the price level is in equilibrium. If, for some reasons, the aggregate expenditure curve shifts to $C' + I' + G' + NX'$, an inflationary gap appears in the output market. The size of the inflationary gap is AB which measures the excess of the aggregate demand over the value of the full employment output; it is given by $C' + I' + G' + NX' - Y_0$. The money value of the real output will be in equilibrium at Y_m. This can be done through the rise in the price level, as the real output is constant at full employment. So long the inflationary gap exists the price level will go on increasing. Inflation goes on without limit unless the inflationary gap is eliminated by actions of fiscal and monetary authorities or by the indirect effect of inflation on real demand. If aggregate demand is less than aggregate supply at full-employment then we have the deflationary gap. When there is a deflationary gap, the economy will settle at a less than full employment situation.

We now examine the indirect effects of the existence of inflationary gap on the components of demand and see whether the inflationary gap can automatically be eliminated as a result of the operation of these indirect effects. First, if money supply remains constant the rate of interest will increase because the price increase will reduce the real money supply. As the rate of interest increases, the investment demand will fall and the aggregate demand will be reduced, thereby eliminating a part of the inflationary gap. Second, as a result of the operation of the Pigou effect, an increase in the price level will reduce the real value of the given supply of money, which will reduce the aggregate real consumption expenditure thus shifting the consumption function— and, consequently, the aggregate demand function—in a downward direction. Third, indirect effect of the price increase would be to redistribute income against fixed income groups (i.e. between wages and profits). If the *MPC* of the fixed income groups is assumed higher than the average of the economy, such redistribution will reduce aggregate consumption expenditure. Fourth effect is that as the tax collection rises faster than prices (especially in the case of income tax) disposable income will fall—which will also reduce consumption expenditure. Fifth effect of higher domestic price will tend to discourage exports and encourage imports which will reduce net exports $(X - M)$. However, Keynes was of the opinion that neither of these indirect effects would be able to eliminate the inflationary gap.

Keynesian theory of inflation suffers from the following limitations. This is a static theory, which does not determine the rate of inflation. This limitation can be removed by dynamising it by assuming that the rate of inflation is proportional to the length of the inflationary gap.

This theory has considered excess demand in the commodity market only. If there is excess demand in the factor market inflation may develop from that market. This possibility has not been considered by Keynes at all. This limitation has been removed by Hansen, who has introduced both goods and factor gaps in the analysis of inflation.

The Keynesian theory assumed that inflation arises only after full employment is reached. So long full employment is not reached, there is no possibility of price increases. But when full employment is reached, the supply of commodity remains stationary and only the price level can increase. But, in reality, the inflation can begin even in a period of unemployment as we have seen in the 1970s and 1980s. Keynes also ignored the cost push inflation. Even when there is unemployment in the labour market, the wage rate may increase due to trade union pressure. If the productivity of labour does not increase with wage increases, unit cost of production will increase. This will push-up prices.

Bent Hansen's Model of Demand-Pull Inflation[1]

Hansen's Model of demand inflation shows that the simultaneous increase in the money wage rate and the price level are the products of the inflationary gaps in both the labour market and the output market. When the aggregate demand for labour exceeds its full employment supply, the inflationary gap appears in the labour market, and when the aggregate demand for output exceeds its full employment supply, the inflationary gap appears in the output market. When the inflationary gap appears in the output market, consequence is a rise in the price level, and when it appears in the labour market, the result is a rise in the money wage rate. The wage rate will increase only if there is excess demand for labour. Even if there is no excess demand for output the price level can go up due to an increase in the wage rate. Hansen points out that, in an inflationary process, there is an interaction between the two markets; inflationary gaps appear in both markets and both prices and money wages rise simultaneously. The existence of inflationary gap in the output market ensures its existence in the labor market, and vice versa. As a consequence, both the money wage rate and the price level rise in such a way as to keep the real wage rate, the real output and the size of the inflationary gaps constant.

If the full employment supply of output is autonomously given, the inflationary gap in the output market can be expressed as the difference between the actual demand and the full employment supply. The inflationary gap in the labour market may be expressed in two ways: the difference between the actual demand for labour and its full employment supply, and the difference between the intended and the actual supply of output. The intended supply of output generates the demand for labour, and it is the second difference which gives a measure of the inflationary gap in the market in terms of the

[1] See B. Hansen, A Study in the Theory of Inflation (George Allen & Unwin Ltd., London, 1953), Ch. 7. A Summary of Hansen's Model can be found in A. J. Hagger, The Theory of Inflation (Melbourne University Press, 1964).

unfulfilled supply plans of the producers. In this analysis, we shall use the second expression of the inflationary gap in the labour market, which enables us to express both the inflationary gap in the same unit.

The aggregate demand for output *(AD)* may be expressed as an increasing function of the real wage rate *(W/P)*. If wage income rises with the rise in the real wage rate and if the marginal propensity to spend of the workers is greater than that of the profit-earners, we can assume that, an increase in the real wage rate will lead to an increase in the aggregate demand for output. The intended supply of output *(AS)* may be assumed to be a decreasing function of the real wage rate. The diminishing marginal productivity of labour and the principle profit-maximisation explain why a rise in the real wage rate leads to a fall in the intended supply of output. It is assumed that the full employment output (S_f) is independent of the real wage rate. The inflationary gap in the output market is defined as $(AD - S_f)$, and the rate of increase in the price level over time is assumed to be a monotonically rising function of the inflationary gap in the output market. Thus, the following functional relation can be written as, $dp/dt = f(AD - S_F)$, where $dp/dt = 0$ for $f(0)$ and the first derivative of the function $f' > 0$. The inflationary gap in the labour market is defined as $AS - S_f$, and the rate of increase in the money wage (W_m) rate over time is assumed to be a monotonically rising function of the inflationary gap in the labour market. Thus, we have the following functional relationship: $dw/dt = F(AS - S_f)$, where $dw/dt = 0$ for $F(0)$ and its first derivative $F' > 0$.

These assumptions of the last paragraph will generate a model of demand inflation in which the simultaneous rises in the money wage rate and the price level can be explained. Diagrammatic presentation of the model is presented in Fig. 16.10. In part 16.10(a), the positively sloped *AD* curve and the vertical S_f line is the full employment supply curve. When the full employment supply curve passes through the point of intersection between the *AD* curve and the intended supply curve, there is equilibrium in both markets. Given the full employment supply curve, the point of intersection between the *AD* curve and the *AS* curve may shift to the right of the S_f line, when conditions of disequilibrium are created in both markets. The rightward shift of the point of intersection is brought about by autonomously produced rightward shifts in the *AD* - curve and the *AS* - curve. These autonomous shifts are the inflation-producing factors that are mainly responsible for the conditions of disequilibrium in the economy. Once the point of intersection between the *AD*-curve and the *AS*-curve goes to the right of the S_f-curve, inflationary gap arise in both markets.

At the real wage rate W'/P' there is no inflationary gap in the labour market, though there is an inflationary gap in the product market. As a result, the price level rises and the real wage rate falls. Thus, at W'/P', the real wage rate is the highest and it is bound to fall. With the fall in the real wage rate below W'/P', an inflationary gap also appears in the labour market. The simultaneous existence of inflationary gaps in both markets leads to rises in prices and wages. Again, at the lowest real wage rate of W''/P'', there is an inflationary gap in the labour market, though no such gap exists in the product market. But, the money wage rate rises leading to a rise in the real wage rate. As a result, inflationary gaps arise in both markets and both P and wage increase. Thus, it follows that the real wage rate must be between these two limits, where it will exactly lie depends on the two functions $dp/dt = f(RD - S_f)$ and $dw/dt = F(AS - S_f)$. If $dp/dt = dw/dt$, both markets are in equilibrium. If they are not equal $[dp/dt \neq dw/dt]$, the real wage rate changes, leading to changes in the respective inflationary gaps in the two markets. As a result, *dp/dt* rises and *dw/dt* falls. Thus, *dp/dt* and *dw/dt* always move forwards equality. If $dp/dt < dw/dt$, the real wage rate rises, and then the inflationary gap in the output market rises and that in the labour market falls. If, on the other

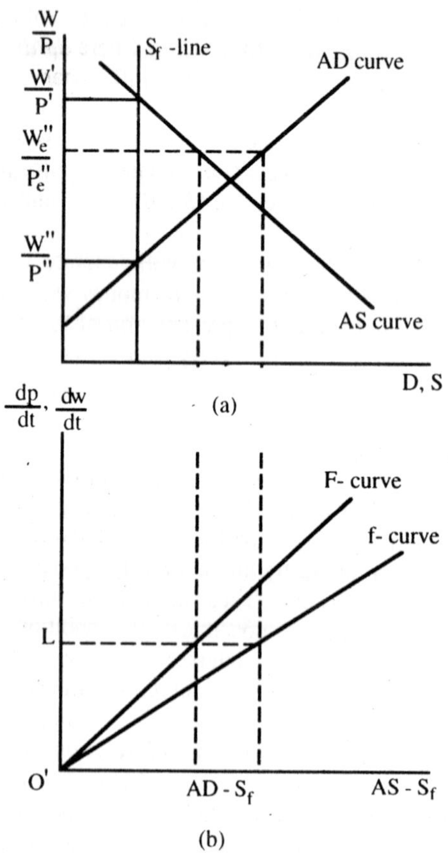

Fig. 16.10 Bent Hansen's Model of Demand-pull Inflation

hand, $dp/dt > dw/dt$, the real wage rate falls and the inflationary gap in the output market falls and that in the labour market rises. Thus, dp/dt falls and dw/dt rises.

This can be seen in Fig. 16.10(b) where the two functions, dp/dt and dw/dt, are presented and shown on the *f*-curve and *F*-curves, respectively. The origin of the figure in 16.10(b) has been placed at a particular point, so that the respective inflationary gaps in it equal to those in 16.10(a). The positions of the two functions in 16.10(b) depends on their sensitivities to the respective inflationary gaps. If dp/dt is more sensitive to $(AD - S_f)$ than dw/dt to $(AS - S_f)$, the *f*-curve will lie to the left of the *F*-curve, meaning that the inflationary gap in the output market will be less than that in the labour market to make $dp/dt = dw/dt$. If, however, the *f*-curve lies to the right of the *F*-curve, then $dp/dt = dw/dt$ would be at a greater inflationary gap in the output market than that in the labour market. In Fig. 16.10(b) the curves have been drawn under the assumption that dp/dt is less sensitive to the inflationary gap in the output market than dw/dt to that in the labour market. During the inflation, a position of quasi-equilibrium is reached, when $dp/dt = dw/dt$. Then, w/p becomes constant and the inflationary gaps remain unchanged, leading to rises in the price level and the money wage rate at a constant rate. In the Fig. 16.10(b) W/P is constant real wage rate which prevails in quasi-equilibrium position. $O'L$ is the rate of increase in P and W. If the *f*-curve lies to the right of the *F*-curve, the position of w_e/p_e will be located above the point of intersection between the *AD*-curve and the *AS*-curve. In the opposite case, it will lie below that point. When dp/dt and dw/dt are equally sensitive to the respective inflationary gaps, the two curves in Fig. 16.10(b) will coincide with each other and W_e/P_e will lie at the point of intersection between the *AD*-curve and the *AS*-curve.

Cost Inflation

Cost inflation arises when there is an increase in the cost of production. A rise in the cost of production may come from various factors, such as labour cost, raw materials, etc. If we assume that labour is the only variable factor in the short-run, then the cost of production will increase if the wage rate rises. Thus, cost inflation may arise, as a result of an increase in the wage rates. Wage rates may increase due to two factors: (1) as a result of collective bargaining or trade union pressure and (2) an increased demand for labour. If the wage rate increases due to increased demand for labour it should not be regarded as cost inflation, because, it is a case of demand inflation where inflationary forces originated in the factor market.

For true cost inflation, wage rate increases must be due to trade union pressure even when there is no excess demand for labour. A theory of cost inflation can be developed under the assumption that the wage rate is not market-determined, which means that the forces of demand and supply do not play any role in wage determination. If an independent role of the trade unions is introduced in the determination of the wage rate, we can build a model in which a rise in the wage rate can take place in the absence of excess demand for labour. Thus, the theory of cost inflation is based on the hypothesis that the wage rate is determined by the trade unions independently of the market force.

It is still assumed that commodity prices are determined by the interaction between the forces of demand and supply. A rise in the level of commodity prices may take place only when there is an excess demand in the commodity market. However, in the theory of cost inflation, we assume that the wage rate is not market determined though the commodity prices are. In the case of a demand inflation, the commodity prices rises when there is excess demand in the output market and the wage rate rise in response to the excess demand in the labour market. The excess demand in the labour market is derived from the excess demand in the commodity market. Whereas, in the case of cost inflation, the wage rate rises independently of the excess demand of the labour market, but the commodity prices rise in response to the excess demand in the output market. Thus, initially, there must not be any excess demand in the output market, when the rise in the wage rate takes place; and the rise in the wage rate must be followed by the emergence of the excess demand in the output market—which will push the commodity prices upward.

Thus, in the theory of a true cost inflation, we must have the following sequence of events : (a) there is an autonomous increase in the wage rate in the absence of any excess demand for labour and output, (b) the rise in the wage rate is followed by changes in the demand and for the supply of output, (c) an excess demand in the output market produce a rise in prices of commodities.

The determination of the wage rate with the interaction of the trade union provides us with the first logical step in the process. Let us assume that the trade union asks for a higher wage rate in the absence of excess demand for labour and that the trade union pressures compel the employers to accept the higher wage demands. It may so happen that the higher wage rate is followed by a rise in productivity, but if the rise in the wage rate exceeds the rise in productivity, this amounts to an autonomous rise in the wage rate. Thus, the wage cost per unit of output is raised thereby.

The second step is the process to see the effects of the rise in the wage rate on demand and supply. We must, now, know the resultant changes in the demand and supply of output. If the guiding principle of the employer is profit maximisation, and, if the law of diminishing returns applies to labour, the autonomous rise in the wage rate will lead to a fall in the level of output and employment. The resultant change in the aggregate demand depends on the changes in the distribution of income and on the marginal propensities to spend of the employers and workers. If the elasticity of demand for labour is less than one, the income of the workers will increase. If it is equal to one, the income of the workers will remain unchanged. However, there may be a fall in the profit income, as the total income has fallen. If the elasticity of demand for labour is greater than one, there will be a fall in the income of the workers. As a result of the change in the distribution of income, there will be a change in the aggregate demand.

When the wage income rises, the expenditure of the workers rises, but, then, the expenditure of the employers falls, as their profit income falls. If the marginal propensity to spend of the profit-earners is lower than that of workers, the aggregate expenditure will rise. In the opposite case, it will fall. When the total wage income remains unchanged, the expenditure of the businessmen falls, but the expenditure of the workers does not change. Thus, the aggregate expenditure falls. If, however, we assume that, the marginal propensity to spend of the economy as a whole is less than one, we can go to the third logical step. If, then, the aggregate demand falls, this fall must be less than the fall in the aggregate supply. The result will be an emergence of excess demand in the output market. Thus, there will be a rise in the price level.

The situation of a cost inflation may also be considered in a slightly different way in which the excess demand is the originating factor, but the role of the trade union may be responsible for the determination of wage rate and the spread of inflation in the whole economy. If there is an excess demand in some sectors of the economy, prices will rise in those sectors. However, because of structural rigidities, it is not possible to transfer labour from other sectors to those sectors. Thus, the wage rate of the workers employed in those sectors will rise, while those in other sectors will not fall. Trade unions in other sectors will put forward higher wage claims in order to maintain the relative position of their members. When they are successful in realising their higher wage claims, there is an autonomous rise in the wage rate in the rest of the economy, even where no excess demand exists. The result is a cost inflation all over the economy. Thus, the inflation has originated from the demand side, but it then spread into the economy by the cost factor through the role of the trade union.

The wage-price spiral can also be explained with the role of the trade unions. The autonomous rise in the wage rate is followed by an increase in the price level and this increases the cost of living of the workers. The price rise leads to a fall in the real wage rate. The trade unions will then demand a higher wage increase. Once this higher wage claim is granted by the businessmen, there is a second round of price inflation caused by the cost factor. This process may continue indefinitely, if it is not checked by other factors.

Distinction between Demand Pull and Cost Push Inflation

The distinction between a demand inflation and a cost inflation is purely theoretical. It is difficult to make this distinction in practice. The wage-price spiral is a normal feature of both types of inflation. In the case of demand inflation, the rise in the price level leads to the rise in the wage rate. In the case of a cost inflation, the rise in the wage rate leads to a rise in the price level. If we can identify what had risen first, we could then say whether it was a demand inflation or a cost inflation. In practice, both prices and wages are unstable over time. This instability can be created either from the demand side or from the cost side. These changes are indicated by the respective index numbers which fail to indicate what has led to what, because the time gap between a price rise and a wage rise is much shorter than a year, whereas the index numbers calculation is limited to annual data. The arbitrary choice of a base period makes a conclusion quite misleading.

It has been suggested that we should see which of the two — the price level or money wage rate — has increased more. If the rise in the price level is greater than the rise in the money wage rate, we can say that it is a case of a demand inflation. In the opposite case, we can say it is a case of cost inflation. Again, it may be argued that the price rise caused by an increase in the aggregate demand leads to a rise in profit and profit rate, until the wage rate is raised by the increased demand for labour. Thus, when the rise in the price level is associated with increase in profit rates and with wage rates lagging behind, we can say that it is the case of a demand inflation. Both the comparisons between the price level and the wage rate and between the wage rate and the profit rate are elusive because of the arbitrary selection of base period.

It may further be argued that if increases in the wage rate are caused by rises in labour productivity, it would not be a cause of inflation. Thus, when the rise in the wage rate exceeds the rise in labour productivity it may be regarded as the case of a cost inflation. However, a demand inflation does not leave the wage rate unchanged; the rise in the wage rate produced by the increase in demand for labour may be so high that it exceeds the rise in labour productivity. Thus, the comparison between the rises in the labour productivity and the wage rate is inconclusive with regard to the distinction between a demand and a cost inflation.

The theoretical models of the two types of inflation developed here suggests a method of distinction which should be examined in detail. There is an excess demand for labour in the case of a demand inflation and, thus, we can expect that a demand inflation should be associated with a condition of full employment in the economy or at least a falling unemployment. Whereas, a cost inflation should be associated with a rise in the level of unemployment. Thus, we need to examine the percentage of labour force unemployed to make a distinction between a demand inflation and a cost inflation. A rising percentage of unemployment indicates a cost inflation, whereas a falling percentage indicates a demand inflation. But this theoretically conclusive test for the distinction fails in practice because of a number of other considerations.

First, most of the governments in the developed economies are committed to the policy of maintaining full employment with the help of suitable fiscal and monetary measures. When a cost inflation threatens to aggravate the employment situation, the expansionary policy of the government counteracts the effects of the cost inflation. Thus, we may not find rise in the percentage of unemployment even at the time of cost inflation.

Second, the theory of cost inflation rests on the hypothesis that the trade unions have powers of raising the wage rate. This hypothesis has been tested and it has been found that there is a positive correlation between the strength of the trade unions and the level of economic activity. The level of economic activity varies inversely with the percentage of unemployment. Trade unions are generally more active at the time of rising level of economic activity. They are also successful in realising their demand at that time. Thus, we find that falling unemployment is associated with rising wage rates. The *"Phillips Curve"* gives a relationship between unemployment and the rate of change of money wage rates in the U.K., between 1861-1957, which shows that, the rate of change of money wage rates would be high when unemployment is low and low or negative when unemployment is high. In view of the difficulties mentioned above, the distinction between a cost and demand inflation becomes unworkable. The *"Phillips Curve"* has been discussed in details above.

The Quantity Theory Approach to Inflation

The neo-classical economists used to believe that inflation is created by the increase in the supply of money. The speed of inflation is determined by the rate of increase of money supply as the quantity theory establishes a direct and proportional relation between the price level and the quantity of money. This approach assumed that there was always full employment in the economy. If there is an increase in money supply in the economy, there will be an expansion of aggregate demand. The inevitable result is an increase in price level as the supply of output is fixed at the full employment level. Thus, the cause of excess demand is the rise in the money supply, which has produced inflationary situation. The disequilibrating factor is an increase in the supply of money.

However, Keynesian economists denied the rigid link between the quantity of money and the price level. Keynes pointed out that even if the quantity of money remains the same inflationary situation may emerge if aggregate demand is greater than aggregate supply. Keynes shifted the link from the relation between the stock of money and the flow of income to the relation between the flow of capital expenditure and income. He regards that the change in the stock of money is of minor importance in times of unemployment and may exercise a significant influence only when there is full employment. Later Keynesians argued that "money does not matter", and that the stock of money was mainly passive of economic change and play no part except as it might affect interest rates.

The new quantity theory formulated by Friedman in the 1950s again emphasizes the rate of the quantity of money in generating inflation. It was first formulated by Morton, who argued that, prices and wages were rising only because the monetary authorities in their attempt to maintain full employment were prepared to create money that was appropriate to full employment. If the objective of full employment was abandoned and the money supply was increased, there might not be an inflationary situation. The monetarists in the reformulation of the quantity theory emphasise the importance of the substitution between goods and money rather than Keynesian substitution between money and other assets. Friedman came to the conclusion on the basis of empirical evidence that, in each case, supply of money changed autonomously first, leading to change in the price level. According to him the supply of money is not a passive factor as described by the Keynesian economists. Changes in the supply of money are caused by factors which has nothing to do with the changes in the price level or in the level of income. In fact, changes in the price level or the level of income are caused by changes in the stock of money in the economy. The price level will remain stable only if the stock of money changes at a fairly steady rate — which is equal to or slightly higher than the average rate of growth in the economy. In short, this approach maintains that money stock — rather than the income flow — determines both the level of economic activity and the price level. Thus, to control inflation, the rate of growth of money supply should be controlled first.

The basic postulate of the quantity theory approach is that there is a stable demand function for money in real terms, into which the rate of inflation enters as a cost of holding real balances which influences the quantity of real balances held. Given this function, the rate of increase of the nominal stock of money determines the rate of inflation. In order to maintain its real balances constant in the face of inflation it is necessary to accumulate money balances at the rate of inflation. This accumulation of money balances in order to preserve real balances is achieved at the cost of sacrificing the consumption of current income. This can be regarded as the cost of holding real balances. This cost or tax on real balances accrues as revenue to the beneficiaries of the inflationary increase in the money supply. This can be represented in the Fig. 16.11, where the rate of inflation is measured in the vertical axis and the ratio of money stock to income in the horizontal axis. DD' is the demand for real money balances as a proportion of real income. The curve is downward sloping, which means that the lower the rate of inflation the greater is the demand for real balances relative to the real income. With zero inflation the ratio of real balances relative to real income is OD'. With the rate of inflation of OP, the demand for real balances falls to OM which is due to increase in the cost of holding real balances. The area $OMP'P$ represents the proportion of real income that holders of real balances are obliged by inflation to accumulate in the form of money balances in order to keep the real balance intact.

The quantity theory approach to inflation differs from Keynesian approach in several ways: (1) In the quantity theory approach it is assumed that the redistribution of income takes place from the community at large to the monetary

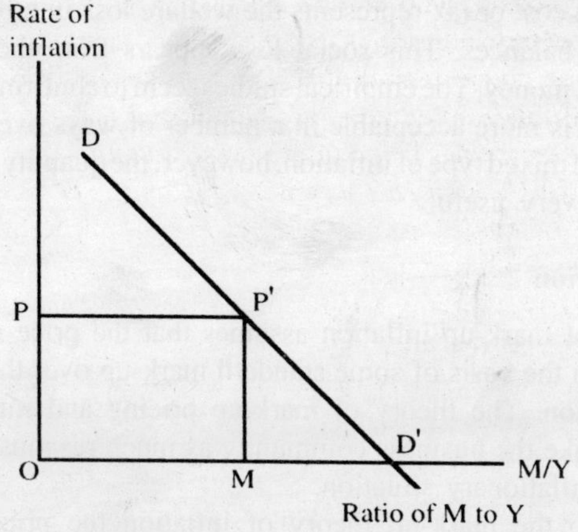

Fig. 16.11 The Quantity Theory Approach to Inflation

authority. But, in the Keynesian theory, redistribution of income takes place during inflation from fixed income earners to profit earners. (2) In the quantity theory, the rate of inflation is determined by the rate of increase in the money supply; whereas, in the Keynesian theory, it is determined by the institutional factors governing the responses of wages and prices to one another. (3) In the quantity theory approach the cost of inflation appears as the waste of resources involved in the efforts of the public to economise on the use of money by substituting real resources for it. On the other hand, in the Keynesian approach, the cost of inflation is taken as the socially undesirable redistribution of income. In. Fig.16.11 the cost of inflation can be measured by the area $P'MD'$ and this area can be approximated by the formula, $\frac{1}{2}P'\frac{M}{Y}\eta$, where P' is the rate of inflation, M/Y is the ratio of money to income and n is the inflation elasticity of the ratio of money to income. This can be shown as follows:

The area $P'MD' = \frac{1}{2} \times MD' \times P'M$. But $\frac{MD'}{P'M} = \frac{d(M/Y)}{d(\dot{P}/P)}$

$$\therefore MD' = \frac{d(M/Y)}{d(\dot{P}/P)} \times P'M = \frac{d(M/Y)}{d(\dot{P}/P)} \times \frac{\dot{P}}{P}$$

$$\therefore P'MD' = \frac{1}{2} \cdot \frac{d(M/Y)}{d(\dot{P}/P)} \times \left(\frac{\dot{P}}{P}\right)^2 = \frac{1}{2} \cdot \frac{\dot{P}}{P} \times \frac{d(M/Y)}{(M/Y)} \cdot \frac{(\dot{P}/P)}{d(\dot{P}/P)} \times \frac{M}{Y}$$

$$= \frac{1}{2} \cdot \frac{\dot{P}}{P} \cdot \eta \cdot \frac{M}{Y} = \frac{1}{2} \cdot P' \cdot \eta \frac{M}{Y}$$

where $P' = \frac{\dot{P}}{P} =$ rate of inflation.

This inflation cost or tax represents the welfare loss in order to economise the use of cash balances. This social loss appears from the substitution of real resources for money. The empirical studies seem to confirm that the quantity theory approach is more acceptable in a number of ways over the Keynesian approach. For the mixed type of inflation, however, the quantity theory approach has not proved very useful.

Mark-up Inflation

The theory of mark-up inflation assumes that the price of a commodity is determined on the basis of some standard mark-up over the average direct cost of production. The theory of mark-up pricing and inflation has been developed to make the business community as much responsible as the trade unions for an inflationary situation.

According to the mark-up theory of inflation the price of product is determined by the seller in the following way; an estimate is made of the average direct cost of labour and raw materials on the basis of their prices and the expected level of production; then a costing margin is added to the average direct cost to cover the overhead expenses and the expected profit; the costing margin is expressed as a percentage of the average direct cost. This is also called the percentage mark-up which, when added to the average cost, gives the price per unit. When the market is dominated by oligopolistic firms, price-formation in this way is the general rule. In the labour market, the trade unions are supposed to follow the same procedure to determine their wage rate. On the basis of the prevailing price level, the average cost is estimated, and, then, a percentage mark-up is added to the average cost of living to determine the wage rate. The percentage mark-up employed by the trade unions for the formation of the wage rate is based on the bargaining strength of the Unions and their expectation of a share in the improvement of productivity in the economy.

Under mark-up pricing theory the cost-push tends to be facilitated for the following reasons. First, the price rise follows directly and, thus, more rapidly upon the wage increases. Second, when prices are not sensitive to demand, profit rates tend to be maintained. The resulting price is fixed at a higher level than short-run profit maximisation. Third, management will put up less resistance to wage claims when mark-up pricing is used.

The mark-up inflation is generalised as income inflation. The basic idea of income inflation is that, at full employment, different groups of people in the economy attempt to improve or maintain their real income by raising their money incomes. If output cannot be increased to satisfy expectations, prices must rise and all groups of people in the economy experience some frustration. The process may continue so long as these frustrated groups try to improve their economic position to suit their monetary objectives. The process will stop when all groups adapt to the new monetary arrangements. This process is shown in Fig. 16.12 below. In this diagram money income is measured on the vertical axis and the price level on the horizontal axis. All combinations of price level and money income lie on the straight line OO' and represents the same real income. Let OB represent the fixed money claims of the rentier group. Let π and W curves represent the claims of profit and wage recipients, respectively. Let $\pi + W + F$ represent total claims (C) which exceeds the total real income available at (Y_1, P_1). This leads to a price rise. These conflicting claims are ultimately resolved by the rise in the price at (Y_2, P_2) where the $\pi + W + F$ curve intersects the OO' line. At this point, prices cease to rise. This stable equilibrium will not be possible if the $W + \pi + F$ curve does not intersect the OO' line at all.

Ackley's mark-up model of inflation is an adaptation of the theory of income inflation. In this mark-up inflation model, Ackley assumes that all business firms set their prices on some mark-up over the material and labour cost, and the labour seeks an increase in money wages that involves some mark-up over the increase in the cost of living. Ackley is of the opinion that inflationary process develops in inter firm transactions which also includes a mark-up price. Ackley's model adds to the income inflation picture in that it relates the price setting process to actual business practice and also that it stresses the insensitivity to demand in the short-run and of administrated wages and prices. Thus, if all wages and prices were set up by mark-up, an inflation could not be originated from excess demand in the short-run, nor be controlled by deficient demand. However, over the long-run, the situation could be different. Eventually, excess demand may induce an increase in the rates of mark-up and, thus, beginning or accelerating an inflation without a cost increase. As there is always a competitive sector in the agricultural commodities and other inputs, excess demand may induce a mark-up inflation via rises in the prices of inputs. The

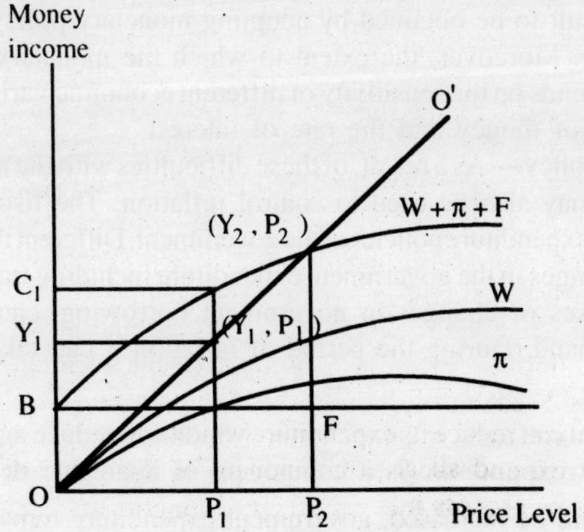

Fig. 16.12 Mark-up inflation

mark-up inflation points out that labour is not solely responsible for cost inflation. It is a combination of wage claims and business pricing policies that may be responsible for producing inflation.

Anti-Inflation Policies

Anti-inflation policies may be grouped as (1) Monetary Policy (2) Fiscal Policy and (3) Non-Monetary Policy. Let us discuss these policies one by one.

(1) Monetary Policy — The monetary policy refers to the Credit Control Policy of the central bank. The central bank can take the following measures to control the volume of credit : (a) Open Market Operations — means that, government can reduce or eliminate the excess purchasing power by selling government securities in the open market. This will reduce the purchasing power of the public as they are buying government securities rather than commodities. This would reduce the quantity of money in the economy. (b) Changes in the Bank Rate — The bank rate should be increased during a period of inflation. The increase in the bank rate will increase the long-run market rate of interest, thereby discouraging investment. This will reduce the inflationary gap. (c) Changes in the reserve ratio to be maintained by the Commercial Banks with the central bank. The reserve ratio of the Commercial Banks will have to be increased during the period of inflation. When the reserve ratio is raised, this will reduce the excess reserves of the commercial banks and thus, reduce the credit creating capacity of the banking system and (d) Selective methods of credit control — to control credit in some selective sectors of the economy the selective methods of credit control like regulation of margin requirements or regulation of consumer credit may be used.

The main difficulty with the monetary policy is that, it works only indirectly. Hence, the result to be obtained by adopting monetary policy would require some time lag. Moreover, the extent to which the monetary policy will be successful depends on the sensitivity of different economic variables to changes in the supply of money and the rate of interest.

(2) Fiscal Policy—As a result, of these difficulties with the monetary policy, fiscal policy may also be used to control inflation. The fiscal policy refers to taxation and expenditure policies of the government. Different fiscal parameters, such as the changes in the government expenditure including transfer payments, changes in taxes or changes in government borrowing, can directly affect aggregate demand. During the period of inflation it can take the following steps :

(a) Government can reduce its expenditure which will reduce aggregate demand as government expenditure is a component of aggregate demand.

(b) Taxes should be increased, government expenditure remaining the same. An increase in taxes will reduce the disposable income and, thereby, reducing consumption expenditure. It should be noted that, as anti-inflationary measures, direct taxes are superior to indirect taxes. Since the impact of indirect taxes can be shifted, imposition of indirect taxes will lead to an increase in the price level.

(c) The government should borrow from the public during a period of inflation by selling bonds. When people buy bonds, they surrender purchasing power, which may, otherwise, have been spent on consumption or investment.

(3) Non-Monetary Policy— Apart from the monetary and fiscal measures, non-monetary policies may also be adopted to control inflationary situation. The most commonly used anti-inflationary measure, other than restricting demand, has been income policies. It refers to a wide range of policies running from the government's setting of voluntary guidelines for wages and price increases, through consultation on wage and price norm between unions, management and government to compulsory controls on wage, price and profit increases. These are basically interventionist policies that call for government action to alter the results, that would otherwise have emerged from private-sector bargaining.

Income policies have been used in Europe in all sorts of circumstances. The non-monetary measures may also include output adjustments and rationing, etc. Inflation may arise because of shortage of output. Thus, to control inflation, the level of output should be increased in real terms. The measures to control price and rationing are actually short-run measures. Price control means fixation of legal upper limit for prices of goods. However, if demand cannot be controlled, mere price control may lead to the creation of black market. Rationing functions as a device of stabilising consumer prices and assuring distributive justice. However, rationing by weak administration may lead to black market and corruption.

Different anti-inflationary policies should not be regarded as competitive. They are rather complementary. All of them should be used together to get the best result.

Exercise

1. Discuss the main causes of the rapid rise in the rate of inflation during the 1970s. Can you account for the simultaneous increase in the rate of unemployment?

2. 'Inflation is always and everywhere a monetary phenomenon'—Critically examine the statement.

3. Discuss the redistribution effects of inflation.

4. According to the monetarist theory, what will be the effect on the rate of inflation if the government attempts to reduce unemployment below its natural rate?

5. How and why may an inflationary process automatically come to an end?

17 THE THEORY OF REAL BUSINESS CYCLES AND ECONOMIC FLUCTUATION

Most èconomists believe that the classical model cannot explain the short-run economic fluctuations because in this model prices are flexible. However, the new classical economists believe that the classical model can explain the short-run economic fluctuations. They believe that it is best to assume that prices are flexible even in the short-run. Almost all microeconomic analysis is based on the assumption that prices adjust to clear markets. New classical economists argue that macroeconomic analysis should be based on the same assumption.

The leading new classical explanation of economic fluctuations is called the theory of real business cycles. According to this analysis, the assumptions that have been used for long-run may also apply for short-run study. Most importantly, real-business-cycle theory holds that the economy obeys the classical dichotomy, nominal variables are assumed not to influence real variables. To explain fluctuations in real variables, real-business-cycle theory emphasises real changes in the economy, such as changes in fiscal policy and production technologies. This theory excludes the nominal variables to explain economic fluctuations.

Here we examine a simple theory of real business cycles.

A Review of the Economy Under Flexible Prices

The real-business-cycle theory is a new theory of fluctuations which requires the *IS-LM* model, under the assumption of flexibility of prices. We then modify it to develop a real model of short-run fluctuations.

In the *IS-LM* model we used the following equations for the goods and money markets:

$$Y = C(Y - T) + I(r) + G \qquad IS$$

$$M/P = L(r, Y) \qquad LM$$

The first equation is the *IS* equation, which states that income Y is the sum of C, I, and G. Consumption, C, depends on disposable income $(Y - T)$, investment depends on the real interest rate, r, and government expenditure, G, which is autonomous. The second equation is the *LM* equation, which states that the supply of real money balances, M/P, equals the demand, which is the function of the interest rate and the level of income. For simplicity, we are assuming that expected inflation is zero, so that, the nominal interest rate equals the real interest rate.

To analyse the short-run fluctuations with the *IS-LM* model, we assume that price level is fixed. If prices are flexible, then the price level adjusts, so that output is at its natural rate : $Y = \overline{Y} = F(\overline{K}, \overline{L})$

These three equations determine three endogenous variables : the level of output *Y*, the real interest rate *r*, and the price level *P*.

Fig. 17.1 shows the equilibrium of the economy with flexible prices. The level of output is at its natural rate $\overline{Y}$ which is determined by the supply of factors of production and the production function. The interest rate is determined by the intersection of the *IS* curve and the vertical line $\overline{Y}$, the natural rate of output. The price level adjusts, so that the *LM* curve crosses the intersection of the other two curves.

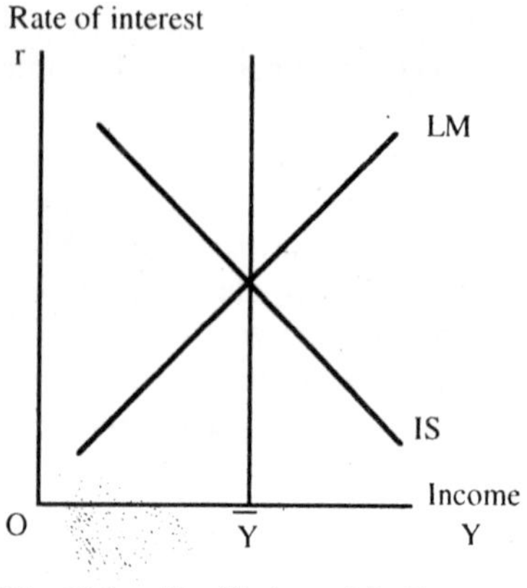

Fig. 17.1 Equilibrium of the Economy with Flexible Prices

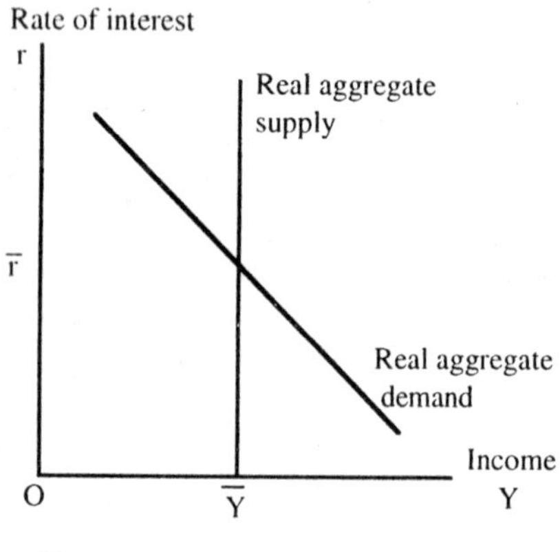

Fig. 17.2 Relationship Between the Real Aggregate Demand (AD) and Aggregate Supply (AS)

It may be noted that the *LM* curve is not very important here, as the prices are flexible and the price level adjusts to equilibrate the money market, where the other two curves intersect. For the purpose of understanding the real variables, such as output and interest rate, we can ignore the money market.

The two key relationships under flexible prices can be shown in Fig.17.2. These two relationships are real aggregate demand and real aggregate supply. The *IS* curve is called here the real aggregate demand curve, which shows that the demand for goods and services is a function of the interest rate. Real aggregate supply shows the supply of goods and services, which is determined by the supply of factors of production and the availability of technology.

In Fig. 17.2, the interest rate is on the vertical axis instead of price level as we have already seen in the case of aggregate demand and aggregate supply curves. In business-cycle theory, we are interested in real variables and not nominal variables, so the price level is unimportant. We are now developing a different theory of economic fluctuations.

A Real-Business-Cycle Model

We now turn our model of the economy under flexible prices into a model of fluctuations. The new feature of the model is the behaviour of labour supply. In a classical model the supply of labour is fixed which determines the level of employment. Yet employment fluctuates over the business cycle. If we maintain classical assumption that labour market clears, as new classical economists do, then we must examine what causes fluctuations in the quantity of labour supplied.

After discussing the determinants of labour supply, we modify classical model, aggregate income to include changes in labour supply. The supply of output depends in part on the supply of labour, which means that the greater the number of hours people are willing to work, the more output the economy can produce. We examine how various events influence labour supply and aggregate income according to real-business-cycle theory.

Intertemporal Substitution of Labour

Real-business-cycle theory states that the quantity of labour supplied depends on the incentives that workers receive at any point in time. When workers are well rewarded, they wish to work more hours, and vice versa. This willingness to reallocate hours of work over time is called the intertemporal substitution of labour. For example, a second year college student has two years summer vacations left before graduation. He wishes to work for one of these summers and to relax during the other summer. How should he choose which summer to work?

Let W_1 be his real wage in the first summer, and W_2 the real wage he expects in the second summer. Choosing which summer to work means comparing these two wages. Since the student can earn interest on money earned earlier, money earned in the first summer is worth more than money earned in the second summer. Let r be the real interest rate. If the student works in the first summer and saves his earnings, he will have $(1 + r)W_1$ a year later. If he works in the second summer, he will have W_2. The intertemporal relative wage is $\frac{(1+r)W_1}{W_2}$. Working in the first summer is more attractive if the interest rate is high or if the wage is high relative to wage expected to prevail in the future.

According to real-business-cycle theory, all workers calculate cost-benefit analysis to decide when to work and when to enjoy leisure. If the wage is temporarily high or if the interest rate is high, it is good time to work. If the wage is temporarily low or if the interest rate is low, it is a good time to enjoy leisure.

Real-business-cycle theory uses the intertemporal substitution of labour to explain why employment and output fluctuate. Shocks to the economy that cause the interest rate to rise or the wage rate to be temporarily high cause people to want to work more—which raises employment and output.

Real Aggregate Demand and Real Aggregate Supply

Real-business-cycle theory incorporates intertemporal substitution of labour into the classical model of the economy. Our analysis of labour supply shows that the interest rate influences the attractiveness of working today. The higher the interest rate, the greater the amount of labour supplied, and the greater the amount of output produced.

Fig. 17.3 shows the real-business-cycle model of the economy. Because of intertemporal substitution of labour, the real aggregate supply curve slopes

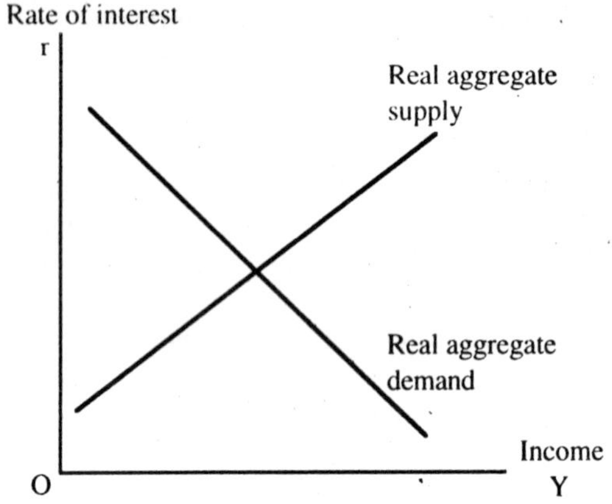

Fig. 17.3 Real Business-cycle Model

upward rather than vertically, which means a higher interest rate makes working more attractive, which increases labour supply and, thus, output. The real interest rate adjusts to equilibrate real aggregate supply and real aggregate demand. We can use this model to explain fluctuations in output. Any shock to the economy that shifts aggregate demand or aggregate supply changes equilibrium output. Intertemporal substitution of labour leads to a corresponding change in the level of employment as well.

To explain shifts in real aggregate demand and supply, real-business-cycle theorists have emphasised changes in fiscal policy and in technology. We now examine these sources of short-run fluctuations.

Fiscal Policy

An increase in government purchases is shown in the real-business-cycle model. Fig. 17.4 shows an increase in government purchases shifts the real aggregate demand curve rightward. The result is higher output and a higher real interest rate.

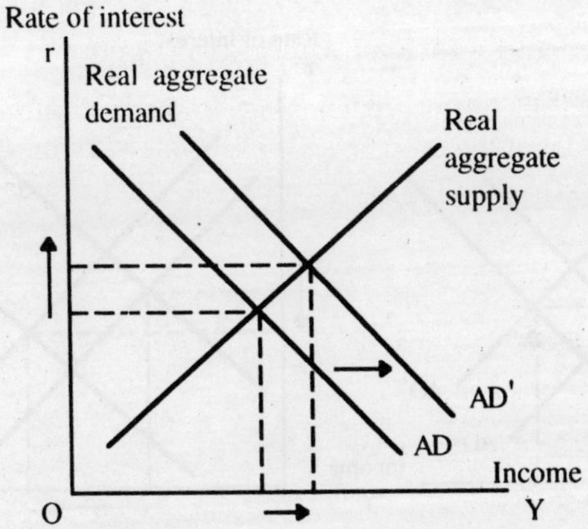

Fig. 17.4 Effect of Fiscal Policy in the Real-Business Cycle

It may be noted that there are similarities between this explanation of the effects of fiscal policy and the one we saw in the *IS-LM* model. An increase in government purchases shifts the real aggregate demand curve outwards for the same reason that it shifts the *IS* curve outwards in the *IS-LM* model. In both cases, the result is higher output and a higher interest rate. Thus, the two models make similar predictions.

However, there are important differences between the two explanations. In the *IS-LM* model, prices are stable, and aggregate demand determines output and employment; labour supply and intertemporal substitution play no role in explaining how fiscal policy influences output. In a real-business-cycle model, prices are flexible, and workers intertemporally substitute labour. The expansion of output results from an increase in labour supply; people respond to the higher interest rate by choosing to work longer hours.

Technology

Many theorists emphasise the role of shocks in technology. To see how technological shocks cause fluctuations, suppose some improvements in technology are available, such as, faster computers. According to this theory, this change affects the economy in two ways.

Firstly, the improved technology increases the supply of goods and services.

As the production function is improved, more output is produced for any given input. The real aggregate supply curve shifts outwards.

Secondly, the availability of the new technology raises the demand for goods. For example, firms wishing to buy these computers will raise their demand for investment goods. The real aggregate demand curve shifts outwards as well.

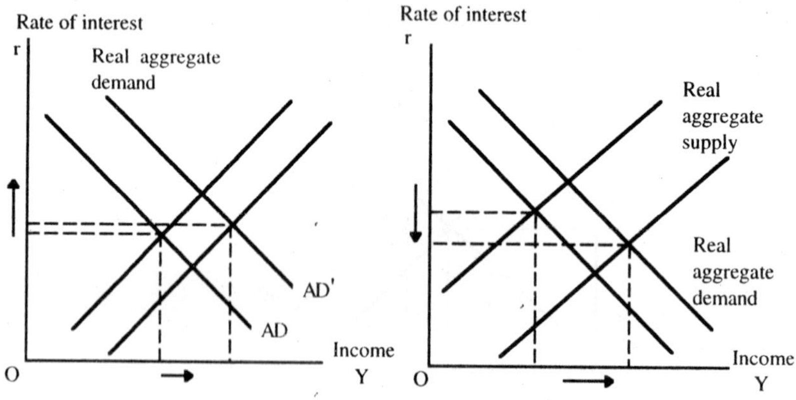

(a) Real aggregate demand shifts more than real aggregate supply

(b) Real aggregate supply shifts more than real aggregate demand

Fig. 17.5 Two Effects of Technological Innovation

Fig. 17.5 shows two effects. A beneficial shock to the technology raises both real aggregate supply and real aggregate demand. In Fig. 17.5(a), demand shifts more than supply. In Fig. 17.5(b), demand shifts less than supply.

The Debate Over Real-Business-Cycle Theory

Economists disagree about the validity of real-business-cycle theory. At the heart of the debate are four basic issues :

a) The importance of technology shocks.
b) The interpretation of unemployment.
c) The neutrality of money.
d) The flexibility of wages and prices.

The Importance of Technological Shocks

Real-business-cycle theory assumes that the economy experiences fluctuations in its ability to turn inputs into outputs, and that these fluctuations in technology cause fluctuations in output and employment. When the available production technology improves, the economy produces more output with the same inputs. Because of intertemporal substitution of labour, the improved technology also leads to greater employment. This theory often explains recessions as periods of technology regress. According to this theory, output and employment fall during recessions because the available production technology deteriorates, which reduces output and the incentive to work.

Critics of this theory are sceptical that the economy experiences large shocks in technology. It is common knowledge that technological progress takes place gradually. It is difficult to think that technology can regress. The technological knowledge may slow down, but it is hard to imagine that it would go into reverse.

Advocates respond by taking a broad view of shocks to technology. They argue that there are many events that—although not literally technological in nature—nevertheless, affect the economy as much as technological shocks do. For example, bad weather or increases in world oil prices have effects similar to adverse changes in technology. Whether such events are sufficiently common to explain the frequency and magnitude of business cycles is open to question.

The Interpretation of Unemployment

Real-business-cycle theory assumes that fluctuations in employment reflect changes in the amount people want to work. Alternatively, it assumes that the economy is always on the labour supply curve: everyone who wants a job at the going wage rate can find one. To explain fluctuations in employment, advocates of this theory argue that changes in wage rates and interest rates cause intertemporal substitution of labour.

Critics of this theory believe that fluctuations in employment do not reflect changes in the amount people want to work. They do not think desired employment is very sensitive to real wage and the real interest rate. They point out that unemployment fluctuates substantially over the business cycle. The high unemployment in recessions suggests that the labour market does not clear: if people were voluntarily choosing not to work in recessions, they are not, in fact, unemployed. These critics conclude that, wages do not adjust to equilibrate labour demand and supply, as the real-business-cycle model assumes.

Advocates of this theory argue that unemployment statistics are difficult to interpret. The mere fact that the unemployment rate is high does not mean that intertemporal substitution of labour is unimportant. Individuals who voluntarily choose not to work may call themselves unemployed to received unemployment benefits. Alternatively, they may call themselves unemployed because they would be willing to work.

The Neutrality of Money

This theory assumes that money is neutral which means monetary policy is assumed not to affect real variables, such as output and employment. The neutrality of money not only gives this theory its name, it is also the most radical feature of the theory.

Critics point out that the evidence does not support the assumption of neutrality of money. They argue that reductions of money growth and inflation are always associated with periods of high unemployment. Monetary policy appears to have a strong influence on the real economy.

Advocates of the theory argue that their critics confuse the direction of causation between money and output. They also claim that money supply is endogenous : fluctuation in output might cause fluctuations in money supply. For example, when output rises—because of beneficial technological shock—the quantity of money demanded rises. The central bank may respond by raising money supply to accommodate the greater demand. This endogenous response of money to economic activity may give the illusion of non-neutrality of money.

The Flexibility of Wages and Prices

Real-business-cycle theory assumes that wages and prices adjust quickly to clear markets. Proponents of this theory believe that the stickiness of wages and prices is unimportant for understanding economic fluctuations. They also believe that the assumption of flexible prices is methodologically superior to the assumption of sticky prices, because it ties microeconomic theory to macroeconomic theory more closely. Most of microeconomic analysis is based on the assumption that prices adjust quickly to equate demand and supply. Advocates of this theory believe that macroeconomists should base the analysis on the same assumption.

Critics argue that money wages and prices are inflexible—which explains both the existence of unemployment and monetary non-neutrality. To explain stickiness of prices, they rely on the various new Keynesian theories.

Conclusion

Real-business-cycle theory reminds us that our understanding of economic fluctuations is not good enough. Fundamental questions about the economy remain open to dispute. Is the stickiness of wages and prices a key to our understanding of economic fluctuations? Does monetary policy have real effects?

The way economists answer these questions influence the way they view the role of the economic policy. Those who believe that wages and prices are sticky often believe that fiscal and monetary policy should be used to try to stabilise the economy. Price stickiness is a type of market imperfection, which leaves open the possibility that government policies can raise economic benefits.

By contrast, the theorists believe that the government's ability to stabilise the economy is limited. They view the business cycle as the efficient and natural response of the economy to technological changes. Most models of this theory do not include any market imperfection and believe that the invisible hand guides the economy to an optimal allocation of resources.

These two views of economic fluctuations are a source of frequent and heated debate. It is this kind of debate that makes macroeconomics an attractive field of study.

Long-Run Economic Fluctuations

Cyclical fluctuations in the level of economic activity can be observed by examining annual changes in real national income over a long period of years. These changes are inversely related to variations in the rate of unemployment. The fluctuations were much reduced, possibly as a result of the adoption of Keynesian demand management policies by all governments in the developed capitalist economies since 1950s. None the less, even in this period, the economy has been subjected to fairly regular cycles of minor expansions and recessions. In the 1970s, the business cycle was marked by world recession—due to the energy crisis—which resulted in an upward trend in the rate of unemployment.

The phases of the business-cycle-slump, recovery, boom and deflation — are illustrated in Fig. 17.6. An economy in a slump is experiencing high demand-deficient unemployment of both labour and capital. A low level of both investment and consumption demand leads firms to cut back on their production, lay off workers and leave capital goods idle. Although money may be available for firms to borrow and interest rates may be low, investment will not increase because of pessimistic expectations.

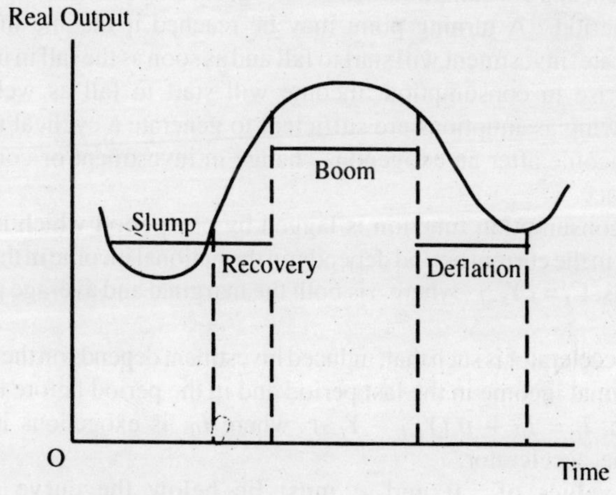

Fig. 17.6 Long-run Economic Fluctuations

In the recovery phase the level of aggregate demand is rising and, thus, businessmen become more optimistic. Generally, this is a period of rising consumer demand, investment demand, expanding output levels and a falling rate of unemployment. Eventually, the economy reached a boom period. This is a time of low unemployment, a high level of demand, high level of output and profits, an increasing rate of inflation and rising interest rates. Finally, in the deflation phase, the demands of both firms and households start to fall, firms' profits dwindle and output and employment levels are reduced. Again, businessmen become pessimistic about the future level of demand for their product and so become extremely reluctant to invest in new capital, even for replacement purposes. Ultimately, this contracting economy reaches the slump again and the whole process is repeated.

The objective here is to consider the possible causes of this cyclical movement in economic activity. We concentrate on the multiplier-accelerator theory to explain the fluctuations.

Multiplier-Accelerator Interaction

Samuelson's trade cycle theory is based on the interaction between the multiplier process and the accelerator principle. This model concentrates on the real sector of the economy and so excludes monetary variables. According to the 'accelerator' principle, investment depends on changes in income, and according to the multiplier, changes in investment cause changes in income. Thus, it is natural that interaction between the two can result in cumulative movements in income— for example, if income is rising at an increasing rate, both investment and consumption will be rising, causing further rises in income in the next period. A turning point may be reached if income increases at a decreasing rate; investment will start to fall and as soon as the fall in investment exceeds the rise in consumption, income will start to fall as well.

The following assumptions are sufficient to generate a cyclical movement in national income after an exogenous change in investment or consumption has taken place.

(1) The consumption function is lagged by one period which means that consumption in the current period depends on the national income in the previous period. That is, $C_t = cY_{t-1}$, where c is both the marginal and average propensity to consume.

(2) The accelerator is such that, induced investment depends on the difference between national income in the last period and in the period before that. Thus, we can write, $I_t = I_0 + \upsilon (Y_{t-1} - Y_{t-2})$ where I_0 is exogenous investment and υ is the accelerator.

(3) The values of υ and c must lie below the curve shown in Fig. 17.7. For example, if the values of c and υ lie in the area *GHJ* (say $c = 0.5$ and $\upsilon = 0.5$) as at point *E*, then any exogenous change in consumption or investment will generate a damped cycle like that given in Fig. 17.8; it is called damped, because the fluctuations in real output become smaller and smaller over time. But if the values of c and υ lie in the area *JHK* (for example, $c = 0.5$ and $\upsilon = 1.5$ at point *F*) then any exogenous change in

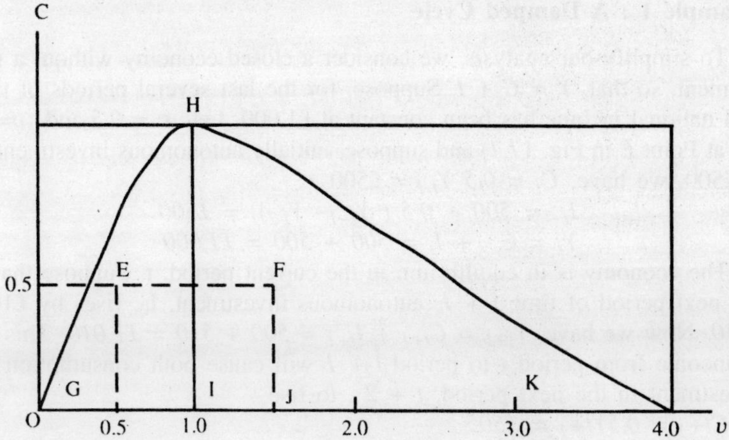

Fig. 17.7

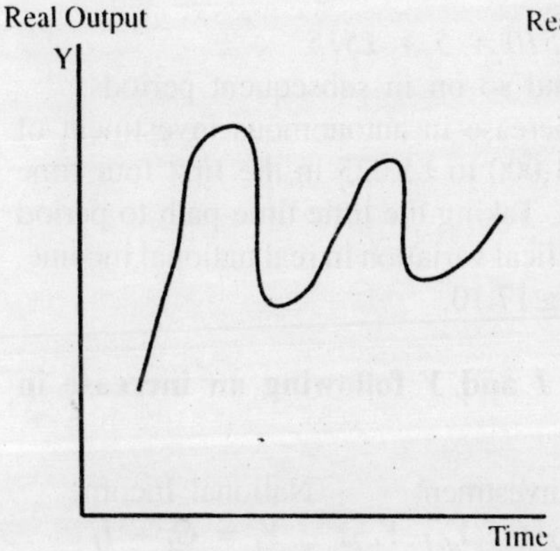

Fig.17.8

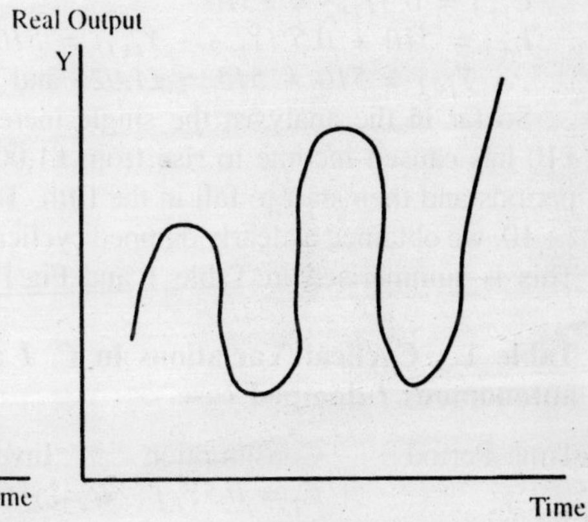

Fig.17.9

Cyclical Movement in National Income, Investment and Consumption

spending will generate an explosive cycle like that, in Fig. 17.9; here the oscillations get larger and larger over time.

There may be various types of cycle between these two extremes depending on values of c and v.

The derivation of the curve in Fig. 17.7 is beyond the scope of this book. However, we can partially demonstrate its validity by means of two simple numerical examples.

Example 1 : A Damped Cycle

To simplify our analysis, we consider a closed economy without a government, so that, $Y = C + I$. Suppose, for the last several periods of time, real national income has been constant at £1,000. Let $c = 0.5$ and $v = 0.5$ (as at Point E in Fig. 17.7) and suppose, initially autonomous investment (I_0) = £500, we have, $C_t = 0.5\ Y_{t-1} =$ £500

$$I_t = 500 + 0.5\ (\ Y_{t-1} - Y_{t-2})) = £500$$
$$Y_t = C_t + I_t = 500 + 500 = £1,000$$

The economy is in equilibrium in the current period, t. Suppose that, in the next period of time $t + 1$, autonomous investment, I_0, rises by £10 to $£510$. Now we have, $Y_{t+1} = C_{t+1} + I_{t+1} = 500 + 510 = £1,010$. This rise in income from period t to period $t + 1$ will cause both consumption and investment in the next period, $t + 2$, to rise :

$Ct+_1 = 0.5Yt+_1 = £505$

$I_{t+1} = 510 + 0.5\ (\ Y_{t-1} - Y_t) = 510 + 5 = £515.$

This means that, $Y_{t+2} = C_{t+2} + I_{t+2} = 505 + 515 = £1,020.$

This further rise in income from period $t + 1$ to $t + 2$ will cause C and I in period $t + 3$ to rise again.

$C_{t+3} = 0.5Y_{t+2} = £510$

$I_{t+3} = 510 + 0.5\ (Y_{t+2} - Y_{t+1}) = 510 + 5 + £515$

$\therefore\ Y_{t+3} = 510 + 515 = £1.025$ and so on in subsequent periods.

So far in the analysis, the single increase in autonomous investment of £10 has caused income to rise from £1,000 to £1,025 in the first four time periods and then start to fall in the fifth. Taking the little time-path to period t + 10, we obtained a clearly damped cyclical variation in real national income. This is summarised in Table 1 and Fig.17.10.

Table 1 : Cyclical Variations in *C, I* and *Y* following an increase in autonomous *I*-damped case.

Time Period	Consumption $C_t = 0.5Y_{t-1}$	Investment $I_t = I_0 + 0.5(Y_{t-1} - Y_{t-2})$	National Income $Y_t = C_t + I_t$
t	500	500	1,000
t + 1	500	510	1,010
t + 2	505	515	1,020
t + 3	510	515	1,025
t + 4	512.5	512.5	1,025
t + 5	512.5	510	1,022.5
t + 6	511.25	508.75	1,020
t + 7	510	508.75	1,018.8
t + 8	509.38	509.38	1,018.8
t + 9	509.38	510	1,019.38
t + 10	509.68	510.31	1,020

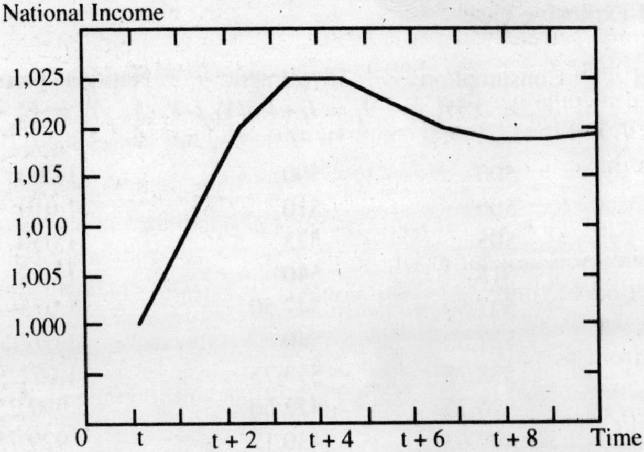

Fig. 17.10 Damped cycle

It may be noted that eventually the cycle will converge on the new equilibrium level of income of £1,020 (since the multiplier is 2 in this example). Only when income settles at £1,020 can we say that, the full multiplier effect has taken place. However, no new equilibrium position is likely to reach in the case of an explosive cycle, As is shown in the next example.

Example II : An Explosive Cycle

Now suppose $c = 0.5$ and $\upsilon = 1.5$ (point *F* in Fig.17.7). Assume, as before, that *Y* has been constant for several time periods at £1,000, and the autonomous *I* is equal to £500. This means that the economy is in equilibrium in period *t*. Now suppose, autonomous *I* rises to *£510* in period $t + 1$. This rise in spending will raise *Y* to £1010 in period $t + 1$ and this will cause both *C* and *I* to increase in the next period, $t + 2 : C_{t+2} = 0.5Y_{t+1} = £505$ $I_{t+2} = £510 + 1.5(Y_{t+1} - Y_t) = 510 + 15 = £525.$

Therefore, $Y_{t+2} = 505 + 525 = £1,030$

It may be noted that *I* and *Y* have already risen above the levels reached in the previous example. The time-path to period $t + 16$ is given in Table 2 and Fig.17.11. An explosive cyclical variation in national income, *Y*, results. Although the arithmetic becomes quite laborious, but it is a worthwhile exercise.

Table 2. Cyclical Variations in *C, I* and *Y* following an increase in autonomous I-explosive case

Time Period	Consumption $C_t = 0.5Y_{t-1}$	Investment $I_t = I_0+1.5(Y_{t-1}-Y_{t-2})$	National Income $Y_t = C_t + I_t$
t	500	500	1,000
t + 1	500	510	1,010
t + 2	505	525	1,030
t + 3	515	540	1,055
t + 4	527.50	547.50	1,075
t + 5	537.50	540	1,077.50
t + 6	538.75	513.75	1,052.50
t + 7	526.75	472.50	999.25
t + 8	499.63	430.12	929.75
t + 9	464.88	405.75	870.63
t + 10	435.31	421.31	856.62
t + 11	428.31	489	917.31
t + 12	458.66	601.03	1,059.69
t + 13	529.84	652.38	1,182.22
t + 14	591.11	693.80	1,284.91
t + 15	642.45	664.03	1,306.48
t + 16	653.24	542.37	1,195.61

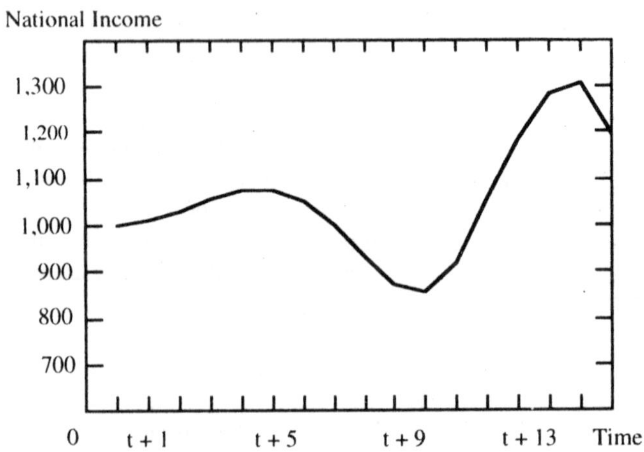

Fig. 17.11 An Explosive Cycle

Ceilings and Floors

We have seen that the multiplier-accelerator model is capable, under certain circumstances, of generating cycles automatically following any change in autonomous spending. Depending on the values assigned to c and v, the cycle may be damped and explosive. Table 1 shows that, cycle in practice displays no obvious tendency either to diminish or increase in amplitude over time, but in the 19th century, the amplitude of the cycle was remarkably constant. A possible explanation is that the cycle is inherently explosive, but is constrained within a band determined by an upper limit, called a ceiling and lower limit,

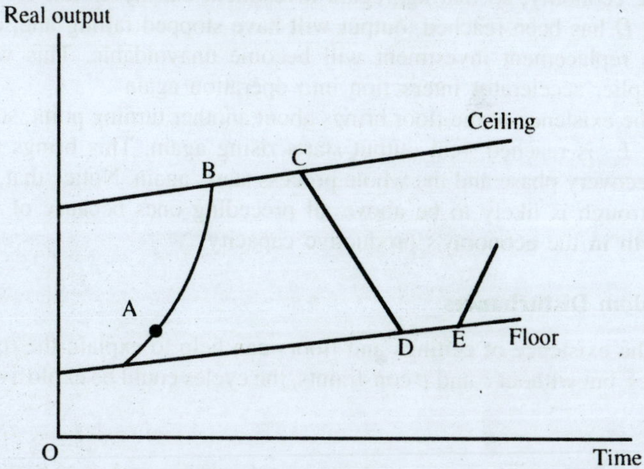

Fig. 17.12 Ceilings and Floors

called a floor. The cycle thus generated will tend to have a constant amplitude determined by ceiling and floor. Such a cyclical movement in real output is illustrated in Fig. 17.12. To explain how such a movement will develop, start at point *A* in Fig. 17.12. This is in the recovery phase. Consequently, demand is increasing, output is expanding and unemployment is falling. In terms of the multiplier-accelerator interaction, rising investment will cause *Y* to rise via the multiplier effect and the rising level of *Y* induces more investment to occur via the accelerator. Soon full employment will be reached (point *B* in Fig.17.12) which determine the ceiling because now real output can only rise as net new investment comes into operation. Firms may want to produce more at point *B* but are unable to do so, because of insufficient resources. This check to the growth of output and income will soon affect firms' investment plans via the accelerator. In fact, since the increase in income has slowed down, induced investment will actually fall and this causes income itself to fall via the multiplier. The existence of the ceiling brings about a turning-point and, after point *C*, real output starts falling.

Real output will continue to fall with multiplier-accelerator interacting with each other until the floor is reached. What determine the position of the floor? As we know, income cannot fall below zero, so that represents an absolute floor. However, investment demand can fall to zero when firms are so pessimistic that they have no demand for either new or replacement capital. Consumption demand must always be positive, if to sustain life. This consumption spending must represent floor below which the level of income cannot be expected to fall. Furthermore, it is likely that some investment will always occur somewhere in the economy, so that aggregate investment can never fall to zero. Once point *D* has been reached, output will have stopped falling and, eventually, some replacement investment will become unavoidable. This will set the multiplier-accelerator interaction into operation again.

The existence of the floor brings about another turning point, so that, after point *E* is reached, real output starts rising again. This brings us back to the recovery phase and the whole process starts again. Notice that, each peak and trough is likely to be above all preceding ones because of underlying growth in the economy's productive capacity.

Random Disturbances

The existence of ceilings and floors can help to explain the regularity of cycles, but without *c* and *υ* constraints, the cycles could be explosive. Suppose

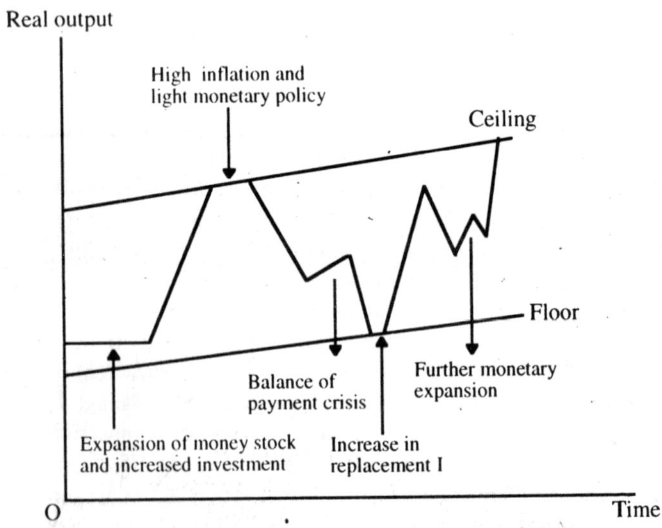

Fig. 17.13 Random Disturbance

c and *v* took on values consistent with damped cycles, how then could we explain the observed regularity of cyclical fluctuations?

One possible answer has been suggested by R. Frisch, who argues that, even though fluctuations around the equilibrium growth path are damped, random disturbances will be occurring continuously to stop the equilibrium path from being achieved and to maintain the cyclical variations in a fairly regular pattern. No sooner has one cycle started to diminish in amplitude than another disturbance occurs, starting off a new cycle. The types of disturbances which could do this are changes in investment, balance of payment crisis, changes in money supply, rapid inflation and policies designed to curb it, industrial disputes, and so on.

Of course, it is possible for more than one disturbance to occur at the same time, thus lengthening the inherently damped cycle. This means that the 'ceiling' and 'floor' analysis may become relevant here as well as in the explosive cycles case. Random disturbances are shown in Fig. 17.13, which give rise to fairly realistic variations in real output.

In this kind of model, real output is volatile, reaching occasionally the ceiling or floor, with each successive random disturbance pushing real income downwards or upwards and with underlying stabilizing influences of the multiplier and accelerator.

Monetary Influences

One of the random disturbances mentioned was a change in the money supply. We now consider to what extent changes in monetary variables may be responsible for cyclical variations in real output.

We know that the monetarists put a great deal of faith in the correlation between changes in the money supply and changes in national income; especially in the study by Friedman and Schwartz emphasises the observation that all major recessions have been preceded by a fall in the money supply and all major inflations by excess money supply. They concluded that the monetary changes were not associated with changes in national income, but the change in the money supply that causes the change in national income.

Non-monetarists also recognise the role of money supply in real output, though they do not assign them such a major role as the monetarists. For example, they recognise that, in the recovery phase of the cycle, the demand for money will increase. If the increased money demand is not accommodated, interest rates will rise this will discourage investment and so contribute to the slowing down in the growth of output and consequently lead to the upper turning-point. Similarly, in the deflationary phase, the money demand will be falling. If the money supply does not fall, interest rates will fall and, thus, encouraging new investment. This will contribute to the lower turning-point. However, its effectiveness depends on the interest-elasticity of investment which is like to be very low in the boom and slump periods of the cycle.

Exercise

1. According to real-business-cycle theory, permanent and transitory shocks should have very different effects on the economy. Let us compare the effects of a transitory technological shock (good weather) and a permanent technological shock (new invention in production process).
   a) Which shock would have the larger impact on the demand for investment goods? Which shock would cause the larger shift in real aggregate demand?
   b) Compare the effects of two shocks on output and the real interest rate.
   c) Which shock would raise the current real wage above the expected future real wage? Which shock would cause the largest shift in real aggregate supply?

2. Suppose that prices are flexible and that the output of the economy fluctuates because of the technological shocks.
   a) If the central bank holds the money supply constant, what will happen to the price level as output fluctuates?
   b) Many economists have observed that fluctuations in the money supply are positively correlated with fluctuations in output. Is this evidence against real-business-cycle theory?
   c) If the central bank adjusts the money supply to stabilise the price level, what will happen to money supply as output fluctuates?

3. Using the multiplier-accelerator model discussed here, trace out the time-path for national income over 10 years when
   a) $c = 0.8$ and $v = 0.1$ b) $c = 0.5$ and $v = 1$

4. An essential characteristic of cyclical behaviour is not only that expansion and contraction follow each other, but that each phase of the cycle contains within itself the seeds to generate the succeeding phase (*R. Levacic*). How can this aspect of the trade cycle be explained ?

18 THEORY OF ECONOMIC GROWTH

The Classical Theory of Growth can be explained in a simple way — given a certain amount of labour (assuming labour theory of value), at a certain level of production, wages will be paid to each worker according to the level of subsistence and any surplus *(TP – TC* = Total Surplus*)* accumulated by the capitalist. Such accumulation will increase the demand for labour and, with a given population, wages will tend to rise. As the wage exceeds temporarily the level of subsistence, the population will increase according to the Malthusian Theory of Population. With a growth of population, the supply of labour will increase and wages will again fall back to the subsistence level. But as wages become equal to the subsistence level a surplus will emerge again to encourage accumulation of demand for labour and the whole process will be repeated again in the next phase. The dynamics of growth ends as the law of diminishing returns sets in and wages eat up the whole production — leaving no surplus for accumulation, expansion and growth of population. The 'magnificent dynamics' ends not with a bang but a whimper as Fig. 18.1 shows.

The vertical axis measures *TP* and the horizontal axis measures *L* = Labour and *OW* line is a subsistence wage line. With ON_1 population, production is *OP*, wage per unit is N_1W_1 and surplus or profit is W_1E_1, when *TP* = Wages + Profits. The emergence of a surplus engenders accumulation which leads

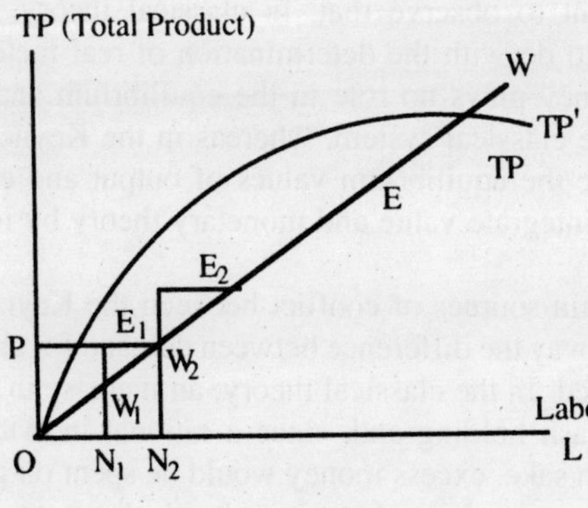

Fig. 18.1 The Classical Theory of Growth

to an increase in the demand for labour. Wages rise to E_1N_1 since the demand for L rises with accumulation but population, and, thus L supply remains constant at ON_1. But once the wages are above the level of subsistence, *i.e.* $N_1E_1 > N_1W_1$, growth of population is stimulated to ON_2. Once the population is ON_2, a surplus emerges again, i.e. W_2E_2, as wages are driven back to the level of subsistence and the whole process is repeated until the economy reaches a point E where the stationary state is reached. As $W = TP$, there is no surplus and the day of doom is reached. If technical progress is introduced (a shift of TP to TP'), then the day of doom is postponed, but not eliminated.

Limitations of the Model

(1) The role of technical progress has been underestimated in the model. The experience has shown that the role of *DR*, as the pointer to the day of doom, has certainly diminished. (2) The iron law of wages, which suggests that wages cannot be above the subsistence level because the Malthusian Law of Population has been discredited as the sole-explanation of wage determination. The iron law of wages is based only on supply, whereas wages are determined both by demand and supply. It does not take into account the role of trade union on wage determination. (3) The Malthusian Theory of Population Growth has been found to be misleading in the light of the experience of economic-development of the economically advanced European countries. The Malthusian argument that, whenever wages are above the subsistence level, people like to have more babies rather than other things seems to be unacceptable, both logically and empirically. (4) The classical model seems to be too simplistic to account for the complex factors which influence growth.

Keynesian Theory and The Classical Theory

It is significant to observe that, in classical theory, money is a 'veil' and has nothing to do with the determination of real factors like output and employment; money plays no role in the equilibrium analysis of value and distribution in the classical system, whereas in the Keynesian model money tends to influence the equilibrium values of output and employment. Later, Patinkin tried to integrate value and monetary theory by introducing the real balance effect.

One of the main sources of conflict between the Keynesian and classical theories lie in the way the difference between demand for and supply of money should be corrected. In the classical theory, an increase in money supply will raise unwanted cash holding and, since a rational individual does not hold money for its own sake, excess money would be spent on goods and services, pushing the price upwards, with a given level of output. The mechanism is explained with the help of the quantity theory : $MV = PT$, where M = quantity of money, V = Velocity, P = Price Level and T = total transaction. It is assumed that V and T are unlikely to change substantially in the short-run.

In such a situation, an expansion of M will have a direct and positive impact on prices. The critics, however, have argued that, if either V or T or both change with the change in M, then the direct relationship between M and P is unlikely to hold. To this 'new monetarists' point out that, as long as the demand for money remains stable, an expansion of M will always lead to a rise in prices, though the effect may not be seen instantaneously. At a higher price the expansion of money supply would be consistent with ordinary transaction demand (k) which is assumed to be fixed proportion of income (Y), or $M = kY$

In the Keynesian theory, an expansion of money supply will raise bond prices and reduce interest rate, increase the level of investment, output and employment and perhaps lead to a secondary effect on prices. Should there be excess capacity, the effect on prices of a rise in money supply will be even less. If we are concerned with an underemployment situation, prices should not be affected so long as the supply of output with respect to money supply is elastic. Thus, the effect could well be on income, output and employment.

Marxist Theory of Economic Growth

Marx rejected some principal features of the Classical theory of economic growth and offered his own theory within a socio-historical framework in which economic forces play a major role. In Marxist theory, the law of diminishing returns has been discarded because Marx believed that the Classical theory of Stationary State was actually a creation of human actions rather than the end product of a natural, immutable law. For a similar reason, Marx also castigated the Malthusian theory of Population.

Marx looked at economic development from a social and historical standpoint. Each stage of economic growth was regarded as the product of Hegelian dialectics of a game of contradictions where a thesis created its anti-thesis and the conflict between the two produced a synthesis. Marx emphasised that, with capitalism, social relations of production are much more important than an exchange relations between goods. The social character of labour has been stressed in particular. Marx argued that labour productivity 'is a gift, not of nature, but of history embracing thousands of centuries'. However, the Marxist concept of relations of production is rather vague. It has been interpreted as an 'organic whole' characterized by labour organisation and skill, the standing of labour in society, technological and scientific knowledge and its use in a certain environment. In the Marxist analysis, these 'relations of production' determine the socio-cultural set-up of a society. Marx believed that capitalism would not end up in a quiet classical 'stationary' state; rather, it would break up with a 'bang' 'when the expropriators are expropriated'. Here we shall only analyse the economic views in the Marxist theory.

The Marxist model of economic growth depends on some major dynamic 'laws' —

(1) The law of capital accumulation, which says that the prime desire of the capitalists is to accumulate more and more capital.

(2) The law of falling tendency of the rate of profit which plays a crucial role in the breakdown of the capitalist system.

(3) The law of increasing centralisation and concentration of capital, which tells us that, with the growth of capitalism, cut-throat competition among capitalists will lead to the annihilation of the smaller firms by bigger ones, which will lead to the growth of monopoly and concentration of economic power.

(4) The law of increasing 'pauperization' which implies the growth of the misery of the working class with the advancement of capitalism, reflected in wages being tied to the subsistence level coupled with a rise in the proportion of unemployed people — or, what Marx called the 'industrial reserved army of labour'— made possible by the substitution of capital for labour in the process of technical change.

The simultaneous working of these laws would generate contradictory forces, which would eventually sharpen the class conflict between capitalists and workers or between 'haves' and 'have-nots'. Capitalism would face a violent death in the final confrontation, when the expropriators would be expropriated. Hence, Marx gave the clarion call : 'workers of the world unite', as they have nothing to lose except their 'chain' and 'the whole world to conquer'.

The Marxist notion of the falling tendency of the rate of profit plays a crucial role in the whole process of change and can now be illustrated. According to Marx, the value of a commodity *(W)* is given by the sum of 'constant capital' *(c)* + the 'variable capital'*(q)* + the 'surplus value'*(s)*. If the working day consists of 8 hours and only 4 hours are required to produce a commodity for subsistence then for the remaining 4 hours, the worker is producing a surplus value, which is expropriated by the capitalists. More formally, $W = c + q + s$ and $X = s/q$ where x is the rate of surplus value or the rate of 'exploitation'. Thus, in the above example,

$$4\ hrs/4\ hrs = 100\% = X$$

The rate of profit *(P)* in the Marxian analysis is given by $P = \dfrac{S}{q+C} = \dfrac{\frac{S}{q}}{1+\frac{C}{q}}$

Let $S/q = X$, i.e. the rate of exploitation, and $c/q = J$ or the 'organic composition of capital'. Then we have $P = \dfrac{X}{1+J}$. Now, it is clear that, if X remained constant, P and J would be inversely correlated. A rise in J would take place as capitalism developed with continuous accumulation. Also, capitalists would substitute capital for labour whenever wages tended to rise above the subsistence level to maintain their rate of profit. The process would lead to higher unemployment among the working class and sharpen the polarization of forces. On the other hand, the crisis of capitalism would be reflected in the periodic fluctuations of growth and a falling tendency of the rate of profit, which would lead to cut-throat competition among the capitalists which, in turn, would lead to monopoly. Eventually, the conflict between the 'immiserized proletarians' and the capitalists would toll the death-knell of capitalism.

It is interesting to observe that the falling tendency of the rate of profit may not always be seen within an economic system. This can easily be demonstrated within the Marxist model. We have $P = \frac{X}{1+J}$. Differentiating P with respect to time we get

$$\frac{dP}{dt} = \frac{1}{1+J}\frac{dX}{dt} - \frac{X}{(1+J)^2}\frac{dj}{dt} \quad or, \quad \frac{dP}{dt} = \frac{1}{1+J}\left(\frac{dX}{dt} - P\frac{dj}{dt}\right)$$

Note that the profit rate will rise if the rate of exploitation rises more rapidly than the organic composition of capital. Even if the rise in the organic composition of capital is higher than that of the rate of exploitation, whether or not profit will fall depends on the difference between *dx/dt* and the product of profit rate and *dj/dt*. For profit rate to fall, *Pdj/dt* (which is *negative*) must be greater than *dx/dt*. But a fixed rate of exploitation and an increase in capital intensity may not go together because a rise in organic composition of capital would raise labour productivity which would either raise the rate of exploitation or raise real wages. Inevitably, the internal consistency of the Marxist model has been questioned. Further, a rise in the organic composition of capital could increase the rate of profit with an increase in productivity and a change in technology. Under such circumstances, the intensity of competition among capitalists declines. Technical progress may be neutral or even labour-using. Thus, the rise in the industrial reserve army of labour and a fall in the wage share in national income may not occur.

Other criticisms usually levelled against Marxist model may also be briefly mentioned. It is contended that Marx's correlation between the growth of the average firm size and an increase in the degree of concentration need not always happen. However, the proportion of unemployment has increased in recent decades.

Empirically, wage share of national income in most developed economies remained fairly constant for a long time and this phenomenon seems to have weakened the Marxist law of increasing pauperization. On the other hand, the Marxist prediction about the increasing concentration and centralisation of capital is not rejected. However, the rise in the output-capital ratios in developed economies probably reflects the growth of both accumulation and real wages, a phenomenon which Marx probably did not envisage within the strict framework of his analysis.

Rostow's 'Stage' Theory of Development

This theory states that the transition of an economy from being less developed to developed is possible through a series of steps. The most important of these is the so-called 'take off' stage when resistance to change in traditional values and, in the social, political and economic institutions of an underdeveloped economy is finally overcome and modern industries begin to expand.

The theory may be criticised for viewing development as simply a matter of higher saving and investment ratios.

Saving and Investment

Physical capital has always been at the centre of economic development. In order to invest, the country must save or, else, must have access to foreign saving through loans and aid. If domestic saving is the prerequisite for capital accumulation, then attention must focus on policies to promote saving.

Saving does depend on the availability of saving instruments — a banking system that offers convenient deposit services. There is evidence that extreme financial instability interferes with saving. When the return on saving becomes negative one of three things happens: households reduce their savings or they shift their saving abroad or they accumulate their saving in unproductive assets, such as gold. The financial environment for saving is thus an important factor in channeling saving from households to investing firms.

In addition to the private sector, the government affects national savings through its budgetary policies. It can also draw foreign savings to finance investment. A developing economy can tap foreign savings in three ways. One possibility is that, foreign firms invest directly in a country. The second way is that a country can tap foreign resources by borrowing in the world capital market or from institutions, such as the World Bank. Third possibility is that a country may receive foreign aid from industrialised countries.

The importance of these three sources of external saving has varied over time and between countries. But, there is no doubt that external saving can supplement domestic saving as it always has done. Of course, foreign saving is all the more important the lower the per capita income.

The amount of saving, whatever, may be its source, determines how much investment will take place in a country. But the productivity of investment may vary widely. The larger differences in productivity of investment across countries focuses attention on development policies and strategies that affect the efficiency of resource utilisation.

Harrod-Domar Growth Model

This model assumes that : (a) The economy is closed with no government. Thus, the condition for equilibrium is that, planned investment is equal to planned savings; (b) There are only two factors of production, Labour *(L)* and

Capital(K), and there is no technical progress; (c) Labour is homogeneous, measured in its own units and grows at the constant natural rate of growth, n.; (d) There are constant returns to scale. This means that, if both L and K are increased by a given proportion, output also increased by that proportion. (e) Savings (S) are a fixed proportion of income (Y). That is, $S = sY$ where s is both APS and MPS. Investment (I) is autonomous and there is no depreciation. (f) The potential national income (Y_P) is proportional to the quantity of K and L. Thus, we can write $L = uY_P$ and $K = \upsilon Y_P$, where υ is a constant capital-output ratio and u is a constant labour-output ratio. This is a fixed proportional production function with L-shaped isoquant as in Fig. 18.2. Both K and L have to be employed in fixed proportions: as the Fig. 18.2 shows, increased capital and labour from OK_1 and OL_1 to OK_2 and OL_2 increased output from Q_1 to Q_2 (from A to B). Increasing only one of the factors would keep output unchanged (from A to C).

In Fig. 18.3, we start from equilibrium A and the initial investment I_1 which is equal to S at the income level OY_1. Over time, the investment adds to the capital stock and so increases the economy's potential output, say to OY_2. The following analysis shows what the increase in potential output (ΔY_P) will be : $K = \upsilon Y_P$, thus, $\Delta K = \upsilon \Delta Y_P$. But $\Delta K + I_1$, so we have $\Delta Y_P = \dfrac{I_1}{\upsilon}$ ....(1)

The new level of income, OY_2, will be an equilibrium Y if AD increases. Assuming that the C and S functions are stable, thus, increase in demand must come from an increase in I. Investment must rise to I_2 as in Fig.18.3, where I_2 intersects the savings line at Point B where OY_2 is an equilibrium income.

As the new K from this extra I comes into operation, potential output will rise yet again, say to OY_3. For this to be an equilibrium Y, investment must rise again — and so on as the growth-process continues.

This is Harrod's warranted rate of growth (g_W) which can be derived as

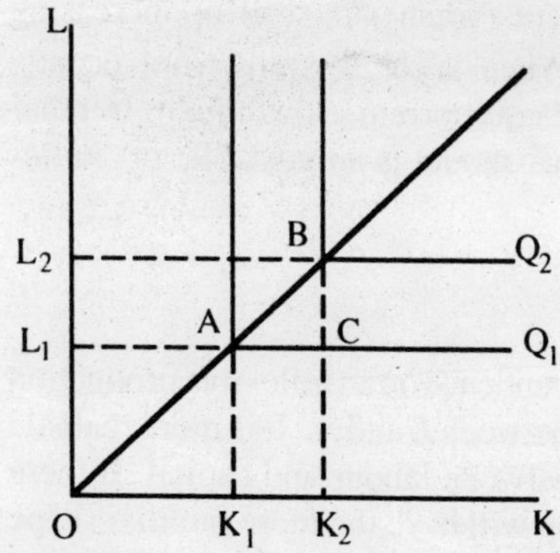

Fig. 18.2 Fixed Proportion Production Function

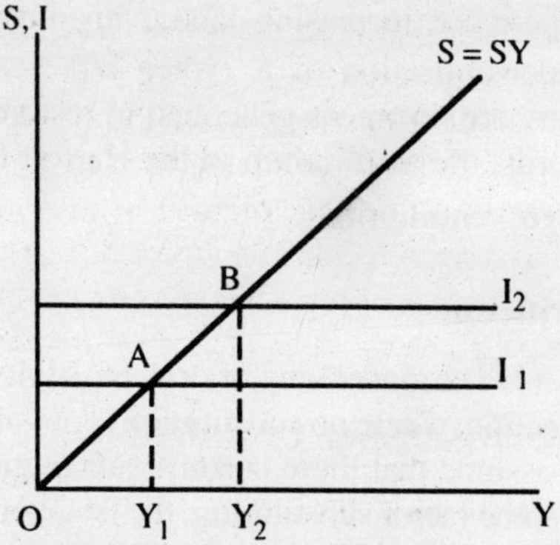

Fig. 18.3 Equilibrium Output changes with Investment

follows : $\Delta Y = \frac{I}{v}$ (from equation 1). In equilibrium, we have $I = S = sY$. By substitution $\Delta Y = \frac{sY}{v}$. Rearranging, $\frac{\Delta Y}{Y} = \frac{s}{v} = g_w$. This is the rate of growth of output required to keep the economy in equilibrium at its potential output level. It is Harrod's warranted rate of growth. For example, suppose $v = 4$ and that the savings proportion, $s = 0.2$. The warranted rate of growth (g_W) would be $g_w = \frac{0.2}{4} = 5\%$.

This means that 5% growth would be necessary to keep the potential and equilibrium output levels equal. Thus, the warranted rate of growth can be increased by policies designed to increase the propensity to save or to reduce the capital-output ratio by measuring the productivity of K.

In this model output can only grow at the warranted rate, s/v, if sufficient labour is made available. It is assumed that the labour force is growing at the constant rate n; if $n > \frac{s}{v}$, the warranted rate can be achieved but will lead to an increasing rate of unemployment; if $n < \frac{s}{v}$, the actual rate of growth will fall short of warranted rate and unemployed capital will be created. Thus, for an equilibrium growth path which maintains full employment of both L and K, the following condition must be satisfied: $n = \frac{s}{v}$. That is, warranted rate of growth must be equal to the natural rate of growth.

Unfortunately, s, v and n are all constants in the Harrod-Domar model and unrelated to one another. It would be a complete 'fluke' if $n = \frac{s}{v}$. We can conclude that the equilibrium rate of growth in this model is highly unlikely to be achieved automatically. Furthermore, when $\frac{s}{v} \neq n$, the economy will either experience increasing labour unemployment (when $s/v < n$) or increasing under-utilisation of K (when $s/v > n$). When such disequilibrium occurs, there are no forces generated to restore the equilibrium growth path. In other words, the equilibrium in the Harrod-Domar model is an unstable, or 'knife-edge', equilibrium.

Criticism

(1) The model's major drawback is its dependence on an inflexible production function, where no substitution is possible between L and K. It is more realistic to assume that there is some substitution between labour and capital. If there is some factor substitution; the isoquant map will have the more familiar shape as in Fig. 18.4. It is now possible to increase output from Q_1 to Q_2 by increasing the capital stock from OK_1 to OK_2, keeping the labour force unchanged, or

by increasing the labour force from OL_1 to OL_2, keeping the capital stock unchanged.

With a production function of this kind, the capital-output ratio (v) can vary. Suppose that the warranted and natural rate of growth are not equal. As an example, let $s/v > n$; this means that the capital stock is growing

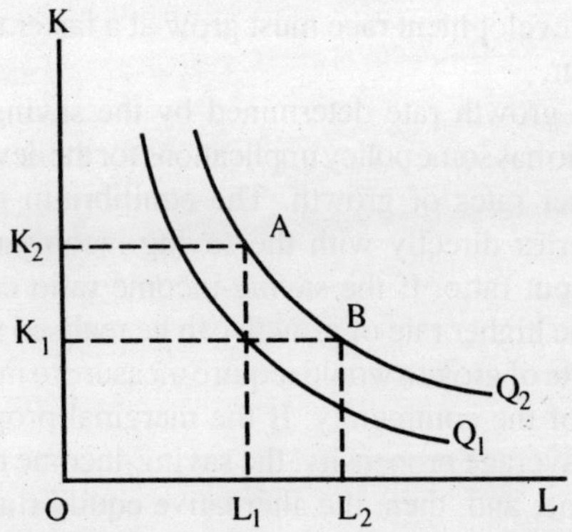

Fig. 18.4 Production Function with Some Factor Substitution

faster than the labour force and also faster than output. Consequently, the capital-output ratio will rise and so s/v will fall. This tendency will continue until $s/v = n$ again, which is the steady state growth, all economic variables grow at the constant proportional rate which is equal to the natural rate of growth. Then the economy is on its long-run equilibrium growth path. This view, that any $\frac{s}{v} \neq n$ will be corrected by a change in v, is the basis of the so-called neo-classical growth model, which will be developed in the latter sections. In the meantime, we shall see some of the interesting uses of the model in the national planning.

Uses of Harrod-Domar Growth Model in National Planning

The central point in the growth theories developed by Harrod-Domar is concerned with the existence of a unique equilibrium rate of growth which may or may not be achieved in practice. Given a community's propensity to save and the state of its technical progress, its income, investment and capital stock have a uniquely determined uniform rate of growth at which the condition of dynamic equilibrium is satisfied. This is the fundamental proposition that goes into this growth model in the post-Keynesian theory.

There are two interesting implications of this type of equilibrium growth model. First, if the two countries have the same equilibrium growth rate, but if income in one country is higher than the other, the absolute gap between the two incomes will increase with the passage of time. Second, if the income in one country is larger than that in other, but if the latter has a slightly higher rate of growth than the former, the income in the latter will catch up with the income of the former in course of time. That is, perhaps, the reason why a late starter in the development race must grow at a faster rate than its already developed neighbour.

The equilibrium growth rate determined by the saving-income ratio and the capital-output ratio has some policy implications for the developing economies, that aspire for higher rates of growth. The equilibrium rate of growth that can be achieved varies directly with the saving-income ratio and inversely with the capital-output ratio. If the saving-income ratio can be raised above the existing level, the higher rate of growth can be realised thereby. The policy of maximising the rate of growth would require measure to increase the marginal propensity to save of the community. If the marginal propensity to save can be raised above the average propensity, the saving-income ratio will rise above the growth of income; and, then, the alternative equilibrium growth rate will also increase over time.

The growth rate may also be maximised by reducing the capital-output ratio. Different commodities have different capital-output ratios, and the same commodity may be produced with different processes that may have different capital-output ratios. Thus, by a suitable choice of processes and composition of output, the over-all capital-output ratio of the whole economy may be reduced to maximise the growth rate. The choice of technique is an important device in the process of economic growth. The macro-economic significance of the choice of technique in increasing the rate of growth with given saving-income ratio is a direct outcome of the Harrod-Domar growth model.

Another application of the Harrod-Domar growth model can be found in the analysis of the role of the foreign aid in the economic development of a developing economy. To start with, a developing economy has a low saving-income ratio which produces a very low rate of growth. It may be possible to increase the rate of growth of an economy by increasing the marginal propensity to save above the average propensity which will raise the saving-income ratio. If the domestic saving is supplemented by foreign aid, the rate of growth may be raised above what is attainable without it. The higher rate of growth may produce a faster rise in the saving-income ratio, and, hence, the higher rate of growth may be achieved at an earlier date.

Now we can fix a target rate of growth which may be higher than presently attainable rate. Domestic saving may be incapable of realising it at the beginning; but if the saving-income ratio rises with the growth of income, the target rate of growth will be possible to realise at some future date even without the foreign aid. If we know the saving function, we can calculate the date of achieving the target rate of growth. If t is the date of realising the target rate of growth without foreign aid, then, with foreign aid, it may be possible to realise the target rate much earlier; and with the rise in the saving-income ratio it will be possible to realise the target rate domestically attainable at a future date when foreign aid may not be available or required. The date of terminating the foreign aid is t^* which must be higher than t as the growth rate with foreign aid is higher than without it. The difference between t^* and t is the contribution of the foreign aid, which may be calculated by the simple Harrod-Domar Model.

Though we have discussed the usefulness of this simple models in examining the various policy implications in the economic development in an under-developed economy, we must emphasise that the problems of economic development are more complex than the simple Harrod-Domar model can handle. Economic development means radical restructuring of the economy. Structural rigidities, socio-economic and many socio-political factors are responsible for economic backwardness. Economic theory alone cannot deal with the structural problems of underdeveloped economies. In fact, the growth models have been developed to deal with the problems of maintaining steady growth in industrially developed economies. The question of development in a developing economy cannot be dealt with by the economic theory alone. It requires the help of other branches of studies, such as sociology, politics, religious inhibitions and so on.

Economic Growth

Our primary task is to develop Solow Growth Model, which shows how saving, population growth and technical progress affect the growth of output over time.

Our second task is to examine how economic policy can influence the level and growth of the standard of living. The model provides a framework with which we can address one of the most important questions in economics — how much of the economy's output should be consumed today and how much should be saved for future? Since saving equals investment, saving determines the amount of capital an economy will have for future production. National saving is influenced by government policies. Evaluating these policies requires an understanding of the costs and benefits to society of alternative rates of saving.

Accumulation of Capital

The Solow Growth Model shows how growth in the capital stock, growth in the labour force, and advance in technology interact, and how they affect output. As a first step in building the model, we examine how the supply and demand for goods determine the accumulation of capital. To do this, we hold the labour and technology fixed. We relax these assumptions later.

Supply and Demand for Goods

The supply and demand for goods play a central role in the Solow Model. The supply of goods determines how much output is produced at any given moment in time, and the demand determines how this output is allocated among alternative uses.

Supply of Goods and Production Function

Supply of goods in the Solow Model is based on the production function $Y = F(K, L)$, output depends on the capital stock and the labour force. The Solow Growth Model assumes that the production function has constant returns to scale. $ZY = F(ZK, ZL)$, for any positive number Z. That is, if we multiply K and L by Z, we also multiply the amount of output by Z.

Production function with constant return to scale are convenient, because output per worker depends only on the amount of capital per worker. For this, set $Z = 1/L$ in the equation above to obtain $Y/L = F(K/L, 1)$. Thus, output per worker Y/L is a function of capital per worker K/L, where $y = Y/L$ is output per worker, and $k = K/L$ is capital per worker. We can now write the production function as $y = f(k)$, where we define $f(k) = F(k,1)$. It is more

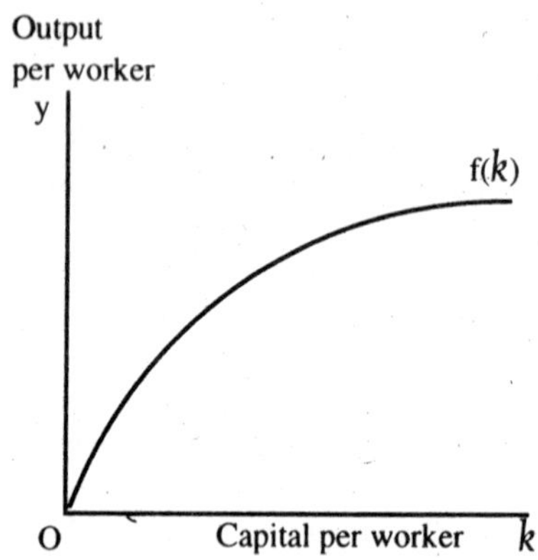

Fig. 18.5 Production Function

convenient to analyze the economy using this production function as Fig. 18.5 shows.

The slope of this production function shows how much extra output per worker is produced from an extra unit of capital per worker. This is the MP_K. Mathematically, we can write : $MP_K = f(k + 1) - f(k)$. The production function becomes flatter as k increases, indicating diminishing MP_K.

Demand for Goods and Consumption Function

The demand for goods in this model comes from consumption and investment. That is, output y is divided between c and i : $y = c + i$ This equation is the national income account identity except government purchases and it expresses y, c and i as per worker.

The model assumes that the consumption function takes the form: $c = (i - s)y$ where s, the saving rate, $O < s < I$. This consumption function states that consumption is proportional to income. Each year a fraction $(I - S)$ of Y is consumed, and a fraction is saved.

Substituting $(I - S)Y$ for C we get the national income identity: $Y = (I - S)Y + i$. Rearranging the terms we obtain : $i = SY$. This states that, investment, like consumption, is proportional to Y. Since $I = S$, the rate of saving S is a fraction of output devoted to investment.

Evolution of Capital and Steady State

Having introduced the production and consumption functions — main ingredients of the model, we can examine how increases in the capital stock over time result in economic growth. Two forces — investment and depreciation — cause the capital stock to change.

The saving rate S determines the allocation of output between consumption and investment. At any level of k, output is $f(k)$, investment is $sf(k)$, and the consumption is $f(k) - sf(k)$.

The higher the level of capital k, the greater the levels of output $f(k)$ and investment i. This equation relates the existing stock of capital k to the accumulation of new capital i, Fig. 18.6 shows how the saving rate determines the allocation of output between c and i for every value of k.

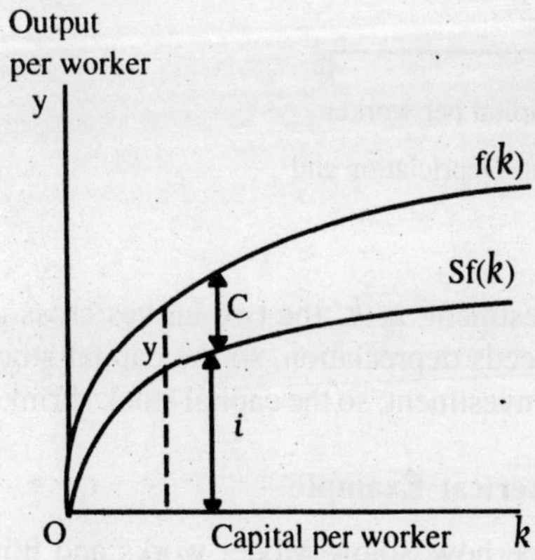

Fig. 18.6 Output, Consumption and Investment

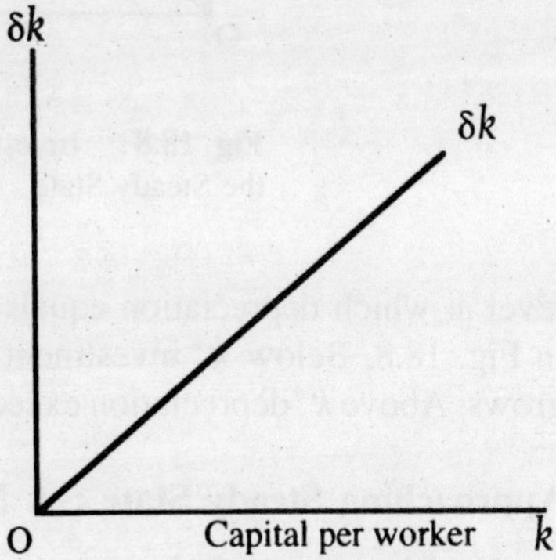

Fig. 18.7 Depreciation

A constant function δ of the capital stock depreciates every year. Depreciation is, therefore, proportional to the capital stock. For example, if capital lasts an average of 25 years, then the depreciation rate is 4% per year. The rate of depreciation is δk. Fig. 18.7 shows how depreciation depends on the capital stock.

We can express the impact of i and δ on the capital stock with this adjustment equation.

Change in capital stock = Investment – Depreciation, $\Delta k = i - \delta k$. Since $s = i$, we can write the change in the capital stock as : $\Delta k = sf(k) - \delta k$. This equation states that the change in capital stock equals investment $sf(k)$ minus the depreciation of existing capital δk.

Investment, Depreciation and The Steady State

Since the rate of saving S is constant and saving equals investment, the amount of investment is $sf(k)$. Since capital depreciates at a constant rate δ, the amount of depreciation is δk. The steady-state level of capital k^* is the

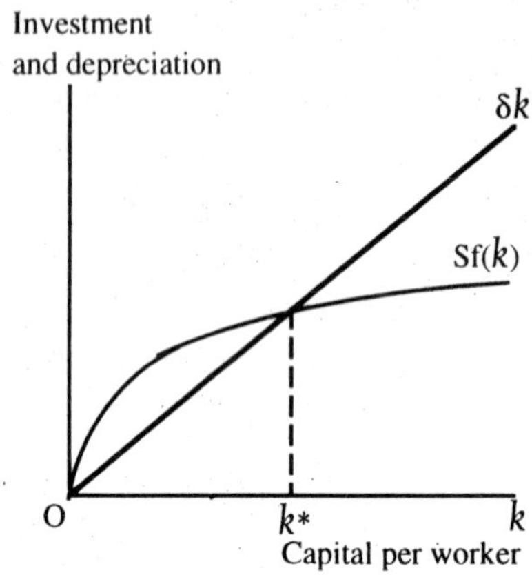

Fig. 18.8 Investment, Depriciation and the Steady State

level at which depreciation equals investment; at k^* the two curves cross as in Fig. 18.8. Below k^* investment exceeds depreciation, so the capital stock grows. Above k^* depreciation exceeds investment, so the capital stock shrinks.

Approaching Steady State : A Numerical Example

We take a numerical example to see how Solow Model works and how the economy approaches the steady state. For example, we assume the production function to be : $Y = K^{1/2}L^{1/2}$.

To derive the per-worker production function $f(k)$, divide both sides by L. $\frac{Y}{L} = \frac{K^{1/2}L^{1/2}}{L}$, substitute $y = \frac{Y}{L}$ and rearrange to obtain $y = \left(\frac{K}{L}\right)^{1/2}$. Since $k = \frac{K}{L}$, this becomes $y = k^{1/2}$.

The equation can also be written as $y = \sqrt{k}$. Output per worker is the square root of capital per worker.

If we assume that $S = 0.3$, $\delta = 0.1$ and the economy starts off with 4 units of capital per worker, $k = 4$. We can examine what happens to the economy over time.

Let us look at the production and allocation of output in the fresh year—our production function tells us that the 4 units of k will produce 2 units of y. Since $C = 0.7$ and $S = 0.3 = i$, in our case $C = 1.4$ and $S = i = 0.6$ and $\delta = 0.4$. With $i = 0.6$ and $\delta = 0.4$, $\Delta k = 0.2$. The second year begins with 4.2 units of capital per worker, $k = 4.2$.

Every year new capital is added and output grows. Over many years, the economy approaches a steady state with $k = 9$. In this steady state, $i = 0.9$ and $\delta = 0.9$, so that the capital stock and output will not grow any more.

Following the progress of the economy for many years is one way to find the steady-state capital stock, but another way requires fewer calculations. Recall that $\Delta k = sf(k) - \delta k$. The equation shows k grows over time. Since $\Delta k = 0$ in the steady-state, we know: $0 = sf(k^*) - \delta k^*$ or, $\frac{k^*}{f(k^*)} = \frac{s}{\delta}$. We can find steady-state from this equation. Substituting in our example, we obtain $\frac{k^*}{\sqrt{k^*}} = \frac{0.3}{0.1}$ or, $k^*=9$. The steady-state capital stock $k^* = 9$.

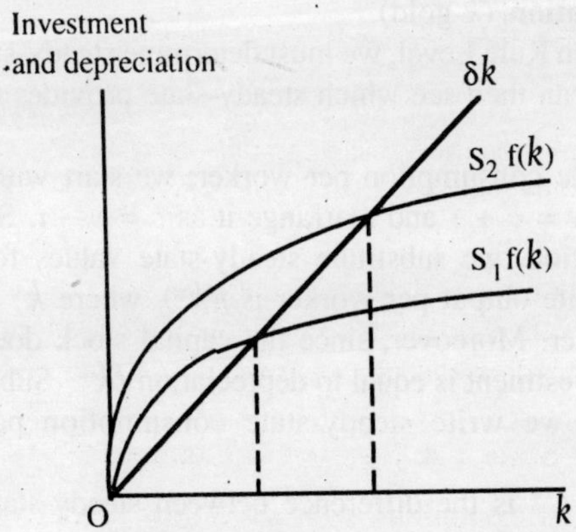

Fig. 18.9 Changes in saving Rate

Changes in Saving Rate

An increase in S implies that, the amount of i for any given stock of capital is higher. It thus shifts the saving function upward. At the old steady state, $i > \delta$, the capital stock rises until the economy reaches a new steady state with more capital and output.

The Solow Model shows that the saving rate is a key determinant of the steady-state capital stock. If S is high, the economy will have a large capital stock and a high level of output. If S is low, the economy will have a small capital stock and a low level of output.

The relationship between saving and economic growth is that a higher saving leads to a higher economic growth, but only in the short-run. However, in the long-run, a high rate of saving will not maintain a high rate of growth.

Golden Rule Level of Capital

Since we have examined the link between the rate of saving and the steady-state levels of capital and income, we can discuss what amount of capital accumulation is optimal. We first present the theory behind government's policy regarding saving rate, which will be discussed later on. We assume, for the moment, that a policymaker can set economy's saving rate at any level. By setting the saving rate, the policymaker determines the steady-state they choose.

Comparing Steady-State

When choosing the steady-state, the policymaker's goal is to maximise the well-being of the society. Individuals in the society may not care about the amount of capital and even output in the economy. They only care about the amount of goods and services they can consume. However, the policymaker would wish to choose the steady-state with the highest consumption level. The steady-state with the highest consumption is called the **Golden Rule Level of Capital Accumulation** (k gold).

To know the Golden Rule Level, we must determine steady-state consumption per worker. We can then see which steady-state provides the most consumption.

To find steady-state consumption per worker, we start with the national Y accounts identity : $y = c + i$ and rearrange it as $c = y - i$. Since we want steady-state consumption, we substitute steady-state values for output and investment. Steady-state output per worker is $f(k^*)$, where k^* is the steady-state capital per worker. Moreover, since the capital stock does not change in the steady-state, investment is equal to depreciation δk^*. Substituting $f(k^*)$ for y and δk^* for i we write steady-state consumption per worker as $C^* = f(k^*) - \delta k^*$.

Thus, steady-state C^* is the difference between steady-state output and depreciation. It shows that increased capital has two effects on C^* : it causes greater output, but more output must be used for δk.

Steady-State Consumption

Fig. 18.10 shows steady-state output and depreciation as a function of the steady-state capital stock. Steady-state C^* is the gap between output of $f(k^*)$ and depreciation δk. The figure shows that, there is one level of capital stock —the Golden Rule level k^*_{gold}—that maximizes consumption. At the Golden Rule level of Capital, the production function and the δk^* line have the same slope, and consumption is at its greatest level.

To make the point somewhat differently, suppose the economy starts at some capital stock k^* and that the policymaker wants to increase the capital stock at $k^* + 1$. The amount of extra output would then be $f(k^* + 1) - f(k^*) = MPK$. The amount of extra depreciation from having one more unit of capital

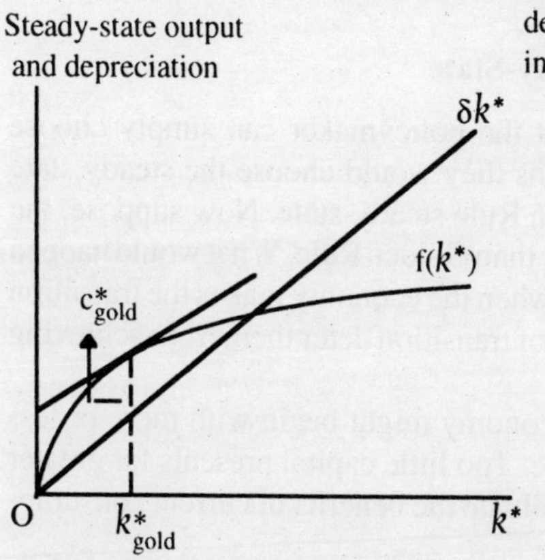

Fig. 18.10 Steady-state Consumption

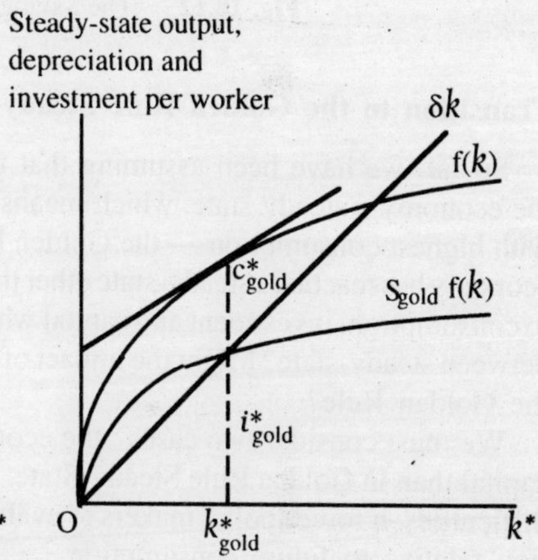

Fig. 18.11 The Saving-Rate and the Golden Rule

is δ. The net effect of this extra unit of capital on consumption is $MPK - \delta$.. If the steady-state capital stock is below the Golden Rule level, increases in capital increase consumption because the $MPK > \delta$. If the steady-state capital stock exceeds the Golden Rule level, increases in capital reduce consumption because the $MPK < \delta$. Thus, the following condition describes the Golden Rule : $MPK = \delta$ or $MPK - \delta = 0$

The Saving Rate and The Golden Rule

Fig.18.11 shows there is one saving rate that produces the Golden Rule level of Capital k^*_{gold}. A change in the saving rate would shift the $sf(k)$ curve, which would move the economy to a steady-state with a lower level of consumption.

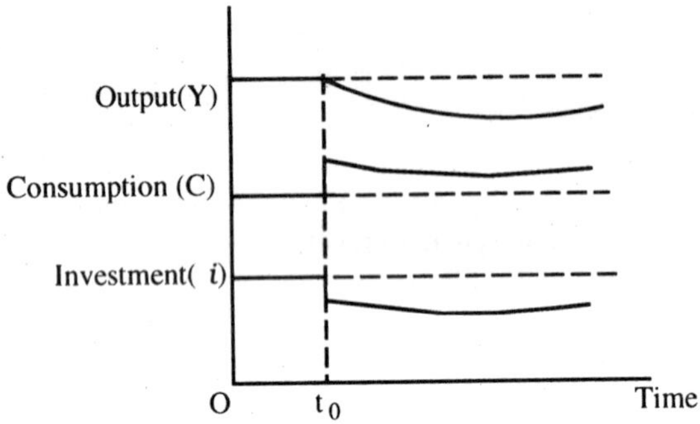

Fig. 18.12 The Saving rate is reduced

Transition to the Golden Rule Steady-State

So far, we have been assuming that the policymaker can simply choose the economy's steady state, which means they would choose the steady state with highest consumption — the Golden Rule steady-state. Now suppose, the economy has reached a steady-state other than Golden Rule. What would happen to consumption, investment and capital when the economy makes the transition between steady-state? Might the impact of transition deter them from achieving the Golden Rule?

We must consider two cases : the economy might begin with more or less capital than in Golden Rule Steady-State. Too little capital presents far greater difficulties, it forces policymakers to evaluate the benefits of current consumption relative to future consumption.

Starting with more capital than in the Golden Rule : Reducing saving — Fig. 18.12 shows what happens over time to output, consumption and investment when economy begins with more capital than the Golden Rule

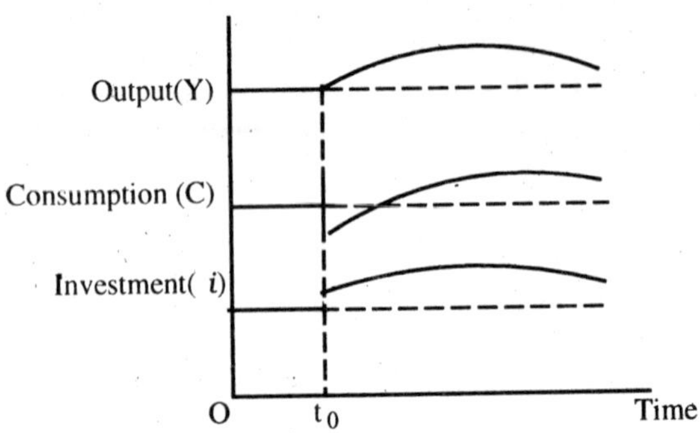

Fig. 18.13 The Saving rate is increased

as the investment saving rate is reduced. The reduction in the saving rate (t_o) causes an immediate increase in consumption and an equal decrease in investment. Over time, as the capital stock falls, output, investment and consumption fall together. Since the economy began with too much capital, the new steady-state has a higher level of consumption than the initial steady-state. The new steady-state is the Golden Rule Steady-State.

Start with less Capital than in the Golden Rule

Saving rate must be raised to reach the Golden Rule: Fig. 18.13 shows what happens to output, consumption and investment over time when the economy begins with less capital than the Golden Rule, and the saving rate is increased. The increase in the saving rate, at time t_0, causes an immediate drop in *c* and equal increase in *i*. Over time, as the stock grows, output *(y)*, consumption*(c)* and investment*(i)* increase together. Since the economy began with less than the Golden Rule Capital, the new steady-state has a higher level of *c* than the initial steady-state.

The Golden Rule Steady-State and Economic Welfare

Does the increase in saving that leads to the Golden Rule Steady-State raise economic welfare? Eventually it does, because the steady-state level of consumption is higher. But to reach the new steady-state requires an initial period of low consumption. If the economy begins above the Golden Rule, the situation would be different. When the economy begins above the Golden Rule, reaching the Golden Rule produces higher consumption at all time. When the economy begins below the Golden Rule, reaching the Golden Rule needs reducing consumption today to increase consumption in the future.

Decision about reaching the Golden Rule Steady-State is difficult when the population changes over time. Reaching the Golden Rule that achieves the highest steady-state level of consumption thus benefits future generations. But reaching the Golden Rule requires raising investment and, thus, lowering the consumption of present generations.

When deciding whether to increase capital accumulation, the policymaker must compare the welfare of different generations. A policymaker who is more interested about the present generation than about the future generations may decide not to pursue policies to reach the Golden Rule Steady-State. Conversely, if a policymaker cares about all generations equally will choose to achieve the Golden Rule. Even though the current generation will consume less, future generations will benefit by moving to the Golden Rule. Thus, optimal capital accumulation depends crucially on how we weigh the interests of different generations.

Population Growth

The basic Solow Model shows that capital accumulation alone cannot explain sustained economic growth. High rate of saving leads to high growth rate temporarily, but eventually, the economy approaches a steady-state in which output and capital are constant. To explain the sustained economic growth, we must expand the Solow Model to include the other two sources of economic growth: population and technological growth. Let us discuss population growth first. We assume that, the population and the labour force grow at a constant rate n.

The Steady-State with Population Growth

Like depreciation, population growth reduces the capital stock per worker. As before, $K = K/L$ and $Y = Y/L$. Now the number of people is growing over time. The change in the capital stock per worker is $\Delta k = i - (\delta + n)k$. If n is the rate of population growth and δ is the rate of depreciation, then $(\delta + n)k$ is the investment necessary to keep the capital stock per worker constant at k. If $n = o$, the equation becomes $\Delta k = i - \delta k$ in the special case of constant population as seen before. Like depreciation, population growth reduces k thus now break-even investment is $(\delta + n)k$.

Now substituting $sf(k)$ for i, the equation can be written as :

$$\Delta k = sf(k) - (\delta + n)k$$

For the economy to be in a steady-state (k^*), investment $sf(k)$ must offset the effect of depreciation and population growth $(\delta + n)k$. This is presented in Fig. 18.14. If $k^* > k$, investment is greater than break-even investment, so k^* rises. If $k^* < k$, investment is less than break-even investment, so k

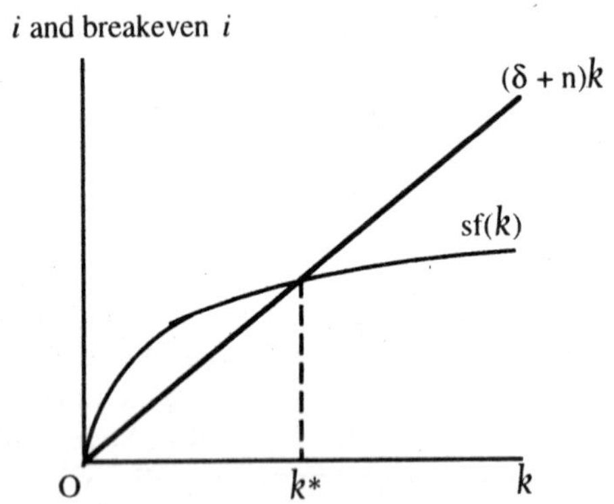

The steady-state capital per worker

Fig. 18.14

falls. Thus, k^*, $\Delta k = 0$ and $i = \delta k^* + nk^*$. Once the economy is in the steady-state, i has two purposes — to replace the depreciated capital, and to provide the new workers with the steady-state amount of capital.

Effects of Population Growth

Population growth alters the basic model in three ways : (1) It brings us closer to explaining sustained economic growth but not the sustained growth in the standard of living, because output per worker is constant in the steady-state. It can explain sustain growth in total output. (2) This model predicts that, economies with higher rate of population growth will have lower levels of capital per worker and, thus, lower income, as the Fig. 18.15 shows.

An increase in the rate of population growth from n_1 to n_2 reduces the steady-state level of capital per worker from k^*_1 to k^*_2. Since k^*_2 is lower, and since $y^* = f(k^*)$, the level of output per worker y^* is also lower.

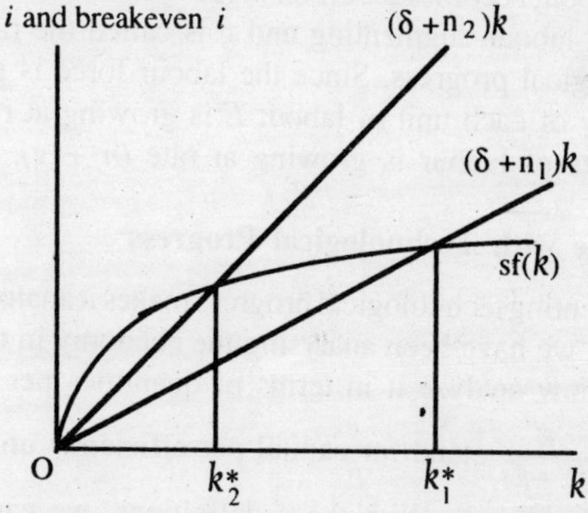

Fig. 18.15 Effect of Population Growth

(3) Population growth affects the condition for determining the Golden Rule Level of capital accumulation. To find this condition in an economy with higher population growth, we proceed as before. Consumption per worker is $c = y - i$. Since the steady-state output is $f(k^*)$ and investment is $(\delta + n)k^*$, we can write steady-state consumption as $C^\pi = f(k^*) - (\delta + n)k^*$. As before, we can conclude that the level of k^* that maximizes consumption is the one at which : $MPK = \delta + n$. In the Golden Rule Steady-State, the $MPK - \delta = n$.

Technological Progress

We now incorporate technological progress — the third source of economic growth — into the Solow Model. So far, we assumed an unchanging relationship between the inputs of capital and labour and the output. Yet the model can be modified to allow for exogenous increases in society's ability to produce.

The Efficiency of Labour

The production function has been written as :

$Y = F(K, L)$ where K is capital, L is labour and total output is Y. New production function is written as : $Y = F(K, L \times E)$ where E is called the efficiency of labour which includes technological progress. The efficiency of labour may also reflect the health, education, and skill of labour force.

This new production function states that total output Y depends on the number of units of capital K and on the number of efficiency units of labour, $L \times E$.

The simplest assumption about technological progress is that it increases the efficiency of labour E at a constant rate g. For example, if $g = 0.02$, then each unit of labour becomes 2% efficient each year. This form of technological progress is called labour-augmenting and g is called the rate of labour-augmenting technological progress. Since the labour force is growing at rate n, and the efficiency of each unit of labour E is growing at rate g, the number of efficiency units of labour is growing at rate $(n + g)$.

The Steady-State with Technological Progress

Labour-augmenting technological progress makes it analogous to population growth. Thus far, we have been analysing the economy in terms of quantities per worker, we now analyze it in terms of quantities per efficiency unit of labour. Let $k = \frac{K}{(L+E)}$ stand for capital per efficiency unit, and $y = \frac{Y}{(L+E)}$, output per efficiency unit. With these definitions, we can write $y = f(k)$.

Our analysis now proceeds just as it did when we examined population growth. The equation now changes to $\Delta k = sf(k) - (\delta + n + g)k$ where g is the rate of technical progress. If g is high, then the number of efficiency units is growing quickly, and the amount of capital per efficiency unit tends to fall.

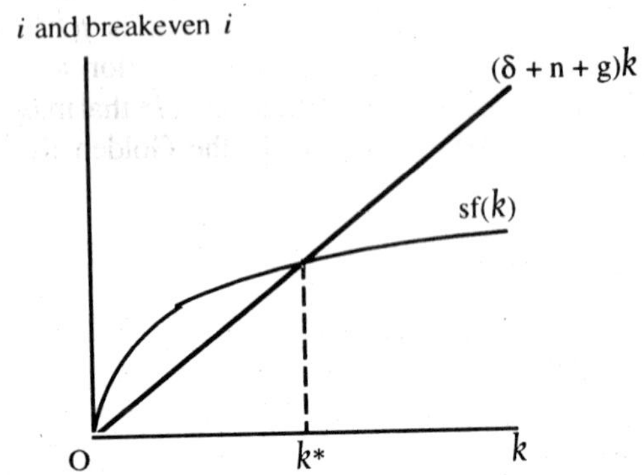

Fig. 18.16 Steady-state with Technical Progress

Fig. 18.16 shows that the inclusion of technological progress does not substantially alter our analysis of the steady-state. There is one level of k, denoted by k^*, at which output per efficiency unit and capital per efficiency unit are constant. The steady-state is the long-run equilibrium of the economy.

Effect of Technological Progress

As we have seen, k, capital per efficiency unit and y, output per efficiency unit, are constant, though the number of efficiency units per worker is growing at rate g. Hence, output per worker $(Y/L = Y \times E)$ also growing at rate g. Total output grows at rate $(n + g)$.

With the addition of technological progress, the model can finally explain the sustained increases in standard of living that we observe. That is, technological progress can lead to sustained growth in output per worker. By contrast, we have seen that a high rate of saving leads to a high rate of growth only until the steady-state is reached. Once the steady-state is reached, the rate of growth of output per worker depends only on g. The Solow Model shows that, only technological progress can explain persistently rising living standards.

The technological progress also modifies the condition for the Golden Rule. The Golden Rule level of capital accumulation is defined as the steady-state that maximizes consumption per efficiency unit of labour. Following the same argument as before, we can show that steady-state consumption per efficiency unit is $C^* = f(k^*) - (\delta + n + g)k^*$.

Steady-State consumption is maximized if : $MPK = \delta + n + g$ or, $MPK - \delta = n + g$.

That is, at the Golden Rule level of capital, the net MPK $(MPK - \delta)$ equals the rate of growth of total output $(n + g)$.

Saving, Growth and Economic Policy

Having discussed the Solow Model and various sources of economic growth, we now want to use the theory to help guide our thinking about economic policy. We address the following policy questions :

(1) Should society save more or less?
(2) How can policy influence the rate of saving?
(3) What investment policy should be encouraged?
(4) How can policy encourage the rate of technical progress?

Evaluate the Rate of Saving

The model shows how the saving rate determines the steady-state levels of capital and output. There is one particular saving rate that produces the Golden Rule Steady-State, which maximises consumption and, thus, economic well-being of the people. These results help us to address the important question for economic policy. Is the rate of saving in the economy just right or above or below that rate? If the $MPK - \delta >$ than the growth rate, the economy has less capital than in the Golden Rule Steady-State. In this situation, increasing the rate of saving will eventually lead to Golden Rule Steady State. If, however, the net $MPK <$ than the growth rate, the economy has too much capital, and the rate of saving should be reduced. To evaluate a economy's rate of capital accumulation, we need to compare the growth rate and the net return to capital.

This requires an estimate of the growth rate $(n + g)$ and the estimate of the net $MPK(MPK - \delta)$. If the real GDP in an economy is on an average 3% per year, $n + g = 0.03$. We can estimate the net MPK from the following: (1) The capital stock is about 2.5 times GDP; (2) Depreciation is about 10% of GDP; and (3) Capital's share is about 30%. From (1) we know that $k = 2.5y$; and from (2) we know that, $\delta k = 0.1y$. Therefore, $\delta = (\delta k)/k = (0.1y)/2.5y = 0.04$. That is, about 4% of the capital stock is depreciated each year. Thus, MPK can be calculated as : Capital's Share $= (MPK \times K)/Y = MPK \times (K/Y)$. Substituting from above; $0.30 = MPK \times 2.5$ or

$$MPK = \frac{0.30}{2.5} = 0.12.$$

Thus, the $MPK = 12\%$ per year, well in excess of the average growth rate of 3% per year.

This high return to capital implies that the capital stock in the economy is well below the Golden Rule level. Thus, policymakers should increase the rate of saving and investment.

Changing the Rate of Saving

Policymakers can influence the rate of saving in two ways : (1) directly through public saving and (2) indirectly through the incentive for private saving.

Public saving $= TR - G$. If the government spending is higher than the tax revenue, it runs budget deficit, which means negative saving which crowds out private investment. On the other hand, if the government spends less than its revenue, it runs a budget surplus which can stimulate investment.

Private saving can be influenced by various policies of the government, such as the higher rate of return on saving, lower tax rate on capital, etc.

Investment Allocation

The Solow Model makes the simplifying assumption that there is only one type of capital. In real world, there are many types. Private businesses invest in many types of capital and the government also invests in various forms of capital, such as infrastructures.

In addition, there is human capital — the knowledge and skill that workers acquire through education and training. Although, the basic Solow Model includes only physical capital and does not try to explain the efficiency of labour. Like physical capital, human capital also raises our ability to produce more.

Policymakers trying to stimulate economic growth must decide the type of capital the economy needs most. That is, the kind of capital yield the highest *MP*. Policymakers can mainly rely on the market-place to allocate the pool of saving to alternative types of investment. Those industries with the highest *MPK* will borrow most at market interest rates to finance new investment. Some economists advocate that the government should treat all forms of capital equally and then rely on the market to allocate capital efficiently.

Other economists suggest that the government should actively encourage particular forms of capital. They argue that technological progress takes place as a beneficial by-product of certain economic activities which is called externality. Some types of capital accumulation may yield greater externalities than others. For example, if installing robots yields greater technological externalities than building a new steel mill, then perhaps the government should use the tax laws to encourage investment in robots. The success of such a technology policy requires that the government be able to measure the externalities of different economic activities which is very difficult.

Encouraging Technological Progress

The Solow Model shows that sustained growth in income per worker must come from technological progress. This model takes technological progress as exogenous. The determinants of technological progress are not well understood.

Despite this limited understanding, many public policies are designed to stimulate technological progress. Proponents of technology policy argue that government should take more active role in promoting rapid technological progress. Most government policies—patent laws, tax code, etc.—encourage individuals to devote resources to technological innovation.

Conclusion

The Solow Model provides the best framework with which to start studying economic growth. But it is only a beginning. The model simplifies many aspects of the economy and it omits many others. Growth economists try to build more sophisticated models that help them to answer a broader range of questions.

The Solow Model takes the rate of saving as exogenous variable. Consumption arises from the decisions of households about how much to consume today and how much to consume tomorrow. Most sophisticated models replace the consumption function of the Solow Model with an explicit theory of household behaviour.

Economists have tried to build models to explain the level and growth of the efficiency of labour. The Solow Model shows that sustained growth in standards of living can arise only from technological progress. Understanding of economic growth will not be complete until we understand how private decisions and public policy affect technological progress.

The Kaldor-Mirrlees Model

Kaldor has developed two models of economic growth (1957,1962). Here we shall briefly concentrate with the one developed by Kaldor and Mirrlees *(KM)* in 1962. The crucial feature of this model is that the saving ratio can be made flexible to obtain a steady-state economic growth. Unlike the neo-classical model, the capital-output ratio remains fixed. Note that the *KM* model discards the production function approach of the neo-classical theory and introduces a technical progress function. The neo-classical school has not specified any investment function; but, in the *KM* model, an investment function is specified which depends upon a fixed pay-off period for investment per worker. The assumptions regarding both full-employment and perfect competition are dropped. Instead, *K* and *M* start off with the assumption that total income Y is equal to the sum of wages W and profits P : $Y = W + P$ ....*(1)*

Total savings $S = S_w + S_p$ ....*(2)*

Note that, $S = S_w W + S_p P$ ......*(3)*

and $S_w = S_w W$ ....*(4)* $S_p = S_p P$ ......*(5)*

where S_w is the propensity to save by wage earners, S_p is the propensity to save by profit earners and S is total savings. Both S_w and S_p are assumed to be constant indicating the equality between marginal and average propensities.

Now $\dot{Y} = W + P$ and $S = S_w W + S_p P$

By substitution, we have $S = S_w(Y - P) + S_p P$ ....*(6)*

$S = (S_p - S_w) + S_w Y$ ......*(7)*

Since it is assumed that $I = S$ ....*(8)*

we have $I = (S_p - S_W) P + S_w Y$....................*(9)*

Dividing both sides of the equation by Y and rearranging we obtain

$$\frac{P}{Y} = \frac{1}{S_p - S_w} \cdot \frac{I}{Y} - \frac{S_w}{S_p - S_w} \quad ....(10)$$

Thus, the profit share of income is given by the share of investment to income. The stability of the model is given by $0 \leq S_w \leq S_p \leq 1$.

Notice that the flexibility of saving is achieved in the *KM* model by the assumption of different propensities to save by wage and profit earners. The specific value of savings necessary to obtain the solution would be given by income distribution between income classes. Given S_p and S_w, I/Y will determine P/Y. If it is assumed that $S_w = 0$, we then obtain $\frac{P}{Y} = \frac{1}{S_w} \cdot \frac{I}{Y}$ ....(11)

Note that, if the capital-output ratio K/Y is fixed as in the *HD* model, we can write

$$\frac{P}{Y} \cdot \frac{Y}{K} = \frac{1}{S_w} \cdot \frac{I}{Y} \cdot \frac{Y}{K} \quad or, \quad \frac{\dot{P}}{K} = \frac{1}{S_p} \cdot \frac{I}{K} \quad ....(12)$$

Since $P/K = Y$, the rate of profit earned on capital, and $I/K = J$, the rate of accumulation, we have $V = \frac{1}{S_p} J$ or, $S_p V = J$ .... (13).

This conclusion betrays remarkable affinity to the Von Neumann case, where Neumann puts $S_p = 1$. Thus, all profits are saved and in equilibrium we obtain $V = J(=n)$ where n is the natural growth rate, which is assumed thus: the rate of growth is given by the rate of profit which is determined by the propensity to save of the profit earners.

Kaldor's introduction of an 'alternative' theory of distribution to analyse the problem of economic growth is interesting. However, several important criticisms have been levelled at the Kaldor's theory. First, Pasinethi mentions a 'logical slip' in Kaldor's argument when he observed that, although he has allowed workers to save, he did not allow these savings to accumulate and generate economic growth. Pasinethi has demonstrated that on a steady-state growth path the profit rate depends only on the growth rate and the propensity to save by the capitalists, it is independent of the propensity to save by the workers. However, if it is assumed that capitalists as a class have been banished and capital is owned by the workers alone, than the relevant variables in the balanced growth path will be given by S_w and n. Second, Kaldor's assumption about the fixed propensities to save disregards the impact of life cycle on save and work. Third, the assumption of a fixed class of income receivers is regarded as unrealistic. Finally, Kaldor's Model fails to exhibit an explicit behavioural mechanism, which will ensure that the actual distribution of income will be such as to maintain the steady-state growth path.

Exercise

1. Do the costs of economic growth outweigh the benefits?

2. What are the major determinants of economic growth? To what extent is a policy for growth incompatible with other macroeconomic policy objectives?

3. Outline the sources of economic growth in the industrialised nations.

4. 'Increases in people's welfare can be measured by increases in the economic growth rate' — Discuss.

5. Can you think of a direct way of measuring the economy's capacity to produce?

19 THE DEBATES OVER GOVERNMENT DEBT

When a government spends more than it collects in taxes, it borrows to finance the deficit. The accumulation of past borrowing is the government debt. All governments have some debt, although the amount varies from country to country. There may be budget surplus and deficit. If a government spends less than it collects in taxes, it pays past borrowing out of the financial surplus. In recent years, most governments have budget deficits rather then surplus. This experience of budget deficits have sparked a renewed interest among economists and policymakers in the economic effects of government debt. Some economists consider these large deficits as worse mistake of economic policy, whereas others think that the deficits matter little.

This chapter discusses the various views of government debt. First, we discuss the traditional view of government debt, according to which government borrowing reduces national saving and crowds out investment. This view is held by most economists.

Secondly, we describe an alternative view, called Ricardian equivalence, which is held by a small number of influential economists. According to this view, government debt does not influence saving and capital accumulation. We will see this disagreement over government debt arises from differences over the theory of consumption. In evaluation whether the tradition or the Ricardian view of the government debt is acceptable, the key question is how fiscal policy affects consumer spending. To analyse the effects of budget deficit on the economy, we must take into consideration whether consumers are short-sighted or forward-looking, or whether they face borrowing constraints or not, and on other aspects of consumer behaviour.

Lastly, we turn to the difficulty of measuring budget deficit. Some economists have argued that traditional measures of budget deficit are misleading and should be ignored.

The Traditional View of Government Debt

Keynesian model shows that a tax cut stimulates consumer spending and reduces national saving. The reduction in saving raises the interest rate, which crowds out investment, as we have seen above. The Solow Growth Model shows that lower investment eventually leads to a lower steady-state capital stock and a lower level of output since the economy starts with less capital than in the Golden Rule steady-state, the reduction in steady-state capital implies lower consumption and reduced economic well-being.

To analyse the short-run effects of the policy change, we turn to the *IS-LM* model. This model shows that a tax cut stimulates consumer spending, which implies an expansionary shift in the *IS* curve. If there is no change in monetary policy, the upward shift in the *IS* curve leads to an expansionary shift of the aggregate demand curve. In the short-run, when prices are sticky, the increase in aggregate demand leads to a higher output and employment. Over time, as prices adjust, the economy returns to the natural rate of output, and the higher aggregate demand results in a higher price level.

To see how international trade affects our analysis, we turn to the open economy model, which shows that reduced national saving causes a trade deficit. Although, the inflow of capital from abroad lessens the effect of the fiscal policy change on capital accumulation, which implies that the economy becomes indebted to foreign countries. The fiscal policy change may cause the domestic currency to appreciate, which makes foreign goods cheaper and domestic goods more expensive abroad. The Mundell-Fleming model shows that this appreciation of domestic currency and fall in net exports reduce the short-run expansionary impact of the fiscal change on output and employment. The tax cut financed by government borrowing would have the following effects on the economy. The immediate impact of the tax cut would be to stimulate consumer spending which affects the economy in both the short-run and the long-run. In the short-run, higher consumer spending would raise the demand for goods and services and, thus, raise output and employment. Interest rate would rise as investors competed for a smaller flow of saving. Higher interest would discourage investment and would encourage capital to flow in from abroad, which would appreciate the value of domestic currency against foreign currencies, which would make domestic product less competitive in the world markets.

In the long-run, the smaller national saving caused by the tax cut would mean smaller capital stock and a greater foreign debt. Thus, the output of the nation would be smaller, and a greater share of that output would be owed to foreigners.

The overall effect of the tax cut on economic well-being would be difficult to judge. Current generations would benefit from higher consumption and employment, although inflation would likely to be higher as well. Future generations would bear the burden of today's budget deficit : they would be born into a nation with a smaller capital stock and a larger foreign debt. However, a 'Ricardian' would reach a quite different conclusion.

We discuss the Ricardian equivalence in the next section.

The Ricardian View of Government Debt

Modern consumption theories emphasize that, because consumers are forward-looking, consumption does not depend on current income alone. Friedman's permanent-income hypothesis and Franco Modigliani's life-cycle hypothesis are based on the forward-looking consumers. The Ricardian view of government debt applies the logic of the forward-looking consumer to study the impact of fiscal policy.

The Basic Logic of Ricardian Equivalence

We consider the response of a forward-looking consumer to the tax cut. The consumer may think that as the government is cutting taxes without reducing its expenditure, so it would not increase their permanent income. The government is financing the tax cut by running a budget deficit, which means, at some point in the future, the government will have to raise taxes to pay-off the debt and accumulated interest. So the policy really means a tax cut today coupled with a tax hike in the future. Thus, the cut merely gives a transitory income that eventually will be taken back. The consumers are not any better off, so they will leave their consumption unchanged.

The forward-looking consumer understands that government borrowing today means higher taxes in the future. A debt-financed tax cut does not reduce the tax burden; it merely reschedules it. It does not raise permanent income of the consumer and, thus, does not increase consumption.

The general principle is that government debt is equivalent to future taxes, and the forward-looking consumers are aware that future taxes are equivalent to current taxes. Hence, financing the government by debt is equivalent to financing it by taxes. This view is known as Ricardian equivalence, named after the famous economist *David Ricardo* who first noted the theoretical argument.

The implication of Ricardian equivalence is that a debt-financed tax cut leaves consumption unaffected. Households save the extra disposable income to pay the future tax liability that the tax cut implies. This increase in private saving just replace the public saving. National saving remains the same. The tax cut has none of the effects that the traditional analysis predicts. The logic of Ricardian equivalence does not imply that all changes in fiscal policy are irrelevant. Changes in fiscal policy do influence consumer spending if they influence government purchases as well. For example, suppose the government cuts taxes today because it plans to reduce government purchases in the future, then only consumer will feel richer and raise his consumption. It may be noted that it is the reduction in government purchases, rather than the reduction in taxes, that stimulates consumption.

The Government Budget Constraint

For better understanding of the link between future taxes and government debt, it is necessary to imagine that, the economy lasts for only two periods — present and future periods. In period one, the government collects taxes T_1 and makes purchases G_1, and in period two, it collect taxes T_2 and makes purchases G_2. Since the government can run a budget deficit or surplus, taxes and purchases need not be equal in any single period.

We wish to see how the government's tax receipts and expenditures in the two periods are related. In the first period, the budget deficit equals government expenditure minus taxes. That is : $D = G_1 - T_1$, where D is the deficit. The government finances the deficit by selling an equal amount of government bonds. In the second period, the government must collect enough taxes to repay the debt including interest, and also pay for its second-period purchases. Thus, $T_2 = (1 + r)D + G_2$ where r is the interest rate.

To derive the equation linking purchases and taxes, we combine the two equations above. Substituting D from the first equation into the second equation we obtain : $T_2 = (1+ r)(G_1 - T_1) + G_2$.

This equation relates purchases in the two periods to taxes in two periods.

After rearranging the terms, we get : $T_1 = \frac{T_2}{(1+r)} = G_1 + \frac{G_2}{(1+r)}$.

This gives us the government budget constraint. It means that, the present value of government purchases must equal the present value of taxes.

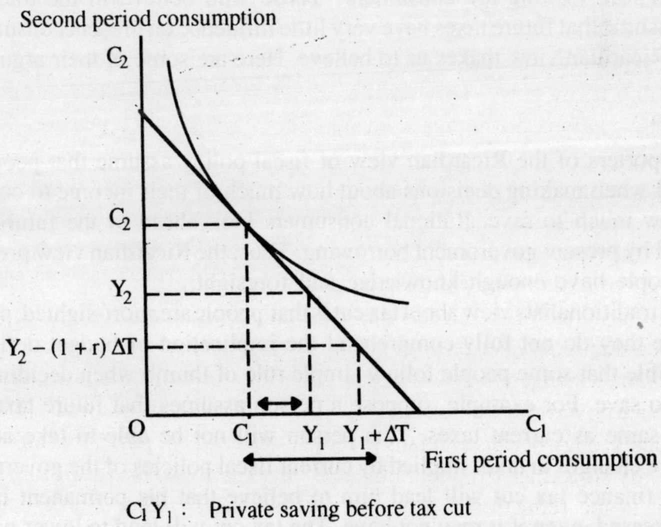

C_1Y_1 : Private saving before tax cut

$C_1 (Y_1+\Delta T)$: Private saving after tax cut

Fig. 19.1 A Debt-financed Tax Cut

The government budget constraint shows how changes in fiscal policy today are related to changes in fiscal policy in the future. If the government cuts first-period taxes without altering first-period expenditure, then it enters the next period owing a debt to the government's bond-holders. This debt forces the government to choose between raising taxes and reducing expenditure. Fig. 19.1 shows a debt-financed tax cut in the Fisher diagram. The cuts in taxes in period one affects consumer under the assumption that it does not alter expenditures in either period. In period one, the government cuts taxes by ΔT and finances this tax cut by borrowing. In period two, the government must raise taxes by $(1+ r)\ \Delta T$ to repay its debt together with interest. Thus, the change in fiscal policy raises the consumer's income by ΔT in period one and reduces it by $(1 + r)\Delta T$ in period two. The consumer's opportunity set remains unchanged because the present value of consumer's lifetime income is the same as before the tax changes. Thus, the consumer does not change the level of consumption even after the change in fiscal policy, which implies that the private saving will rise as a result of the tax cut. Therefore, by combining the government budget constraint and Fisher's model of intertemporal choice, we get the Ricardian result that a debt-financed tax cut does not change consumption.

Consumers and Future Taxes

The Ricardian view is that, when people decide their consumption, they rationally look ahead to the future taxes implied by government debt. But how forward-looking are consumers? Those who believe in the traditional view assume that future taxes have very little influence on present consumption as the Ricardian view makes us to believe. Here are some of their arguments.

Myòpia

Supporters of the Ricardian view of fiscal policy assume that people are rational when making decisions about how much of their income to consume and how much to save. Rational consumers look ahead to the future taxes implied by present government borrowing. Thus, the Ricardian view presumes that people have enough knowledge and foresight.

The traditionalists view about tax cut is that people are short-sighted, perhaps because they do not fully comprehend the implication of budget deficits. It is possible that some people follow simple rule of thumb when deciding how much to save. For example, suppose a person assumes that future taxes will be the same as current taxes. This person will not be able to take account of future changes in taxes implied by current fiscal policies of the government. A debt-finance tax cut will lead him to believe that his permanent income has increased, even if it may not have. The tax cut will lead to lower national saving and higher consumption.

How a Debt-Finance Tax Cut Relaxes a Borrowing Constraint

The Ricardian view of government debt depends on the permanent income hypothesis, which is that consumption does not depend on current income, but on permanent income, which includes both current and expected future income. According to the Ricardian view, a debt-financed tax cut increases current income, but it leaves permanent income and consumption unchanged.

Supporter of the traditional view argue that we should not rely on the permanent-income hypothesis because some consumers face borrowing constraint. Those who face borrowing constraint can consume only his current income. For this person, current income rather than permanent income determines consumption. A debt-financed tax cut increases his current income and thus consumption, even though future income is lower. When the government cuts current taxes and raises future taxes, essentially it is giving taxpayers a loan. For individuals who wanted to obtain loan, but were unable to, the tax cut raises consumption.

A debt-financed tax cut raises consumption for a consumer facing a borrowing constraint. A debt-financed tax cut of ΔT raises first-period income by ΔT and reduces second-period income by $(1 + r)\ \Delta T$. Since the present value of income is unchanged, the budget constraint does not change consumption. Yet, as the first-period income is higher, the borrowing constraint allows a higher level of first-period consumption. Hence, Ricardian equivalence does not hold.

Future Generation

Besides these two arguments presented above, there is a third argument for the traditional view that consumers expect the future taxes not to fall on them, but on future generations. For example, suppose the government cuts taxes today, issues 50-year bonds to finance the budget deficit, and then raises taxes in 50 years to repay the loan. This means that the government debt represents a transfer of wealth from the next generation to the current generation of taxpayers. This transfer increases the lifetime resources of the current generation, so it raises their consumption. It means that, a debt-financed tax cut stimulates consumption because it gives the current generation the opportunity to consume more at the expense of the future generation.

Economist Robert Barro argued in support of the Ricardian view that because the future generations are the children and grand-children of the present generation, we should not consider them as independent economic actors. Instead, he argues that present generations care about future generations. This altruism between generations is evidenced by the gifts that many people give their children, sometimes in the form of bequests at the time of their death. The existence of gifts or bequests demonstrates that people are not willing to take advantage of the opportunities to consume more at the expense of their children.

According to Robert Barro's analysis, the relevant decision making unit is not the individual who lives only a limited number of years, but the family which continues indefinitely. In other words, an individual decides how much to consume not on the basis of his income only but also on the basis of the income of future members of his family. A debt-financed tax cut may raise the income an individual receives in his lifetime, but it does not raise the permanent income of his family. Instead of consuming the extra income from the tax cut, the individual saves it and leaves it as a bequest to his children, who will bear the future tax liability.

Again, we see that the argument about government debt is really an argument over consumer behaviour. The Ricardian view assumes that consumers have a long time horizon. Barro's analysis of the family implies that the consumer's time horizon is infinite. If, however, the consumers do not look ahead to the tax liabilities of future generations, because they do not care enough about their children to leave them a bequest? In this case a debt-financed tax cut can alter consumption by redistributing wealth among generations.

Making a Choice

Having considered the traditional and Ricardian views of government debt, we should ask ourselves two sets of questions.

First, which view do you agree with? How a debt-financed tax cuts affect the economy? Will it stimulate consumption, as the traditional view holds? or, Will it offset the budget deficit with higher private saving?

Second, why do you hold the view that you do? If you agree with the traditional view of government debt, what is the reason? Do consumers fail to understand that higher government borrowing today means higher taxes tomorrow? or, Do they ignore future taxes, because future taxes fall on future generations with whom they do not feel an economic link? If you hold Ricardian view, do you believe that consumers have the foresight to see that government borrowing today implies more taxes tomorrow? Do you believe that consumer will save extra income to offset that future tax liability?

One might have hoped that we could turn to the evidence to decide between the two views. Yet, when economists examine historical episodes of large budget deficits, the evidence is inconclusive.

For example, let us consider the experience of the 1980s. The large budget deficits seem to offer a natural experiment to test the two views of government debt. At first glance, this episode appears to support the traditional view. The large budget deficits coincided with low national saving, high interest rates, and a large trade deficit. Indeed, advocates of the traditional view of government debt often claim that the experience of the 1980s confirms their position.

However, those who believe in the Ricardian view of government debt interpret the events of the 1980s differently because people were optimistic about future economic growth. Or perhaps, saving was low because people expected that the tax cut would not lead to higher taxes but to lower government expenditure. Because it is hard to rule out any of these interpretations, both views survive.

Can the Budget Deficit be Correctly Measured

The disagreement between the traditional and Ricardian views of government debt is only the source of controversy. Even economists who hold the traditional view argue among themselves about how best to evaluate fiscal policy.

Other disagreement among the economists is about the measurement of budget deficit. Some economists believe that the current measurement of deficit is not a good enough indicator of the stance of fiscal policy. They believe that the budget deficit does not accurately measure either the impact of fiscal policy on the economy today or the burden being placed on the future generations. Here we discuss three problems with the usual measure of the budget deficit.

The general principle is that the budget deficit should accurately measure the change of government's overall indebtedness. This principle is not difficult at all. But its application is not so simple as one might expect.

Measurement Problem Number One : Inflation

There is unanimity among the economists that the government's indebtedness should be measured in real terms, not in nominal terms which means that the measurement issues need the correction for inflation. The measured deficit should equal the change in the government's real debt, not its nominal debt. The budget deficit normally does not correct for inflation. This induces large error in the measurement of debt. The following example will give us some idea. Suppose, the real government debt is not changing in real terms, the budget is always balanced. But the nominal debt must be rising at the rate of inflation. That is: $\Delta D/D = \Pi$, where Π is the inflation rate and D is the stock of government debt. This implies $\Delta D = \Pi D$.

The government would look at the change in the nominal debt ΔD and would present a budget deficit of ΠD which most economists believe that the reported budget deficit is overstated by ΠD. In other words, the deficit in government expenditure minus government revenue. Part of government expenditure is the interest paid on the government debt. Expenditure should include only the real interest paid on the debt, rD, but not the nominal interest paid, iD. The difference between the nominal and the real interest rate is the inflation rate, Π, the budget deficit is overstated by ΠD.

This correction for inflation can be large, especially when inflation is high, and it can often change one's evaluation of fiscal policy.

Measurement Problem Number Two : Uncounted Liabilities

Many economists believe that the measured budget deficit is not accurate, because it does not include some important government liabilities. For example, consider the pension of civil servants. These civil servants provide services to the government today, but part of their compensation is deferred to the future. Their future pension benefits represents a liability to the government not very different from other government debt. But this accumulated liability is not included as part of the budget deficit of the government.

Similarly, consider the Social Security System which is not significantly different from a pension plan. People contribute some of their income into the system when young and expect to receive benefits when they are old. Thus, accumulated future Social Security benefits should also be included in the government's liabilities.

One might argue that Social Security Liabilities may not be regarded as government debt, because the government can always change the laws determining Social Security benefits. Yet the government could always choose not to repay all its debt; the government honours its debt only because it decides to do so. To pay the holders of government debt may not be fundamentally different from promises to pay the recipients of Social Security benefits.

A special form of government liability is to measure the contingent liability — the liability that is due only if a special event occurs. For example, if the government guarantees some form of private credit, such as student loans, mortgages, etc. If the borrower repays the loan, the government may not have to pay anything; if the borrower defaults, the government may have to make repayment. When the government provides this guarantee, it undertakes the responsibility to repay the debt if the borrowers default. This contingent liability is not reflected in the budget deficit.

Measurement Problem Three : Capital Assets

Some economists argue that an accurate measurement of budget deficit requires accounting for its assets and its liabilities. In making particular measure of the government's overall indebtedness, we must exclude government assets from its debt. Thus, the budget deficit should include the change in debt minus the change in assets.

Assets and liabilities are treated simultaneously by firms and individuals. For example, when a person borrows to buy a house, we do not consider his liability only. Instead, we should consider his assets (house) against his liability (mortgage) and record no change in net wealth. Perhaps we should treat the government's deficit in the same way. A budget procedure that treats both assets as well as liabilities is called capital budgeting, because it takes into consideration changes in capital. For example, suppose the government privatises its companies or sells its land or office building to reduce its debts. Under present budget procedures, the reported deficit would be lowered. Under capital budgeting, the revenue received from the privatisation of government assets would not lower the deficit because the reduction of debt would be offset by a reduction in assets. Similarly, under capital budgeting, government borrowing to purchase a capital asset would not increase the deficit.

The main difficulty with capital budgeting is that it is difficult to decide which government expenditures should be included as capital expenditure. For example, should the stockpile of nuclear weapons be considered as an asset? If so, how to evaluate these weapons? Should spending on education be treated as expenditure on human capital? To adopt a system of capital budgeting, these difficult questions must be answered by the government, Economists and policymakers do not agree about whether or not the system of capital budgeting should be used by the government. Opponents of capital budgeting argue that it may be a better method than the current system, but it is too difficult to implement in practice. Those who support capital budgeting hold that even an imperfect treatment of capital assets would be better than ignoring them altogether.

Whither the Budget Deficit

Economists differ about the importance of these measurement problems. Some believe that the problems are really very important. Most consider these measurement problems seriously but still view the measured budget deficit as a useful indication of fiscal policy.

The important lesson is that, to evaluate fully the course of fiscal policy, economists must look at more than just the measured budget deficit. In fact, they do. The budget documents prepared annually contain much detailed information about the government's finances.

Conclusion

Fiscal policy and government debt have been central to political debate in many countries over the past decade. As we have seen, economists disagree about how fiscal policy affects the economy and how fiscal policy is best measured. These are among the most important and disputed questions facing policymakers today. We are confident that these debates will continue, as long as fiscal deficit continues!

Exercise

1. According to the traditional view, how does a debt-financed tax cut affect private saving, public saving and national saving?
2. According to the Ricardian view, how does a debt-financed tax cut affect public saving, private saving and national saving?
3. Do you believe in the traditional or the Ricardian view of government debt? Why?
4. Describe some of the problems affecting measurement of the government budget deficit.

20 INTERNATIONAL INSTITUTIONS

At Bretton Woods, USA, in 1944, a conference took place to establish the pattern of post-war-monetary system. The aim was to achieve *free convertibility* and improve international liquidity. Keynes dominated the conference and submitted a plan for an international unit of currency against which all other currencies would be measured. This would be administered by a world bank with which all countries would have an account. Cheques would be written out to settle international debt. Money would be created to finance trade and overdrafts could be provided to those countries in need. The bank would be allowed to determine each country's exchange rate. The plan did not receive the approval of the participating countries including the U.K., because they were unwilling to allow an international institution to determine the value of their currency. The result was the establishment of two compromise institutions : The International Monetary Fund (IMF-1947) and The International Bank for Reconstruction and Development (IBRD -1946) or World Bank as it is called.

The Bretton Woods International Monetary System was an adjustable peg system, and the ultimate international money was gold. Countries held much of their exchange reserves in the form of US dollar, which they could convert into gold.

The International Monetary Fund (IMF) or Adjustable Peg System

It was the IMF system which dominated the pattern of international monetary payments from 1947-72. The objectives of the fund were to achieve free convertibility and to promote stability in international monetary system. These objectives were satisfied until 1972. In 1988 the IMF had 146 members.

Quotas

Each member country was required to contribute its quota depending upon the national income of the country and upon its share in world trade. The quota was made up of 75% in the country's own currency and 25% in gold or foreign currencies. In this way it was hoped that there would be enough of any currency in the pool for any member to draw on should there be any balance of payments difficulties.

Voting power in the IMF is related to the size of the quota. Thus, the

USA and the other industrialised countries have managed to dominate the fund for most of its life. It has been necessary to revise the quotas seven times, firstly to increase the overall size of quotas to take account of the growth of world trade and of inflation, and, secondly, to revise the relative size of members' quotas.

Borrowing

Originally each member of the fund could borrow in tranches (slices) equivalent to 25% of their quotas, taking up to five consecutive tranches, i.e., it was possible to borrow the equivalent of 125% of one's quota. Today it is possible to borrow up to the equivalent of 450% of one's quota over a three year period. This is not an unconditional right to borrow and the fund imposes conditions of increasing severity upon a member as it increases its borrowing.

The borrowing methods from the Fund has received modifications and some of the methods are given below:

a) **Stand-by Arrangements** : This method of borrowing has become the most normal form of assistance by the Fund. Resources are made available to a member, which they may draw if they wish. The stand-by facility is often enough to stabilise a member's balance of payments without actually drawing it. It is necessary for a member to agree to IMF conditions.

b) **General Agreement to Borrow (GAB):** In 1962, the group of 10 industrialised nations agreed to make a pool of $6 billion available to each other through the IMF. Since 1984 the size of the pool has been increased to $17 billion and it has been agreed to help less developed countries.

c) **Compensatory Finance Scheme :** In 1963, it was decided to give loans with fewer conditions to members experiencing temporary difficulties because of delays in the receipt of their export credits. By the early 1980s this accounted for almost 1/3 of all the Fund's lending.

d) **Buffer Stock Facilities :** In 1969, it was decided to give loans to members to allow them to pay for the buffer stock schemes.

e) **The Supplementary Financing Facilities :** In 1979, the scheme was started to give long-term assistance to less developed countries. It has a special fund of SDR $7.8 billion made available by 14 richer countries.

f) **The Extended Fund Facilities :** In 1974, this scheme was introduced to help those members with long-term assistance experiencing more protracted balance of payments difficulties.

Special Drawing Rights (SDR)

In 1969, it was decided to create international liquidity for the first time. This was developed by giving members an allocation of special drawing right at the IMF. This is not tied to the currency of any country but merely as booking entries. When it was first introduced they were linked to dollar and, thus, to gold. However, since 1974, the value of a unit of SDR has been calculated by combining the value of 5 leading currencies. SDRs could be used without prior consultation with the Fund, but only to cope with balance of payment difficulties. The functions of SDRs can be summarised as follows :

a) **A means of exchange :** SDRs can be used to settle indebtedness between nations, but with the consent of the fund only.

b) **A Unit of Account :** All IMF transactions are now denominated in SDRs.

c) **A Store of Value :** In 1976 it was decided to reduce the role of gold and make the SDR the principal asset of the IMF. It can be seen that the SDR fulfils the store of value function of money to some extent. It can thus be described as quasi-money.

The Adjustable Peg System

The object of the IMF system was to create a *set of rules* that would maintain *fixed exchange rate* against short-run fluctuations. It guaranteed that changes in exchange rates would occur only in the face of persistent quasi-equilibrium in the balance of payments. It was also ensured that when such changes did occur they would not spark a series of competitive devaluation.

The basic characteristics of the IMF system was that US dollar held by foreign monetary authorities were made directly convertible into gold as a fixed rate ($35 an ounce) by the US Government, while foreign government fixed the rates at which their currencies were convertible into US dollar. It was this characteristics that made the system a Gold Exchange standard.

The rate at which each country's currency was convertible into dollar was fixed or pegged. The pegged rate could be changed from time to time in the face of 'fundamental disequilibrium' in the balance of payments. A system with these two characteristics: a rate that is pegged against short-term fluctuations but that can be changed from time to time, is referred to as an Adjustable Peg System.

In order to maintain convertibility of their currencies at fixed exchange rates, the monetary authorities of each country had to be ready to intervene in the foreign exchange market. In order to be able to do this, they had to have stocks of gold and foreign currencies — such as dollar or sterling. When a country's currency is in excess supply, their authorities could sell foreign currency or gold in exchange of their own currency. When a country's currency was in excess demand, their authorities would buy foreign currency and sell their own currencies. If they wished to increase their gold reserves they would exchange dollar for gold from the Federal Reserve System, thus, depleting the US gold stock. The problem for the US was to have enough gold to maintain fixed convertibility of the dollar into gold. The problem for the other countries was to maintain fixed convertibility between their currency and the US dollar.

Thus, the IMF system was an adjustable peg, *gold exchange standard* where the ultimate international currency was gold. Countries hold much of their foreign exchange reserves in the form of US dollars, which they could convert into gold.

However, the 1970s saw a collapse of the adjustable peg system despite the Smithsonian agreement of 1971 to patch-up the system.

The Collapse of the IMF System

It was not realised at the time of the 1967 U.K.-devaluation that it was the beginning of the end for the adjustable peg system. The basis of world economic power had changed since 1947 when the Fund was set up. At that time the economies of the then West Germany and Japan were in ruins, but no changes came about in the IMF system to take account of their subsequent development.

The US dollar was not devalued in 1967. The lower prices of the devalued currencies and increasing *Vietnam War* expenditures by the US combined to produce growing deficit in the US balance of payments. This deficit convinced the speculators that the dollar was seriously overvalued. Speculators rushed to buy gold because a devaluation of the dollar would take the form of raising its gold price.

The first break in the IMF system came when the major trading countries were forced to stop pegging the market price of gold. Speculative pressure to buy gold could not be resisted and the market price was allowed to go free in 1968. From that time a two-tier rate of gold was established; one was the official price of gold — for monetary purposes — was maintained at $35 while the price of gold for commercial purposes was allowed to float upwards.

Once the free-market price of gold was allowed to be determined independently of the official price, speculation against the dollar shifted to those currencies, that were clearly undervalued relative to the dollar. The German Mark and Japanese Yen were particularly popular targets, and billions of dollars flowed into speculative holdings of these currencies. The ability of central banks to maintain pegged exchange rates were in doubt.

The US Leaves the Gold Standards (1971)

The announcement of the US government in 1971 was that it would not be possible to exchange dollars for gold at the official price ended the gold standard. This was caused by a massive balance of payments deficit in the US and realignment of the economic power in the world which had led to massive and continuing surpluses and the accumulation of vast reserves by Germany and Japan. However, the situation was made worse for the USA by its high rate of inflation. This system worked reasonably well while the US price level was relatively stable. Countries that were inflating a bit too fast could occasionally devalue their exchange rates, and countries that were inflated even more slowly than the US could occasionally revalue their exchange rates. Occasional upward and downward readjustments relative to the dollar served to keep the system near equilibrium.

But if the US began to inflate rapidly, it became necessary to devalue the US dollar relative to most other currencies. The only way the required US devaluation could be brought about was for all other countries to reduce their currencies against dollar.

Prompted by continuous speculation against the dollar, the US government first suspended the gold convertibility of dollar in August 1971 and then made a de facto devaluation of the dollar by persuading those nations whose balance of payments were in surplus to allow their rates to float upward against the dollar.

The Smithsonian Agreement 1971

As mentioned above, the abandonment of the gold standard swept away the adjustable peg system. But the Smithsonian agreement of December 1971 was an attempt to reestablish the adjustable peg. This agreement put the value of gold at $38 per ounce, an effective devaluation of dollar of 8%. The new rate for the pound was therefore, £1 = $2.60. Since then Smithsonian agreement, the world has been on a de facto Dollar System. It allowed a $2\frac{1}{4}\%$ variation in the value of a currency. The variation was unacceptable to the EEC countries and, therefore, on 24th April 1972, they established a variation between their own currencies of half that of the Smithsonian variation. The Smithsonian variation was said to provide the tunnel within which the smaller European snake moved. The U.K. joined the *snake system* on 1 June 1972 but left it later, when the government announced that the pound was to float.

The Smithsonian agreement did not last long, as most countries were obliged to float their currencies in 1972 and 1973. However, two legacies remain. Since it was the last time when currencies were fixed against each other it is a reference point. The other legacy is the European Currency snake which became the EMS in 1979.

The Oil Crisis

The mobility started in 1971 was made much worse by the oil crisis of 1973. A fourfold rise in oil price resulted in a transfer of money from the developed countries to OPEC nations which brought about a most fundamental shift in economic power. This cost the oil importing countries an extra £100 billion per year.

Oil prices were doubled again in 1978 causing a liquidity problem even greater than that of 1973. This price rise was an important factor in the subsequent world depression. This hit the industrial countries hard but was disastrous to the oil-importing developing countries. The subsequent slump in oil prices left some less developed oil exporters with large debts which they found almost impossible to service.

The Plaza Agreement -1985 and Louvre Accord of 1987

In the Plaza Agreement of 1985, there was a consensus of opinion among the G-5 — the USA, the U.K., the then West Germany, Japan, France — industrial nations that they would like to establish a more stable system of exchange rates and they decided to bring about an orderly decline in the value of dollar, which was considered to be overvalued.

The Louvre Accord (Paris) was an agreement among the G-7 nations to stabilize variations in their exchange rates within certain limits which were not published. However, they could be deduced from the subsequent actions of the central banks of these countries. For example, since March 1988 it became obvious that the Bank of England was commited to hold the pound at or below the level of £1 = DM3.

These agreements illustrate the urge to return to a more orderly pattern of exchange rates. The fact that they were not arrived at through the IMF shows its decline.

The Problem of International Liquidity and IMF

International liquidity problem refers to the lack of universally acceptable means of payment. Since the World War II, the dollar and, to a certain extent, the pound, have attempted to fulfil this role. The floating exchange rate regime has made the situation worse. However, we can summarise the stock of official international liquidity as being gold and foreign currency reserves held by nations, plus their IMF quotas and also their SDR allocations. It could be argued that there has been an excess of unofficial liquidity. The expansion of Eurocurrency in the 1970s left many developing countries hopelessly in debt and they found it impossible even to borrow on the commercial market today. However, the scale of the problem was so great that the resources of the IMF and other international agencies were inadequate to deal with it.

The annual conference of the IMF in 1976 officially recognised the end of *fixed exchange rate system.* This *Jamaica Agreement* also 'demonetised' gold and member countries were no longer required to use gold as part of their quota to the IMF. The IMF also agreed to get rid of its gold stocks.

The IMF role declined significantly during the 1980s. Many LDCs were considered uncreditworthy by the IMF and some countries decided not to borrow from the IMF, because of the *austerity programme* laid down by it when giving loans, such as the role of the IMF with industrialised nations was also reduced. The floating exchange rates regime reduced the need to borrow foreign currency for official purposes. In addition to this, fall in oil prices have reduced or eliminated the current deficit of many countries.

(IBRD) The World Bank

The International Bank of Reconstruction and Development was set up in 1946 as the sister organisation to the IMF. Its original aim was to help develop the war-devastated economies of Europe. One of the important problems facing the World Bank was its lack of funds. Funds came from three sources :

a) **Quotas :** The membership of the World Bank is the same as that of the IMF. Members make contributions in relation to their IMF quotas. Of the quotas, 10% is subscribed while the other 90% is promised as a guarantee for the Bank's loans.

b) **Bonds :** It can sell bonds on the capital market.

c) **Income :** A very small proportion of the Bank's funds come from its income.

The World Bank gradually turned its attention from Europe to the less developed countries (LDCs) of the world. Today it is almost wholly concerned with helping LDCs. It gives advices and information, besides making loans.

The World Bank has increased its operations by forming the following new organisations :

i) The International Financial Corporation (IFC). This was set up in 1956 to enable the Bank to give loans to Private Companies and Governments.

ii) The International Development Association (IDA). This was established in 1960. Its objective was to make loans for longer periods and on preferential terms to the LDCs. The IDA has become known as the 'soft loan window'.

iii) The Multilateral Investment Guarantee Agency (MIGA). This was set up by the G7 nations in 1988 and is controlled by the World Bank. The object of the agency is to guarantee long-term private investment in LDCs. The political instability in many countries make it difficult and expensive for them to borrow. The agency guarantees investors' funds against political risks but not against normal business risks. The effect of this guarantee is to level the degree of risk in investments with that in other advanced or stable nations.

Like IMF, its role is now limited. The limitation comes both from lack of funds and from political disagreement. The role of the World Bank is increasingly overshadowed by that of the commercial lending.

The General Agreement on Trade and Tariff (GATT)

GATT has been an important organisation for the promotion of free trade. It came into existence as a result of the Havana Charter in 1948. The main aims of GATT are the following :

a) **Most favoured nation :** Every signatory of the GATT was to be treated as 'a most favoured nation'. Existing systems of preference were allowed to continue but could not be increased.

b) **Tariffs and quotas :** Members agreed to work towards the reduction of tariffs and the abolition of quotas. In the first 20/30 years of its existence GATT was by and large successful but in recent years protectionism has once again become widespread (i.e. JAPAN/EEC/the USA)

c) **Trading blocs :** The establishment of common market-type agreement such as EEC and EFTA were allowed, but they were encouraged to be outward looking rather than insular.

Progress in GATT was achieved through a series of rounds of talks, the most famous of which was the Kennedy round of the 1960s. In recent years there has been north-south dialogue. The forum for these discussions is the United Nations Conference on Trade and Development (UNCTAD). The object of the LDCs can be summed up in a phrase 'trade not aid'. The poor countries are mainly producers of primary products, but they are not allowed to trade freely with the rich countries because they are discriminated against by protectionist policies of the rich. The depression of the 1970s and early 1980s and increased protectionism of the rich had made the plight of the LDCs worse. The economic condition of the LDCs is really desperate but the high ideals of international cooperation of the immediate post-war period seems to be receding.

The Organisation for Economic Cooperation and Development (OECD)

The Organisation for European Economic Cooperation (OEEC) came into existence in 1947 to administer the European recovery programme (Marshall Aid). This was an important institution, which helped to establish the European Payments Union (EPU). The OEEC became the OECD in 1961. Its objectives are :

a) to encourage economic growth, high employment and financial stability amongst members;

b) to aid the economic development of less developed non-member countries.

Now the OECD has 21 members including its non-European members such as, the USA, Canada, Australia and Japan, who joined in 1965. One of the most important functions of the OECD is to provide statistical information of the economies of its members.

The Bank of International Settlements (BIS)

The purpose of this Switzerland-based institution (formed in 1930) was to enable central banks to coordinate their international payments and receipts. It was originally established to regulate German reparations. It is one of the oldest and most successful of international institutions and also it is profit-making institution.

Since the World Wwar II, the BIS has acted like a central bank for central banks. The board of the BIS was made up of representatives of the central banks of the U.K., France, Germany, Belgium, Italy, Sweden, Netherlands and Switzerland. Other countries, such as, the USA and Japan regularly attend its meetings.

The main functions of the BIS are :

(a) promotion of cooperation between central banks
(b) monitoring euro-currency market
(c) provide export advice to other institutions and
(d) organise finance for countries with payments difficulties.

The European Economic Community (EEC)

The origin of the EEC can be traced back to the European Coal and Steel Community (ECSC), which was established in 1948 by few members—France, Italy, Belgium, Holland and Luxembourg. West Germany later joined the ECSC but the U.K. declined to join. Its objective was to abolish trade restrictions on Coal and Steel between member countries and to coordinate pricing and production policies. The EEC was finally established on 1st January 1958 by the Treaty of Rome. Once again the U.K. did not join the EEC. The U.K. finally joined the EEC in 1972/1973 together with Ireland and Denmark. Greece became member in 1981 and Spain and Portugal in 1986. The introduction of the single European Act in 1987 should complete the process by which these twelve members function as one (i.e. Single Market).

The Main Features of the EEC

There are two main features of the EEC :

a) **Customs Union**

The establishment of Customs Union involves both *the abolition of tariffs between members* and *the erection of a common external tariff* to the rest of the world. Each country must have some external tariff, otherwise imports would flood into the community through the member state, with the lowest tariffs. In some cases—*e.g.* the imports of products from France's ex-colonies' — the lowest duty was adopted and several old colonial states have associate status with the EEC. The original arrangements for these states was superseded by the *Lome Convention* in 1975. Under this arrangements, some 46 developing nations in Africa, the Caribbean and the Pacific are allowed to send all their exports to the EEC duty free.

However, the U.K. was not allowed to join the EEC until she agreed to erect considerable tariff barriers against her Commonwealth Partners.

b) **Common Market**

The EEC is generally known as common market, which refers to the running of the economies of the members as if they were one, i.e. they have common price and production policy (of the ECSC) in all industries. A common market agreement implies the free movement of labour, capital and enterprise within the EEC. Apart from agriculture (CAP), there is no common policy yet in other areas. Despite its formation since 1958 it is only in 1992 that, a true common market was created.

The Structure of the EEC

The Treaty of Rome envisaged that the EEC would eventually lead to economic and political unity. So far it has become possible to have four essential components of state organisation :

a) **The Council of Ministers**

This is the executive or cabinet of the EEC. It consists of one minister from each state, which minister it is to be depends on what is being discussed. For instance, if the issue were agriculture then it would be the minister of agriculture who would attend. Voting in the council is weighted; for example, the U.K. has ten votes while Luxembourg has only two. The Council is assisted by a committee of permanent representatives.

b) **The European Parliament**

It is an embryonic legislature of the EEC and meets at Strasbourg. Since 1979, its members have been directly elected. There are 518 members of the parliament of which 81 are elected from the U.K. At the moment, it has very little power and authority. Its main function today is to monitor the activities of community institutes.

c) **The European Commission**

The commission is the secretariat of the EEC. It consists of 17 permanent members of which 2 come from each of the 5 largest countries and one from each of the other 7. There are 2,500 staffs working for the commission in Brussels. The Commission is responsible for the day-to-day running of the Community and for the development of EEC policy.

d) **The European Court of Justice**

The function of the court is to 'ensure that the law is observed in the interpretation of the treaty of Rome.' It is the final arbiter of the interpretation of the EEC treaties and it deals with disputes between member states and the Commission. It is, thus, the judiciary of the EEC.

The U.K. and the EEC

By joining the EEC the U.K. has become a part of a community of 320 million people. It is claimed that the economic advantages which the U.K. gained were enormous and fundamental — those of increased specialisation and comparative advantage. The gains from the EEC may not be readily appreciated by the average citizen. Real advantages are likely to be increased rate of growth of *GDP* despite some minor changes, it is called trade creation.

However, the common tariff of the EEC prevents Britain from benefiting from comparative advantage worldwide. The most obvious example is foodstuffs, whereby the U.K. is required to consume expensive European food, when it could be imported more cheaply from outside Europe. This diminution of comparative advantage is called *trade diversion.*

Despite the 1992 changes complete economic unity is still far away. Meanwhile, the EEC aims at the harmonisation of the economies of the member countries. Some of the implications of this for the U.K. are given below:

a) **Taxes**

It is the EEC policy that there should be no significant differences between rates and methods of taxation. One of the reasons why *VAT* was introduced in the U.K. was to bring it at par with the EEC. Differences in taxes would be discriminatory. For example, France claims that high excise duty on wine in the U.K. discriminates against French exports of wine.

b) **Metrication**

Most of the EEC countries have always used similar weights and measures, but for the U.K. this meant abandoning the old standards in favour of metric units, e.g. in 1981 petrol began to be sold in litres rather than gallons.

c) **Social Security**

It is EEC policy that social security benefits and payments be similar and transferable. This will enable people to work more easily in different EEC countries.

d) **Competition**

EEC law is aimed at regulating competition throughout the EEC.

e) **Free Movement of Labour, Capital and Enterprise**

It is part of EEC policy that its citizens should be free to work anywhere in the EEC. There is supposed to be free movement of capital and enterprise as well anywhere in the EEC. But many barriers to the movement of capital are still there.

Again it is believed that the 1992 changes will lead to a much free movement of capital and enterprise.

f) **Monetary Union**

It is an objective of the EEC that, there should be free convertibility of members currencies and a European Monetary Union be established as soon as possible (see below).

In joining the EEC the U.K. has simply followed the trend of her own trade, the European market have occupied a larger and larger share of her trade since the World War II. While the EEC may be beneficial to the U.K., many LDCs have described it as 'a rich man's club'. This is because the common external tariff seems to keep out primary products from the LDCs.

The European Monetary System (EMS)

In the later 1970s, dissatisfied with the validity of floating exchange rates led most of the member countries of the EEC (except the U.K.) to form the EMS. This system is viewed as a tentative step back towards fixed exchange rates.

Members of the EMS *agree to fix their exchange rates* relative to each other but to float as a bloc against the currencies of the rest of the world. *Although harmonization* was not a precondition to establish EMS, this remains the *ultimate objective* of those most committed to the European ideal. It has now been agreed that, they will establish a common currency and a single central bank and harmonize monetary and fiscal policy within the 1990s. The EMS is based on a newly devised unit of account called the European Currency Unit (ECU). The value of one unit is determined by taking a weighted basket of all member currencies. The value of members' currencies is allowed to fluctuate by + or – 2.25% of the central rate established by the value of the ECU (the U.K. joined the EMS on October 1990 and pound was allowed to fluctuate by ±6% initially.

The EMS was an attempt to deal with exchange rate volatility in a fairly pragmatic way. The agreement committed the central banks of member countries to intervene whenever any of the currencies threatened to deviate from its par value against other currencies by more than an agreed amount. Since harmonization of domestic macroeconomic policies was not achieved, member countries continued to have different inflation rates. Since, there have been frequent devaluations and revaluations of the agreed parties between member countries, they have usually been of relatively small magnitudes. This may be one of the reasons why speculative pressures have not been intense. Two other features tend to keep speculative pressure under control. First, by intervening collectively, the central banks of the member countries have a larger clout against the speculators. Second, since the group of currencies as a whole floats against the rest of the world, some of the advantages of the flexible exchange rate system have been retained.

The single European Act to abolish all barriers of movement between members of the community by 1992. It was intended that all major obstacles to trade between EEC countries should be removed.

This meant that goods and services should be free to pass between EEC countries. In addition, obstacles to the movement of capital (such as exchange control) would be abolished. Maastricht agreement paved the way for harmonization of monetary, fiscal and other policies within the EEC countries.

The Gains

The gains of a unified market should be those resulting from the benefit of competitive advantage across the whole of the community. The 1992 measures would bring bigger gains than the mere abolition of tariffs.

It was estimated by the Cecchini Report (1988), that, the potential gains of the 1992 changes were about £150 billion. However, the practical difficulties of abolishing tariffs and harmonizing taxes and so on may well reduce this.

European Union (EU) : After Maastricht Treaty of 1992

The flagging course of the EU showed signs of renewal in 1994 which dominated the year when member-states began setting out their views for the forthcoming review of the Maastricht Treaty, schedule for 1996. The promise of the talks was for a renewed advance towards monetary Union, closer cooperation on defense and foreign policy, and important reforms of the European institutions aimed at realigning their relationships and introducing greater levels of democratic control.

The increasing confidence behind the EU's developing foreign and security policy began to be reflected on the economic front during the year when Europe began to move out of economic recession while inflation continued at a low levels. There was evidence of remarkable currency stability despite abandoning of the narrow band limits of the European exchange-rate mechanism in 1993.

Much hope for reinforcing economic recovery was pinned on the signing of the GATT in April in Morocco. The achievement of an agreement after 8 years of difficult negotiations came despite some reservations, especially in France. The only question remained was whether the agreement would be ratified by national parliaments.

Politically the year was dominated by the European parliament elections in June, 1994, the first since the institution was given wider powers under the Maastricht Treaty. Against a background of recession and political disagreement, opposition to integration appeared to be growing in Italy and France, and it continued unabated in the UK. In Germany also increasing numbers of citizens questioned the desirability of abandoning their strong Deutsche Mark in favour of a single European Currency. Although the singing of the Maastricht Treaty on political, economic, and monetary union had introduced the principle of subsidiarity, allowing member states greater control over their own affairs, an underlying suspicion of centralized government remained. Elected members would have to deal with the questions of integrating new member states into the EU beginning January 1, 1995.

Jacques Delors, outgoing president of the European Commission, pointed out that governments would have to step up the fight against unemployment, promote economic growth, and prepare the EU for the next century. The European economy was at a crossroad between survival and decline. Government leaders would have to focus on 4 main areas: on growth, Competitiveness, employment, and economic guidelines for the second stage of European economic and monetary Union.

The talk on Europe's economic future were overshadowed by the difficulty in agreeing on Delors's successor as president of the European Commission. Ultimately, they chose the prime minister of Luxembourg, Jacques Santer, who would take office in 1995. After a long and bitter debate, the MEPs approved his nomination.

Then came the controversial debate about "a two-speed Europe"—a possible "hard core" of EU countries committed to comprehensive economic, political and defense integration and others outside.

For the EU, 1995 was a year marked by introspection and internal debate about both its future constitutional development and its role in international affairs. However, the year began with the formal accession of three new members — Austria, Finland and Sweden — bringing the number to 15 states, but it ended on a note of uncertainty about the pace of further integration.

The declared objective of full monetary union and a single currency by 1999 provided the focus for much of the discussion about future European integration. Uncertainty about the single-currency was underscored with evidence of the economic difficulties facing a majority of EU members during 1995. These suggested that several EU countries might not satisfy the economic conditions laid down in the Maastricht Treaty for participation in the single-currency. However, at a special meeting of EU finance ministers, there was broad agreement for introducing a single currency in stages after January 1999. At the EU summit in December, 1995, the single currency was given a name, the Euro, and the timetable for its introduction was extended to 2002, though a final decision to participate would be undertaken in 1998.

There were disagreements between the EU countries about the speed with which the EU should open its doors to new members. There was also disagreement about the extent to which any enlargement should be preceded and balanced by steps toward closer political and monetary Union.

Many of these issues were due to be resolved in a special conference of the 15 EU governments in 1996 to review the Maastricht Treaty. By late summer it was clear that major differences still separated members about any radical changes in the EU decision-making institutions. At one end of the spectrum, the German government pressed for qualified majority voting instead of unanimity for almost all areas of policy. Germany and other supporters of closer integration argued that the EU itself should take more responsibility for some policy areas still being decided by national governments alone. These included foreign and security policy and some aspects of immigration, justice, and police cooperation. At the other end of the spectrum, the British government continued to resist any moves to closer political union. Prime Minister, John Major also refuse to commit himself to taking part in an eventual single currency even if the UK met the economic conditions.

Apart from the 1996 intergovernmental conference **(IGC),** the political agenda of the EU during 1995 was dominated by two important issues: the continuing war in Bosnia and Herzegovina and concern about unemployment and the competitiveness of the European economics. At the end of the year, there was guarded optimism that the war in Bosnia was over, but the future role of EU countries in the Balkans was far from clear.

EMU of European Union

The drive to achieve economic and monetary Union by 1999 and to work for the enlargement of the EU dominated its political agenda in 1996. The debate about economic and monetary (EMU) and the introduction of single European currency were apparently overshadowed for sometime by the effects of recession and high unemployment in many EU countries raised doubts as to whether it would be in a position to meet such challenges.

There were fears even in most enthusiastic EU member states that they may find great difficulty in meeting some of the conditions for taking part in the planned move to a single currency in January, 1, 1999. The tough criteria — including limits on budget deficits and government debt levels — as well as the 1999 time table for monetary union has been set out in the Maastricht Treaty in 1992.

The attitude of the financial markets was also skeptical because of the serious problems being faced by some European economies at that time including the French economy and it appears that the French franc may have to be devalued against the Deutsche Mark and thus break an important criterion for monetary union.

However, the mood began to change after a meeting of the EU finance ministers in Verona, Italy, in April 1996 where it became clear that almost all members were determined to make the goal of EMU their overriding economic and political priority. They also agreed to maintain a strategy that would commit all the participants in the single currency to maintain long-term policies that would be oriented toward establishing stable economics. At a meeting in June, same year, in Florence, the EU heads of government reinforced this approach which became clear that the political will existed to achieve a single currency despite domestic political difficulties for the governments concerned.

The extent of those difficulties became clear during the summer and after, when one government after another announced austerity measures designed to reduce their budget deficits and meet the Maastricht criteria for a single currency. During the summer, mass trade-union demonstrations took place in France against the social security reforms and discontentment with the governments economic strategy continued to the end of the year as economic recovery brought little or no reduction in unemployment.

There were similar protests in other countries through the year, as anger about persistent high unemployment led to questions about the wisdom of the EU governments' economic and social policies to prepare for monetary union. In Germany the unions organised strikes and demonstrations against planned cuts in welfare benefits, and similar protests continued in Belgium and Spain. In Italy, however, it was mainly the middle classes who opposed the government's proposals to meet the budget deficits with new taxes and spending cuts.

In spite of these problems, the EU appeared to be significantly closer to its target of a single currency. During the winter of 1997, an agreement has been reached by the EU member states on the details of the ways in which the new EMU system would operate. A formal agreement on the stability pact, on the legal status of the proposed new single currency (the Euro), and on the operation of a reformed European exchange-rate system (to link the Euro with those EU currencies outside monetary union) was finalised at a summit in Dublin in December, 1996.

Reflecting this tremendous political determination to achieve the single currency, the European financial markets gradually become less skeptical about the prospects for accomplishing it. This was shown by a remarkable narrowing of interest rates between the main EU countries—namely, France and Germany. Despite this remarkable progress that had been made, the European Monetary Institute warned that governments needed to act further to achieve economic convergence, without which monetary union might fail. Simultaneously the European Commission, the executive body of the EU, published forecasts of improvement in economic growth in 1997, which was to be the base year for judging the economic performance of countries to determine whether they could join the single currency. The commission also predicted that 12 or 13 out of 15 EU countries might qualify for the EMU. Of these 15, two countries —Denmark and the United Kingdom while expected to qualify economically, had negotiated a political right to opt out of the single-currency. Most doubt was focused on the commissions belief that even relatively less-prosperous countries, such as, Portugal, Spain and Italy might qualified to join the single currency.

For all the growing optimism about monetary union, the German government and its central bank, the Bundesbank, expressed concern that the rigour of the EMU conditions might be in danger of being diluted. Thus, debate focused on issues such as the scale of penalties a government might face if it began to break the rules governing budget limits, debt, and inflation. Despite evidence that the worst of the European recession had passed, with the EU economics expecting a recovery, concern remained about unemployment. The commission warned that the economic upturn risked becoming a jobless recovery. There was growing debate about whether the answer to unemployment depended on radical restructuring of the European labour markets and the abandonment of the European social security system. There is growing consciensious among the EU governments that the European welfare model had to be reformed but not scrapped.

The other major institutional issue dominated the EU politics was the inter-governmental conference (IGC) to review the Maastricht Treaty which involved measures to strengthen the supranational decision making authority of the EU institutions. It not only set out the goal of monetary union but also envisioned further steps to full political union, including a common European foreign, security and defence policy.

The commission president, Jacques Santer, told the European parliament that unless radical institutional reforms were agreed upon to improve the effectiveness and accountability of the EU, it would be difficult, if not impossible, to open its doors to new members. The EU promised to begin negotiations with at least some of the would be new members six months after the completion of the IGC. As the discussion in the IGC dragged on through the whole year, however, with little concrete agreement on the key issues, doubts were raised about the likely date of any new treaty.

It may not be out of place to mention that significant progress had already been made in reducing areas of disagreement between most countries on such sensitive questions as voting in the council of ministers, a reduction in the national right of veto on decisions, extensions of the role of the European parliament, a stronger common foreign and security policy, and a bigger role for the EU in such issues as immigration and political asylum.

The major difficulty facing the IGC until 1997 election in Britain was the opposition of the British conservative government to any further strengthening of the EU or any more to what London described as "a federal superstate." British conservative Prime Minister reiterated that he would veto any further extension of majority voting or any weakening of the national veto in EU matters.

Relations between the U.K. and the other European nations worsened when Mr. Major demanded withdrawal of ban on exports of British beef and beef products, which was thought to have a link with BSE or "mad-cow" disease and also wanted to reverse a decision of the European court obliging the U.K. to introduce 48-hour limit for the workweek.

After May 1 elections and victory of the Labour pasty has significantly changed the relationship between the other members of the EU and British Labour government under Tony Blair. British government's present position on EMU is that it is in favour of joining, but not until after the next election, and then not until after a referendum.

The main point is that when, and if, Britain does join, it will have to go through a process of economic convergence. This means that British economic fundamentals must be brought into line with Europe's. For borrowers, the key statistics are that the U.K. base rate is 7.25% and the likely euro interest rate is widely expected to be about 4%, that is a lot less than U.K. borrowers are paying at the moment.

For the 11 of the 15 countries likely to be in the first-wave of EMU, the euro rate will apply from January 1, 1999. British government policy suggests that sterling might not be replaced by the euro and its lower interest rate until well after May 6, 2002, the last possible date for the next general election. But convergence has to start happening long before that if the country and the currency are to be ready to act on a "yes" vote. Therefore, British interest rate will have to move downwards.

It is also government policy that sterling should enter EMU at an exchange rate to the euro weaker than prevails against European Currencies at present which will be a boost for the manufacturing sector and smaller companies.

For equity investors, the key statistics are that while the U.K. equity market has risen by 16% this year, first-wave EMU countries have done better. Germany have gone up by 28%, France by 30%, Spain by 45% and Italy by 47%.

It is likely that U.K. equities will benefit from convergence, as will be the bond market. Investors should continue to hold U.K. gilts rather than European bonds as they currently offer better value then European equities. Britain may not be going into EMU now, but its relative underperformance against Europe, combined with a widespread expectation that it will eventually join EMU, makes it attractive to investors who want to buy into Europe cheaply, and who are not in a hurry.

The stage is set for the long-awaited EMU drama. For the triumphal launch for the single currency, nothing has been left to chance. It has long been clear that 11 of the European Union's 15 members will be declared eligible, despite the underlying divergence between their economics. And the British government is more determined than any other governments to ensure the success of this historic occasion on May 1, 1998. There is only one snag. There is total deadlock on the question of who is to be appointed president of the European Central Bank, the independent institution created under the Maastricht treaty to run the new currency. Germany is adamant that Wim Duisenberg, Dutch head of the interim European Monetary Institute, must have the job, whereas France wants Jean-claude Trichet, head of the Banque de France, to be head of the ECB.

The decision must be unanimous and, since the bank opens for business on July 1, six months before EMU goes into operations, further delay may unsettled the markets. The pressure on the British Presidency to manufacture a compromise is thus considerable because delay will be undesirable, but much greater damage could be done if this battle is settle through the kind of horse-trading that is the trademark of EU politics.

May 2 send-off for the EU single currency will be considered by EU leaders in Brussels as the dawn of a new age, but their historic will not mask anxiety over this gambles attempted by a group of sovereign states.

The euro will be seen by many of the continental political establishment as an historic leap towards political union. However, the territory is so uncharted that the experts and many of its supporters are at odds over the benefits and danger that lie ahead. Forecasts range from the birth of a glorious "European Century" to continental upheaval.

The "Europhobic" scenario, backed by the federalists and the European Commission runs like this : the currency will galvanise the 11 economics of EU countries unleashing the economic power of 270 million people which will reap the benefits of years of fiscal sacrifice. It will be fuelled by low interest rates, set by ECB.

Economic frontiers will wither along with exchange risks and costs, consolidating a richer single market than the USA. Consumers and business will benefit from the transparency that will allow easy comparison of prices in a various new world that will create millions of jobs.

The optimists say the euro will swiftly rival the dollar as the worlds reserve currency, boosting exports from the biggest trading zone and equipping the EU with the global influence. The unity of EU will bring national taxes into line and help to save the "European social model", the welfare system that is now under threat. The euro would not just create a European political space, but also "stop Europe's slide towards a simple free trade zone".

The gloomier forecasts run like this : the continental recovery fatters because it has failed to tackle the underlying structural problems of high taxes and rigid labour laws that have held back growth and kept unemployment above 10%. European "one-size-fits-all" interest rates make life difficult for some countries as performance diverges. Intensifying the tension an the widely diverge tax policies among the European states, which is likely to retain fiscal sovereignty. However, the famous "asymmetric" effect kicks in. Without a true political union with a central authority, economic trouble in one depressed region may not be relieved by the migration of labour or capital transfers, the safety value that operates in the USA. This will sharpen the pain of the suffering regions, fuelling further unemployment. Frankfurt and the EU will likely to be a popular scapegoats, feeding political tension that could blow the euro system apart.

The arguments in favour and against are not going to stop euro becoming the official of the first-wave 11 members, although national currencies may also be used at their euro values until January 1, 2002 when euro notes and coins enter circulation. By July 1, 2002, the national currencies cease to be legal tender. This is the likely timetable for the euro which will be started in January 1, 1999.

The euro is and always was political project, designed to propel the nations of western Europe towards union. Political will has ensured that the dream of Jean Monnet, the architect of post-war economic cooperation, have at last become a reality. But political will cannot solve the region's chronic unemployment problem. It cannot raise its growth rate.

Euro-enthusiasts are in no doubt that there will be big economic benefit. Curbs on inflation and spending have brought lower interest rates to several countries, although there remains the question of their sustainability. The single currency means different things to different groups. To some it means a bulwork against foreign exchange speculators. To bosses of multinational corporations it is a cost cutting exercise. They also argue that the euro will prompt the creation of genuinely pan-European business, with the loss of the devaluation option leading to elimination of the weak and inefficient. It will see the benefits of the economics of scale offered by the single market. It would also "force the governments to introduce more flexible labour markets and reduce the cost of employing people". They also believe that it can meet varying expectations and that policies of low inflation and sound public finance will provide the background for growth and sustainable jobs. Opponents say any benefits may outweighed by potential costs. They have a range of objections. To some the main argument is that the politically unacceptable European Central Bank will be far too hawkish. To them it is a "disaster waiting to happen on the scale of 1914. Instead of using the weapon of mass destruction, we are using shouldering the arms of job destruction.". To others, it is like a building without fire-exits : no escape if it goes wrong. It has also been pointed out that it is unlikely to lubricate structural reform. "People say the shocks will force these countries to make the supply-side reforms that will be needed. That must be a gamble, and a politically naive one ....".

Economists argue that conditions are not right for monetary union to work. In particular, the leak of a common language means labour-market mobility is limited, wages are not flexible and there is no fiscal mechanism for moving money from richer to poorer areas. On balance, it may be added that monetary union could either work badly or well, if the dangers could be guarded against, competition and integration would promote efficiency and growth.

Appendix

Notes on Figures

Fig. 1.1 : Simple Circular Flow Diagram (Page 5)
Firms produce output which the households consume with the income received from firms by selling the factor inputs which they own. Thus, there is a flow of goods and services.

Fig. 2.1 : Okun's Law (Page 14)
Shows the relationship between te percentage change in the rate of growth of unemployment and the percentage change *GDP* growth rate.

Fig. 2.2 : Production Possibility Frontier with Constant Opportunity Cost (Page 19)
This figure shows all efficient combinations of outputs. Point *C* shows that all resources have not been utilized or used efficiently. Point *D* is not attainable with the existing resources and technology. The straight line Production Possibility frontier shows constant opportunity cost.

Fig. 2.3 : Production Possibility Frontier with Increasing Opportunity Cost (Page 20)
Shows the increasing opportunity cost.

Fig. 2.4 : Natural Rate of Unemployment (Page 22)
Shows the demand for labour, DD_L, equals supply of labour, SS_L, at *e* with equilibrium employment *OL*, however actual employment is at *OA*. Thus, *AL* — which is the difference between actual employment *(OA)* and equilibrium level of employment *(OL)*, is the natural rate of unemployment.

Fig. 3.1 : Extended Circular Flow (Page 26)
The figure shows the flow of goods and services from the firm and the money flow from households in exchange for goods. The households receive income from firms in exchange for inputs services.Part of the households' income is either saved, spent on imports or is taken away by the government in the form of taxes.

This tax revenue is spent to finance the services provided by the government including transfer payments.Output produced by firms are sold to the households or to foreigners in the form of exports.

Fig. 4.1 : Equilibrium in the Economy (Page 45)

The figure shows equilibrium in the economy where the *AD* curve intersects the $45°$ line at point *E*. This is stable equilibrium because any deviation from the equilibrium will generate forces to bring it back to equilibrium.

Fig. 4.2 : Income Determination in a Simple Keynesian Model (Page 48)

Figure shows that same equilibrium income, Y_e , can be achieved from the consumption function and from the equality of saving and investment.

Fig. 4.3 : Multiplier Relationship (Page 50)

This figure shows the multiplier relationship where there is an increase in autonomous investment the *AD* schedule shifts from *AD* to *AD'* and the equilibrium moves from *E* to *E'*. The multiplier is greater than 1 because consumption demand increases with output,

so $\Delta Y = \frac{1}{1-b}\Delta \bar{I}$.

Fig. 4.4 : Income Determination with Consumption and Investment as a Function of Income (Page 51)

The figure shows that $C(Y) + I(Y) = AD$. The equilibrium solution is given at the point of intersection between AD and the $45°$ line. The same equilibrium is obtained by the intersection of *S(Y)* and *I(Y)*.

Fig. 4.5 : Actual Path of Income (Page 54)

This figure shows how the actual path of income tends towards equilibrium over time when the *MPC* lies between zero and one. If the income in period *O* is less than Y_e (equilibrium), it rises in the subsequent periods and approaches the equilibrium value. Conversely, if income in period *O* is greater than Y_e , it falls in the subsequent periods and again approaches the equilibrium value.

Fig. 4.6 : Investment Function (Page 59)

This figure gives us the inverse relationship between investment and interest rate i.e. when interest rate increases, investment decreases and when interest rate falls investment increases.

Fig. 4.7 : Derivation of *IS* curve (Page 60)

In this four-quadrant diagram, the real income is measured on the right horizontal and bottom vertical axis. Along the top vertical axis the interest rate is measured and along the left horizontal axis we measure both saving and investment per unit of time. The second quadrant represents the investment function. The third quadrant represents the consumption as well as saving function, while the fourth quadrant represents the *45°* line which allows the transcription of income from the vertical to horizontal axis. In the first quadrant, we derive the *IS* curve which represents the equilibrium condition in the goods sector.

Fig. 4.8 : Saving-Investment Equality and Equilibrium Properties of *IS* curve (Page 61)

This figure shows the top part of Fig. 4.7. Here the three points *A, B, C* all represent the same income Y_0 but different interest rates. Given the assumption that consumption and savings depend on income only. Savings are the same in all the three points, but point *B* shows combination of income and interest rate at which $S = I$. At point *A*, $I_A < I_B$ and at point *C*, $I_C > I_B$, but savings are the same in all points as income is the same as Y_0. This shows that the *IS* curve represents the combination of income and interest rate at which the goods sector is in equilibrium.

Fig. 4.9 : A Shift of the IS Curve (Page 63)

The figure shows that any change in autonomous spending such as government expenditure of investment expenditure will cause a shift in the IS curve. The degree of shifting will depend on the multiplier times the amount of autonomous spending.

Fig. 5.1 : Average Money Holdings (Page 70)

This figure shows that average money holdings over the year depend on the number of withdrawals in each year.

Fig. 5.2 : Average Money Holding which minimises Total Cost (Page 71)

The figure shows how to minimise the total cost which depends on *N*, the number of trips. The optimal value of *N* is *N**.

Fig. 5.3 : Preference Function of Investors (Page 73)

The figure shows the equilibrium solution for the investor who is a diversifier — in the sense that he holds both cash and bonds. This equilibrium is reached where the highest attainable indifference is tangential with the opportunity locus at a given interest rate.

Fig. 5.4 : Equilibrium Solution of Highest Risk-taker (Page 74)
This figure shows the corner solution for an investor who keeps bonds only and no cash.

Fig. 5.5 : Equilibrium Solution of Investor who takes No Risk (Page 74)
This figure shows the corner solution where the investor holds all cash and no bonds.

Fig. 5.6 : Equilibrium of a Standard Investor at Different Interest Rates (Page 74)
This figure gives us the optimum portfolio curve at different interest rates i.e. as the interest rate increases, so also the portfolio of bond held increases and cash holding decreases. Thus, the portfolio balance approach explains the downward sloping liquidity preference function.

Fig. 5.7 : Equilibrium at Different Rates of Interest (Page 75)
This figure shows a downward sloping optimum portfolio curve i.e. as the interest rate goes up, so also the proportion invested in bonds decreases.

Fig. 5.8 : Optimal Money Holding (Page 78)
The figure shows that the demand for money increases as the interest rate decreases. A reduction in interest rate shifts the *MC* curve to MC' and, thereby, increases money demand from M* to M_1*.

Fig. 5.9 : Demand For Active Balances (Page 85)
The figure shows that the demand for active balances (M_t) is an increasing function of income. As income increases, so the demand for active money balance also increases.

Fig. 5.10 : Demand for Idle Balances (Page 85)
The figure shows that the demand for idle balances is a decreasing function of interest rates. As interest rates decrease, so the demand for idle balances increases. At a very low rate of interest, such as r_{min}, demand for money may be infinitely elastic as shown in the figure.

Fig. 5.11 : Determination of the Equilibrium Rate of Interest (Page 86)
This figure shows the demand $[L(r, Y_0)]$ and supply of money (MM_0), when the level of income is constant at Y_0, the demand function for money is *CE*, the supply of money is constant at OM_0 and the money supply function is MM_0. The supply curve intersects the demand curve to give an equilibrium rate of interest which is Or_0

in this case. At a higher interest rate Or_1, the supply of money exceeds the demand for money and interest rates fall. On the other hand, at a lower interest rate of interest, Or_2, the demand is greater than supply and the interest rate rises. At interest rate Or_0, the demand for money equals the supply of money and equilibrium is achieved at that rate.

Fig. 5.12 : Derivation of *LM* curve (Page 89)
The figure shows that at different combinations of r and Y we can have the money demand function equal to the money supply function. The locus of such combinations gives us the *LM* curve or the money market equilibrium. From the given level of income, we know how much money will be demanded for transaction purposes and the rest of the money supply is available for speculative purposes to determine the rate of interest which gives equilibrium in the money market. Thus, corresponding to each level of income, there is a rate of interest which produces equilibrium in the money market. With a given quantity of money, we get a relation between Y and r which gives us the *LM* curve. The *LM* curve gives the relationship where a rise in income leads to an increase in the transaction demand for money which requires that the rate of interest be increased to achieve equilibrium in the money market.

Fig. 5.13 : Shift of the LM curve (Page 91)
The figure 5.13(b) shows the demand for real money balances for a given level of income, say, Y_1. With the initial money supply of $\left(\overline{M}/\overline{P}\right)$, the equilibrium is at E_1 at an interest rate of r_1. The corresponding point on the *LM* curve is E_1. If the money supply now increases to $\left(\overline{M}/\overline{P}\right)'$, to restore equilibrium in a given level of income, Y_1, the interest rate has to decline to r_2 and the equilibrium will be reached at E_2. The new equilibrium is at E_2 and the *LM* curve has shifted to *LM*′.

Fig. 6.1 : General Equilibrium (Page 93)
The figure shows that goods market *(IS)* and money market *(LM)* are simultaneously in equilibrium at point *E*, where interest rate is r_e and income is Y_e. Thus, point *E* gives us general equilibrium.

Fig. 6.2 : Derivation of General Equilibrium Condition (Page 94)
Figure 6.2(c) shows the money sector from which the *LM* curve in Fig. 6.2(b) is derived and Fig. 6.2(a) shows the desired investment function which, together with the consumption function, will help

us to derive the *IS* curve in Fig. 6.2(b). These two curves intersect at point *A* to give us the general equilibrium for the economy at income Y_2 and interest rate r_e.

Fig. 6.3 : General Equilibrium is Stable (Page 95)

Figure 6.3shows that the general equilibrium described here is indeed a stable one. For all points to the left of the *IS* curve, there is an excess demand for goods and, thus, there is pressure on income to rise. Similarly, for all points to the right of the *IS* curve, there is pressure on *Y* to fall.

Now consider points above the *LM* curve, where the interest rate is too high for money market to be in equilibrium, where the supply of money exceeds the demand for money and so downward pressure is exerted on the interest rate. Similarly, upward pressure will be exerted on interest rates at all points below the *LM* curve as there is excess demand for money. Thus, at any disequilibrium point, economic forces will be generated to bring the market towards the general equilibrium position.

Fig. 6.4 : New Equilibrium when *IS* curve Shifts (Page 96)

Figure 6.4 shows that when the IS curve shifts as a result of an increase in desired expenditure, the economy is no longer in equilibrium at A because the goods market is no longer in equilibrium. But the money sector is still in equilibrium as there is no change in behavioural function of the money sector. With the new *IS* curve *(I'S')*, desired expenditures are greater than total output and thus there is an increase in *Y*. As real *Y* rises, A no longer represents equilibrium in the money sector either, because the increase in *Y* affects the quantity of money demanded; hence equilibrium in the money sector will also change. This will increase interest rate and will reduce desired *I* and real *Y*. This process will continue until a new equilibrium is reached at *B* with interest rate r_B and rest income at Y_B.

Fig. 6.5 : New Equilibrium when *LM* curve Shifts (Page 97)

Figure 6.5 shows that when the LM curve shifts as a result of a change in money demand or money supply, the economy is no longer in equilibrium at point A because the money market is not in equilibrium. Suppose that there is an increase in the supply of money brought about by the monetary authority which causes a shift of the *LM* curve to the right to $L'M'$. But the goods sector is still in equilibrium at *A*. However, at *A*, the quantity of money supplied is greater than the quantity of money demanded as the situation in the money sector represented by $L'M'$ which drives the interest rate down. The fall in interest rates also affects the goods sector via its effects on desired I; thus, point A will not remain an equilibrium point for the goods sector either. The changes in the goods sector thus generated will have repercussions on the monetary sector. The process continue until a new equilibrium is reached at point B at which both the sectors are in equilibrium again.

Fig. 6.6 : Perfectly Elastic Demand For Money or the Liquidity Trap Situation (Page 98)

Figure 6.6 shows the perfectly elastic demand for money at the interest rate r_L and 3 demand curves for three different incomes where $Y_1 < Y_2 < Y_3$. At the interest rate, r_L, people are willing to hold all their wealth in the form of money. If the money supply is increased from MS_1 to MS_2, this affects the elastic part of the LM curve only as in Fig. 6.6(b) and has no effect on the interest rate.

Fig. 6.7 : General Equilibrium at the Liquidity Trap Situation (Page 99)

Figure 6.7 shows that a general equilibrium situation is reached by the intersection of IS at the horizontal part of the LM curve at Y_e and r_L, respectively. Increase in money supply has no effect on the equilibrium value of real Y and the interest rate because the part of the LM curve affected by this change is not relevant to the determination of equilibrium.

Fig. 6.8 : Perfectly Elastic Money Supply (Page 100)

Figure 6.8 demonstrates what happens when the monetary authority fixes the interest rate at some given level. For this, the authority will have to supply whatever quantity of money is demanded at that rate, otherwise the interest rate will change. Thus, the figure shows that the supply of money is perfectly elastic at the interest rate, r_f, and the LM curve is horizontal. The general equilibrium is reached by the intersection of IS and horizontal LM curve at r_f and Y_f.

Fig. 6.9 : The Perfectly Inelastic Investment Function (Page 100)

Figure 6.9 gives a perfectly elastic IS curve when we assume that the interest rate has no affect on the investment function and real Y is the only variable which affects AD. The Perfectly interest elastic IS function intersects two LM curves giving the same income but different interest rates.

Fig. 6.10 : The Real Balance Effect (Page 101)

Pigou's argument against the Keynesian Liquidity Trap has been demonstrated in this figure. With a constant nominal money supply, a general deflation of wages and prices tends to increase the real value of people's holdings of money above their desired levels. In such a situation, people will reduce their savings and increase their consumption in an attempt to reduce their real balances. If there is unemployment in the economy, as wages and prices fall, the *LM* curve shifts to the right and the *IS* curve also shifts to the right as consumption expenditure increases. With both curves now shifting to the right, the equilibrium levels of income and employment must increase and there is nothing to stop full employment from being reached.

Fig. 7.1 : Full-employment Equilibrium (Page 105)
Figure 7.1 shows the equilibrium level of employment, the equilibrium real wage rate and the equilibrium level of output. This is classical full-employment equilibrium. The upper part of the diagram shows the equilibrium in the labour market and the lower part of the diagram gives the equilibrium employment and income.

Fig. 7.2 : Inverse Relationship between *Y* and *P* (Page 106)
Figure 7.2 shows the inverse relationship between *Y* and *P* which means that as *Y* increases *P* must decrease.

Fig. 7.3 : Graphic Presentation of the Complete Classical Model (Page 108)
In part I of the figure, we draw the demand and supply curves of labour which gives us equilibrium employment of labour and equilibrium wage rate. In part II, we determine the equilibrium level of output, whereas, in part III, we determine equilibrium price level. Part IV determines the equilibrium money wage rate and in part V, equilibrium rate of interest is determined which is not connected with the determination of the equilibrium values of other variables.

Fig. 7.4 : Effects of a Rightward Shift of the Labour Supply Curve (Page 110)
Figure 7.4 shows the effects of a rightward shift of the labour supply curve in the classical model. This has the effect of increasing the equilibrium level of employment and reducing the equilibrium real wage rate in part I. In part II, we can see that when the level of employment has increased, the level of output has also increased. Whereas, in part III, we can see that as the level of output increases, the equilibrium price decreases. Thus, the effect of an increase in the supply of labour lowers real wage, increases employment and output, and reduces prices.

Fig. 7.5 : Equilibrium Rate of Interest (Page 112)

Figure 7.5 shows that the intersection between the savings and investment functions determines the equilibrium rate of interest, r_f.

Fig. 7.6 : No Positive Intersection between Savings and Investment Functions (Page 114)

The figure shows that the savings function intersects the investment function at full employment to produce a negative rate of interest, r_f. Since there cannot be a negative rate of interest, full employment cannot be achieved under these circumstances.

Fig. 7.7 : Liquidity Trap prevents Full-employment (Page 114)

Figure 7.7shows that there is a lower limit below which interest rate may not fall which is set by the liquidity trap where the speculative demand for money becomes horizontal. Now suppose that, the interest rate required to achieve full-employment is less than the rate of interest permitted by the liquidity trap situation; then full-employment cannot be achieved.

Fig. 8.1 : General Equilibrium (Page 119)

Figure 8.1 shows the general equilibrium at point *E* where the goods sector represented by the *IS* curve and the money sector represented by the *LM* curve intersect.

Fig. 8.2 : General Equilibrium is Stable (Page 119)

The figure explains the stability condition of this general equilibrium.

Fig. 8.3 : Effect of Change in Money Supply on Equilibrium (Page 121)

Figure 8.3 demonstrates the effect of a change in money supply on the equilibrium level of income and interest rates.

Fig. 8.4 : No change of Equilibrium (Page 121)

The figure demonstrates that there will be no change in the equilibrium level of income and interest rates when the *IS* curve intersects the *LM* curve at the latter's horizontal part and the money supply is changed.

Fig. 8.5 : Money Supply with completely Interest-Inelastic Investment Function (Page 122)

Figure 8.5 demonstrates the effect of a change of money supply on the interest rate when the investment function is completely interest-inelastic and the level of income remains unchanged.

Fig. 8.6 : Effect of a change in Autonomous Investment on the Equilibrium Level of Income and Interest Rates (Page 125)

Figure 8.6 demonstrates that the effect of a change in autonomous investment on the equilibrium level of income and interest rate depends on where the *IS*-curve intersects the *LM* curve. Firstly, if the *IS* curve intersects the *LM* curve at its horizontal part, the level of income increases by the full multiplier effect, but the interest rate remains unchanged. Secondly, suppose the *IS*-curve intersects the *LM* curve at its rising part, here the equilibrium level of income and the interest rate change. In this range the multiplier effect will be less than the previous case. Thirdly, if the *IS*-curve intersects the *LM* curve at its vertical range, the equilibrium level of income will remain unchanged, but only the interest rate will change.

Fig. 8.7 : The Total Product Curve (Page 127)

Figure 8.7 gives us the total product curve which shows that the *MP* of labour increases at a decreasing rate when more labour is employed with a given capital stock. The slope of the total product curve gives the *MP* of labour and the shape of the curve reflects the assumption of the diminishing marginal product of labour.

Fig. 8.8 : Demand and Supply Curves of Labour (Page 127)

Figure 8.8 shows that conditions of perfect competition and profit maximisation will give us the demand curve for labour where the value of MP_L = wage rate. The labour demand curve is determined from the aggregate production function which is downward sloping. For each price we get one labour demand curve. If the price level rises, the labour demand curve shifts to the right.

Fig. 8.9 : Volume of Employment and Wage Rate (Page 128)

Figure 8.9 shows that if the volume of employment is greater than the full-employment level, the wage rate will rise as employment increases. The money wage rate is constant at W_0 up to full-employment level, N_f, thereafter, it increases as employment increases.

Fig. 8.10 : Change in Price Level produces New Equilibrium (Page 130)

The figure shows that we get one *LM* curve for each price level and one equilibrium level of income is determined by the intersection of *IS* and *LM* curves. When the price level changes in a given money supply, we get one *LM* curve and one equilibrium level of income.

Fig. 8.11 : Downward-sloping Aggregate Demand Curve (Page 130)

If the supply of money remains constant but the price level changes, we get a different equilibrium levels of income. When the price level decreases, the equilibrium level of income increases. On the other hand, if the price level increases, the equilibrium level of income decreases. Thus, we get a downward-sloping aggregate demand curve.

Fig. 8.12 : Downward-sloping Aggregate Demand Curve and Upwar-sloping Aggregate Supply Curve (Page 131)

They are drawn in this figure to satisfy the equilibrium condition in three markets — labour, commodity and money.

Fig. 8.13 : Complete Keynesian Model (Page 133)

In the figure, we first draw the aggregate demand curve *AD*, on the assumption of a constant money supply M_0 and then draw the aggregate supply curve, *AS*, which intersects the *AD* curve to produce equilibrium price level $\overline{P}$ and the equilibrium income $\overline{Y}$. When the level of output is known, the corresponding level of employment, $\overline{N}$, can be obtained from the production function. The labour demand and supply curves are drawn on the left hand side of the production function. The labour demand curve drawn for the price level, $\overline{P}$, intersects the labour supply curve at its horizontal part to give equilibrium employment which includes involuntary unemployment. The equilibrium money wage rate is W_0. We also draw the *IS* and *LM* curves above the *AD* and *AS* curves. At the intersection of the *IS* and *LM* curves the equilibrium interest rate, *r*, is determined. From this figure we can determine all important variables of the system.

Fig. 8.14 : Change in Money supply with Flexible Prices (Page 136)

In the Keynesian system, the equilibrium price level is determined by the intersection of *AD* and *AS*. When the *AD* curve is drawn, money supply is assumed to be constant. Thus, when the money supply increases, the *AD* curve shifts to the right. The *AS* curve is not affected by money supply.

Now we can see that as the supply of money increases, the *LM* curve shifts to the right at each price level and hence the level of income also increases at each price level from Y_0 to Y_1 when the price level changes from P_0 to P_1.

Fig. 8.15 : Money Supply and *AD* curve (Page 136)

Figure shows how the *AD* curve is affected when the money supply is increased. Thus, when the money supply increases, at each price level, a higher level of income is required to have equilibrium in commodity and money markets. This means that the *AD* curve will shift to the right.

Fig. 8.16 : *AD* Curve has its effect on Equilibrium Price Level and Income (Page 136)

Figure 8.16 demonstrates that as the *AD* curve shifts to the right, the equilibrium price level increases from P_0 to P_1 and the equilibrium also increases from Y_0 to Y_1.

Fig. 9.1 : Full-employment and Price Flexibility (Page 147)

In this figure we start from full-employment equilibrium at $Y_F r_F$ for some price level P_0 and the interest rate r_F at which full-employment saving is equal to investment. Now, suppose, that everybody wants to save more than previously, which shifts the *IS* curve to *IS*′. The new equilibrium interest rate is r_m at which new equilibrium $S = I$ at full-employment and price level P_1. If there is no change in the price level, the interest rate will be r_m and the aggregate demand will be Y_m less than full employment output Y_F. To achieve full employment again, the interest rate must fall and investment must rise.

Fig. 9.2 : Inflexibility of Interest Rate and the Liquidity Trap (Page 148)

In this figure we demonstrate inherent inflexibility in the interest rate because the interest rate in a money economy could never fall below zero (the liquidity trap situation). We start with a full-employment equilibrium at Y_F and r_F. Now, suppose, people want to save more at every level of income, shown by the shift of the *IS* curve to *IS*′ and the equilibrium interest rate is now r'_F at which full-employment savings are equal to investment which is negative and is, thus, unacceptable in a money economy. Thus, in this figure there is an excess of full-employment saving over investment, which will lead to a fall in the price level, but will not result in a fall in the interest rate at the required level. Flexibility of price does not imply the necessary flexibility of the interest rate, especially at the liquidity trap situation.

Fig. 9.3 : Under-employment Equilibrium (Page 150)

Figure 9.3 shows that if investment is I_1, the equilibrium level of income is Y_1. If investment is I_2, the equilibrium level of income is Y_2, and so on. Suppose, full-employment will be achieved only if investment is I_2. There is no reason to believe that the investment schedule will always be I_2. Thus, there is no automatic mechanism to achieve full-employment.

Fig. 9.4 : Full-employment will be achieved by the Interest Rate Flexibility (Page 150)

Against the Keynesian argument, classical economists pointed out that saving and investment are functions of both the rate of interest and the level of income. If saving at full-employment is not equal to investment, the rate of interest will change and this flexibility of the interest rate will ensure the $S = I$ at full-employment as is given in the figure.

Fig. 9.5 : Full-employment is prevented by Negative Interest Rates (Page 151)
The figure shows that savings and investment schedules intersect to produce a negative rate of interest at full-employment. In such a situation, full-employment cannot be achieved because a negative rate of interest is not feasible in a money economy. Whether the system will generate full-employment or not, depends on whether full-employment S and I functions intersect at a positive rate of interest or not.

Fig. 9.6 : Pigou Effect And Full-employment (Page 152)
Figure 9.6 demonstrates that through the Pigou or real balance effect, full employment will be automatically achieved. The argument of negative rates are invalid, if we accept complete flexibility of prices.

Fig. 10.1 : Downward-sloping Aggregate Demand Curve (Page 154)
The aggregate demand curve slopes downwards because, for any fixed money supply, the quantity equation fixes the nominal value of output, *PY*. Thus, if the price level goes up, output must go down and vice versa.

Fig. 10.2 : Changes in Money Supply shifts the Aggregate DemandCurve (Page 155)
The *ADC* is drawn on the assumption of fixed money supply. However, if the money supply changes, the *ADC* shifts. If money supply is increased, there is an increase in *PY*. For any price level, the amount of output is higher. Similarly, if the money supply is reduced, there is a proportionate reduction in the nominal value of output, *PY*. Thus, for any price level, the amount of output is lower.

Fig. 10.3 : Long-run Aggregate Supply Curve is Vertical (Page 156)
According to the classical view, output does not depend on the price level. It depends on the amount of capital, labour, and the available technology. Thus, the long-run aggregate supply curve *(LRASC)* is vertical. The intersection of the *AD* curve with the vertical *LRASC* determines the price level.

Fig. 10.4 : Short-run Aggregate Supply Curve is Horizontal (Page 157)
The classical model applies only in the long run. In the short run, some prices are sticky and do not adjust to changes in demand. This price stickiness implies that the *SRASC* is likely to be horizontal.

Fig. 10.5 : From Short-run Equilibrium to Long-run Equilibrium (Page 157)
Over short periods, prices are sticky, the *SRASC* is horizontal, and thus, the economy moves from *A* to *B*, as in Fig. 10.5. Output and employment increases above the natural levels, which means the economy is in boom. Overtime wages and prices will rise. The gradual increase in the price level moves the economy upward along the *ADC* to point *C*, which is the new long-run equilibrium; output and employment are back again to their natural levels.

Fig. 10.6 : Shift in Aggregate Demand Curve (Page 158)
ADC summarises the results of the *IS-LM* model, shocks that shifts the *ISC* or *LMC* cause the *ADC* to shift. Expansionary fiscal or monetary policy raises income in the *IS-LM* model and, thus, shifts the *ADC* outwards. Similarly, contractionary fiscal or monetary policy lowers income and thus shifts the *ADC* downward.

Fig. 10.7 : Adverse Supply Shock push up Costs and Prices (Page 159)
Supply shock alters the cost of production and, thus, the price level. Adverse supply shocks push up costs and prices. A favourable supply shock reduces costs and prices, as the figure shows.

Fig. 10.8 : Aggregate Demand Curve from *IS-LM* Model (Page 160)
IS-LM model can be used to derive the *ADC*. *IS-LM* model may be used to show that *Y* falls as the price level rises; the downward-sloping *ADC* expresses this relationship. It slopes downward because in a given nominal money supply, increase in price level causes a lower supply of real balances which shifts *LMC* upward, which raises the interest rate and lowers *Y* as in Fig. 10.6(a). Thus, when the price level rises from P_1 to P_2, *Y* falls from Y_1 to Y_2, which is plotted in Fig. 10.6(b).

Fig. 10.9 : Monetary Policy and Shift of Aggregate Demand (Page 161)
Given the price level, an increase in the money supply raises real money balances, shifts the *LMC* downwards and raises income and vice versa. Thus, changes in the *MS* shifts the *ADC*.

Fig. 10.10 : Fiscal Policy and Shift of Aggregate Demand (Page 161)
The fiscal expansion shifts the *ISC* outwards and fiscal contraction

shifts *ISC* inward and, for any given price level, raises or reduces income. Hence, a fiscal change shifts the *ADC* as shown.

Fig. 10.11 : From Short-run to Long-run Equilibrium (Page 162)

Figure 10.11(a) shows the three curves that are necessary to understand the short-run and long-run equilibrium. The short-run equilibrium of the economy is at K, where the *LMC* (P_1) intersects the ISC. Figure 10.11(b) shows the same situation for *AD* and *AS*. At price level P_1, the quantity of output demanded is below the full-employment level. We examine the short-run equilibrium at which the economy finds itself and the long-run equilibrium towards which the economy moves. Point *K* is the short-run equilibrium, where the price level is P_1. Eventually, the low demand for output causes the price to fall, which moves the economy towards the long-run full-employment level at *C*.

Fig. 10.12 : General Equilibrium with Flexible Wages (Page 164)

The *IS* and *LM* curves summarize the condition of equilibrium in the goods and money markets, respectively. The Y_F line shows the one level of output at which the labour market is in equilibrium.

Fig. 10.13 : Disequilibrium and Adjustment in the Economy (Page 164)

Two possible disequilibriums are shown in the diagram. With *IS* and *LM′* curves, the money and goods sectors are in equilibrium at *A* where the *AD* is at $Y_A > Y_F$ which will lead to a rise in prices. We can use our analysis to see how this rise in prices will affect the economy. The rise in prices has no effect on the *ISC* but the price-rise does affect equilibrium in the money market and will shift the *LMC* to the left. The rise in price will continue as long as there is excess demand which means as long as the *IS* and *LM* curves intersect to the right of *E*, when the real quantity of money is such that *LM′* coincides with *LM″* and all sectors will be in equilibrium again. Similarly, if the economy is at *B*, prices will fall and all sectors will be in equilibrium at *E* again.

Fig. 10.14 : Disequilibrium and its Implications (Page 166)

The top right quadrant gives all the sectors of the economy : the *IS*, *LM* and Y_F curves. The bottom right quadrant shows the production function relating output to employment and the bottom left quadrant represents the labour market. Two types of disequilibriums represented by point *B* depend on whether employment at *B* is L_B or L_F. If employment is L_F, the labour market is in equilibrium and output is Y_F. This means that $AD < Y_F$. All prices fall; given the nominal stock of money, the real quantity of money rises, thus leading to a fall in the interest rate and a rise in desired I. This will shift the LMC to the right and ultimately equilibrium will be reached again at E. If, however, employment is L_B and output Y_B, the point B represents equilibrium in the goods market where $AD = Y_B$, and disequilibrium in the labour market. The employment and output will increase until $AD = Y_F$.

Fig. 10.15 : Equilibrium with Flexible Wages (Page 167)

In the previous diagram, we have seen that price levels and wage rates play a crucial role in equilibrating the system. Changes in the price level produces equilibrium in the goods sector, changes in the wage rate produces equilibrium in the employment sector. Thus, wages and prices have to be flexible to be effective in equilibrating the system. They have to react to disequilibrium and the links by which changes in these two variables affect Y and AD have to be operative. If the disequilibrium in the goods market affects the price level but conditions in the money market are such that changes in the price level do not have any effect on the r and I, then the prevailing level will not have any effect on Y and AD. This situation will prival where money supply is perfectly elastic and, thus, LMC is horizontal, as in figure 10.15. With flexible wages, total output will always be Y_F. But if the AD is $Y_A > Y_F$, prices will start rising which may not be able to eliminate disequilibrium because the price rise has no effect on the employment sector as the employment sector is in equilibrium and, thus, output and employment remains unchanged. The rise in prices has no effect on AD; the LMC and r remain unchanged. Thus, even though the disequilibrium in the goods market results in changes in the price level, these changes cannot remove the disequilibrium because the condition in the money market is such that the link between the price level and AD has been broken.

Fig. 10.16 : Fixed Money Wage and Disequilibrium (Page 169)

We assume here that the wage rate is not flexible in a downwards direction which means that no labour will be supplied below some fixed money wage. In the figure, the demand for labour is still a function of real wage, whereas, the supply of labour is now different at a different level, because of the assumption of fixed money wages of W_0. When the price level is P_1 the real wage rate is $\frac{W_0}{P_1}$ and the maximum amount of labour supplied is $L^S{}_1$. Given the price level P_1, our present assumption means that no labour will be supplied below the real wage of $\frac{W_0}{P_1}$ and so on at price level P_2 and P_3.

Equilibrium in the labour market in which the money wage rate is fixed at W_0 and the price level P_1 and as in the figure, the real wage rate is $\frac{W_0}{P_1}$. At this real wage the quantity of labour demanded is $L^D{}_1$ and labour supplied is $L^S{}_1$. There is, thus, an excess supply of labour which has no effect on the wage rate and employment. For the given money wage of W_0 and price level P_1, the labour market is in equilibrium at $L^D{}_1$. Similarly at $L^D{}_2$ and $L^D{}_3$ and so on. Thus, employment becomes a function of the fixed money wage and the price level. Fig. 10.16(b) shows a production function and relating output to employment for various price levels and given money wage W_0. This is similar for other price levels.

Fig. 10.17 : General Equilibrium with a Fixed Money Wage (Page 170) The top right quadrant gives all sectors of the economy : the *IM*, *IS* and Y_F curves. The bottom right quadrant shows the production function relating output to employment and the bottom left quadrant represents the labour market with the real wage rate. Let us examine the situation at point *B* on the assumption that *LMC* passing through this point represents equilibrium in the money market for the price level P_B. Thus $AD = Y_B$. With the money wages fixed at *W* and the price level P_B, the real wage = $\frac{W^0}{P_B}$ and output and employment are equal to Y_B and L_B, respectively. Output is equal to *AD* and both the labour and goods sectors are in equilibrium. Now, suppose, that the *LMC* passing through *B* represents equilibrium in the money sector for the price level P_F, employment is L_F and output $Y_F > AD$. This will lead to a fall in prices, an increase in the real quantity of money, a fall in interest rate and, thus, increase in *AD*. However, the fall in prices also raises the real wage rate and, hence, employment and output fall. This process will continue as long as $Y > AD$ until point *C* is reached with the price level P_C where $AD = Y_C$ and all sectors are in equilibrium.

Fig. 10.18 : Price Level and Aggregate Demand *(AD)* (Page 172) The figure shows various equilibriums in the goods sector for a given *IS* curve and given quantity of nominal money M^0 at various price levels $P_1 > P_2 > P_3$. We can see the relationship between price level and *AD* in the bottom half of figure 10.18(b). The curve is drawn on the assumed conditions in the goods and the money sectors in Fig. 10.18(a). A shift in the *ISC* or the supply curve of nominal money will shift the *ADC*. The *ISC* and *LMC* for the price level P_3 are shown in the top half of Fig.10.18(b).

Fig. 10.19 : Price Level and Aggregate Supply *(AS)* (Page 172)

Figure 10.19 shows the relationship between the price level and *AS*. If the wage rate is flexible, employment is determined independently of the price level and *AS* is independent of the price level as well. If, however, the money wage is fixed, output and employment becomes a function of the price level as shown in the figure. In the bottom two quadrants the labour market and production are shown and the top left quadrant shows the relationship between the real wage rate and the price level for some money wage. Thus W^0 curve shows the relationship between the price level and the real wage when the money wage is fixed at W^0. Similarly, W' curve represents a money wage greater than W^0. We derive the relationship between *AS* and the price level in the top right quadrant.

Fig. 10.20 : Flexible Wages and Interaction Between Aggregate Demand and Aggregate Supply (Page 174)

Figure 10.20 shows the interaction between *AD* and *AS* for flexible wages. If wages are flexible the *AS* is represented by Y_FY_F curve and the *AD* by *AD* curve for the *ISC* shown and the quantity of nominal money M^0. Equilibrium is Y_F, P_F and r_F. If the quantity of money changes to $M^1 > M^0$, *AD* shifts to AD', the new equilibrium will be at Y_F, r_F and P'. Thus, the only effect of the change in the quantity of money is a change in the equilibrium price level.

Fig. 10.21 : Fixed Wages and Aggregate Demand and Aggregate Supply (Page 174)

With fixed wages *AS* curve is W_0Y_F and *AD* curve is AD_0, general equilibrium will be Y_0, P_0 and r_0. At any price level above P_0, $AS > AD$, and prices will fall, increasing *AD* via its effect on *r*, and decreasing *AS* via its effect on the wage rate; the opposite will occur at any price below P_0. If fixed money wage is W', the new equilibrium will be Y_1, P_1, r_1. The fixed money wage affect output and the prices level by interaction of *AD* and *AS*.

Fig. 10.22 : Equilibrium when the Link between Sectors are Broken (Page 175)

The figure examines the effect on equilibrium when the links between the monetary sector and the goods sector are broken, either because the *LMC* is perfectly elastic or because the *ISC* is perfectly inelastic. Both of these would lead to a perfectly inelastic *ADC*. The figure shows a situation in which the money sector is characterised by a perfectly elastic *LMC* as in Fig. 10.21. If we assume that the employment sector is one with flexible wages, the Y_FY_F curve is the one representing the output sector. With the *ADC* as *AD*, we see that AD at any price level is Y_1 and output at any price level is $Y_F > AD$, prices will fall without affecting any of the variables in the system and there is no way to achieve equilibrium in the system. If the AD cuts the Y-axis to the right of Y_FY_F, prices would start rising and continue to do so without affecting the system. If we assume a fixed money wage of W^0, the AS is shown by the curve W^0Y_F. With the ADC, AD equilibrium would be at price OP. At any price above OP_0, output is greater than AD, prices will fall, raising real wages and reducing employment and output. A rise of the fixed money wages to W' would raise the price level to P_1, leaving the real wage rate, output and employment unchanged. This is the situation in which price level can operate to equilibrate the economy.

Fig. 11.1 : Balanced Budget Multiplier (Page 186)

The figure represents the balanced budget multiplier. In the case of lumpsum tax, the slope of the consumption function remains unchanged, while the vertical intercept changes from OC to OA and equilibrium income from ON to OH. Thus, the balanced budget multiplier holds good for 1:1 expansion in income.

Fig. 11.2 : Balanced Budget Multiplier for Income Tax *(BBM)* (Page 187)

We assume that tax yield depends on income and we also assume linear proportional tax function : $T = t.Y$, where t is the rate of tax. The consumption function is assumed to be linear. In the case of income tax, the slope of the consumption function is changed but the intercept remains unchanged. We consider the effect of change in G, assuming that tax yield remains unchanged. Again, we assume that G remains unchanged and the tax yield changes. Thus, the effect of change in both T and G can be obtained by adding the separate effects of change in G and T, i.e., $\frac{dY}{dG} + \frac{dY}{dT} = \frac{1}{1-b} + \frac{-b}{(1-b)} = \frac{(1-b)}{(1-b)}$, where $dG = dT$. Hence, the BBM in the case of income is also as the figure shows. Tax rate is $\frac{N'H'}{ON'}$ where public expenditure is increased by $L'G' = M'L'$ which shifts the AD function to $D'E'$, whereas, the consumption expenditure remains unchanged at $M'N' = L'H'$. Thus, increase in income is equal to increase in government expenditure $N'H' = L'G' = M'L'$. The balanced budget multiplier for income tax is also obtained.

Fig. 11.3 : Government Budget in the *IS-LM* Model (Page 193)

The figure shows that the equilibrium income and interest rate are obtained by the equality between *IS* and *LM*. Since, *G* and *T* enter into the equation of the IS curve, the position of the *IS* curve will shift if *G* and *T* change. Thus, in our model, the tax expenditure policy of the government will change the equilibrium level of income and interest rate by affecting the *IS* curve.

Fig. 11.4 : Government Budget in the Liquidity Trap Situation (Page 193)
In a liquidity trap situation, the *LM* curve is horizontal. Now, if the *IS* curve cuts the horizontal part of the *LM* curve and *IS* curve shifts to the left or right, the national income will change, but the interest rate remains unchanged. If *G* increases (*T* remaining unchanged), the equilibrium level of income increases from Y_0 to Y_2, but the rate of interest remains the same.

Fig. 11.5 : Expansionary Effect of Government Budget (Page 195)
The expansionary effect of an increase in *G* financed by an equal amount of an increase in money supply will be higher than the expansionary effect of an increase in *G* financed by an equal increase in *T*, as Fig.11.5(a) and 11.5(b) show. In the first case, income increases from Y_0 to Y_1 and r_0 remains unchanged as in (a). But, in the second case, only the *ISC* shifts to the right by a small amount when the *LMC* remains unchanged. Thus, *Y* increase from Y_0 to Y_1 and *r* increases from r_0 to r_1, as in (b).

Fig. 11.6 : Fiscal Policy and Crowding-out Effects (Page 197)
When *G* increases the levels of income and interest rate increase. At unchanged *r*, increases in *G* increases the level of *AD*. To meet the increased demand, output must rise as shown by the shift in the *IS* schedule. At each rate of interest, equilibrium income must rise by multiplier times G. If the economy is initially in equilibrium at *E* as in Fig. 11.6 and *G* rises, we would move to E'' with unchanged *r*. At E'', goods market is in equilibrium where planned spending equals output. But the asset market is not in equilibrium. Since income has increased, the quantity of money demanded is higher. As there is excess demand for money, the interest rate rises. Firm's planned I spending declines at higher interest rates and, thus, *AD* decreases.

Fig. 11.7 : Crowding out in Two Extreme Cases : (a) Liquidity Trap Situation; (b) Classical Case (Page 199)
Fig.11.7(a) is the liquidity trap situation where the *LMC* is horizontal; an increase in *G* has its full multiplier effect on the equilibrium level of income. There is no change in the interest rate associated with ΔG, and hence no investment spending is crowded-out as in the figure where *LMC* is horizontal, monetary policy has no impact, whereas, the fiscal policy has full effect on the economy.

However, if the *LMC* is vertical, then an increase in *G* has no effect on the equilibrium level of income and it increases the interest rate only. If the demand for money is interest-inelastic, the *LMC* is vertical, there is a unique level of income at which the money market is in equilibrium. In this situation, there will be complete crowding-out.

Fig. 11.8 : Fiscal Expansion and Crowding-out Effect (Page 200)

To consider the possibility of crowding-out three points, must be made. The first point is that, if we consider an economy below full-employment and given prices, then fiscal expansion will increase output. But when we consider a fully-employed economy, crowding-out becomes a possibility because output cannot be increased. Second point is that in an economy with unemployed resources there cannot be fully crowding output because the *LMC* cannot be vertical. A fiscal expansion will raise interest rates and income. Crowding-out is thus a matter of degree.

The third point is that, with unemployment, interest rates may not rise at all when the fiscal expansion is accommodated by the monetary authority by increasing money supply so that interest rates cannot be increased. This accommodation policy is referred to as monitizing budget deficit which shifts the *IS* and *LM* curves to the right which increases income without increasing interest rates and, thus, private investment will not be adversely affected, as in the figure.

Fig. 11.9 : Effectiveness of Monetary Policy (Page 201)

Monetary policy will affect the position of the *LMC* through changes in money supply. An increase in the real money stock shifts the *LM* to LM_1 and the asset market adjusts immediately through decline in r from r_0 to r_1. The lower interest rates stimulate investment and other expenditures and increase income until a new equilibrium is reached at E_2. Thus, monetary policy is effective in increasing income and reducing interest rates. However, the effectiveness of monetary policy will depend on the point of intersection of the *ISC* with different range of the *LMC* as in Fig. 11.10.

Fig. 11.10 : Effectiveness of Fiscal Policy (Page 201)

Pure fiscal policy affects the *IS* with no effect on the *LMC* as Fig. 11.9 shows, when IS_0 shifts to IS_1 and LM_0 remains unchanged and both income and interest rates increase to Y_2 and r_2, respectively. In the Keynesian range, only fiscal policy is effective and in the classical range only monetary policy is effective and in the intermediate range both monetary and fiscal policy are effective.

Fig. 11.11 : Effectiveness of Fiscal Policy at Different Stages of the *LM* curve (Page 202)

The effectiveness of fiscal expansion will depend on the intersection of the *IS* and *LM* curves, as the three situations are explained in Fig. 11.11. If the IS'_0C intersects the *LMC*, the level of income rises by the full amount of the multiplier effect. The rate of interest remains unchanged and the fiscal policy is perfectly effective. If, however, *ISC* intersects the *LMC* in the classical range and *ISC* shifts from IS_2 to IS'_2, the level of income remains unchanged at Y_2 and the r increases from r_2 to r'_2. In this range, fiscal policy is ineffective. In the intermediate range, both policies are effective.

Fig. 12.1 : Simple Consumption Function (Page 210)

The Keynesian consumption function shows that real consumption is a function of real income which can be written as $C > C(Y)$. The straight line consumption function has a constant slope at all points. The consumption function, *PQ*, is a straight line and *OT* is a $45°$-line which intersects the consumption function from below at point *T*. The slope of the straight line consumption function is constant at all points and this is the *MPC*.

Fig. 12.2 : Consumption *(C)* and Saving *(S)* Functions together (Page 217)

PQ is the consumption function which intersects the $45°$-line at point A. By taking the vertical differences between the $45°$-line and consumption, we get the saving function, when $Y = 0$, consumption is equal to *OP*, and which means that saving is equal to $OP' (= - OP)$. When $Y = OB$, consumption equals income and hence $S = 0$. To the left of *B*, saving is negative as income is less than consumption and to the right of *B*, income is greater than consumption and, thus, *S* is positive. Therefore, we get the saving function $P'Q'$ from the consumption function *PQ*.

Fig. 12.3 : The Long-run Consumption and Saving Functions (Page 218)

The saving function is derived from the consumption function. If the consumption function is proportional, the saving function is also proportional. The proportional consumption function can be written as $C = bY$ and the proportional saving function can be written as $S = (1 - b)Y$. If consumption is proportional to income, the consumption function is a straight line passing through the origin. So will be the saving function. Thus, $APC = MPC$ and $APS = MPS$. Therefore, the long-run consumption and the saving function will be straight lines through the origin as shown.

Fig. 12.4 : Paradox of Thrift (Page 218)

It is an important factor to be considered in an economy. In the Keynesian model, national income is demand-determined. More saving means less spending and, thus, reduces, the aggregate (spending) demand. Less saving means more spending and this means an increase in *AD*.

If people's saving habits have changed and people become more thrifty than before, the result will be more saving at each level of *Y* which means that the saving function will shift to the left and its effect on equilibrium level of income and saving can be seen in Fig. 12.4.

Fig. 12.5 : Short-run and Long-run Consumption Function (Page 220)

When people decide how much to consume and save, they must consider both the present and the future. The more consumption today, the less they will be able to consume tomorrow. In making this trade-off, households must look ahead to their expected future income and the consumption of goods and services they could afford.

Fisher developed the model to analyze how rational, forward-looking consumers make intertemporal choices i.e. choices involving different periods of time. Fisher's model shows the constraint consumers face and how they choose *C* and *S*.

Fig. 12.6 : Budget Constraint (Page 222)

The figure shows the combinations of first-period and second-period consumptions that the consumer can choose. If he chooses more now, he will have less to consume in the next period and vice versa.

Fig. 12.7 : Consumer Preferences (Page 222)

A consumer's preferences in the two periods can be represented by the indifference curve *(IC)*. IC_1 shows combinations of two-periods consumptions that make him equally happy. IC_2 is preferred to IC_1. The consumer is equally happy at points *W, X, Y*, but prefers point *Z* to *W, X, Y* because *Z* is a higher *IC*.

Fig. 12.8 : Optimisation of Consumption (Page 222)

The figure shows that the consumer achieves the highest level of satisfaction by choosing a point *O* which is on the budget constraint and also on the highest *IC (i.e.,* IC_3*)*, where IC_3 is tangential to the budget constraint. At point *O*, $MRS = 1 + r$.

Fig. 12.9 : Change in Income Effect on Consumption (Page 223)

Increase in both periods consumption when the budget constraint shifts outward. If consumption in periods 1 and 2 are normal goods, this increase in income raises consumption in both periods.

Fig. 12.10 : Interest Rate Effect on Consumption (Page 223)

An increase in the interest rate tilts the budget constraint around the point (Y_1, Y_2). The figure shows the higher interest rate reduces first-period consumption and raises second-period consumption because of income and substitution effects. The income effect tends to make the consumer choose more consumption in both periods. But the substitution effect makes consumption in period two become less expensive relative to the consumption in period one when interest rates rise.

Fig. 12.11 : Borrowing Constraint and Consumer's Choice (Page 224)

The figure shows how this borrowing constraint restricts the consumer's set of choices. The consumer's choice must satisfy both the intertemporal budget constraint and the borrowing constraint. The area under the budget constraint represents the combinations of first and second-period consumptions.

Fig. 12.12 : Consumer's Optimum with a Borrowing Constraint (Page 225)

A borrowing constraint can impose two possible conditions. Fig. 12(a) shows that the consumer chooses first-period consumption to be less than first-period income, so that the borrowing constraint is not binding and does not affect consumption.

Fig. 12(b) shows when the borrowing constraint is binding. The consumer would like to borrow more and choose point *D*. If borrowing is not allowed, the best available choice is *E*.

Fig. 12.13 : The Life-cycle Consumption Function (Page 226)

This model shows that consumption depends on wealth, *W*, and also on income, *Y*. The intercept of consumption function, including wealth, is shown in Fig. 12.13, which holds only in short-periods when wealth is constant.

Fig. 12.14 : The Life-cycle Model to Predict Saving Behaviour (Page 227)

This life-cycle model predicts saving behaviour. If implies that saving varies over a person's life in a predictable way. It the consumer smooths consumption over his lifetime, he will save and accumulate wealth during his working life and then dis-save and may even run down his wealth during his retirement period.

Fig. 13.1 : The Equilibrium Price of Capital (Page 232)

Figure 13.1 shows the equilibrium in the rental market for capital. The MP_K determines the demand curve which is downward-sloping because the MP_K decreases as capital increases and, after a point, the amount of capital is fixed, so the supply curve is vertical. The real rental price of capital adjusts to equilibrate supply and demand.

Fig. 13.2 : Investment is a Function of Interest Rate (Page 234)
This model shows that there is an inverse relationship between interest rates and investment. The model also shows that the investment schedule shifts upward when the marginal productivity of capital increases from $I_1(r)$ to $I_2(r)$.

Fig. 13.3 : The Stock Equilibrium and Supply of Houses (Page 237)
Two aspects are shown in the model. First, the market for the existing stock of houses determines the equilibrium price for houses. Second, the price of houses determines the flow of residential investment. The relative price of housing, P_H/P, is determined by the demand and supply of the existing stock of housing as in Fig. (a). The relative price of housing determines the supply of new houses as in Fig. (b).

Fig. 13.4 : Change in Demand and Equilibrium Price of Houses (Page 238)
Fig. (a) shows that an expansionary shift in demand raises the equilibrium price of houses, which shows in Fig. (b) that the increase in housing price increases residential investment.

Fig. 13.5 : Marginal Efficiency of Capital (Page 243)
At point *A*, where $C = V$, the *MEC* is determined.

Fig. 13.6 : Profit-maximising Employment of Capital (Page 244)
MEC the schedule is downward-slopping and it can determine the optimum stock of capital. If the market interest rate is r_0, the firm would be able to maximise profit by employing K_0 units of capital goods where $MFC = r_0$. Similarly, at an interest rate of r_1, the profit-maximising employment of capital would be K_1 and so on. Thus, the *MEC* can give us the optimum stock of capital.

Fig. 13.7 : Supply Price of Capital is Determined by the Replacement Level of Investment (Page 246)
In calculating the *MEC* we assume that, the supply price of capital is constant and it is determined by the replacement level of investment. SS' is the supply price of capital. Ox is the amount of capital required for replacement and xy is the supply price for this level of capital stock.

Fig. 13.8 : Relationship between *MEC* & *MEI* (Page 247)
If net investment is positive, the amount of capital stock required is greater than Ox, as in Fig. 13.7 and, hence, the supply price is greater than xy. Further, the supply price would be different for

different levels of investment. However, the expected yields of the *MEI* is calculated on the assumption of the variability of supply price. The *MEI* will be different for different levels of investment. As the rate of investment increases, supply price increases and the *MEI* decreases. So, we can get the *MEI* schedule like the *MEC* schedule. While the *MEC* schedule refers to the stock of capital, the *MEI* schedule refers to the flow of investment. The relationship between them is shown in Fig. 13.8. If the market rate of r is Or_2, the optimum stock of capital is OK_m. Now if the actual stock of capital is $K_0 < K_m$, there is slope for more investment.

Fig. 13.9 : *MEI* Schedule (Page 248)

The figure shows the *MEI* schedule. The investment schedule can be obtained if we know the interest rate. If the interest rate is Or_0, the volume of investment would be OI_0 and the *MEI* is equal to the rate of interest. The rate of investment is determined by the *MEI* schedule and the optimum capital is determined by the *MFC* schedule.

Fig. 13.10 : Net Present Value Criterion of Investment (Page 249)

The yields and the cost of capital goods are taken as given. Hence, given the rate of discount or interest, we can determine the *NPV*. On the basis of this criterion, a project will be accepted if its *NPV* is positive. If the *NPV* of a project is negative, it would be rejected. Now, we assume that the rate of interest is constant at r_0. At this rate of interest, the *NPV* of different units of capital is calculated and has been ranked in descending value of *NPV*. The *NPV* is V_0I_0 when the rate of interest is r_0. If the rate of interest increases to r_1, the *NPV* for each project will be lower at a given price and yield.

Fig. 13.11 : Comparison between the *MEC* and the *NPV* Methods (Page 251)

A conflict may arise between the *MEC* and the *NPV* when ranking mutually exclusive projects as in the Fig. Suppose the two mutually exclusive projects x and y have their *NPV* of VV' and WW', respectively. Given the yields and the cost of the project, the *NPV* of any project is a function of the r. For different r_s we can have different NPV_s which give us the different *NPV* curves. The *NPV* curves are downward-sloping for conventional investments. The discount rates OP and OQ will give *NPV* of zero for x and y projects and also the *MEC* for these projects, respectively.

Fig. 14.1 : The Equilibrium Level of Income (Page 257)

The equilibrium income can be obtained graphically as in the

Keynesian model for income determination in a closed economy. Now the aggregate demand curve would be different for a closed economy. The aggregate demand is $C + I_0 + X_0 - m(Y)$ which intersects the $45°$-line gives the equilibrium at Y_0.

Fig. 14.2 : The Alternative Way to Express the Equilibrium Income (Page 257)
Withdrawal and injection will give us the same equilibrium as in previous figure $W = S + m = I + X = J$. The intersection between W and J gives the same equilibrium as the intersection between aggregate demand and the $45°$-line.

Fig. 14.3 : Equilibrium Income by Equating the Trade Difference and the Saving Investment Expenditure (Page 258)
The balance trade difference is a falling function of income and the saving-investment expenditure is a rising function of income. The intersection between them gives us the same equilibrium Y_0.

Fig. 14.4 : Balance of Payments and the Domestic Economy (Page 265)
Figure 14.4 shows the balance of payments equilibrium with or without capital inflows. Point Y_A shows that the balance of trade is in balance and net capital inflows are equal to zero. At any other points, balance of payments are in balance with positive or negative capital inflows.

Fig. 14.5 : Fixed Exchange Rate with or without some Capital Mobility (Page 267)
F_1F_1 = No Capital Mobility; F_0F_0 = Perfect Capital Mobility; F_2F_2 & F_3F_3 = Some Capital Mobility.

The figure shows that both the domestic and the balance of payments are in equilibrium with income Y^* and interest rate r^*. Any attempt to increase income will be frustrated and, ultimately, either the expansionary fiscal policy has to be reversed or some other policy to reduce income has to be undertaken. If the foreign currency flows are not stabilized, the deficit will cause an outflow of foreign currency and an automatic fall in the quantity of domestic money which will shift the *LMC* to the left until it intersects the $IS'C$ at a point *A*, where we have, again, domestic and balance of payments in equilibrium.

Figure shows the Balance of Payments and the Domestic Economy—In a Fixed Exchange Rate Regime, with Perfect Capital Mobility, with no Capital Mobility and with some Capital Mobility.

Fig. 14.6 : Fixed Exchange Rate with Perfect Capital Mobility (Page 269)

Figure 14.6 starts from initial domestic and *BOP* equilibrium at Y^* and $r = r_w$, with perfect capital mobility, where r_w is the world interest rate. An expansionary fiscal policy is now carried out which shifts the *ISC* to IS'. The domestic interest rate, r', is now above the world interest rate, r_w, which will cause massive capital inflows. To achieve *BOP* equilibrium at the higher income, Y_P, the *MS* will have to be increased until the $L'M'$ intersects $I'S'$ at r_w. This happens automatically with perfect capital mobility until $r^* = r_w$. Any attempt by the monetary authorities to change money supply without any associated changes in fiscal policy will result in capital outflows/ inflows, which, via their effect on money supply, will reverse the original change. Starting from Y^*, r_w, increased money supply will shift the *LMC* to $L'M'$ and the interest rate will fall to r'' as in Fig. 14.6. This will cause massive capital outflows until money supply falls back to its original level and r'' rises to r_w.

Fig. 14.7 : The Balance of Payments and the Domestic Economy with Flexible Exchange Rate (Page 271)

Equilibrium in the goods sector depends on the exchange rate, as Fig. 14.7(a) demonstrates. Three *IS* curves are shown for three exchange rates with one *LMC*. This shows that domestic equilibrium incomes and interest rates depend on the exchange rate. We, thus, derive the relationship between *AD* and exchange rate in *DD* curve in Fig. 14.7(b).

Fig. 14.8 : The *BOP* Equilibrium and Money Supply (Page 272)

Increased money supply is shown in the figure by a downward shift of the *BB* curve from *BB* to $B'B'$. Any change in monetary policy can be shown by shifts in the *LMC* which will also shift the *BB* curve. We, thus, have to hold the quantity of money constant along the *BB* curve.

Fig. 14.9 : The *BB* curve would be upward-sloping if the *FF* curve is flatterthan *LMC* (Page 272)

In case the *FF* curve is flatter than *LMC*, the *BB* curve, which is derived from the *FF* curve, will be upward-sloping. Thus, an increase in money supply will shift the *BB* curve to the right as $B'B'$.

Fig. 14.10 : The *BB* curve with Perfect Capital Mobility (Page 273)

In the case of perfect capital mobility, the *FF* curve is perfectly elastic. The *BB* curve with perfect capital mobility will be perfectly inelastic. An increase in money supply will shift the *BB* curve to the right from *BB* to $B'B'$.

Fig. 14.11 : Interactions between Domestic and *BOP* Equilibrium (Page 273)

Here we combine the domestic and *BOP* equilibrium for a downward-sloping *BB* curve. At point *A,* we have both domestic and *BOP* equilibrium with income Y^* and exchange rate e^*. *AD* for commodities, including exports, is equal to the *AS,* including imports, where the inflow of foreign currency is equal to outflow. At points *B* and *C,* the *BOP* and the domestic economy is in disequilibrium.

Fig. 14.12 : Expansionary Fiscal Policy — Flexible Exchange Rates (Page 274)

The figure shows an initial domestic and *BOP* equilibrium at Y^* and E^*. With *AD* curve, *DD.* Three *BB* curves are shown for three cases. An expansionary fiscal policy will shift the *DD* curve to $D'D'$. We now examine the effect of such a policy in the three cases. In the case of perfect capital mobility shown in B_1B_1, the expansionary fiscal policy has no effect on income, whereas, the exchange rate rises from E^* to E_1. Thus, fiscal policy is totally ineffective. With B_2B_2, the expansionary fiscal policy results in an increase in *Y* with a rise in exchange rate to E_2. With B_3B_3 curve there is an increase in *Y* with a fall in the exchange rate to E_3.

Fig. 14.13 : Effect of Monetary Policy: Flexible Exchange Rate (Page 274)

Fig. 14.13(a) shows the effect of monetary policy in the case of perfect capital mobility and Fig. 14.13(b) shows a downward-sloping *BB* curve. In both cases, we start from initial equilibrium at Y_0 and E_0. And in both cases, expansionary monetary policy increases *Y* and reduces the exchange rate, *E.*

Fig. 15.1 : The Mundell-Fleming Model on a *Y–E* Graph (Page 278)

The figure is drawn holding the interest rate constant at the world interest rate, Ir^*. The equilibrium of the economy is found by the intersection of IS^* and LM^* curves which determines the level of income and the exchange rate.

Fig. 15.2 : Net Exports Schedule combined with Keynesian Model (Page 279)

The IS^* curve slopes downward because a higher exchange rate lowers net exports and, thus, lowers aggregate income. Fig. 15.2(a) shows the net exports schedule: an increase in exchange rate lowers net exports. Fig. 15.2(b) shows the Keynesian Model : a decrease in net exports reduces income. Fig. 15.2(c) shows the IS^* curve which summarizes this inverse relationship between income and exchange rate.

Fig. 15.3 : Fiscal Policy in an Open Economy : Floating Exchange Rates (Page 280)

A government stimulates the economy by expansionary fiscal policy which shifts the IS^*_1 to IS^*_2. This policy increases the exchange rate, but the level of income remains unchanged. This is in stark contrast to the conclusion reached at by the closed economy, *IS-LM* model, where a fiscal expansion increases income. However, in an open economy with a flexible exchange rate, a fiscal expansion leaves income unchanged.

Fig. 15.4 : Effect of Monetary Policy in an Open Economy (Page 281)

An increase in the money supply in a fixed price level increases real balance and, thus, shifts the *LM** curve to the right which lowers the exchange rate and increases income. Although monetary policy increases income in a closed as well as in an open economy, the monetary transaction mechanism works differently.

Fig. 15.5 : Effect of Trade Policy on Income and Exchange Rate (Page 281)

A government may wish to reduce the demand for imports by imposing a quota or a tariff which would have an effect on the exchange rate without any effect on income. A reduction of imports will mean an increase in net exports which will shift the IS^*_1 to IS^*_2. Thus, a trade restriction raises the exchange rate and has no effect on income.

Fig. 15.6 : The Equilibrium Exchange Rate is greater than Fixed Exchange Rate (Page 282)

The figure shows that if the equilibrium exchange rate exceeds the fixed exchange rate, arbitrageurs will buy foreign currency in foreign exchange markets and sell it to the central bank for a profit. This process automatically increases the money supply and thereby shifts the *LM** curve to the right and lowers the exchange rate.

Fig. 15.7 : The Equilibrium Exchange Rate is less than Fixed Exchange Rate (Page 282)

The figure shows that if the equilibrium exchange rate is below the fixed exchange rate, arbitrageurs will buy pounds in foreign exchange market and use them to buy foreign currency from the central bank. This process automatically reduces the money supply and shift the *LM** curve to the left raising the exchange rate above the equilibrium rate.

Fig. 15.8 : Fiscal Policy and Fixed Exchange Rate (Page 284)

A fiscal expansion shifts the IS*C to the right and to maintain the fixed exchange rate, the Central Bank must increase money supply to shift the *LM*C* to the right as well, as shown. Thus, under a fixed exchange rate, fiscal policy is effective.

Fig. 15.9 : Monetary Policy and Fixed Exchange Rate (Page 284)

If the Central Bank increases money supply it will shift the *LM*C* to the right, lowering the exchange rate, as the figure shows. Since the central bank is commited to maintain a fixed exchange rate, arbitrageurs sell pounds to the Bank of England, causing the money supply to fall and the *LM*C* to return to its original position. Thus, monetary policy is ineffective under a fixed exchange rate.

Fig. 15.10 : Trade Policy Under Fixed Exchange Rate (Page 284)

A tariff or a quota reduces imports and shifts the net exports outwards and, hence, shifts the *IS*C* to the right as well. This will raise the exchange rate. To keep the exchange rate fixed, the money supply must rise which shifts the *LM*C* to the right. Under a fixed exchange rate, a trade restriction raises income and net exports, which also increases savings.

Fig. 15.11 : The Mundell-Fleming Model with a Change in Price Level (Page 286)

The figure shows what happens when the price level falls. As lower price levels imply a higher level of real balances, the *LM*C* shifts to the right. The real exchange rate depreciates and the equilibrium level of income rises. The negative relationship between the price level and the income level is shown in the *AD* curve in Fig.(b). Thus, the Mundell-Fleming Model is similar to that implied by the *IS-LM* Model.

Fig. 15.12 : The Short-run and Long-run Equilibrium (Page 287)

The short-run and long-run equilibrium, *IS** and *LM**, intersection at K shows equilibrium under the Keynesian assumption where the price level is fixed at P_1. At this equilibrium, the demand for goods and services is too low to keep the economy producing at its natural rate. The low demand causes the price to fall in the long-run which increases real money balances and, thus, shifts the *LMC* to the right. The real exchange rate depreciates, which stimulates net exports.

Fig. 16.1 : Short-run Trade-off between Inflation and Unemployment (Page 295)

The policymaker can manipulate *AD* to choose a combination of unemployment and inflation on the curve known as the short-run Phillips curve. The short-run Phillips curve depends on expected inflation. If expected inflation rises, the curve shifts upward, and the policy maker's trade-off becomes less favourable : inflation is higher for any level of unemployment. The curve is higher when expected inflation is higher.

Fig. 16.2 : Unemployment and Inflation (Page 297)

Here we start with an equilibrium of less than full-employment arising from a fixed money wage of W^0, price level P_0 and real income of Y_0. Now, suppose that the government has a policy of maintaining full-employment which it can do with some expansionary fiscal and monetary policy. This is shown in the diagram by the shift of the AD curve from AD to AD'. If this was the end of the story, the result of this policy would be to raise Y_0 to Y' and the price level to P' and to lower unemployment by some percentage. However, given the fixed money wages and the rise in prices induced by the government policy, there is a fall in real wages. If workers wish to maintain their real wage, they would raise their money wage to W'. The effect would be to raise the price level to P' and income to Y_0 and unemployment to what it was before. Under the circumstances, the government's attempt to maintain full-employment will end in continuous increase in prices and money wages, whereas, income and unemployment will remain unchanged.

Fig. 16.3 : Labour Market Equilibrium (Page 299)

The figure represents the labour markets with demand and supply of labour as a function of real wages, which is measured by a money wage divided by a price level, which, for the moment is assumed given. Assume that we have flexible money wages. At the real wage $W_f = \frac{W}{P}$, we have full-employment in the sense that there is no excess demand or supply of labour. However, this does not mean that there is no unemployment. Let us assume that unemployment is U_f.

Fig. 16.4 : Phillips Curve — Relationship between Unemployment and Inflation (Page 300)

In the figure, full-employment is represented by U_f, where there is no tendency for money wage to change, even though there is some unemployment which is known as natural rate of unemployment. Any level of unemployment less than U_f implies that money wages will rise because there is an excess demand for labour, and the rate at which they will rise depends on the excess demand for labour.

Fig. 16.5 : Unemployment and Inflation (Page 300)

We assume that there is a positive relationship between the change in money wages and a change in prices. We can then translate Fig. 16.4 into Fig. 16.5 where we measure the rate of change of price *(P)* on the vertical axis and unemployment on the horizontal axis. The government now wishes to maintain unemployment at $U' < U_f$. To do that, the government has to induce a rate of price change, P', which means that the government has a choice between two goals — inflation and unemployment.

Fig. 16.6 : Labour Market : Relationship between the Quantity of Labour Supplied and the Real Wage (Page 303)

Here the supply of labour is not the function of the current real wage, but the expected real wage. If the expected change in the real wage is zero, then the current real wage is the correct variable for the supply of labour. This is shown by the middle supply curve of labour where the expected rate of inflation is equal to the actual rate of inflation. At an initial equilibrium, in which the actual inflation rate is equal to the expected inflation rate, assume that both are zero (no inflation). The equilibrium in the labour market is at *A* where real wage is W_0 and employment is L_0 and there is a natural rate of unemployment at this full-employment level.

Fig. 16.7 : Phillips Curve : Short-run and Long-run (Page 303)

The figure measures the rate of change of prices on the vertical axis and unemployment on the horizontal axis. When the rate of ΔP is zero and expected rate is also zero, equilibrium in the labour market is at W_0, L_0 with unemployment at U_f, as in Fig. 16.7. Assuming that now prices start rising at the rate P' though people still expect inflation to be at zero. The workers receive higher money wages and mistakenly believe that they are receiving higher real wages. Labour market equilibrium is now at W_1L_1. Unemployment is smaller at U' as in Fig. 16.7. If change in prices and money wages is higher, say, P'', the unemployment will be smaller at U''. Thus, we get a downward-sloping Phillips curve. This Phillips curve has been on the assumption that expected inflation is zero. Now, assume that people begin to expect a positive rate of inflation and the difference between the expected and actual rate of inflation will decrease and eventually unemployment will start rising which is shown in the figure by the shifting of the Phillips curve. The vertical Phillips curve at U_f shows that the trade-off relationship has been broken, which is known as the long-run Phillips curve.

Fig. 16.8 : Expectation-adjusted Phillips Curve *(PC)* (Page 304)

The figure shows that expectation-adjusted *PC* gives some insight not only into the effect of inflation, but also into the effects of reducing inflation. In the figure we assume that there has been an ongoing inflation at the rate of P'' to which everyone has adjusted and the expected rate of inflation is also equal to P''. Now assume that the rate of inflation is reduced to P'. People expect the rate of inflation to remain at the higher level, so we move along the solid *PC*. Unemployment thus rises to U'. Only after expectations become adjusted to the lower inflation rates does the *PC* start shifting to the left, and unemployment starts falling. When full adjustment has taken place, unemployment will be back at U_f.

Fig. 16.9 : The Inflationary Gap Analysis (Page 310)

The figure shows the full-employed output of Y_0 which has been found by the interaction of *AD* and *45°* line and the price level is in equilibrium at this point. If the *AD* curve shifts, for some reason, to $C' + I' + G' + NX'$, an inflationary gap appears in the output market. The size of the inflationary gap is *AB* which measures the excess of the *AD* over the full-employment output and it is given by $C' + I' + G' + NX' - Y_0$. The money value of the real output will be at Y_m. This is done through the rise in the price level, as the real output is constant at full-employment level.

Fig. 16.10 : Bent Hansen's Model of Demand-Pull Inflation (Page 314)

Figure shows the positively-sloped *AD* curve and the vertical S_f line is the full-employment supply curve. When the full-employment supply curve passes through the point of intersection between the *AD* curve and the intended supply curve, there is equilibrium in both markets. Given the full-employment supply curve, the point of intersection between the *AD* curve and the *AS* curve may shift to the right of the S_f line, when conditions of disequilibrium are created in both markets. The rightward shift of the point of intersection is brought about by autonomously produced shift of the *AD* and *AS* curves. These autonomous shifts are the inflation-producing factors.

Fig. 16.11 : The Quantity Theory Approach to Inflation (Page 321)

The figure demonstrates that DD' is the demand for real money balance as a proportion of real income. The curve is downward-sloping, which means that the lower the rate of inflation, the greater is the demand for real balances relative to the real income. With zero inflation the ratio of real balances to real income is OD'. With the rate of inflation of *OP*, the demand for real balances fall to

OM, which is due to increase in the cost of holding real balances. The area $OMP'P$ represents the proportion of real income that people are obliged by inflation to accumulate in the form of money balances in order to keep the real balance intact.

Fig. 16.12 : Mark-up Inflation (Page 323)

Mark-up or income inflation is that, at full-employment, different groups of people attempt to improve or maintain their real income by raising their money incomes. If output cannot be increased to satisfy expectations, prices must rise and all groups of people experience some frustration. The process may continue so long as these groups try to improve their economic position to suit their monetary objectives. The process stops when all groups adapt to the new monetary arrangements which is shown in this figure. All combinations of price level and money income lie on the straight line OO' which represents the same real income. *OB* represents the fixed money claims of the rentier group and π and the *W* curves represent the claim of profit and wage recipients, respectively. $\pi + W + F$ represents total claim *(C)* which exceeds the total real income (Y_1P_1). This leads to a price rise. These conflicting claims are resolved by the rise in the price at (Y_2P_2).

Fig. 17.1 : Equilibrium of the Economy with Flexible Prices (Page 328)

The figure shows the natural rate of output, $\overline{Y}$, which is determined by the supply of inputs and the production function. The interest rate is determined by the intersection of the *ISC* and the natural rate of output, $\overline{Y}$. The price level adjusts, so that the *LMC* intersects the other two curves.

Fig. 17.2 : Relationship between the Real Aggregate Demand (AD) and Aggregate Supply *(AS)*) (Page 328)

The real aggregate demand curve for goods and services is a function of the interest rate and the real aggregate supply of goods and services is determined by the supply of factors of production and the availability of technology.

Fig. 17.3 : Real Business-cycle Model (Page 330)

The real aggregate supply curve slopes upwards rather than vertically, which means a higher interest rate makes working more attractive, which increases labour supply and, hence, output. The real interest rate adjusts to equilibrate real aggregate demand and supply. Any shock to the economy that shifts aggregate demand or aggregate supply changes equilibrium output and hence explains fluctuations.

Fig. 17.4 : Effect of Fiscal Policy in the Real Business-cycle (Page 331)

An increase in fiscal expansion shifts the *AD* curve rightward which results in higher output and higher real interest rate.

It may be noted here that there are similarities between this explanation of the effect of fiscal policy and the one we saw in the *IS-LM* model. An increase in government expenditure here shifts the real *ADC* outwards for the same reason as the shifts in the *ISC* in the *IS-LM* model. In both cases, the result is a higher interest rate and a higher output. Thus, the two models make similar predictions.

Fig. 17.5 : Two Effects of Technological Innovation (Page 332)

The figure shows two beneficial effects of technical improvement. A beneficial shock to technology raises both real aggregate demand and real aggregate supply. In Fig. (a), demand shifts more than supply and in Fig. (b), supply shifts more than demand.

Fig. 17.6 : Long-run Economic Fluctuations (Page 335

Figure 17.6 illustrates the different phases of the long-run business cycle, such as slump, recovery, boom and deflation in the economy.

Fig. 17.7 to 17.9 : Cyclical Movement in National Income, Investment and Consumption (Page 337)

The figures demonstrate what happens when the values of *v* and *c* lie below the curve. For example, if the values of *c* and *v* lie in the area *GHJ* (say $c = 0.5$ and $v = 0.5$) as at point *E,* then any exogenous change in consumption or investment will generate a damped cycle, as in Fig. 17.8, which means that the fluctuations in real output become smaller and smaller over time. But, on the other hand, if the values of *c* and *v* lie in the area *JHK* (i.e., $c = 0.5$ and $v = 1.5$ at point *F*) then, any exogenous change in spending will generate an explosive cycle such as that shown in Fig. 17.9.

Fig. 17.10 : Damped Cyclical Variation (Page 339)

So far we have seen that an autonomous increase in investment of £10 has caused income to rise from £1,000 to £1,025 in the first 4 time periods and then start to fall in the fifth. Taking the little time-path to period $t + 10$, we obtain a clearly damped cyclical variation in real national income as summarised in Fig.17.10.

Fig. 17.11 : An Explosive Cycle (Page340)

The figure shows that *I* and *Y* have already risen above the levels reached in the previous example, as given in the favour. An explosive cyclical variation in *Y* results.

Fig. 17.12 : Ceilings and Floors (Page 341)

The cycle here will generate a constant amplitude determined by the ceiling and floor. Such a cyclical movement in real output is given in this figure. Movements like this will develop from point A which may be identified as a recovery phase, consequently demand is increasing, output is expanding and unemployment is falling. In terms of the multiplier-accelerator intersecting, raising *I* will cause *Y* to rise via multiplier effect and the rising level of *Y* induces more *I* to occur via the accelerator. Soon full-employment will be reached at a point which determines the ceiling as real output can only rise as new investment comes into operation. Firms may be interested to produce more at point *B* but are unable to do so, because of insufficient resources. This checks the growth of output which will soon affect the firms' *I*-plan via the accelerator.

Fig. 17.13 : Random Disturbance (Page 342)

The existence of a ceiling and floor can help to explain the regularity of cycles, but without *c* and *v* constraints the cycles could be explosive.

Fig. 18.1 : The Classical Theory of Growth (Page 345)

The dynamics of growth ends as the law of diminishing returns sets in and wages eat up the whole production leaving no surplus for accumulation, expanstion and growth. The dynamics of growth ends at *E*. The vertical axis measures total product and the horizontal axis measures labour, and *OW* is a subsistence wage line. With ON_1 population, *OP* production wages per unit is N_1W_1 and surplus is W_1E_1.

Fig. 18.2 : Fixed Proportion Production Function (Page 351)

The figure shows increased capital and labour from OK_1 and OL_1 to OK_2 and OL_2 increased output from Q_1 to Q_2 (from *A* to *B*). Increasing only one of the factors would keep output unchanged (from *A* to *C*).

Fig. 18.3 : Equilibrium Output Changes with Investment (Page 351)

We start from equilibrium *A* and initial investment I_1 which is equal to *S* at the income level OY_1. Over time the investment adds to the capital stock and so increases the economy's potential output, say, to OY_2.

Fig. 18.4 : Production Function with some Factor Substitution (Page 353)

It is more realistic to assume that there is some substitution between labour and capital. If there is some factor substitution, the isoquant map will have a more familiar shape, as in this figure. Now it is possible to increase output from Q_1 to Q_2 by increasing the capital stock from OK_1 to OK_2, keeping labour force unchanged, or by increasing the labour force from OL_1 to OL_2, keeping capital stock unchanged.

Fig. 18.5 : Production Function (Page 356)

Production function with constant returns to scale are convenient, because output per worker depends only on the amount of capital per worker. The slope of this production function shows how much extra output per worker is produced from one extra unit of capital per worker. This is the MP_K. The production function becomes flatter as k increases, indicating deminishing MP_K.

Fig. 18.6 : Output, Consumption and Investment (Page 357)

The figure shows how the saving rates determines the allocation of output between consumption (c) and investment (i) for every value of k.

Fig. 18.7 : Depreciation (Page 357)

The figure shows that depreciation depends on the capital stock where the rate of depreciation is δk.

Fig. 18.8 : Investment, Depreciation and the Steady State (Page 358)

Since S is constant and $S = I = sf(k)$, and the amount of depreciation is δk. The steady-state level of capital k^* is the level at which $\delta = sf(k)$. At k^*, the two curve cross as in figure. Below k^*, $sf(k) > \delta$, so capital stock grows and abovek^*, $\delta > sf(k)$, so the capital stock shrinks.

Fig. 18.9 : Change in Saving Rate (Page 359)

An increase in saving implies that the amount of investment for any given stock of capital is higher. It has shifted the saving function upward. At the old steady state, investment is greater than δL, the capital stock rises until the economy reaches a new steady state with more capital and output.

Fig. 18.10 : Steady-State Consumption (Page 361)

The figure shows steady-state output and depreciation as a function of the steady-state capital stock. Steady-state c^* is the gap between output of $f(k^*)$ and depreciation δk. The figure shows that there is one level of capital stock, the Golden Rule level k^* gold, that maximises consumption.

Fig. 18.11 : The Saving Rate and the Golden Rule (Page 361)

The Figure shows that there is one saving rate that produces the Golden Rule level of capital k^* gold. A change in the saving rate would shift the $sf(k)$ curve, which would move the economy to a steady-state with a lower level of consumption.

Fig. 18.12 : The Saving Rate is Reduced (Page 362)

The figure shows what happens over time to output, consumption and investment when economy begins with more capital than the Golden Rule as the investment saving rate is reduced. This reduction in saving rate (t_0) causes an immediate increase in consumption and equal decrease in investment.

Fig. 18.13 : The Saving Rate is Increased (Page 362)

The figure shows what happens to output, consumption and investment over time when the economy begins with less capital than the Golden Rule, and the saving rate is increased. This increase in saving rate, causes immediate decrease in consumption and equal increase in i.

Fig. 18.14 : The Steady-State Capital per Worker (Page 364)

The figure shows that if $k^* > k$, investment is greater then break-even investment, so k^* rises. If $k^* < k$, investment is less then break-even investment, so k falls. Thus, $k^* \quad \Delta k = 0$ and $i = \delta k^* + nk^*$. Once the economy is in the steady-state, i has two purposes—to replace the depreciated K, and to provide the new workers with the steady-state amount of capital.

Fig. 18.15 : Effect of Population Growth (Page 365)

An increase in the rate of population growth reduces the steady-state level of capital per worker.

Fig. 18.16 : Steady-State with Technical Progress (Page 366)

The figure shows that the inclusion of technological progress does not substantially alter our analysis of the steady-state. There is one level of k, denoted by k^*, at which output per efficiency unit and capital per efficiency unit are constant. The steady-state is the long-run equilibrium of the economy.

Fig. 19.1 : A Debt-Financed Tax Cut (Page 375)

The cut in taxes in period one affects the consumer under the assumption that it does not alter expenditure in either period. In period one, the government cuts taxes by ΔT, and finances this by borrowing. In period two, the government must raise taxes by $(1 + r)\,\Delta T$ to repay its debt together with interest. Thus, the change in fiscal policy raises the consumer's income by ΔT in period one and reduces it by $(1 + r)\,\Delta T$ in period two.

Glossary

Accelerator model : The model according to which investment depends on the change in output.

Accommodating policy : A policy that yields to the effect of a shock and thereby prevents the shock from being disruptive; for example, a policy that raises aggregate demand in response to an adverse supply shock, sustaining the effect of the shock on prices and keeping output at the natural rate.

Accounting profit : The amount of revenue remaining for the owners of a firm after all the factors of production except capital have been compensated. (Cf. economic profit, profit.)

Acyclical : Moving in no consistent direction over the business cycle. (Cf. countercyclical, procyclical.)

Adaptive expectations : An approach that assumes that people form their expectation of a variable based on recently observed values of the variable. (Cf. rational expectations.)

Adverse Selection : An unfavourable sorting of individuals by their own choices; for example, in efficiency-wage theory, when a wage cut induces good workers to quit and bad workers to remain with the firm.

Aggregate : Total for the whole economy.

Aggregate demand curve : The negative relationship between the price level and the aggregate quantity of output demanded that arises from the interaction between the goods market and the money market.

Aggregate demand externality : The macro-economic impact of one firm's price adjustment on the demand for all other firms' products.

Aggregate supply curve : The relationship between the price level and the aggregate quantity of output firms produce.

Animal spirits : Exogenous and perhaps self-fulfilling waves of optimism and pessimism about the state of the economy which, according to some economists, influence the level of investment.

Appreciation : A rise in the value of a currency relative to other currencies in the market for foreign exchange. (Cf. depreciation.)

Arbitrage : The act of buying an item in one market and selling it at a higher price in another market in order to profit from the price differential in the two markets.

Automatic stabilizer : A policy that reduces the amplitude of economic fluctuations without regular and deliberate changes in economic policy; for example, an income tax system which automatically reduces taxes when income falls.

Average propensity to consume *(APC)* : The ratio of consumption to income(C/Y).

Balance sheet : An accounting statement that shows assets and liabilities.

Balanced budget : A budget in which receipts equal expenditures.

Baumol-Tobin model : A model of money demand positing that people choose optimal money holdings by comparing the opportunity cost of the forgone interest from holding money and the benefit of making less frequent trips to the bank.

Bond : A document representing an interest bearing debt of the issuer, usually a corporation or the government.

Borrowing constraint : A restriction on the amount a person can borrow from financial institutions, limiting that person's ability to spend his or her future income today; also called a liquidity constraint.

Budget constraint : The limit that income places on expenditure. (Cf. intertemporal budget constraint.)

Budget deficit : A shortfall of receipts from expenditure.

Budget surplus : An excess of receipts over expenditure.

Business cycle : Economy-wide fluctuations in output, incomes, and employment.

Business fixed investment : Equipment and structures that businesses buy for use in future production.

Capital : 1. The stock of equipment and structures used in production. 2. The funds to finance the accumulation of equipment and structures.

Capital budgeting : An accounting procedure that measures both assets and liabilities.

Central Bank : The institution responsible for the conduct of monetary policy, such as the Federal Reserve in the United States.

Classical dichotomy : The theoretical separation of real and nominal variables in the classical model, which implies that nominal variables do not influence real variables. (Cf. neutrality of money.)

Classical model : A model of the economy derived from the ideas of the classical, or pre-Keynesian economists; a model based on the assumptions that wages and prices adjust to clear markets and that monetary policy does not influence real variables. (Cf. Keynesian model).

Closed economy : An economy that does not engage in international trade. (Cf. open economy.)

Cobb-Douglas production function: A production function of the form $F(K, L) = AK^{\alpha}L^{1-\alpha}$,where K is capital, L is labour, and A and α are parameters.

Commodity money : Money that is intrinsically useful and would be valued even if it did not serve as money. (Cf. fiat money, money.)

Competition : A situation in which there are many individuals or firms so that the actions of any one of them do not influence market prices.

Constant returns to scale : A property of a production function whereby a proportionate increase in all factors of production leads to an increase in output of the same proportion.

Consumer price index (CPI) : A measure of the overall level of prices that shows the cost of a fixed basket of consumer goods relative to the cost of the same basket in a base year.

Consumption : Goods and services purchased by consumers.

Consumption function : A relationship showing the determinants of consumption; for example, a relationship between consumption and disposable income, $C = C(Y - T)$.

Contractionary policy : Policy that reduces aggregate demand, real income, and employment. (Cf. expansionary policy).

Coordination failure : A situation in which decision-makers reach an outcome that is inferior for all of them because of their inability to jointly choose strategies that would result in a preferred outcome.

Corporate income tax : The tax levied on the accounting profit of corporations.

Cost of capital : The amount forgone by holding a unit of capital for one period, including interest, depreciation, and the gain or loss from the change in the price of capital.

Cost-push inflation : Inflation resulting from shocks to aggregate supply. (Cf. demand-pull inflation.)

Countercyclical : Moving in the opposite direction from output, incomes, and employment over the business cycle; rising during recessions and falling during recoveries. (Cf. acyclical, procyclical.)

CPI : *See* consumer price index.

Crowding out : The reduction in investment that results when expansionary fiscal policy raises the interest rate.

Currency : The sum of outstanding paper money and coins.

Cyclical unemployment : The employment associated with short-run economic fluctuations; the deviation of the unemployment rate from the natural rate.

Debt-deflation : A theory according to which an unexpected fall in the price level redistributes real wealth from debtors to creditors and, therefore, reduces total spending in the economy.

Deflation : A decrease in the overall level of prices. (Cf. disinflation, inflation.)

Deflator : *See GDP* deflator.

Demand deposits : Assets that are held in banks and can be used on demand to make transactions, such as checking accounts.

Demand-pull inflation : Inflation resulting from shocks to aggregate demand. (Cf. cost-push inflation.)

Depreciation : 1. The reduction in the capital stock that occurs over time because of aging and use. 2. A fall in the value of a currency relative to other currencies in the market for foreign exchange. (Cf. appreciation.)

Depression : A very severe recession.

Devaluation : An action by the central bank to decrease the value of a currency under a system of fixed exchange rates. (Cf. revaluation).

Diminishing marginal product : A characteristic of a production function whereby the marginal product of a factor falls as the amount of the factor increases while all other factors are held constant.

Discount rate : The interest rate that the Fed. charges when it makes loans to banks.

Discounting : The reduction in value of future expenditure and receipts, compared to current expenditure and receipts, resulting from the presence of a positive interest rate.

Discouraged workers : Individuals who have left the labour force because they believe that there is little hope of finding a job.

Disinflation : A reduction in the rate at which prices are rising. (Cf. deflation, inflation.)

Disposable income : Income remaining after the payment of taxes.

Dominated asset : An asset that offers an inferior return compared to another asset in all possible realizations of future uncertainty.

Double coincidence of wants : A situation in which two individuals each have precisely the good that the other wants.

Economic profit : The amount of revenue remaining for the owners of a firm after all the factors of production have been compensated. (Cf. accounting profit, profit.)

Efficiency of labor : A variable in the Solow growth model that measures the health, education, skills, and knowledge of the labor force.

Efficiency units of labor : A measure of the labor force that incorporates both the number of workers and the efficiency of each worker.

Efficiency-wage theories : Theories of real-wage rigidity and unemployment according to which firms raise labor productivity and profits by keeping real wages above the equilibrium level.

Elasticity : The percent change in a variable caused by a 1 percent change in another variable.

Endogenous variable : A variable that is explained by a particular model; a variable whose value is determined by the model's solution. (Cf. exogenous variable.)

Equilibrium : A state of balance between opposing forces, such as the balance of supply and demand in a market.

Euler's theorem : The mathematical result economists use to show that economic profit must be zero if the production function has constant returns to scale and if factors are paid their marginal products.

Ex ante real interest rate : The real interest rate anticipated when a loan is made; the nominal interest rate minus expected inflation. (Cf. ex post real interest rate.)

Ex post real interest rate : The real interest rate actually realized; the nominal interest rate minus actual inflation. (Cf. ex ante real interest rate.)

Excess reserves : Reserves held by banks above the amount mandated by reserve requirements.

Exchange rate : The rate at which a country makes exchanges in world markets. (Cf. nominal exchange rate, real exchange rate.)

Exchange-rate union : A group of countries that agree to limit exchange-rate fluctuations among their currencies.

Exogenous variable : A variable that a particular model takes as given; a variable whose value is independent of the model's solution. (Cf. endogenous variable.)

Expansionary policy : Policy that raises aggregate demand, real income, and employment. (Cf. contractionary policy.)

Exports : Goods and services sold to other countries.

Factor of production : An input used to produce goods and services; for example, capital or labor.

Factor price : The amount paid for one unit of a factor of production.

Factor share : The proportion of total income being paid to a factor of production.

Federal Reserve (the Fed.) : The central bank of the United States.

Fiat money : Money that is not intrinsically useful and is valued only because it is used as money. (Cf. commodity money, money.)

Financial intermediation : The process by which resources are allocated from those individuals who wish to save some of their income for future consumption to those individuals and firms who wish to borrow to buy investment goods for future production.

Financing constraint : A limit on the quantity of funds a firm can raise—such as through borrowing—in order to buy capital.

Fiscal policy : The government's choice regarding levels of spending and taxation.

Fisher effect : The one-for-one influence of expected inflation on the nominal interest rate.

Fisher equation : The equation stating that the nominal interest rate is the sum of the real interest rate and expected inflation ($i = r + \pi^e$).

Fixed exchange rate : An exchange rate that is set by the central bank's willingness to buy and sell the domestic currency for foreign currencies at a predetermined price. (Cf. floating exchange rate.)

Flexible prices : Prices that adjust quickly to equilibrate supply and demand. (Cf. sticky prices.)

Floating exchange rate : An exchange rate that the central bank allows to change in response to changing economic conditions and economic policies. (Cf. fixed exchange rate.)

Flow : A variable measured as a quantity per unit of time. (Cf. stock.)

Fractional-reserve banking : A system in which banks keep only some of their deposits on reserve. (Cf. 100-percent-reserve banking.)

Frictional unemployment : The unemployment that results because it takes time for workers to search for the jobs that best suit their skills and tastes. (Cf. wait unemployment.)

GDP : *See* gross domestic product.

GDP deflator : The ratio of nominal *GDP* to real *GDP*; a measure of the overall level of prices that shows the cost of the currently produced basket of goods relative to the cost of that basket in a base year.

General equilibrium : The simultaneous equilibrium of all the markets in the economy.

GNP : See gross national product.

Gold standard : A monetary system in which gold serves as money or in which all money is convertible into gold.

Golden rule : The saving rate in the Solow growth model that leads to the steady state in which consumption per worker (or consumption per efficiency unit of labor) is maximized.

Government purchases : Goods and services bought by the government. (Cf. transfer payments.)

Government-purchases multiplier: The change in aggregate income resulting from a one-dollar change in government purchases.

Gross domestic product (GDP) : The total income earned domestically, including the income earned by foreign-owned factors of production; the total expenditure on domestically produced goods and services.

Gross national product (GNP) : The total income of all residents of a nation, including the income from factors of production used abroad; the total expenditure on the nation's output of goods and services.

High-powered money : The sum of currency and bank reserves: also called the monetary base.

Hyperinflation : Extremely high inflation.

Hysteresis : The long-lasting influence of history, such as on the natural rate of unemployment.

Identification problem : The difficulty of isolating a particular relationship in data when two or more variables are related in more than one way.

Imperfect-information model : The model of aggregate supply emphasizing that individuals do not always know the overall price level because they cannot observe the prices of all goods and services in the economy.

Import quota : A legal limit on the amount of a good that can be imported.

Imports : Goods and services bought from other countries.

Imputed value : An estimate of the value of a good or service that is not sold in the market place and therefore does not have a market price.

Income effect : The change in consumption of a good resulting from a movement to a higher or lower indifference curve, holding the relative price constant. (Cf. substitution effect.)

Index of leading indicators : *See* leading indicators.

Indifference curves : A graphical representation of preferences that shows different combinations of goods producing the same level of satisfaction.

Inflation : An increase in the overall level of prices. (Cf. deflation, disinflation.)

Inflation tax : The revenue raised by the government through the creation of money; seigniorage.

Inside lag : The time between a shock hitting the economy and the policy action taken to respond to the shock. (Cf. outside lag.)

Insiders : Workers who are already employed and therefore have an influence on wage bargaining. (Cf. outsiders).

Interest rate : The market price at which resources are transferred between the present and the future; the return to saving and the cost of borrowing.

Intermediation : *See* financial intermediation.

Intertemporal budget constraint : The budget constraint applying to expenditure and income in more than one period of time. (Cf. budget constraint.)

Intertemporal substitution of labor: The willingness of people to trade off working in one period for working in future periods.

Inventory investment : The change in the quantity of goods that firms hold in storage, including materials and supplies, work in process, and finished goods.

Investment : Goods purchased by individuals and firms to add to their stock of capital.

Investment tax credit : A provision of the corporate income tax that reduces a firm's tax when it buys new capital goods.

IS curve : The negative relationship between the interest rate and the level of income that arises in the market for goods and services. (Cf. *IS-LM* model, *LM* curve.)

IS-LM model : A model of aggregate demand that shows what determines aggregate income for a given price level by analyzing the interaction between the goods market and the money market. (Cf. IS curve, LM curve.)

Keynesian cross : A simple model of income determination, based on the ideas in Keynes's General Theory, which shows how changes in spending can have a multiplied effect on aggregate income.

Keynesian model : A model derived from the ideas of Keynes's General Theory; a model based on the assumptions that wages and prices do not adjust to clear markets and that aggregate demand determines the economy's output and employment. (Cf. classical model.)

Labor-augmenting technological progress : Advances in productive capability that raise the efficiency of labor.

Labor force : Those in the population who have a job or are looking for a job.

Labor-force participation rate : The percent of the adult population in the labor force.

Labor hoarding : The phenomenon of firms employing workers whom they do not need when the demand for their products is low, so that they will still have these workers when demand recovers.

Large open economy : An open economy that can influence its domestic interest rate; an economy that, by virtue of its size, can have a substantial impact on world markets and, in particular, on the world interest rate. (Cf. small open economy.)

Laspeyres price index : A measure of the level of prices based on a fixed basket of goods. (Cf. Paasche price index.)

Leading indicators : Economic variables that fluctuate in advance of the economy's output and thus signal the direction of economic fluctuations.

Life-cycle hypothesis : The theory of consumption that emphasizes the role of saving and borrowing as transferring resources from those times in life when income is high to those times in life when income is low, such as from working years to retirement.

Liquid : Readily convertible into the medium of exchange; easily used to make transactions.

Liquidity constraint : A restriction on the amount a person can borrow from a financial institution, which limits and person's ability to spend his future income today; also called a borrowing constraint.

Liquidity-preference theory : A simple model of the interest rate, based on the ideas in Keynes's General Theory, which says that the interest rate adjusts to equilibrate the supply and demand for real money balances.

LM curve : The positive relationship between the interest rate and the level of income (while holding the price level fixed) that arises in the market for real money balances. (Cf. *IS-LM* model, *IS* curve.)

Loanable funds : The flow of resources available to finance capital accumulation.

Lucas critique : The argument that traditional policy analysis does not adequately take into account the impact of policy changes on people's expectations.

M1, M2, M3 : Various measures of the stock of money, where larger numbers signify a broader definition of money.

Macroeconometric model : A model that uses data and statistical techniques to describe the economy quantitatively, rather than just qualitatively.

Macroeconomics : The study of the economy as a whole. (Cf. microeconomics.)

Marginal product of capital (MPK): The amount of extra output produced when the capital input is increased by one unit.

Marginal product of labor (MPL): The amount of extra output produced when the labor input is increased by one unit.

Marginal propensity to consume (MPC) : The increase in consumption resulting from a one-dollar increase in disposable income.

Marginal rate of substitution (MRS): The rate at which a consumer is willing to give up some of one good in exchange for more of another; the slope of the indifference curve.

Market-clearing model : A model that assumes that prices freely adjust to equilibrate supply and demand.

Medium of exchange: The item widely accepted in transactions for goods and services; one of the functions of money. (Cf. store of value, unit of account.)

Menu cost : The cost of changing a price.

Microeconomics : The study of individual markets and decisionmakers. (Cf. macroeconomics.)

Model : A simplified representation of reality, often using diagrams or equations, that show how variables interact.

Monetarism : The doctrine according to which changes in the money supply are the primary cause of economic fluctuations, implying that a stable money supply would lead to a stable economy.

Monetary base : The sum of currency and bank reserves; also called high-powered money.

Monetary neutrality : *See* neutrality of money.

Monetary policy : The central bank's choice regarding the supply of money.

Monetary transmission mechanism: The process by which changes in the money supply influence the amount that households and firms wish to spend on goods and services.

Money : The stock of assets used for transactions. (Cf. commodity money, fiat money.)

Money demand function : A function showing the determinants of the demand for real money balances; for example, $(M/P)^d = L(i, Y)$.

Money multiplier : The increase in the money supply resulting from a one-dollar increase in the monetary base.

Moral hazard : The possibility of dishonest behaviour in situations in which behavior is imperfectly monitored; for example, in efficiency-wage theory, the possibility that low-wage workers may shirk their responsibilities and risk getting caught and fired.

Multiplier : *See* government-purchases multiplier, money multiplier, or tax multiplier.

Mundell-Fleming model : The *IS-LM* model for a small open economy.

Mundell-Tobin effect : The fall in the real interest rate that results when an increase in expected inflation raises the nominal interest rate, lowers real money balances and real wealth, and thereby reduces consumption and raises saving.

National income accounting : The accounting system that measures *GDP* and many other related statistics.

National income accounts identity: The equation showing that *GDP* is the sum of consumption, investment, government purchases, and net exports.

National saving : A nation's income minus consumption and government purchases; the sum of private and public saving.

Natural rate of unemployment : The steady-state rate of unemployment; the rate of unemployment toward which the economy gravitates in the long run.

Natural-rate hypothesis : The premise that fluctuations in aggregate demand influence output, employment, and unemployment only in the short run, and that in the long run these variables return to the levels implied by the classical model.

Near Money : Assets that are almost as useful as money for engaging in transactions and, therefore, are close substitutes for money.

Neoclassical model of investment: The theory according to which investment depends on the deviation of the marginal product of capital from the cost of capital.

Net exports : Exports minus imports.

Net foreign investment : The net flow of funds being invested abroad; domestic saving minus domestic investment.

Net investment : The amount of investment after the replacement of depreciated capital; the change in the capital stock.

Neutrality of money : The property that a change in the money supply does not influence real variables. (Cf. classical dichotomy.)

New classical economics : The school of thought according to which economic fluctuations can be explained while maintaining the assumptions of the classical model. (Cf. new Keynesian economics.)

New Keynesian economics : The school of thought according to which economic fluctuations can be explained only by admitting a role for some microeconomic imperfection, such as sticky wages or prices. (Cf. new classical economics.)

Nominal : Measured in current dollars; not adjusted for inflation. (Cf. real.)

Nominal exchange rate : The rate at which one country's currency trades for another country's currency. (Cf. exchange rate, real exchange rate.)

Nominal interest rate : The return to saving and the cost of borrowing without adjustment for inflation. (Cf. real interest rate.)

Normal good : A good that a consumer demands in greater quantity when his or her income rises.

Okun's law : The negative relationship between unemployment and real *GDP*, according to which a decrease in unemployment of one percentage point is associated with additional growth in real *GDP* of approximately two percent.

100-percent-reserve banking : A system in which banks keep all deposits on reserve. (Cf. fractional-reserve banking.)

Open economy : An economy in which people can freely engage in international trade in goods and capital. (Cf. closed economy.)

Open-market operations : The purchase or sale of government bonds by the central bank for the purpose of increasing or decreasing the money supply.

Outside lag: The time between a policy action and its influence on the economy. (Cf. inside lag.)

Outsiders: Workers who are not employed and therefore have no influence on wage bargaining. (Cf. insiders.)

Paasche price index : A measure of the level of prices based on a changing basket of goods. (Cf. Laspeyres price index.)

Permanent income : Income that people expect to persist into the future; normal income. (Cf. transitory income.)

Permanent-income hypothesis : The theory of consumption according to which people choose consumption based on their permanent income, and use saving and borrowing to smooth consumption in response to transitory variations in income.

Phillips curve : A negative relationship between inflation and unemployment; in its modern form, a relationship among inflation, cyclical unemployment, expected inflation, and supply shocks, derived from the short-run aggregate supply curve.

Pigou effect : The increase in consumer spending that results when a fall in the price level raises real money balances and, thereby, consumers' wealth.

Political business cycle : The fluctuations in output and employment resulting from the manipulation of the economy for electoral gain.

Portfolio theories of money demand : Theories that explain how much money people choose to hold and that stress the role of money as a store of value. (Cf. transactions theories of money demand.)

Precautionary saving : The extra saving that results from uncertainty regarding, for example, longevity or future income.

Present value : The amount today that is equivalent to an amount to be received in the future, taking into account the interest that could be earned over the interval of time.

Private saving : Disposable income minus consumption.

Procyclical : Moving in the same direction as output, incomes, and employment over the business cycle; falling during recessions and rising during recoveries. (Cf. acyclical, counter-cyclical.)

Production function : The mathematical relationship showing how the quantities of the factors of production determine the quantity of goods and services produced; for example, $Y = F(K, L)$.

Production smoothing : The motive for holding inventories according to which a firm can reduce its costs by keeping the amount of output it produces steady and allowing its stock of inventories to respond to fluctuating sales.

Profit : The income of firm's owners: firm revenue minus firm costs. (Cf. accounting profit, economic profit.)

Public saving: Government receipts minus government spending; the budget surplus.

Purchasing-power parity : The doctrine according to which goods must sell for the same price in every country, implying that the nominal exchange rate reflects differences in price levels.

q-theory of investment : The theory according to which expenditure on capital goods depends on the ratio of the market value of installed capital to its replacement cost.

Quantity equation : The identity stating that the product of the money supply and the velocity of money equals nominal expenditure *(MV = PY)*; coupled with the assumption of stable velocity, an explanation of nominal expenditure called the quantity theory of money.

Quantity theory of money : The doctrine emphasizing that changes in the quantity of money lead to changes in nominal expenditure.

Quota : *See* import quota.

Random walk: The path of a variable whose changes over time are unpredictable.

Rational expectations : An approach that assumes that people optimally use all available information — including information about current and prospective policies — to forecast the future. (Cf. adaptive expectations.)

Real : Measured in constant dollars; adjusted for inflation. (Cf. nominal.)

Real aggregate demand curve : In real-business-cycle theory, the negative relationship arising from the goods market between the real interest rate and the aggregate quantity of output demanded.

Real aggregate supply curve : In real-business-cycle theory, the positive relationship arising from intertem-poral substitution in the labor market between the real interest rate and the aggregate quantity of output supplied.

Real-business-cycle theory : The theory according to which economic fluctuations can be explained by real changes in the economy (such as changes in technology) and without any role for nominal variables (such as the money supply).

Real exchange rate : The rate at which one country's goods trade for another country's goods. (Cf. exchange rate, nominal exchange rate.)

Real interest rate : The return to saving and the cost of borrowing after adjustment for inflation (Cf. nominal interest rate.)

Real money balances : The quantity of money expressed in terms of the quantity of goods and services it can buy; the quantity of money divided by the price level *(M/P)*.

Recession : A sustained period of falling real income.

Rental price of capital : The amount paid to rent one unit of capital.

Reserve requirements : Regulations imposed on banks by the central bank that specify a minimum reserve-deposit ratio.

Reserves : The money that banks have received from depositors but have not used to make loans.

Residential investment : New housing bought by people to live in and by landlords to rent out.

Revaluation : An action undertaken by the central bank to raise the value of a currency under a system of fixed exchange rates. (Cf. devaluation.)

Ricardian equivalence : The theory according to which forward-looking consumers fully anticipate the future taxes implied by government debt, so that government borrowing today coupled with a tax increase in the future to repay the debt has the same effect on the economy as a tax increase today.

Sacrifice ratio : The number of percentage points of a year's real *GDP* that must be forgone to reduce inflation by one percentage point.

Saving : See national saving, private saving, and public saving.

Seasonal adjustment : The removal of the regular fluctuations in an economic variable that occurs as a function of the time of year.

Sectoral shift : A change in the composition of demand among industries or regions.

Seigniorage : The revenue raised by the government through the creation of money; the inflation tax.

Shock : An exogenous change in an economic relationship, such as the aggregate demand or aggregate supply curve.

Shoe-leather cost : The cost of inflation from reducing real money balances, such as the inconvenience of needing to make more frequent trips to the bank.

Small open economy : An open economy that takes its interest rate as given by world financial markets; an economy that, by virtue of its size, has a negligible impact on world markets and, in particular, on the world interest rate. (Cf. large open economy.)

Solow growth model : A model showing how saving, population growth, and technological progress determine the level of and growth in the standard of living.

Solow residual : The growth in total factor productivity, measured as the percentage change in output minus the percentage change in inputs, where the inputs are weighted by their factor shares. (Cf. total factor productivity.)

Stabilization policy : Public policy aimed at keeping output and employment at their natural-rate levels.

Stagflation : A situation of falling output and rising prices; combination of stagnation and inflation.

Steady state : A condition in which key variables are not changing.

Sticky prices : Prices that adjust sluggishly and, therefore, do not always equilibrate supply and demand.

Sticky-price model : The model of aggregate supply emphasizing the slow adjustment of the prices of goods and services.

Sticky-wage model : The model of aggregate supply emphasizing the slow adjustment of nominal wages.

Stock : 1. A variable measured as a quantity at a point in time. (Cf. flow.) 2. Shares of ownership in a corporation.

Stock market : A market in which shares of ownership in corporations are bought and sold.

Stock-out avoidance : The motive for holding inventories according to which firms keep extra goods on hand to prevent running out if sales are unexpectedly high.

Store of value : A way of transferring purchasing power from the present to the future; one of the functions of money. (Cf. medium of exchange, unit of account.)

Substitution effect : The change in consumption of a good resulting from a movement along an indifference curve because of a change in the relative price. (Cf. income effect.)

Tariff : A tax on imported goods.

Tax multiplier : The change in aggregate income resulting from a one-dollar change in taxes.

Time inconsistency : The tendency of policy-makers to announce policies in advance in order to influence the expectations of private decision-makers, and then to follow different policies after those expectations have been formed and acted upon.

Tobin's q : The ratio of the market value of installed capital to its replacement cost.

Total factor productivity : A measure of the level of technology; the amount of output per unit of input, where different inputs are combined on the basis of their factor shares. (Cf. Solow residual.)

Trade balance : The receipts from exports minus the payments for imports.

Transactions theories of money demand : Theories that explain how much money people choose to hold and that stress the role of money as a medium of exchange. (Cf. portfolio theories of money demand.)

Transfer payments : Payments from the government to individuals that are not in exchange for goods and services, such as Social Security payments.

Transitory income : Income that people do not expect to persist into the future; current income minus normal income. (Cf. permanent income.)

Underground economy : Economic transactions that are hidden in order to evade taxes or conceal illegal activity.

Unemployment insurance : A government program under which unemployed workers can collect benefits for a certain period of time after losing their jobs.

Unemployment rate : The percentage of those in the labor force who do not have jobs.

Unit of account : The measure in which prices and other accounting records are recorded; one of the functions of money. (Cf. medium of exchange, store of value.)

Value-added : The value of a firm's output minus the value of the intermediate goods the firm purchased.

Velocity of money : The ratio of nominal expenditure to the money supply; the rate at which money changes hands.

Wage : The amount paid for one unit of labor.

Wage rigidity : The failure of wages to adjust to equilibrate labor supply and labor demand.

Wait unemployment : The unemployment resulting from wage rigidity and job rationing. (Cf. frictional unemployment.)

Work in process : Goods in inventory that are in the process of being completed.

Worker-misperception model : The model of aggregate supply emphasizing that workers sometimes perceive incorrectly the overall level of prices.

World interest rate : The interest rate prevailing in world financial markets.

Bibliography

1. Ackley, G. (1961), Macroeconomic Theory.
2. Ackley, G. (1978), Macroeconomic Theory and Policy.
3. Allen, G. R. D. (1967), Macroeconomic Theory — A Mathematical treatment.
4. Audo and Modigliani (1963), "The Life cycle Hypothesis of saving", AER.
5. Baumol, W. J. (1980), Economic Theory and Operational Analysis.
6. Beckerman, W. (1976), National Income Analysis.
7. Black, J. (1979), The Economics of modern Britain.
8. Brooman, F. S. (1977), macroeconomics.
9. Branson, W. H. (1979), Macroeconomic Theory and policy.
10. Barro, R. J. and Grossman, H. I (1978), Money, Employment and Inflation.
11. Crouch, R. L. (1972), Macroeconomics.
12. Deruburg, T. F. and McDougall D. M. (1976), Macroeconomics.
13. Domar, E. D. (1957), Essays in the Theory of Economic Growth.
14. Dorabusch, R. and Fishers, S (1978), Macroeconomics.
15. Duesenberry, J. (1949), Income, Saving and the theory of Consumer Behaviour.
16. Evans, M. K. (1969), Macroeconomic Activity.
17. Friedman, M. (1957), A Theory of the Consumption Function.
18. Friedman, M. (1956) ed. Studies in the Quantity theory of Money.
19. Friedman and Schwastz (1963), A monetary History of the United States, 1867-1960.
20. Friedman, M. (1969), The Optimum Quantity of Money.
21. Háberler, G (1960), Prosperity and Depression.
22. Hahn, F. H and Mathews, RCO (1964), The Theory of Economic Growth.
23. Hicks, J. R. (1937), Mr. Keynes and the classics.
24. Hicks, J. R. (1950), A contribution to the Theory of Trade Cycle.
25. Johnson, H. J. (1969), Essays in Monetary Economics.

26. Keynes, J. M. (1936), The General Theory of Employment, Interest and Money.

27. Kurihara (ed) (1954), Post-Keneysian Economics.

28. Kurihara (ed) (1954), An Introduction to Keynesian Dynamics.

29. Kurihara (ed) (1954), Monetary Theory and Public Policy.

30. Laidler, D. (1969), The demand for money; Theories and Evidence.

31. Leijouhufvud, A (1968), On Keynesian Economics and the Economics of Keynes.

32. Levacic, R. (1976), Macroeconomics.

33. Lipsey, R. ((1983), An Introduction to positive Economics.

34. Lucas, R.E., Models of Business Cycles.

35. Metzler, L.A. (1951), Wealth, Saving and the Rate of Interest.

36. Mathews, R. C. O. (1959), The Trade Cycle.

37. Muller, M. G. (1966) (ed.) Reading in Macroeconomics.

38.. Mundell, R. A. (1968), International Economics.

39. Mankiw, N. G. (1994), Macroeconomics.

40. Musgrave, R. A. (1978), The Theory of Public Finance.

41. Newlyn & Bootle (1978), Theory of Money.

42. Patinkin, D. (1965), Money, Interest and Prices.

43. Patinkin, D. (1948), Price flexibility and full employment.

44. Patinkin, D. (1972), Studeis in Monetary Economics.

45. Phillips, A.W. (1958), "The Relation between Unemployment and the rate of change of money wage Rates in the U.K. 1886-1957", Economics.

46. Pigou, A. C. (1917), The Value of Money.

47. Rowan, D. C. (1983), Output, Inflation and Growth.

48. Rees, A (1970), 'The Phillips Curve as a Menu for policy choice' Economics.

49. Pigou, A.C. (1943), 'The classical stationary state' E. J.

50. Samulson & Nordhaus (1985), Economics.

51. Samulson (1974), Foundations of Economic Analysis.

52. Samulson (1948), The Simple Mathematics of Income Determination.

53. Samulson & Nordhaus (1939), Interaction Between The Multiplier and the Principle of accelerator RES statistics.

54. Solow, R.M. (1970), Growth Theory an Exposition.

55. Schumpeter, J.A. (1954), History of Economic Analysis.

56. Smith, W.L. (1966) 'A Graphic Exposition of the complete Keynesian System', in M.G. Muller (ed.) Readings in Macroeconics.

57. Smith, W. L. (1970), Macroeconomics.

58. Shaw and Gurdey (1960), Money in a Theory of Finance.

59. Silber, W.L. (1970) Fiscal Policy in IS-LM Analysis.

60. Tobin, J. (1956) "The interest elasticity of transaction demand for cash", RES statistics.

61. Tobin, J. (1958) "Liquidity Preference as a behaviour towards risk" RES.

62. Tobin, J. (1972) "Inflation and Unemployment", AER.

63. White, W.M. (1956), Interest Elasticity of Investment Demand, AER.

64. Wrightman, D. (1971), An Introduction to Monetary Theory and Policy.

Index

Acceleration Principle, 239, 254, 336
Accelerator
  defined, 336
  interaction with multiplier, 336, 341-343
Acceleration Theory, 253
Active balances, 85
Adjustable page system, 382, 386
Age, and consumption, 221
Aggregate demand and supply, 9, 45-47, 132-35, 154, 156
  equilibrium of, 21, 48, 116, 129, 162-164, 307-308, 328
Aggregate demand function, 48, 51, 165-68, 176
Aggregates, use of, 46
Anti-inflation policy, 324, 325
Autonomous demand, 50
Autonomous investment, 52, 55, 56
  and accelerator-multiplier interaction, 341-343
Average Propensity to Consume, 58, 210, 211, 214, 215, 226, 336
Average Propensity to Save 216, 351, 354

Balance of payments, 4, 261-267, 343, 382, 384, 385
Balance of trade, 8, 258, 259, 270
Balanced-budget theorem, 182-184
Bank deposits, 67, 79
Bank of England, 67, 78, 282, 284, 387
Bank Rate, 324
Banknotes, 67
Baumol, W. J., 69,
Bonds, Prices and yields of, 179, 212, 236, 325, 347
Brumberg, R., 225
Budget, 179-191, 193, 375
  deficit, 189, 372, 373, 375, 375-381, 396
  surplus, 188, 372, 375
Built-in stabilisers, 187, 190
Business-motive, 254
Business-cycle, 138, 241, 327, 329, 333, 335

Capital coefficient, 156
Capital formation, 219, 220
Capital gains, 24, 72, 233
Capital mobility, 264
Capital-output ratio, 349, 351, 353, 354
Capital Stock, influence on investment, 103, 112, 127, 138, 233, 234, 351, 357, 358
Capital Stock Adjustment Principle, 164
Comparative statics, 258, 293, 297, 301
Compensatory finance, 383
Consumer behaviour, 378
Consumer credit, 213, 324
Consumers' durables, 213
Consumers' expenditure, 180, 256, 311, 325
Consumer price index, 33
Consumption Function, 48, 51, 53, 55, 96, 118, 139, 149, 150, 181, 209, 210, 226, 228, 230, 311, 357
  and interest rates, 212, 223
Consumption lags, 53, 57, 336
Corporate saving, 214
Cross-section, 213, 214
Corporate Profits, 235
Cost-inflation, 295, 305, 306, 315-319, 321
Crowding out effect, 97, 196-200, 309, 312
Cyclical fluctuation, 335, 343

Damped cycles, 336, 338, 343
Debt, 179
Deflationary gap, 311
Demand for labour, 104, 115, 118, 127-129, 131, 137, 299, 315
Demand for money, 69, 72, 87-90, 96, 111, 118, 138, 139
Demand-deficiency unemployment, 116
Demand-inflation, 312, 313, 315, 319
Depreciation, 351, 357, 358, 360, 361, 364
  in, 232, 233, 235, 246, 247, 253, 286
Depreciation allowances, 28
Devaluation, 262, 284, 384, 385, 386, 393
Difference equations, 55, 124, 139
Discount rate, 82, 249, 251
Diversifier, 74
Dividends, 214
Domar, E. D., 350
Dynamic analysis, 15, 53, 56, 93, 345, 348
Dynamic income determination, 53, 55

Economic fluctuation, 327, 329, 334, 335
Elasticity : (*see* Price-elasticity, Income-elasticity)
  elastic money demand, 98
  elastic money supply, 98
Equilibrium, 4, 9, 42, 45-47, 58, 131, 145, 180
  of aggregate demand and supply, 42, 45-50, 56-59, 114, 115
  of ex ante saving and investment, 106, 114, 115, 117, 129, 130
  stable, 49, 95, 119, 129, 130
  unstable, 352
  in labour market, 103, 104, 115, 128-130
  of interest rate, 86, 87, 120-121
  money market, 83, 90, 103
  of price-level, 107, 113, 117, 156, 297
  general, 93-96, 119, 130-131, 163, 164, 170
European monetary union, 396
European union, 394
Ex ante and *ex post,* 305
Exchange control, 393
Exchange rate, 256, 261-275, 281, 285, 382, 384, 385, 387, 397
  appreciation, 260, 280, 291, 373
  depreciation, 259, 287
  fixed, 264, 269, 282-83, 285, 384, 393
  flexible, 260-270, 274, 280, 282-283, 285
  quasi, 315, 384
Expectations, 72, 212, 228, 251
  and consumption, 205, 228, 229
  and investment, 205
  and prices, 294, 298
  in inflation, 293-95, 296, 302, 304, 305
  rational, 228, 229, 296
Explosive cycle, 337, 339, 343
Ex-port, 256, 270
Ex-post, 286, 306

Factor cost, 24, 30
Factor market, 315
Final products, 20, 22, 24, 25
Financial intermediaries, 80
Fiscal policy, 160, 162, 196, 197, 200, 203, 205, 263, 267-272, 274, 280, 283, 285, 290, 324, 331, 373, 374, 376, 379, 381
Fleming, M., 277
Flexibility of money-wages and prices, 298, 334
'Floor-and-ceiling' models of the trade cycle, 341-343
Foreign currency, 262-264, 382, 384
Foreign trade, 256
Foreign trade multiplier, 259, 260
Fractional reserve banking, 79
Frictional unemployment, 104, 156
Friedman, M., 220, 227, 319, 320, 374
Frisch, R., 4, 227, 343
Full employment, 103, 104, 112-114, 117, 127-129, 132, 146-148, 151, 299, 311, 312, 319
GDP deflator, 32, 68

Golden rule, 360-365, 367, 368
Gross Domestic Product, 6, 24, 29
Gross National Income (GNI), 29, 27
Gross National Product (GNP), 6, 29
Growth, 137-139, 343, 345, 346, 348, 367

Hansen, A. H., 9, 312
Harrod, Sir Roy, 350
Houses, imputed rent of owner-occupied, 238
House purchase, loans for, 238
Housewives' services, 19-20
Housing, investment in, 237

Idle balances, 85, 88
Illiquid, 76
Imports, 26, 256, 270, 311
Import controls, 282
Import Function, 257
Imputed rent, 19
Income, concept of, 29-30
Income effect, 75
Income
- of persons, 29
- of enterprises, 29-30
- of public authorities, 30-1
- of 'collective persons', 31
- disposable, 36, 57, 311, 324, 327

Income-determination, 45-49, 117, 150, 219, 257
Income-distribution and consumption, 213, 306, 311, 316, 317, 370
Income-tax multiplier, 183-187
Income-velocity, 68, 154
Index-numbers, 307, 318
Index-number problem, 33
Indifference curve, 74
Indirect taxes, 36-37
Induced investment, 341
Industrial result, 348
Inflation, 3, 76, 137-139, 159, 203, 233, 293, 298, 311, 312, 379
- cost-push, 295, 308, 311, 312, 317, 322
- demand-pull, 295, 308, 317
- inertia, 294
- mark-up, 322, 324

Inflationary gap, 311-315, 324
Inflexibility of prices and money wages, 116, 147
Input-output tables, 307
Insensitivity of investment to interest rate, 98, 100, 101, 114
Interest rates, 58, 60, 83, 87, 96, 97, 108, 115, 117, 146, 209, 256, 372
- and demand for money, 80, 96-101
- and fixed investment, 114, 231, 234
- and investment in housing, 237
- and investment in stocks, 106, 121
- and prices of long-term bonds, 122
- and real income, 209

Interest-cost of fixed investment, 93-97, 108, 117, 148, 241
International monetary fund, 382
Investment, 144, 148, 325
IS curve, 59-61, 93-97-102, 118-175, 163-165, 191-202, 269-272, 327
Investment–*continued*
- autonomous, 50, 54, 123-25, 137, 241, 256, 338 351
- expenditure in 1960, 58, 180, 256
- *ex ante,* equilibrium with saving, 106, 115, 150
- *ex post,* identity with saving, 106, 150
- gross and net, 234, 235, 246, 247
- induced, 124, 125, 241
- and interest-rates, 93; 114, 234, 343
- and share issues, 236

Investment Function, 48, 51, 60, 107, 111-114, 118, 122, 131, 137, 139, 153, 180, 181, 231, 234, 370
Investment multiplier, 50, 123, 259
Involuntary unemployment, 117-130, 134, 298

Kaldor, N., 370

Labour efficiency, 366
Labour market, 298, 302, 315
Lag
- inside, outside, 204

Laspeyres index, 35
Lerner, A. P., 248

Life-cycle hypothesis, 213, 220, 225, 374
LM curve, 87-97-102, 118, 163-165, 191-202, 269-272, 327
  derivation of, 88
  slope of, 90
  shift of, 91
Liquidity of assets, 83
Liquidity-preference
  and demand for money, 72, 93, 94
  function, 75, 77, 87, 111
  precautionary-motive, 83
  transactions-motive, 90-91
  transaction motive theory, 76, 118
  speculative-motive, 84, 85
  and interest-rates, 118
Liquidity-trap, 87, 98-99, 114, 115, 122, 134, 141, 149, 193, 198-200

Marginal Efficiency of Capital (MEC), 241, 242, 248
  schedule, 168
Marginal Efficiency of Invest (MEI), 246-48
Marginal product of capital, 231, 232, 242, 244, 368
Marginal productivity of labour, 103, 104, 109, 127, 300, 313
Marginal Propensity to Consume (MPC) 47-49, 52, 182, 210-212, 214-217
Marginal Propensity to Import (MPM), 256-258
Marginal Propensity to Invest (MPI), 51, 218, 241
Marginal Propensity to Save (MPS), 47, 52, 258, 351, 354
Marginal Propensity to Spend, 52, 182, 216, 313, 316, 317
Marginal rates of tax, 183-191
Market prices, 24, 30
Marshall, A., 103
Marxist theory, 347
Maastricht treaty, 396
Microeconomics, 3, 327, 334
Modigliani, F., 3, 9, 220, 225, 227, 374
Monetary policy, 66, 82, 87, 138, 141, 160, 161, 200-203, 205, 263-272, 275, 281, 282,. 284, 285, 290, 292, 324
Monetarist, 13, 76, 138, 320, 343
Money, functions of, 65, 68, 146
Money illusion, 68, 128
Money, quantity of, 66, 88
  and inflation, 76, 137, 138
  and interest-rate, 96, 101
  multiplier, 81, 82
  and prices, 128
Money, Quantity Theory of, 66
Money-wages 297, 299, 301
  in inflation, 304
  flexibility of, 298, 334
Multiplier, 50, 342
  budget, 182
  export, 259-262
  public expenditure, 182
  static, 51
  dynamic, 54
  simple, 50, 55, 124-126
  and balanced budget, 182-194

National Expenditure, 25, 27, 28
  Gross and Net, 29
  identical with National Income and National Product, 28
National Income, 23, 27
  Gross and Net, 24, 29
  identical with National Product, 29, 357
National income identity, 39
National income and economic welfare, 40
National Product, 27
'Natural' rate of growth, 353, 371
Net income from abroad, 27, 32
Net investment abroad, 280
Net National Product (NNP), 29
Neutrality of money, 333, 334
Nominal GDP, 31, 69

Okun's law, 294
Opportunity cost, 240
Open economy, 38, 58, 71, 76
Open inflation, 307
Optimum portfolio curve, 75

Paasche index, 35

Paradox of thrift, 4, 218
Patinkin, D., 151, 346
Pay-out period, 252
Permanent Income, 77, 374
    theory, 220, 227, 374
Personal disposable income, 36, 37
Phillips, A. W., 300
Phillips curve, 293, 295, 296, 297, 300, 319
Pigou effect, 139, 149, 150, 152, 153, 213, 311
Pigou, A. C., 101, 149, 151
Policy debate, 203
Population growth, 345, 363, 365
Precautionary demand, 78
Precautionary-motive, 69, 77, 145
Present value, 59, 77, 242, 249
    net present value, 249-251
Price-level, 105, 113, 120, 137, 146, 148, 154, 156, 160, 171-175, 256, 346
Price-elasticity of demand for exports and imports, 261
Private sector, 179
Production function, 109, 328, 356, 357, 358, 359, 370
Productivity of labour, 312, 318, 349
Profit, 139, 214, 233, 234
Profit-expectations, 237
Profit tax, 235
Progressive income tax, 57, 179-187
Public expenditure, 63, 161, 179, 324
    effects of changes in, 161-162
Public sector, 179, 350, 372

Quantity equation, 68, 69
    Fisher version, 304, 305
Quantity of money, 68, 79, 146, 173, 213, 302, 309, 346
Quantity Theory of money, 67, 76, 154, 160, 305, 309, 319, 320, 346

Random disturbances, 342, 343
Rate-of-income-tax' multiplier, 57, 184, 185
Real and money wage-rates, 297
Real balance effect, 68, 98, 101, 102, 139, 152, 155, 213, 320, 327
Real GDP, 31
'Real' rate of interest, 240
Real price index, 33
Relevant rate of interest, 72
Replacement investment, 234, 336, 342
Reserve requirement, 82
Rostow's stage theory, 350

Samuelson, P. A., 336
Saving
    defined, 26, 27, 367
    investment, 14, 47, 51, 61, 115
    ex post, identity with investment, 14, 93, 94
Saving function, 48, 61, 111, 114, 118, 131, 146, 153, 216, 257, 354, 360
Single currency, 396, 397
Speculative balances, 88
Speculative demand for money, 72, 90-94, 134, 145, 310
Speculative-motive, 69, 84, 85
Stability, 187, 204, 258, 269, 397
Stagflation, 159
Static analysis, 15, 49, 52, 138, 311
Stationary economy, 347
Steady state, 357-59, 368, 370-71
'Stickiness' of money-wages, 334
Stock appreciation, 30
Stock of capital, and investment, 233-35, 241-42
Stocks, 45
    investment in additions to, 45, 237
Stock market, 81, 235-236
Sterilization policy, 260
Structural unemployment, 307, 308
Subsidies, 36, 37
Substitution effect, 75
Supply curve
    perfectly elastic, 126
Supply of labour, 104, 110, 115, 118, 127, 128, 131, 137, 299, 302, 345
Supply, Aggregate, and National Product, 293
Suppressed inflation, 307
Supply of Money, 57, 66, 69, 78, 120, 135, 155, 269-272, 310, 319

function, 94, 96
perfectly elastic, 99, 100

Taxation, 179-181
of incomes, 57, 179-181, 187, 235
direct, 36, 37, 325
indirect, 36, 37, 325
lump-sum, 182-185, 197
Technological progress, 248, 346, 349, 351, 365-367-369
Technology, 331
Time Series Data, 214, 215, 228
Tobin, J., 235
Trade policy, 281, 284
Trade unions, 128, 312, 315-319, 322, 346, 396
Transactions-demand for money, 69, 77, 145, 310, 347
Transactions-motive, 83, 85, 90, 91, 137
Transfer incomes,
payments 36, 180, 214
Transitory income and consumption, 227

Underemployment equilibrium, 117, 146, 347
Unemployment, 3, 104, 105, 203, 293-95, 299, 312, 396
cyclical, 293-295
demand-deficiency, 335
frictional, 87
involuntary, 117
natural, 138, 293, 300, 302
Unemployment Rate, 335, 336
technological, 331
Unemployment benefit, as a built-in, 205, 333
Utility function, 74

Value added, 28
Velocity of circulation, 346
in inflation, 228

Wage-price spiral, 312, 317
Wage-rates, money, 103, 128-134, 139, 145, 168, 174, 175, 256, 313
flexibility of, 105, 106, 112, 113, 145, 147
determination of, 107, 316, 317
inflexibility or 'Sticky', 128, 147, 168-175
Wage-rates, real
and demand and supply of labour, 104, 105, 108, 117, 134, 145, 313, 316
World bank, 382
World trade, 383

Yields
on shares, 236
negative and non-negative, 243